7th Workshop on Innovative Use of NLP for Building Educational Applications 2012

Held at the 2012 Conference of the North American Chapter of the Association for Computational Linguistics: Human Language Technologies (NAACL-HLT 2012)

Montreal, Quebec, Canada
3-8 June 2012

ISBN: 978-1-62276-548-5

Printed from e-media with permission by:

Curran Associates, Inc.
57 Morehouse Lane
Red Hook, NY 12571

Some format issues inherent in the e-media version may also appear in this print version.

Printed by Curran Associates, Inc. (2013)

For permission requests, please contact the Association for Computational Linguistics at the address below.

Association for Computational Linguistics
209 N. Eighth Street
Stroudsburg, Pennsylvania 18360

Phone: 1-570-476-8006
Fax: 1-570-476-0860

acl@aclweb.org

Additional copies of this publication are available from:

Curran Associates, Inc.
57 Morehouse Lane
Red Hook, NY 12571 USA
Phone: 845-758-0400
Fax: 845-758-2634
Email: curran@proceedings.com
Web: www.proceedings.com

Preface

Research in natural language processing (NLP) applications for education has continued to progress using innovative statistical and rule-based NLP methods, or most commonly, a combination of the two. As a community, we continue to improve existing capabilities and to identify and generate innovative ways to use NLP in applications for writing, reading, speaking, critical thinking, curriculum development, and assessment. Steady growth in the development of NLP-based applications for education has prompted an increased number of workshops, typically focusing on a single subfield. In this workshop, researchers present papers from many subfields: tools for automated scoring of text and speech, intelligent tutoring, readability measures, use of corpora, grammatical error detection, and tools for teachers and test developers. These focus on contributions to the three core educational problem spaces: development of curriculum and assessment (e.g., applications that help teachers develop reading materials), delivery of curriculum and assessments (e.g., applications where the student receives instruction and interacts with the system), and reporting of assessment outcomes (e.g., automated essay and other constructed response scoring).

NLP-based educational applications continue to develop in order to serve the learning and assessment needs of students, teachers, schools, and assessment organizations. The practical need for language-analysis capabilities has been motivated even further by increased requirements for state and national assessments, and a growing population of foreign and second language learners. There are currently a number of commercial systems that handle automated scoring of free-text and speech as well as systems that address linguistic complexity in text – commonly referred to as readability measures. More recently, the need for language analysis tools is, in part, driven by a new influence in the educational landscape in the United States: the Common Core State Standards initiative (http://www.corestandards.org/). The initiative has been adopted by 46 states for use in Kindergarten through 12th grade (K-12) classrooms and is likely to have a strong influence on teaching standards, as well as how NLP research and applications are applied in the classroom.

This workshop is the seventh in a series related to Building NLP Applications for Education. The series began at NAACL/HLT (2003), and continued at ACL 2005 (Ann Arbor), ACL/HLT 2008 (Columbus), NAACL/HLT 2009 (Boulder), NAACL/HLT 2010 (Los Angeles), ACL/HLT 2011 (Portland), and now NAACL/HLT 2012 (Montréal). This year, we received a record 42 submissions and accepted 8 full papers as oral presentations and 16 papers as poster presentations, as well as an invited talk by Robert Dale describing the *HOO2012 Shared Task*. The acceptance rate is 57%. All of the papers are published in these proceedings. Each paper was carefully reviewed by at least three members of the Program Committee. We carefully selected reviewers most appropriate for each paper so as to get knowledgeable reviews. This workshop offers an opportunity to present and publish work that is highly relevant to NAACL/HLT, but is also specialized. Thus, the BEA workshop is often a more appropriate venue for such work. We believe that the workshop framework designed to introduce works in progress and new ideas needs to be revived, and we hope that we have achieved this with the breadth and variety of research accepted presented here.

While the field is growing, we do recognize that there is a core group of institutions and researchers who work in this area. With a higher acceptance rate, we were able to include papers from a broad range of topics and institutions. We continue to have a strong policy to avoid conflicts of interest. We did not assign papers to reviewers if the paper had an author from the same institution. Second, with respect to the organizing committee, authors of papers where there was a conflict of interest did not participate in the discussion.

The papers accepted to this workshop were selected on the basis of several factors, including the relevance to a core educational problem space, the novelty of the approach or domain, and the strength of the research. The final set of 24 papers fall under several main themes:

Assessing Speech: Four papers focus on assessing spoken language of non-native speakers of English (Chen; Chen and Zechner; Huant et al, and Yoon et al.).

Automated Scoring Tools: Six papers focus on aspects of scoring textual responses, such as short answer scoring (Hahn and Meurers; Rus and Lintean; and Ziai et al.), measuring coherence in learner essays (Yannakoudakis and Briscoe), measuring the use of factual information (Beigman-Klebanov and Higgins), and automatically grading responses to science questions (Sil et al.).

Generation: Two papers (both Perez-Beltrachini et al.) present work into generation cloze questions and grammar exercises.

Grammatical Error Detection: Three papers target grammatical error detection. Madnina et al. discuss novel techniques for error correction and Ferraro et al. judge grammatically. The third paper (Flor and Futagi) focuses on automatic spell correction in student essays.

Intelligent Tutoring: Two papers discuss issues related to intelligent tutoring systems (Becker et al.; and Bethard et al.).

Readability and Reading Assistance Tools: Four papers investigate aspects of readability ranging from developing tools for student reading assistance to detecting a document's reading level (Talukdar and Cohen; Eom et al.; Maamouri et al.; and Vajjala and Meurers).

Other Learning Assistance Research: Finally, we have three papers on other topics. Xiong et al., present a tool for peer-review exploration. Dickinson et al. present a method for predicting which college level Hebrew class a student should place into. And Chen et al. present an approach to generating paraphrases for language learning.

This year, we are pleased to host the *Helping Our Own* (HOO-2012) shared task on grammatical error detection (http://www.correcttext.org/hoo2012), organized by Robert Dale et al. In its second year, this instantiation of the shared task focuses on the detection and correction of determiner and preposition errors in texts written by non-native speakers of English. These error types are two of the most frequent, and nettlesome, ones for English learners. 14 teams took part in the shared task and descriptions of their submitted systems are found in these proceedings and are presented as posters in conjunction with the BEA7 poster session.

We wish to thank everyone who showed interest and submitted a paper, all of the authors for their contributions, the members of the Program Committee for their thoughtful reviews, and everyone who attended this workshop. All of these factors contribute to a truly enriching event!

Joel Tetreault, Educational Testing Service
Jill Burstein, Educational Testing Service
Claudia Leacock, CTB McGraw-Hill

Organizers:

Joel Tetreault, Educational Testing Service
Jill Burstein, Educational Testing Service
Claudia Leacock, CTB McGraw-Hill

Program Committee:

Andrea Abel, EURAC, Italy
Shane Bergsma, Johns Hopkins University, USA
Delphine Bernhard, Université de Strasbourg, France
Jared Bernstein, Pearson, USA
Daniel Blanchard, Educational Testing Service, USA
Kristy Boyer, North Carolina State University, USA
Chris Brew, Educational Testing Service, USA
Chris Brockett, Microsoft Research, USA
Aoife Cahill, Educational Testing Service, USA
Martin Chodorow, Hunter College of CUNY, USA
Mark Core, USC Institute for Creative Technologies, USA
Daniel Dahlmeier, National University of Singapore, Singapore
Markus Dickinson, Indiana University, USA
Robert Dale, Macquarie University, Australia
Bill Dolan, Microsoft Research, USA
Maxine Eskenazi, Carnegie Mellon University, USA
Keelan Evanini, Educational Testing Service, USA
Jennifer Foster, Dublin City University, Ireland
Annette Frank, University of Heidelberg, Germany
Michael Gamon, Microsoft Research, USA
Caroline Gasperin, TouchType, Brazil
Kallirroi Georgila, USC Institute for Creative Technologies, USA
Iryna Gurevych, University of Darmstadt, Germany
Na-Rae Han, University of Pittsburgh, USA
Trude Heift, Simon Frasier University, Canada
Michael Heilman, Educational Testing Service, USA
Derrick Higgins, Educational Testing Service, USA
Heng Ji, Queens College of CUNY, USA
Pamela Jordan, University of Pittsburgh, USA
Ola Knutsson, Stockholm University, Sweden
John Lee, City University of Hong Kong, China
Xiaofei Lu, Penn State University, USA
Roger Levy, University of California San Diego, USA
Jackson Liscombe, SpeechCycle, USA
Diane Litman, University of Pittsburgh, USA

Annie Louis, University of Pennsylvania, USA
Nitin Madnani, Educational Testing Service, USA
Montse Maritxalar, University of the Basque Country, Spain
Aurélien Max, LIMSI-CNRS, France
Detmar Meurers, University of Tübingen, Germany
Lisa Michaud, Merrimack College, USA
Rada Mihalcea, University of North Texas, USA
Michael Mohler, University of North Texas, USA
Jack Mostow, Carnegie Mellon University, USA
Smaranda Muresan, Rutgers University, USA
Ani Nenkova, University of Pennsylvania, USA
Rodney Nielsen, University of Colorado, USA
Hwee Tou Ng, National University of Singapore, USA
Matt Post, Johns Hopkins University, USA
Patti Price, PPRICE Speech and Language Technology, USA
Andrew Rosenberg, Queens College of CUNY, USA
Mihai Rotaru, TextKernel, the Netherlands
Dan Roth, University of Illinois Urbana-Champagne, USA
Alla Rozovskaya, University of Illinois Urbana-Champagne, USA
Mathias Schulze, University of Waterloo, Canada
Stephanie Seneff, Massachusetts Institute of Technology, USA
Izhak Shafran, Oregon Health and Science University, USA
Serge Sharoff, University of Leeds, UK
Svetlana Stenchikova, Open University, UK
Helmer Strik, Radboud University Nijmegen, the Netherlands
Joseph Tepperman, Rosetta Stone, USA
Nai-Lung Tsao, National Central University, Taiwan
Benjamin Van Durme, Johns Hopkins University, USA
Arthur Ward, University of Pittsburgh, USA
Monica Ward, Dublin City University, Ireland
David Wible, National Central University, Taiwan
Sze Wong, Macquarie University, Australia
Peter Wood, University of Saskatchewan in Saskatoon, Canada
Klaus Zechner, Educational Testing Service, USA

Table of Contents

Conference Program

Thursday, June 7, 2012

8:45–9:00 Load Presentations

9:00–9:15 Opening Remarks

\+ 9:15–9:40

Question Ranking and Selection in Tutorial Dialogues
Lee Becker, Martha Palmer, Sarel van Vuuren and Wayne Ward

\+ 9:40–10:05

Identifying science concepts and student misconceptions in an interactive essay writing tutor
Steven Bethard, Ifeyinwa Okoye, Md. Arafat Sultan, Haojie Hang, James H. Martin and Tamara Sumner

\+ 10:05–10:30

Automatic Grading of Scientific Inquiry
Avirup Sil, Angela Shelton, Diane Jass Ketelhut and Alexander Yates

10:30–11:00 **Break**

\+ 11:00–11:25

Modeling coherence in ESOL learner texts
Helen Yannakoudakis and Ted Briscoe

\+ 11:25–11:50

Exploring Grammatical Error Correction with Not-So-Crummy Machine Translation
Nitin Madnani, Joel Tetreault and Martin Chodorow

\+ 11:50–12:15

HOO 2012: A Report on the Preposition and Determiner Error Correction Shared Task
Robert Dale, Ilya Anisimoff and George Narroway

Thursday, June 7, 2012 (continued)

12:15–1:45 **Lunch**

1:45–3:30 **Poster Session**

+ BEA7 Posters

Measuring the Use of Factual Information in Test-Taker Essays
Beata Beigman Klebanov and Derrick Higgins

Utilizing Cumulative Logit Model and Human Computation on Automated Speech Assessment
Lei Chen

PREFER: Using a Graph-Based Approach to Generate Paraphrases for Language Learning
Mei-Hua Chen, Shi-Ting Huang, Chung-Chi Huang, Hsien-Chin Liou and Jason S. Chang

Using an Ontology for Improved Automated Content Scoring of Spontaneous Non-Native Speech
Miao Chen and Klaus Zechner

Predicting Learner Levels for Online Exercises of Hebrew
Markus Dickinson, Sandra Kübler and Anthony Meyer

On using context for automatic correction of non-word misspellings in student essays
Michael Flor and Yoko Futagi

Judging Grammaticality with Count-Induced Tree Substitution Grammars
Francis Ferraro, Matt Post and Benjamin Van Durme

Scoring Spoken Responses Based on Content Accuracy
Fei Huang, Lei Chen and Jana Sukkarieh

Developing ARET: An NLP-based Educational Tool Set for Arabic Reading Enhancement
Mohammed Maamouri, Wajdi Zaghouani, Violetta Cavalli-Sforza, Dave Graff and Mike Ciul

Generating Diagnostic Multiple Choice Comprehension Cloze Questions
Jack Mostow and Hyeju Jang

Thursday, June 7, 2012 (continued)

Thursday, June 7, 2012 (continued)

Korea University System in the HOO 2012 Shared Task
Jieun Lee, Jung-Tae Lee and Hae-Chang Rim

A Naive Bayes classifier for automatic correction of preposition and determiner errors in ESL text
Gerard Lynch, Erwan Moreau and Carl Vogel

KU Leuven at HOO-2012: A Hybrid Approach to Detection and Correction of Determiner and Preposition Errors in Non-native English Text
Li Quan, Oleksandr Kolomiyets and Marie-Francine Moens

The UI System in the HOO 2012 Shared Task on Error Correction
Alla Rozovskaya, Mark Sammons and Dan Roth

NAIST at the HOO 2012 Shared Task
Keisuke Sakaguchi, Yuta Hayashibe, Shuhei Kondo, Lis Kanashiro, Tomoya Mizumoto, Mamoru Komachi and Yuji Matsumoto

Memory-based text correction for preposition and determiner errors
Antal van den Bosch and Peter Berck

Helping Our Own: NTHU NLPLAB System Description
Jian-Cheng Wu, Joseph Chang, Yi-Chun Chen, Shih-Ting Huang, Mei-Hua Chen and Jason S. Chang

HOO 2012 Shared Task: UKP Lab System Description
Torsten Zesch and Jens Haase

3:30–4:00 **Break**

\+ 4:00–4:25

Crowdsourced Comprehension: Predicting Prerequisite Structure in Wikipedia
Partha Talukdar and William Cohen

\+ 4:25–4:50

Sense-Specific Lexical Information for Reading Assistance
Soojeong Eom, Markus Dickinson and Rebecca Sachs

Thursday, June 7, 2012 (continued)

+ 4:50–5:15

Evaluating the Meaning of Answers to Reading Comprehension Questions: A Semantics-Based Approach
Michael Hahn and Detmar Meurers

5:15–5:30 Closing Remarks

Question Ranking and Selection in Tutorial Dialogues

Lee Becker[a] and **Martha Palmer 2**[a] and **Sarel van Vuuren 3**[a] and **Wayne Ward 4**[a,b]
[a]The Center for Computational Language and Education Research (CLEAR)
University of Colorado Boulder
[b]Boulder Language Technologies
{lee.becker,martha.palmer,sarel.vanvuuren}@colorado.edu
wward@bltek.com

Abstract

A key challenge for dialogue-based intelligent tutoring systems lies in selecting follow-up questions that are not only context relevant but also encourage self-expression and stimulate learning. This paper presents an approach to ranking candidate questions for a given dialogue context and introduces an evaluation framework for this task. We learn to rank using judgments collected from expert human tutors, and we show that adding features derived from a rich, multi-layer dialogue act representation improves system performance over baseline lexical and syntactic features to a level in agreement with the judges. The experimental results highlight the important factors in modeling the questioning process. This work provides a framework for future work in automatic question generation and it represents a step toward the larger goal of directly learning tutorial dialogue policies directly from human examples.

1 Introduction

Socratic tutoring styles place an emphasis on eliciting information from the learner to help them build their own connections to the material. The role of a tutor in a Socratic dialogue is to scaffold the material and present questions that ultimately lead the student to an "A-ha!" moment. Numerous studies have illustrated the effectiveness of Socratic-style tutoring (VanLehn et al., 2007; Rose et al., 2001; Collins and Stevens, 1982); consequently recreating the behavior on a computer has long been a goal of research in Intelligent Tutoring Systems (ITS). Recent successes have shown the efficacy of conversational ITS (Graesser et al., 2005; Litman and Silliman, 2004; Ward et al., 2011b), however these systems are still not as effective as human tutors, and much improvement is needed before they can truly claim to be Socratic. Furthermore, development and tuning of tutorial dialogue behavior requires significant human effort.

While our overarching goal is to improve ITS by automatically learning tutorial dialogue strategies directly from expert tutor behavior, we focus on the crucial subtask of selecting follow-up questions. Although asking questions is only a subset of the overall tutoring process, it is still a complex process that requires understanding of the dialogue state, the student's ability, and the learning goals.

This work frames question selection as a task of scoring and ranking candidate questions for a specific point in the tutorial dialogue. Since dialogue is a dynamic process with multiple correct possibilities, we do not restrict ourselves only to the moves and questions found in a corpus of transcripts. Instead we posit "What if we had a fully automatic question generation system?" and subsequently use candidate questions hand-authored for each dialogue context. To explore the mechanisms involved in ranking follow-up questions against one other, we pair these questions with judgments of quality from expert human tutors and extract surface form and dialogue-based features to train machine learning classification models to rank the appropriateness of questions for specific points in a dialogue.

Our results show promise with our best question

ranking models exhibiting performance on par with expert human tutors. Furthermore these experiments demonstrate the utility and importance of rich dialogue move annotation for modeling decision making in conversation and tutoring.

2 Background and Related Works

Learning tutorial dialogue policies from corpora is a growing area of research in natural language processing and intelligent tutoring systems. Past studies have made use of hidden Markov models (Boyer et al., 2009a) and reinforcement learning (Chi et al., 2010; Chi et al., 2009; Chi et al., 2008) to discover tutoring strategies. However, these approaches are typically optimized to maximize learning gains, and are not necessarily focused on replicating human tutor behavior. Other work has explored specific factors in questioning such as when to ask "why" questions (Rose et al., 2003), provide hints (Tsovaltzi and Matheson, 2001), or insert discourse markers (Kim et al., 2000).

There is also an expanding body of work that applies ranking algorithms toward the task of question generation (QG) using approaches such as overgeneration-and-ranking (Heilman and Smith, 2010), language model ranking (Yao, 2010), and heuristics-based ranking (Agarwal and Mannem, 2011). While the focus of these efforts centers on issues of grammaticality, fluency, and content selection for automatic creation of standalone questions, we move to the higher level task of choosing context appropriate questions. Our work merges aspects of these QG approaches with the sentence planning tradition from natural language generation (Walker et al., 2001; Rambow et al., 2001). In sentence planning the goal is to select lexico-structural resources that encode communicative action. Rather than selecting representations, we use them directly as part of the feature space for learning functions to rank the questions' actual surface form realization. To our knowledge there has been no research in ranking the quality and suitability of questions within a tutorial dialogue context.

Because questioning tactics depend heavily on the curriculum and choice of pedagogy, we ground our investigations within the context of the My Science Tutor (MyST) intelligent tutoring system (Ward et al., 2011b), a conversational virtual tutor designed to improve science learning and understanding for students in grades 3-5 (ages 8-11). Students using MyST investigate and discuss science through natural spoken dialogues and multimedia interactions with a virtual tutor named Marni. The MyST dialogue design and tutoring style is based on a pedagogy called Questioning the Author (QtA) (Beck et al., 1996) which emphasizes open-ended questions and keying in on student language to promote self-explanation of concepts, and its curriculum is based on the Full Option Science System (FOSS) [1] a proven system for inquiry based learning.

3 Data Collection

3.1 MyST Logfiles and Transcripts

For these experiments, we use MyST transcripts collected in a Wizard-of-Oz (WoZ) condition with a human tutor inserted into the interaction loop. Project tutors trained in both QtA and in the tutorial subject matter served as the wizards. During a session tutors were responsible for accepting, overriding, and/or authoring system actions. Tutor wizards were also responsible for setting the current dialogue frame to indicate which of the learning goals was currently in focus. Students talked to MyST via microphone while MyST communicates using Text-to-Speech (TTS) in the WoZ setting. A typical MyST session revolves around a single FOSS lesson and lasts approximately 15 minutes. To obtain a dialogue transcript, tutor moves are taken directly from the system logfile, while student speech is manually transcribed from audio. In addition to the dialogue text, MyST records additional information such as timestamps and the current dialogue frame (i.e. learning goal). In total we make use of transcripts from 122 WoZ dialogues covering 10 units on magnetism and electricity and 2 in measurement and standards.

3.2 Dialogue Annotation

Lesson-independent analysis of dialogue requires a level of abstraction that reduces a dialogue to its underlying actions and intentions. To address this need we use the Dialogue Schema Unifying Speech and Semantics (DISCUSS) (Becker et al.,

[1] http://www.fossweb.com

2011), a multidimensional dialogue move taxonomy that captures both the pragmatic and semantic interpretation of an utterance. Instead of using one label, a DISCUSS move is a tuple composed of three dimensions: *Dialogue Act, Rhetorical Form, Predicate Type*. Together these labels account for the action, function, and content of an utterance. This scheme draws from past work in task-oriented dialogue acts (Bunt, 2009; Core and Allen, 1997), tutorial act taxonomies (Pilkington, 1999; Tsovaltzi and Karagjosova, 2004; Buckley and Wolska, 2008; Boyer et al., 2009b) discourse relations (Mann and Thompson, 1986) and question taxonomies (Graesser and Person, 1994; Nielsen et al., 2008).

Dialogue Act (22 tags): The dialogue act dimension is the top-level dimension in DISCUSS, and its values govern the possible values for the other dimensions. Though the DISCUSS dialogue act layer seeks to replicate the learnings from other well-established taxonomies like DIT++ (Bunt, 2009) or DAMSL (Core and Allen, 1997) wherever possible, the QtA style of pedagogy driving our tutoring sessions dictated the addition of two tutorial specific acts: marking and revoicing. A *mark* act highlights key words from the student's speech to draw attention to a particular term or concept. Like with marking, *revoicing* keys in on student language, but instead of highlighting specific words, a *revoice* act will summarize or refine the student's language to bring clarity to a concept.

Rhetorical Form (22 tags): Although the dialogue act is useful for identifying the speaker's intent, it gives no indication of how the speaker is advancing the conversation. The rhetorical form refines the dialogue act by providing a link to its surface form realization. Consider the questions "What is the battery doing?" and "Which one is the battery?". They would both be labeled with *Ask* dialogue acts, but they elicit two very different kinds of responses. The former, which elicits some form of description, would be labeled with a *Describe* rhetorical form, while the latter is seeking to *Identify* an object. Similarly an *Assert* act from a tutor could be coupled with a *Describe* rhetorical form to introduce new information or with a *Recap* to reconvey a major point.

Predicate Type (19 tags): Beyond knowing the propositional content of an utterance, it is useful to know how the entities and predicates in a response relate to one another. A student may mention several keywords that are semantically similar to the learning goals, but it is important for a tutor to recognize whether the student's language provides a deeper description of some phenomena or if it is simply a superficial observation. The Predicate Type aims to categorize the semantic relationships a student may talk about; whether it is a *Procedure*, a *Function*, a *Causal Relation*, or some other predicate type.

Reliability Metric	DA	RF	PT
Cohen's Kappa	0.75	0.72	0.63
Exact Agreement	0.80	0.66	0.56
Partial Agreement	0.89	0.77	0.68

Table 1: Inter-annotator agreement for DISCUSS types (DA=Dialogue Act, RF=Rhetorical Form, PT=Predicate Type)

3.2.1 Annotation

All transcripts used in this experiment have been annotated with DISCUSS labels at the turn level. A reliability study using 15% of the transcripts was conducted to assess inter-rater agreement of DISCUSS tagging. This consisted of 18 doubly annotated transcripts comprised of 828 dialogue utterances.

To assess inter-rater reliability we use Cohen's Kappa (κ) (Carletta, 1996). Because DISCUSS permits multiple labels per instance, we compute a κ value for each label and provide a mean for each DISCUSS dimension. To get an additional sense of agreement, we use two other metrics: exact agreement and partial agreement. For each of these metrics, we treat each annotators' annotations as a per class bag-of-labels. For exact agreement, each annotators' set of labels must match exactly to receive credit. Partial agreement is defined as the number of intersecting labels divided by the total number of unique labels. Together these statistics help to bound the reliability of the DISCUSS annotation. Table 1 lists all three metrics broken down by DISCUSS dimension. The κ values show fair agreement for the dialogue act and rhetorical form dimensions, whereas the predicate type shows more moderate agreement. This difference reflects the relative difficulty in labeling each dimension, and the agreement as a whole illustrates the open-endedness of the task.

3.3 Question Authoring

While the long-term plan for this work is to integrate fully automatic question generation into a tutoring system, for this study we opted to use manually authored questions. This allows us to remain focused on learning to identify context appropriate questions rather than confounding our experiments with issues of question grammaticality and well-formedness. Even though using multiple authors would provide greater diversity of questions, to avoid repeated effort and to maintain consistency in authoring we trained a single question author in both the FOSS material and MyST QtA techniques. Although he was free to author any question he found appropriate, our guidelines primarily emphasized authoring by making permutations aligned with DISCUSS dimensions while also permitting the author to incorporate changes in wording, learning-goal content, and tutoring tactics. For example, we taught him to consider how QtA moves such as *Revoicing*, *Marking*, or *Recapping* could alter otherwise similar questions. To minimize the risk of rater bias, we explicitly told our author to avoid using positive feedback expressions such as "Good job!" or "Great!". Table 2 illustrates how the combinations of DISCUSS labels, QtA tactics, and dialogue context drives the question generation process.

To simulate the conditions available to both the human WoZ and computer MyST tutors, the author was presented with the entire dialogue history preceding the decision point, the current dialogue frame (learning goal), and any visuals that may be on-screen. Question authoring contexts were manually selected to capture points where students provided responses to tutor questions. This eliminated the need to account for other dialogue behavior such as greetings, closings, or meta-behavior, and allowed us to focus on follow-up style questions. Because these question authoring contexts came from actual tutorial dialogues, we also extracted the original turn provided by the tutor, and we filtered out turns that did not contain questions related to the lesson content. Our corpus has 205 question authoring contexts comprised of 1025 manually authored questions and 131 questions extracted from the original transcript yielding 1156 questions in total.

3.4 Ratings Collection

To rate questions, we enlisted the help of four tutors who had previously served as project tutors and wizards. The raters were presented with much of the same information used during question authoring. The interface included the entire dialogue history preceding the question decision point and a list of up to 6 candidate questions (5 manually authored, 1 taken from the original transcript if applicable). To give a more complete tutoring context, raters also had access to the lessons' learning goals and the interactive visuals used by MyST.

Previous studies in rating questions (Becker et al., 2009) have found poor inter-rater agreement when rating questions in isolation. To decrease the task's difficulty we instead ask raters to simultaneously score all candidate questions. Because we did not want to bias raters, we did not specify specific criteria for question quality. Instead we instructed the raters to consider the question's role in assisting student understanding of the learning goals and to think about factors such as tutorial pacing, context appropriateness, and content. Scores were collected using an ordinal 10-point scale ranging from 1 (lowest/worst) to 10 (highest/best).

Each set of questions was rated by at least three tutors, and rater assignments were selected to ensure raters never score questions from sessions they tutored themselves. In total we collected ratings for 1156 question representing a total of 205 question contexts distributed across 30 transcripts.

3.4.1 Rater Agreement

Because these judgments are subjective, a key challenge in this work centers on understanding to what degree the tutors agree with one another. Since our goal is to rank questions and not to score questions, we convert each tutors scores for a given context into a rank-ordered list. To compute inter-rater agreement in ranking, we use Kendall's-Tau (τ) rank correlation coefficient. This measure is a non-parametric statistic that quantifies the similarity in orderings of data, and it is closely tied to AUC, the area under the receiver operating characteristics (ROC) curve. Though Kendall's-τ can vary from -1 to 1, its value is highly task dependent, and it is typ-

	...			
T:	*Tell me more about what is happening with the electricity in a complete circuit.*			
S:	*Well the battery sends all the electricity in a circuit to the motor so the motor starts to go.*			
	Candidate Question	Frame	Element	DISCUSS
Q1	Roll over the switch and then in your own words, tell me again what a complete or closed circuit is all about.	Same	Same	Direct/Task/Visual Ask/Describe/Configuration
Q2	How is this circuit setup? Is it open or closed?	Same	Same	Ask/Select/Configuration
Q3	To summarize, a closed circuit allows the electricity to flow and the motor to spin. Now in this circuit, we have a new component. The switch. What is the switch all about?	Diff	Diff	Assert/Recap/Proposition Direct/Task/Visual Ask/Describe/Function
Q4	You said something about the motor spinning in a complete circuit. Tell me more about that.	Same	Same	Revoice/None/None Ask/Elaborate/CausalRelation

Table 2: Example dialogue context snippet and a collection of candidate questions. The frame, element, and DISCUSS columns show how the questions vary from one another.

ically lower when the range of possible choices is narrow as it is in this task. To get a single score we average τ values across all sets of questions (contexts) and all pairs of raters. The mean value for all pairs of raters and contexts is $\tau = 0.1478$. The inter-rater statistics are shown in table 3. While inter-rater agreement is fairly modest, we do see lots of variation between different pairs of tutors. Additionally, we found that a pair of raters agreed on the top rated question 33% of the time. This suggests that despite their common training and experience, the raters may be using different criteria in rating.

To assess the tutors' internal consistency, we had each tutor re-rate 60 sets of questions approximately two months after their first trial, and we computed self-agreement Kendall's-τ values using the method above. These statistics are listed in the bottom row of table 3. In contrast with the inter-rater agreement, self-agreement is much more consistent giving further evidence for a difference in criteria. Together self and inter-rater agreement help bound expected system performance in ranking.

	rater A	rater B	rater C	rater D
rater A	X	0.2590	0.1418	0.0075
rater B	0.2590	X	0.1217	0.2370
rater C	0.1418	0.1217	X	0.0540
rater D	0.0075	0.2370	0.0540	X
mean	0.1361	0.2059	0.1058	0.0995
self	0.4802	0.4022	0.2327	0.3531

Table 3: Inter-rater rank agreement (Kendall's-τ). The bottom row is the self-agreement for contexts they rated in two separate trials.

4 Automatic Ranking

Because we are more interested in learning to predict which questions are more suitable for a given tutoring scenario than we are in assigning specific scores to questions, we approach the task of question selection as a ranking task. To create a gold-standard for training and evaluation we first need to convert the collective ratings for a set of questions into a rank-ordered list. While the most straightforward way to make this conversion is to average the ratings for each item, this approach assumes all raters operate on the same scale. Furthermore, a single score does not account for how a question relates to other candidate questions. Instead we create a single rank-order by tabulating pairwise wins for all pairs of questions $q_i, q_j, (i \neq j)$ within a given dialogue context C. If $rating(q_i) > rating(q_j)$, questions q_i receives a win. This is summed across all raters for the context. The question(s) with the most wins has rank 1. Questions with an equal number of wins are considered tied and are given the average ranking of their ordinal positions. For example if two questions are tied for second place, they are each assigned a ranking of 2.5.

Using this rank-ordering we then train a pairwise classifier to learn a preferences function (Cohen et al., 1998) that determines if one question has a better rank than another. For each question q_i within a context C, we construct a vector of features ϕ_i. For a pair of questions q_i and q_j, we then create a new vector using the difference of features: $\Phi(q_i, q_j, C) = \phi_i - \phi_j$. For training, if $rank(q_i) < rank(q_j)$, the classification is positive otherwise it is negative. To account for the possibility of ties, and to make the difference measure appear symmetric, we train both combinations (q_i, q_j) and (q_j, q_i). During decoding, we run the trained classifier on all pairs and tabulate wins using the approach described above.

For our experiments we train pairwise classifiers using Mallet's Maximum Entropy (McCallum, 2002) and SVM^{Light}'s Support Vector Machines models (Joachims, 1999). We also use SVM^{Rank} (Joachims, 1999), which performs the same maximum margin separation as SVM^{Light}, but uses Kendall's-τ as a loss function to optimize for rank ordering. We run SVM^{Rank} with a linear kernel and model parameters of $c = 2.0$ and $\epsilon = 0.0156$. For MaxEnt, we use Mallet's default model parameters. Training and evaluation are carried out using 10-fold cross validation (3 transcripts per fold, approximately 7 dialogue contexts per transcript). Folds are partitioned by FOSS unit, to ensure training and evaluation are on different lessons. To explore the impact of DISCUSS representations on this question ranking task, we train and evaluate models by incrementally adding additional information extracted from the DISCUSS annotation.

4.1 Features

When designing features for this task, we wanted to capture the factors that may play a role in the tutor's decision making process during question selection. When rating, scorers may consider factors such as the question's surface form, lesson relevance, contextual relevance. The subsections below detail the motivations and intuitions behind these factors.

4.1.1 Surface Form Features

When presented with a list of questions, a rater likely bases the decision on his or her initial reaction to the questions' wording. In some cases, wording may supercede any other decisions regarding educational value or dialogue cohesiveness. Question verbosity is captured by the *number of words in the question* feature. Analysis of rater comments also suggested that preferences are often tied to the question's form and structure. A rough measure of form comes from the *Wh-word* features to mark the presence of the following question words: who, what, why, where, when, which, and how. Additionally we use the *bag-of-part-of-speech-tags (POS)* features to provide another aspect of the question's structure.

4.1.2 Lexical Similarity Features

Past work (Ward et al., 2011a) has shown that entrainment, the process of automatic alignment between dialogue partners, is a useful predictor of learning and is a key factor in facilitating a successful conversation. For question selection, we hypothesize that successful tutors ask questions that display some degree of semantic entrainment with student utterances. In MyST-based tutoring, dialogue actions are driven by the goal of eliciting student responses that address the learning goals for the lesson. Consequently, choosing an appropriate question may depend on how closely student responses align with the learning goals. To model both entrainment and lexical similarity we extract features for unigram and bigram overlap of words, word-lemmas, and part-of-speech tags between the pairs below.

- The candidate question and the student's last utterance
- The candidate question and the last tutor's utterance
- The candidate question and the text of the current learning goal
- The candidate question and the text of the other learning goals

Example learning goals for a lesson on circuits are provided in table 4. The current learning goal is simply the learning goal in focus at the point of question asking according to the MyST logfile. Other learning goals are all other goals for the lesson. Using the example from the table, if goal 2 is the current learning goal, then goals 1 and 3 are the other goals.

Goal 1:	*Wires carry electricity and can connect components*
Goal 2:	*Bulb receives electricity and transforms electricity into heat*
Goal 3:	*A circuit provides a pathway for energy to flow*

Table 4: Example learning goals

4.1.3 DISCUSS Features

The lexical and surface form features provide some cues about the content of the question, but they do not account for the action or intent in tutoring. The DISCUSS annotation allows us to bridge between the question's semantics and pragmatically and focus on what differentiates one question from another. Basic DISCUSS features include bags of Dialogue Acts (DA), Rhetorical Forms (RF), and Predicate types (PT) found in the question's DISCUSS annotation. We capture the question's dialogue cohesiveness with binary features indicating whether or not the question's RF and PT match those found in the previous student and tutor turns.

4.1.4 Contextualized DISCUSS Features

In tutoring, follow-up questions are licensed by the questions that precede them. For example a tutor may be less likely to ask how an object functions until after the object has first been identified by the student. Along a different dimension, a tutor's line of questioning may change to match a student's understanding of the material. Struggling students may require additional opportunities to explain themselves, while advanced students may benefit more from a more rapid pace of instruction.

We model the conditional relevance of moves by computing dialogue act transition probabilities from our corpus of DISCUSS annotated tutorial dialogues. Although DISCUSS allows multiple tags per dialogue turn, we simplify probability calculations by treating each DISCUSS tuple as a separate event, and tallying all pairs of turn-turn labels. A DISCUSS tuple consists of a Dialogue Act (DA), Rhetorical Form (RF), and Predicate Type (PT), and we use different subsets of the tuple to compute the transition probabilities listed in equations 1-3. All probabilities are computed using Laplace-smoothing. When extracting features, we sum the log of the probabilities for each DISCUSS label present in the question.

MyST models dialogue as a sequence of semantic frames which correspond to specific learning goals. For natural language understanding, MyST uses Phoenix semantic grammars (Ward, 1994) to identify which elements within these frames have been filled. To account for student progress in question asking, we compute the conditional probability of a DISCUSS label given the percentage of elements filled in the current dialogue frame (equation 4). This progress percentage is discretized into bins of 0-25%, 25-50%, 50-75%, and 75-100%.

$$p(DA, RF, PT_{question}|DA, RF, PT_{stud.\ turn}) \quad (1)$$

$$p(DA, RF_{question}|DA, RF_{student\ turn}) \quad (2)$$

$$p(PT_{question}|PT_{student\ turn}) \quad (3)$$

$$p(DA, RF, PT_{ques.}|\%\ elements\ filled) \quad (4)$$

4.2 Evaluation

To evaluate our systems' performance in ranking, we use two measures commonly used in information retrieval: the Mean Kendall's-τ measure described in section 3.4.1 and Mean Reciprocal Rank (MRR). MRR is the average of the multiplicative inverse of the rank of the highest ranking question across all contexts. To account for ties we use the Tau-b variant of Kendall's-τ , and for MRR we compute reciprocal rank by averaging the system rankings for all of the questions tied for first. To obtain a gold-standard ranking for comparison, we combine individual raters' ratings using the approached described in section 4.

5 Results and Discussion

We trained several models to investigate how different feature classes influence overall performance in ranking. The results for these experiments are listed in Table 5. Because we found comparable performance between MaxEnt and SVM^{Light}, we only report results for MaxEnt and SVM^{Rank} models. In addition to MRR and Kendall's-τ , we list the number of concordances and discordances in pairwise classification to give the reader another sense of the accuracy associated with rank agreement.

Random Baseline: On average, assigning random ranks will yield mean τ=0 and MRR=0.408.

Model	Features	Mean Kendall's-τ	Num. Concord.	Num. Discord.	Pairwise Accuracy	MRR
MaxEnt	CONTEXT+DA+PT+MATCH+POS-	**0.211**	1560	**974**	**0.616**	0.516
SVM^{Rank}	CONTEXT+DA+PT+MATCH+POS-	0.190	**1725**	1154	0.599	**0.555**
MaxEnt	CONTEXT+DA+RF+PT+MATCH+POS-	0.185	1529	1014	0.601	0.512
MaxEnt	DA+RF+PT+MATCH+POS-	0.179	1510	1009	0.599	0.503
MaxEnt	DA+RF+PT+MATCH+	0.163	1506	1044	0.591	0.485
MaxEnt	DA+RF+PT+	0.147	1500	1075	0.583	0.480
MaxEnt	DA+RF+	0.130	1458	1082	0.574	0.476
MaxEnt	DA+	0.120	1417	1076	0.568	0.458
SVM^{Rank}	Baseline	0.108	1601	1278	0.556	0.473
MaxEnt	Baseline	0.105	1410	1115	0.558	0.448

Table 5: System scores by feature set and and machine learning model. Presence or absence of specific features is denoted with a '+' or '-' otherwise the label refers to a set of features. The **Baseline** features consist of the Surface Form and Lexical Similarity features described in sections 4.1.1 and 4.1.2. **POS** are the bag-of-POS surface form features. **DA**, **RF**, and **PT** refer to the DISCUSS presence features for the Dialogue Act, Rhetorical Form, and Predicate Type dimensions described in section 4.1.3. **MATCH** refers specifically to the RF and PT match features. **CONTEXT** refers to the Contextualized DISCUSS features described in section 4.1.4. The best scores for each column appear in boldface.

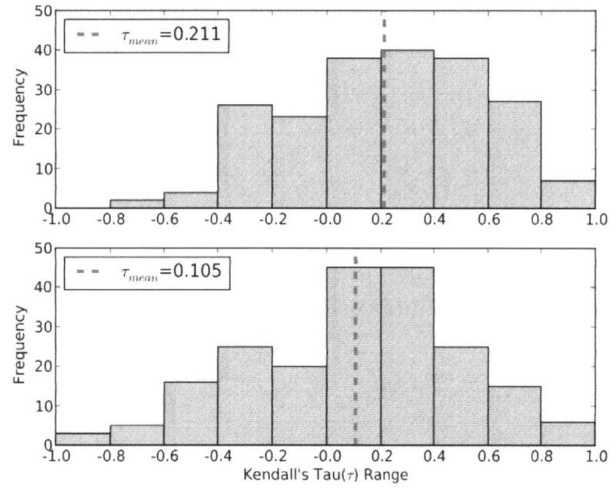

Figure 1: Distribution of per-context Kendall's-τ values for the top-scoring system (top), and the baseline system (bottom).

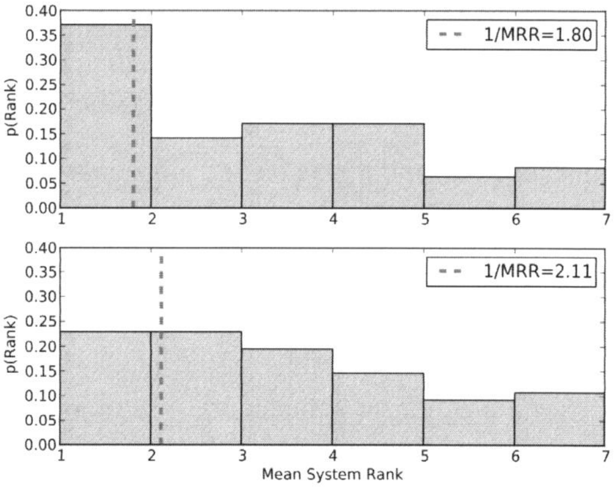

Figure 2: Distribution of per-context system ranks for the highest rated question for the top-scoring system (top), and the baseline system (bottom). These ranks are the inverse of the reciprocal rank used to calculate MRR.

Baseline System: Our baseline system used all of the surface form and lexical similarity features described above. This set of features achieves the highest rank agreement ($\tau = 0.105$) using maximum entropy and the highest MRR (0.473) with SVM^{Rank} . This improvement over the random baseline suggests there is a correlation between a question's ranking and its surface form.

DISCUSS System: Table 5 shows system performance steadily improves as additional DISCUSS features are included in the model. When using DISCUSS features, removing the part-of-speech features gives an additional bump in performance suggesting that there is an overlap in information between DISCUSS representations and POS tags. Finally, adding contextualized DISCUSS features pushes our ranking models to their highest level of agreement with $\tau = 0.211$ using MaxEnt and MRR=0.555 using SVM^{Rank} . Inspection of the MRR values shows that without taking into account the possibility of ties the baseline system selects the top-ranked question in 44/205 (21.4%) contexts. While the system with the best MRR score, correctly chooses the top-ranked question in 71/205 (34.6%) contexts – a rate comparable to how often a pair of raters agreed on the number-one item (33.4%).

Application of the Wilcoxon signed-rank test shows the DISCUSS system exhibits statistically significant improvement over the baseline system in its distribution of Kendall's-τ values ($n = 205, z = 7350, p < 0.001$) and distribution of reciprocal ranks ($n = 205, z = 3739, p < 0.001$). Figures 1 and 2 give visual confirmation of this improvement, and highlight the overall reduction in negative τ values as well as the greater-than-50% increase in likelihood of selecting the best question first.

To get another perspective on system performance, we evaluated our human raters on the gold-standard rankings from the subset of questions used for assessing internal agreement. This yielded a mean τ between 0.2589 and 0.3619. If we remove ratings so that the gold-standard does not include the rater under evaluation, tutor performance drops to a range of 0.1523 to 0.2432, which is roughly centered around the agreement exhibited by our best-performing system.

Looking at the impact of learning algorithms we see that SVM^{Rank} tends to perform better on MRR while the pairwise maximum entropy models yield higher τ's. One possible explanation for this discrepancy may stem from the ranking algorithms' different treatment of ties. The pairwise model permits ties, whereas the scores produced by SVM^{Rank} produce a strict order. Without ties, it is difficult to exactly match the raters' orderings which had numerous ties, which can in turn produce an overall higher number of concordances and discordances than the pairwise classification model.

6 Conclusions and Future Work

We have introduced a framework for learning and evaluating models for ranking and selecting questions for a given point in a tutorial dialogue. Furthermore these experiments show that it is feasible to learn this behavior by coupling predefined questions with ratings from trained tutors. Supplementing our baseline surface form and lexical similarity features with additional features extracted from the dialogue context and DISCUSS dialogue act annotation improves system performance in ranking to a level on par with expert human tutors. These results illustrate how question asking depends not only on the form of the question but also on the underlying dialogue action, function and content.

In the near future we plan to train models on individual tutors to investigate which factors drive individual preferences in question asking. We also plan to characterize system performance using automatically labeled DISCUSS annotation. Lastly, we feel these results provide a natural starting point to explore automatic generation of questions from the DISCUSS dialogue move representation.

Acknowledgments

This work was supported by grants from the NSF (DRL-0733322, DRL-0733323), the IES (R3053070434) and the DARPA GALE program (Contract No. HR0011-06-C-0022, a supplement for VerbNet attached to the subcontract from the BBN-AGILE Team). Any findings, recommendations, or conclusions are those of the author and do not necessarily represent the views of NSF, IES, or DARPA.

References

Manish Agarwal and Prashanth Mannem. 2011. Automatic gap-fill question generation from text books automatic gap-fill question generation from text books automatic gap-fill questions from text books. In *Proceedings of the Sixth Workshop on Innovative Use of NLP for Building Educational Applications*.

I. L. Beck, M. G. McKeown, J. Worthy, C. A. Sandora, and L. Kucan. 1996. Questioning the author: A year-long classroom implementation to engage students with text. *The Elementary School Journal*, 96(4):387–416.

L. Becker, R. D. Nielsen, and W. Ward. 2009. What a pilot study says about running a question generation challenge. In *Proceedings of the Second Workshop on Question Generation*, Brighton, England, July.

L. Becker, W. Ward, S. van Vuuren, and M. Palmer. 2011. Discuss: A dialogue move taxonomy layered over semantic representations. In *In Proceedings of the International Conference on Computational Semantics (IWCS) 2011*, Oxford, England, January 12-14.

K.E. Boyer, E.Y. Ha, M. Wallis, R. Phillips, M.A. Vouk, and J.C. Lester. 2009a. Discovering tutorial dialogue strategies with hidden markov models. In *Proceedings of the 14th International Conference on Artificial Intelligence in Education (AIED '09)*, pages 141–148, Brighton, U.K.

K.E. Boyer, W.J. Lahti, R. Phillips, M. D. Wallis, M. A. Vouk, and J. C. Lester. 2009b. An empirically derived question taxonomy for task-oriented tutorial dialogue. In *Proceedings of the Second Workshop on Question Generation*, pages 9–16, Brighton, U.K.

M. Buckley and M. Wolska. 2008. A classification of dialogue actions in tutorial dialogue. In *Proceedings of COLING 2008*, pages 73–80. ACL.

H. C. Bunt. 2009. The DIT++ taxonomy for functional dialogue markup. In *Proc. EDAML 2009*.

Jean Carletta. 1996. Assessing agreement on classification tasks: The kappa statistic. *Computational Linguistics*, 22(2):pp. 249–254.

M. Chi, P. Jordan, K. VanLehn, and M. Hall. 2008. Reinforcement learning-based feature selection for developing pedagogically effective tutorial dialogue tactics. In Ryan S. Baker, Tiffany Barnes, and Joseph Becker, editors, *Proceedings of the 1st International Conference on Educational Data Mining*, pages pp258–265.

M. Chi, P. W. Jordan, K. VanLehn, and D. J. Litman. 2009. To elicit or to tell: Does it matter? In *Artificial Intelligence in Education*, pages 197–204.

M. Chi, K. VanLehn, and D. Litman. 2010. Do micro-level tutorial decisions matter: Applying reinforcement learning to induce do micro-level tutorial decisions matter. In Vincent Aleven, Judy Kay, and Jack Mostow, editors, *Preceedings of the 10th Internation Confernce on Intelligent Tutoring Systems (ITS 2010)*.

William W. Cohen, Robert E. Schapire, and Yoram Singer. 1998. Learning to order things. In *Advances in Neural Information Processing Systems 10 (NIPS 1998)*.

A. Collins and A. Stevens. 1982. Goals and methods for inquiry teachers. *Advances in Instructional Psychology*, 2.

M. G. Core and J.F. Allen. 1997. Coding dialogs with the DAMSL annotation scheme. In *AAAI Fall Symposium*, pages 28–35.

A.C. Graesser and N.K. Person. 1994. Question asking during tutoring. *American Educational Research Journal*, 31:104–137.

A.C. Graesser, P. Chipman, B.C Haynes, and A. Olney. 2005. Autotutor: An intelligent tutoring system with mixed-initiative dialogue. *IEEE Transactions in Education*, 48:612–618.

M. Heilman and N. A. Smith. 2010. Good question! statistical ranking for question generation. In *Proceedings of NAACL/HLT 2010*.

T. Joachims. 1999. Making large-scale svm learning practical. In B. Schölkopf, C. Burges, and A. Smola, editors, *Advances in Kernel Methods - Support Vector Learning*. MIT-Press.

J.H. Kim, M. Glass, R. Freedman, and M.W. Evens. 2000. Learning the use of discourse markers in tutorial dialogue learning the use of discourse markers in tutorial dialogue. In *Proceedings of the 22nd Annual Conference of the Cognitive Science Society*.

D. Litman and S. Silliman. 2004. Itspoke: An intelligent tutoring spoken dialogue system. In *Companion Proceedings of the Human Language Technology Conference: 4th Meeting of the North American Chapter of the Association for Computational Linguistics (HLT/NAACL)*.

W.C. Mann and S.A Thompson. 1986. Rhetorical structure theory: Description and construction of text structures. In *In Proceedings of the Third International Workshop on Text Generation*, August.

A. K. McCallum, 2002. *MALLET: A Machine Learning for Language Toolkit*. http://mallet.cs.umass.edu.

R. D. Nielsen, J. Buckingham, G. Knoll, B. Marsh, and L. Palen. 2008. A taxonomy of questions for question generation. In *Proceedings of the Workshop on the Question Generation Shared Task and Evaluation Challenge*, September.

R.M. Pilkington. 1999. Analysing educational discourse: The discount scheme. Technical Report 99/2, Computer Based Learning Unit, University of Leeds.

Owen Rambow, Monica Rogati, and Marilyn A. Walker. 2001. Evaluating a trainable sentence planner for a spoken dialogue system evaluating a trainable sentence planner for a spoken dialogue system. In *Proceedings of the 39th Annual Meeting of the Association for Computational Linguistics (ACL 2001)*.

C.P. Rose, P. Jordan, M. Ringenberg, S. Siler, K. VanLehn, and A. Weinstein. 2001. A comparative evaluation of socratic versus didactic tutoring. In *Proceedings of Cognitive Sciences Society*.

C.P. Rose, D. Bhembe, S. Siler, R. Srivastava, and K. VanLehn. 2003. The role of why questions in effective human tutoring. In *Proceedings of Artificial Intelligence in Education (AIED 2003)*.

D. Tsovaltzi and E. Karagjosova. 2004. A view on dialogue move taxonomies for tutorial dialogues. In *Proceedings of SIGDIAL 2004*, pages 35–38. ACL.

D. Tsovaltzi and C. Matheson. 2001. Formalising hinting in tutorial dialogues. In *In EDILOG: 6th workshop on the semantics and pragmatics of dialogue*, pages 185–192.

K. VanLehn, A.C. Graesser, G.T. Jackson, P. Jordan, A. Olney, and C.P. Rose. 2007. When are tutorial dialogues more effective than reading? *Cognitive Science*, 31(1):3–62.

Marilyn A. Walker, Owen Rambow, and Monica Rogati. 2001. SPOT: A trainable sentence planner. In *Proceedings of the North American Meeting of the Association for Computational Linguistics (NAACL)*.

A. Ward, D. Litman, and M. Eskenazi. 2011a. Predicting change in student motivation by measuring cohesion between predicting change in student motivation by measuring cohesion between tutor and student. In *Proceedings of the Sixth Workshop on Innovative Use of NLP for Building Educational Applications*, pages 136–141.

W. Ward, R. Cole, D. Bolaños, C. Buchenroth-Martin, E. Svirsky, S. van Vuuren, T. Weston, J. Zheng, and L. Becker. 2011b. My science tutor: A conversational multi-media virtual tutor for elementary school science. *ACM Transactions on Speech and Language Processing (TSLP)*, 7(4), August.

W. Ward. 1994. Extracting information from spontaneous speech. In *Proceedings of the International Conference on Speech and Language Processing (ICSLP)*.

Xuchen Yao. 2010. Question generation with minimal recursion semantics. Master's thesis, Saarland University.

Identifying science concepts and student misconceptions in an interactive essay writing tutor

Steven Bethard
University of Colorado
Boulder, Colorado, USA
steven.bethard@colorado.edu

Ifeyinwa Okoye
University of Colorado
Boulder, Colorado, USA
ifeyinwa.okoye@colorado.edu

Md. Arafat Sultan
University of Colorado
Boulder, Colorado, USA
arafat.sultan@colorado.edu

Haojie Hang
University of Colorado
Boulder, Colorado, USA
haojie.hang@colorado.edu

James H. Martin
University of Colorado
Boulder, Colorado, USA
james.martin@colorado.edu

Tamara Sumner
University of Colorado
Boulder, Colorado, USA
tamara.sumner@colorado.edu

Abstract

We present initial steps towards an interactive essay writing tutor that improves science knowledge by analyzing student essays for misconceptions and recommending science webpages that help correct those misconceptions. We describe the five components in this system: identifying core science concepts, determining appropriate pedagogical sequences for the science concepts, identifying student misconceptions in essays, aligning student misconceptions to science concepts, and recommending webpages to address misconceptions. We provide initial models and evaluations of the models for each component.

1 Introduction

Students come to class with a variety of misconceptions present in their science knowledge. For example, science assessments developed by the American Association for the Advancement of Science (AAAS)[1] showed that 49% of American 6th-8th graders believe that the Earth's tectonic plates are only feet thick (while in fact they are miles thick) and that 48% of American 6th-8th graders believe that atoms of a solid are not moving (while in fact all atoms are in constant motion). A key challenge for interactive tutoring systems is thus to identify and correct such student misconceptions.

In this article, we develop an interactive essay writing tutor that tries to address these challenges. The tutor first examines a set of science webpages to identify key concepts (Section 4) and attempts to order the science concepts in a pedagogically appropriate learning path (Section 5). Then the tutor examines a student essay and identifies misconception sentences (Section 6) and aligns these misconceptions to the true science concepts (Section 7). Finally, the tutor suggests science webpages that can help the student address each of the misconceptions (Section 8).

The key contributions of this work are:

- Demonstrating that a summarization approach can identify core science concepts
- Showing how a learning path model can be bootstrapped from webpages with grade metadata
- Developing models for misconception identification based on textual entailment techniques
- Presenting an information retrieval approach to aligning misconceptions to science concepts
- Designing a system that recommends webpages to address student misconceptions

2 Related work

Interactive tutoring systems have been designed for a variety of domains and applications. Dialog-based tutoring systems, such as Why2-Atlas (VanLehn et al., 2002), AutoTutor (Graesser et al., 2004) and MetaTutor (Azevedo et al., 2008), interact with students via questions and answers. Student knowledge is judged by comparing student responses to knowledge bases of domain concepts and misconceptions. These knowledge bases are typically manually curated, and a new knowledge base must be constructed for each new domain where the tutor is to be used.

[1] http://assessment.aaas.org/

Essay-based tutoring systems, such as Summary Street (Wade-Stein and Kintsch, 2004) or CLICK (de la Chica et al., 2008b), interact with students who are writing a summary or essay. They compare what the student has written to domain knowledge in the form of textbooks or webpages. They typically do not require a knowledge base to be manually constructed, instead using natural language processing techniques to compare the student's essay to the information in the textbooks or webpages.

The current work is inspired by these essay-based tutoring systems, where interaction revolves around essay writing. However, where Summary Street relies primarily upon measuring how much of a textbook a student essay has "covered", we aim to give more detailed assessments that pinpoint specific student misconceptions. CLICK targets a similar goal to ours, but assumes that accurate knowledge maps can be generated for both the domain knowledge and for each student essay. Our approach does not require the automatic generation of knowledge maps, instead working directly with the sentences in the student essays and the webpages of science domain knowledge.

3 System overview

Our system is composed of five key components. First, a core concept identifier examines domain knowledge (webpages) and identifies key concepts (sentences) that describe the most important pieces of knowledge in the domain. Second, a concept sequencer assigns a pedagogically appropriate order in which a student should learn the identified core concepts. Third, a misconception identifier examines the student essay and identifies sentences that describe misconceptions the student has about the domain. Fourth, a misconception-concept aligner finds a core concept that can be used to correct each misconception. Finally, a recommender takes all the information about core concepts and student misconceptions, decides what order to address the misconceptions in, and identifies a set of resources (webpages) for the student to read.

To assemble this system, we draw on a variety of existing datasets (and some data collection of our own). For example, we use data from an annotation study of concept coreness to evaluate our model for identifying domain concepts, and we use data from science assessments of the American Association for the Advancement of Science to train and evaluate our model for identifying misconceptions. We use this disparate data to establish baseline models for each of the tutor's components. In the near future, this baseline tutoring system will be used to collect student essays and other data that will allow us to develop more sophisticated model for each component.

4 Identifying core concepts

This first module aims at automatically identifying a set of *core concepts* in a given set of digital library resources or webpages. Core concepts in a subject domain are critical ideas necessary to support deep science learning and transfer in that domain. From a digital learning perspective, availability of such concepts helps in providing pedagogical feedback to learners to support robust learning and also in prioritizing instructional intervention (e.g., deciding the order in which to treat student misconceptions). A concept can be materialized using different levels of linguistic expressions (e.g. phrases, sentences or paragraphs), but for this work, we focus only on individual sentences as expressions of concepts.

We used COGENT (de la Chica et al., 2008a), a multi-document summarization system to extract concepts (i.e. sentences) from a given set of resources. In the following two subsections, we describe the COGENT system, discuss how we used it for core concept extraction and report the results of its evaluation of effectiveness.

4.1 Model

COGENT is a text summarizer that builds on MEAD (Radev et al., 2004), a multidocument summarization and evaluation platform . MEAD was originally developed to summarize news articles. COGENT aims to generate pedagogically useful summaries from educational resources.

COGENT extends MEAD by incorporating new features in the summarization process. MEAD uses a set of generic (i.e. domain-independent) features to evaluate each sentence in the given set of documents. These features include the length of the sentence, the distance from the sentence to the beginning of the document, etc. Individual scores of a sentence along these dimensions are combined to assign a total score to the sentence. After removing redundant sentences, MEAD then generates a summary using the sentences that had the highest scores. A user-specified parameter determines the number of sentences included in the summary.

COGENT extends this framework by incorporating new domain-general and domain-specific features in the sentence scoring process. The domain-general features include a *document structure* feature, which takes into account a sentence's level in terms of HTML headings, and a *content word density* feature, which computes the ratio of content words to function words. The domain-specific features include an *educational standards* feature, which uses a TF-IDF based textual similarity score between a sentence and nationally recognized educational goals from the American Association for the Advancement of Science (AAAS) Benchmarks (Project2061., 1993) and the associated National Science Education Standards (NRC, 1996), and a *gazetteer* feature, which scores sentences highly that mention many unique names from a gazetteer of named entities.

While in the past, COGENT was used primarily as a summarization system, in the current work, we evaluate its utility as a means of identifying core concepts. That is, are the top sentences selected by COGENT also the sentences describing the key science concepts in the domain?

4.2 Evaluation

We evaluate the core concept extraction module by assessing the extracted concepts against human expert annotations. We ran an annotation study where two human experts assigned "coreness" ratings to a selected set of sentences collected from digital resources in three science domains: *Plate Tectonics*, *Weather and Climate*, and *Biological Evolution*. These experts had been recruited based on their training and expertise in the selected subject domains.

First, a set of digital resources was selected from the Digital Library for Earth System Education (DLESE) [2] across the three subject domains. Then COGENT was used to extract the top 5% sentences for each domain. The experts then annotated each extracted sentence with its coreness rating on a scale

	Extraction %			
	0.5%	1.0%	2.5%	5.0%
Plate Tectonics	3.33	3.27	3.00	2.81
Weather and Climate	3.13	2.97	3.07	2.99
Biological Evolution	2.00	2.13	2.46	2.25

Table 1: Average coreness of sentences extracted at different percentages in each domain

of 1 to 4, 4 being the highest. Human annotation is a time-consuming process and this is why we had to limit the number of extracted sentences to a moderate 5% (which is still more than 400 sentences). 17% of the sentences were double annotated and the inter-rater reliability, measured by Spearman's rho, was 0.38. These expert ratings of sentences form the basis of our evaluation.

Table 1 shows the average coreness assigned by the experts to sentences extracted by COGENT in each domain, for different extraction percentages. For example, if COGENT is used to extract the top 1% of sentences from all the *Plate Tectonics* resources, then the average of their coreness ratings (as assigned by the experts) is 3.27, representing a high level of coreness. This is essentially a measure of the precision of COGENT at 1% extraction. Note that we cannot calculate a measure of recall without asking experts to annotate all of the domain sentences, a time consuming task which was outside of the scope of this study.

The performance of COGENT was the best in the *Plate Tectonics* domain since the domain-aware features (e.g. the gazetteer features) used to train COGENT were selected from this domain. In the "near domain" of *Weather and Climate*, the performance is still good, but performance falls in the "far domain" of *Biological Evolution*, because of the significant differences between the training domain and the test domain. In the two latter domains, the performance of COGENT was also inconsistent in that with an increase in the extraction percentage, the average coreness increased in some cases and decreased in others. This inconsistency and overall degradation in performance in the two latter domains are indicative of the importance of introducing domain-aware features into COGENT.

It is evident from the values in Table 1 that the core concepts extraction module does a decent job,

[2] http://www.dlese.org

especially when trained with appropriate domain-aware features.

5 Sequencing core concepts

The goal of this next component is to take a set of core science concepts (sentences), as produced by the preceding module, and predict an appropriate sequence in which those concepts should be learned by the student. Some concepts serve as building blocks for other concepts, and thus it is essential to learn the basic concepts first (and address any misconceptions associated with them) before moving on to other concepts that depend on the basic concepts. For example, a student must first understand the concept of tectonic plates before they can understand the concept of a convergent plate boundary. The sequence of core concepts that results from this module will serve as input for the later module that prioritizes a student's misconceptions.

There may exist several different but reasonable concept sequences (also known as *learning paths*) – the goal of this component is to recommend at least one of these. As a first step, we focus on generating a single concept sequence that represents a general path through the learning goals, much like textbooks and curriculums do.

5.1 Models

Our model for concept sequencing is a pair-wise ordering model, that takes two concepts c_1 and c_2, and predicts whether c_1 should come before or after c_2 in the recommended learning path. Formally,

$$\text{SEQUENCE}(c_1, c_2) = \begin{cases} 0 & \text{if } c_1 < c_2 \\ 1 & \text{if } c_1 \geq c_2 \end{cases}$$

To generate a complete ordering of concepts, we construct a precedence table from these pair-wise judgments and generate a path that is consistent with these judgments.

We learn the SEQUENCE model as a supervised classifier, where a feature vector is extracted for each of the two concepts and the two feature vectors, concatenated, serve as the input to the classifier. For each word in each concept, we include the following two features:

- **local word count** - the number of times the word appeared in this concept
- **global word count** - the log of the ratio between the number of times the word occurred in the concept and the number of times it occurred in a background corpus, Gigaword (Graff, 2002)

These features are motivated by the work of Tanaka-ishii et al (2010) that showed that local and global word count features were sufficient to build a pair-wise readability classifier that achieved 90% accuracy.

For the supervised classifier, we consider naive Bayes, decision trees, and support vector machines.

5.2 Evaluation

To evaluate our concept sequencing model, we gathered learning paths from experts in high school earth science. Using the model from Section 4, we selected 30 core concepts for the domain of plate tectonics. We asked two earth science experts to each come up with two learning paths for these core concepts, with the first path following an *evidence or research based* and second path following a *traditional* learning path.

An *evidence or research based* learning path, is a pedagogy where students are encouraged to use the scientific method to learn about a phenomena, i.e they gather information by observing the phenomena, form a hypothesis, perform experiment, collect and analyze data and then interpret the data and draw conclusions that hopefully align with the current understanding about the phenomena. A teacher that uses this learning path acts as a *guide on the side*. A *traditional* learning path on the other hand, is the pedagogy where teachers are simply trying to pass on the correct information to students rather than letting the students discover the information themselves. In a classroom environment, a teacher using this learning path would be seen as the classical *sage on stage*.

We used the learning paths collected from the experts to form two test sets, one for the *evidence-based* pedagogy, and one for the *traditional* pedagogy. For each pedagogy, we asked which of all the possible pair-wise orderings our experts agreed upon. For example, if the first expert said that $A < B < C$ and the second expert said that $A < C < B$, then both experts agreed that $A < B$ and $A < C$, while they disagreed on whether $B < C$ or $C < B$. Note that we evaluate pair-wise orderings here, not a complete ranking of the concepts, because the experts did not

Pedagogy	*Pairs (%)*	$c_1 < c_2$	$c_1 \geq c_2$
Evidence	637 (68%)	48.5%	51.5%
Traditional	613 (70%)	48.5%	51.5%

Table 2: Test sets for sequencing concepts. The *Pairs* column shows how many pairs the experts agreed upon (out of a total of $30 * 29 = 870$ pairs).

	Baseline	*NaiveBayes*	*SVM*
Evidence	51.5%	60.8%	53.3%
Traditional	51.5%	56.6%	49.7%

Table 3: Accuracy result from Naive Bayes and SVM for classifying the core concepts

produce a total ordering of the concepts, only a partial tree-like ordering. The experts put the concepts in levels, with concepts in the same level having no precedence relationship, while a concept in a lower level preceded a concept in a higher level.

For our test sets, we selected only the pairs on which both experts agreed. Table 2 shows that experts agreed on 68-70% of the pair-wise orderings. Table 2 also shows the percentage of each type of pair-wise ordering ($c_1 < c_2$ vs. $c_1 \geq c_2$) present in the data. Note that even though all concepts are paired with all other concepts, because the experts do not produce complete orderings, the number of agreements for each type of ordering may not be the same. Consider the case where expert E_1 says that concepts A and B are on the same level (i.e., $A = B$) and expert E_2 says that concept A is in a lower level than concept B (i.e., $A < B$). Then for the pair (A, B), they disagree on the relation (E_1 says $A \geq B$ while E_2 says $A < B$) but for the pair (B, A) they agree on the relation (they both say $B \geq A$). As a result, the $c_1 \geq c_2$ class is slightly larger than the $c_1 < c_2$ class.

Since these data sets were small, we reserved them for testing, and trained our pair-wise classification model using a proxy task: ordering sentences by grade. In this task, the model is given two sentences s_1 and s_2, one written for middle school and written for high school, and asked to decide whether $s_1 < s_2$ (i.e. s_1 is the middle school sentence) or $s_2 < s_1$ (i.e. s_2 is the middle school sentence). We expect that a model for ordering sentences by grade should also be a reasonable model for ordering concepts for a pedagogical learning path. And importantly, getting grade ordering data automatically is easy: the Digital Library for Earth System Education (DLESE) contains a variety of earth science resources with metadata about the grade level they were written for.

To construct the training data, we searched the DLESE website for text resources that contained the words *earthquake* or *plate tectonics*. We collected 10 such resources for each of the two grade cohorts, middle school (we allowed anything K-8) and high school (we allowed anything 9+). We downloaded the webpage for each resource, and used COGENT to extract the 20 most important sentences from each. This resulted in 200 sentences for each of the two grade cohorts. To create pairs of grade-ordered sentences, we paired up middle and high school concepts both ways: middle school first (i.e. $\text{SEQUENCE}(c_m, c_h) = 0$) and high school first (i.e. $\text{SEQUENCE}(c_h, c_m) = 1$). This resulted in 40,000 grade-ordered sentence pairs for training.

We then used this proxy-task training data to train our models. We extracted 1702 unique non-stopwords from the training data, resulting in 3404 features per concept, and 6808 features per concept pair (i.e. per classification instance). On the grade-ordering task, we evaluated three models using WEKA[3], a naive Bayes model, a decision tree (J48) model, and a support vector machine (SVM) model. Using a stratified 50/50 split of the training data, we found that the naive Bayes and SVM models both achieved an accuracy of 80.2%, while the decision tree achieved only 62%. So, we selected the naive Bayes and SVM models for our real task, concept sequencing.

Table 3 shows the performance of the two models on the expert judgments of concept sequencing. We find that the naive Bayes model produces more expert-like concept sequences than would be generated by chance and also outperforms the SVM model on the concept sequencing task. For the final output of the module, we combine the pair-wise judgments into a complete concept sequence, breaking any ties in the pair-wise judgments by preferring the order of the concepts in the output of the core concept identifier.

[3]http://www.cs.waikato.ac.nz/ml/weka/

6 Identifying student misconceptions

The previous components have focused on analyzing the background knowledge – finding core concepts in the domain and selecting an appropriate learning sequence for these concepts. The current component focuses on the student essay, using the collected background knowledge to help analyze the essay and give feedback.

Given a student essay, the goal of this component is to identify which sentences in the essay are most likely to be misconceptions. The task of misconception identification is closely related to the task of textual entailment (Dagan et al., 2006), in which the goal is to predict if a hypothesis sentence, H, can be reasonably concluded given another sentence, T. In misconception identification, the goal is to predict if a student sentence can be concluded from any combination of the sentences in the domain knowledge, similar to a textual entailment task with a single H but many Ts. A student sentence that can not be concluded from the domain knowledge is likely a misconception.

6.1 Models

We developed two models for identifying student misconceptions, inspired by work in textual entailment that showed that a model that simply counts the words in H that appeared in T, after expanding the words in T using WordNet, achieves state-of-the-art performance (Shnarch et al., 2011)[4].

The **Coverage** model scores a student sentence by counting the number of its words that are also in some domain sentence. Low-scoring sentences are likely misconceptions. Formally:

$$\text{SCORE}(s) = \frac{|s \cap d|}{|s|} \qquad d = \bigcup_{s' \in D} \text{EXPAND}(s')$$

where s is a student sentence (a list of words), D is the set of domain sentences, and EXPAND performs lexical expansion on the words of a sentence.

The **Retrieval** model indexes the domain sentences with an information retrieval system (we use Lucene[5]), and scores a student sentence by querying the index and summing the scores. Formally:

$$\text{SCORE}(s) = \sum_{s' \in D} \text{SCORE}_{\text{lucene}}(s, \text{EXPAND}(s'))$$

where s, D and EXPAND are defined as before, and $\text{SCORE}_{\text{lucene}}$ is a cosine over TF-IDF vectors[6].

For both the **Coverage** and **Retrieval** models, we consider the following lexical expansion techniques for defining the EXPAND function:

- **tokens** – words in the sentence (no expansion)
- **tokens, synsets** – words in the sentence, plus all lemmas of all WordNet synsets of each word
- **tokens, synsets$_{\textbf{expanded}}$** – words in the sentence, plus all lemmas of all WordNet synsets of each word, plus all lemmas of derived forms, hyponyms or meroynms of the WordNet synsets
- **tokens, synsets$_{\textbf{expanded}\times 4}$** – words in the sentence, plus all lemmas of all WordNet synsets of each word, plus all lemmas of WordNet synsets reachable by a path of no more than 4 links through derived forms, hyponyms or meroynms

6.2 Evaluation

We evaluate the quality of our misconception identification models using data collected from the American Association for the Advancement of Science's Project 2061 Science Assessment Website[7]. This website identifies the main ideas in various topics under Life Science, Physical Science and Earth Science, and for each idea provides several sentences of description along with its individual concepts and common student misconceptions.

We used 3 topics (17 ideas, averaging 6.2 description sentences, 7.1 concept sentences and 9.9 misconception sentences each) as a development set:

CE Cells
AM Atoms, Molecules, and States of Matter
PT Plate Tectonics

We used 11 topics (64 ideas, averaging 5.9 description sentences, 9.4 concept sentences and 8.6 misconception sentences each) as the test set:

[4]The paper also proposes a more elaborate probabilistic model, but shows that the "lexical coverage" model we adopt here is quite competitive both with their probabilistic model and with the top-performing systems of RTE5 and RTE6.

[5]`http://lucene.apache.org`

[6]See org.apache.lucene.search.Similarity javadoc for details.

[7]`http://assessment.aaas.org/`

Model	*MAP*	*P@1*
Randomly ordered	0.607	0.607
Coverage - tokens	0.647	0.471
Coverage - tokens, synsets	0.633	0.529
Coverage - tokens, synsets$_{\text{expanded}}$	0.650	0.471
Coverage - tokens, synsets$_{\text{expanded}\times 4}$	**0.690**	**0.706**
Retrieval - tokens	0.665	0.529
Retrieval - tokens, synsets	0.641	0.471
Retrieval - tokens, synsets$_{\text{expanded}}$	0.650	0.529
Retrieval - tokens, synsets$_{\text{expanded}\times 4}$	**0.684**	**0.647**

Table 4: Development set results for identifying misconceptions.

EN	Evolution and Natural Selection
BF	Human Body Systems
IE	Interdependence in Ecosystems
ME	Matter and Energy in Living Systems
RH	Reproduction, Genes, and Heredity
EG	Energy: Forms, Transformation, Transfer...
FM	Force and Motion
SC	Substances, Chemical Reactions...
WC	Weather and Climate: Basic Elements
CL	Weather and Climate: Seasonal Differences
WE	Weathering, Erosion, and Deposition

For the evaluation, we provide all of the idea's description sentences as the domain knowledge, and combine all of an idea's concepts and misconceptions into a "student essay"[8]. We then ask the system to rank the sentences in the essay, placing misconceptions above true concepts. Accuracy at placing misconceptions at the top of the ranked list is then measured using mean average precision (MAP) and precision at the first item (P@1).

The models were compared to a chance baseline: the expected MAP and P@1 if the concept and misconception sentences were ordered randomly. Table 4 shows that on the development set, while all models outperformed the random ordering baseline's MAP (0.607), only models with lexical expansion from 4-link WordNet chains outperformed the baseline's P@1 (0.607). The Coverage and Retrieval models using this expansion technique had comparable MAPs (0.690 vs. 0.684), but the Coverage model had a higher P@1 (0.706 vs. 0.647). These top two misconception identification models were evaluated on the test set. Table 5 shows that both models again outperformed the random ordering baseline, and the Retrieval model outperformed the Coverage model (0.644 vs. 0.603 MAP, 0.625 vs. 0.578 P@1).

[8]These "student essays" are a naive approximation of real essays, but the sentences are at least drawn from real student errors. In the future, we hope to create an evaluation corpus where real student essays have been annotated for misconceptions.

Model	*MAP*	*P@1*
Randomly ordered	0.487	0.487
Coverage - tokens, synsets$_{\text{expanded}\times 4}$	0.603	0.578
Retrieval - tokens, synsets$_{\text{expanded}\times 4}$	**0.644**	**0.625**

Table 5: Test set results for identifying misconceptions.

7 Aligning misconceptions to concepts

The goal of this component is to take the misconception sentences identified in a student essay and align them to the core science concepts identified for the domain. For example, a student misconception like *Earth's plates cannot bend* would be aligned to a science concept like *Mountains form when plate material slowly bends over time*.

7.1 Models

The model for misconception-concept alignment takes a similar approach to that of the Retrieval model for misconception identification. The alignment model applies lexical expansion to each word in a core science concept, indexes the expanded concepts with an information retrieval system, and scores each concept for its relevance to a student misconception by querying the index with the misconception and returning the index's score for that concept. Formally:

$$\text{SCORE}(c) = \text{SCORE}_{\text{lucene}}(m, \text{EXPAND}(c))$$

where m is the query misconception, c is the science concept, and EXPAND and $\text{SCORE}_{\text{lucene}}$ are defined as in the Retrieval model for misconception identification. The concept with the highest score is the concept that best aligns to the student misconception according to the model.

For lexical expansion, we consider the same definitions of EXPAND as for misconception identification: **tokens**; **tokens, synsets**; **tokens, synsets$_{\text{expanded}}$**; and **tokens, synsets$_{\text{expanded}\times 4}$**.

Model	*MAP*	*P@1*
Randomly ordered	0.276	0.276
Alignment - Tokens	0.731	0.639
Alignment - Tokens, synsets	**0.813**	**0.734**
Alignment - tokens, $\text{synsets}_{\text{expanded}}$	0.790	0.698
Alignment - Tokens, $\text{synsets}_{\text{expanded}\times 4}$	0.762	0.639

Table 6: Development set results for aligning concepts to misconceptions.

7.2 Evaluation

We again leverage the AAAS Science Assessments to evaluate the misconception-concept alignment models. In addition to identifying key science ideas, and the concepts and common misconceptions within each idea, the AAAS Science Assessments provide links between the misconceptions and the concepts. Usually there is a single concept to which each misconception is aligned, but the AAAS data aligns as many as 16 concepts to a misconception in some cases.

For the evaluation, we give the system one misconception from an idea, and the list of all concepts from that idea, and ask the system to rank the concepts[9]. If the system performs well, the concepts that are aligned to the misconception should be ranked above the other concepts. Accuracy at placing the aligned concepts at the top of the ranked list is then measured using mean average precision (MAP) and precision at the first item (P@1).

The models were compared to a chance baseline: the expected MAP and P@1 if the concept and misconception sentences were ordered randomly. Table 6 shows that on the development set, all models outperformed the random ordering baseline. Lexical expansion with tokens and synsets achieved the highest performance, 0.813 MAP and 0.734 P@1. This model was evaluated on the test set, and Table 7 shows that the model again outperformed the random ordering baseline, achieving 0.704 MAP and 0.611 P@1. Overall, these are promising results – given a student misconception, the model's first choice for a concept to address the misconception is helpful more than 60% of the time.

[9] As discussed in Section 6.2, there are on average 9.4 concepts per item. This is not too far off from the 10-20 core concepts we typically expect the tutor to extract for each domain.

Model	*MAP*	*P@1*
Randomly ordered	0.259	0.259
Alignment - Tokens, synsets	**0.704**	**0.611**

Table 7: Test set results for aligning concepts to misconceptions.

8 Recommending resources

The goal of this component is to take a set of student misconceptions, the core science concepts to which each misconception is aligned, and the pedagogical ordering of the core science concepts, and recommend digital resources (webpages) to address the most important of the misconceptions. For example, a student that believes that *water evaporates into the air only when the air is very warm* might be directed to websites about evaporation and condensation. The recommended resources are intended to help the student quickly locate the concept knowledge necessary to correct each of their misconceptions.

8.1 Models

The intuition behind our model is simple: sentences from recommended resources should contain the same or lexically related terminology as both the misconception sentences and their aligned concepts. As a first approach to this problem, we focus on the overlap between recommended sentences and the misconception sentences, and use an information retrieval approach to build a resource recommender.

First, the user gives the model a set of domain knowledge webpages, and we use an information retrieval system (Lucene) to index each sentence from each of the webpages. (Note that we index all sentences, not just core concept sentences.) Given a student misconception, we query the index and identify the source URL for each sentence that is returned. We then return the list of the recommended URLs, keeping only the first instance of each URL if duplicates exist. Formally:

$$\text{SCORE}(url) = \max_{s \in url} \text{SCORE}_{\text{lucene}}(m, s)$$

where url is a domain resource, s is a sentence from a domain resource and m is the student misconception. URLs are ranked by score and the top k URLs are returned as recommendations.

8.2 Evaluation

As a preliminary evaluation of the resource recommendation model, we obtained student misconception sentences that had been aligned to concepts in a knowledge map of plate tectonics (Ahmad, 2009). The concepts in the knowledge map were originally drawn from 37 domain webpages, thus each concept could serve as a link between a student misconception and a recommended webpage. For evaluation, we took all 11 misconceptions for a single student, where each misconception had been aligned through the concepts to on average 3.4 URLs. For each misconception, we asked the recommender model to rank the 37 domain URLs in order of their relevance to the student misconception.

We expect the final interactive essay writing system to return up to $k = 5$ resources for each misconception, so we evaluated the performance of the recommender model in terms of precision at five (P@5). That is, of the top five URLs recommended by the system, how many were also recommended by the experts? Averaging over the 11 student misconception queries, the current model achieves P@5 of 32%, an acceptable initial baseline as randomly recommending resources would achieve only P@5 of 9%.

9 Discussion

In this article, we have presented our initial steps towards an interactive essay writing system that can help students identify and remedy misconceptions in their science knowledge. The system relies on techniques drawn from a variety of areas of natural language processing research, including multi-document summarization, textual entailment and information retrieval. Each component has been evaluated independently and demonstrated promising initial performance.

A variety of challenges remain for this effort. The core concept identification system performs well on the plate tectonics domain that it was originally developed for, but poorer on more distant domains, suggesting the need for more domain-independent features. The model for sequencing science concepts pedagogically uses only the most basic of word-based features, and could potentially benefit from features drawn from other research areas such as text readability. The misconception identification and alignment models perform well on the AAAS science assessments but have not yet been evaluated on real student essays, which may require moving from lexical coverage models to more sophisticated entailment models. Finally, the recommender model considers only information about the misconception sentence (not the aligned core concept nor the pedagogical ordering of concepts) and recommends entire resources instead of directing students to specifically relevant sentences or paragraphs.

Perhaps the most important challenge for this work will be moving from evaluating the components independently to a whole-system evaluation in the context of a real essay writing task. We are currently designing a study to gather data on students using the system, from which we hope to derive information about which components are most reliable or useful to the students. This information will help guide our research to focus on improving the components that yield the greatest benefits to the students.

References

[Ahmad2009] Faisal Ahmad. 2009. *Generating conceptually personalized interactions for educational digital libraries using concept maps*. Ph.D. thesis, University of Colorado at Boulder.

[Azevedo et al.2008] Roger Azevedo, Amy Witherspoon, Arthur Graesser, Danielle McNamara, Vasile Rus, Zhiqiang Cai, Mihai Lintean, and Emily Siler. 2008. MetaTutor: An adaptive hypermedia system for training and fostering self-regulated learning about complex science topics. In *Meeting of Society for Computers in Psychology*, November.

[Dagan et al.2006] Ido Dagan, Oren Glickman, and Bernardo Magnini. 2006. The PASCAL recognising textual entailment challenge. In Joaquin Quiñonero Candela, Ido Dagan, Bernardo Magnini, and Florence d'Alché Buc, editors, *Machine Learning Challenges. Evaluating Predictive Uncertainty, Visual Object Classification, and Recognising Tectual Entailment*, volume 3944 of *Lecture Notes in Computer Science*, pages 177–190. Springer Berlin / Heidelberg.

[de la Chica et al.2008a] Sebastian de la Chica, Faisal Ahmad, James H. Martin, and Tamara Sumner. 2008a. Pedagogically useful extractive summaries for science education. In *Proceedings of the 22nd International Conference on Computational Linguistics - Volume 1*, COLING '08, pages 177–184, Stroudsburg, PA, USA. Association for Computational Linguistics.

[de la Chica et al.2008b] Sebastian de la Chica, Faisal Ahmad, Tamara Sumner, James H. Martin, and Kirsten Butcher. 2008b. Computational foundations for personalizing instruction with digital libraries. *International Journal on Digital Libraries*, 9(1):3–18, July.

[Graesser et al.2004] Arthur Graesser, Shulan Lu, George Jackson, Heather Mitchell, Mathew Ventura, Andrew Olney, and Max Louwerse. 2004. AutoTutor: A tutor with dialogue in natural language. *Behavior Research Methods*, 36:180–192.

[Graff2002] David Graff. 2002. English Gigaword. *Linguistic Data Consortium.*

[NRC1996] National Research Council NRC. 1996. *National Science Education Standards.* National Academy Press, Washington DC.

[Project2061.1993] Project2061. 1993. *Benchmarks for Science Literacy.* Oxford University Press, New York, United States.

[Radev et al.2004] Dragomir R. Radev, Hongyan Jing, Małgorzata Styś, and Daniel Tam. 2004. Centroid-based summarization of multiple documents. *Inf. Process. Manage.*, 40(6):919–938, November.

[Shnarch et al.2011] Eyal Shnarch, Jacob Goldberger, and Ido Dagan. 2011. A probabilistic modeling framework for lexical entailment. In *Proceedings of the 49th Annual Meeting of the Association for Computational Linguistics: Human Language Technologies*, pages 558–563, Portland, Oregon, USA, June. Association for Computational Linguistics.

[Tanaka-Ishii et al.2010] K. Tanaka-Ishii, S. Tezuka, and H. Terada. 2010. Sorting texts by readability. *Computational Linguistics*, 36(2):203–227.

[VanLehn et al.2002] Kurt VanLehn, Pamela Jordan, Carolyn Rosé, Dumisizwe Bhembe, Michael Böttner, Andy Gaydos, Maxim Makatchev, Umarani Pappuswamy, Michael Ringenberg, Antonio Roque, Stephanie Siler, and Ramesh Srivastava. 2002. The architecture of Why2-Atlas: A coach for qualitative physics essay writing. In Stefano Cerri, Guy Gouardères, and Fábio Paraguaçu, editors, *Intelligent Tutoring Systems*, volume 2363 of *Lecture Notes in Computer Science*, pages 158–167. Springer Berlin / Heidelberg.

[Wade-Stein and Kintsch2004] David Wade-Stein and Eileen Kintsch. 2004. Summary Street: Interactive computer support for writing. *Cognition and Instruction*, 22(3):333–362.

Automatic Grading of Scientific Inquiry

Avirup Sil
Computer and Information Sciences
Temple University
Philadelphia, PA
avirup.sil@temple.edu

Angela Shelton
College of Education
Temple University
Philadelphia, PA
angi@temple.edu

Diane Jass Ketelhut
Teaching and Learning, Policy and Leadership
University of Maryland
College Park, MD
djk@umd.edu

Alexander Yates
Computer and Information Sciences
Temple University
Philadelphia, PA
yates@temple.edu

Abstract

The SAVE Science project is an attempt to address the shortcomings of current assessments of science. The project has developed two virtual worlds that each have a mystery or natural phenomenon requiring scientific explanation; by recording students' behavior as they investigate the mystery, these worlds can be used to assess their understanding of the scientific method. Currently, however, the scoring of the assessment depends either on manual grading of students' written responses, or, on multiple choice questions. This paper presents an automated grader that can combine with SAVE Science's virtual worlds to provide a cheap mechanism for assessments of the ability to apply scientific methodology. In experiments on over 300 middle school students, our best automated grader improves by over 50% relative to the closest system from previous work in predicting grades supplied by human judges.

1 Introduction

Education researchers criticize current standardized tests of science on many grounds. First, they lack context (Behrens et al., 2007), which complicates a student's task of applying classroom-based learning, as the theory of situated cognition suggests (Brown et al., 1989). Second, many have criticized such tests for failing to engage students long enough to apply their understanding to the question. Furthermore and perhaps worst of all, standardized tests fail to assess scientific inquiry—the ability of students to apply the scientific method—authentically rather than as scientific content (National Research Council, 2005; Singley and Taft, 1995).

We consider an assessment conducted by the Situated Assessment using Virtual Environments for Science Content and Inquiry (SAVE Science) project (Ketelhut et al., 2010; Ketelhut et al., 2009), whose long-term goal is to address the shortcomings of current standardized tests of science. The assessments from SAVE Science have produced an abundance of data on how students interact with a virtual world, when trying to conduct scientific inquiry. Observing student behavior in virtual environments offers the potential for new insights into both how students learn and what they know. However, this benefit can only be realized if we can make sense of the stream of data and text produced by the students.

In this paper, we attempt to automate the process of grading students in SAVE Science assessments, to make the evaluations as cost-effective as standardized tests. Unlike most previous systems for automated grading (Sukkarieh and Stoyanchev, 2009; Sukkarieh et al., 2004; Higgins et al., 2004; Wang et al., 2008), the data for this task includes a short paragraph (usually 50-60 words) natural language response stating a hypothesis and evidence in support of it. In addition, there is a wealth of relational data about student behavior in a virtual environment. We develop novel predictors for automatically grading the written responses using a wide variety of natural language features, as well as features from the data on student behavior in the virtual world. On student data from two virtual worlds, our best automated grader has correlations of $r = 0.58$ and 0.44 with human judgments, improving over the closest technique from previous work by 56% for the first world, and by 120% for the second.

The rest of the paper is organized as follows. The next section contrasts this project with previous work. Section 3 describes the SAVE Science project and the student data it has produced. Section 4 details our automated grading models. Section 5 reports on experiments, and Section 6 concludes.

2 Previous Work

Wang et al. (2008) have previously conducted a study on assessing creative problem-solving in science education by automatically grading student essays. Our techniques improve substantially over theirs, as we demonstrate empirically. In part, we improve by including more sophisticated language-processing features in our model than the unigram and bigram features they use; as others have noted, bag-of-words representations and latent semantic indexing become less useful as word order and causal relationships become important for judging an essay's quality (Malatesta et al., 2002; Wiemer-Hastings et al., 2005). A secondary reason for our improvement is that we also have access to non-linguistic data about the students that we can mine for additional patterns.

Most previous research on automated grading of written text focuses on short, factual text (Wiemer-Hastings et al., 1999; Mohler and Mihalcea, 2009; Leacock and Chodorow, 2003; Sukkarieh and Stoyanchev, 2009; Sukkarieh et al., 2004; Mitchell et al., 2002; Pulman and Sukkarieh, 2005), whereas SAVE Science's texts are only partly factual. Responses are meant to convey a scientific explanation of a mystery, and therefore, correct responses contain inferences, observations of the world, and causal links between observations and inferences.

Automatic systems for grading longer responses typically grade essays for coherence and discourse structure (Burstein et al., 2001; Higgins et al., 2004), but these global discourse criteria are only partially indicative of the quality of a student's response to the SAVE Science assessments. To be considered fully correct in these tests, student responses must contain factually correct information, as well as causal relationships that justify the student's inferences, such as "The balls don't bounce outside because it's cold, and lower temperatures decrease pressure."

3 Assessing Scientific Inquiry Using Virtual Worlds

We now give a brief overview of SAVE Science, which aims to complement (or even replace) current standardized tests for evaluating students' understanding of science. We first present the project's goals and methodology, and then describe the challenges involved in creating an automated evaluation of student performance for this new assessment paradigm.

3.1 The SAVE Science Project

SAVE Science (Ketelhut et al., 2010; Ketelhut et al., 2009; Ketelhut et al., 2012) is a novel project for evaluating students' understanding of the scientific method — problem identification, gathering data, analyzing data, developing a hypothesis, and communicating results — by asking students to solve a mystery in a virtual world through the application of the scientific method to a content-based problem. Using immersive virtual environments for assessments is a current area of focus among education researchers (Clarke-Midura, 2010); SAVE Science is unique in its attempt to assess understanding of both *inquiry* as well as *content*. That is, the test is designed to assess students' ability to apply their knowledge of the scientific inquiry processes to a problem they have never seen before, but within a content area they have just studied. To be successful, students must explore a virtual environment, collect appropriate data about it, and find evidence that supports their inference about the cause of the mystery. Part of the reasoning for a particular conclusion draws on scientific knowledge learned in the classroom, but for these mysteries such knowledge of scientific content is insufficient. Students must also be able to explore the virtual world and create a hypothesis about the cause of the problem, based on their observations and analysis of collected data.

For this study, we concentrate on two virtual worlds produced by the SAVE Science project team, Basketball and Weather Trouble. Screenshots of the two virtual worlds are shown in Figure 1. Students are represented by an *avatar*, or virtual character, whom they can control in the virtual world

Figure 1: Screenshots from SAVE Science's virtual environments. Left: the Basketball module. Right: the Weather Trouble module. The bar of icons along the bottom of the screen shows various tools that students may choose to use in the world, including a map, compass, graphing tool, note pad, and instruments like a barometer and thermometer, among others. Glowing green arrows indicate "objects" (sometimes including people) with which the student's avatar may interact, by making observations, by taking measurements, or through conversation.

with a mouse or key presses. When the test begins, one character in the world informs the student of a mystery that the student needs to explain. In the Weather Trouble world, citizens of Scientopolis are concerned with the lack of rain recently, and ask the avatar to determine whether it will rain soon. In the Basketball world, a basketball tournament staffer is concerned that students cannot play basketball on the outdoor playground, because the balls will not bounce high enough outdoors, even though the same balls bounce just fine indoors.

Once informed of the mission, the student (through her or his avatar) explores the world, and interacts with objects or other characters in the virtual world by "colliding" with them. Interactions with characters mostly involve the character telling the avatar some part of the story of the world through their eyes (*e.g.*, "It hasn't rained here in weeks; I hope it rains soon!"). The conversation may yield useful clues, or it may be "folk science" (*e.g.*, "The sheep are lying down, so it is probably going to rain soon"). When the avatar interacts with an object, the student can choose from a set of tools to determine measurements of the object. Measurements that a student deems interesting can be recorded in the student's clipboard, and a graphing tool allows students to construct charts from the data in the clipboard.

Once students have finished exploring, collecting data, and analyzing the data, they are asked to communicate the results by writing a brief explanation for the cause of the mystery for the world. In addition, students are asked to provide what they consider to be the top three pieces of evidence for their explanation. Both the explanation and the ranked evidence are written in freeform text, consisting of 48.5 words on average for Basketball, and 62.4 for Weather Trouble. We refer to the explanation and ranked evidence collectively as the student's *freeform response*. These texts are critical components of the overall data about the student, as they can be used to assess the student's ability to communicate findings.

3.2 Assessing the ability to make scientific inquiries

The virtual worlds from SAVE Science provide an abundance of data about each student's ability to apply the scientific method, as well as their understanding of content, but the current assessment scheme involves either manual grading of freeform responses, or multiple choice questions. The first is problematic because of the effort and expense involved; the second is problematic because of the difficulty in designing multiple choice questions that accurately assess everything a student has learned (Wang et al., 2008; Chang and Chiu, 2005; Singley and Taft, 1995). The focus of this paper is to provide an automated way of assessing students' ability to perform scientific inquiry based on their behavior in the virtual world and their freeform responses. We first describe the current assessment mechanisms available in SAVE Science's data, which we then use

Score	Criteria
4	Provides a correct hypothesis with supporting data gathered from within the world
3	Provides a correct hypothesis with only folk or incorrect evidence
2	Provides a somewhat correct answer
1	Provides a hypothesis
0	No hypothesis, or nonsense

Table 1: Rubric for manual scoring of freeform responses.

Score	Example
3	it's because the air outside is more colder than the air inside here the cold air causes the air molecules to gather up toghter tight toghter causeing the ball to deflate and have less bounce ...
1	the wieght isnt up to regulations but the bouce is ok everyball i bouce it bouced according to regulartion but almost every ball has the weight of 1.25 ...

Figure 2: Example portions of two freeform responses from Basketball, presented as written by the students.

below as gold standards for automated predictors for assessment.

Manual grading of the freeform responses uses a rubric of integer scores from 0 to 4. Guidelines for the rubric scores are shown in Table 1, and two example responses are shown in Figure 2. Two annotators, the first holding a PhD in education and the second a PhD student in computer science, independently judged each response, achieving a high inter-annotator agreement — for Basketball, Cohen's $\kappa = 0.95$, Pearson's $\rho = 0.98$; and for Weather Trouble $\kappa = 0.8$, $\rho = 0.93$. For our experiments, we use the judgments of the first annotator, who helped design the virtual worlds and has experience in grading student essays, but the choice of which annotator's judgments to use makes little difference to the results.

The multiple choice questions, which we call *quiz questions*, consist of two types, as shown in Table 2. The first type, which we call *contextualized questions*, directly test students' understanding of the scientific issues that arise in the virtual environment of the module. *Non-contextualized questions* are related to the topic of the module, but they can be answered correctly using general scientific knowledge rather than specific knowledge gleaned from exploration of the virtual world. The non-contextualized questions are taken from the benchmark exams of a major urban school district.

4 Predictors for Scientific Inquiry Grades

We now focus on the task of building automated predictors for assessing students' ability to make scientific inquiries. To do this, we turn the grading task into a classical machine learning problem, in which the system must learn from a set of training data (students and their grades) how to predict a grade for new students included in separate test data. We focus on two main types of models: ones that can grade by predicting how many multiple-choice questions (contextualized, non-contextualized, or both) a student will answer correctly, and ones that can predict the manual grade assigned to a freeform response.

Unlike typical automated-grading systems for grading written or spoken natural language, our task includes a large additional source of evidence for the predictions: data about the students' behavior in the virtual world. Our prediction models therefore make extensive use of both the freeform response and data from the students' behavior in the world, which we refer to as world data.

4.1 Models

We use Support Vector Machines with Radial Basis Function kernels (RBF-SVM) (Pang-Ning et al., 2006; Smola and Schölkopf, 1998) for learning non-linear regression models of grading. Let S be the set of students evaluated through SAVE Science's virtual environment, and let $\mathbf{f}\colon S \rightarrow \mathbb{R}^n$ be a vector-valued feature function providing n real-valued features for each student, based on the student's freeform response and behavior in the virtual world. Let $g\colon S \rightarrow \mathbb{R}$ be the target grading function, which provides a real-valued grade for each student. The hypothesis space $\mathcal{H}$ for RBF-SVMs includes functions $h\colon S \rightarrow \mathbb{R}$ of the form

$$h(s) = \sum_{i=1}^{m} \alpha_i K(\mathbf{x}_i, \mathbf{f}(s)) + b \qquad (1)$$

Contextualized Questions	Non-Contextualized Questions
What variable would you change to correct this basketball problem? 1. Temperature A. **Make it 75°F** B. Make it 55°F C. Make it 35°F 2. Court Type A. Concrete only B. Wood only C. **Court Type makes little to no difference** 3. Basketball used A. Replace one Wade Park ball with one Jordan Gym ball B. Purchase a new set of balls for Wade Park C. **New basketballs will not help this problem**	1. A child riding a bicycle notices that the tires are more inflated on hot days than on cold days, even though no air is being added or removed. How can this be explained? A. A higher temperature of the air in the tires causes the particles in the air to stick together and take up more space. B. A higher temperature of the air in the tires causes the number of particles in the air to increase. C. A higher temperature of the air in the tires causes the pressure of the air to drop and the volume of the air to increase. D. **A higher temperature of the air in the tires causes both the pressure and volume of the air to increase.** 2. A sample of oxygen is being stored in a closed container at a constant temperature. What will happen to the gas if it is transferred to a container with a smaller volume? A. Its weight will increase B. Its weight will decrease C. **Its pressure will increase** D. The size of its particles will decrease

Table 2: Complete list of Basketball contextualized and non-contextualized quiz questions. **Bold** indicates the correct answer.

where the $\mathbf{x}_i$ are the support vectors, and K is the RBF kernel function, given by:

$$K(\mathbf{x}, \mathbf{x}') = \exp(-\gamma \|\mathbf{x} - \mathbf{x}'\|^2) \qquad (2)$$

Here, $\alpha_i, b, \gamma \in \mathbb{R}$ are parameters to be learned from the training data. We use the Weka (Hall et al., 2009) toolkit for running standard training and prediction algorithms with the SVM.

We train models for four distinct prediction tasks, each defined by a different grading function $g(s)$: 1) $g(s)$ is the manually-assessed grade on student s's freeform responses; 2) $g(s)$ is the number of correctly-answered contextualized questions; 3) $g(s)$ is the number of correctly-answered non-contextualized questions; and 4) $g(s)$ is the total number of correctly-answered quiz questions (the sum of $g(s)$ from 2 and 3). We use the same feature function $\mathbf{f}$ for all models, which we describe next.

4.2 World Features

From the database that records a student's activity in the immersive virtual environment, we extract features describing the frequency and types of activities in which students engaged. For both modules, we include features for the number of object interactions, the number of distinct objects interacted with, the total number of measurements made, the number of measurements saved in the student's clipboard, and the number of graphs made. We also include module-specific features: for example, in the Basketball assessment module, we counted how many distinct basketballs were interacted with, how many measurements were made using each type of tool available in the Basketball world, whether a given student created graphs of temperature inside vs. outside, or graphs of temperature vs. pressure, *etc.* In total, the model contains 69 world features in the Weather module, and 65 in the Basketball module. All features conform to the pattern of counts over particular types of actions the avatar might take. We call the features from the virtual environment *world features*.

We note that the relational data in this world is large and complex, containing temporal and sequential information which these features currently ignore. This feature set serves as an initial exploration of the world data, but we fully expect that future investigation will improve on this representation. For this paper we are primarily interested in features of the freeform responses, which we now turn to.

4.3 Natural Language Features

We investigate standard text mining features from bag-of-words representations and Latent Semantic Analysis, as well as a variety of features tailored to the grading task. Spelling is a major problem for this type of prediction task, but spelling-correctors are investigated elsewhere (Kernighan et al., 1990) and are not a focus of this research. We therefore manually corrected spelling errors throughout the texts before extracting features and conducting experiments. No correction of grammar or punctuation was performed.

4.3.1 Latent Semantic Analysis Features

After removing 34 common stopwords, we extract a bag-of-words representation from the freeform responses (Manning and Schütze, 1999). We apply Latent Semantic Analysis (LSA) (Landauer and Dumais, 1997; Steyvers and Griffiths, 2006) to this set of features to produce a smaller set of 72 latent features for Basketball, and 94 for Weather Trouble, based on a threshold of retaining 90% of the variance in the data.

4.3.2 Features from Hidden Markov Models

LSA and other topic models identify latent structure based on document-level cooccurrence statistics, but the "documents" in our data are short for topic-modeling purposes, and we have less than 200 of them for each world. As a result, standard topic modeling techniques may have difficulty identifying the appropriate structure. We therefore also consider Hidden Markov Models (HMMs) (Rabiner, 1989), generative models which rely both on cooccurrence within a sentence and on sequence information for determining model parameters. Following recent work by Huang et al. (2011) on using HMMs to build representations, we estimate parameters for a fully-connected HMM with 100 latent states over the freeform responses using Expectation-Maximization. We then decode the HMM over the corpus to produce a Viterbi-optimal latent state for each word. Finally, we use counts of these 100 latent states to produce 100 new features for each freeform response.

4.3.3 Detecting disengagement

A small number of students show little enthusiasm for the test, and their responses and general performance are quite poor. Often their freeform responses are short, or they repeat the same text multiple times. We include three features that help identify such cases: the overall length of the response, the number of times a full sentence is repeated exactly, and the number of tokens that are repeated across multiple sentences.

4.3.4 Ngram and Pattern Features

While HMM and LSA features help combat sparsity in the predictive model, they may ignore the strong signal from a few expressions that are particularly important for a domain. By soliciting advice from domain experts, we selected important unigrams, bigrams, and trigrams for each module, and created features that count each of these. Likewise, we selected important two-word and three-word sets, which we call *loose patterns*, that weakly indicate that a student understood the problem, if they all occur in the same response but not necessarily near one another. Again, these words were selected as a result of combination of empirical observations and expert domain knowledge from designers. For instance, if a response contains the three words "temperature," "pressure," and "because," it would match one of these loose patterns. For each pattern, we create a feature to count the number of matches in a response.

The selected patterns and ngrams both consist of three kinds of words: ones that indicate types of measurable phenomena or properties (*e.g.*, "temperature"), locations (*e.g.*, "outside"), or causal or comparative words (*e.g.*, "causes," "higher," "than," or "decrease"). Because the responses discuss numerical observations like temperature and pressure values, we also allow a wildcard for matching any number as part of the loose patterns.

4.3.5 Semantic Features

We use the Senna[1] semantic role labeling (SRL) system (Collobert et al., 2011) to automatically identify predicate-argument relationships in the freeform responses. In general, the SRL system is only able

[1] http://ml.nec-labs.com/senna/

to identify predicate-argument structures in well-crafted sentences, which on its own is a good indicator that the student will do well in the evaluation. In addition, we extract *semantic features* (SFs) that count how often certain predicate-argument structures appear which are indicative of a good answer:

SF1 Count how often the freeform response contains any predicate.

SF2 Count how often the response contains predicates that involve causality, such as "causes" or change-of-value predicates like "increase."

SF3 Count how often measurement words (*e.g.*, temperature, pressure) appear as arguments to any predicate.

SF4 Count how often measurement words appear as arguments to the predicates related to causality.

4.4 Feature Selection

We perform feature selection using a correlation-based technique that tries to identify maximally-relevant and minimally-redundant features (Hall, 1998; Deng and Moore, 1998). The algorithm evaluates the value of a subset of features by considering the individual correlation between each feature and the gold standard, as well as the correlation between features. We use the default parameter settings for feature selection, as specified in Weka.

5 Experiments

5.1 Experimental Setup

We use a dataset collected by the SAVE Science project, consisting of the world data, freeform responses, and quiz answers from public middle-school students in a major urban area of the United States. 120 students completed the Weather Trouble module, and 184 students completed Basketball. After manually correcting spelling errors in the freeform responses, we extracted features as described above.

Following Wang et al. (2008), we evaluate our regression models using Pearson correlation between the predicted outcome and the gold standard outcome. Four different gold standards are considered for each module: manually-assigned grades for the freeform text, and three versions of the number of correctly-answered quiz questions (contextualized only, non-contextualized only, and all). We use a χ^2 test with a threshold of $p < 0.05$ to determine statistical significance. We train and test models using 10-fold cross-validation to reduce variability, and the results are averaged over the folds.

We evaluate several variants of our system, including a World variant that only includes features from the world data; an NLP variant that only includes features from the freeform responses; and a combined World+NLP variant that includes all features before feature selection is performed.

Our evaluation compares against the essay grading technique by Wang et al. Like ours, their system uses RBF-SVM regression with default parameter settings as implemented in Weka, and like ours the system is trained on student texts proposing solutions to a science problem (in their case, a high school chemistry problem). The system is trained on human judgments of the quality of the student answers. The major difference between our technique and theirs lies in the representation of the data; Wang et al. use two types of features: unigrams, and bigrams that occur at least five times during training. In our implementation of their technique, we use a lower threshold for bigrams — they must occur at least twice. This is because we have less text to work with, and the higher threshold yields too few bigrams. Using the lower threshold improved performance slightly, so we report only those results below.

5.2 Results and Discussion

The full system for automatic grading is accurate, across both worlds and all gold standards. Figure 3 shows the results of predicting human judgments of the freeform responses, where the World+NLP system achieves a correlation of 0.58 for Basketball and 0.44 for Weather Trouble. The same system achieves 0.55 and 0.54 on the World questions of Basketball and Weather Trouble, respectively (Figures 4 and 5). Our best models are statistically significantly different from the Wang et al. model (for predicting contextualized questions for basketball: $p = .009, \chi^2 = 6.87162$; for grading freeform responses: $p \approx 0, \chi^2 = 14.21725$). Correlations from World+NLP for other quiz types —

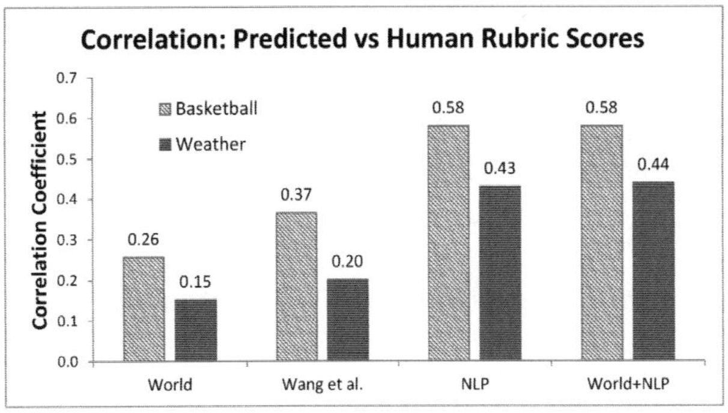

Figure 3: Our NLP features dramatically improve prediction over the Wang et al. model for grading freeform science essays, by a margin of 0.21 on Basketball and 0.23 on Weather Trouble.

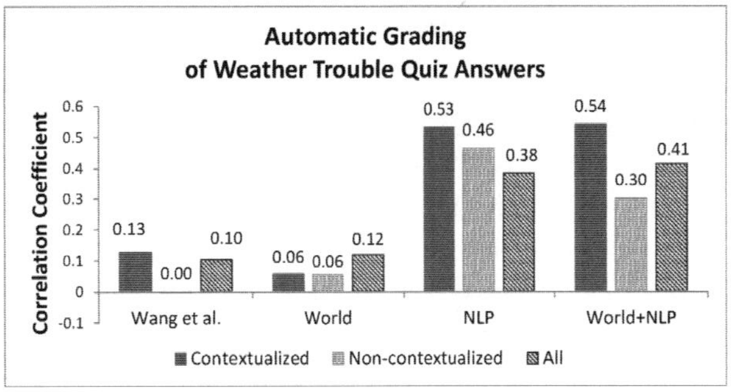

Figure 5: The NLP model substantially outperforms World and Wang et al. on predicting quiz questions for Weather Trouble, and the combined World+NLP model achieves a 0.54 correlation for contextualized questions.

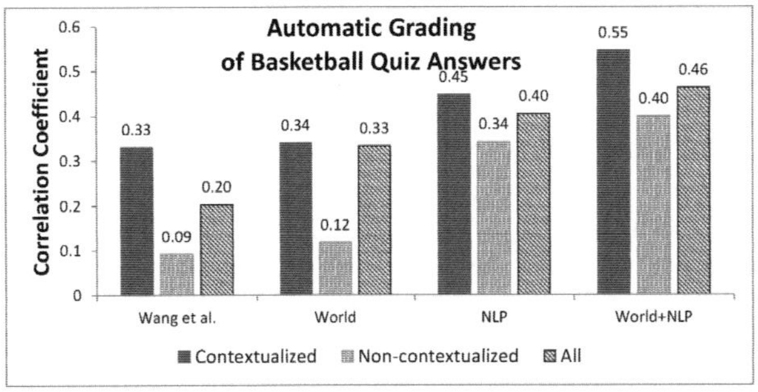

Figure 4: The World+NLP model outperforms both World and NLP, and substantially outperforms the Wang et al. system.

non-contextualized and all questions — were somewhat lower, but still statistically significant ($p = .002, \chi^2 = 10.05986$).

The language features are currently the major factor in the predictive models for automated grading. The NLP model substantially outperforms both the simpler Wang et al. model and the World-only model in predicting quiz answers for both worlds. It achieves correlations that are statistically significantly different from the baseline, for all gold standards and both worlds.

The story in the case of grading freeform essays is similar. Our NLP model beats the Wang et al. model and the World-only model. Our full model World+NLP, however, outperforms the NLP model by only a small fraction. Also, the Wang et al. model performs slightly better than the World-only model on freeform responses. For Basketball, the correlation coefficient of their model is greater by 0.11 and for Weather by 0.05. We believe that the NLP-based models, including Wang et al.'s, are outperforming the World model because the current representation of the World data fails to capture all of the pertinent information from students' behavior in the virtual environments. Our plans for future work include the development of features that can capture temporal patterns in student activity.

Each type of language feature appears to provide a beneficial and complementary source of evidence. We tested the model using only individual subsets of the NLP features, such as HMM features only, LSA features only, ngrams and loose patterns only, and features from semantic role labeling only. On their own, each set of features provides only a small improvement over the mean predictor. When combined with the world features, each subset of the NLP features again provides only a small improvement over the World-only model. For example, for predicting Basketball world quiz questions, World features achieve $r = 0.34$, World+HMM and World+LSA achieve 0.35, and World+(ngrams and loose patterns) achieves 0.39. The relative ranking of these subsets of features is not consistent across different tasks; for Weather contextualized questions, World+HMM is best, and for Weather non-contextualized questions, World+LSA is best. Features selected by the feature selection algorithm also indicate that the different types of language features complement one another. The feature selection algorithm for the World+NLP model selects some features for every different type we presented, although the HMM, LSA, loose pattern, and unigram features dominate. We believe that the best procedure for developing grading systems for science essays is therefore to construct a large number of possible features using a variety of techniques, and then train a model for a particular task and gold standard. Including significantly more varieties of features, perhaps from additional kinds of language models or NLP pipeline tools, is an important future direction for further improving the grading accuracy.

While the accuracies of the models for contextualized and non-contextualized questions are broadly similar, the models themselves are not. For the contextualized questions, 4 important world behavior features were deemed important and non-redundant by the feature selection algorithm: the number of distinct collisions, the number of people collided with, the number of distinct objects (basketballs or balloons) whose pressure was measured, and the number of distinct temperature measurements that were recorded into clipboards. The essential task in this virtual world is to discover that a decrease in the temperature of several gas systems (basketballs and balloons filled with air) is causing their pressure to decrease. The model for the contextualized questions thus includes variables that are highly relevant to a student's understanding of the core problem in the world, which in turn indicates that automated data mining techniques are capable of identifying when students are learning to practice the scientific method, by observing student behavior. On the other hand, the model for the non-contextualized questions includes only 2 world features: The number of collisions made and number of different objects whose circumference was measured. The first one is an indicator of the activity level of a student and the second variable is an indicator for whether the student has identified the problem (the basketballs are not bouncing because they are deflated), but not for the underlying cause of the problem (the outside temperature causes a drop in pressure, which causes the basketball circumference to decrease). Thus the model that predicts non-contextualized questions very accurately has little information about whether the student understood the core problem of the world or not; instead, it has information about whether the student is active in the world. These observations lend some support to the criticism that the standardized tests are not properly assessing inquiry.

Performance on the Weather Trouble module is consistently lower than on Basketball. In part, this reflects the increased difficulty of this world; human inter-annotator agreement is a bit lower ($\kappa = 0.8$ vs. 0.95 on Basketball). However, another large part of the difference is that the world features provide far less information in Weather Trouble — the World-only model has less than half the correlation on Weather than on Basketball, for all quiz question types. We suspect that the cause is the nature of the task on the Weather Trouble world, where temporal information plays a bigger role as measurements of air pressure and wind direction may change over time. Investigating world features that can distinguish different patterns of student behavior over time is an important area for further investigation.

6 Conclusion

Our automated grader uses a wide variety of NLP pipeline tools to produce features for students' essays on the answers to scientific mysteries. The grader achieves significant correlation with human judges and multiple choice quiz evaluations, substantially outperforming a simpler grader from prior work. The findings of this research suggest that authentic assessments of scientific inquiry through virtual environments can be graded purely automatically, like high stakes multiple choice tests. Ongoing work on SAVE Science is investigating the differences in how students respond to standard multiple-choice tests and tests based on virtual environments. But the contextualized assessments from SAVE Science provide evaluation of scientific inquiry that multiple choice tests currently do not, and they can now be graded just as cheaply.

Acknowledgments

This material is based upon work supported under National Science Foundation Grant No. 0822308/1157534. Any opinions, findings, and conclusions or recommendations expressed in this material are those of the authors and do not necessarily reflect the views of the NSF. We would like to thank Catherine Schifter and the rest of the SAVE Science team for their help and support. We also wish to thank the anonymous reviewers for their helpful comments.

References

J. T. Behrens, D. Frezzo, R. Mislevy, M. Kroopnick, and D. Wise. 2007. Structural, Functional, and Semiotic Symmetries in Simulation-based Games and Assessments. In E. Baker, J. Dickieson, W. Wulfeck, and H. O'Neil, editors, *Assessment of Problem Solving Using Simulations*. Lawrence Erlbaum Associates.

J. S. Brown, A. Collins, , and P. Duguid. 1989. Situated cognition and the culture of learning. *Educational Researcher*, 18(1):32–41.

J. Burstein, C. Leacock, and R. Swartz. 2001. Automated evaluation of essays and short answers. In *5th International Computer Assisted Assessment Conference. Loughborough University*.

S.-N. Chang and M.-H. Chiu. 2005. The development of authentic assessment to investigate ninth graders scientific literacy: In the case of scientific cognition concerning the concepts of chemistry and physics. *International Journal of Science and Mathematics Education*, 3:117–140.

J. Clarke-Midura. 2010. The Role of Technology in Science Assessments. *Better: Evidence-based Education*, 3(1).

R. Collobert, J. Weston, L. Bottou, M. Karlen, K. Kavukcuoglu, and P. Kuksa. 2011. Natural language processing (almost) from scratch. *Journal of Machine Learning Research*, 12:2493–2537.

Kan Deng and Andrew Moore. 1998. On the greediness of feature selection algorithms. In *Proc. International Conference on Machine Learning (ICML), June 1998*.

Mark Hall, Eibe Frank, Geoffrey Holmes, Bernhard Pfahringer, Peter Reutemann, and Ian H. Witten. 2009. The WEKA Data Mining Software: An Update. *SIGKDD Explorations*, 11(1).

M. A. Hall. 1998. Correlation-based feature subset selection for machine learning. In *Hamilton, New Zealand*.

D. Higgins, J. Burstein, D. Marcu, and C. Gentile. 2004. Evaluating multiple aspects of coherence in student essays. In *Proceedings of the annual meeting of the North American Chapter of the Association for Computational Linguistics, Boston, MA*.

Fei Huang, Alexander Yates, Arun Ahuja, and Doug Downey. 2011. Language Models as Representations for Weakly Supervised NLP Tasks. In *Conference on Computational Natural Language Learning (CoNLL)*.

Mark D. Kernighan, Kenneth W. Church, and William A. Gale. 1990. A spelling correction program based on a noisy channel model. In *Proceedings of the 13th Conference on Computational Linguistics*, pages 205–210.

D.J. Ketelhut, B. Nelson, and C. Schifter. 2009. Virtual Environments for Situated Science Assessment. In *Proceedings of the International Conference on Cognition and Exploratory Learning in the Digital Age*, pages 507–508.

D.J. Ketelhut, B. Nelson, C. Schifter, and Y. Kim. 2010. Using Immersive Virtual Environments to Assess Science Content Understanding: The Impact of Context. In D. G. Kinshuk, J. M. Sampson, P. Spector, D. Isaas, Ifenthaler, and R. Vasiu, editors, *Proceedings of the IADIS International Conference on Cognition and Exploratory Learning in the Digital Age (CELDA)*, pages 227–230.

Diane Jass Ketelhut, Alexander Yates, Avirup Sil, and Michael Timms. 2012. Applying Educational Data mining in E-learning environments. In *Section within the New Measurement Paradigm Report, p 47-52*.

T.K. Landauer and S.T. Dumais. 1997. A solution to Platos problem: The latent semantic analysis theory of acquisition, induction, and representation of knowledge. In *Psychological Review, 104*.

C. Leacock and M. Chodorow. 2003. C-rater: Automated scoring of short-answer questions. In *Computers and the Humanities, 37(4):389405*.

K.I. Malatesta, P. Wiemer-Hastings, and J. Robertson. 2002. Beyond the short answer question with research methods tutor. In *Proceedings of the Intelligent Tutoring Systems Conference*.

Chris Manning and Hinrich Schütze. 1999. *Foundations of Statistical Natural Language Processings*. MIT Press.

T. Mitchell, T. Russell, P. Broomhead, and N. Aldridge. 2002. Towards robust computerised marking of free-text responses. In *Proceedings of the 6th International Computer Assisted Assessment (CAA) Conference*.

Michael Mohler and Rada Mihalcea. 2009. Text-to-text semantic similarity for automatic short answer grading. In *Proceedings of the 12th Conference of the European Chapter of the Association for Computational Linguistics, EACL*.

National Research Council. 2005. *America's Lab Report: Investigations in High School Science*. National Academies Press.

T. Pang-Ning, M. Steinbach, and V. Kumar. 2006. *Introduction to Data Mining*. Pearson Addison-Wesley.

S.G. Pulman and J.Z. Sukkarieh. 2005. Automatic short answer marking. In *Proceedings of the Second workshop on Building Educational Applications Using NLP*.

Lawrence R. Rabiner. 1989. A tutorial on hidden Markov models and selected applications in speech recognition. *Proceedings of the IEEE*, 77(2):257–285.

M.K. Singley and H.L. Taft. 1995. Open-ended approaches to science assessment using computers. *Journal of Science Education and Technology*, 4(1):7–20.

A. Smola and B. Schölkopf. 1998. A tutorial on support vector regression. Technical report, Royal Holloway College, University of London, UK.

Mark Steyvers and Tom Griffiths. 2006. Probabilistic topic models. In T. Landauer, D. McNamara, S. Dennis, and W. Kintsch, editors, *Latent Semantic Analysis: A Road to Meaning*, pages 427–448. Lawrence Erlbaum Associates.

J. Sukkarieh and S. Stoyanchev. 2009. Automating model building in C-rater. In *Proceedings of the 2009 Workshop on Applied Textual Inference, pages 6169, Suntec, Singapore, August.*

J.Z. Sukkarieh, S.G. Pulman, and N. Raikes. 2004. Automarking 2: An update on the ucles-oxford university research into using computational linguistics to score short, free text responses. In *International Association of Educational Assessment, Philadephia.*

H-C. Wang, C-Y. Chang, and T-Y Li. 2008. Assessing creative problem solving with automated text grading. In *Computers and Education.*

P. Wiemer-Hastings, K. Wiemer-Hastings, and A. Graesser. 1999. Improving an intelligent tutors comprehension of students with latent semantic analysis. In *Artificial Intelligence in Education, pages 535542.*

P. Wiemer-Hastings, E. Arnott, and D. Allbritton. 2005. Initial results and mixed directions for research methods tutor. In *AIED2005 - Supplementary Proceedings of the 12th International Conference on Artificial Intelligence in Education, Amsterdam.*

Modeling coherence in ESOL learner texts

Helen Yannakoudakis
Computer Laboratory
University of Cambridge
United Kingdom
Helen.Yannakoudakis@cl.cam.ac.uk

Ted Briscoe
Computer Laboratory
University of Cambridge
United Kingdom
Ted.Briscoe@cl.cam.ac.uk

Abstract

To date, few attempts have been made to develop new methods and validate existing ones for automatic evaluation of discourse coherence in the noisy domain of learner texts. We present the first systematic analysis of several methods for assessing coherence under the framework of automated assessment (AA) of learner free-text responses. We examine the predictive power of different coherence models by measuring the effect on performance when combined with an AA system that achieves competitive results, but does not use discourse coherence features, which are also strong indicators of a learner's level of attainment. Additionally, we identify new techniques that outperform previously developed ones and improve on the best published result for AA on a publically-available dataset of English learner free-text examination scripts.

1 Introduction

Automated assessment (hereafter AA) systems of English learner text assign grades based on textual features which attempt to balance evidence of writing competence against evidence of performance errors. Previous work has mostly treated AA as a supervised text classification or regression task. A number of techniques have been investigated, including cosine similarity of feature vectors (Attali and Burstein, 2006), often combined with dimensionality reduction techniques such as Latent Semantic Analysis (LSA) (Landauer et al., 2003), and generative machine learning models (Rudner and Liang, 2002) as well as discriminative ones (Yannakoudakis et al., 2011). As multiple factors influence the linguistic quality of texts, such systems exploit features that correspond to different properties of texts, such as grammar, style, vocabulary usage, topic similarity, and discourse coherence and cohesion.

Cohesion refers to the use of explicit linguistic cohesive devices (e.g., anaphora, lexical semantic relatedness, discourse markers, etc.) within a text that can signal primarily suprasentential discourse relations between textual units (Halliday and Hasan, 1976). Cohesion is not the only mechanism of discourse coherence, which may also be inferred from meaning without presence of explicit linguistic cues. Coherence can be assessed locally in terms of transitions between adjacent clauses, parentheticals, and other textual units capable of standing in discourse relations, or more globally in terms of the overall topical coherence of text passages.

There is a large body of work that has investigated a number of different coherence models on news texts (e.g., Lin et al. (2011), Elsner and Charniak (2008), and Soricut and Marcu (2006)). Recently, Pitler et al. (2010) presented a detailed survey of current techniques in coherence analysis of extractive summaries. To date, however, few attempts have been made to develop new methods and validate existing ones for automatic evaluation of discourse coherence and cohesion in the noisy domain of learner texts, where spelling and grammatical errors are common.

Coherence quality is typically present in marking criteria for evaluating learner texts, and it is identified by examiners as a determinant of the overall score. Thus we expect that adding a coherence metric to the feature set of an AA system would better reflect the evaluation performed by examiners and improve performance. The goal of the experiments presented in this paper is to measure the effect a number of (previously-developed and new) coherence models have on performance when combined with an AA system that achieves competitive results, but does not use discourse coherence features.

Our contribution is threefold: 1) we present the first systematic analysis of several methods for assessing discourse coherence in the framework of AA of learner free-text responses, 2) we identify new discourse features that serve as proxies for the level of (in)coherence in texts and outperform previously developed techniques, and 3) we improve the best results reported by Yannakoudakis et al. (2011) on the publically available 'English as a Second or Other Language' (ESOL) corpus of learner texts (to date, this is the only public-domain corpus that contains grades). Finally, we explore the utility of our best model for assessing the incoherent 'outlier' texts used in Yannakoudakis et al. (2011).

2 Experimental Design & Background

We examine the predictive power of a number of different coherence models by measuring the effect on performance when combined with an AA system that achieves state-of-the-art results, but does not use discourse coherence features. Specifically, we describe a number of different experiments improving on the AA system presented in Yannakoudakis et al. (2011); AA is treated as a rank preference supervised learning problem and ranking Support Vector Machines (SVMs) (Joachims, 2002) are used to explicitly model the grade relationships between scripts. This system uses a number of different linguistic features that achieve good performance on the AA task. However, these features only focus on lexical and grammatical properties, as well as errors within individual sentences, ignoring discourse coherence, which is also present in marking criteria for evaluating learner texts, as well as a strong indicator of a writer's understanding of a language.

Also, in Yannakoudakis et al. (2011), experiments are presented that test the validity of the system using a number of automatically-created 'outlier' texts. The results showed that the model is vulnerable to input where individually high-scoring sentences are randomly ordered within a text. Failing to identify such pathological cases makes AA systems vulnerable to subversion by writers who understand something of its workings, thus posing a threat to their validity. For example, an examinee might learn by rote a set of well-formed sentences and reproduce these in an exam in the knowledge that an AA system is not checking for prompt relevance or coherence[1].

3 Dataset & Experimental Setup

We use the First Certificate in English (FCE) ESOL examination scripts[2] (upper-intermediate level assessment) described in detail in Yannakoudakis et al. (2011), extracted from the Cambridge Learner Corpus[3] (CLC). The dataset consists of 1,238 texts between 200 and 400 words produced by 1,238 distinct learners in response to two different prompts. An overall mark has been assigned in the range 1–40.

For all experiments, we use a series of 5-fold cross-validation runs on 1,141 texts from the examination year 2000 to evaluate performance as well as generalization of numerous models. Moreover, we identify the best model on year 2000 and we also test it on 97 texts from the examination year 2001, previously used in Yannakoudakis et al. (2011) to report the best published results. Validating the results on a different examination year tests generalization to some prompts not used in 2000, and also allows us to test correlation between examiners and the AA system. Again, we treat AA as a rank preference learning problem and use SVMs, utilizing the SVM^{light} package (Joachims, 2002), to facilitate comparison with Yannakoudakis et al. (2011).

4 Discourse Coherence

We focus on the development and evaluation of (automated) methods for assessing coherence in learner

[1]Powers et al. (2002) report the results of a related experiment with the AA system e-Rater, in which experts tried to subvert the system by submitting essays they believed would be inaccurately scored.

[2]http://ilexir.co.uk/applications/clc-fce-dataset/

[3]http://www.cup.cam.ac.uk/gb/elt/catalogue/subject/custom /item3646603/

texts under the framework of AA. Most of the methods we investigate require syntactic analysis. As in Yannakoudakis et al. (2011), we analyze all texts using the RASP toolkit (Briscoe et al., 2006)[4].

4.1 'Superficial' Proxies

In this section we introduce diverse classes of 'superficial' cohesive features that serve as proxies for coherence. Surface text properties have been assessed in the framework of automatic summary evaluation (Pitler et al., 2010), and have been shown to significantly correlate with the fluency of machine-translated sentences (Chae and Nenkova, 2009).

4.1.1 Part-of-Speech (POS) Distribution

The AA system described in Yannakoudakis et al. (2011) exploited features based on POS tag sequences, but did not consider the distribution of POS types across grades. In coherent texts, constituent clauses and sentences are related and depend on each other for their interpretation. Anaphors such as pronouns link the current sentence to those where the entities were previously mentioned. Pronouns can be directly related to (lack of) coherence and make intuitive sense as cohesive devices. We compute the number of pronouns in a text and use it as a shallow feature for capturing coherence.

4.1.2 Discourse Connectives

Discourse connectives (such as *but* or *because*) relate propositions expressed by different clauses or sentences. The presence of such items in a text should be indicative of (better) coherence. We thus compute a number of shallow cohesive features as proxies for coherence, based on fixed lists of words belonging to the following categories: (a) Addition (e.g., *additionally*), (b) Comparison (e.g., *likewise*), (c) Contrast (e.g., *whereas*) and (d) Conclusion (e.g., *therefore*), and use the frequencies of these four categories as features.

4.1.3 Word Length

The previous AA system treated script length as a normalizing feature, but otherwise avoided such 'superficial' proxies of text quality. However, many cohesive words are longer than average, especially for the closed-class functional component of English vocabulary. We thus assess the minimum, maximum and average word length as a superficial proxy for coherence.

[4]http://ilexir.co.uk/applications/rasp/

4.2 Semantic Similarity

We explore the utility of inter-sentential feature types for assessing discourse coherence. Among the features used in Yannakoudakis et al. (2011), none explicitly captures coherence and none models inter-sentential relationships. Incremental Semantic analysis (ISA) (Baroni et al., 2007) is a word-level distributional model that induces a semantic space from input texts. ISA is a fully-incremental variation of Random Indexing (RI) (Sahlgren, 2005), which can efficiently capture second-order effects in common with other dimensionality-reduction methods based on singular value decomposition, but does not rely on stoplists or global statistics for weighting purposes.

Utilizing the S-Space package (Jurgens and Stevens, 2010), we trained an ISA model[5] using a subset of ukWaC (Ferraresi et al., 2008), a large corpus of English containing more than 2 billion tokens. We used the POS tagger lexicon provided with the RASP system to discard documents whose proportion of valid English words to total words is less than 0.4; 78,000 documents were extracted in total and were then preprocessed replacing URLs, email addresses, IP addresses, numbers and emoticons with special markers. To measure local coherence we define the similarity between two sentences s_i and s_{i+1} as the maximum cosine similarity between the history vectors of the words they contain. The overall coherence of a text T is then measured by taking the mean of all sentence-pair scores:

$$\text{coherence}(T) = \frac{\sum_{i=1}^{n-1} \max_{k,j} \text{sim}(s_i^k, s_{i+1}^j)}{n-1} \quad (1)$$

where $\text{sim}(s_i^k, s_{i+1}^j)$ is the cosine similarity between the history vectors of the kth word in s_i and the jth word in s_{i+1}, and n is the total number of sentences[6]. We investigate the efficacy of ISA by adding this coherence score, as well as the maximum

[5]The parameters of our ISA model are fairly standard: 1800 dimensions, a context window of 3 words, impact rate $i = 0.0003$ and decay rate $k_m = 50$.

[6]We exclude articles, conjunctions, prepositions and auxiliary verbs from the calculation of sentence similarity.

sim value found over the entire text, to the vectors of features associated with a text. The hypothesis is that the degree of semantic relatedness between adjoining sentences serves as a proxy for local discourse coherence; that is, coherent text units contain semantically-related words.

Higgins et al. (2004) and Higgins and Burstein (2007) use RI to determine the semantic similarity between sentences of same/different discourse segments (e.g., from the essay thesis and conclusion, or between sentences and the essay prompt), and assess the percentage of sentences that are correctly classified as related or unrelated. The main differences from our approach are that we assess the utility of semantic space models for predicting the overall grade for a text, in contrast to binary classification at the sentence-level, and we use ISA rather than RI[7].

4.3 Entity-based Coherence

The entity-based coherence model, proposed by Barzilay and Lapata (2008), is one of the most popular statistical models of inter-sentential coherence, and learns coherence properties similar to those employed by Centering Theory (Grosz et al., 1995). Local coherence is modeled on the basis of sequences of entity mentions that are labeled with their syntactic roles (e.g., subject, object). We construct the entity grids using the Brown Coherence Toolkit[8,9] (Elsner and Charniak, 2011b), and use as features the probabilities of different entity transition types, defined in terms of their role in adjacent sentences[10]. Burstein et al. (2010) show how the entity-grid can be used to discriminate high-coherence from low-coherence learner texts. The main difference with our approach is that we evaluate the entity-grid model in the context of AA text grading, rather than binary classification.

[7]We also used RI in addition to ISA, and found that it did not yield significantly different results. In particular, we trained a RI model with 2,000 dimensions and a context window of 3 on the same ukWaC data. Below we only report results for the fully-incremental ISA model.

[8]https://bitbucket.org/melsner/browncoherence

[9]The tool does not perform full coreference resolution; instead, coreference is approximated by linking entities that share a head noun.

[10]We represent entities with specified roles (Subject, Object, Neither, Absent), use transition probabilities of length 2, 3 and 4, and a salience option of 2.

4.4 Pronoun Coreference Model

Pronominal anaphora is another important aspect of coherence. Charniak and Elsner (2009) present an unsupervised generative model of pronominal anaphora for coherence modeling. In their implementation, they model each pronoun as generated by an antecedent somewhere in the previous two sentences. If a 'good' antecedent is found, the probability of a pronoun will be high; otherwise, the probability will be low. The overall probability of a text is then calculated as the probability of the resulting sequence of pronoun assignments. In our experiments, we use the pre-trained model distributed by Charniak and Elsner (2009) for news text to estimate the probability of a text and include it as a feature. However, this model is trained on high-quality texts, so performance may deteriorate when applied to learner texts. It is not obvious how to train such a model on learner texts and we leave this for future research.

4.5 Discourse-new Model

Elsner and Charniak (2008) apply a discourse-new classifier to model coherence. Their classifier distinguishes NPs whose referents have not been previously mentioned in the discourse from those that have been already introduced, using a number of syntactic and lexical features. To model coherence, they assign each NP in a text a label $L_{np} \in \{new, old\}$[11], and calculate the probability of a text as $\Pi_{np:NPs} P(L_{np}|np)$. Again, we use the pre-trained model distributed by Charniak and Elsner (2009) for news text to find the probability of a text following Elsner and Charniak (2008) and include it as a feature.

4.6 IBM Coherence Model

Soricut and Marcu (2006) adapted the IBM model 1 (Brown et al., 1994) used in machine translation (MT) to model local discourse coherence. The intuition behind the IBM model in MT is that the use of certain words in a source language is likely to trigger the use of certain words in a target language. Instead, they hypothesized that the use of certain words in a sentence tends to trigger the use of certain words in an adjoining sentence. In contrast to

[11]NPs with the same head are considered to be coreferent.

semantic space models such as ISA or RI (discussed above), this method models the intuition that local coherence is signaled by the identification of word co-occurrence patterns across adjacent sentences.

We compute two features introduced by Soricut and Marcu (2006): the *forward likelihood* and the *backward likelihood*. The first refers to the likelihood of observing the words in sentence s_{i+1} conditioned on s_i, and the latter to the likelihood of observing the words in s_i conditioned on s_{i+1}. We extract 3 million adjacent sentences from ukWaC[12], and use the GIZA++ (Och and Ney, 2000) implementation of IBM model 1 to obtain the probabilities of recurring patterns. The forward and backward probabilities are calculated over the entire text, and their values are used as features in our feature vectors[13]. We further extend the above model and incorporate syntactic aspects of text coherence by training on POS tags instead of lexical items. We try to model the intuition that local coherence is signaled by the identification of POS co-occurrence patterns across adjacent sentences, where the use of certain POS tags in a sentence tends to trigger the use of other POS tags in an adjacent sentence. We analyze 3 million adjacent sentences using the RASP POS tagger and train the same IBM model to obtain the probabilities of recurring POS patterns.

4.7 Lemma/POS Cosine Similarity

A simple method of incorporating (syntactic) aspects of text coherence is to use cosine similarity between vectors of lemma and/or POS-tag counts in adjacent sentences. We experiment with both: each sentence is represented by a vector whose dimension depends on the total number of lemmas/POS-types. The sentence vectors are weighted using lemma/POS frequency, and the cosine similarity between adjacent sentences is calculated. The coherence of a text T is then calculated as the average value of cosine similarity over the entire text[14]:

$$\text{coherence}(T) = \frac{\sum_{i=1}^{n-1} \text{sim}(s_i, s_{i+1})}{n-1} \quad (2)$$

[12]We use the same subset of documents as the ones used to train our ISA model in Section 4.2.

[13]Pitler et al. (2010) have also investigated the IBM model to measure text quality in automatically-generated texts.

[14]Pitler et al. (2010) use POS cosine similarity to measure continuity in automatically-generated texts.

4.8 Locally-Weighted Bag-of-Words

The popular bag-of-words (BOW) assumption represents a text as a histogram of word occurrences. While computationally efficient, such a representation is unable to maintain any sequential information. The locally-weighted bag-of-words (LOWBOW) framework, introduced by Lebanon et al. (2007), is a sequentially-sensitive alternative to BOW. In BOW, we represent a text as a histogram over the vocabulary used to generate that text. In LOWBOW, a text is represented by a set of local histograms computed across the whole text, but smoothed by kernels centered on different locations.

More specifically, a smoothed characterization of the local histogram is obtained by integrating a length-normalized document with respect to a non-uniform measure that is concentrated around a particular location $\mu \in [0, 1]$. In accordance with the statistical literature on non-parametric smoothing, we refer to such a measure as a smoothing kernel. The kernel parameters μ and σ specify the local histogram's position in the text (i.e., where it is centered) and its scale (i.e., to what extent it is smoothed over the surrounding region) respectively. In contrast to BOW or n-grams, which keep track of frequently occurring patterns independent of their positions, this representation is able to robustly capture medium and long range sequential trends in a text by keeping track of changes in the histograms from its beginning to end.

Geometrically, LOWBOW uses local smoothing to embed texts as smooth curves in the multinomial simplex. These curves summarize the progression of semantic and/or statistical trends through the text. By varying the amount of smoothing we obtain a family of sequential representations possessing different sequential resolutions or scales. Low resolution representations capture topic trends and shifts while ignoring finer details. High resolution representations capture fine sequential details but make it difficult to grasp the general trends within the text[15].

Since coherence involves both cohesive lexical devices and sequential progression within a text, we believe that LOWBOW can be used to assess the sequential content and the global structure and coher-

[15]For more details regarding LOWBOW and its geometric properties see Lebanon et al. (2007).

ence of texts. We use a publically-available LOWBOW implementation[16] to create local histograms over word unigrams. For the LOWBOW kernel smoothing function (see above), we use the Gaussian probability density function restricted to $[0, 1]$ and re-normalized, and a smoothing σ value of 0.02. Additionally, we consider a total number of 9 local histograms (discourse segments). We further extend the above model and incorporate syntactic aspects of text coherence by using local histograms over POS unigrams. This representation is able to capture sequential trends abstracted into POS tags. We try to model the hypothesis that coherence is signaled by sequential, mostly inter-sentential progression of POS types.

Since each text is represented by a set of local histrograms/vectors, and standard SVM kernels cannot work with such input spaces, we use instead a kernel defined over sets of vectors: the diffusion kernel (Lafferty and Lebanon, 2005) compares local histograms in a one-to-one fashion (i.e., histograms at the same locations are compared to each other), and has proven to be useful for related tasks (Lebanon et al., 2007; Escalante et al., 2011). To the best of our knowledge, LOWBOW representations have not been investigated for coherence evaluation (under the AA framework). So far, they have been applied to discourse segmentation (AMIDA, 2007), text categorization (Lebanon et al., 2007), and authorship attribution (Escalante et al., 2011).

5 Evaluation

We examine the predictive power of each of the coherence models/features described in Section 4 by measuring the effect on performance when combined with an AA system that achieves state-of-the-art results on the FCE dataset, but does not use discourse coherence features. In particular, we use the system described in Yannakoudakis et al. (2011) as our baseline AA system. Discourse coherence is a strong indicator of thorough knowledge of a second language and thus we expect coherence features to further improve performance of AA systems.

We evaluate the grade predictions of our models against the gold standard grades in the dataset using Pearson's product-moment correlation coefficient (r) and Spearman's rank correlation coefficient (ρ) as is standard in AA research (Briscoe et al., 2010). Table 1 gives results obtained by augmenting the baseline model with each of the coherence features described above. In each of these experiments, we perform 5-fold cross-validation[17] using all 1,141 texts from the exam year 2000 (see Section 3).

Most of the resulting models have minimal effect on performance[18]. However, word length, ISA, $\text{LOWBOW}_{\text{lex}}$, and the IBM $\text{model}_{\text{POS}_\text{f}}$ derived models all improve performance, while larger differences are observed in r. The highest performance – 0.675 and 0.678 – is obtained with ISA, while the second best feature is word length. The entity-grid, the pronoun model and the discourse-new model do not improve on the baseline. Although these models have been successfully used as components in state-of-the-art systems for discriminating coherent from incoherent news documents (Elsner and Charniak, 2011b), and the entity-grid model has also been successfully applied to learner text (Burstein et al., 2010), they seem to have minimal impact on performance, while the discourse-new model decreases ρ by~0.01. On the other hand, $\text{LOWBOW}_{\text{lex}}$ and $\text{LOWBOW}_{\text{POS}}$ give an increase in performance, which confirms our hypothesis that local histograms are useful. Also, the former seems to perform slightly better than the latter.

Our adapted version of the IBM model – IBM $\text{model}_{\text{POS}}$ – performs better than its lexicalized version, which does not have an impact on performance, while larger differences are observed in r. Additionally, the increase in performance is larger than the one obtained with the entity-grid, pronoun or discourse-new model. The forward version of IBM $\text{model}_{\text{POS}}$ seems to perform slightly better than the backward one, while the results are comparable to $\text{LOWBOW}_{\text{POS}}$ and outperformed by $\text{LOWBOW}_{\text{lex}}$. The rest of the models do not perform as well; the number of pronouns or discourse connectives gives low results, while lemma and POS cosine similarity between adjacent sentences are also

[16] http://goo.gl/yQ0Q0

[17] We compute mean values of correlation coefficients by first applying the r-to-Z Fisher transformation, and then using the Fisher weighted mean correlation coefficient (Faller, 1981).

[18] Significance tests in averaged correlations are omitted as variable estimates are produced, whose variance is hard to be estimated unbiasedly.

		r	ρ
0	Baseline	0.651	0.670
1	POS distr.	0.653	0.670
2	Disc. connectives	0.648	0.668
3	Word length	**0.667**	**0.676**
4	ISA	**0.675**	**0.678**
5	EGrid	0.650	0.668
6	Pronoun	0.650	0.668
7	Disc-new	0.646	0.662
8	$\text{LOWBOW}_{\text{lex}}$	**0.663**	**0.677**
9	$\text{LOWBOW}_{\text{POS}}$	0.659	0.674
10	IBM $\text{model}_{\text{lex}_\text{f}}$	0.649	0.668
11	IBM $\text{model}_{\text{lex}_\text{b}}$	0.649	0.667
12	IBM $\text{model}_{\text{POS}_\text{f}}$	**0.661**	**0.672**
13	IBM $\text{model}_{\text{POS}_\text{b}}$	0.658	0.669
14	Lemma cosine	0.651	0.667
15	POS cosine	0.650	0.665
16	5+6+7+10+11	0.648	0.665
17	All	0.677	0.671

Table 1: 5-fold cross-validation performance on texts from year 2000 when adding different coherence features on top of the baseline AA system.

among the weakest predictors.

Elsner and Charniak (2011b) have shown that combining the entity-grid with the pronoun, discourse-new and lexicalized IBM models gives state-of-the-art results for discriminating news documents and their random permutations. We also combine these models and assess their performance under the AA framework. Row 16 of Table 1 shows that the combination does not give an improvement over the individual models. Moreover, combining all feature classes together in row 17 does not yield higher results than those obtained with ISA, while ρ is no better than the baseline.

In the following experiments, we evaluate the best model identified on year 2000 on a set of 97 texts from the exam year 2001, previously used in Yannakoudakis et al. (2011) to report results of the final best system. Validating the model on a different exam year also shows us the extent to which it generalizes between years. Table 2 presents the results. The published correlations on this dataset are 0.741 and 0.773 r and ρ respectively. Adding ISA on top of the previous system significantly improves[19] the

	r	ρ
Baseline	0.741	0.773
ISA	**0.749**	**0.790***

Table 2: Performance on the exam scripts drawn from the examination year 2001. $\star$ indicates a significant improvement at $\alpha = 0.05$.

published results on the 2001 texts, getting closer to the upper-bound. The upper-bound on this dataset[20] is 0.796 and 0.792 r and ρ respectively, calculated by taking the average correlation between the FCE grades and the ones provided by 4 senior ESOL examiners[21]. Table 3 also presents the average correlation between our extended AA system's predicted grades and the 4 examiners' grades, in addition to the original FCE grades from the dataset. Again, our extended model improves over the baseline.

Finally, we explore the utility of our best model for assessing the publically available 'outlier' texts used in Yannakoudakis et al. (2011). The previous AA system is unable to downgrade appropriately 'outlier' scripts containing individually high-scoring sentences with poor overall coherence, created by randomly ordering a set of highly-marked texts. To test our best system, we train an SVM rank preference model with the ISA-derived coherence feature, which can explicitly capture such sequential trends. A generic model for flagging putative 'outlier' texts – whose predicted score is lower than a predefined threshold – for manual checking might be used as the first stage of a deployed AA system. The ISA model improves r and ρ by 0.320 and 0.463 respectively for predicting a score on this type of 'outlier' texts and their original version (Table 4).

6 Analysis & Discussion

In the previous section, we evaluated various cohesion and coherence features on learner data, and found different patterns of performance compared to those previously reported on news texts (see Section 7 for more details). Although most of the models examined gave a minimal effect on AA performance, ISA, $\text{LOWBOW}_{\text{lex}}$, IBM $\text{model}_{\text{POS}_\text{f}}$ and word length

[19]Calculated using one-tailed tests for the difference between dependent correlations (Williams, 1959; Steiger, 1980).

[20]See Yannakoudakis et al. (2011) for details.

[21]The examiners' scores are also distributed with the FCE dataset.

	r	ρ
Baseline	0.723	0.721
ISA	**0.727**	**0.736**

Table 3: Average correlation between the AA model, the FCE dataset grades, and 4 examiners on the exam scripts from year 2000.

	r	ρ
Baseline	0.08	0.163
ISA	**0.400**	**0.626**

Table 4: Performance of the ISA AA model on outliers.

gave a clear improvement in correlation, with larger differences in r. Our results indicate that coherence metrics further improve the performance of a competitive AA system. More specifically, we found the ISA-derived feature to be the most effective contributor to the prediction of text quality. This suggests that incoherence in FCE texts might be due to topic discontinuities. Also, the improvement obtained by LOWBOW suggests that patterns of sequential progression within a text can be useful: coherent texts appear to use similar token distributions at similar locations across different documents.

The word length feature was successfully used as a proxy for coherence, perhaps because many cohesive words are longer than average. However, such a feature can also capture further aspects of texts, such as lexical complexity, so further investigation is needed to identify the extent to which it measures different properties. On the other hand, the minimal effect of the entity-grid, pronoun and discourse-new model suggests that infelicitous use of pronominal forms or sequences of entities may not be an issue in FCE texts. Preliminary investigation of the scripts showed that learners tend to repeat the same entity names or descriptions rather than use pronouns or shorter descriptions.

A possible explanation for the difference in performance between the lexicalized and POS IBM model is that the latter abstracts away from lexical information and thus avoids misspellings and reduces sparsity. Also, our discourse connective classes do not seem to have a predictive power. This may be because our manually-built word lists do not have sufficient coverage.

7 Previous Work

Comparatively few metrics have been investigated for evaluating coherence in (ESOL) learner texts. Miltsakaki and Kukich (2004) employ e-Rater (Attali and Burstein, 2006), an essay scoring system, and show that Centering Theory's Rough-Shift transitions (Grosz et al., 1995) contribute significantly to the assessment of learner texts. Higgins et al. (2004) and Higgins and Burstein (2007) use RI to determine the semantic similarity between sentences of same/different discourse segments. Their model is based on a number of different semantic similarity scores and assesses the percentage of sentences that are correctly classified as (un)related. Among their results, they found that it is hard to beat the baseline (as 98.1% of the sentences were annotated as 'highly related') and identify sentences which are not related to other ones in the same discourse segment. We demonstrate that the related fully-incremental ISA model can be used to improve AA grading accuracy on the FCE dataset, as opposed to classifying the (non-)relatedness of sentences.

Burstein et al. (2010) show how the entity-grid can be used to discriminate high-coherence from low-coherence learner texts. They augment this model with additional features related to writing quality and word usage, and show a positive effect in performance for automated coherence prediction of student essays of different populations. On the FCE dataset used here, entity-grids do not improve AA grading accuracy. This may be because the texts are shorter or because grading is a more difficult task than binary classification. Application of their augmented entity-grid model to FCE texts would be an interesting avenue for future research.

Foltz et al. (1998) examine local coherence in textbooks and articles using Latent Semantic Analysis (LSA) (Landauer et al., 2003). They assess semantic relatedness using vector-based similarity between adjacent sentences. They argue that LSA may be more appropriate for comparing the relative quality of texts; for determining the overall text coherence it may be difficult to set a criterion for the coherence value since it depends on a variety of different factors, such as the size of the text units to be compared. Nevertheless, our results show that ISA, a similar distributional semantic model with dimensionality reduction, improves FCE grading accuracy.

Barzilay and Lee (2004) implement lexicalized content models that represent global text properties on news articles and narratives using Hidden Markov Models (HMMs). In the HMM, states correspond to distinct topics, and transitions between states represent the probability of moving from one topic to another. This approach has the advantage of capturing the order in which different topics appear in texts; however, the HMMs are highly domain specific and would probably need retraining for each distinct essay prompt.

Soricut and Marcu (2006) use a log-linear model that combines local and global models of coherence and show that it outperforms each of the individual ones on news articles and accident reports. Their global model is based on the document content model proposed by Barzilay and Lee (2004). Their local model of discourse coherence is based on the entity-grid (Barzilay and Lapata, 2008), as well as on the lexicalized IBM model (see Section 4.6 above); we have experimented with both, and showed that they have a minimal effect on grading performance with the FCE dataset.

Elsner and Charniak (2008;2011a) apply a discourse-new classifier and a pronoun coreference system to model coherence (see Section 4) on dialogue and news texts. They found that combining these models with the entity-grid achieves state-of-the-art performance. We found that such a combination, as well as the individual models do not perform well for grading the FCE texts.

Recently, Elsner and Charniak (2011a) proposed a variation of the entity-grid intended to integrate topical information. They use Latent Dirichlet Allocation (Blei et al., 2003) to learn topic-to-word distributions, and model coherence by generalizing the binary history features of the entity-grid and computing a real-valued feature which represents the similarity between an entity and the subject(s) of the previous sentence. Also, Lin et al. (2011) proposed a model that assesses the coherence of a text based on discourse relation transitions. The underlying idea is that coherent texts exhibit measurable preferences for specific intra- and inter-discourse relation ordering. They found their model to be complementary to the entity-grid, as it encodes the notion of preferential ordering of discourse relations, and thus tackles local coherence from a different perspective. Applying the above models to AA on learner texts would also be an interesting avenue for future work.

8 Conclusion

We presented the first systematic analysis of a wide variety of models for assessing discourse coherence on learner data, and evaluated their individual performance as well as their combinations for the AA grading task. We adapted the LOWBOW model for assessing sequential content in texts, and showed evidence supporting our hypothesis that local histograms are useful. We also successfully adapted ISA, an efficient and incremental variant distributional semantic model, to this task. ISA, LOWBOW, the POS IBM model and word length are the best individual features for assessing coherence.

A significant improvement over the AA system presented in Yannakoudakis et al. (2011) and the best published result on the FCE dataset was obtained by augmenting the system with an ISA-based local coherence feature. However, it is quite likely that further experimentation with LOWBOW features, given the large range of possible parameter settings, would yield better results too.

We also explored the robustness of the ISA model of local coherence on 'outlier' texts and achieved much better correlations with the examiner's grades for these texts in the FCE dataset. This should facilitate development of an automated system to detect essays consisting of high-quality but incoherent sequences of sentences.

All our results are specific to ESOL FCE texts and may not generalize to other genres or ESOL attainment levels. Future work should also investigate a wider range of (learner) texts and further coherence models, such as that of Elsner and Charniak (2011a) and Lin et al. (2011).

Acknowledgments

We are grateful to Cambridge ESOL, a division of Cambridge Assessment, for supporting this research. We would like to thank Marek Rei and Øistein Andersen for their valuable comments and suggestions, Yi Mao for giving us access to her code, as well as the anonymous reviewers for their useful feedback.

References

AMIDA. 2007. Augmented multi-party interaction with distance access. Available from www. amidaproject.org/, AMIDA Report.

Yigal Attali and Jill Burstein. 2006. Automated essay scoring with e-rater v.2. *Journal of Technology, Learning, and Assessment*, 4(3):1–30.

Marco Baroni, Alessandro Lenci, and Luca Onnis. 2007. ISA meets Lara: An incremental word space model for cognitively plausible simulations of semantic learning. In *Proceedings of the Association for Computational Linguistics*.

Regina Barzilay and Mirella Lapata. 2008. Modeling Local Coherence: An Entity-Based Approach. *Computational Linguistics*, 34(1):1–34.

Regina Barzilay and Lillian Lee. 2004. Catching the drift: Probabilistic content models, with applications to generation and summarization. In *Proceedings of the Human Language Technology Conference of the North American Chapter of the Association for Computational Linguistics*.

David M. Blei, Andrew Y. Ng, and Michael I. Jordan. 2003. Latent dirichlet allocation. *Journal of Machine Learning Research*.

Ted Briscoe, John Carroll, and Rebecca Watson. 2006. The second release of the RASP system. In *Proceedings of the COLING/ACL*, volume 6.

Ted Briscoe, Ben Medlock, and Øistein Andersen. 2010. Automated assessment of ESOL free text examinations. Technical Report UCAM-CL-TR-790, University of Cambridge, Computer Laboratory, November.

Peter F. Brown, Stephen A. Della Pietra, Vincent J. Della Pietra, and Robert L. Mercer. 1994. The mathematic of statistical machine translation: Parameter estimation. *Computational linguistics*, 19(2):263–311.

Jill Burstein, Joel Tetreault, and Slava Andreyev. 2010. Using entity-based features to model coherence in student essays. In *Proceedings of the Human Language Technology Conference of the North American Chapter of the Association for Computational Linguistics*, pages 681–684.

Jieun Chae and Ani Nenkova. 2009. Predicting the fluency of text with shallow structural features: case studies of machine translation and human-written text. In *Proceedings of the 12th Conference of the European Chapter of the Association for Computational Linguistics*, pages 139–147.

Eugene Charniak and Micha Elsner. 2009. EM works for pronoun anaphora resolution. In *Proceedings of the 12th Conference of the European Chapter of the Association for Computational Linguistics*, pages 148–156.

Micha Elsner and Eugene Charniak. 2008. Coreference-inspired coherence modeling. In *Proceedings of the 46th Annual Meeting of the Association for Computational Linguistics on Human Language Technologies*, pages 41–44.

Micha Elsner and Eugene Charniak. 2011a. Disentangling chat with local coherence models. In *Proceedings of the 49th Annual Meeting of the Association for Computational Linguistics: Human Language Technologies*, pages 1179–1189.

Micha Elsner and Eugene Charniak. 2011b. Extending the entity grid with entity-specific features. In *Proceedings of the 49th Annual Meeting of the Association for Computational Linguistics: Human Language Technologies*, pages 125–129.

Hugo J. Escalante, Thamar Solorio, and Manuel Montes-y Gómez. 2011. Local Histograms of Character N-grams for Authorship Attribution. In *Proceedings of the 49th Annual Meeting on Association for Computational Linguistics*, pages 288–298.

Alan J. Faller. 1981. An Average Correlation Coefficient. *Journal of Applied Meteorology*.

Adriano Ferraresi, Eros Zanchetta, Marco Baroni, and Silvia Bernardini. 2008. Introducing and evaluating ukWaC, a very large web-derived corpus of English. In S. Evert, A. Kilgarriff, and S. Sharoff, editors, *Proceedings of the 4th Web as Corpus Workshop*.

Peter W. Foltz, Walter Kintsch, and Thomas K. Landauer. 1998. The measurement of textual coherence with latent semantic analysis. *Discourse processes*, 25(2):285–308.

Barbara J. Grosz, Scott Weinstein, and Aravind K. Joshi. 1995. Centering: A framework for modeling the local coherence of discourse. *Computational linguistics*, 21(2):203–225.

Michael A. K. Halliday and Ruqaiya Hasan. 1976. *Cohesion in English* . Longman Pub Group.

Derrick Higgins and Jill Burstein. 2007. Sentence similarity measures for essay coherence. In *Proceedings of the 7th International Workshop on Computational Semantics*, pages 1–12.

Derrick Higgins, Jill Burstein, Daniel Marcu, and Claudia Gentile. 2004. Evaluating multiple aspects of coherence in student essays. In *Proceedings of the Human Language Technology Conference of the North American Chapter of the Association for Computational Linguistics*.

Thorsten Joachims. 2002. Optimizing search engines using clickthrough data. In *Proceedings of the ACM Conference on Knowledge Discovery and Data Mining*, pages 133–142.

David Jurgens and Keith Stevens. 2010. The S-Space package: an open source package for word space models. In *Proceedings of the Association for Computational Linguistics 2010 System Demonstrations*, pages 30–35.

John Lafferty and Guy Lebanon. 2005. Diffusion kernels on statistical manifolds. *Journal of Machine Learning Research*, 6:129–163.

Thomas K. Landauer, Darrell Laham, and Peter W. Foltz. 2003. Automated scoring and annotation of essays with the Intelligent Essay Assessor. In M.D. Shermis and J.C. Burstein, editors, *Automated essay scoring: A cross-disciplinary perspective*, pages 87–112.

Guy Lebanon, Yi Mao, and Joshua Dillon. 2007. The locally weighted bag-of-words framework for document representation. *Journal of Machine Learning Research*, 8(10):2405–2441.

Ziheng Lin, Hwee T. Ng, and Min-Yen Kan. 2011. Automatically Evaluating Text Coherence Using Discourse Relations. In *Proceedings of the 49th Annual Meeting on Association for Computational Linguistics*.

Eleni Miltsakaki and Karen Kukich. 2004. Evaluation of text coherence for electronic essay scoring systems. *Natural Language Engineering*, 10(01):25–55.

Franz J. Och and Hermann Ney. 2000. Improved statistical alignment models. In *Proceedings of the 38th Annual Meeting on Association for Computational Linguistics*, pages 440–447.

Emily Pitler, Annie Louis, and Ani Nenkova. 2010. Automatic evaluation of linguistic quality in multi-document summarization. In *Proceedings of the 48th Annual Meeting of the Association for Computational Linguistics*, pages 544–554.

Donald E. Powers, Jill C. Burstein, Martin Chodorow, Mary E. Fowles, and Karen Kukich. 2002. Stumping e-rater: challenging the validity of automated essay scoring. *Computers in Human Behavior*, 18(2):103–134.

Lawrence M. Rudner and Tahung Liang. 2002. Automated essay scoring using Bayes' theorem. *The Journal of Technology, Learning and Assessment*, 1(2):3–21.

Magnus Sahlgren. 2005. An introduction to random indexing. In *Methods and Applications of Semantic Indexing Workshop at the 7th International Conference on Terminology and Knowledge Engineering*, pages 1–9. Citeseer.

Radu Soricut and Daniel Marcu. 2006. Discourse generation using utility-trained coherence models. In *Proceedings of the COLING/ACL on Main conference poster sessions*, pages 803–810.

James H. Steiger. 1980. Tests for comparing elements of a correlation matrix. *Psychological Bulletin*, 87(2):245–251.

Evan J. Williams. 1959. The Comparison of Regression Variables. *Journal of the Royal Statistical Society. Series B (Methodological)*, 21(2):396–399.

Helen Yannakoudakis, Ted Briscoe, and Ben Medlock. 2011. A New Dataset and Method for Automatically Grading ESOL Texts. In *The 49th Annual Meeting of the Association for Computational Linguistics: Human Language Technologies*.

Exploring Grammatical Error Correction with Not-So-Crummy Machine Translation*

Nitin Madnani **Joel Tetreault**
Educational Testing Service
Princeton, NJ, USA
{nmadnani,jtetreault}@ets.org

Martin Chodorow
Hunter College of CUNY
New York, NY, USA
martin.chodorow@hunter.cuny.edu

Abstract

To date, most work in grammatical error correction has focused on targeting specific error types. We present a probe study into whether we can use round-trip translations obtained from Google Translate via 8 different pivot languages for **whole-sentence** grammatical error correction. We develop a novel alignment algorithm for combining multiple round-trip translations into a lattice using the TERp machine translation metric. We further implement six different methods for extracting whole-sentence corrections from the lattice. Our preliminary experiments yield fairly satisfactory results but leave significant room for improvement. Most importantly, though, they make it clear the methods we propose have strong potential and require further study.

1 Introduction

Given the large and growing number of non-native English speakers around the world, detecting and correcting grammatical errors in learner text currently ranks as one of the most popular educational NLP applications. Previously published work has explored the effectiveness of using **round-trip machine translation** (translating an English sentence to some foreign language F, called the *pivot*, and then translating the F language sentence back to English) for correcting preposition errors (Hermet and Désilets, 2009). In this paper, we present a pilot study that explores the effectiveness of extending this approach to whole-sentence grammatical error correction.

Specifically, we explore whether using the concept of round-trip machine translation via *multiple*—rather than single—pivot languages has the potential of correcting most, if not all, grammatical errors present in a sentence. To do so, we develop a round-trip translation framework using the Google Translate API. Furthermore, we propose a novel combination algorithm that can combine the evidence present in multiple round-trip translations and increase the likelihood of producing a whole-sentence correction. Details of our methodology are presented in §3 and of the dataset we use in §4. Since this work is of an exploratory nature, we conduct a detailed error analysis and present the results in §5. Finally, §6 summarizes the contributions of this pilot study and provides a discussion of possible future work.

2 Related Work

To date, most work in grammatical error detection has focused on targeting specific error types (usually prepositions or article errors) by using rule-based methods or statistical machine-learning classification algorithms, or a combination of the two. Leacock et al. (2010) present a survey of the common approaches. However, targeted errors such as preposition and determiner errors are just two of the many types of grammatical errors present in non-native writing. One of the anonymous reviewers for this paper makes the point eloquently: *"Given the frequent complexity of learner errors, less holistic, error-type specific approaches are often unable to*

*cf. *Good Applications for Crummy Machine Translation.* Ken Church & Ed Hovy. Machine Translation, 8(4). 1993

disentangle compounded errors of style and grammar." Below we discuss related work that uses machine translation to address targeted errors and some recent work that also focused on whole-sentence error correction.

Brockett et al. (2006) use information about mass noun errors from a Chinese learner corpus to engineer a "parallel" corpus with sentences containing mass noun errors on one side and their corrected counterparts on the other. With this parallel corpus, the authors use standard statistical machine translation (SMT) framework to learn a translation (correction) model which can then be applied to unseen sentences containing mass noun errors. This approach was able to correct almost 62% of the errors found in a test set of 150 errors. In our approach, we do not treat correction directly as a translation problem but instead rely on an MT system to round-trip translate an English sentence back to English.

Park and Levy (2011) use a noisy channel model to achieve whole-sentence grammar correction; they learn a noise model from a dataset of errorful sentences but do not rely on SMT. They show that the corrections produced by their model generally have higher n-gram overlap with human-authored reference corrections than the original errorful sentences.

The previous work that is most directly relevant to our approach is that of Hermet and Désilets (2009) who focused only on sentences containing pre-marked preposition errors and generated a *single* round-trip translation for such sentences via a single pivot language (French). They then simply posited this round-trip translation as the "correction" for the original sentence. In their evaluation on sentences containing 133 unique preposition errors, their round-trip translation system was able to correct 66.4% of the cases. However, this was outperformed by a simple method based on web counts (68.7%). They also found that combining the round-trip method with the web counts method into a hybrid system yielded higher performance (82.1%).

In contrast, we use multiple pivot languages to generate several round-trip translations. In addition, we use a novel alignment algorithm that allows us to combine different parts of different round-trip translations and explore a whole new set of corrections that go beyond the translations themselves. Finally, we do not restrict our analysis to any single type of error. In fact, our test sentences contain several different types of grammatical errors.

Outside of the literature on grammatical error detection, our combination approach is directly related to the research on machine translation system combination wherein translation hypotheses produced by different SMT systems are combined to allow the extraction of a better, combined hypothesis (Bangalore et al., 2001; Rosti et al., 2007; Feng et al., 2009). However, our combination approach is different in that all the round-trip translations are produced by a single system but via different pivot languages.

Finally, the idea of combining multiple surface renderings with the same meaning has also been explored in paraphrase generation. Pang et al. (2003) propose an algorithm to align sets of parallel sentences driven entirely by the syntactic representations of the sentences. The alignment algorithm outputs a merged lattice from which lexical, phrasal, and sentential paraphrases could simply be read off. Barzilay and Lee (2003) cluster topically related sentences into slotted word lattices by using multiple sequence alignment for the purpose of downstream paraphrase generation from comparable corpora. More recently, Zhao et al. (2010) perform round-trip translation of English sentences via different pivot languages and different off-the-shelf SMT systems to generate candidate paraphrases. However, they do not combine the candidate paraphrases in any way. A detailed survey of paraphrase generation techniques can be found in (Androutsopoulos and Malakasiotis, 2010) and (Madnani and Dorr, 2010).

3 Methodology

The basic idea underlying our error correction technique is quite simple: if we can automatically generate alternative surface renderings of the meaning expressed in the original sentence and then pick the one that is most fluent, we are likely to have picked a version of the sentence in which the original grammatical errors have been fixed.

In this paper, we propose generating such alternative formulations using statistical machine translation. For example, we take the original sentence E and translate it to Chinese using the Google Trans-

Original	Both experience and books are very important *about living*.
Swedish	Both experience and books are very important in live.
Italian	Both books are very important experience and life.
Russian	**And the experience, and a very important book about life.**
French	Both experience and the books are very important in life.
German	Both experience and books are very important about life.
Chinese	Related to the life experiences and the books are very important.
Spanish	Both experience and the books are very important about life.
Arabic	Both experience and books are very important for life.

Figure 1: Illustrating the deficiency in using an n-gram language model to select one of the 8 round-trip translations as the correction for the Original sentence. The grammatical errors in the Original sentence are shown in italics. The round-trip translation via Russian is chosen by a 5-gram language model trained on the English gigaword corpus even though it changes the meaning of the original sentence entirely.

late API. We then take the resulting Chinese sentence C and translate it back to English. Since the translation process is designed to be meaning-preserving, the resulting **round-trip translation** E' can be seen as an alternative formulation of the original sentence E. Furthermore, if additional pivot languages besides Chinese are used, several alternative formulations of E can be generated. We use 8 different pivot languages: Arabic, Chinese, Spanish, French, Italian, German, Swedish, Russian. We chose these eight languages since they are frequently used in SMT research and shared translation tasks. To obtain the eight round-trip translations via each of these pivot languages, we use the Google Translate research API.[1]

3.1 Round-Trip Translation Combination

Once the translations are generated, an obvious solution is to pick the most fluent alternative, e.g., using an n-gram language model. However, since the language model has no incentive to preserve the meaning of the sentence, it is possible that it might pick a translation that changes the meaning of the original sentence entirely. For example, consider the sentence and its round-trip translations shown in Figure 1. For this sentence, a 5-gram language model trained on gigaword picks the Russian round-trip translation simply because it has n-grams that were seen more frequently in the English gigaword corpus.

Given the deficiencies in statistical phrase-based translation, it is also possible that no single round-trip translation fixes all of the errors. Again, consider Figure 1. None of the 8 round-trip translations is error-free itself. Therefore, the task is more complex than simply selecting the right round-trip translation. We posit that a better approach will be to combine the evidence of correction produced by each independent translation model and increase the likelihood of producing a final whole-sentence correction. Additionally, by engineering such a combination, we increase the likelihood that the final correction will preserve the meaning of the original sentence.

In order to combine the round-trip translations, we developed a heuristic alignment algorithm that uses the TERp machine translation metric (Snover et al., 2009). The TERp metric takes a pair of sentences and computes the least number of edit operations that can be employed to turn one sentence into the other.[2] As a by-product of computing the edit sequence, TERp produces an *alignment* between the two sentences where each alignment link is defined by an edit operation. Figure 2 shows an example of the alignment produced by TERp between the original sentence from Figure 1 and its Russian round-trip translation. Note that TERp also allows shifting words and phrases in the second sentence in order to obtain a smaller edit cost (as indicated by the asterisk next to the word *book* which has shifted from its original position in the Russian round-trip translation).

Our algorithm starts by treating the original sentence as the backbone of a lattice. First, it cre-

[1] `http://research.google.com/university/translate/`

[2] Edit operations in TERp include matches, substitutions, insertion, deletions, paraphrase, synonymy and stemming.

ates a node for each word in the original sentence and creates edges between them with a weight of 1. Then, for each of the round-trip translations, it computes its TERp alignment with the original sentence and aligns it to the backbone based on the edit operations in the alignment. Specifically, each insertion, substitution, stemming, synonymy and paraphrase operation lead to creation of new nodes that essentially provide an alternative formulation for the aligned substring from the backbone. Any duplicate nodes are merged. Finally, edges produced by different translations between the same pairs of nodes are merged and their weights added. Figure 3(a) shows how our algorithm aligns the Russian round-trip translation from Figure 1 to the original sentence using the TERp alignment from Figure 2. Figure 3(b) shows the final lattice produced by our algorithm for the sentence and all the round-trip translations from Figure 1.

```
           -- and        [I]
      both -- the        [S]
experience -- experience [M]
           -- ,          [I]
       and -- and        [M]
     books -- book       [T] [*]
       are -- a          [S]
      very -- very       [M]
 important -- important  [M]
     about -- about      [M]
    living -- life       [Y]
         . -- .          [M]
```

Figure 2: The alignment produced by TERp between the original sentence from Figure 1 and its Russian round-trip translation. The alignment operations are indicated in square brackets after each alignment link: **I**=insertion, **M**=match, **S**=substitution, **T**=stemming and **Y**=WordNet synonymy. The asterisk next to the work *book* denotes that TERp chose to shift its position before computing an edit operation for it.

3.2 Correction Generation

For each original sentence, we computed six possible corrections from the round-trip translations and the combined lattice:

1. **Baseline LM (B)**. The most fluent round-trip translation out of the eight as measured by a 5-gram language model trained on the English gigaword corpus.

2. **Greedy (G)**. A path is extracted from the TERp lattice using a greedy best-first strategy at each node, i.e., at each node, the outgoing edge with the largest weight is followed.

3. **1-Best (1)**: The shortest path is extracted from the TERp lattice by using the OpenFST toolkit.[3]. This method assumes that, like **G**, the combined evidence from the round-trip translations itself is enough to produce a good final correction and no external method for measuring fluency is required.[4]

4. **LM Re-ranked (L)**. An n-best (n=20) list is extracted from the lattice using the OpenFST toolkit and re-ranked using the 5-gram gigaword language model. The 1-best reranked item is then extracted as the correction. This method assumes that an external method of measuring fluency—the 5-gram language model—can help to bring the most grammatical correction to the top of the n-best list.

5. **Product Re-ranked (P)**. Same as L except the re-ranking is done based on the product of the cost of each hypothesis in the n-best list and the language model score, i.e., both the evidence from the round-trip translations and the language model is weighted equally.

6. **Full LM Composition (C)**. The edge weights in the TERp lattice are converted to probabilities. The lattice is then composed with a tri-gram finite state language model (trained on a corpus of $100,000$ high-scoring student essays).[5] The shortest path through the composed lattice is then extracted as the correction. This method assumes that using an n-gram language model during the actual search process is better than using it as a post-processing tool on an already extracted n-best list, such as for **L** and **P**.

[3]http://www.openfst.org/

[4]Note that the edge weights in the lattice must be converted into costs for this method (we do so by multiplying the weights by -1).

[5]We adapted the code available at http://www.ling.ohio-state.edu/~bromberg/ngramcount/ngramcount.html to perform the LM composition.

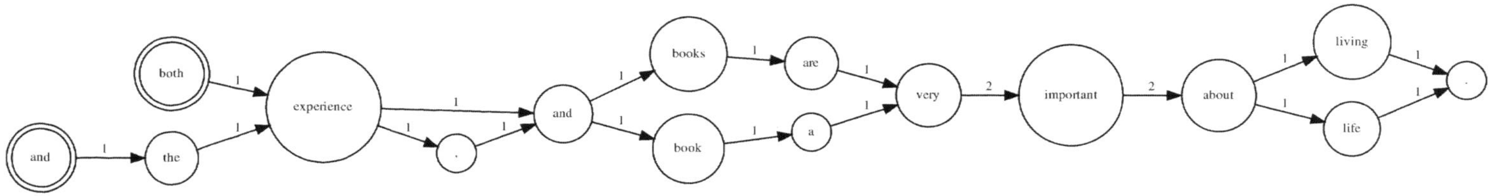

(a)

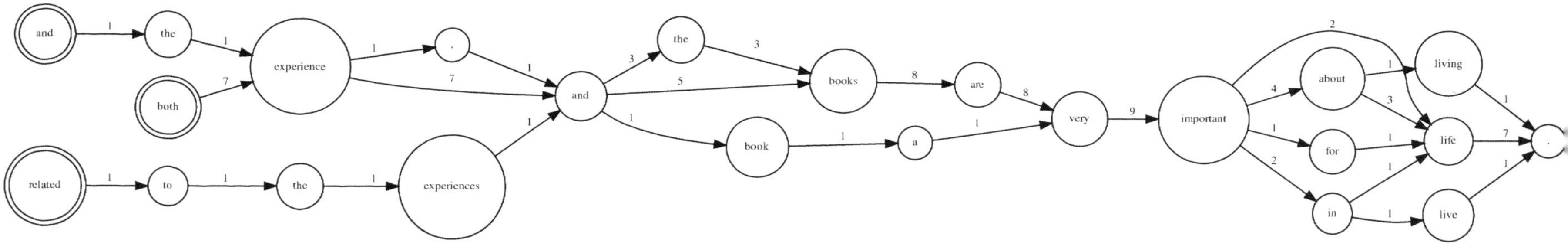

(b)

Original (O)	Both experience and books are very important *about living*.
Baseline LM (B)	And the experience, and a very important book about life.
Greedy (G)	Both experience and books are very important about life.
1-best (1)	Both experience and the books are very important about life.
LM Re-ranked (L)	And the experience and the books are very important in life.
Product Re-ranked (P)	Both experience and books are very important about life.
LM Composition (C)	**Both experience and books are very important in life.**

(c)

Figure 3: (a) shows the output of our alignment algorithm for the Russian round-trip translation from Figure 1. (b) shows the final TERp lattice after aligning all eight round-trip translations from Figure 1. (c) shows the corrections for the original sentence (O) produced by the six techniques discussed in 3.2. The correction produced by the Full LM Composition technique (C) fixes both the errors in the original sentence.

No. of Errors	Sentences	Avg. Length
1	61	14.4
2	45	19.9
3	29	24.2
4	14	29.4
>4	13	38.0

Table 1: The distribution of grammatical errors for the 162 errorful sentences.

Figure 3(c) shows these six corrections as computed for the sentence from Figure 1.

4 Corpus

To assess our system, we manually selected 200 sentences from a corpus of essays written by non-native English speakers for a college-level English proficiency exam. In addition to sentences containing grammatical errors, we also deliberately sampled sentences that contained no grammatical errors in order to determine how our techniques perform in those cases. In total, 162 of the sentences contained at least one error, and the remaining 38 were perfectly grammatical. For both errorful as well as grammatical sentences, we sampled sentences of different lengths (under 10 words, 10-20 words, 20-30 words, 30-40 words, and over 40 words). The 162 errorful sentences varied in the number and type of errors present. Table 1 shows the distribution of the number of errors across these 162 sentences.

Specifically, the error types found in these sentences included prepositions, articles, punctuation, agreement, collocations, confused words, etc. Some only contained a handful of straightforward errors, such as "*In recent day, transportation is one of the most important thing to support human activity*", where *day* and *thing* should be pluralized. On the other hand, others were quite garbled to the point where it was difficult to understand the meaning, such as "*Sometimes reading a book is give me information about the knowledge of life so that I can prevent future happened but who knows that when it will happen and how fastly can react to that happen.*" During development, we noticed that the round-trip translation process could not handle misspelled words, so we manually corrected all spelling mistakes which did *not* result in a real word.[6]

[6]A total of 82 spelling errors were manually corrected.

5 Evaluation

In order to evaluate the six techniques for generating corrections, we designed an evaluation task where the annotators would be shown a correction along with the original sentence for which it was generated. Since there are 6 corrections for each of the 200 sentences, this yields a total of 1,200 units for pairwise preference judgments. We chose two annotators, both native English speakers, each of whom annotated half of the judgment units.

Given the idiosyncrasies of the statistical machine translation process underlying our correction techniques, it is quite possible that:

- A correction may fix some, but not all, of the grammatical errors present in the original sentence, and
- A correction may be more fluent but might change the meaning of the original sentence.
- A correction may introduce a new disfluency, even though other errors in the sentence have been largely corrected. This is especially likely to be the case for longer sentences.

Therefore, the pairwise preference judgment task is non-trivial in that it expects the annotators to consider two dimensions: that of grammaticality and of meaning. To accommodate these considerations, we designed the evaluation task such that it asked the annotators to answer the following two questions:

1. **Grammaticality**. The annotators were asked to choose between three options: "*Original sentence sounds better*", "*Correction sounds better*" and "*Both sound about the same*".
2. **Meaning**. The annotators were asked to choose between two options: "*Correction preserves the original meaning*" and "*Correction changes the original meaning*". It should be noted that determining change in or preservation of meaning was treated as a very strict judgment. Subtle changes such as the omission of a determiner were deemed to change the meaning. In some cases, the original sentences were too garbled to determine the original meaning itself.

	$C > O$	$C = O$	$C < O$
Meaning = 1	S	D	F
Meaning = 0	F	F	F

Table 2: A matrix illustrating the Success-Failure-Draw evaluation criterion for the 162 errorful sentences. The rows represent the meaning dimension (1 = meaning preserved, 0 = meaning changed) and the columns represent the grammaticality dimension ($C > O$ denotes correction being more grammatical than the original, $C = O$ denotes they are about the same and $C < O$ denotes that the correction is worse). Such a matrix is computed for each of the six techniques.

5.1 Effectiveness

First, we concentrate our analysis on the original sentences which contain at least one grammatical error. We aggregated the results of the pairwise preference judgments for each of the six specific correction generation techniques and applied the strictest evaluation criterion by computing the following, for each technique:

- **Successes.** Only those sentences for which the correction generated by method is not only more grammatical but also preserves the meaning.

- **Failures.** All those sentences for which the correction is either less grammatical or changes the original meaning.

- **Draws.** Those sentences for which the correction preserves the meaning but sounds about the same as the original.

Table 2 shows a matrix of the six possible combinations of grammaticality and meaning for each method and demonstrates which cells of the matrix contribute to which of the above three measures: Successes (S), Failures (F) and Draws (D).

In addition to the six techniques, we also posit an oracle in order to determine the upper bound on the performance of our round-trip translation approach. The oracle picks the most accurate correction generation method for each individual sentence out of the 6 that are available. For sentences where none of the six techniques produce an adequate correction, the oracle just picks the original sentence. Table 3 shows how the various techniques (including the oracle) perform on the 162 errorful sentences as measured by this criterion. Based on this criterion, the greedy technique performs the best compared to the others since it has a higher success rate (36%) and a lower failure rate (31%). The oracle shows that 60% of the errorful sentences are fixed by at least one of the six correction generation techniques. We show examples of success and failure for the greedy technique in Figure 4.

5.2 Effect of sentence length

From our observations on development data (not part of the test set), we noticed that Google Translate, like most statistical machine translation systems, performs significantly better on shorter sentences. Therefore, we wanted to measure whether the successes for the best method were biased towards shorter sentences and the failures towards longer ones. To do so, we measured the mean and standard deviation of lengths of sentences comprising the successes and failures of the greedy technique. Successful sentences had an average length of approximately 18 words with a standard deviation of 9.5. Failed sentences had an average length of 23 words with a standard deviation of 12.31. These numbers indicate that although the failures are somewhat correlated with larger sentence length, there is no evidence of a significant length bias.

5.3 Effect on grammatical sentences

Finally, we also carried out the same Success-Failure-Draw analysis for the 38 sentences in our test set that were perfectly grammatical to begin with. The analysis differs from that of errorful sentences in one key aspect: since the sentences are already free of any grammatical errors, no correction can be grammatically better. Therefore, sentences for which the correction preserves the meaning and is not grammaticality worse will count as successes and all other cases will count as failures. There are no draws. Table 4 illustrates this difference and Table 5 presents the success and failure rates for all six methods. The greedy technique again performs the best out of all six methods and successfully retains the meaning and grammaticality for almost 80% of

Method	Success	Draw	Failure
Baseline LM (B)	21% (34)	9% (15)	70% (113)
Greedy (G)	36% (59)	33% (52)	31% (51)
1-best (1)	32% (52)	30% (48)	38% (62)
LM Re-ranked (L)	30% (48)	17% (27)	54% (87)
Product Re-ranked (P)	23% (37)	38% (61)	40% (64)
LM Composition (C)	19% (31)	12% (20)	69% (111)
Oracle	60% (97)	40% (65)	-

Table 3: The success, draw and failure rates for the six correction generation techniques and the oracle as computed for the 162 errorful sentences from the test set. The oracle picks the method that produces the most meaning-preserving and grammatical correction for each sentence. For sentences that have no adequate correction, it picks the original sentence. Numbers in parentheses represent counts.

Success	That's why I like to *make travel by* using my own car. **That's why I like to travel using my own car.**
	Having discuss all this I must say that I *must rather prefer* to be a leader than just a member. **After discussing all this, I must say that I would prefer to be a leader than a member.**
Failure	And simply *there* is fantastic for everyone **All magical and simply there is fantastic for all**
	I hope that *share a room with she can be certainly kindle*, because she *is likely me* and so *will not be problems with she.* **I hope that sharing a room with her can be certainly kindle, because it is likely that I and so there will be no problems with it.**

Figure 4: Two examples of success and failure for the Greedy (G) technique. Original sentences are shown first followed by the corrections in bold. Grammatical errors in the original sentences are in italics.

the grammatical sentences.[7]

	$C > O$	$C = O$	$C < O$
Meaning = 1	-	S	F
Meaning = 0	-	F	F

Table 4: A matrix illustrating the Success-Draw-Failure evaluation criterion for the 38 grammatical sentences. There are no draws and sentences for which corrections preserve meaning and are not grammatically worse count as successes. The rest are failures.

Method	Success	Failure
Baseline LM (B)	26% (10)	74% (28)
Greedy (G)	79% (30)	21% (8)
1-best (1)	61% (23)	39% (15)
LM Re-ranked (L)	34% (13)	66% (25)
Product Re-ranked (P)	42% (16)	58% (22)
LM Composition (C)	29% (11)	71% (25)

Table 5: The success and failure rates for the six correction generation techniques as computed for the 38 grammatical sentences from the test set.

6 Discussion & Future Work

In this paper, we explored the potential of a novel technique based on round-trip machine translation for the more ambitious and realistic task of whole-sentence grammatical error correction. Although the idea of round-trip machine translation (via a single pivot language) has been explored before in the context of just preposition errors, we expanded on it significantly by combining multiple round-trip translations and developed several new methods for producing whole-sentence error corrections. Our oracle experiments show that the ideas we explore have the potential to produce whole-sentence corrections for a variety of sentences though there is clearly room for improvement.

An important point needs to be made regarding the motivation for the round-trip translation approach. We claim that this approach is useful not just because it can produce alternative renderings of a given sentence but primarily because each of those

[7] An oracle for this setup is uninteresting since it will simply return the original sentence for every sentence.

renderings is likely to retain at least some of meaning of the original sentence.

Most of the problems with our techniques arise due to the introduction of new errors by Google Translate. One could use an error detection system (or a human) to explicitly identify spans containing grammatical errors and constrain the SMT system to translate only these errorful spans while still retaining the rest of the words in the sentence. This approach should minimize the introduction of new errors. Note that Google Translate does not currently provide a way to perform such **selective translation**. However, other open-source SMT systems such as Moses[8] and Joshua[9] do. Furthermore, it might also be useful to exploit n-best translation outputs instead of just relying on the 1-best as we currently do.

As an alternative to selective translation, one could simply extract the identified errorful spans and round-trip translate each of them individually. For example, consider the sentence: "*Most of all, luck is* null prep *no use without* a *hard work.*" where the preposition *of* is omitted and there is an extraneous article *a* before "hard work". With this approach, one would simply provide Google Translate with the two phrasal spans containing the errors, instead of the entire sentence.

More generally, although we use Google Translate for this pilot study due to its easy availability, it might be more practical and useful to rely on an inhouse SMT system that trades-off translation quality for additional features.

We also found that the language-model based techniques performed quite poorly compared to the other techniques. We suspect that this is due to the fact that Google Translate already employs large-order language models trained on trillions of words. Using lower-order models trained on much smaller corpora might simply introduce noise. However, a detailed analysis is certainly warranted.

In conclusion, we claim that our preliminary exploration of large-scale round-trip translation based techniques yielded fairly reasonable results. However, more importantly, it makes it clear that, with additional research, these techniques have the potential to be very effective at whole-sentence grammatical error correction.

[8] `http://www.statmt.org/moses`

[9] `https://github.com/joshua-decoder`

Acknowledgments

We would like to thank Aoife Cahill, Michael Heilman and the three anonymous reviewers for their useful comments and suggestions. We would also like to thank Melissa Lopez and Matthew Mulholland for helping with the annotation.

References

Ion Androutsopoulos and Prodromos Malakasiotis. 2010. A Survey of Paraphrasing and Textual Entailment Methods. *J. Artif. Int. Res.*, 38(1):135–187.

Srinivas Bangalore, German Bordel, and Giuseppe Riccardi. 2001. Computing Consensus Translation from Multiple Machine Translation Systems. In *Proceedings of ASRU*, pages 351–354.

Regina Barzilay and Lillian Lee. 2003. Learning to Paraphrase: An Unsupervised Approach Using Multiple-Sequence Alignment. In *Proceedings of HLT-NAACL 2003*, pages 16–23.

Chris Brockett, William B. Dolan, and Michael Gamon. 2006. Correcting ESL Errors Using Phrasal SMT Techniques. In *Proceedings of the 21st International Conference on Computational Linguistics and 44th Annual Meeting of the Association for Computational Linguistics*, pages 249–256.

Yang Feng, Yang Liu, Haitao Mi, Qun Liu, and Yajuan Lü. 2009. Lattice-based System Combination for Statistical Machine Translation. In *Proceedings of the 2009 Conference on Empirical Methods in Natural Language Processing: Volume 3 - Volume 3*, pages 1105–1113.

Matthieu Hermet and Alain Désilets. 2009. Using First and Second Language Models to Correct Preposition Errors in Second Language Authoring. In *Proceedings of the Fourth Workshop on Innovative Use of NLP for Building Educational Applications*, pages 64–72.

Claudia Leacock, Martin Chodorow, Michael Gamon, and Joel Tetreault. 2010. *Automated Grammatical Error Detection for Language Learners*. Synthesis Lectures on Human Language Technologies. Morgan Claypool.

Nitin Madnani and Bonnie J. Dorr. 2010. Generating Phrasal and Sentential Paraphrases: A Survey of Data-driven Methods. *Computational Linguistics*, 36(3).

Bo Pang, Kevin Knight, and Daniel Marcu. 2003. Syntax-based Alignment of Multiple Translations: Extracting Paraphrases and Generating New Sentences. In *Proceedings of HLT-NAACL*, pages 102–109.

Y. Albert Park and Roger Levy. 2011. Automated Whole Sentence Grammar Correction using a Noisy Channel Model. In *Proceedings of the 49th Annual Meeting of the Association for Computational Linguistics: Human Language Technologies - Volume 1*, pages 934–944.

Antti-Veikko Rosti, Necip Fazil Ayan, Bing Xiang, Spyros Matsoukas, Richard Schwartz, and Bonnie Dorr. 2007. Combining Outputs from Multiple Machine Translation Systems. In *Human Language Technologies 2007: The Conference of the North American Chapter of the Association for Computational Linguistics; Proceedings of the Main Conference*, pages 228–235.

Matthew Snover, Nitin Madnani, Bonnie Dorr, and Richard Schwartz. 2009. Fluency, Adequacy, or HTER? Exploring Different Human Judgments with a Tunable MT Metric. In *Proceedings of the Fourth Workshop on Statistical Machine Translation at the 12th Meeting of the European Chapter of the Association for Computational Linguistics (EACL-2009)*.

Shiqi Zhao, Haifeng Wang, Xiang Lan, and Ting Liu. 2010. Leveraging Multiple MT Engines for Paraphrase Generation. In *COLING*, pages 1326–1334.

HOO 2012:
A Report on the Preposition and Determiner Error Correction Shared Task

Robert Dale, Ilya Anisimoff and George Narroway
Centre for Language Technology
Macquarie University
Sydney NSW 2109
Australia
rdale@acm.org, anisimoff@gmail.com, george.narroway@me.com

Abstract

Incorrect usage of prepositions and determiners constitute the most common types of errors made by non-native speakers of English. It is not surprising, then, that there has been a significant amount of work directed towards the automated detection and correction of such errors. However, to date, the use of different data sets and different task definitions has made it difficult to compare work on the topic. This paper reports on the HOO 2012 shared task on error detection and correction in the use of prepositions and determiners, where systems developed by 14 teams from around the world were evaluated on the same previously unseen errorful text.

1 Introduction

It is widely recognized that the correct usage of determiners and prepositions in English is a major problem area for non-native speakers of the language.[1] The issues here have been explored and discussed extensively in the literature; an excellent and up-to-date summary is available in (Leacock et al., 2010). However, the various teams that have attempted to tackle these problems so far have tended to use slightly different task specifications, and different data sets for evaluation; this makes it very difficult to compare the results achieved using different approaches.

To address this problem, the aim of the HOO 2012 Shared Task was to provide a forum for the comparative evaluation of different approaches to the correction of these errors.[2] The shared task provides a common training dataset, a shared evaluation framework, and a set of previously unseen test data.

These proceedings contain detailed reports by all 14 teams who participated in HOO 2012. The present paper provides a summary of the task and its evaluation, and a report on the results of that evaluation.

Section 2 provides an overview of the task and the timeline across which it was carried out; Section 3 provides details of the participating teams; Section 4 describes the training and test data in more detail; Section 5 presents the results of the evaluation; and Section 6 provides some concluding remarks and discussion, reflecting on lessons learned.

2 The Task

Non-native speakers who are learning English find prepositions and determiners particularly problematic. The selection of the appropriate preposition in a given context often appears to be a matter of idiom or convention rather than being governed by a consistent set of rules; and selecting a determiner

[1] We use the broad term 'non-native speaker', abbreviated 'NNS', in this paper; other work makes a distinction between ESL (English as a Second Language) speakers (who live and speak in a primarily English-speaking environment) or EFL (English as a Foreign Language) speakers (who are learning English in a non-English-speaking country.

[2] HOO stands for 'Helping Our Own', a reflection of the historical origins of the exercise as an attempt to develop tools to help researchers in natural language processing to write better papers: see (Dale and Kilgarriff, 2010) for the background to this enterprise and (Dale and Kilgarriff, 2011) for a report on the pilot round of the task held in 2011.

Team ID	Group or Institution	Subtasks	Runs
CU	Computer Laboratory, University of Cambridge, UK	DRC	8
ET	Educational Testing Service, New Jersey, USA	DR	3
JU	Jadavpur University, Kolkata, India	DRC	1
KU	Natural Language Processing Lab, Korea University, Seoul, Korea	DRC	10
LE	KU Leuven, Belgium	DRC	2
NA	NAIST, Japan	DRC	8
NU	National University of Singapore, Singapore	DRC	1
TC	Department of Computer Science and Statistics, Trinity College Dublin, Ireland	DRC	10
TH	NLPLAB, National Tsing Hua University, Hsinchu, Taiwan	DRC	4
UD	UKP Lab, Technische Universität Darmstadt, Germany	DRC	3
UI	Cognitive Computation Group, University of Illinois, USA	DRC	10
UT	Theoretical Computational Linguistics Group, University of Tübingen, Germany	DRC	10
VA	Valkuil.net, The Netherlands	DRC	6
VT	VTEX, Vilnius, Lithuania	DRC	9

Table 1: Participating teams

depends on a complex of contextual factors which is particularly challenging for those whose native language does not make use of determiners. The literature suggests that mistakes in the use of the determiners and prepositions account for 20–50% of grammar and usage errors; the extent to which a learner has problems with determiners varies depending on their native language, while the degree of difficulty experienced with prepositions is less varied (see Chapter 3 in (Leacock et al., 2010)).

For the shared task, we made use of data drawn from the CLC FCE Dataset, a set of 1,244 exam scripts written by candidates sitting the Cambridge ESOL First Certificate in English (FCE) examination in 2000 and 2001, and made available by Cambridge Universiy Press; see (Yannakoudakis et al., 2011). This data is described in more detail below.

The version of the data we provided to teams as training data consisted of the original text as written by the examination subjects, so it contains many errors besides the preposition and determiner errors; it thus provides a quite realistic challenge, as opposed to artificial data sets where the only errors present are the particular errors of interest. The training data we provided consisted of the raw, errorful texts, and for each text file a set of gold-standard standoff annotations indicating the locations of the preposition and determiner errors and their corrections, which we extracted from the CUP data annotations.

The task consisted in attempting to generate sets of standoff annotations that matched those in the gold standard. Teams were to be evaluated on three subtasks: *detection*, *recognition* and *correction*. The first of these is a measure of a system's success in determining that something is wrong in a text and that it requires fixing; the second requires also that the precise extent of the error be identified, and the correct type assigned; and the third requires that a correction matching that in the gold standard be offered. Scores on each of these subtasks were computed for preposition and determiner errors combined, and for preposition and determiner errors separately; thus, each participating system run could generate up to nine distinct scores. In addition, we also provided teams with detection, recognition and correction scores for each of the six base error types (see Table 2); some teams report on these statistics in their individual reports.

The training data and evaluation tools were made available on 27th January 2012; test data was released on April 6th 2012, with submissions of results from teams due on April 13th 2012. Teams therefore had 10 weeks to develop a system that could handle the training data, and one week to provide results on the test data.

3 The Participants

At the time we released the training data, 26 teams registered interest in the task. The test data, receipt of which required a signed agreement with Cambridge University Press, was requested by 15 teams; one of these teams subsequently withdrew

Type	Tag	Original	Correction
Replacement Preposition	RT	I could only travel *on* July	I could only travel *in* July
Missing Preposition	MT	I am looking forward your reply	I am looking forward *to* your reply
Unwanted Preposition	UT	I have booked a flight *to* home	I have booked a flight home
Replacement Determiner	RD	wich was situeded on *a* seaside	wich was situeded on *the* seaside
Missing Determiner	MD	I will give you all information	I will give you all *the* information
Unwanted Determiner	UD	One of my hobbies is *the* photography	One of my hobbies is photography

Table 2: Examples of the six base error types

from the competition. The 14 teams who completed the shared task are listed in Table 1.[3]

4 The Data

4.1 Basic Statistics

The training data consisted of 1000 files drawn from the publicly available FCE dataset. These were converted from the native FCE format into the HOO data format, which was slightly revised from the version used in HOO 2011 (see (Dale and Kilgarriff, 2011)). The original data was marked up with all the errors found by the CUP annotator, but we discarded annotations of errors other than the six base types we were interested in, and converted the remaining errors into standoff annotations. The six types, with examples of each, are shown in Table 2;[4] Figure 1 shows a fragment of an FCE data file, and Figure 2 shows a standoff annotation example extracted from this file in the HOO format.

Elements of some of these files were removed to dispose of nested edits and other phenomena that caused difficulties in the preprocessing of the data.[5] The resulting set of training data comprised a total of 374680 words, for an average of 375 words per file.

The test data consisted of a further 100 previously unseen files provided to us for this shared task by CUP. These were processed in the same manner as the training data. The test data comprised 18013 words, for an average of 180 words per file. Counts of the different error types in the training and test data are provided in Table 3, demonstrating that the error rate remained fairly constant across training and test data. However, whereas the training data included information on author's first language (L1) and age range, the L1 information was not present in the test data, thus removing a potentially useful feature that some teams may have hoped to exploit.

```
<p>
First I must say that most <#UT>of</#UT>
people don't see any problems with
<#RV>growing|increasing</#RV>
<#RD>a|the</#RD> list of
<#UP>car's|car</#UP> owners.
Some of them think that it shows how
<#SX>reach|rich</#SX> our country is.
</p>
```

Figure 1: A fragment of an FCE data file

```
<edit type="RD" index="0005"
      file="0006" part="1"
      start="427" end="428">
   <original>a</original>
   <corrections>
      <correction>the</correction>
   </corrections>
</edit>
```

Figure 2: A standoff error annotation

4.2 Revisions to the Gold-Standard Data

Note that Table 3 shows counts for two versions of the gold-standard test data: the original version as derived from the CUP-provided data set ('Test A'), and a revised version ('Test B') which incorporates corrections to errors found in the annotations.

The evaluation process quickly revealed that there appeared to be cases of annotation error in the original test data. This concerned us because it meant that system performance was being under-reported:

[3]The 'Subtasks' column indicates which subtasks the team took part in: detection (D), recognition (R) and correction (C). The 'Runs' column is explained later.

[4]For the present exercise we used the preposition and determiner error tags as provided in the CLE tagset. The full CLE tagset is described in (Nicholls, 2003).

[5]This preprocessing step was not perfect, and we subsequently discovered it had introduced some noise into the data.

Type	# Training	# Test A	# Test B
UT	822	43	39
MT	1105	57	56
RT	2618	136	148
Prep	4545	236	243
UD	1048	53	62
MD	2230	125	131
RD	609	39	37
Det	3887	217	230
Total	8432	453	473
Words/Error	44.18	39.77	38.08

Table 3: Data statistics

Team	Requested	Acted On
CU	51	30
ET	22	18
LE	5	5
NU	83	59
UI	151	54
UT	45	39
Totals	357	205

Table 4: Requests for corrections to the gold-standard data

in particular, systems were identifying real errors in the source texts which had not been annotated in the gold standard, and were consequently being penalised for finding spurious errors which were not in fact spurious.

To address this problem, once teams had submitted their results, we allowed a brief period where teams could review the gold-standard data to identify possible corrections to that data. Table 4 shows the number of revisions requested by each team, and the number of these revisions that were accepted. Note that there were a significant number of revisions (99) that were requested by more than one team, so the total count of revision requests is larger than the actual number of revisions considered. Of the total 357 requests, 205 were acted on, in some cases not in the manner requested by the team; 152 requests led to no changes being made to the annotations.

Note that the teams' original sets of submitted edits were compared against this revised gold standard, so there was no sense in which a system's behaviour could be tuned to the test data. However, clearly any given team might stand to benefit from identifying particular errors their system had identified that were not in the gold standard, effectively tuning the test data to system behaviour. Consequently, we provide results below for both the original and the revised data sets, and briefly discuss the impact of these corrections.

5 Results

Each team was allowed to submit up to 10 separate 'runs' over the test data, thus allowing them to have different configurations of their systems evaluated; the number of runs submitted by each team is shown in Table 1. We report here only on the best-performing runs from each team.

Teams were asked to indicate whether they had used only publicly-available data to train their systems, or whether they had made use of privately-held data: only the ET and CU teams used privately-held data, and in the latter case only for a subset of their runs. In the tabulated results provided here, reported runs that involve privately-held data are marked with an asterisk.

The results of the evaluation are provided here in six tables. Tables 5 and 6 provide results for preposition and determiner errors combined; Tables 7 and 8 provide results for preposition errors only; and Tables 9 and 10 provide results for determiner errors only. In each pair, the first table shows results before the revisions described in Section 4.2 were carried out, and the second table shows the results using the revised gold-standard data. Each table shows precision, recall and F-score (computed as the harmonic mean) for each of detection, recognition and correction; for each of these, the best score is shown in bold.[6] Note that team ET did not participate in the correction subtask.

The scores for all teams improve as a consequence of the revisions being made to the data. The result of a paired t-test on the 'before' and 'after' combined preposition and determiner scores across teams was statistically significant ($t = -3.17$, $df(12)$, $p < .01$);

[6] The precise definitions of these measures as implemented in the evaluation tool, and further details on the evaluation process, are provided in (Dale and Narroway, 2012) and elaborated on at the HOO website at www.correcttext.org/hoo2012.

F-scores improved by a mean value of 2.32. The same analyses for preposition scores also resulted in significant improvement ($t = -3.29$, *df*(12), $p < .01$), with a mean improvement in F-scores of 2.6. A smaller (but still statistically significant) improvement in determiner scores was also present ($t = -2.86$, *df*(12), $p < .05$), with a mean improvement in F-scores of 1.99.

There are also positive correlations between the rankings before and after revisions. Pearson correlation coefficients for the 'before' and 'after' scores for prepositions and determiners combined, prepositions only, and determiners only (respectively) are .993, .985 and .996. All correlation coefficients are significant at $p < .001$, $n = 13$ (teams).

However, some systems improve more than others. An obvious question to ask, then, is whether the benefit that a team achieves is positively correlated with the number of accepted corrections they proposed; a calculation of Pearson's correlation coefficient suggests that this is indeed the case ($r = 0.821$, $p = 0.044$ (one-tailed)).[7] This suggests, then, that the 'before' results may be a more reliable indicator of comparative performance.

6 Discussion and Conclusions

In this section, we make some observations on lessons learned with regard to various aspects of the shared task.

6.1 Data Acquisition

Data annotated with non-native speaker errors has significant commercial value, and so is not easy to find in the public domain. We were fortunate to be able to take advantage of the recently-made-available FCE dataset as training data, but this left us with the problem of acquiring previously unseen test data. To address this, we entered into negotiation with Cambridge University Press with the aim of acquiring some additional previously unreleased data. We started this process in December 2011, but it quickly became apparent that some of the legal aspects would necessarily make this a slow process.

[7]Computed here on the combined preposition and determiner scores, and taking account only of the five teams that proposed corrections, these being UI, NU, LE, UT and CU. ET was not included in this calculation since they did not submit to the corrections subtask.

As a back-up plan, we informed teams that we might have to fall back on some of the already-available FCE data as test data; to this end, we asked teams only to use versions and subsets of the FCE data that we made directly available. We thus selected 1000 files from the 1200 that make up the public FCE data set as training data, and reserved the remainder as a source of possible test data.

This is clearly not an ideal situation; fortunately, we finally signed agreements for the use of a new set of FCE data in the week before the test data was due to be released, but this was leaving things rather tight. The moral here is that one needs to be confident of one's data sources early on in the process.

6.2 Data Quality

As discussed above, it became apparent that there were what appeared to be annotation errors in our data. This is perhaps inevitable given the nature of the source data, which was annotated by only one annotator (subsequent to some prior automatic processing). The issue of reliability of annotation in this area has been noted by others (see, for example, the discussion in Chapter 5 in (Leacock et al., 2010)). Assuming that we agree an error is present—and this is not always in itself straightforward—there is often more than one way to correct that error; however, the FCE annotation scheme does not permit multiple possible corrections, so in the source data we used, there was only ever one correction per error. Our revision process identified a number of cases where alternative corrections were equally acceptable, and fortunately the HOO annotation scheme allowed us to incorporate multiple possible corrections; but it's quite clear that we did not identify all cases where multiple corrections were valid.[8]

This is a significant issue. If we cannot entirely trust our gold-standard data, then we cannot place too much trust in the results of evaluations carried out using that data. Of course, annotation quality is a problem in any task, but it may be more severe in cases like the present one because the judgements here are often less clear cut: whereas there is rarely dispute as to whether a given string constitutes a named entity, it is not always so clear that

[8]The HOO scheme also allows optional edits, but we did not make use of these here since it complicates the scoring process; see (Dale and Kilgarriff, 2011) for discussion.

	Detection				Recognition				Correction			
Team	Run	P	R	F	Run	P	R	F	Run	P	R	F
CU	2	13.12	34.88	19.07	7	8.13	41.5	13.6	0	**70.0**	4.64	8.7
ET	1	33.59*	37.97*	35.65*	1	30.27*	34.22*	32.12*	–	–	–	–
JU	1	6.93	7.28	7.1	1	6.3	6.62	6.46	1	2.52	2.65	2.58
KU	0	4.61	**49.23**	8.43	0	2.67	28.48	4.88	0	1.45	15.45	2.65
LE	0	37.38	26.49	31.01	0	33.33	23.62	27.65	0	31.15	22.08	25.84
NA	3	40.19	28.04	33.03	3	36.39	25.39	29.91	3	29.43	20.53	24.19
NU	0	**57.42**	26.49	36.25	0	**55.98**	25.83	35.35	0	45.45	20.97	**28.7**
TC	9	5.33	25.61	8.82	9	4.18	20.09	6.92	9	2.66	12.8	4.41
TH	1	17.74	48.12	25.92	1	15.38	**41.72**	22.47	1	9.44	25.61	13.79
UD	2	8.94	31.13	13.88	2	5.51	19.21	8.57	2	1.2	4.19	1.87
UI	8	37.22	43.71	**40.2**	1	34.23	36.64	**35.39**	1	26.39	**28.26**	27.29
UT	6	37.46	25.39	30.26	7	32.01	23.18	26.89	7	21.95	15.89	18.44
VA	3	12.5	15.23	13.73	3	10.87	13.25	11.94	3	6.16	7.51	6.77
VT	5	10.6	5.08	6.87	5	10.14	4.86	6.57	5	8.76	4.19	5.67

Table 5: Results before revisions, all errors

	Detection				Recognition				Correction			
Team	Run	P	R	F	Run	P	R	F	Run	P	R	F
CU	2	14.04	35.73	20.16	7	8.69	42.49	14.43	6	5.73	28.54	9.54
ET	1	38.09*	41.23*	39.59*	1	35.55*	38.48*	36.95*	–	–	–	–
JU	1	8.19	8.25	8.22	1	7.56	7.61	7.59	1	3.15	3.17	3.16
KU	0	5.01	**51.16**	9.12	0	3.04	31.08	5.54	0	1.86	19.03	3.39
LE	0	41.12	27.91	33.25	0	36.45	24.74	29.47	0	34.27	23.26	27.71
NA	3	45.25	30.23	36.25	3	40.82	27.27	32.7	3	33.86	22.62	27.12
NU	0	**70.33**	31.08	43.11	0	**69.38**	30.66	**42.52**	0	**61.72**	27.27	**37.83**
TC	8	6.56	26.0	10.48	8	4.91	19.45	7.84	8	3.09	12.26	4.94
TH	1	19.2	49.89	27.73	1	17.33	**45.03**	25.03	1	10.82	28.12	15.63
UD	2	9.95	33.19	15.31	2	5.77	19.24	8.87	2	1.33	4.44	2.05
UI	2	43.56	42.92	**43.24**	1	38.97	39.96	39.46	1	32.58	**33.4**	32.99
UT	7	39.94	27.7	32.71	7	35.67	24.74	29.21	5	31.58	17.76	22.73
VA	3	13.22	15.43	14.24	3	11.59	13.53	12.49	3	7.25	8.46	7.8
VT	5	11.52	5.29	7.25	5	11.06	5.07	6.96	5	9.68	4.44	6.09

Table 6: Results after revisions, all errors

something is an error, or where that error should be located. The incorporation of optional and multiple corrections in the HOO framework was intended to address this kind of problem, but the value of these features is only delivered if the scheme is used during annotation, rather than being applied after annotation has already been carried out.

6.3 The Annotation Scheme and Evaluation Tools

Given real non-native speaker data that contains a wide range of errors other than those that we were particularly concerned with in this shared task, we were faced with three alternatives in how we prepared the data for use in the task.

1. We could provide the data with all original errors in place.
2. We could provide the data with all but the preposition and determiner errors corrected.
3. We could provide the data with selected errors corrected or replaced.

The problem with the first of these options, of course, is that other errors that appear in the context

	Detection				Recognition				Correction			
Team	Run	P	R	F	Run	P	R	F	Run	P	R	F
CU	2	14.88	59.32	23.79	2	9.99	39.83	15.97	0	**61.11**	4.66	8.66
ET	1	31.95*	42.37*	36.43*	1	27.16*	36.02*	30.97*	–	–	–	–
JU	1	6.1	7.63	6.78	1	5.42	6.78	6.03	1	3.05	3.81	3.39
KU	0	3.39	**66.95**	6.46	0	2.51	**49.58**	4.79	0	1.27	25.0	2.41
LE	0	32.81	17.8	23.08	0	27.34	14.83	19.23	0	25.78	13.98	18.13
NA	6	41.13	24.58	30.77	3	36.43	19.92	25.75	3	30.23	16.53	21.37
NU	0	**56.99**	22.46	32.22	0	**53.76**	21.19	30.4	0	41.94	16.53	**23.71**
TC	9	6.49	29.66	10.65	9	5.19	23.73	8.52	9	3.06	13.98	5.02
TH	1	17.39	59.32	26.9	1	14.16	48.31	21.9	1	9.19	**31.36**	14.22
UD	2	11.84	36.86	17.92	2	9.66	30.08	14.62	1	7.63	4.24	5.45
UI	1	38.21	45.34	**41.47**	5	31.05	40.25	**35.06**	1	20.36	24.15	22.09
UT	2	39.35	25.85	31.2	7	35.76	22.88	27.91	0	25.45	11.86	16.18
VA	0	13.44	14.41	13.91	0	11.46	12.29	11.86	0	7.51	8.05	7.77
VT	7	12.24	2.54	4.21	7	12.24	2.54	4.21	7	12.24	2.54	4.21

Table 7: Results before revisions, preposition errors only

	Detection				Recognition				Correction			
Team	Run	P	R	F	Run	P	R	F	Run	P	R	F
CU	2	15.41	59.43	24.47	2	10.63	40.98	16.88	0	**66.67**	4.92	9.16
ET	1	35.14*	45.08*	39.5*	1	32.27*	41.39*	36.27*	–	–	–	–
JU	1	7.12	8.61	7.79	1	6.44	7.79	7.05	1	3.73	4.51	4.08
KU	0	3.67	**70.08**	6.98	0	2.9	**55.33**	5.51	0	1.7	32.38	3.23
LE	0	35.16	18.44	24.19	0	29.69	15.57	20.43	0	28.13	14.75	19.35
NA	6	48.23	27.87	35.32	6	41.84	24.18	30.65	6	33.33	19.26	24.42
NU	0	**72.04**	27.46	39.76	0	**70.97**	27.05	39.17	0	60.22	22.95	**33.23**
TC	8	7.72	29.92	12.27	8	5.92	22.95	9.41	9	3.34	14.75	5.45
TH	1	18.76	61.89	28.79	1	16.27	53.69	24.98	1	10.68	**35.25**	16.4
UD	2	12.65	38.11	19.0	2	10.2	30.74	15.32	1	9.16	4.92	6.4
UI	1	41.43	47.54	**44.27**	1	37.14	42.62	**39.69**	1	26.79	30.74	28.63
UT	2	41.94	26.64	32.58	2	39.35	25.0	30.58	0	35.45	15.98	22.03
VA	0	14.23	14.75	14.49	0	12.65	13.11	12.88	0	8.7	9.02	8.85
VT	7	16.33	3.28	5.46	7	16.33	3.28	5.46	7	16.33	3.28	5.46

Table 8: Results after revisions, preposition errors only

of a preposition or determiner error could confuse a system focussed only on preposition or determiner errors; if the surrounding context contains errors, then it cannot be relied upon to deliver the kinds of features that one would expect to find in well-formed text. To partially address this, many teams ran a spelling correction process on the texts prior to applying their techniques; but this only catches a small proportion of the potential problems.

However, the second option has the opposite problem: by removing all the other errors from the text, we would be providing a very artificial dataset where one assumes some other process has fixed all the other errors before the errors of interest here are addressed. While there are some types of errors that might sensibly be addressed before others in a pipeline, in general this is not a very plausible model; any real system is going to have to address noisy data containing many different kinds of errors simultaneously.

A third alternative, that of selectively removing or correcting errors, is something of a middle road, and has been used in other work using the CLC data: in particular, Gamon (2010) removes from the data sentences where some other error appears immediately next to a preposition or determiner error.

	Detection				Recognition				Correction			
Team	Run	P	R	F	Run	P	R	F	Run	P	R	F
CU	6	7.8	**49.31**	13.48	6	6.86	**43.32**	11.84	6	5.25	33.18	9.07
ET	0	51.67*	28.57*	36.8*	0	50.83*	28.11*	36.2*	–	–	–	–
JU	1	7.73	6.45	7.04	1	7.73	6.45	7.04	1	1.66	1.38	1.51
KU	0	12.85	10.6	11.62	0	6.7	5.53	6.06	0	6.15	5.07	5.56
LE	0	40.41	35.94	38.05	0	37.31	33.18	35.12	0	34.72	30.88	32.68
NA	1	37.43	32.26	34.65	1	36.36	31.34	33.66	1	28.88	24.88	26.73
NU	0	**57.76**	30.88	**40.24**	0	**57.76**	30.88	**40.24**	0	**48.28**	25.81	33.63
TC	3	8.68	8.76	8.72	3	7.76	7.83	7.8	3	4.11	4.15	4.13
TH	1	17.69	34.56	23.4	1	17.69	34.56	23.4	1	9.91	19.35	13.1
UD	2	6.41	24.88	10.19	1	1.98	6.45	3.03	0	0.0	0.0	0.0
UI	0	40.0	37.79	38.86	0	38.05	35.94	36.97	0	35.61	**33.64**	**34.6**
UT	5	34.38	25.35	29.18	5	31.87	23.5	27.06	6	25.75	19.82	22.4
VA	3	11.04	15.21	12.79	3	10.37	14.29	12.02	3	5.02	6.91	5.81
VT	5	9.82	7.37	8.42	5	9.82	7.37	8.42	5	7.98	5.99	6.84

Table 9: Results before revisions, determiner errors only

	Detection				Recognition				Correction			
Team	Run	P	R	F	Run	P	R	F	Run	P	R	F
CU	6	8.53	**51.09**	14.63	6	7.37	**44.1**	12.63	6	5.91	35.37	10.13
ET	0	57.5*	30.13*	39.54*	0	56.67*	29.69*	38.97*	–	–	–	–
JU	1	9.39	7.42	8.29	1	9.39	7.42	8.29	1	2.21	1.75	1.95
KU	0	14.53	11.35	12.75	0	6.7	5.24	5.88	0	6.15	4.8	5.39
LE	0	44.56	37.55	40.76	0	40.93	34.5	37.44	0	38.34	32.31	35.07
NA	1	41.18	33.62	37.02	1	39.57	32.31	35.58	1	33.16	27.07	29.81
NU	0	**68.1**	34.5	**45.8**	0	**68.1**	34.5	**45.8**	0	**62.93**	31.88	**42.32**
TC	8	5.17	20.96	8.3	3	7.31	6.99	7.14	8	2.8	11.35	4.49
TH	1	19.34	35.81	25.11	1	19.34	35.81	25.11	1	11.08	20.52	14.4
UD	1	8.07	24.89	12.19	1	1.98	6.11	2.99	0	0.0	0.0	0.0
UI	0	43.9	39.3	41.47	2	45.98	34.93	39.7	0	41.46	**37.12**	39.17
UT	5	39.38	27.51	32.39	5	35.63	24.89	29.31	6	30.54	22.27	25.76
VA	3	11.71	15.28	13.26	3	10.7	13.97	12.12	3	6.02	7.86	6.82
VT	5	9.82	6.99	8.16	5	9.82	6.99	8.16	5	7.98	5.68	6.63

Table 10: Results after revisions, determiner errors only

In the end, we opted for the first alternative here, on the grounds that this is the best approximation to the real task of non-native speaker error correction. The third alternative would also have been possible, but we were concerned about the impact on the size of our test data set that would result from carrying out this process across the board. However, in the revision step described in Section 4.2, we did remove instances of a particular error type, where a preposition error was immediately followed by a verb error; consider the following sentence and its correction.

(1) a. What do you do *for trying* to save the wild life?

b. What do you do *to try* to save the wild life?

The compound nature of these errors meant that teams were unlikely to correct them; and it might be argued that they are not preposition errors in the conventional sense. However, we did not remove these instances uniformly, so some still remain in the test data.

An orthogonal issue with regard to the HOO annotation scheme is that we require precise identification of error locations and accurate specification of these locations at a character-offset level in our standoff edit notation. It is often inaccuracies at this level that contribute to the differences between a team's detection score and the corresponding recognition score. While precise character offset information is important for some error correction tasks (for example, one would not want an automated corrector to insert corrections misplaced by one character), arguably it is too strict in the present circumstances. Dahlmeier and Ng (2012) propose an alternative evaluation scheme which, along with other properties, overcomes this by operating in terms of tokens rather than character offsets.

6.4 Summary

Overall, we were immensely pleased with the level of interest in this shared task. The HOO 2012 training data and evaluation tools are publicly available, so interested parties who did not take part in the shared task can still try their hand retrospectively; unfortunately, our contract with CUP means that the test data used in this round is not publicly available. Our future plans include packaging a subset of the initially held-out public FCE data set as a new test set, with the aim of establishing a standardised training and testing setup in the same way as Section 23 of the Wall Street Journal corpus is conventionally used as a test set. We have strongly encouraged the use of publicly available data sets, and have asked teams to be as detailed as possible in their reports in the interests of replicability; we hope this will make it possible for new entrants to the area to get up to speed quickly.

Of course, the FCE data also supports work on many other kinds of errors. We expect to address subsets of these in future HOO rounds.

Acknowledgements

We'd like to acknowledge the kind assistance of various people in making this shared task possible: Ted Briscoe for seeding the enterprise by working to make the FCE data publicly available; Diane Nicholls and Adam Kilgarriff for encouragement and advice along the way; Ann Fiddes at Cambridge University Press for providing the previously unseen test data; Richard Cox for statistics; and Joel Tetreault, Claudia Leacock and Jill Burstein for agreeing to host the shared task at the Building Educational Applications Workshop. Macquarie University provided financial support via a Research Development Grant. Finally, of course, we'd like to thank all the teams for participating.

References

Daniel Dahlmeier and Hwee Tou Ng. 2012. Better evaluation for grammatical error correction. In *Proceedings of the 2012 Conference of the North American Chapter of the Association for Computational Linguistics: Human Language Technologies*, Montréal, Canada, 3rd–8th June 2012.

Robert Dale and Adam Kilgarriff. 2010. Helping Our Own: Text massaging for computational linguistics as a new shared task. In *Proceedings of the 6th International Natural Language Generation Conference*, pages 261–266, Dublin, Ireland, 7th–9th July 2010.

Robert Dale and Adam Kilgarriff. 2011. Helping our own: The HOO 2011 pilot shared task. In *Proceedings of the 13th European Workshop on Natural Language Generation*, Nancy, France, 28th–30th September 2011.

Robert Dale and George Narroway. 2012. A framework for evaluating text correction. In *Proceedings of the Eighth International Conference on Language Resources and Evaluation (LREC2012)*, Istanbul, Turkey, 21st–27th May 2012.

Michael Gamon. 2010. Using mostly native data to correct errors in learners writing. In *Proceedings of the Eleventh Annual Conference of the North American Chapter of the Association for Computational Linguistics (NAACL)*, pages 163–171, Los Angeles, USA.

Claudia Leacock, Martin Chodorow, Michael Gamon, and Joel Tetreault. 2010. *Automated Grammatical Error Detection for Language Learners*. Synthesis Lectures on Human Language Technologies. Morgan and Claypool.

Diane Nicholls. 2003. The Cambridge Learner Corpus—error coding and analysis for lexicography and ELT. In D Archer, P Rayson, A Wilson, and T McEnery, editors, *Proceedings of the Corpus Linguistics 2003 Conference*, pages 572–581, Lancaster, UK, 29th March–2nd April 2001.

Helen Yannakoudakis, Ted Briscoe, and Ben Medlock. 2011. A new dataset and method for automatically grading esol texts. In *Proceedings of the 49th Annual Meeting of the Association for Computational Linguistics: Human Language Technologies*, Portland, Oregon, USA, 19th–24th June 2011.

Measuring the Use of Factual Information in Test-Taker Essays

Beata Beigman Klebanov
Educational Testing Service
660 Rosedale Road
Princeton, NJ 08541, USA
bbeigmanklebanov@ets.org

Derrick Higgins
Educational Testing Service
660 Rosedale Road
Princeton, NJ 08541, USA
dhiggins@ets.org

Abstract

We describe a study aimed at measuring the use of factual information in test-taker essays and assessing its effectiveness for predicting essay scores. We found medium correlations with the proposed measures, that remained significant after the effect of essay length was factored out. The correlations did not differ substantionally between a simple, relatively robust measure vs a more sophisticated measure with better construct validity. Implications for development of automated essay scoring systems are discussed.

1 Introduction

Automated scoring of essays deals with various aspects of writing, such as grammar, usage, mechanics, as well as organization and content (Attali and Burstein, 2006). For assessment of content, the focus is traditionally on topical appropriateness of the vocabulary (Attali and Burstein, 2006; Landauer et al., 2003; Louis and Higgins, 2010; Chen et al., 2010; De and Kopparapu, 2011; Higgins et al., 2006; Ishioka and Kameda, 2006; Kakkonen et al., 2005; Kakkonen and Sutinen, 2004; Lemaire and Dessus, 2001; Rosé et al., 2003; Larkey, 1998), although recently other aspects, such as detection of sentiment or figurative language, have started to attract attention (Beigman Klebanov et al., 2012; Chang et al., 2006).

The nature of factual information used in an essay has not so far been addressed, to our knowledge; yet a misleading premise, insufficient factual basis, or an example that flies in the face of the reader's knowledge clearly detract from an essay's quality.

This paper presents a study on assessing the use of factual knowledge in argumentative essays on general topics written for a graduate school entrance exam. We propose a definition of fact, and an operationalization thereof. We find that the proposed measure has positive medium-strength correlation with essay grade, which remains significant after the impact of essay length is factored out. In order to quantify which aspects of the measure drive the observed correlations, we gradually relax the measurement procedure, down to a simple and robust proxy measure. Surprisingly, we find that the correlations do not change throughout the relaxation process. We discuss the findings in the context of validity vs reliability of measurement, and point out implications for automated essay scoring.

2 What is a Fact?

To help articulate the notion of fact, we use the following definition from a seminal text in argumentation theory: "... in the context of argumentation, the notion of fact is uniquely characterized by the idea that is held of agreements of a certain type relating to certain data, those which refer to an objective reality, and, in Poincare's words, designate essentially "what is common to several thinking beings, and could be common to all" (Perelman and Olbrechts-Tyteca, 1969, 67). Factuality is thus a matter of selecting certain kinds of data and securing a certain type of agreement over those data.

Of the different statements that refer to objective reality, the term *facts* is used to "designate objects of precise, limited agreement" (Perelman and Olbrechts-Tyteca, 1969, 69). These are contrasted with *presumptions* – statements connected to what is normal and likely (*ibid.*). We suggest that the distinctions in the scope of the required agreement can be related to the referential device used in a statement: If the reference is more rigid (Kripke, 1980), that is, less prone to change in time and to indeterminacy of the boundaries, the scope of the necessary agreement is likely to be more precise and limited. With proper names prototypically being the most rigid designators, we will focus our efforts on statements about named entities.[1]

Perhaps the simplest model of the universal audience is an encyclopedia – a body of knowledge that is verified by experts, and is, therefore, "common to several thinking beings, and could be common to all" by virtue of the authority of the experts and the wide availability of the resource. However, many facts known to various groups of people that could be known to all are absent from any encyclopedia. The knowledge contained in the WWW at large, reaching not only statements explicitly contributed to an encyclopedia but also those made by people on their blogs – is perhaps as close as it gets to a working model of the universal audience.

Recent developments in Open Information Extraction make it possible to tap into this vast knowledge resource. Indeed, fact-checking is one of the applications the developers of OpenIE have in mind for their emergent technology (Etzioni et al., 2008).

3 Open Information Extraction

Traditionally, the goal of an information extraction system is automated population of structured databases of events or concepts of interest and their properties by analyzing large corpora of text (Chinchor et al., 1993; Onyshkevych, 1993; Grishman and Sundheim, 1995; Ravichandran and Hovy, 2002; Agichtein and Gravano, 2000; Davidov and Rappoport, 2009).

[1]For example, *Barack Obama* picks out precisely one person, and the same one in 2010 as it did in 1990. In contrast, *the current US president* picks out different people every 4-8 years. For indeteminacy of boundaries, consider a statement like *US officials are wealthy*. To determine its truth, one must first secure agreement on acceptable referents of *US officials*.

In contrast, the recently proposed Open Information Extraction paradigm aims to detect related pairs of entities without knowing in advance what kinds of relations exist between entities in the source data and without any seeding (Banko and Etzioni, 2008). The possibility of such extraction in English is attributed by the authors to a small number of syntactic patterns that realize binary relations between entities. In particular, they found that almost 40% of such relations are realized by the argument-verb-argument pattern (henceforth, **AVA**) (see Table 1 in Banko and Etzioni (2008)).

The TextRunner system (Banko and Etzioni, 2008) is trained using a CRF classifier on S-V-O tuples from a parsed corpus as positive examples, and tuples that violate phrasal structure as negative ones. The examples are described using features that do not require parsing or semantic role labeling. Features include part-of-speech tags, regular expressions (detecting capitalization, punctuation, etc.), context words belonging to closed classes, and conjunctions of features occurring in adjacent positions within six words of the current word.

TextRunner achieves P=0.94, R=0.65, and F-Score=0.77 on the AVA pattern (Banko and Etzioni, 2008). We note that all relations in the test sentences involve a predicate connecting two named entities, or a named entity and a date.[2] The authors kindly made available to us for research purposes a database of about 2 bln AVA extractions produced by TextRunner; this database was used in the experiments reported below.

4 Data

We randomly sampled essays written on 10 different prompts, 200 essays per prompt. Essays are graded on the scale of 1-6; the distribution of grades is shown in table 1.

Grade	**1**	**2**	**3**	**4**	**5**	**6**
%	0.6	4.9	23.5	42.6	23.8	4.7

Table 1: The distribution of grades for 2,000 essays.

[2]http://www.cs.washington.edu/research/knowitall/hlt-naacl08-data.txt

5 Building Queries from Essays

We define a query as a 3-tuple <NE,?,NP>,[3] where NE is a named entity and NP is a noun phrase from the same or neighboring sentence in a test-taker essay (the selection process is described in section 5.2). We use the pattern of predicate matches against the TextRunner database to assess the degree and the equivocality of the connection between NE and NP.

5.1 Named Entities in Test-Taker Essay

We use the Stanford Named Entity Recognizer (Finkel et al., 2005) that tags named entities as people, locations, organizations, and miscellaneous. We annotated a sample of 90 essays for named entities; the sample yielded 442 tokens, which we classified as shown in Table 2. The Enamex classes (people, locations, organizations) account for 58% of all the entities in the sample. The recognizer's recall of people and locations is excellent (though they are not always classified correctly – see caption of Table 2), although test-taker essays feature additional entity types that are not detected as well.

Category	Recall	Examples
Location	0.98	Iraq, USA
Person	0.96	George W. Bush, Freud
Org.	0.87	Guggenheim Foundation
Gov.	0.79	No Child Left Behind
Awards	0.79	Nobel Prize
Events	0.68	Civil War, World War I
Sci & Tech	0.59	GPS, Windows 3.11
Art	0.44	Beowulf, Little Women

Table 2: Recall of the Stanford NER by category. Note that an entity is counted as recalled as long as it is identified as belonging to any NE category, even if it is misclassified. For example, *Freud* is tagged as location, but we count it towards the recall of people.

In terms of precision, we observed that the tagger made few clear mistakes, such as tagging sentence-initial adverbs and their mis-spelled versions as named entities (*Eventhough*, *Afterall*). The bulk of the 96 items over-generated by the tagger are in the "grey area" – while we haven't marked them, they are not clearly mistakes. A common case are names of national and religious groups, such as *Muslim* or *Turkish*, or capitalizations of otherwise common nouns for emphasis and elevation, such as *Arts* or *Masters*. Given our objective to ground the queries in items with specific referents, these are less suitable. If all such cases are counted as mistakes, the tagger's precision is 82%.

5.2 Selection of NPs

We employ a grammar-based approach for selecting NPs. We use the Stanford dependency parser (de Marneffe et al., 2006; Klein and Manning, 2003) to determine dependency relations.

In order to find out which dependency paths connect between named entities and clearly related NPs in essays, we manually marked concepts related to 95 NEs in 10 randomly sampled essays. We marked 210 query-able concepts in total. The resulting 210 dependency paths were classified according to the direction of the movement.

Out of the 210 paths, 51 (24%) contain a single upward or downard step, that is, are cases where the NE is the head of the constituent in which the NP is embedded, or the other way around. Some examples are shown in Figure 1. Note that the predicate connecting NE and NP is not lexicalized, but the existence of connection is signaled by the close-knit grammatical pattern.

The most prolific family of paths starts with an upward step, followed by a sequences of 1-4 downwards steps; 71 (34%) of all paths are of this type. Most typically, the first upward move connects the NE to the predicate of which it is an argument, and, down from there, to either the head of another argument ($\uparrow\downarrow$) or to an argument's head's modifier ($\uparrow\downarrow\downarrow$). These are explicit relations, where the relation is typically lexicalized by the predicate.

We expand the context of extraction beyond a single sentence only for NEs classified as PERSON. We apply a gazetteer of private names by gender from US Census 2010 to expand a NE of a given gender with the appropriate personal pronouns; a word that is a part of the original name (only surname, for

[3] We do not attempt matching the predicate, as (1) in many cases there is no clearly lexicalized predicate (see the discussion of single step patterns in section 5.2) and (2) adding a predicate field would make matches against the database sparser (see section 6.1).

[4] NE=Kroemer; NP=Heterojunction Bipolar Transitor

↓ a Nobel Prize in a science field

↓ Chaucer, in the 14 century, ...

↑ the prestige of the Nobel Prize

↑ Kidman's talent

↑↓ Kroemer received the Nobel Prize

↑↓↓ Kroemer received the Nobel Prize for his work on the Heterojunction Bipolar Transitor[4]

Figure 1: Examples of dependency paths used for query construction.

example), is also considered an anaphor and a candidate for expansion. We expand the context of the PERSON entity as long as the subsequent sentence uses any of the anaphors for the name. This way, we hope to capture an extended discussion of a named entity and construct queries around its anaphoric mentions just as we do around the regular, NE mention. A name that is not predominantly male or female is not expanded with personal pronouns. Table 3 shows the distribution of queries automatically generated from the sample of 2,000 essays.

↑	2,817	15.9%
↓	798	4.5%
↑↑	813	4.6%
↓↓	372	2.1%
↑↓	4,940	27.8%
↑↓↓	2,691	15.1%
↑↓↓↓	1,568	8.8%
↑↑↓	3,772	21.2%
total	17,771	100%

Table 3: Distribution of queries by path type.

6 Matching and Filtering Queries

6.1 Relaxation for improved matching

To estimate the coverage of the fact repository with respect to the queries extracted from essays, we submit each query to the TextRunner repository in the <NE,?,NP> format and record the number of times the repository returned any matches at all. The percentage of matched queries is 21%. To increase the chances of finding a match, we process the NP to remove determiners and pre-modifiers of the head that are very frequent words, such as removing *a very* from *a very beautiful photograph*.

Additionally, we produce three variants of the NP. The first, NP_1, contains only the sequence of nouns ending with the head noun; in the example, NP_1 would be *photograph*. The second variant, NP_2, contains only the word that is rarest in the whole of NP. All capitalized words are given the lowest frequency of 1. Thus, if any of the NP words are capitalized, the NP_2 would either contain an out of vocabulary word to the left of the first capitalized word, or the leftmost capitalized word. This means that names would typically be split such that only the first name is taken. For example, the NP *the author Orhan Phamuk* would generate NP_2 *Orhan*. When no capitalized words exist, we take the rarest one, thus a NP *category 3 hurricane* would yield NP_2 *hurricane*. The third variant only applies to NPs with capitalized parts, and takes the rightmost capitalized word in the query. Thus, the NP *the actress Nicole Kidman* would yield NP_3 *Kidman*.

Applying these procedures to every NP inflates the number of actual queries posed to the TextRunner repository by almost two-fold (31,211 instead of 17,771), while yielding a 50% increase in the number of cases where at least one variant of the original query had at least one match against the repository (from 21% to 35%).

6.2 Match-specific filters

In order to zero in on matches that correpond to factual statements and indeed pertain to the queried arguments, we implement a number of filters.

Predicate filters

We filter out modal and hedged predicates, using lists of relevant markers. We remove predicates like *might turn out to be* or *possibly attended*, as well as future tense predicates (marked with *will*).

Argument filters

For matches that passed the predicate filters, we check the arguments. Let **mARG** be the actual string that matched ARG (ARG $\in$\{NE,NP\}). Let **EC** (Essay Context) refer to source sentence(s) in the essay.[5] We filter out the following matches:

- Capitalized words follow ARG in mARG that are not in EC;
- >1 capitalized or rare words precede ARG in mARG that are not in EC and not honorifics;
- mARG is longer than 8 words;
- More than 3 words follow ARG in mARG.

The filters target cases where mARG is more specific than ARG, and so the connection to ARG might be tenuous, such as ARG=*Harriet Beecher Stowe*, mARG = *Harriet Beecher Stowe Center*.

6.3 Filters based on overall pattern of matches

6.3.1 Negation filter

For all matches for a given query that passed the filters in section 6.2, we tally positive vs negative predicates.[6] If the ratio of negative to positive is above a threshold (we use 0.1), we consider the query an unsuitable candidate for being "potentially common to all," and therefore do not credit the author with having mentioned a fact.

This criterion of potential acceptance by a universal audience fails a query such as <Barack Obama,?,US citizen>, based on the following pattern of matches:

Count	Predicate
10	is not
4	is
2	was always
1	is really
1	isn't
1	was not

In a similar fashion, an essay writer's statement that "The beating of Rodney King in Los Angeles ... made for tense race relations" is not quite in accord with the 16 hits garnered by the statement "The Los Angeles riots were not caused by the Rodney King verdict," against other hits with predicates like *erupted after*, *occurred after*, *resulted from*, *were sparked by*, *followed*.

[5]A single sentence, unless anaphor-based expansion was carried out; see section 5.2.

[6]We use a list of negation markers to detect those.

Somewhat more subtly, the connection between *Albert Einstein* and *atomic bomb*, articulated as "For example, Albert Einstein's accidental development of the atomic bomb has created a belligerent technological front" by a test-taker, is opposed by 6 hits with the predicate *did not build* against matches with predicates such as *paved the way to*, *led indirectly to*, *helped in*, *created the theory of*. The conflicting accounts seem to reflect a lack of consensus on the degree of Einstein's responsibility.

The cases above clearly demonstrate the implications of the *argumentative* notion of facts used in our project. Facts are statements that the audience is prepared to accept without further justification, differently from arguments, and even from presumptions (statements about what is normal and likely), for which, as Perelman and Olbrechts-Tyteca (1969) observe, "additional justification is beneficial for strengthening the audience's adherence." Certainly in the Obama case and possibly in others, a different notion of factuality, for example, a notion that emphasizes availability of legally acceptable supporting evidence, would have led to a different result. Yet, in an ongoing instance of argumentation, the mere *need* to resort to such a proof is already a sign that the audience is not prepared to accept a statement as a fact.

6.4 Additional filters

We also implemented a number of filters aimed at detecting excessive diversity in the matches, which could suggest that there is no clear and systematic relation between the NE and the NP. The filters are conjunctions of thresholds operating over measures such as purity of matches (percentage of exact matches in NE or NP), degree of overlap of non-pure matches with the context of the query in the essay, clustering of the predicates (recurrence of the same predicates across matches), general frequencies of NE and NP.

7 Evaluation

7.1 Manual check of queries

A manual check of a small subset of queries was initially intended as an interim evaluation of the query construction process, to see how often the produced queries are deficient candidates for later verification.

However, we also decided to include a human fact-check of the queries that were found to be verifiable, to see the kinds of factual mistakes made in essays.

A research assistant was asked to classify 500 queries into **W**rong (the NE and NP are not related in the essay), **T**rivial (almost any NE could be substituted, as in <WWI,?, Historians>), **S**ubjective (<T.S.Eliot,?,the most frightening poet of all time>), **VC** – verifiable and correct, **VI** – verifiable and incorrect. Table 4 shows the distribution.

W	**T**	**S**	**VC**	**VI**
18%	13%	13%	54%	2%

Table 4: The distribution of query types for 500 queries.

Queries classified as Wrong (18%) mostly correspond to parser mistakes. Trivial and Subjective queries, while not attributing to the author connections that she has not made, are of questionable value as far as fact-checking goes. Perhaps the most surprising figure is the meager amount of verifiable and incorrect queries. Examples of relevant statements from essays include (NE and NP are boldfaced):

- For example, **Paul Gaugin** who was a **sucessful business man**, with a respectable wife and family, suddenly gave in to the calling of the arts and left his life. (He was a *failing* businessman immediately before leaving family.)
- For example, in **Jane Austin**'s **Little Women**, she portrays the image of a lovely family and the wonders of womenhood. (The book is by Louisa May Alcott.)
- This occurrence can be seen with the **Rodney King** problem in California during the **late 1980's**. (The Rodney King incident occurred on March 3, 1991).
- We see the philosophers Aristotle, Plato, **Socrates** and their **practical writings** of the political problems and issues of the day. (Socrates is not known to have left writings.)

First, we observe that factual mistakes are rare. Furthermore, they seem to pertain to one in a series of related facts, most of which are correct and testify to the author's substantial knowledge about the matter – consider Paul Gaugin's biography or the contents of "Little Women" in the examples above. It is therefore unclear how detrimental the occasional factual "glitches" are to the quality of the essay.

8 Application to Essay Scoring

We show Pearson correlations between human scores given to essays and a number of characteristics derived from the work described here, as well as the partial correlations when the effect of essay length is factored out. We calculated both the correlations using raw numbers and on a logarithmic scale, with the latter generally producing higher correaltions. Therefore, we are reporting the correlations between grade and the logarithm of the relevant characteristic. The characteristics are:

#NE The number of NE tokens in an essay.

#Queries The number of queries generated by the system from the given essay (as described in section 5.2).

#Matched Queries The number of queries for which a match was found in the TextRunner database. If the original query or any of its expansion variants (see section 6.1) had matches, the query contributes a count of 1.

#Filtered Matches The number of queries that passed the filters introduced in section 6. If the original query or any of its expansion variants passed the filters, the query contributes a count of 1.

Table 5 shows the results. First, we find that all correlations are significant at p=0.05, as well as the partial correlations exluding the effect of length for 7 out of 10 prompts. All correlations are positive, that is, the more factual information a writer employs in an essay, the higher the grade – beyond the oft reported correlations between the grade and the length of an essay (Powers, 2005).

Second, we notice that all characteristics – from the number of named entities to the number of filtered matches – produce similar correlation figures.

Third, there are large differences between average numbers of named entities per essay across prompts.

Prompt	NE	Pearson Corr. with Grade				Partial Corr. Removing Length			
		#NE	#Q	#Mat.	# Filt.	#NE	#Q	#Mat.	# Filt.
P1	280	0.144	0.154	0.182	0.185	0.006	0.019	0.058	0.076
P2	406	0.265	0.259	0.274	0.225	0.039	0.053	0.072	0.069
P3	452	0.245	0.225	0.188	0.203	0.049	0.033	0.009	0.051
P4	658	0.327	0.302	0.335	0.327	0.165	0.159	0.177	0.160
P5	704	0.470	0.477	0.473	0.471	0.287	0.294	0.304	0.305
P6	750	0.429	0.415	0.388	0.373	0.271	0.242	0.244	0.257
P7	785	0.470	0.463	0.479	0.469	0.302	0.302	0.341	0.326
P8	838	0.423	0.390	0.406	0.363	0.264	0.228	0.266	0.225
P9	919	0.398	0.445	0.426	0.393	0.158	0.209	0.233	0.219
P10	986	0.455	0.438	0.375	0.336	0.261	0.257	0.170	0.175
AV.	678	0.363	0.357	0.353	0.335	0.180	0.180	0.187	0.186

Table 5: Pearson correlation and partial correlation removing the effect of length between a number of characteristics (all on a log scale) and the grade. The second column shows the total number of identified named entities in the 200-essay sample from the given prompt. The prompts are sorted by the second column.

Generally, the higher the number, the better the number of named entities in the essay predicts its grade (the more NEs the higher the grade). This suggests that the use of named entities might be relatively irrelevant for some prompts, and much more relevant for others. For example, prompt P10 reads "The arts (painting, music, literature, etc.) reveal the otherwise hidden ideas and impulses of a society," thus practically inviting exemplification using specific works of art or art movements, while success with prompt P1 – "The human mind will always be superior to machines because machines are only tools of human minds" – is apparently not as dependent on named entity based exemplification. Excluding prompts with smaller than average total number of named entities (<678), the correlations average 0.40-0.44 across the various characteristics, with partial correlations averaging 0.25-0.26.

9 Discussion and Conclusion

9.1 Summary of the main result

In this article, we proposed a way to measure the use of factual information in text-taker essays. We demonstrated that the use of factual information is indicative of essay quality, observing positive correlations between the count of instances of fact-use in essays and the grade of the essay, beyond what can be attributed to a correlation between the total number of words in an essay and the grade.

9.2 What is driving the correlations?

We also investigated which of the components of the fact-use measure were responsible for the observed correlations. Specifically, we considered (a) the number instances of fact-use that were verified against a database of human-produced assertions, filtered for controversy and excessive diversity; (b) the number of instances of fact-use that were verified against the database, without subsequent filtering; (c) the number of instances of fact-use identified in an essay (without checking against the database); (d) the number of named entities used in an essay (without constructing queries around the entity). These steps correspond to a gradual relaxation of the full fact-checking procedure all the way to a proxy measure that counts the number of named entities.

We observed similar correlations throughout the relaxation procedure. We therefore conclude that the number of named entities is the driving force behind the correlations, with no observed effect of the query construction and verification procedures.[7] This result could be explained by two factors.

First, a manual check of 500 queries showed that factual mistakes are rare – only 2% of the queries corresponded to factually incorrect statements. Furthermore, mistakes were often accompanied by the

[7]While the trend is in the direction of an increase in Pearson correlations from (a) to (d), the differences are not statistically significant.

test-taker's use of additional facts about the same entity which were correct; this might alleviate the impact of a mistake in the eyes of a grader.

Second, the query verification procedure applied to only about 35% of the queries – those for which at least one match was found in the database, that is, 65% of the queries could not be assessed using the database of 2 bln extractions. The verification procedure is thus much less robust than the procedure for detecting named entities, which performs at above >80% recall and precision.

9.3 Implications for automated scoring

Our results suggest that essays on a general topic written by adults for a high-stakes exam contain few incorrect facts, so the potential for a full fact-checking system to improve correlations with grades beyond merely detecting the potential for a factual statement using a named entity recognizer is not large. While a measure based on the number of "verified" facts found in an essay demonstrated a significant correlation with human scores beyond the contribution of essay length, a simpler measure based only on the number of named entities in the essay demonstrated a similar relationship with human scores.

Given the similarity in the two features' empirical usefulness, it would seem that the feature that counts the number of named entities in an essay is a better candidate, due to its simplicity and robustness. However, there is another perspective from which a feature based only on the number of named entities in an essay may be less suitable for use in scoring: the perspective of *construct validity*, the degree to which a test (or, in this case, a scoring system) actually measures what it purports to. As mentioned above, the number of named entities in an essay is, at best, a proxy measure,[8] roughly indicative of the referencing of factual statements in support of an argument within an essay. Because the measure itself is not directly sensitive to how named entities are used in the essay, though, even entities with no connection to the essay topic would tend to contribute to the score, and the measure is therefore vulnerable to manipulation by test-takers.

[8]For a discussion of *proxes* vs *trins* in essay grading, see (Page and Petersen, 1995).

An obvious strategy to exploit this scoring mechanism would be to simply include more named entities in an essay, either interspersing them randomly throughout the text, or including them in long lists of examples to illustrate a single point. Such a blatant approach could potentially be detected by the use of a filter or *advisory* (Higgins et al., 2006; Landauer et al., 2003) designed to identify anomalous writing strategies. However, there could be more subtle approaches to exploiting such a feature. For example, it is possible that test-takers might be inclined to increase their use of named entities by adducing more facts in support of an argument, and would go beyond the comfort zone of their actual factual knowledge, thus making more factual mistakes. Test gaming strategies have been recognized as a threat to automated scoring systems for some time (Powers et al., 2001), and there is evidence based on test takers' own self-reported behavior that this threat is real (Powers, 2011). This is one major reason why large-scale operational testing programs (such as GRE or TOEFL) use automated essay scoring only in combination with human ratings. In sum, the degree to which a linguistic feature is predictive of human essay scores is not the only criterion for evaluation; the washback effects of using the feature (on writing behavior and on instruction) must also be considered.

The second finding of this study is that the effectiveness of fact-checking for essay assessment is compromised by the limited coverage of the wealth of factual statements made by essay writers, with only 35% of queries garnering any hits at all in a large general-purpose database of assertions. It is possible, however, that OpenIE technology can be used to collect more focused repositories on specific topics, such as the history of the American Civil War, which could be used to assess responses to tasks related to that particular subject matter. This is one of the directions of our future research.

References

Eugene Agichtein and Luis Gravano. 2000. Snowball: Extracting relations from large plain-text collections. In *Proceedings of the 5th ACM conference on Digital Libraries*, pages 85–94. ACM.

Yigal Attali and Jill Burstein. 2006. Automated Essay Scoring With e-rater®V.2. *Journal of Technology, Learning, and Assessment*, 4(3).

Michele Banko and Oren Etzioni. 2008. The Tradeoffs Between Open and Traditional Relation Extraction. In *Proceedings of the 46th Annual Meeting of the Association for Computational Linguistics*, pages 28–36, Columbus, OH, June. Association for Computational Linguistics.

Beata Beigman Klebanov, Jill Burstein, Nitin Madnani, Adam Faulkner, and Joel Tetreault. 2012. Building Subjectivity Lexicon(s) From Scratch For Essay Data. In *Proceedings of CICLING*, New Delhi, India.

Tao-Hsing Chang, Chia-Hoang Lee, and Yu-Ming Chang. 2006. Enhancing Automatic Chinese Essay Scoring System from Figures-of-Speech. In *Proceedings of the 20th Pacific Asia Conference on Language, Information and Computation*, pages 28–34.

Yen-Yu Chen, Chien-Liang Liu, Chia-Hoang Lee, and Tao-Hsing Chang. 2010. An Unsupervised Automated Essay Scoring System. *IEEE Transactions on Intelligent Systems*, 25(5):61–67.

Nancy Chinchor, Lynette Hirschman, and David Lewis. 1993. Evaluating Message Understanding Systems: An Analysis of the Third Message Understanding Conference (MUC-3). *Computational Linguistics*, 19(3):409–449.

Dmitry Davidov and Ari Rappoport. 2009. Geo-mining: Discovery of Road and Transport Networks Using Directional Patterns. In *Proceedings of EMNLP*, pages 267–275.

Arijit De and Sunil Kopparapu. 2011. An unsupervised approach to automated selection of good essays. In *Recent Advances in Intelligent Computational Systems (RAICS), 2011 IEEE*, pages 662 –666.

Marie-Catherine de Marneffe, Bill MacCartney, and Christopher Manning. 2006. Generating Typed Dependency Parses from Phrase Structure Parses. In *Proceedings of LREC*, pages 449–454, Genoa, Italy, May.

Oren Etzioni, Michele Banko, Stephen Soderland, and Daniel Weld. 2008. Open information extraction from the web. *Commun. ACM*, 51(12):68–74.

Jenny Finkel, Trond Grenager, and Christopher Manning. 2005. Incorporating Non-local Information into Information Extraction Systems by Gibbs Sampling. In *Proceedings of the 43rd Annual Meeting of the Association for Computational Linguistics*, pages 363–370, Ann Arbor, MI, June. Association for Computational Linguistics.

Ralph Grishman and Beth Sundheim. 1995. Design of the MUC-6 evaluation. In *Proceedings of MUC*, pages 1–11.

Derrick Higgins, Jill Burstein, and Yigal Attali. 2006. Identifying off-topic student essays without topic-specific training data. *Natural Language Engineering*, 12(2):145–159.

Tsunenori Ishioka and Masayuki Kameda. 2006. Automated Japanese Essay Scoring System based on Articles Written by Experts. In *Proceedings of the 21st International Conference on Computational Linguistics and 44th Annual Meeting of the Association for Computational Linguistics*, pages 233–240, Sydney, Australia, July. Association for Computational Linguistics.

Tuomo Kakkonen and Erkki Sutinen. 2004. Automatic assessment of the content of essays based on course materials. In *Proceedings of the International Conference on Information Technology: Research and Education*, pages 126–130, London, UK.

Tuomo Kakkonen, Niko Myller, Jari Timonen, and Erkki Sutinen. 2005. Automatic Essay Grading with Probabilistic Latent Semantic Analysis. In *Proceedings of the Second Workshop on Building Educational Applications Using NLP*, pages 29–36, Ann Arbor, Michigan, June. Association for Computational Linguistics.

Dan Klein and Christopher Manning. 2003. Accurate Unlexicalized Parsing. In *Proceedings of the 41st Annual Meeting of the Association for Computational Linguistics*, pages 423–430, Sapporo, Japan, July. Association for Computational Linguistics.

Saul Kripke. 1980. *Naming and Necessity*. Harvard University Press.

Thomas Landauer, Darrell Laham, and Peter Foltz. 2003. Automated scoring and annotation of essays with the Intelligent Essay Assessor. In Mark Shermis and Jill Burstein, editors, *Automated essay scoring: A cross-disciplinary perspective*, pages 87–112. Lawrence Erlbaum Associates, Mahwah, New Jersey.

Leah Larkey. 1998. Automatic essay grading using text categorization techniques. In *Proceedings of SIGIR*, pages 90–95, Melbourne, AU.

Benoît Lemaire and Philippe Dessus. 2001. A System to Assess the Semantic Content of Student Essays. *Journal of Educational Computing Research*, 24:305–320.

Annie Louis and Derrick Higgins. 2010. Off-topic essay detection using short prompt texts. In *Proceedings of the NAACL HLT 2010 Fifth Workshop on Innovative Use of NLP for Building Educational Applications*, pages 92–95, Los Angeles, California, June. Association for Computational Linguistics.

Boyan Onyshkevych. 1993. Template design for information extraction. In *Proceedings of MUC*, pages 19–23.

Ellis Page and Nancy Petersen. 1995. The computer moves into essay grading: Updating the ancient test. *Phi Delta Kappan*, 76:561–565.

Chaïm Perelman and Lucie Olbrechts-Tyteca. 1969. *The New Rhetoric: A Treatise on Argumentation*. Notre

Dame, Indiana: University of Notre Dame Press. Translated by John Wilkinson and Purcell Weaver from French original published in 1958.

Donald Powers, Jill Burstein, Martin Chodorow, Mary Fowles, and Karen Kukich. 2001. Stumping E-Rater: Challenging the Validity of Automated Essay Scoring. *ETS research report RR-01-03*, http://www.ets.org/research/policy_research_reports/rr-01-03.

Donald Powers. 2005. "Wordiness": A selective review of its influence, and suggestions for investigating its relevance in tests requiring extended written responses. *ETS research memorandum RM-04-08*, http://www.ets.org/research/policy_research_reports/rm-04-08.

Donald Powers. 2011. Scoring the TOEFL Independent Essay Automatically: Reactions of Test Takers and Test Score Users. *ETS research manuscript RM-11-34*, http://www.ets.org/research/policy_research_reports/rm-11-34.

Deepak Ravichandran and Eduard Hovy. 2002. Learning surface text patterns for a Question Answering System. In *Proceedings of ACL*, pages 41–47.

Carolyn Rosé, Antonio Roqueand, Dumisizwe Bhembe, and Kurt VanLehn. 2003. A hybrid text classification approach for analysis of student essays. In *Proceedings of the Second Workshop on Building Educational Applications Using NLP*, pages 29–36.

Utilizing Cumulative Logit Models and Human Computation on Automated Speech Assessment

Lei Chen
Educational Testing Service (ETS)
Princeton, NJ, 08541
lchen@ets.org

Abstract

We report two new approaches for building scoring models used by automated speech scoring systems. First, we introduce the Cumulative Logit Model (CLM), which has been widely used in modeling categorical outcomes in statistics. On a large set of responses to an English proficiency test, we systematically compare the CLM with two other scoring models that have been widely used, i.e., linear regression and decision trees. Our experiments suggest that the CLM has advantages in its scoring performance and its robustness to limited-sized training data. Second, we propose a novel way to utilize human rating processes in automated speech scoring. Applying accurate human ratings on a small set of responses can improve the whole scoring system's performance while meeting cost and score-reporting time requirements. We find that the scoring difficulty of each speech response, which could be modeled by the degree to which it challenged human raters, could provide a way to select an optimal set of responses for the application of human scoring. In a simulation, we show that focusing on challenging responses can achieve a larger scoring performance improvement than simply applying human scoring on the same number of randomly selected responses.

1 Introduction

Automated assessment is a process by which computer algorithms are used to score test-taker inputs, which could be essays, short-text descriptions, read-aloud sentences, or spontaneous speech responses to open-end questions. Until recently, human scoring has been predominantly used for scoring these types of inputs. Several limitations of the human scoring process have been identified in previous research (Bennett, 2006). First, the human scoring process is influenced by many hidden factors, such as human raters' mood and fatigue conditions. In addition, human raters may not strictly follow the rubrics designed to guide the scoring process in their practical scoring sessions. Furthermore, human rating is also an expensive and slow process, especially for large-scale tests.

There has been an increasing number of studies concerning the use of speech processing and natural language processing (NLP) technologies to automatically score spoken responses (Eskenazi, 2009). In these machine scoring systems, a set of features related to multiple aspects of human speaking capabilities, e.g., fluency, pronunciation, intonation, vocabulary usage, grammatical accuracy, and content, is extracted automatically. Then, statistical models, such as the widely used linear regression models, classification and regression trees (CART), are trained based on human ratings and these features. For new responses, the trained statistical models are applied to predict machine scores.

The performance of current automated speech scoring systems, especially for spontaneous speech responses, still lags markedly behind the performance of human scoring. To improve the performance of automated speech scoring, an increasing number of research studies have been undertaken (Jang, 2009; Chen and Zechner, 2011; Chen and Yoon, 2011). However, these studies have mostly focused on exploring additional speech features, not on building alternative scoring models. Hence, in this paper, we will report on two new lines of research focusing on the scoring model part of automated speech scoring systems. In particular, we will introduce the Cumulative Logit Model (CLM), which is not widely used in NLP, and compare it systematically with other widely-used modeling methods. In addition, we will propose a hybrid scoring system inspired by the recent trend of involving human computation in machine learning tasks (Quinn et al., 2010), which consists of both human scoring and machine scoring to achieve a balance of scoring accuracy, speed, and cost.

The remainder of the paper is organized as follows: Section 2 reviews the previous research efforts; Section 3 describes both the test from which our experimental data were collected and the automated speech scoring system; Section 4 introduces the Cumulative Logit Model (CLM) and reports a systematic comparison with two other widely used modeling approaches; Section 5 proposes using both human scoring and machine scoring to achieve a trade-off between scoring accuracy, speed, and cost, and shows a simulation. Finally, Section 6 concludes the paper and describes our plans for future research.

2 Related Work

In the language testing field, it is critical how easily a score can be interpreted by test takers and stakeholders. Therefore, "white-box" machine learning methods (mostly from the field of statistics) are favored over black-box systems (e.g., neural networks) and widely used in automated scoring systems. For example, SRI's EduSpeak system (Franco et al., 2010) used a decision-tree model to automatically produce a speaking score from a set of discrete score labels. Linear Discrimination Analysis (LDA) has been used in pronunciation evaluation (Hacker et al., 2005). In a speech scoring system described by Zechner et al. (2009), a linear regression (LR) model was used to predict human scores.

Applying linear regression, which is designed for continuous outcomes, on ordinal outcomes, such as discrete human rated scores, is questioned by some statisticians.

> A linear regression model does not exploit the fact that the scores can assume only a limited number of values and hence may provide inefficient approximations to essay scores obtained by raters. Consequently, estimation based on a model that assumes that the response is categorical will be more accurate than linear regression. A cumulative logit model, sometimes called a proportional odds model, is one such model (Haberman and Sinharay, 2010).

The CLM was compared systematically with an ordinary linear regression model in terms of automated essay scoring (Haberman and Sinharay, 2010). Based on their experiment on a large variety of TOEFL prompts, they suggested that the CLM should be considered a very attractive alternative to regression analysis.

In recent years, a new trend of research in the machine learning field is to use human computation to provide additional help, especially on difficult tasks. For example, after the ESP game (Von Ahn, 2006), an increasing number of human computation based games emerged to use a large number of human participants to solve many machine learning problems, such as human identification for image processing and sentiment annotation in natural language processing (NLP). Quinn and Bederson (2011) review research in this area. Furthermore, Quinn et al. (2010) proposed a hybrid mechanism to integrate both human computation and machine learning to achieve a balance between speed, cost, and quality.

In this paper, we will follow the advances in the two directions mentioned above, including using CML as a modeling method and obtaining complementary computing by integrating machine scoring with human scoring to further improve the scoring models in automated speech scoring systems.

3 Data and Automated Scoring System

3.1 Data

AEST is a large-scale English test for assessing test-takers' English proficiency in reading, writing, listening, and speaking. The data used in our experiments was collected from operational AEST tests. In each test session, test takers were required to respond to six speaking test questions to provide information or express their opinions.

Each spoken response was assigned a score in the range of 1 to 4, or 0 if the candidate either made no attempt to answer the item or produced a few words totally unrelated to the topic. Each spoken response could also receive a "technical difficulty" (TD) label when technical issues may have degraded the audio quality to such degree that a fair evaluation was not possible. Note that in the experiments reported in this paper, we excluded both 0 and TD responses from our analyses. The human scoring process used the scoring rules designed for the AEST test. From a large pool of certified human raters, two human raters were randomly selected to score each response in parallel. If two raters' scores had a discrepancy larger than one point, a third rater with more experience in human scoring was asked to give a final score. Otherwise, the final scores used were taken from the first human rater in each rater pair.

The Pearson correlation r among human raters was calculated as 0.64. The second human scores had a correlation of 0.63 to the final scores while the first human scores had a correlation of 0.99. This is due to the fact that only in about 2% of the cases, two human scores have a discrepancy larger than one point. Table 1 describes the data size and final score distribution of the four score levels.

N	1(%)	2(%)	3(%)	4 (%)
49813	4.56	37.96	47.74	9.74

Table 1: Human score distribution of the AEST datasets

3.2 Automated scoring system

To automatically score spontaneous speech, we used the method proposed in Chen et al. (2009). In this method, a speech recognizer is used to recognize non-native speech and a forced alignment is conducted based on the obtained recognition hypotheses. From the recognition and alignment outputs, a number of features were extracted from multiple aspects, such as the timing profiles, recognition confidence scores, alignment likelihoods, etc. For speech recognition and forced alignment, we used a gender-independent, fully continuous Hidden Markov Model (HMM) speech recognizer. Our ASR system was trained from about 800 hours of non-native speech data and its corresponding word transcriptions. We extracted the following two types of features, including (1) fluency and intonation features based on the speech recognition output as described in Xi et al. (2008) and (2) pronunciation features that indicated the quality of phonemes and phoneme durations as described in Chen et al. (2009).

4 A comparison of three machine learning methods in automated speech scoring

We will briefly introduce CLM and then compare it with two other widely used scoring methods, i.e., linear regression and CART. In most of the related previous investigations, several machine learning algorithms were compared using a fixed number of instances. However, as shown in recent studies, such as Rozovskaya and Roth (2011), judging an algorithm requires consideration of the impact of the size of the training data set. Therefore, in our experiment, we compared three algorithms on different sizes of training samples.

Let the response's holistic score be $Y = 1, 2, ...J$ (J is 4 in our study on the AEST data) and let the associated probabilities be $\pi_1, \pi_2, ...\pi_J$. Therefore the probability of a predicted score is not larger than j

$$P(Y \leq j) = \pi_1 + \pi_2 + ... + \pi_j \qquad (1)$$

The logit of this probability can be estimated as

$$log\frac{P(Y \leq j)}{1 - P(Y \leq j)} = \alpha_j + \sum_{k=1}^{K} \beta_k X_k \qquad (2)$$

where K is the number of speech features. We can see that a CLM contains K βs where each β is associated with one feature. In addition, for each score j, there is an intercept α_j. The CLM is a special case of multinomial logistic regression, which is named Maximum Entropy (MaxEnt) model (Berger et al., 1996) and is well known by NLP researchers. In CLM, the ranking order of the labels being predicted is emphasized. However, in MaxEnt models, there is no assumption about the relationship of the labels being predicted.

For CLM, we used the Ye's VGAM R package (Yee, 2010) as our implementation. For ordinary linear regression and CART methods, we used corresponding implementations in the WEKA toolkit (Hall et al., 2009), i.e., *lm* and *J48* tree, through the RWeka package (Hornik et al., 2009) so that we could run these three algorithms inside R.

From the available speech features, we first run an inter-correlation analysis among these features. Then, two feature selection approaches implemented in the caret R package (Kuhn, 2008) were used to select useful features from about 80 features. First, all feature-pairs whose inter-correlation was higher than 0.80 were analyzed and one feature for each pair was removed. Next, a recursive feature elimination (RFE) based on a linear regression model was utilized to reduce the feature size to just 20.

Using a stratified sampling based on the final scores, the whole data set was split into a training set (with 44,830 instances) and a test set (with 4,980 instances). Then, on a log_{10} scale, we tried using increasing number of training samples from 100 to $10^{4.5}$. For each training data set size, we randomly selected the size of training samples from the training set, built the three models, and evaluated the models on the entire test data. For each data set size, such process was repeated 10 times. The evaluation result is the averaged values from these 10 iterations. We repeated the same experiment on the top 5, 10, 15, and 20 features. The evaluation metrics include widely used measures in the field of automated scoring, including Pearson correlation r and quadratic weighted Kappa κ (hereafter weighted κ) between the machine predicted scores and human final scores in this data set.

Figure 1 shows the Pearson r and weighted κ values of the three methods vs. an increasing numbers of training samples. We find that the CLM always has the highest weighted κ value among these three methods for each data size level. The CART performs poorly, especially facing a limited number of training samples. However, when the training data size is large enough, the performance gap between the CART and other regression models becomes smaller. For two regression models, when working on 20 features, both Pearson r and weighted κ values plateaued after reaching 1000 training samples. More importantly, we find that the CLM still can provide a quite high value of weighted κ even just using 100 training samples. This is very important for automated assessments in cases where there are not enough pre-test responses to fully train the scoring model. When using other feature selections (5, 10, and 15), we also observed the same trend as shown in the Figure 1.

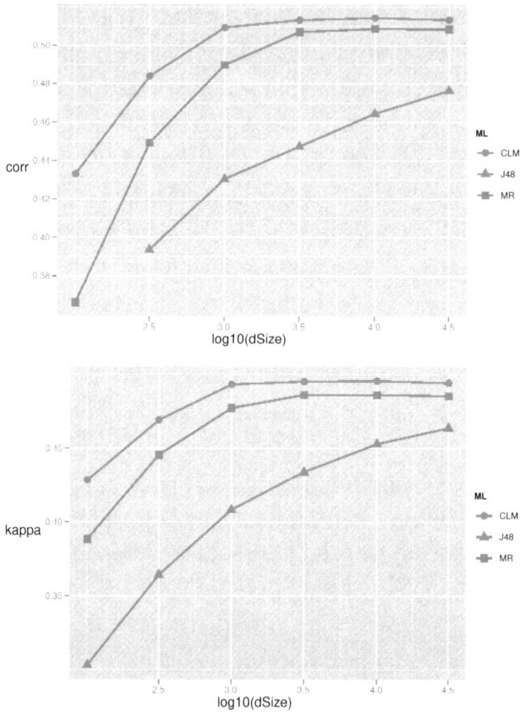

Figure 1: Weighted κ and Pearson correlation r of LR, CART, and CLM vs. an increasing number of training samples when using 20 features.

5 Utilizing human computation to support automated speech scoring

On spontaneous speech responses, the performance of automated scoring still lags behind human ratings. For example, on the test set (4,098 samples), among human raters both the Pearson r and the weighted κ values are about 0.6, much higher than the best automated scoring results we saw in the previous section (around 0.5). There are many possible reasons for such a big performance gap between automated speech scoring and human scoring. For example, the automated features' lack of a measurement of content accuracy and relevance might provide an explanation for part of the performance gap. As a result, to our knowledge, there has not been any commercial application of automated speech scoring on high-stakes speaking tests to open-ended questions.

To further improve the speech scoring system's performance, inspired by Quinn et al. (2010), we propose to include human computation — human rating of speech responses — in the automated speech scoring system. Previously, there have been some efforts to use human computation in automated speech scoring systems. For example, it is well known that human scores were used to train automated scoring models. For essay scoring, an automated scoring system, e-rater, has been used to validate the human rating process (Enright and Quinlan, 2010). One advantage of using both human and e-rater to score is that about 10% of human rating requests for double-scoring required in operational essay scoring could be saved. However, there has been no previous work investigating the joint use of human scoring and machine scoring. By using these two scoring methods together, we hope to achieve a balance among scoring accuracy, speed, and cost.

From a total of N test responses, we need ask humans to score m, where $m << N$. Therefore, an important question concerning the joint use of human scoring and machine scoring is how to find these m responses so that the expensive and slow human scoring process can provide a large performance gain. In this paper, we will report our preliminary research results of focusing on the responses challenging to machine scoring process.

Since the responses used in this paper were selected to be double-scored responses from a very large pool of AEST responses, we use the rating condition of each doubly-scored response to predict how challenging any given response is. For speech responses for which two human raters gave different holistic scores, we assumed that these responses were not only difficult to score for human beings, but also for the machine learning method, which has been trained from human scores in a supervised learning way. We call the responses on which two human raters agreed *easy-case* responses and the responses on which two human raters disagreed *hard-case* ones. Table 2 reports on the application of trained automated speech assessment systems to these two types of responses. From the entire testing set, human raters agreed on $3,128$ responses, but disagreed on $1,852$ responses. From the training set described in the previous section, we randomly sampled $1,000$ responses to train a CLM model using those 20 features used in Section 4. Then, the trained CLM model was evaluated on these two types of responses, respectively. Table 2 reports the evaluation metrics averaged on 20 trials of using different training set portions. We can clearly see that the machine scoring has a significantly better performance on the easy-case responses than the hard-case responses. Therefore, it is natural to focus expensive/slow human computation efforts on these hard-case responses.

metric	easy-case	hard-case
agreement(%)	68.16	48.08
r	0.594	0.377
weighted κ	0.582	0.355

Table 2: Evaluation of automated speech assessment systems on two types of speech responses. For the responses on which two human raters agreed, the machine has a statistically significantly better performance.

Suppose that we can obtain the type of each response, hard-case vs. easy-case, in some way, we then can focus our human scoring efforts on hard-case responses only since machine scoring performs much worse on them. Figure 2 depicts the results of one trial of using human scoring to replace an increasing number of machine scores. Among $4,980$ responses in the test set, the blue curve shows the weighted κ values after replacing an increasing number of machine scores with human scores. Here, we used the scores provided by the second rater from each rater pair. This set of human scores had a Pearson r of 0.626 with the final scores. We also replaced the same number of responses, but without distinguishing easy- and hard-case responses by the corresponding human scores. The results are shown in the red curve. We can observe that the weighted κ values increased from about 0.50, which was obtained by using only machine scoring, to about 0.58 by asking humans to score all hard-case responses, about 33% of all responses. Among the two methods to select the responses for using human scoring, we can clearly see that the strategy of focusing on *hard-case* responses can achieve higher weighted κ when spending the same amount of human efforts as the strategy of randomly selecting responses.

6 Discussions

In this paper, we reported on two experiments for improving the scoring model in automated sponta-

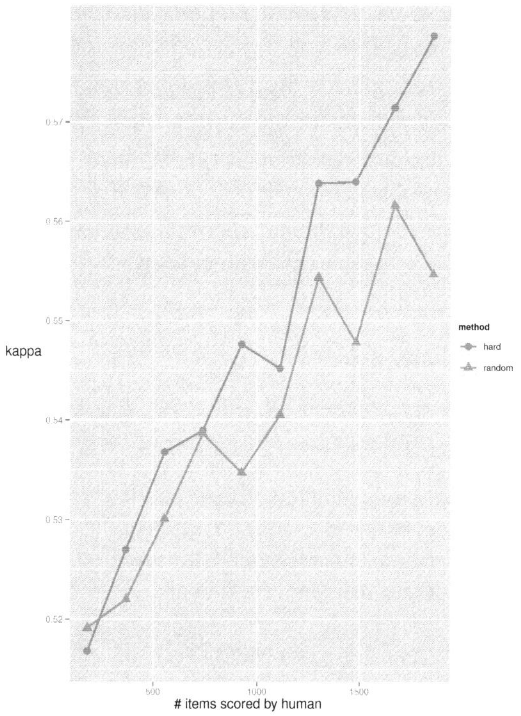

Figure 2: Weighted κ values when using human rating results to replace machine-predicted scores on hard-case responses or a similar number of responses that are randomly selected.

neous speech assessment. In the first experiment, we systematically compared a new modeling method, Cumulative Logit Model (CLM), which has been widely used in statistics, with other two widely used modeling methods, linear regression and CART. We compared these three modeling methods on a large test data set (containing $4,980$ responses) and evaluated these methods on a series of training data sizes. The experimental results suggest that the CLM model consistently achieves the best performance (measured in Pearson r and quadratic weighted κ between the predicted scores and human rated scores). More importantly, we find that the CLM can work quite well even when just using hundreds of responses in the training stage. This finding is especially important for building scoring models when pre-test data is limited.

Although automated scoring has been designed to overcome several disadvantages of the human rating process, our experiments are meant to initiate scientific debate on how best to combine the strengths of human and automated scoringto achieve an optimal compromise of scoring accuracy, cost, and time. At least for current automated scoring systems for spontaneous speech, the machine performance lags behind the reliability of the human rating process. We also found that the automated system performed worse on hard-case responses on which even two human raters did not agree. In a simulation study, we showed that jointly using human scoring and machine scoring can further improve the scoring performance obtained by just using automated speech scoring. By focusing human scoring, which is expensive, slow, but more accurate, on a set of responses specially selected from the entire set of responses, we can achieve larger gains of scoring performance than randomly assigning the same amount of responses for human scoring. Therefore, from an engineering point of view of building more accurate scoring systems, it is promising to design a hybrid system consisting of both human scoring and machine scoring.

For future research, given the automated speech scoring system's large performance variation on two types of responses, it is worthwhile finding a reliable way to automatically predict a responses' condition, i.e., whether it is hard or easy to score for humans or for machines. We need to consider both proficiency features we used in this paper and other features measuring audio quality. Finding such information can help us decide when to use machine scoring and when to rely on human raters. In addition, other applications of human computation, such as asking humans to adjust machine predicted scores or using human rated scores accumulated in scoring operations to routinely update the machine scoring system will be explored.

References

R.E. Bennett. 2006. Moving the field forward: Some thoughts on validity and automated scoring. *Automated scoring of complex tasks in computer-based testing*, pages 403–412.

A. Berger, S. Pietra, and V. Pietra. 1996. A maximum entropy approach to natural language processing. *Computational Linguistics*, 22:39–72.

L. Chen and S. Yoon. 2011. Detecting structural event for assessing non-native speech. In *6th Workshop on Innovative Use of NLP for Building Educational Applications*, page 74.

Miao Chen and Klaus Zechner. 2011. Computing and evaluating syntactic complexity features for automated scoring of spontaneous non-native speech. In *ACL'11*, pages 722–731.

L. Chen, K. Zechner, and X Xi. 2009. Improved pronunciation features for construct-driven assessment of non-native spontaneous speech. In *NAACL-HLT*.

M.K. Enright and T. Quinlan. 2010. Complementing human judgment of essays written by english language learners with e-rater scoring. *Language Testing*, 27(3):317–334.

M. Eskenazi. 2009. An overview of spoken language technology for education. *Speech Communication*, 51(10):832–844.

H. Franco, H. Bratt, R. Rossier, V. Rao Gadde, E. Shriberg, V. Abrash, and K. Precoda. 2010. EduSpeak: a speech recognition and pronunciation scoring toolkit for computer-aided language learning applications. *Language Testing*, 27(3):401.

S.J. Haberman and S. Sinharay. 2010. The application of the cumulative logistic regression model to automated essay scoring. *Journal of Educational and Behavioral Statistics*, 35(5):586.

C. Hacker, T. Cincarek, R. Grubn, S. Steidl, E. Noth, and H. Niemann. 2005. Pronunciation Feature Extraction. In *Proceedings of DAGM 2005*.

M. Hall, E. Frank, G. Holmes, B. Pfahringer, P. Reutemann, and I. H Witten. 2009. The WEKA data mining software: An update. *ACM SIGKDD Explorations Newsletter*, 11(1):10–18.

K. Hornik, C. Buchta, and A. Zeileis. 2009. Open-source machine learning: R meets weka. *Computational Statistics*, 24(2):225–232.

T. Y Jang. 2009. Automatic assessment of non-native prosody using rhythm metrics: Focusing on korean speakers' english pronunciation. In *Proc. of the 2nd International Conference on East Asian Linguistics*.

M. Kuhn. 2008. Building predictive models in r using the caret package. *Journal of Statistical Software*, 28(5):1–26.

A.J. Quinn and B.B. Bederson. 2011. Human computation: a survey and taxonomy of a growing field. In *Proceedings of the 2011 annual conference on Human factors in computing systems*, page 14031412.

A.J. Quinn, B.B. Bederson, T. Yeh, and J. Lin. 2010. CrowdFlow: integrating machine learning with mechanical turk for speed-cost-quality flexibility. *Better performance over iterations*.

A. Rozovskaya and D. Roth. 2011. Algorithm selection and model adaptation for ESL correction tasks. *Urbana*, 51:61801.

L. Von Ahn. 2006. Games with a purpose. *Computer*, 39(6):92–94.

X. Xi, D. Higgins, K. Zechner, and D. Williamson. 2008. Automated Scoring of Spontaneous Speech Using SpeechRater v1.0. Technical report, Educational Testing Service.

Thomas W. Yee. 2010. The VGAM package for categorical data analysis. *J. Statist. Soft.*, 32(10):1–34.

Klaus Zechner, Derrick Higgins, Xiaoming Xi, and David M. Williamson. 2009. Automatic scoring of non-native spontaneous speech in tests of spoken english. *Speech Communication*, 51:883–895, October.

PREFER: Using a Graph-Based Approach to Generate Paraphrases for Language Learning

Mei-Hua Chen*, Shih-Ting Huang+, Chung-Chi Huang*, Hsien-Chin Liou, Jason S. Chang+**

*Institute of Information Systems and Applications

+Department of Computer Science

** Department of Foreign Languages and Literature

National Tsing Hua University

HsinChu, Taiwan, R.O.C. 30013

{chen.meihua,koromiko1104,u901571,hsienchin,jason.jschang}@gmail.com

Abstract

Paraphrasing is an important aspect of language competence; however, EFL learners have long had difficulty paraphrasing in their writing owing to their limited language proficiency. Therefore, automatic paraphrase suggestion systems can be useful for writers. In this paper, we present PREFER[1], a paraphrase reference tool for helping language learners improve their writing skills. In this paper, we attempt to transform the paraphrase generation problem into a graphical problem in which the phrases are treated as nodes and translation similarities as edges. We adopt the PageRank algorithm to rank and filter the paraphrases generated by the pivot-based paraphrase generation method. We manually evaluate the performance of our method and assess the effectiveness of PREFER in language learning. The results show that our method successfully preserves both the semantic meaning and syntactic structure of the query phrase. Moreover, the students' writing performance improve most with the assistance of PREFER.

1. Introduction

Paraphrasing, or restating information using different words, is an essential part of productive language competence (Fuchs, 1980; Mel'čuk, 1992; Martinot, 2003). However, EFL learners have difficulty paraphrasing in their writing partly because of their insufficient lexical knowledge (Abasi et al. 2006; Chandrasoma et al. 2004). If they are provided with direct and substantial support while writing, they may be able to express their thoughts more fluently. Unfortunately, few paraphrase reference tools have been developed to provide instant assistance to learners in their writing process. In the light of the pressing need for paraphrase reference tools, we develop PREFER, a paraphrasing assistant system to help EFL learners vary their expression during writing.

Over the past decade, paraphrasing techniques have played an important role in many areas of Natural Language Processing, such as machine translation, and question answering. However, very few studies have been conducted concerning the application of automatic paraphrase generation techniques in language learning and teaching.

In this paper, we treat the paraphrase generation problem as a graph-related problem. We adopt the PageRank algorithm (Page et al., 1999) to generate paraphrases based on the assumption that a page with more incoming links is likely to receive a higher rank. Meanwhile, a page which is linked by a higher ranked page should transitively be ranked higher. We take advantage of transitivity of relevance to rank and filter the paraphrases generated by the pivot-based method (i.e., phrase are treated as paraphrases if they share the same translations) of Bannard and Callison-Burch (2005).

The advantage of the pivot approach is that the generated paraphrases are exactly semantically equivalent to the query phrase. However, its

[1] http://140.114.89.231/PREFER

quality of the paraphrases highly correlates with that of the techniques of bilingual alignment. To overcome such limitation, we use the PageRank algorithm to refine the generated paraphrases. In other words, we leverage the PageRank algorithm to find more relevant paraphrases that preserve both meaning and grammaticality for language learners. The results of a manual evaluation and a system assessment show that our approach and system perform well.

2. Related Work

A number of studies have investigated EFL leaners' paraphrase competence. For example, Campbell (1987) reveals that language proficiency significantly affects paraphrasing competence. McInnis (2009) reports that paraphrasing task is more difficult for L2 students than that for L1 students. According to Milicevic (2011), L2 learners propose less valid paraphrases than native speakers. These findings indicate that EFL students have problems in paraphrasing. In view of this, we develop PREFER, a paraphrase reference tool, for helping English learners with their writing.

Paraphrase generation, on the other hand, has been an area of active research and the related work has been thoroughly surveyed in Androutsopoulos and Malakasiotis (2010) as well as in Madnani and Dorr (2010). In the rest of this section, we focus on reviewing the methods related to our work.

One prominent approach to paraphrase generation is based on bilingual parallel corpora. For example, Bannard and Callison-Burch (2005) propose the pivot approach to generate phrasal paraphrases from an English-German parallel corpus. With the advantage of its parallel and bilingual natures of such a corpus, the output paraphrases do preserve semantic similarity. Callison-Burch (2008) further places syntactic constraints on generated paraphrases to improve the quality of the paraphrases. In this paper, we generate paraphrases adopting the pivot-based method proposed by Bannard and Callison-Burch (2005) in the first round. Then we use a graph-based approach to further ensure paraphrase candidates preserve *both* meaning *and* grammaticality.

In a study more closely related to our work, Kok and Brockett (2010) take a graphical view of the pivot-based approach. They propose the Hitting Time Paraphrase algorithm (HTP) to measure similarities between phrases. The smaller the number of steps a random walker goes from one node to the other, the more likely these two nodes are paraphrases. The main difference between their work and ours lies in the definition of the graph. While they treat multilingual phrases as nodes, we treat only English phrases as nodes. Besides, we define the edges between nodes as semantic relation instead of bilingual alignment.

In contrast to the previous work, we present a graph-based method for refining the paraphrases generated by the pivoting approach. Our goal is to consolidate the relation between paraphrases to provide learners with more and better paraphrases which are helpful in expanding their lexical knowledge.

3. Graph-Based Paraphrase Generation

In this section, we describe how we use the PageRank algorithm to rank and filter the paraphrases generated by the pivot-based method.

3.1 Graph Construction

We first exploit the pivot-based method proposed by Bannard and Callison-Burch (2005) to populate our graph G using of candidate paraphrases $cP = \{cp_1, cp_2, \ldots, cp_n\}$ from a bilingual parallel corpus B for a query phrase q. Each phrase in *cP* is also represented as a node in *G*. Note that the query phrase *q* is excluded from *cP*.

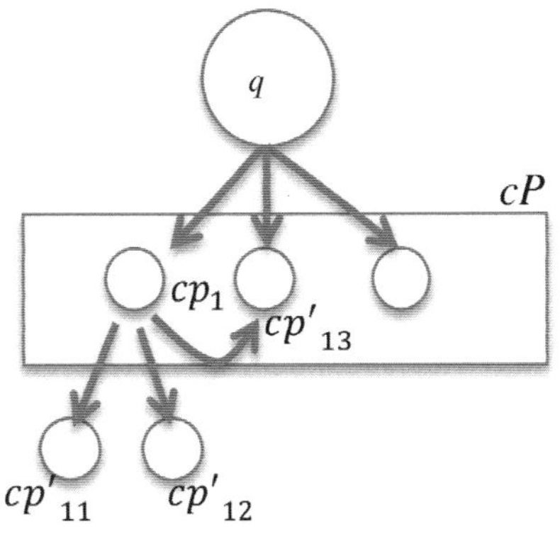

Figure 1. A simple graph *G*. Note that the cp_1 and cp'_{13} will be linked iff cp'_{13} is the paraphrase of *q* and is also the paraphrase of cp_1.

Graph G only contains the paraphrases cp_i whose probabilities are higher than a certain threshold ε^2 as nodes. In addition, each cp_i is linked to the query phrase q with edge e which is weighted by the probability $P(cp_i|q)$. Furthermore, we establish the edges among the phrases in cP. An example graph is shown in Figure 1. By repeating the previous steps, for each phrase cp_1, cp_2,... in cP, we find their corresponding paraphrases, $cp'_{11}, cp'_{12}, cp'_{13}, \ldots$ and $cp'_{21}, cp'_{22}, cp'_{23}, \ldots$, and discard the paraphrases that are not in cP. Once the phrases are linked with their paraphrases, the graph G is created.

In this paper, we also place a constraint that a paraphrase of a phrase q must neither be a substring nor a superstring of q. These strings are usually aligned with the same foreign language phrase while they are not paraphrases at all. For example, "*play an important*" and "*play an important role in*" are excluded for "*play an important role*". This has the effect of reducing some of the noise generated by the pivot-based method.

3.2 Graph-Based Paraphrase Generation

We then refine the generated paraphrases adopting the PageRank algorithm proposed by Page et al. (1999). Consider a graph consisting of a set of webpages on the Web V and a set of hyperlinks E. The PageRank algorithm assigns a value PR to each webpage as their importance measurement. The PR value of a certain page u is defined iteratively as the following equation:

$$PR(u) = \sum_{v \in B_u} \frac{PR(v)}{L(v)} \quad (1)$$

where B_u is a set of pages linked to u and $L(.)$ denotes the number of *outbound links* from a page v.

Intuitively, by using formula (1) iteratively, we are able to calculate the PR values for all nodes and thus extract relatively important paraphrases. However, the original PageRank algorithm does not take the weight of each edge into consideration. That is, the PageRank algorithm treats all links equally when distributing rank scores. Treating all links equally in paraphrase generation task might lose some linguistic properties. For this, we consider the importance of edges of the nodes and weight the edges based on the paraphrase probability in the pivot-based approach using

$$w(u, v) = \sum_{f} P(f|v)P(u|f) \quad (2).$$

Formula (2) represents the probability that the phrase u is the paraphrase of the phrase v. f refers to shared translations of v and u. Then for each iteration of the PageRank calculation, we reassign the PR value for all u in V to be $PR'(u)$ as:

$$PR'(u) = \sum_{v \in B_u} \frac{w(u,v)PR(v)}{L(v)} \quad (3)$$

Instead of treating all edges equally, formula (3) integrates the weights of inbound link and outbound link edges (see Section 4 for the performance differences with and without weighting edges).

4. Results

In this section, we first present our experimental setting. Then evaluation results are reported.

4.1 Experimental Setting

In this paper, word alignments were produced by Giza++ toolkit (Och and Ney, 2003) over a set of Danish-English section (containing 1,236,427 sentences) of the Europarl corpus, version 2 (Koehn, 2002).

We compared our graph-based approach with a strong baseline, the pivot-based method with syntactic constraint (SBP) (Callison-Burch, 2008) utilizing the same Danish-English corpus. We also investigate the contribution of adding the edge weights to the PageRank algorithm by building two models, **PR** representing the method of the PageRank algorithm without weights and **PRw** representing the method of the weighted PageRank algorithm, for comparison.

To assess the performance of our method, we conducted a manual evaluation. We asked an experienced English lecturer to randomly select 100 most commonly used and meaningful phrases from 30 research articles in the discipline of Computer-Assisted Language Learning (CALL). A total of 88 unique phrases were used as our test set for evaluation excluding 12 phrases not existing in the Europarl corpus. For each phrase, we extracted

[2] We set ε to be 0.01.

the corresponding candidate paraphrases and chose top 5 for evaluation. Two raters, provided with a simplified scoring standard used by Callison-Burch (2008), manually evaluate the accuracy of the top ranked paraphrases of each phrase by score 0, 1 and 2. It is worth noting that the raters were asked to score each paraphrase candidate by considering its appropriateness in various contexts. In this evaluation, we strictly deemed a paraphrase to be correct if and only if both raters scored 2. The inter-annotator agreement was 0.63.

The coverage was measured by the number of correct answers within top 5 candidates. The precision was measured by the number of correct answers within the returned answers.

On the other hand, to assess the effectiveness of PREFER in language learning, we carried out an experiment with 55 Chinese-speaking EFL college freshmen, who had at least six years of formal instruction from junior to senior high schools and were estimated to be at the intermediate level regarding their overall English competence. The students were randomly divided into three groups. They were asked to paraphrase seven short paragraphs in the pre-test with no system support, and then paraphrase another seven short paragraphs in the post-test using three different tools: PREFER (P), *LONGMAN Dictionary of Contemporary English Online* (L), and *Thesaurus.com* (T). A total of 22 default phrases (http://140.114.75.22/share/examples.htm) were embedded in the paragraphs in the pre- and post-tests, targeted at comparing the quality and quantity of students' paraphrasing performance. Students were not restricted to paraphrase these embedded phrases. Instead, they were encouraged to replace any possible phrases or even restructure sentences. We had two experienced native-speaker TESL (Teaching English as a Second Language) lecturers to score the students' paraphrasing performance.

4.2 Experimental Results

4.2.1 Manual Evaluation

As shown in Table 1, **PRw** achieved both good precision and coverage. Moreover, **PR** and **PRw** performed better than **SBP** in both coverage and precision. Also, the result that the performance of **PRw** is better than that of **PR** implies that **PRw** is able to generate more semantically and syntactically correct paraphrases. However, the precision of 0.19 indicates that there is still room to improve the paraphrase generation model.

	PR	**PRw**	**SBP**
Coverage	0.17	**0.18**	0.07
Precision	0.17	**0.19**	0.10

Table 1: The measurement of paraphrases.

Additionally, Mean Reciprocal Rank (MRR) is also reported. Here, MRR is defined as a measure of how much effort needed to locate the first appropriate paraphrase for the given phrase in the ranked list of paraphrases. The MRR score of **PRw** (0.53) outperformed **PR** (0.51) and **SBP** (0.47). It demonstrated that the **PRw** model facilitates the high ranking of good paraphrases (i.e., paraphrases with meaning and grammaticality preserved would be ranked high).

4.2.2. Evaluation on Language Learning

The second evaluation is to assess the effectiveness of PREFER applied to CALL. We used a comparison method to measure the extent to which EFL learners achieved good performance in paraphrasing.

		P	L	T
improvement of paraphrasing task		**38.2%**	-31.6%	-6.2%
all paraphrasable phrases	rephrased	**38.4%**	-23.2%	9.5%
	correct	**53.3%**	-17.5%	4.6%
	correctness rate	**7.9%**	4.9%	-3.1%
22 default phrases	rephrased	**68%**	-16%	28%
	correct	**100%**	-5%	31%
	correctness rate	**13.6%**	7.9%	1.5%

Table 2. Comparison of paraphrasing performance among students using three different reference tools.

As seen in the first row of Table 2, the students' writing performance improved most with the assistance of PREFER (i.e., group P), compared with group L and group T. We further analyzed and compared the number of the rephrased phrases and the correct paraphrases, and the rate of correctness students achieved using different reference tools among our testing paraphrase candidates (see the middle and bottom panels of Table 2). Obviously, the students consulting PREFER achieved substantial paraphrasing improvement in all three aspects of both all and default phrases. But the other two groups seemed unable to manage well the paraphrasing task with traditional way of phrase information. This limited information seems insufficient to enable students to familiarize themselves with proper usages of phrases which might lead to improper paraphrasing.

In short, PREFER outperformed the other two reference tools in assisting EFL learners in their paraphrasing task.

5. Conclusion and Future Work

In this paper, we treat the paraphrase generation problem as a graphical problem. We utilize the PageRank algorithm to rank and filter the paraphrases generated using the pivot-based method. The results show that our method significantly produces better paraphrases in both precision and coverage compared with the syntactically-constrained pivot method of Callison-Burch (2008). Additionally, PREFER does benefit learners' writing performance.

In order to conduct a more comprehensive evaluation, we plan to adapt the in-context evaluation metric introduced by Callison-Burch et. al (2008). A larger test set would be generated manually to evaluate the performance of our paraphrase system. In addition, we will implement various kinds of baseline systems such as Kok and Brockett (2010) and Chan et al. (2011) to provide a more competitive comparison.

Many avenues exist for future research and improvement. For example, we would like to extend paraphrasing consecutive n-gram phrases to inconsecutive ones such as ones with incomplete transitive verbs (e.g., "***provide*** *someone* ***with*** *something*"). Besides, we are interested in weighting edges using syntactic and semantic relation in our graph-based method to further improve the quality of generated paraphrases.

References

Ali R. Abasi, Nahal Akbari, and Barbara Graves. 2006. Discourse appropriation, construction of identities, and the complex issue of plagiarism: ESL students writing in graduate school. *Journal of Second Language Writing*, 15, 102–117.

Ion Androutsopoulos and Prodromos Malakasiotis. 2010. A Survey of Paraphrasing and Textual Entailment Methods. *Journal of Artificial Intelligence Research* 38, 135–187.

Colin Bannard and Chris Callison-Burch. 2005. Paraphrasing with bilingual parallel corpora. In *Proceedings of ACL*, pp. 597-604.

Chris Callison-Burch. 2008. Syntactic constraints on paraphrases extracted from parallel corpora. In *Proceedings of EMNLP*, pp. 196–205.

Chris Callison-Burch, Trevor Cohn, and Mirella Lapata. 2008. ParaMetric: an automatic evaluation metric for paraphrasing. In *Proceedings of the 22nd International Conference on Computational Linguistics*, pp. 97-104.

Cherry Campbell. 1990. Writing with others' words: Using background reading text in academic compositions. In B. Kroll (Ed.), *Second language writing: Research insights for the classroom* (pp. 211-30). Cambridge, UK: Cambridge University Press.

Tsz Ping Chan, Chris Callison-Burch and Benjamin Van Durme. 2011. Reranking Bilingually Extracted Paraphrases Using Monolingual Distributional Similarity. In *Proceedings of the GEMS 2011 Workshop on GEometrical Models of Natural Language Semantics*, pp. 33-42.

Ranamukalage Chandrasoma, Celia Thompson, and Alastair Pennycook. 2004. Beyond plagiarism: Transgressive and nontransgressive intertextuality. *Journal of Language, Identity, and Education*, *3*(3), 171–194.

Catherine Fuchs. 1980. *Paraphrase et théorie du langage. Contribition à une histoire des theories linguistiques contemporaines et à la construction d'une théorie énonciative de la paraphraase*. Thèse de doctorat. Paris: Université Paris VII.

Philipp Koehn. 2002. Europarl: A multilingual corpus for evaluation of machine translation. Unpublished, http://www.isi.edu/~koehn/europarl/.

Stanley Kok and Chris Brockett. 2010. Hitting the right paraphrases in good time. In *Proceedings of NAACL/HLT*, pp. 145-153.

Nitin Madnani and Bonnie J. Dorr. 2010. Generating phrasal and sentential paraphrases: A survey of data-driven methods. *Computational Linguistics*, 36(3):341–388.

Claire Martinot. 2003. Pour une linguistique de l'acquisition. La reformulation: du concept descriptif au concept explicatif. *Langage et Société*, 2(104); 147-151.

Lara McInnis. 2009. *Analyzing English L1 and L2 Paraphrasing Strategies through Concurrent Verbal Report and Stimulated Recall Protocols*. MA Thesis. Toronto: University of Toronto.

Igor Mel'čuk. 1992. Paraphrase et lexique: la théorie Sens-Texte et le Dictionnaire explicatif et combinatoire. In: Mel'čuk, I. et al., *Dictionnaire explicatif et combinatoire du français contemporain. Recherches lexico-sémantiques III*. Montréal: Presses de l'Université de Montréal; 9-59.

Jasmina Milićević and Alexandra Tsedryk. 2011. Assessing and Improving Paraphrasing Competence in FSL. In *Proceedings of the 5th International Conference on Meaning- Text Theory*, pp. 175-184.

Franz Josef Och and Hermann Ney. 2003. A systematic comparison of various statistical alignment models. *Computational Linguistics*, 29(1): 19-51.

Lawrence Page, Sergey Brin, Rajeev Motwani, Terry Winograd. 1999. The PageRank Citation Ranking: Bringing Order to the Web. *Technical Report*. pp. 1999-66, Stanford University InfoLab.

Using an Ontology for Improved Automated Content Scoring of Spontaneous Non-Native Speech

Miao Chen
School of Information Studies
Syracuse University
Syracuse, NY 13244, USA
mchen14@syr.edu

Klaus Zechner
Educational Testing Service
660 Rosedale Road
Princeton, NJ 08541, USA
kzechner@ets.org

Abstract

This paper presents an exploration into automated content scoring of non-native spontaneous speech using ontology-based information to enhance a vector space approach. We use content vector analysis as a baseline and evaluate the correlations between human rater proficiency scores and two cosine-similarity-based features, previously used in the context of automated essay scoring. We use two ontology-facilitated approaches to improve feature correlations by exploiting the semantic knowledge encoded in WordNet: (1) extending word vectors with semantic concepts from the WordNet ontology (synsets); and (2) using a reasoning approach for estimating the concept weights of concepts not present in the set of training responses by exploiting the hierarchical structure of WordNet. Furthermore, we compare features computed from human transcriptions of spoken responses with features based on output from an automatic speech recognizer. We find that (1) for one of the two features, both ontologically based approaches improve average feature correlations with human scores, and that (2) the correlations for both features decrease only marginally when moving from human speech transcriptions to speech recognizer output.

1 Introduction

Currently, automated speech scoring systems mainly utilize features related to the acoustic aspects of a spoken response of a test taker, for example, fluency, pronunciation, and prosody features (Cucchiarini et al., 2000, 2002; Franco et al., 2010; Zechner et al., 2009). In terms of the content aspect of speech, for highly predictable speech, such as reading a passage aloud, scoring of content reduces to measuring the reading accuracy of the read passage which is typically achieved by computing the string edit distance between the target passage and the actual text read by the test taker, using the speech recognizer hypothesis as a proxy (Alwan et al., 2007; Balogh et al., 2007). For high entropy speech whose content is difficult to predict such as spontaneous speech in this study, on the other hand, content scoring has not been investigated much so far, mostly due to the difficulty of obtaining accurate word hypotheses for spontaneous non-native speech by Automated Speech Recognition (ASR) systems.

In this paper, we use spoken responses from an English language spoken proficiency test where candidates, all non-native speakers of English, respond to four different prompts[1] with a speaking time of one minute per response.

For this study, we decide to use a baseline approach for content scoring of spontaneous speech that was previously employed for a similar task in the context of automated essay scoring (Attali & Burstein, 2006), namely Content Vector Analysis (CVA) where every document is represented as a vector of word weights, based on their frequencies in a document or document collection. However, there are two issues with the CVA vector of words representation that we want to address with this study: (1) Similar words are treated in isolation and not grouped together. Words with similar meaning should be treated in the same way in an automated scoring system, so grouping word synonyms into semantic concepts can help with this issue. (2) The vector of word representation is based on an exist-

[1] Prompts are test tasks assigned to test takers to elicit spoken responses.

ing corpus of training documents. When encountering a word or concept in a test document that is not contained in the training set, it is difficult to decide the relevance of that word or concept.

We propose to use ontology-facilitated approaches as solutions to these two issues, aiming at enriching speech content representations to improve speech content scoring. Specifically, to address issue (1), we represent speech content by concept-level vectors, using the *synsets* (lists of synonymous words) of the WordNet ontology (Fellbaum, 1998; WordNet 3.0, 2010). As for issue (2), we expand the vector representation by inferring the importance (weight) of concepts not present in the training vectors based on their path distance to known concepts or words in the hierarchical structure of the WordNet ontology.

Since we only look at the content aspect of speech without considering the acoustic features in this study, we work on speech transcripts exclusively, both from human transcribers as well as from a state-of-the-art automated speech recognition system, and compare results between the ideal human transcripts and the imperfect transcripts generated by the speech recognizer. For the purpose of simplified illustration, speech transcripts are often referred to as "documents" in the paper as they are a special type of textual documents.

The remainder of this paper is organized as follows: in Section 2, we review related research in content scoring of texts, particularly student essays; Section 3 describes the data set we use for this study and the ASR system; and Section 4 presents the ontologically-facilitated methods we are using in detail. In Section 5, we present our experiments along with their results, followed by a discussion in Section 6, and we conclude the paper with a summary and outlook in Section 7.

2 Related Work

There have been some effective approaches for test takers' written responses in language tests, namely in the area of Automated Essay Scoring (AES).

AES has employed content vector analysis, i.e., vectors of words to represent text, for example, the e-rater system (Burstein, 2003; Attali & Burstein, 2006) and the experimental system in Larkey and Croft (2003). Representations in the BETSY system (Bayesian Essay Test Scoring System) also involve words, such as the frequency of content words, and also include specific phrases as well (Dikli, 2006). AES has also used latent concepts for text representation, such as the Intelligent Essay Assessor system (Landauer et al., 2003). The latent concepts are generated by a statistical approach called Latent Semantic Analysis (LSA), which constructs a semantic vector space and projects essays to the new space.

Representing texts by vectors of words has also been a common practice in many research areas beyond AES, including information retrieval (Salton et al., 1975; Croft et al., 2010). One of its weaknesses, however, is its difficulty in addressing issues such as synonyms and related terms. Different words, such as lawyer, attorney, counsel etc. can share similar meaning, while in a word vector representation they are treated as different dimensions; however, because they are conceptually similar, it makes more sense to group them into the same vector dimension. Ontologies are in a good position to resolve this issue because they organize words and terms under structured concepts, group terms with similar meaning together and also maintain various semantic relations between concepts. Therefore, text can be represented on a concept level by using ontology concepts as features. Recognizing concepts in documents can further reveal semantic relations between documents (Hotho et al., 2003a), thus can facilitate further text-related tasks such as clustering, information retrieval, as well as our speech scoring task. This type of representation has been tried in several studies (e.g., Hotho et al., 2003a; Hotho et al., 2003b; Bloehdorn & Hotho, 2004).

Hotho et al. (2003a; 2003b) use ontology concepts to represent text and use the representation for document clustering. The studies employ the WordNet ontology, a general domain ontology. The experiments test three parameters of using an ontology for text representation: (1) whether concept features should be used alone or replace word features or be used together with word features; (2) word sense disambiguation strategies when using concepts; and (3) investigating the optimal level of word generalization in terms of the hierarchical structure of the ontology, i.e., how general the concepts should be. Some options of the first two parameters will be implemented and tested in our experiment design below.

The vector representation approach of text documents, either using words or concepts, can be used to measure the content similarity between essays. E-rater, for example, measures the similarity between test essays and training essays by computing the cosine similarity of their word vectors and by generating two content features based on this similarity metric. It uses multiple regression as its final scoring model, using both content features, as well as features related to other aspects of the essay, such as grammar and vocabulary usage (Burstein, 2003; Attali & Burstein, 2006). Intelligent Essay Assessor also employs cosine similarity between to-be-scored essays and training essays as basis of one content feature, and models the scoring process by normalization and regression analysis (Landauer et al., 2003). The IntelliMetric system uses a nonlinear and multidimensional modeling approach to reflect the complexity of the writing process as opposed to the general linear model (Dikli, 2006). Larkey and Croft (2003) employ Bayesian classifiers for modeling, which is a type of text categorization technique. It treats essay scoring as a text categorization task, the purpose of which is to classify essays into score categories based on content features (i.e., if the scores range from 1-4, then there are four score categories).

Zechner and Xi (2008) report on experiments related to scoring of spontaneous speech responses where content vector analysis was used as one of several features in scoring models for two different item types. They found that while these content features performed reasonably well by themselves, they were not able to increase the overall scoring model performance over a baseline that did not use content features.

This paper will use CVA as a baseline for our experiment and investigate two ontology-based approaches to enhance the content representation and improve content feature performance.

3 Data

We use data from a test for English proficiency for non-native speakers of English. Candidates are asked to provide spontaneous speech responses to four prompts, with each of the responses being one minute in length. The four prompts are all integrated prompts, meaning candidates are first given some materials to read or listen and then are asked to respond with their opinions or arguments towards the materials. The responses are scored holistically by human raters on a scale of 1 to 4, 4 being the highest score. For holistic scoring, the human raters use a speech scoring rubric as the guideline of expected performance on aspects such as fluency, pronunciation, and content for each score level.

Our data set contains 1243 speech samples in total as responses to four different prompts, obtained from 327 speakers (note that not all speakers responded to all prompts). Each response is verbatim transcribed by a human transcriber. The responses are grouped by their prompts since our experiments are prompt-specific. For responses of each prompt, we randomly split the responses into a training set (44%) and a test set (56%), making sure that response scores are distributed in a similar proportion in both training and test sets. Each response is considered as a single document here. Table 1 shows the size of the two data sets.

Prompt	Training Set	Test Set	Total
A	143	176	319 (4/79/158/78)
B	140	168	308 (7/86/146/69)
C	139	172	311 (4/74/154/79)
D	137	168	305 (8/75/141/81)

Table 1. Size of training and test data sets. The numbers in parentheses are the number of documents on score levels 1-4.

The training set is used for generating representative vectors of a prompt on different score levels, which are to be compared with test documents. The test set is primarily used to compute content features for test documents and examine performance of approaches under different experiment setups.

Besides human transcriptions of the speech files, we also obtained ASR output of the files, in order to examine performance of the proposed approaches on imperfect output, in a fully automated operational scenario where no human transcribers would be in the loop. Since the training set is used for deriving representative vectors for the four different prompts and we would like to generate accurate vectors based on human transcriptions, we do not use a separate training set for ASR data. Thus, we only obtain corresponding ASR output for the test set of each prompt.

The ASR system we use for our experiments in this paper is a state-of-the-art gender-independent continuous density Hidden Markov Model speech recognizer, trained on about 30 hours of non-native spontaneous speech. Its word error rate on the test set used here is about 12.8%.

4 Method

We employ one baseline approach for word-level features and two experimental approaches for concept-level features to examine the effect of the WordNet ontology and concept-level features on content feature correlations.

4.1 Baseline Approach: Content Vector Analysis (CVA)

We decide to use the two content features used by e-rater based on CVA analysis, called "max.cos" and "cos.w4" here (Attali & Burstein, 2006). The assumption behind this approach is that essays with similar human scores contain similar words; thus, they should share similar vector representations in CVA. For our data, this assumption is held for the spoken test documents in the same way. Moreover, we conjecture this assumption is mostly true for high score responses as opposed to low score responses, because we expect high vocabulary uniformity in high score responses and more irrelevant and more diverse vocabulary in low score responses.

Before feature computation, some preprocessing is conducted on the speech transcripts. For each prompt, we group its training set into four groups according to their score levels ("score-level documents"). Then we use the score-level documents of each prompt to generate a super vector as a representation for documents on this score level of this specific prompt. As a result, we have four score-level vectors under each prompt, generated from their training sets. While the score-level training vectors are produced using multiple documents of the same score level, vectors of test documents are generated on an individual document level. Given a test document that needs to be scored, we first convert it into the vector representation. Then we are ready to compute the two content features. Equation 1 provides the exact formula for the cosine similarity measure used in all of our methods.

$$(1)\quad \frac{\sum_{i=1}^{n} w_{t,i} * w_{sl,i}}{\sqrt{\sum_{i=1}^{n} w_{t,i}^2} * \sqrt{\sum_{i=1}^{n} w_{sl,i}^2}}$$

where n is the number of words and/or concepts in the score-level vector (from the training set documents), $w_{sl,i}$ are the word or concept weights of a score-level vector and $w_{t,i}$ are the word or concept weights of a test document (response transcription). $w_{t,i}$ are computed by term frequency and $w_{sl,i}$ are computed in the same way after concatenating documents of the same score level as one large document.

The max.cos feature. This feature measures which score level of documents the test document is most similar to in vector space by computing the cosine similarity with each score-level vector and then selecting the score level which has the largest cosine similarity to the test vector as feature value. Thus, this feature assumes integer values from 1 to 4 only.

The cos.w4 feature[2]. This feature measures content similarity between the test document and the best quality documents in vector space. Since score 4 is the highest level in our data set of spoken responses, we compute the cosine similarity between the test vector and the score level 4 vector as an indicator of how similar the test document is to the speech content of the test takers with highest proficiency.

The two features are evaluated based on their Pearson r correlation to human assigned scores. We evaluate the features in all experiments, as a way to observe how the two features' predictiveness varies among different experiment setups. Note that since the max.cos feature assumes integer values but the cos.w4 feature is real valued, we expect correlations to be higher for cos.w4 due to this difference, all other things being equal.

4.2 Ontology-facilitated Approaches

We use two ontology-facilitated document representation approaches, which represent documents based on the WordNet ontology. The first approach matches words in a document to concepts and represents documents by vectors of concepts, whereas the second one addresses the unknown word issue by inferring their weight based on the structure of the WordNet ontology.

[2] The feature is referred to as "cos.w/6" in Attali and Burstein (2006) because there are usually 6 score levels, while here our data has 4 score levels therefore it is written as "cos.w4".

4.2.1 Ontology-facilitated representation approach

This representation uses concepts instead of the words as elements in the document vectors. Given a document, we map words in the document to concepts, using the synsets in WordNet. For example, *chance* and *opportunity* are different words, however they belong to the same WordNet synset (*'opportunity.n.01'*). This concept-level representation groups words of similar meaning in the same vector dimension, thus making the vector space more succinct and semantically meaningful. The weighting scheme of concepts follows the one in the CVA approach. In this study, we focus on single words and match them to WordNet synsets; in future work, we consider matching multi-word expressions to ontologies like Wikipedia (Wikipedia, 2011). Experiments show that including words and their corresponding WordNet synsets as vector dimensions has better performance than only including WordNet synsets for text clustering tasks (Hotho et al., 2003a) and the same result also occurs in our preliminary experiments. Therefore, we include both WordNet synsets and words in the vector representation.

4.2.2 Ontology-facilitated reasoning approach

This approach is based on the ontology-facilitated representation and goes further to resolve the unknown word issue, i.e., handling words in test documents that have not been seen in the training documents.

First, test documents are converted to vectors of concepts plus words. If a concept in the test vector does not appear in the score level vector, its weight therefore is unknown, as well. We then estimate its weight based on structural information contained in the WordNet ontology. More specifically, given an unknown concept in the test document, we find the N most similar concepts to that unknown concept from the set of all concepts contained in the score level vector. We use a WordNet-based similarity estimate to measure similarity between concepts, namely the edge-based Path Similarity, which measures the length of a path from one concept to another concept in WordNet by computing the inverse of the shortest path between the two concepts (Pedersen et al., 2004). We submit that the estimated weight of the unknown concept in the test document vector should be close to the weights of its most similar concepts in the score level vector derived from the training documents. From this assumption, we propose estimating the unknown concept's weight by averaging the weights of the N most similar concepts:

(2) $w_{unk}=(\sum_{i=1}^{N} w_i)/N$

with N denoting the number of similar concepts in a score level vector, w_i denoting the weights of these similar concepts, and w_{unk} standing for the resulting concept weight for the unknown concept in a test document.

For example, a test document may be "so radio also create a great impact on this uh people communication". The words are matched to WordNet concepts, and we find that the concept synset *'impact.n.01'* is an unknown concept to the score level 4 vector. From the dimensions of the score level 4 vector we find these three most similar concepts to the unknown concept: *'happening.n.01'*, *'event.n.01'*, and *'change.n.01'*. We now can average the weights of these three concepts in the score-level vector to use it as a weight estimate for the unknown concept *'impact.n.01'*.

We want to note that while this approach can estimate weights for test document words or concepts contained in WordNet (but not in the training vectors), it cannot handle words that are not included in WordNet at all, such as many proper names, foreign words, etc. To address the latter as well, we would have to use a much larger and more comprehensive ontology, e.g., the online encyclopedia Wikipedia.

5 Experiments and Results

We design experiments according to the above approaches. The first experiment group is the baseline system using two features employed by e-rater, max.cos and cos.w4. The second and third experiment groups implement the two ontology-facilitated approaches, respectively. We first run CVA and compare several different parameter setups to optimize them for further experiments.

5.1 Parameter Optimization in CVA Experiments

For the CVA method, we need to decide (1) which term weighting scheme to use, and (2) whether or not to use a list of stopwords to exclude common non-content words such as determiners or prepositions from consideration. We compare five commonly used term weighting schemes, each one with or without using a stoplist, based on averaged correlations with human scores across all four prompts. The best results are obtained for the weighting scheme (TF/EDL)*IDF, where TF is the frequency of a term in a document, EDL is the Euclidean document length[3], and IDF is the inverse document frequency of a term based on a collection of documents. For this scheme, as for most others, there is almost no difference between using vs. not using a stoplist and we decide to use a stoplist for our experiments based on the tradition in the field. The selected term weighting scheme is applied in the same way for both the score-level vectors as well as the test document vectors.

5.2 Experiment Groups

5.2.1 Group 1: CVA

As described above, we first convert the training sets to score level vectors and the test documents into test vectors with the TF/EDL*IDF weighting, and compute the max.cos and cos.w4 features for each test document.

5.2.2 Group 2: Ontology-facilitated Representation

We first match words in documents to WordNet concepts. There are several ways to achieve this (Hotho et al., 2003a). Given a word, it may correspond to multiple concepts in WordNet, in which each possibility is called a "sense" in WordNet, and we need to decide which sense to use.

WordNet-Sense-1. In this study we employ a simple word sense disambiguation method by using the first sense returned by WordNet. We send a word to WordNet synset search function, which returns all synstes of the word, and we select to use the first result because it is also the most frequently used sense for the word.

After obtaining the senses and concepts for the words, the training sets and test documents are converted to vectors of WordNet concepts plus words, using TF/EDL*IDF weighting, the same one used by the CVA approach. We compute the max.cos and cos.w4 features in the same way as for the baseline CVA method.

5.2.3 Group 3: Ontology-facilitated Reasoning

This approach, called here "WordNet-Reasoning", also extracts vectors of WordNet concepts plus words with the same term weighting scheme as before. For matching words to concepts, we still employ the WordNet–Sense-1 sense selection method. For unknown concepts, which appear in a test vector but not in any score level vectors, we infer their weights by using the reasoning approach proposed in section 4.2.2 with N=5 as the number of most similar concepts to the unknown concept[4], located in the WordNet hierarchy. The score level vectors are expanded by the inferred unknown concepts. When we obtain the expanded score level vectors, we compute the two content features from the vectors in the same way as before, and finally calculate feature correlations with human scores.

5.3 Results

We run the three experiment groups on human and ASR transcriptions respectively and obtain the max.cos and cos.w4 feature values of test documents in the experiments. As stated in 4.1, we compute the correlations between the two features and the human assigned scores for evaluating the approaches.

Tables 2 and 3 (next page) list correlations of the two content features with human scores under different experiment setups. Significant differences on individual prompts between correlations of the two WordNet-based methods WordNet-Sense-1 and WordNet-Reasoning and the CVA baseline are denoted with * ($p<0.05$) and ** ($p<0.01$).

[3] Given a vector of raw term frequencies ($rtf_1, rtf_2, \ldots, rtf_n$), its Euclidean length is computed in this way:

$$\sqrt{\sum_{i=1}^{n} rtf_i^{\,2}}$$

[4] We manually inspected some of the similar concepts of the unknown concepts and found the first 5 similar concepts were relevant to the unknown concepts, and thus made the decision of N=5.

Prompt	Hum, CVA	Hum, WordNet-Sense-1	Hum, Word-Net-Reasoning	ASR, CVA	ASR, Word-Net-Sense-1	ASR, Word-Net-Reasoning
A	0.320	0.333	0.038**	0.293	0.286	0.014**
B	0.348	0.352	0.350	0.308	0.338	0.339
C	0.366	0.373	0.074**	0.396	0.386	0.106**
D	0.343	0.323	0.265	0.309	0.309	0.265
Average	0.344	0.345	0.182	0.327	0.330	0.181

Table 2. Correlations between the max.cos feature and human scores (Hum=using human transcriptions; ASR=using ASR hypotheses).

Prompt	Hum, CVA	Hum, WordNet-Sense-1	Hum, Word-Net-Reasoning	ASR, CVA	ASR, Word-Net-Sense-1	ASR, Word-Net-Reasoning
A	0.427	0.429	0.434	0.409	0.416	0.411
B	0.295	0.303	0.327*	0.259	0.278	0.292*
C	0.352	0.385*	0.402**	0.338	0.366	0.380**
D	0.368	0.385	0.389	0.360	0.379	0.374
Average	0.360	0.376	0.388	0.342	0.360	0.364

Table 3. Correlations between the cos.w4 feature and human scores (Hum=using human transcriptions; ASR=using ASR hypotheses)

6 Discussion

6.1 Results on Human Transcriptions

On human transcriptions, Table 2 shows that the max.cos feature correlations increase, albeit not significantly, when using the method WordNet–Sense-1 on all prompts except for prompt D but decrease sometimes significantly when using the WordNet-Reasoning approach.

The cos.w4 feature correlations, on the other hand, exhibit constant increases on all four prompts when using WordNet-Sense-1 and the increase on prompt C is significant. The average correlations further increase for all prompts when using WordNet-Reasoning and the increase is significant on prompts B and C (Table 3).

6.2 Results on ASR Output

On the ASR output, for the max.cos feature, the average correlation barely changes when using the WordNet-Sense-1 method but decreases when using WordNet-Reasoning with significant decrease on prompts A and C (Table 2).

For the cos.w4 feature, however, WordNet-Sense-1 improves correlations on all four prompts with 0.018 correlation increase on average but increases are not statistically significant on a prompt level. WordNet-Reasoning does not further improve correlations much beyond the correlations of WordNet-Sense-1, with a further 0.004 increase in average correlation. Compared to CVA, though, correlations for WordNet-Reasoning are significantly higher on prompts B and C (Table 3).

6.3 Overall Discussion

Based on these observations, we find that for cos.w4, the WordNet-Sense-1 approach can improve average correlations compared to the CVA baseline on both ASR and human transcriptions. Hence, the extension of the document vectors by WordNet synsets has a positive impact on the accuracy of content scoring of the spoken responses by non-native speakers.

Again looking at the cos.w4 feature, while the WordNet Reasoning approach works well on human transcriptions to further improve correlations compared to WordNet-Sense-1, it does not consistently improve correlations on ASR output. This may indicate that WordNet-Reasoning is more sensitive to ASR errors than WordNet-Sense-1.

For the max.cos feature, the correlation of WordNet-Reasoning decreases significantly from WordNet-Sense-1 on prompts A and C for both human and ASR transcriptions; moreover, in the WordNet-Reasoning approach the max.cos correlations vary greatly on the four prompts (Table 2). We conjecture that one reason for this finding may lie in the rather small sample size of the data set, as this is an exploratory study, and the differences across prompts may be smaller when using a substantially larger data set.

Comparing the average reduction in correlation between human and ASR transcriptions, we find an absolute drop in correlations of 0.017 between the CVA baseline for the max.cos and of 0.019 for the cos.w4 feature. Looking at the WordNet-Sense-1 approach for the cos.w4 feature, the average correlation of 0.376 for human transcriptions is reduced by 0.016 to 0.360 for ASR hypotheses. Hence, we observe that the imperfect speech recognition output does not cause a major degradation for this content feature; the degradations observed are all in the range of 5% relative (the ASR word error rate on the test set is about 13%.)

Overall, the ontology-facilitated approaches are effective for the cos.w4 feature and seem to be less appropriate for the max.cos feature. We conjecture that the characteristics of the max.cos feature may be the reason for the poor performance of the ontology-facilitated approaches on this feature. To compute this feature, we need to compare a test vector with vectors for each score level, and it is assumed that these vectors are representative vectors for documents at these score levels. In reality though, while the score level 4 vector is quite a good representative for the prompt topic (highest proficiency speakers), score level vectors of less proficient speakers are less uniform and more diverse. The reason is that there are only a few ways to appropriately represent the correct topic in a good quality spoken response but there can be many different ways of generating responses that are not on topic. For example, the score level 1 vector contains vectors generated from score 1 documents, whose words are considered mostly irrelevant for the prompt. Then, given a test document, which also contains irrelevant words for the prompt but with little overlap to the level 1 score vector, the similarity between them would be very small. Thus, any ontological approach has to face this heterogeneous distribution of words in the score level vectors for responses with lower scores; any semantic generalizations are inherently more difficult compared to those on higher scoring responses. For the cos.w4 feature, in contrast, only score level 4 vectors are used, and this problem does not surface here.

Finally, we observe that average correlations of both features based on ASR hypotheses (except for WordNet-Reasoning for the max.cos feature) fall in the range of 0.32-0.37. This range is well in line with our better performing features in other dimensions of spontaneous speech responses, e.g., fluency, pronunciation, and prosody.

7 Conclusion and Future Work

In this paper, we propose using ontology-facilitated approaches for content scoring of non-native spontaneous speech due to specific merits of ontologies. Two ontology-facilitated approaches are proposed and evaluated, and their results are compared against a CVA baseline. The results indicate that the ontology approaches can improve content feature correlations in some circumstances. As a summary, concept-level features and reasoning-based approaches work well on the cos.w4 content feature where test documents are compared against a vector representing all training set documents with the highest human score.

For future work, we plan to investigate more sophisticated reasoning approaches. For this study, we use a simple averaging method to infer the concept importance based on hierarchy-inferred similarity metrics. As a next step, we plan to infer weights according to different similarity metrics and differential weighting of the N closest terms. Another avenue for future research is to employ different ontologies, for example, Wikipedia, which contains more concepts and entities than WordNet and has a structure that has grown more organically and less from first principles. Wikipedia also has a larger pool of multi-word expressions and we would like to explore how representations based on the Wikipedia ontology affects automated speech scoring performance.

References

Alwan, A., Bai, Y., Black, M., Casey, L., Gerosa, M., Heritage, M., & Wang, S. (2007). A system for technology based assessment of language and literacy in young children: The role of multiple information sources. *Proceedings of the IEEE International Workshop on Multimedia signal Processing*, Greece.

Attali, Y., & Burstein, J. (2006). Automated essay scoring with e-rater® V. 2. *The Journal of Technology, Learning and Assessment*, 4(3).

Balogh, J., Bernstein, J., Cheng, J., & Townshend, B. (2007). Automatic evaluation of reading accuracy: Assessing machine scores. *Proceedings of the ISCA-SLaTE-2007 Workshop, Farmington, PA, October.*

Bloehdorn, S., & Hotho, A. (2004). Boosting for text classification with semantic features. *Workshop on mining for and from the semantic web at the 10th*

ACM SIGKDD conference on knowledge discovery and data mining (KDD 2004).

Burstein, J. (2003). The E-rater® scoring engine: Automated essay scoring with natural language processing. In M. D. Shermis, Burstein, J.C. (Ed.), *Automated essay scoring: A cross-disciplinary perspective* (pp. 113-121). Mahwah, NJ: Lawrence Erlbaum Associates, Inc.

Croft, W. B., Metzler, D., & Strohman, T. (2010). *Search engines: Information retrieval in practice.* Boston, MA: Addison-Wesley.

Cucchiarini, C., Strik, H., & Boves, L. (2000). Quantitative assessment of second language learners' fluency by means of automatic speech recognition technology. *Journal of the Acoustical Society of America,* 107(2), 989-999.

Cucchiarini, C., Strik, H., & Boves, L. (2002). Quantitative assessment of second language learners' fluency: Comparisons between read and spontaneous speech. *Journal of the Acoustical Society of America,* 111(6), 2862-2873.

Dikli, S. (2006). An overview of automated scoring of essays. *The Journal of Technology, Learning and Assessment*, 5(1), 1-35.

Fellbaum, C. (Ed.). (1998). *WordNet: An electronic lexical database*. Cambridge, MA: The MIT press.

Franco, H., Bratt, H., Rossier, R., Gadde, V. R., Shriberg, E., Abrash, V., & Precoda, K. (2010). EduSpeak: A speech recognition and pronunciation scoring toolkit for computer-aided language learning applications. *Language Testing*, 27(3), 401-418.

Hotho, A., Staab, S., & Stumme, G. (2003a). Ontologies improve text document clustering. *Proceedings of the Third IEEE International Conference on Data Mining (ICDM'03).*

Hotho, A., Staab, S., & Stumme, G. (2003b*). Text clustering based on background knowledge* (Technical report, no.425.): Institute of Applied Informatics and Formal Description Methods AIFB, University of Karlsruche.

Landauer, T. K., Laham, D., & Foltz, P. W. (2003). Automated scoring and annotation of essays with the Intelligent Essay Assessor. In M. D. Shermis, Burstein, J.C. (Ed.), *Automated essay scoring: A cross-disciplinary perspective* (pp. 87–112). Mahwah, NJ: Lawrence Erlbaum Associates, Inc.

Larkey, L. S., & Croft, W. B. (2003). A Text Categorization Approach to Automated Essay Grading. In M. D. Shermis & J. C. Burstein (Eds.), *Automated Essay Scoring: A Cross-discipline Perspective*: Mahwah, NJ, Lawrence Erlbaum.

Pedersen, T., Patwardhan, S., & Michelizzi, J. (2004). WordNet:: Similarity: measuring the relatedness of concepts. *Proceedings of the Fifth Annual Meeting of the North American Chapter of the Association for Computational Linguistics (NAACL-04).*

Salton, G., Wong, A., & Yang, C. S. (1975). A vector space model for automatic indexing. *Communications of the ACM*, 18(11), 613-620.

Wikipedia: The free encyclopedia (2011). FL: Wikimedia Foundation, Inc. Retrieved Apr 26, 2012, from http://www.wikipedia.org

WordNet 3.0 Reference Manual. (2010). Retrieved Apr 26, 2012 from http://wordnet.princeton.edu/wordnet/documentation/

Zechner, K., Higgins, D., Xi, X, & D. M. Williamson (2009). Automatic scoring of non-native spontaneous speech in tests of spoken English. *Speech Communication, 51(10)*, 883-895.

Zechner, K., & X. Xi (2008). Towards Automatic Scoring of a Test of Spoken Language with Heterogeneous Task Types. Proceedings of the ACL Workshop on Innovative Use of NLP for Building Educational Applications, Columbus, OH, June.

Predicting Learner Levels for Online Exercises of Hebrew

Markus Dickinson, Sandra Kübler, Anthony Meyer
Indiana University
Bloomington, IN, USA
{md7,skuebler,antmeyer}@indiana.edu

Abstract

We develop a system for predicting the level of language learners, using only a small amount of targeted language data. In particular, we focus on learners of Hebrew and predict level based on restricted placement exam exercises. As with many language teaching situations, a major problem is data sparsity, which we account for in our feature selection, learning algorithm, and in the setup. Specifically, we define a two-phase classification process, isolating individual errors and linguistic constructions which are then aggregated into a second phase; such a two-step process allows for easy integration of other exercises and features in the future. The aggregation of information also allows us to smooth over sparse features.

1 Introduction and Motivation

Several strands of research in intelligent computer-assisted language learning (ICALL) focus on determining learner ability (Attali and Burstein, 2006; Yannakoudakis et al., 2011). One of the tasks, detecting errors in a range of languages and for a range of types of errors, is becoming an increasingly popular topic (Rozovskaya and Roth, 2011; Tetreault and Chodorow, 2008); see, for example, the recent HOO (Helping Our Own) Challenge for Automated Writing Assistance (Dale and Kilgarriff, 2011). Only rarely has there been work on detecting errors in more morphologically-complex languages (Dickinson et al., 2011).

In our work, we extend the task to predicting the learner's level based on the errors, focusing on Hebrew. Our system is targeted to be used in a university setting where incoming students need to be placed into the appropriate language level—i.e., the appropriate course—based on their proficiency in the language. Such a level prediction system for Hebrew faces a number of challenges: 1) unclear correspondence between errors and levels, 2) missing NLP resources, and, most critically, 3) data sparsity.

Placing learners into levels is generally done by a human, based on a written exam (e.g. (Fulcher, 1997)). To model the decision process automatically, we need to understand how the types of errors, as well as their frequencies, correspond to learner levels. There is only little work investigating this correspondence formally (see (Hawkins and Filipović, 2010; Alexopoulou et al., 2010) for discussion) and only on error-annotated English learner corpora. For this reason, we follow a data-driven approach to learn the correspondence between errors and levels, based on exercises from written placement exams. Although the exact exercises will vary across languages and language programs, the methodology is widely applicable, as developing a small set of exercises requires minimal effort—effort already largely expended for paper exams. Currently, we focus on an exercise in which the learner has to order a set of words into a grammatical sentence. Our goal is to move towards freer language production and to analyze language proficiency through more variables, but, in the interest of practicality, we start in a more restricted way.

For lesser-resourced languages, there is generally little data and few NLP resources available. For Hebrew, for example, we must create our own pool of learner data, and while NLP tools and resources exist (Goldberg and Elhadad, 2011; Yona and Wintner, 2008; Itai and Wintner, 2008), they are not adapted for dealing with potentially ill-formed learner productions. For this reason, we are performing linguistic analysis on the gold standard answers to obtain optimal linguistic analyses. Then, the system aligns the learner answer to the gold standard answer and determines the types of deviations.

Since Hebrew is a less commonly taught language (LCTL), we have few placement exams from which to learn correspondences. Compounding the data sparsity problem is that each piece of data is complex: if a learner produces an erroneous answer, there are potentially a number of ways to analyze it (cf. e.g. (Dickinson, 2011)). An error could feature, for instance, a letter inserted in an irregular verb stem, or between two nouns; any of these properties may be relevant to describing the error (cf. how errors are described in different taxonomies, e.g. (Díaz-Negrillo and Fernández-Domínguez, 2006; Boyd, 2010)). Specific error types are unlikely to recur, making sparsity even more of a concern. We thus need to develop methods which generalize well, finding the most useful aspects of the data.

Our system is an online system to be used at the Hebrew Language Program at our university. The system is intended to semi-automatically place incoming students into the appropriate Hebrew course, i.e., level. As with many exams, the main purpose is to "reduce the number of students who attend an oral interview" (Fulcher, 1997).

2 The Data

Exercise type We focus on a scrambled sentence exercise, in which learners are given a set of well-formed words and must put them into the correct order. For example, given (1), they must produce one of the correct choices in (2). This gives them the opportunity to practice skills in syntactic ordering.[1]

(1) *barC beph dibrw hybrit ieral la tmid*

(2) a. *la tmid dibrw beph*
not always spoke in-the-language
hybrit barC ieral .
the-Hebrew in-land-of Israel .
'They did not always speak in the Hebrew language in the land of Israel.'

b. *barC ieral la dibrw tmid beph hybrit* .

c. *la tmid dibrw barC ieral beph hybrit* .

(3) *barC ieral* ***la tmid*** *dibrw beph* ***hybriM*** .

[1] We follow the transliteration scheme of the Hebrew Treebank (Sima'an et al., 2001).

Although the lexical choice is restricted—in that learners are to select from a set of words—learners must write the words. Thus, in addition to syntactic errors, there is possible variation in word form, as in (3), where *hybrit* is misspelled as *hybriM*.

This exercise was chosen because: a) it has been used on Hebrew placement exams for many years; and b) the amount of expected answers is constrained. Starting here also allows us to focus less on the NLP preprocessing and more on designing a machine learning set-up to analyze proficiency. It is important to note that the proficiency level is determined by experts looking at the whole exam, whereas we are currently predicting the proficiency level on the basis of a single exercise.

Placement exams The data for training and testing is pooled from previous placement exams at our university. Students who intend to take Hebrew have in past years been given written placement exams, covering a range of question types, including scrambled sentences. The learners are grouped into the first to the sixth semester, or they test out. We are using the following levels: the first four semesters (100, 150, 200, 250), and anything above (300+).

We use a small set of data—38 learners covering 128 sentences across 11 exercises—all the data that is available. While this is very small, it is indicative of the type of situation we expect for resource-poor languages, and it underscores the need to develop methods appropriate for data-scarce situations.

(Manual) annotation For each of the 11 unique exercises, we annotate an ordered list of correct answers, ranked from best to worst. Since Hebrew possesses free word order, there are between 1 and 10 correct answers per exercise, with an average of 3.4 gold standard answers. The sentences have between 8 and 15 words, with an average of 9.7 words per exercise. This annotation concerns only the gold standard answers. It requires minimal effort and needs to be performed only once per exercise.

```
T09:      SURFACE qnw
          SEGMENTATION (VB-BR3V qnw)
          PRE_PARTICLES    -
          MAIN_WORD:
              INDICES    0,1,2,
              TAG     VB-BR3V
              BINYAN    PAAL
              INFL_PREFIX     -
              STEM    0,1,
              ROOT    0,1,h,
              INFL_SUFFIX     2,
          PRO_SUFFIX    -
```

Figure 1: An example annotated word for *qnw* ('bought'), token T09 in one particular exercise

To annotate, we note that all the correct answers share the same set of words, varying in word order and not in morphological properties. Thus, we store word orders separately from morphological annotation, annotating morphology once for all possible word orders. An example of morphological annotation is given in fig. 1 for the verb *qnw* ('bought'). Segmentation information is provided by referring to indices (e.g., STEM 0,1), while TAG and BINYAN provide morphosyntactic properties.

Since the annotation is on controlled, correct data, i.e., not potentially malformed learner data, we can explore automatically annotating exercises in the future, as we expect relatively high accuracy.

3 System overview

The overall system architecture is given in fig. 2; the individual modules are described below. In brief, we align a learner sentence with the gold standard; use three specialized classifiers to classify individual phenomena; and then combine the information from these classifiers into an overall classifier for the learner level. This means the classification is performed in two phases: the first phase looks at individual phenomena (i.e., errors and other properties); the second phase aggregates all phenomena of one learner over all exercises and makes a final decision.

4 Feature extraction

To categorize learners into levels, we first need to extract relevant information from each sentence. That is, we need to perform a linguistic and/or error analysis on each sentence, which can be used for classification (sec. 5). Although we extract features for classification, this analysis could also be used for other purposes, such as providing feedback.

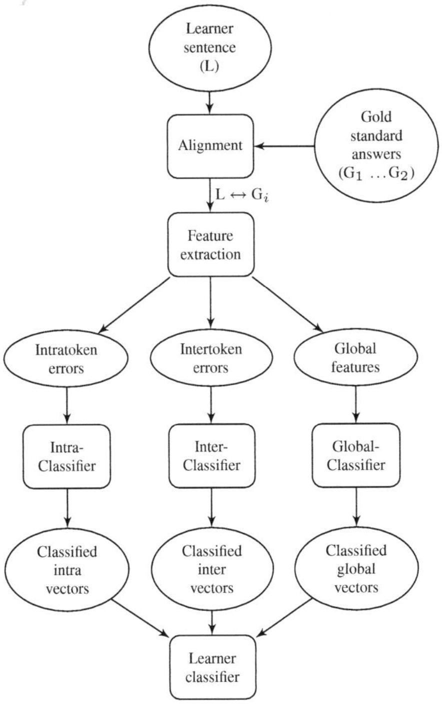

Figure 2: Overall system architecture (boxes = system components, circles = data)

4.1 Phenomena of interest

We extract features capturing *individual phenomena*. These can be at the level of individual words, bigrams of words, or anything up to a whole sentence; and they may represent errors or correctly-produced language. Importantly, at this stage, each phenomenon is treated uniquely and is not combined or aggregated until the second phase (see sec. 5).

While features can be based on individual phenomena of any type, we base our extracted features largely upon learner errors. Errors have been shown to have a significant impact on predicting learner level (Yannakoudakis et al., 2011). To detect errors, we align the learner sentence with a gold standard and extract the features. Although we focus on errors, we model some correct language (sec. 4.3.3).

4.2 Token alignment

With a listing of correct answers, we align the learner sentence to the answer which matches best:

We iterate over the correct answers and align learner tokens with correct tokens, based on the *cost* of mapping one to the other. The aligned sentence is the one with the lowest overall cost. The cost between a source token w_s and target token w_t accounts for:

1. Levenshtein distance between w_s & w_t (Lev)
2. similiarity between w_s & w_t (longest common subsequence ($LCSq$) & substring ($LCSt$))
3. displacement between w_s & w_t ($Displ$)

This method is reminiscent of alignment approaches in paraphrasing (e.g. (Grigonytè et al., 2010)), but note that our problem is more restricted in that we have the same number of words, and in most cases identical words. We use different distance and similarity metrics, to ensure robustness across different kinds of errors. The third metric is the least important, as learners can shift tokens far from their original slot, and thus it is given a low weight. The only reason to use it at all is to distinguish cases where more than one target word is a strong possibility, favoring the closer one.

The formula for the cost between source and target words w_s and w_t is given in (4), where the distance metrics are averaged and normalized by the length of the target word w_t. This length is also used to convert the similarity measures into distances, as in (5). We non-exhaustively tested different weight distributions on about half the data, and our final set is given in (6), where slightly less weight is given for the longest common substring and only a minor amount for the displacement score.

(4) $cost(w_s, w_t) = \theta_1 Displ(w_s, w_t) + \frac{\theta_2 Lev(w_s,w_t)+\theta_3 d_{LCSq}(w_s,w_t)+\theta_4 d_{LCSt}(w_s,w_t)}{3 \times len(w_t)}$

(5) $d_{LCS}(w_s, w_t) = len(w_t) - LCS(w_s, w_t)$

(6) $\theta_1 = 0.05; \theta_2 = 1.0; \theta_3 = 1.0; \theta_4 = 0.7$

In calculating Levenshtein distance, we hand-created a small table of weights for insertions, deletions, and substitutions, to reflect likely modifications in Hebrew. All weights can be tweaked in the future, but we have observed good results thus far.

The total alignment is the one which minimizes the total cost (7). A is an alignment between the learner sentence s and a given correct sentence t. Alignments to NULL have a cost of 0.6, so that words with high costs can instead align to nothing.

(7) $align = \arg\min_A \sum_{(w_s,w_t)\in A} cost(w_s, w_t)$

4.3 Extracted features

We extract three different types of features; as these have different feature sets, we correspondingly have three different classifiers, as detailed in sec. 5.1. They are followed by a fourth classifier that tallies up the results of these three classifiers.

4.3.1 Intra-token features

Based on the token alignments, it is straightforward to calculate differences within the tokens and thus to determine values for many features (e.g., a deleted letter in a prefix). We calculate such *intra-token* feature vectors for each word-internal error.

For instance, consider the learner attempt (8b) for the target in (8a). We find in the learner answer two intra-token errors: one in *hmtnwt* (cf. *hmtnh*), where the fem.pl. suffix *-wt* has been substituted for the fem.sg. ending *-h*, and another in *hnw* (cf. *qnw*), where *h* has been substituted for *q*. These two errors yield the feature vectors presented as example cases in table 1.

(8) a. *haM hN eilmw hrbh ksP*
Q they.FEM paid much money
bebil hmtnh$_1$ *ehN qnw*$_2$ *?*
for the-gift which-they.FEM bought ?
'Did they pay much money for the gift that they bought?'

b. *haM hN eilmw hrbh ksP bebil* ***hmtnwt***$_1$ *ehN* ***hnw***$_2$ *?*

Features 1 and 11 in table 1 are the POS tags of the morphemes *preceding* and *following* the erroneous morpheme, respectively. The POS tag of the morpheme containing the error is given by feature 2, and its person, gender, and number by feature 3. The remaining features describe the error itself (f. 6–8), as well as its word-internal context, i.e., both its left (f. 4–5) and right (f. 9–10) contexts.

The context features refer to individual character slots, which may or may not be occupied by actual characters. For example, since the error in ***hmtnwt*** is word-final, its two right-context slots are empty, hence the '#' symbol for both features 9 and 10.

The feature values for these character slots are generally not literal characters, but rather abstract labels representing various categories, most of which

	Features	*hnw*	*hmtnwt*
1.	Preceding POS	PRP	H
2.	Current POS	VB	NN
3.	Per.Gen.Num.	3cp	-fs
4.	Left Context (2)	#	R2
5.	Left Context (1)	#	R3
6.	Source String	h	wt
7.	Target String	q	h
8.	Anomaly	h→q	wt→h
9.	Right Context (1)	R2	#
10.	Right Context (2)	INFL-SFX	#
11.	Following POS	yyQM	REL

Table 1: Intra-token feature categories

	Features	**Seq. 1**	**Seq. 2**
1.	Anomaly	TRNS	SHFT
2.	Sequence Label	RB↔VP	PP
3.	Head Per.Gen.Num.	3cp	---
4.	Head POS.(Binyan)	VB.PIEL	IN
5.	Sequence-Initial POS	VB	IN
6.	Sequence-Final POS	RB	JJ
7.	Left POS (Learner)	RB	NNP
8.	Right POS (Learner)	IN	RB
9.	Left POS (Target)	RB	RB
10.	Right POS (Target)	IN	yyDOT
11.	Sequence Length	2	2
12.	Normalized Error Cost	0.625	0.250
13.	Sent-Level@Rank	200@2	200@2

Table 2: Inter-token feature categories

are morphological in nature. In *hmtnwt*, for example, the two left-context characters *t* and *n* are the second and third radicals of the root, hence the feature values R2 and R3, respectively.

4.3.2 Inter-token features

The inter-token features encode anomalies whose scope is not confined to a particular token. Such anomalies include token displacements and missing tokens. We again use the Levenshtein algorithm to detect inter-token anomalies, but we disable the substitution operation here so that we can link up corresponding deletions and insertions to yield "shifts."

For example, suppose the target is A B C D, and the learner has D A B C. Without substitutions, the minimal cost edit sequence is to delete D from the beginning of the learner's input and insert D at the end. Merging the two operations results in a D shift.

The learner sentence in (9b) shows two inter-token anomalies with respect to the target in (9a). First, the learner has transposed the two tokens in sequence 1, namely the verb *dibrw* ('speak-PAST') and the adverb *tmid* ('always'). Second, sequence 2 (the PP *beph hybrit*, 'in the Hebrew language') has been shifted from its position in the target sentence.

(9) a. *barC ieral la* ***dibrw***$_1$
in-land-of Israel not speak-PAST
tmid$_1$ ***beph***$_2$ ***hybrit***$_2$.
always in-the-language the-Hebrew .

b. *barC ieral* ***beph***$_2$ ***hybrit***$_2$ *la* ***tmid***$_1$ ***dibrw***$_1$.

Table 2 presents the inter-token feature vectors for the two anomalies in (9b). After *Anomaly*, the next three features provide approximations of phrasal properties, e.g., the phrasal category and head, based on a few syntactically-motivated heuristics. *Sequence Label* identifies the lexical or phrasal category of the shifted token/token-sequence (e.g., PP). Note that sequence labels for transpositions are special cases consisting of two category labels separated by an arrow. *Head Per.Gen.Num* and *Head POS.(Binyan)* represent the morphosyntactic properties of the sequence's (approximate) head word, namely its person, gender, and number, and its POS tag. If the head is a verb, the POS tag is followed by the verb's *binyan* (i.e., verb class), as in VB.PIEL.

The cost feature, *Normalized Error Cost*, is computed as follows: for missing, extra, and transposed sequences, the cost is simply the sequence length divided by the sentence length. For shifts, the sequence length and the shift distance are summed and then divided by the sentence length. *Sent-Level@Rank* indicates both the difficulty level of the exercise and the word-order rank of target sentence to which the learner sentence has been matched.

4.3.3 Global features

In addition to errors, we also look at *global features* capturing global trends in a sentence, in order to integrate information about the learner's overall performance on a sentence. For example, we note the percentage of target POS bigrams present in the learner sentence (*POS recall*). Table 3 presents the global features. The two example feature vectors are those for the sentences (8b) and (9b) above.

	Features	Ex. (8b)	Ex. (9b)
1.	POS Bigram Recall	2.000	1.273
2.	LCSeq Ratio	2.000	1.250
3.	LCStr Ratio	1.200	0.500
4.	Relaxed LCStr Ratio	2.000	0.500
5.	Intra-token Error Count	1.500	0.000
6.	Inter-token Error Count	0.000	1.500
7.	Intra-token Net Cost	1.875	0.000
8.	Norm. Aggregate Displ.	0.000	0.422
9.	Sentence Level	200	200

Table 3: Global feature categories

Except for feature 9 (*Sentence Level*), every feature in table 3 is multiplied by a weight derived from the sentence level. These weights serve either to penalize or compensate for a sentence's difficulty, depending on the feature type. Because features 1–4 are "positive" measures, they are multiplied by a factor proportional to the sentence level, namely $l = 1 \ldots 4$, whose values correspond directly to the levels 150–300+, respectively. Features 5–8, in contrast, are "negative" measures, so they are multiplied by a factor *inversely* proportional to l, namely $\frac{5-l}{4}$.

Among the positive features, *LCSeq* looks for the longest common subsequence between the learner sentence and the target, while *LCStr Ratio* and *Relaxed LCStr Ratio* both look for longest common substrings. However, *Relaxed LCStr Ratio* allows for token-internal anomalies (as long as the token itself is present) while *LCStr Ratio* does not.

As for the negative features, the two *Error Count* features simply tally up the errors of each type present in the sentence. The *Intra-token Net Cost* sums over the token-internal Levenshtein distances between corresponding learner and target tokens. *Normalized Aggregate Displacement* is the sum of insertions and deletions carried out during inter-token alignment, normalized by sentence length.

5 Two-phase classification

To combine the features for individual phenomena, we run a two-phase classifier. In the first phase, we classify each feature vector for each phenomenon into a level. In the second phase, we aggregate over this output to classify the overall learner level.

We use two-phase classification in order to: 1) modularize each individual phenomenon, meaning that new phenomena are more easily incorporated into future models; 2) better capture sparsely-represented phenomena, by aggregating over them; and 3) easily integrate other exercise types simply by having more specialized phase 1 classifiers and by then integrating the results into phase 2.

One potential drawback of two-phase classification is that of not having gold standard annotation of phase 1 levels or even knowing for sure whether individual phenomena can be classified into consistent and useful categories. That is, even if a 200-level learner makes an error, that error is not necessarily a 200-level *error*. We discuss this next.

5.1 Classifying individual phenomena

With our three sets of features (sec. 4), we set up three classifiers. Depending upon the type, the appropriate classifier is used to categorize each phase 1 vector. For classification, every phase 1 vector is assigned a single learner level. However, this assumes that each error indicates a unique level, which is not always true. A substitution of *i* for *w*, for example, may largely be made by 250-level (intermediate) learners, but also by learners of other levels.

One approach is to thus view each phenomenon as mapping to a set of levels, and for a new vector, classification predicts the *set* of appropriate levels, and their likelihood. Another approach to overcome the fact that each uniquely-classified phenomenon can be indicative of many levels is to rely on phase 2 to aggregate over different phenomena. The advantage of the first approach is that it makes no assumptions about individual phenomena being indicative of a single level, but the disadvantage is that one may start to add confusion for phase 2 by including less relevant levels, especially when using little training data. The second approach counteracts this confusion by selecting the most prototypical level for an individual phenomenon (cf. criterial features in (Hawkins and Buttery, 2010)), giving less noise to phase 2. We may lose important non-best level information, but as we show in sec. 6, with a range of classifications from phase 1, the second phase can learn the proper learner level.

In either case, from the perspective of training, an individual phenomenon can be seen, in terms of level, as the set of learners who produced such a phenomenon. We thus approximate the level of each

Feature type	Feature type
1. 100-level classes	7. Intra-token error sum
2. 150-level classes	8. Inter-token error sum
3. 200-level classes	9. Sentences attempted
4. 250-level classes	10. 250-level attempts
5. 300-level classes	11. 300-level attempts
6. Composite error	

Table 4: Feature categories for learner level prediction

phenomenon by using the level of the learner from the gold standard training data. This allows us not to make a theoretical classification of phenomena (as opposed to taxonomically labeling phenomena).

5.2 Predicting learner level

We aggregate the information from phase 1 classification to classify overall learner levels. We assume that the set of all individual phenomena and their quantities (e.g., proportion of phenomena classified as 200-level in phase 1) characterize a learner's level (Hawkins and Buttery, 2010). The feature types are given in table 4. Features 1–6 are discussed in sec. 6.1; features 7–8 are (normalized) sums; and the rest record the number of sentences attempted, broken down by intended level of the sentence. Lower-level attempts are not included, as they are the same values for nearly all students. When we incorporate other exercise types in the future, additional features can be added—and the current features modified—to fold in information from those exercise types.

An example To take an example, one of our (300+) learners attempts four sentences, giving four sets of global features, and makes four errors, for a total of eight phase 1 individual phenomena. One phenomenon is automatically classified as 100-level, one as 150, four as 200, one as 250, and one as 300+. Taking the 1-best phase 1 output (see section 6.3), the phase 2 vector in this case is as in (10a), corresponding directly to the features in table 4.

(10) a. 0.25, 0.25, 1.00, 0.25, 0.25, 2.00, 0.50, 0.50, 4, 1, 0

b. 0.25, 0.00, 1.00, 0.25, 0.00, 1.625, 0.00, 0.50, 4, 1, 0

In training, we find a 300+-level learner with a very similar vector, namely that of (10b). Depending upon the exact experimental set-up (e.g., $k_2 = 1$, see section 6.3), then, this vector helps the system to correctly classify our learner as 300+.

6 Evaluation

6.1 Details of the experiments

We use TiMBL (Daelemans et al., 2010; Daelemans et al., 1999), a memory-based learner (MBL), for both phases. We use TiMBL because MBL has been shown to work well with small data sets (Banko and Brill, 2001); allows for the use of both text-based and numeric features; and does not suffer from a fragmented class space. We mostly use the default settings of TiMBL—the IB1 learning algorithm and overlap comparison metric between instances—and experiment with different values of k.

For prediction of phenomenon level (phase 1) and learner level (phase 2), the system is trained on data from placement exams previously collected in a Hebrew language program, as described in sec. 2. With only 38 learners, we use leave-one-out testing, training on the data from the 37 other learners in order to run a model on each learner's sentences. All of phase 1 is completed (i.e., automatically analyzed) before training the phase 2 models. As a baseline, we use the majority class (level 150); choosing this for all learners gives an accuracy of 34.2% (13/38).[2]

Phase 1 probability distributions Because TiMBL retrieves all neighbor with the k nearest distances rather than the k nearest neighbors, we can use the number of neighbors in phase 1 to adjust the values of, e.g., *150-level classes*. For example, the output from phase 1 for two different vectors might be as in (11). Both have a distribution of $\frac{2}{3}$ 150-level and $\frac{1}{3}$ 200-level; however, in one case, this is based on 6 neighbors, whereas for the other, there are 12 neighbors within the nearest distance.

(11) a) 150:4, 200:2 b) 150:8, 200:4

With more data, we may have more confidence in the prediction of the second case. The *classes* features (f_x) of table 4 are thus calculated as in (12), multiplying counts of each class ($c(x)$) by their probabilities ($p(x)$).

[2]We are aware that the baseline is not very strong, but the only alternative would be to use a classifier since we observed no direct correlation between level and number of errors.

k	Intra	Inter	Global	Overall
1	28.1%	38.6%	34.4%	34.7%
3	34.2%	44.6%	44.6%	**41.9%**
5	34.2%	37.1%	36.7%	36.3%

Table 5: Phase 1 accuracies

(12) $f_x = \sum_{phase1} c(x)p(x)$

The *Composite error* feature combines all *classes* features into one score, inversely weighing them by level, so that more low-level errors give a high value.

6.2 Predicting phenomena levels

We first evaluate phase 1 accuracy, as in table 5. Using $k = 3$ gives the best phase 1 result, 41.9%. We evaluate with respect to the single-best class, i.e., the level of the learner of interest. Accuracy is the percentage of correctly-classified instances out of all instances. We assume an instance is classified correctly if its class corresponds to the learner level.

Accuracy is rather low, at 41.9%. However, we must bear in mind that we cannot expect 100% accuracy, given that individual phenomena do not clearly belong to a single level. Intra-token classification is lowest, likely due to greater issues of sparsity: random typos are unlikely to occur more than once.

6.3 Predicting learner level

For the second phase, we use different settings for phase 1 instances. The results are shown in table 6. The overall best results are reached using single-best classification for phase 1 and $k = 1$ for phase 2, giving an accuracy of 60.5%. Note that the best result does not use the best performing setting for phase 1 but rather the one with the lowest performance for phase 1. This shows clearly that optimizing the two phases individually is not feasible. We obtain the same accuracy using $k = 5$ for both phases.

Since we are interested in how these two settings differ, we extract confusion matrices for them; they are shown in table 7. The matrices show that the inherent smoothing via the k nearest neighbors leads to a good performance for lower levels, to the exclusion of levels higher than 200. The higher levels are also the least frequent: the $k_1 = 5/k_2 = 5$ case shows a bias towards the overall distribution of levels, whereas the 1-best/$k_2 = 1$ setting is more

		Phase 1			
		1-best	$k_1 = 1$	$k_1 = 3$	$k_1 = 5$
Phase 2	Max	42.1	47.4	57.9	42.1
	$k_2 = 1$	**60.5**	57.9	36.8	39.5
	$k_2 = 3$	42.1	44.7	44.7	42.1
	$k_2 = 5$	39.5	42.1	44.7	**60.5**

Table 6: Phase 2 accuracies for different phase 1 settings

		System					
	1-best	100	150	200	250	300+	Acc.
Gold	100	6	1				6/7
	150	2	7	3		1	7/13
	200		2	7	1	1	7/11
	250			1		1	0/2
	300+			1	1	3	3/5
	k=5	100	150	200	250	300+	Acc.
Gold	100	5	2				5/7
	150	2	9	2			9/13
	200		2	9			9/11
	250			2			0/2
	300+		1	4			0/5

Table 7: Classification confusion matrices

likely to guess neighboring classes. In order to better account for incorrect classifications which are close to the correct answer (e.g., 250 for 200), we also calculated weighted kappa for all the results in table 6. Based on kappa, the best result is based on the setting $k_1 = 1/k_2 = 1$ (0.647), followed by 1-best/$k_2 = 1$ (0.639). The weighted kappa for $k_1 = 5/k_2 = 5$ is significantly lower (0.503).

We are also interested in whether we need such a complex system: phase 1 can outputs a distribution of senses ($k_1 = n$), or we can use the single best class as input to phase 2 (*1-best*). In a different vein, phase 2 is a machine learner ($k_2 = n$) trained on phase 1 classified data, but could be simplified to take the maximum phase 1 class (*Max*). The results in table 6 show that using the single-best result from phase 1 in combination with $k_2 = 1$ provides the best results, indicating that phase 2 can properly aggregate over individual phenomena (see sec. 5.1). However, for all other phase 2 settings, adding the distribution over phase 1 results increases accuracy. Using the maximum class rather than the machine learner in phase 2 generally works best in combination with more nearest neighbors in phase 1, providing a type of smoothing. However, using the maximum has an overall detrimental effect.

While the results may not be robust enough to deploy, they are high, given that this is only *one* type of exercise, and we have used a very small set of training data. When performing the error analysis, we found one student who had attempted only half of the sentences—generally a sign of a low level—who was put into level 300. We assume this student performed better on other exercises in the exam. Given this picture, it is not surprising that our system consistently groups this student into a lower level.

6.4 Ablation studies

We are particularly interested in how the different phases interact, 1) because one major way to expand the system is to add different exercises and incorporate them into the second phase, and 2) because the results in table 6 show a strong interdependence between phases. We thus performed a set of experiments to gauge the effect of different types of features. By running ablation studies—i.e., removing one or more sets of features (cf. e.g. (Yannakoudakis et al., 2011))–we can determine their relative importance and usefulness. We run phase 2 ($k = 1$) using different combinations of phase 1 classifiers (1-best) as input. The results are presented in table 8.

Intra	Inter	Global	Acc.
Y	Y	Y	**60.5%**
Y	Y	N	47.4%
Y	N	N	42.1%
N	Y	Y	42.1%
N	Y	N	42.1%
Y	N	Y	36.8%
N	N	Y	34.2%

Table 8: Ablation studies, evaluating on phase 2 accuracy

Perhaps unsurprisingly, the combination of all feature types results in the highest results of 60.5%. Also, using only one type of features results in the lowest performance, with the global features being the least informative set, on par with the baseline of 34.2%. If we use only two feature sets, removing the global features results in the least deterioration. Since these features do not directly model errors but rather global sentence trends, this is to be expected. However, leaving out inter-token features results in the second-lowest results (36.8%), thus showing that this set is extremely important—again not surprising given that we are working with an exercise designed to test word order skills.

7 Summary and Outlook

We have developed a system for predicting the level of Hebrew language learners, using only a small amount of targeted language data. We have predicted level based on a single placement exam exercise, finding a surprising degree of accuracy despite missing much of the information normally used on such exams. We accounted for the problem of data sparsity by breaking the problem into a two-phase classification and through our choice of learning algorithm. The classification process isolates individual errors and linguistic constructions which are then aggregated into a second phase; such a two-step process allows for easy integration of other exercises and features in the future. The aggregation of information allows us to smooth over sparse features.

In the immediate future, we are integrating other exercises, to improve the overall accuracy of level prediction (i.e., the second phase) and make automatic testing more valid (cf. e.g. (Fulcher, 1997)), while at the same time incorporating more linguistic processing for more complex input. For example, with question formation exercises, no closed set of correct answers exists, and one must use parse tree distance to delineate features. With multiple exercises, we have plans to test the system with incoming students to the Hebrew program at our university.

Acknowledgments

We would like to thank Ayelet Weiss for help throughout, as well as Chris Riley and Amber Smith. Part of this work was funded by the IU Jewish Studies Center, as well as by the Institute for Digital Arts and Humanities and the Data to Insight Center at IU. We also thank Stephanie Dickinson from the Indiana Statistical Consulting Center (ISCC) for analysis assistance and the three anonymous reviewers for their comments.

References

Dora Alexopoulou, Helen Yannakoudakis, and Ted Briscoe. 2010. From discriminative features to learner grammars: a data driven approach to learner corpora. Talk given at *Second Language Research Forum*, University of Maryland, October 2010.

Yigal Attali and Jill Burstein. 2006. Automated essay scoring with e-rater v.2. *Journal of Technology, Learning, and Assessment*, 4(3), February.

Michele Banko and Eric Brill. 2001. Mitigating the paucity-of-data problem: Exploring the effect of training corpus size on classifier performance for natural language processing. In *Proceedings of HLT 2001, First International Conference on Human Language Technology Research*, pages 253–257, San Diego, CA.

Adriane Boyd. 2010. EAGLE: an error-annotated corpus of beginning learner German. In *Proceedings of LREC-10*, Valetta, Malta.

Walter Daelemans, Antal van den Bosch, and Jakub Zavrel. 1999. Forgetting exceptions is harmful in language learning. *Machine Learning*, 34:11–41.

Walter Daelemans, Jakub Zavrel, Ko van der Sloot, and Antal van den Bosch. 2010. Timbl: Tilburg memory based learner, version 6.3, reference guide. Technical report, ILK Research Group. Technical Report Series no. 10-01.

Robert Dale and Adam Kilgarriff. 2011. Helping our own: The HOO 2011 pilot shared task. In *Proceedings of the Generation Challenges Session at the 13th European Workshop on Natural Language Generation*, pages 242–249, Nancy, France, September.

Ana Díaz-Negrillo and Jesús Fernández-Domínguez. 2006. Error tagging systems for learner corpora. *Spanish Journal of Applied Linguistics (RESLA)*, 19:83–102.

Markus Dickinson, Ross Israel, and Sun-Hee Lee. 2011. Developing methodology for Korean particle error detection. In *Proceedings of the Sixth Workshop on Innovative Use of NLP for Building Educational Applications*, pages 81–86, Portland, OR, June.

Markus Dickinson. 2011. On morphological analysis for learner language, focusing on Russian. *Research on Language and Computation*, 8(4):273–298.

Glenn Fulcher. 1997. An English language placement test: issues in reliability and validity. *Language Testing*, 14(2):113–138.

Yoav Goldberg and Michael Elhadad. 2011. Joint Hebrew segmentation and parsing using a PCFGLA lattice parser. In *Proceedings of ACL-HLT*, pages 704–709, Portland, OR, June.

Gintarė Grigonytė, João Paulo Cordeiro, Gaël Dias, Rumen Moraliyski, and Pavel Brazdil. 2010. Paraphrase alignment for synonym evidence discovery. In *Proceedings of the 23rd International Conference on Computational Linguistics (COLING)*, pages 403–411, Beijing, China.

John A. Hawkins and Paula Buttery. 2010. Criterial features in learner corpora: Theory and illustrations. *English Profile Journal*, 1(1):1–23.

John A. Hawkins and Luna Filipović. 2010. *Criterial Features in L2 English: Specifying the Reference Levels of the Common European Framework*. Cambridge University Press.

Alon Itai and Shuly Wintner. 2008. Language resources for Hebrew. *Language Resources and Evaluation*, 42(1):75–98.

Alla Rozovskaya and Dan Roth. 2011. Algorithm selection and model adaptation for ESL correction tasks. In *Proceedings of the 49th Annual Meeting of the Association for Computational Linguistics: Human Language Technologies*, pages 924–933, Portland, OR, June.

Khalil Sima'an, Alon Itai, Yoad Winter, Alon Altman, and N. Nativ. 2001. Building a tree-bank of Modern Hebrew text. *Traitment Automatique des Langues*, 42(2).

Joel Tetreault and Martin Chodorow. 2008. The ups and downs of preposition error detection in ESL writing. In *Proceedings of COLING-08*, Manchester.

Helen Yannakoudakis, Ted Briscoe, and Ben Medlock. 2011. A new dataset and method for automatically grading ESOL texts. In *Proceedings of the 49th Annual Meeting of the Association for Computational Linguistics: Human Language Technologies*, pages 180–189, Portland, OR, June.

Shlomo Yona and Shuly Wintner. 2008. A finite-state morphological grammar of Hebrew. *Natural Language Engineering*, 14(2):173–190.

On using context for automatic correction of non-word misspellings in student essays

Michael Flor
Educational Testing Service
Rosedale Road
Princeton, NJ, 08541, USA
mflor@ets.org

Yoko Futagi
Educational Testing Service
Rosedale Road
Princeton, NJ, 08541, USA
yfutagi@ets.org

Abstract

In this paper we present a new spell-checking system that utilizes contextual information for automatic correction of non-word misspellings. The system is evaluated with a large corpus of essays written by native and non-native speakers of English to the writing prompts of high-stakes standardized tests (TOEFL® and GRE®). We also present comparative evaluations with Aspell and the speller from Microsoft Office 2007. Using context-informed re-ranking of candidate suggestions, our system exhibits superior error-correction results overall and also corrects errors generated by non-native English writers with almost same rate of success as it does for writers who are native English speakers.

1 Introduction

Misspellings are ubiquitous in student writing. Connors and Lunsford (1988) have found that spelling errors accounted for about one quarter of all errors found in a random sample of 300 student essays. Desmet and Balthazor (2006) found that spelling errors are among the five most frequent errors in first-year college composition of US students. Lunsford and Lunsford (2008) found that spelling errors constituted about 6.5% of all errors found in a US national sample of 3000 college composition essays, despite the fact that writers had access to spellcheckers.

Misspellings are even more ubiquitous in texts written by non-native speakers of English, especially English Language Learners (ELL). The types of misspellings produced by L2 writers are typically different from errors produced by native speakers (Hovermale, 2010; Al-Jarf, 2010; Okada, 2005).

In the area of automatic assessment of writing, detection of misspellings is utilized in computer-aided language learning applications and in some automatic scoring systems, especially when feedback to users is involved (Dikli, 2006; Warschauer and Ware, 2006). Yet spelling errors may have a deeper influence on automated text assessment. As noted by Nagata, et al. (2011), sub-optimal automatic detection of grammar and mechanics errors may be attributed to poor performance of NLP tools over noisy text.

Presence of spelling errors also hinders systems that require only lexical analysis of text (Landauer, et al. , 2003; Pérez, et al., 2004). Granger and Wynne (1999) have shown that spelling errors can affect automated estimates of lexical variation, which in turn are used as predictors of text quality (Crossley, et al., 2008; Yu, 2010). In the context of automated preposition and determiner error correction in L2 English, De Felice and Pulman (2008) noted that the process is often disrupted by misspellings. Futagi (2010) described how misspellings pose problems in development of a tool for detection of phraseological collocation errors.

Given this state of affairs, it is only natural for automatic text assessment systems to utilize automatic spellchecking components. However, generic spellcheckers are typically oriented for errors produced by writers who are native speakers of a language. Rimrott and Heift (2008, 2005) have demonstrated that a generic speller has poor performance on data from German language learners.

Bestgen and Granger (2011) and Hovermale (2010) have demonstrated similar results on data from ELL.

Many researchers have suggested that spellcheckers for L2 users need to be adapted for the particular patterns of errors that characterize each native language (L1), by studying patterns of interference and influence from L1 to L2 (Mitton and Okada, 2007; Mitton, 1996; Rimrott and Heift, 2008, 2005; Bestgen and Granger, 2011; Hovermale, 2010). We have set up to explore a different path, in the context of automated text assessment. Our goal in the present study is to examine to what extent detection and automatic correction of non-word misspellings can be improved by utilizing essay context, for data from both native and non-native English speakers.

The rest of this paper is organized as follows. Section 2 provides a description of the corpus of texts and misspellings that was used in this study. Section 3 describes the ConSpel automatic spell-checking system. Section 4 presents results from a comparative evaluation of our system, ConSpel, the popular Aspell speller and the Microsoft Office 2007 speller. Section 5 compares our findings with some recent studies and discusses implications for further development of automatic spell-checking systems.

2 Corpus

The corpus used in this study is a collection of essays, annotated for misspellings by trained annotators. It is developed for evaluation of automatic spellcheckers, and for research on patterns of misspellings produced by both native English speakers and ELL.

2.1 Texts

The corpus comprises essays written by examinees on the writing sections of GRE® (Graduate Record Examinations) and TOEFL® (Test of English as a Foreign Language) (ETS, 2011a,b). The TOEFL test includes two different writing tasks: a short opinion essay, on a pre-assigned topic, and a summary essay that compares arguments from two different sources (both supplied during the test). GRE also includes two different writing tasks: one is a short argumentative essay taking a position on an assigned topic, the other is an essay evaluating the soundness of arguments presented in prompt. Both tests are delivered on computer (at test centers around the world and via Internet), always using the standard English language computer keyboard (QWERTY). Editing tools such as a spellchecker are not provided in the test-delivery software (ETS, 2011a). All writing tasks have time constraints.

In the current phase of the project, the corpus includes 3000 essays, for a total of 963,428 words. The essays were selected equally from the two tests (4 tasks, 10 prompts per task, 75 essays per prompt), also covering full range of scores (as a proxy for English proficiency levels) for each task. The majority of essays in this collection were written by examinees for whom English is not the first language (98.73% of TOEFL essays, 57.86% of GRE essays).

2.2 Annotation

Each text was independently reviewed by two annotators, who are native English speakers experienced in linguistic annotation. Annotators were asked to identify all non-word misspellings and provide the adequate correction for each one. Inter-annotator agreement was quite high - annotators agreed in 82.6% of the cases (Cohen's Kappa=0.8, $p<.001$). All disagreements were resolved by a third annotator (adjudicator). For details of the annotation procedure, see Flor and Futagi (2011).

The Annotation Scheme for this project provides three classes of misspellings, as summarized in Table 1. Classification of annotated misspellings was automatic.

Type	Description	Count in corpus
1	single token non-word (e.g. "businees", "inthe")	21,160
2	single token non-word for which no plausible correction was found	52
3	multi-token non-word misspelling (e.g. "mor efun" for "more fun")	383
	Total	21,595

Table 1. Classification of misspellings annotated in the study corpus.

The annotation effort focused specifically on misspellings, rather than on a wider category of orthographic errors in general. The annotation ignored repeated words, missing spaces[1] and improper capitalization. Many of the essays have inconsistent capitalization and essays written fully in capital letters are not uncommon (not only in our corpus). In addition, different spelling variants were acceptable. This consideration stems from the international nature of the two tests – the examinees come from all around the world, being accustomed to either British, American, or some other English spelling standard; so, it is only fair to accept all of them.

Overall, the annotated corpus of 3,000 essays has the following statistics. Average essay length is 321 words (the range is 28-798 words). 148 essays turned out to have no misspellings at all. Total spelling error counts are given in Table 1; 2.24% of the words in the corpus are non-word misspellings.

3 Spelling correction systems

3.1 Background

Classic approaches to the problem of spelling correction of non-word errors were reviewed by Kukich (1992). The typical approach for error detection is using good spelling dictionaries. The typical approach for correction of non-word errors is to include modules for computing edit distance (Damerau, 1964; Levenshtein, 1966) and phonetic similarity. These are used for ranking suggestions by their orthographic and phonetic similarity to the misspelled word. A more recent feature utilizes word frequency data for candidate ranking. Mitton (2009) and Deorowicz and Ciura (2005) describe state of the art approaches to non-word correction without contextual information.

The use of context for spelling correction was initially proposed by Mayes, et al. (1991) only for 'contextual spelling' – correcting real-word errors (e.g. writing *'fig'* instead of *'fog'*). A common strategy for this task is using pre-defined confusion sets, which makes it more amenable to classifier-based approaches (Golding and Roth, 1999). Several recent studies used a web-scale language model (Google Web1T n-gram corpus – Brants and Franz, 2006) for "context-sensitive" (i.e. real-words) spelling correction (Bergsma, et al., 2009; Islam and Inkpen, 2009; Carlson and Fette, 2007). Chen, et al. (2007) used a LM for pruning candidate corrections for non-words in web queries. Whitelaw, et al. (2009) used a LM for correcting non-word and real-word errors without a dictionary and using a statistically trained error model. Our study extends the use of language models to automatic correction of non-word errors, with a dictionary, but without any explicit error model.

3.2 ConSpel system

The ConSpel system was designed and implemented as a fully automatic system for detection and correction of spelling errors. The current version is focused on non-word misspellings. The system has two intended uses. One is to serve as a component in NLP systems for automatic evaluation of student essays. The other use is to facilitate automation for research on patterns of misspellings in ELL essays.

In ConSpel, detection policy is quite simple. A token in a text is potentially a misspelling if the string is not in the system dictionaries. A text may include some non-dictionary tokens that systematically are not misspellings. ConSpel has several parameterized options to handle such cases. By default, the system will ignore numbers, dates, web and email addresses, and mixed alpha-numeric strings (e.g. 'RV400'). The system can be instructed to ignore capitalized words (e.g. 'London') and/or words in all uppercase (e.g. 'ROME').

ConSpel spelling dictionaries include about 360,000 entries. The core set includes 245,000 entries, providing a comprehensive coverage of modern English vocabulary. This lexicon includes all inflectional variants for a given word (e.g. 'love', 'loved', 'loves', 'loving'), and international spelling variants (e.g. American and British English). Additional dictionaries include about 120,000 entries for international surnames and first names, and names for geographical places.

Dictionaries are also the source of suggested corrections. Candidate suggestions for each detected misspelling are generated by returning all dictionary words that have an edit distance up to a given threshold. With the default threshold of 5, a

[1] Annotation ignored missing spaces around punctuation (e.g. "*chairs,tables*", but all cases where missing spaces result in fused words were marked in annotation (e.g. "*inthe*").

misspelling can easily get hundreds of correction candidates. Since ConSpel is intended to work on ELL data, and ELL misspellings can be quite dissimilar from the intended words, starting with a large number of candidates is a deliberate strategy to ensure that the adequate correction will be included in the candidate set. Candidates are pruned during the re-ranking process, so that only a few candidates from the initial set survive to the final decision making stage.

Candidate suggestions for each detected misspelling are ranked using a set of algorithms. An edit distance module is used to compute orthographic similarity between each candidate and the original misspelling. Phonetic similarity is computed using the Double Metaphone algorithm (Philips, 2000). Word frequency is computed for each candidate using a very large word-frequency data source.

The main thrust of our new spelling correction system is the conjecture that non-word misspellings can be corrected better when their context is taken into account.

Local context (several words around the misspelled word in the text) provides lots of information for choosing the adequate correction. For each candidate, we check the frequency of its co-occurrence (in a language model) with the adjacent words in the text. This approach borrows from the family of noisy-channel error-correction models (Zhang, et al., 2006; Cucerzan and Brill, 2004; Kernigham, et al., 1990). With the advent of very large word n-gram language models, we can utilize large contexts (about 4 words on each side of a misspelling). Our current language model uses a filtered version of the Google Web1T collection, containing 1,881,244,352 n-gram types of size 1-5, with punctuation included.[2] Notably, ConSpel does not use any statistical error model.

A second context-sensitive algorithm utilizes non-local context in the essay. The idea is quite simple – given a misspelled token in a text and a set of correction-candidates for that word, for each candidate we check whether that candidate string occurs elsewhere in the text. Since content words have some tendency of recurrence in same text, the misspelled token might be such a case, and the candidate should be strengthened. The idea is somewhat similar to cache-based language model adaptation (Kuhn and De Mori, 1990), though there are considerable differences. First, our system looks not only in preceding context, but over the whole essay text. Second, and unique to our system, ConSpel looks not only in the text, but also into the k-best candidate correction lists of the other misspelled words. Thus, if a word is systematically misspelled in a document, ConSpel will strengthen a candidate correction that appears as a candidate for multiple misspelled instances.[3]

For each misspelling found in a text, each algorithm produces ranking scores for each candidate. We use a linear-weighted ensemble method to combine scores from different algorithms. First, scores for all candidates of a given misspelling are normalized into a 0-1 range, separately for each ranker. Normalized scores are then summed using a set of constant weights.[4]

The ConSpel system is implemented as a flexible configurable system. Configuration settings include choice of dictionaries, choice of algorithms and weights for computing the final ranking, and choice of the output formats.

4 Comparative evaluation

In this section we report the results of evaluation on data from our gold-standard corpus of 3,000 essays described in section 2. This evaluation focuses on detection and correction of the 21,212 single-token non-word misspellings (types 1 and 2 in Table 1) as well as false alarms raised by spellcheckers.

Evaluation included three systems. In addition to ConSpel, we tested Aspell (version 0.60.6), a popular open-source spell checking library (Atkinson, 2011). The third system is spellchecker included in Microsoft Office 2007 (hereafter 'MS Word').

All evaluations were performed "in full context" (rather than word-by-word) – each essay in the corpus was submitted to each system separately, as a simple text file. All evaluations used standard

[2] ConSpel system uses the TrendStream n-gram compression software library (Flor, 2012) for fast and memory efficient retrieval of n-gram data. As a result, the ConSpel system runs even on modest hardware (e.g. a 4GB RAM laptop), concurrently with other applications.

[3] A detailed comparative study of different context utilization methods is under way.

[4] The current weights were found experimentally, prior to the annotation effort described in this article. We intend to use machine learning methods in future research, using the annotated corpus for this purpose.

measures of recall, precision and F-score (Leacock, et al., 2010).

Evaluations for Aspell and MS Word were conducted twice – once with their original dictionaries[5] and once with the ConSpel spelling dictionary of about 360,000 word forms. Evaluations where Aspell and MS Word were bundled with ConSpel dictionary are marked below as Aspell+ and MS Word+.

4.1 Error Detection

Detection results for non-word misspellings are presented in Table 2. All systems show very strong recall rates, above 99%. There is more variability when precision of error detection is concerned. Both MS Word and Aspell benefit from using the larger dictionary – they raise much less false alarms than with original dictionaries (Aspell improves precision by about 4% and MS Word by about 6%). ConSpel shows best precision, the difference with second-best (MS Word+) is statistically significant at p<.01.

System	Recall	Precision	F-score
Aspell	99.45	86.66	92.62
Aspell+	99.14	90.92	94.85
ConSpel	99.40	98.43	98.91
MS Word	99.55	90.26	94.68
MS Word+	99.32	96.16	97.71

Table 2. Evaluation results: non-word error detection

4.2 Error Correction

For evaluating spelling correction, we again use the measures of recall, precision and F-score. Note that precision of error correction is defined as proportion of adequately corrected misspellings out of total number of misspellings that a system tried to correct (this excludes cases missed in detection).

We conducted error-correction evaluations with ConSpel in two variants. The baseline variant, ConSpel-A, ranks candidate suggestions using edit distance, phonetic similarity and word-frequency. The contextual variant, ConSpel-B, adds contextual information in the ranking process.

Results of error-correction evaluations are shown in Table 3. While MS Word speller provided the adequate correction (top ranked suggestion) in about 73% of annotated cases, its precision is only about 67-69%, due to large number of false alarms. Aspell has markedly lower accuracy – both in recall and precision. ConSpel-A has approximately same recall as MS-Word, but better precision (due to low rate of false alarms). ConSpel-B, which uses contextual information in ranking candidate suggestions, shows markedly better recall and precision than either ConSpel-A or MS Word (statistically significant at p<.01).

For Aspell, use of the larger spelling dictionary improved detection precision (fewer false alarms – see Table 2), but it has led to degradation in error correction – as shown in Table 3 (possibly ranking of candidates is affected by larger dictionaries).

System	Recall	Precision	F-score
Aspell	61.53	53.62	57.30
Aspell+	54.17	49.68	51.83
ConSpel-A	72.65	71.94	72.29
ConSpel-B	**78.32**	**77.55**	**77.93**
MS Word	73.34	66.49	69.74
MS Word+	71.71	69.44	70.56

Table 3. Evaluation results: non-word error correction (top ranked candidates only)

An additional way to evaluate automatic spelling correction is to consider how often the adequate target correction is found among the k-best of the candidate suggestions (Mitton, 2009; Brill and Moore, 2000). Figure 1 shows error-correction recall and precision results for four systems[6] using k-best values 1-5 and 10.

When two-or-more best-ranked candidates are considered for each misspelling, the baseline ConSpel-A system shows better performance than MS Word. Aspell results lag significantly below the other systems, although it catches up with MS-Word beyond k=5. ConSpel-B system outperforms all other systems, in both recall and precision. It

[5] Notably, both Aspell and MS Word in this evaluation came with respective default dictionaries for US spelling, and generated many false alarms when flagging words that are British and other international spelling variants. Such false alarm cases were discounted from the evaluation statistics.

[6] 'MS Word' and 'MS Word+' overlap for all values of k, except for k=1, thus only 'MS Word' is shown in Figure 1.

places the target correction among the top two candidates in 88% of cases, and among top three or more candidates in beyond 90% of cases.

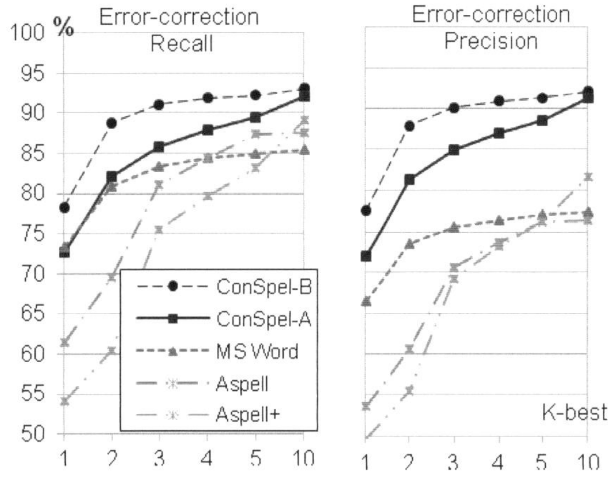

Figure 1. Error correction recall and precision for four systems, with different k-best cutoffs.

4.3 Evaluation with data from native and non-native English speakers

In this section we report the results of spell-check evaluation with data breakdown by native and non-native English speakers. Out of 21,212 single-token non-word misspellings in our corpus, 2,859 came from 570 essays written by native English speakers (NS) and 18,353 misspellings came from 2,282 essays written by test-takers who are not native speakers of English (NNS).

Comparison of error-detection for five systems is presented in Table 4. All systems show very strong recall results for both types of populations (all values are above 99%). The results are a bit different for error-detection precision. ConSpel achieves best results in both populations (the differences with second-best, MS Word+, are statistically significant at $p<.01$). MS Word has precision around 91%, approximately same in both populations. Compared to MS Word, MS Word+ has better recall rates, in both populations – due to a larger dictionary, it raises much less false alarms. Aspell lags behind in this comparison. Using a larger dictionary helps, as Aspell+ precision is better than that of Aspell in both populations; improvement is manifest for NNS data and only 2% for NS data. Aspell detection precision on NS data (77%) is lower than its precision on NNS data (88%). This may be due to Aspell having a problem with possessive forms (80% of the false alarms on NS data are possessives, but only 70% for NNS data).[7]

System		Recall	Precision	F-score
Aspell	ns:	99.7	76.7	86.7
	nns:	99.4	88.5	93.6
Aspell+	ns:	99.6	78.7	87.9
	nns:	99.3	93.3	96.3
ConSpel	ns:	99.5	96.2	97.9
	nns:	99.4	98.8	99.1
MS Word	ns:	99.6	91.1	95.1
	nns:	99.6	90.1	94.6
MS Word+	ns:	99.2	94.4	96.7
	nns:	99.3	96.5	97.9

Table 4. Evaluation results: percent correct for non-word error detection, with breakdown for data from native (ns) and non-native (nns) English speakers

Results of error-correction recall, with k-best levels 1-5 and 10, are presented in Figure 2. In comparisons of recall, with k=1, on NS data (right panel), MS Word (81.3%) and ConSpel-B (80.7%) show best results (the difference is not significant). For larger k-values, MS Word correction rate[8] improves to a ceiling of about 88.5% and both ConSpel variants have better improvement than MS Word. The context-informed ConSpel-B system has error-correction recall above 90% for $k \geq 2$ and reaches 94.2% at k=5.

On NNS data, ConSpel-B has a clear advantage over all other systems. At k=1, ConSpel-A and MS Word show equal correction performance (72%). For $k \geq 2$, ConSpel-A shows constant improvement, while MS Word improves to a ceiling of about 85%. For both NS and NNS populations, Aspell error-correction performance lags considerably behind the other systems, although it catches up with and even outperforms MS Word for $k \geq 3$. Interestingly, Aspell+ performs consistently worse than Aspell; the larger dictionary has detrimental effect on error-correction for Aspell, but not for MS Word.

[7] ConSpel dictionary does not contain possessive forms.

[8] Results for 'MS Word' and 'MS Word+' on this data overlap for all values of k, in both populations.

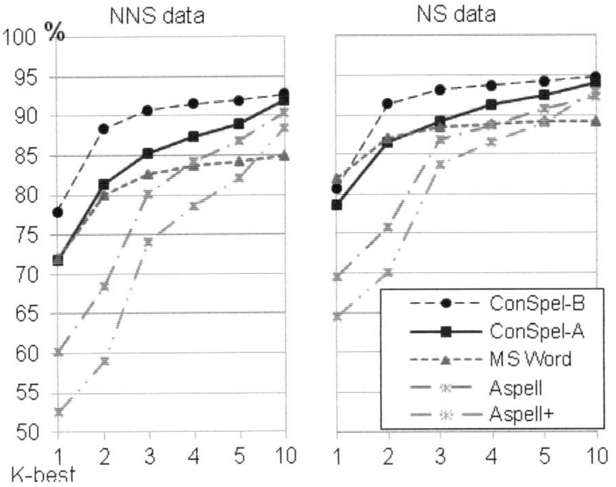

Figure 2. Error-correction recall for five systems, data from native (ns) and non-native (nns) English speakers.

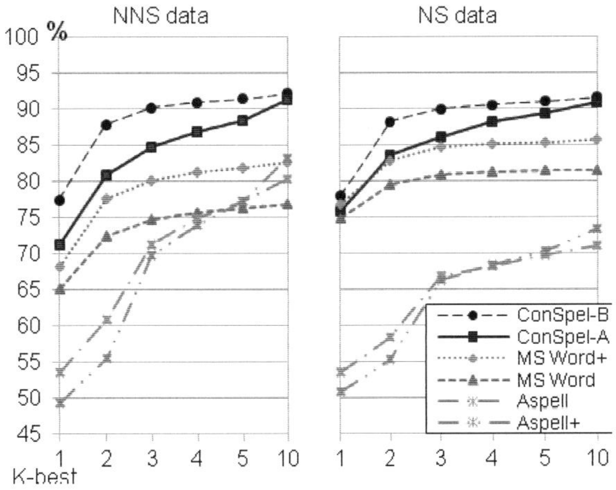

Figure 3. Error-correction precision for six systems, for native (ns) and non-native (nns) English speakers.

Error-correction precision results are shown in Figure 3. Overall, ConSpel-B outperforms all other systems, for both NS and NNS populations. On NS data, for k=1, MS Word+ (77%), ConSpel-A (76%) and MS Word (75%) are very close. For k≥2, ConSpel-A shows better improvement, reaching 89.4% at k=5, while MS Word+ reaches a ceiling of about 85% (81% for MS Word). Aspell performance lags clearly behind the other systems, although it also improves considerably with larger k-values. For NNS data, the separation between systems is even clearer. Aspell lags behind, although it catches up to MS Word at k≥5.

Except for ConSpel-B, all systems have manifestly better error-correction precision on NS data than on NNS data – misspellings made by non-native English speakers are harder to correct. ConSpel-B, with context-informed ranking of spelling suggestions, performs almost equally well for both populations. For k=1, its error-correction precision is 77.5% for NNS data and 78% for NS data. For k=2, precision is 87.9% for NNS and 88.2% for NS data. These differences are not statistically significant. For both populations, precision rises beyond 90% for k≥3. ConSpel-B also shows remarkably close error-correction recall in both populations: at k=1, recall is 77.9% for NNS and 80.7% for NS; at k=2, recall is 88.4% for NNS, 91.4% for NS (the differences are statistically significant). For k≥3, recall is beyond 90% for both populations, with about 2% advantage for NS population.

Table 5 presents F-scores for error-correction evaluation results, for six systems, for k-best values 1-5 and 10, for NS and NNS data. For each value of k, the ConSpel-B system has best values for both NS and NNS data. For each cell in Table 5, we calculated the absolute difference between the NS and NNS F-scores. The results are shown in Figure 4. Except for ConSpel-B, all systems have marked differences in performance on NS and NNS data. The differences tend to diminish for larger k-values. ConSpel-B is the only system for which the differences in error-correction between NS and NNS data are consistently below 2%, even for k=1.

K-best:	1	2	3	4	5	10
Aspell	60.6	65.9	75.6	77.0	78.9	80.3
	54.9	62.3	72.8	76.5	78.9	81.8
Aspell+	56.9	61.8	74.0	76.4	78.5	82.4
	49.6	55.6	69.8	74.0	77.3	82.9
MS Word	78.2	83.2	84.4	84.9	85.1	85.2
	68.4	76.0	78.5	79.5	80.1	80.6
MS Word+	78.7	84.8	86.9	87.3	87.5	87.9
	69.3	78.7	81.4	82.4	83.0	83.9
ConSpel-A	77.2	85.1	87.7	89.7	90.9	92.4
	71.5	81.2	85.0	87.0	88.7	91.6
ConSpel-B	79.3	89.8	91.6	92.1	92.6	93.2
	77.7	88.1	90.5	91.3	91.7	92.5

Table 5. Error-correction evaluation results: F-scores for six systems, data from native (upper value in each cell) and non-native English speakers

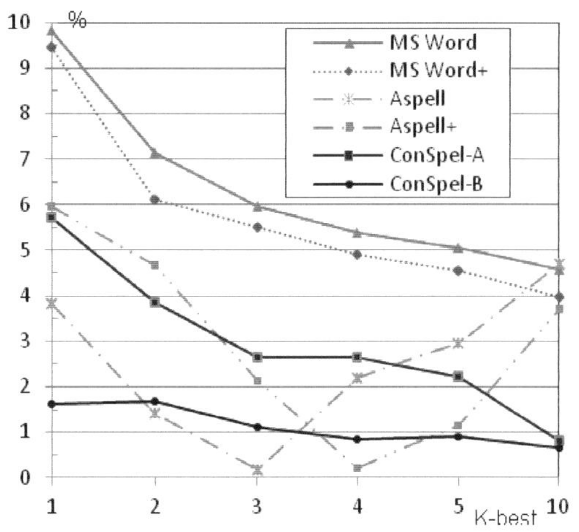

Figure 4. Error-correction F-scores absolute differences

A question we need to address is whether there are any real differences in misspellings produced by NS and NNS writers in our corpus. Our initial analyses show that there are some distinguishing characteristics.

One characterization is obtained when we look at the 'complexity' of the error, defining it as the edit distance between misspelling and correct word. The data is presented in Table 6. Native English speakers make significantly more simple errors (edit distance 1) than non-native speakers, while the latter make more complex errors (edit distance 4+).

Edit distance between misspelling and correct form	NS	NNS
1	83.3%	*79.9%
2	13.0%	14.0%
3	3.1%	3.9%
4+	0.6%	*2.1%

Table 6. Percent of non-word misspellings (tokens) by edit distance to correct word, for native and non-native populations.
* difference significant at p<.01

Another difference we found in our data is the length (number of characters) of the correct word that was misspelled, for each population (Figure 5). For words of length 2 to 7, non-native speakers produce relatively more misspellings than native speakers. For words of length 8 and longer, native speakers produce relatively more misspellings than non-native speakers.

ConSpel-B performs about the same on NS and NNS data, and better than the other systems. Given the above differences of NS and NNS misspellings in our corpus, and given that all evaluated systems, except ConSpel-B, show better correction on NS data, we conclude that ConSpel-B shows this real advantage due to utilization of contextual data.

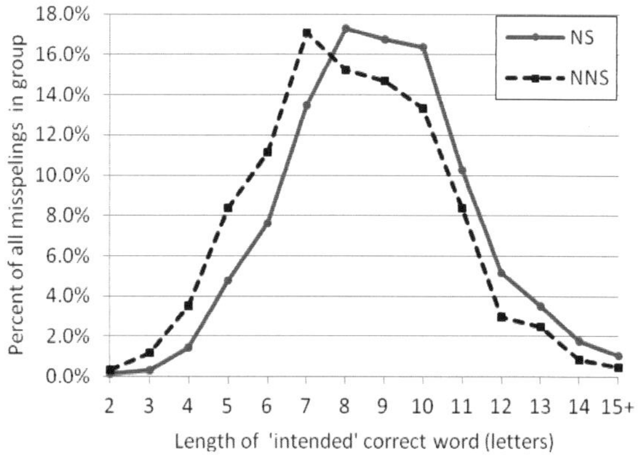

Figure 5. Percent of non-word misspellings (tokens) by length of the 'intended' correct word, for native and non-native populations.

5 Discussion

Large scale comparative studies of spellchecker performance on data from non-native language speakers are scarce, possibly due to large amount of effort required for expert annotation of data.

Hovermale (2010) analyzed 500 spelling errors from a corpus of essays produced by ELL in Japan. In that study, MS Word 2007 successfully corrected 72% of non-word errors, while Aspell had a success rate of 81% (presumably at k=1). In our study, with data from an international sample of non-native English speakers, Aspell error-correction precision rate is only 52% at k=1, and rises to 78% for k=5. MS Word and ConSpel-A (no-context) begin with precision of about 75-77% at k=1. At k=5, MS Word improves to about 85%, and ConSpel-A to above 89%.

Bestgen and Granger (2011) analyzed 222 argumentative essays from the ICLE corpus (Granger et al., 2009), written by European EFL students across different levels of English proficiency. Their sample included about 150,000 words and had 1,549 spelling errors. This amounts to spelling-error rate of about 1%, compared to 2.2% in our data. In that study, MS Word 2007 had detection recall of 80.43%, and detection precision of 82.35%. In our study, MS Word had 99.6% recall and 90.1% precision in error detection. The difference may be attributed to the fact that we focus on single-token non-word misspellings, while Bestgen and Granger included other categories, specifically multi-token errors. Error-correction recall was 71% and precision 59% (at k=1). In our study, at k=1, MS Word achieved 72% recall and 65% precision, which is quite close to the above figures.

Given that our context-informed system has error-correction F-score of 77.9% at k=1, and 91.8% at k=5, it is obvious that the system picks up the right corrections. There is a potential for improvement, possibly by better ranking. Why doesn't the context help even more? Could the system perform with 90% at k=1? We have tentatively identified three major types of influences that detract the system from better performance. Those are a) local error density; b) poor grammar; and c) competition among inflectional variants. Local error density means simply that adjacent words are misspelled so there is not enough reliable context to use n-grams in such cases.

Poor grammar is also problematic for n-gram-based approach. In a fragment "*If docter want to operate, he...*", the intended word was '*doctor*', but '*doctor want*' is a subject-verb agreement error, which is not frequent in the normative n-gram data. Thus, under n-gram frequency influence, the system prefers '*doctors*' as top ranked candidate. There is competition of inflectional variants in presence of grammatical errors.

We have observed that even in absence of grammatical errors, sometimes an inadequate top ranked candidate is an inflectional variant of the adequate correction. For example: "*They received fresh air, interacte with other youth their age, solved problems...*". The adequate correction is '*interacted*', but ConSpel ranks it third, while '*interacts*' comes second and '*interact*' is ranked first. Notably, non-local context is not always beneficial – for a example, the presence of word '*interact*' elsewhere in the essay will strengthen the wrong candidate. Possibly, additional linguistic information could help improve ranking in such cases, e.g. by observing that all verbs in this sentence come in past tense.

Mitton (1996) suggested that it should be possible to adapt a spellchecker to cope specifically with L1-characteristic errors of English learners. Granger and Wynne (1999) analyzed misspellings produced by students with several different L1 backgrounds and have also suggested that it might be "useful to adapt tools such as spellcheckers to the needs of non-native users." Mitton and Okada (2007) have demonstrated a successful adaptation of a spellchecker (oriented for native English speakers) to Japanese learners of English.[9] However, adaptation to each specific L1 would require considerable resources. As noted by Hovermale (2010), it is not clear whether it is worthwhile to customize spellchecker heuristics for each learner population or better to just have one ELL spellchecker. Results from our study indicate that it is at least feasible to produce a general-purpose spellchecker that can successfully correct misspellings produced by non-native English speakers, almost as well as it does for native English speakers. A key for such development is utilization of essay context for re-ranking of spelling suggestions.

6 Conclusions

In this paper we presented a method for context-informed correction of single-token non-word spelling errors. Our results with ConSpel system demonstrate that utilizing contextual information helps improve automatic correction of non-word misspellings, for both native and non-native speakers of English, at least for essays written by test takers on standardized English proficiency tests. In future work we intend to produce a detailed study of the different ways of context utilization. We also intend to expand the system to handle multi-word spelling errors.

Acknowledgments

Many thanks to Chong Min Lee and Daniel Blanchard for assisting in evaluation with Aspell and Microsoft Office 2007; to our annotators, Nicole DiCrecchio, Julia Farnum, Melissa Lopez, Susanne Miller, Matthew Mulholland, Sarah Ohls, and Waverely VanWinkle. The manuscript has also benefited from the comments of three anonymous reviewers.

[9] Boyd (2009) used non-native (Japanese ELL) pronunciation modeling to improve a speller that uses just an orthographic error-model. Her combined system achieved 65% correction precision at k=1, and 82.6% at k=5. Our context-informed system achieves 77.5% and 91.4% respectively.

References

Reima Al-Jarf. 2010. Spelling error corpora in EFL. *Sino-US English Teaching*, 7(1):6-15.

Kevin Atkinson. 2011. GNU Aspell. Software available at http://aspell.net.

Shane Bergsma, Dekang Lin and Randy Goebel. 2009. Web-Scale N-gram Models for Lexical Disambiguation. In *Proceedings of International Joint Conference on Artificial Intelligence* (IJCAI-2009), pages 1507-1512.

Yves Bestgen and Sylviane Granger. 2011. Categorising spelling errors to assess L2 writing. *International Journal of Continuing Engineering Education and Life-Long Learning*, 21(2/3):235-252.

Adriane Boyd. 2009. Pronunciation Modeling in Spelling Correction for Writers of English as a Foreign Language. In *Proceedings of the NAACL HLT 2009 Student Research Workshop and Doctoral Consortium*, pages 31–36.

Torsten Brants and Alex Franz. 2006. *Web 1T 5-gram Version 1*. LDC2006T13. Philadelphia, PA, USA: Linguistic Data Consortium.

Eric Brill and Robert C. Moore. 2000. An improved error model for noisy channel spelling correction. In *Proceedings of the 38th Annual Meeting of ACL*, pages 286-293

Andrew Carlson and Ian Fette. 2007. Memory-Based Context-Sensitive Spelling Correction at Web Scale. In *Proceedings of the Sixth International Conference on Machine Learning and Applications*, pages 166-171.

Qing Chen, Mu Li and Ming Zhou. 2007. Improving query spelling correction using web search results. In *Proceedings of the 2007 Conference on Empirical Methods in Natural Language* (EMNLP 2007), pages 181-189.

Robert Connors and Andrea A. Lunsford. 1988. Frequency of Formal Error in Current College Writing, or Ma and Pa Kettle Do Research. *College Composition and Communication*, 39(4):395–409.

Scott A. Crossley, Tom Salsbury, Philip McCarthy and Danielle S. McNamara. 2008. Using latent semantic analysis to explore second language lexical development. In Wilson, D. and Chad Lane, H. (Eds.): *Proceedings of the 21st International Florida Artificial Intelligence Research Society Conference*, pages 136–141.

Silviu Cucerzan and Eric Brill. 2004. Spelling correction as an iterative process that exploits the collective knowledge of web users. In *Proceedings of the Conference on Empirical Methods in Natural Language Processing* (EMNLP-2004), pages 293–300.

Frederick Damerau. 1964. A technique for computer detection and correction of spelling errors. *Communications of the ACM*, 7(3): 659-664.

Rachele De Felice and Stephen G. Pulman. 2008. A Classifier-Based Approach to Preposition and Determiner Error Correction in L2 English. In *Proceedings of the 22nd International Conference on Computational Linguistics* (COLING 2008), pages 69-176.

Sebastian Deorowicz and Marcin G. Ciura. 2005. Correcting spelling errors by modelling their causes. *International Journal of Applied Mathematics and Computer Science*, 15(2), pages 275–285.

Christy Desmet and Ron Balthazor. 2006. Finding Patterns in Textual Corpora: Data Mining, Research, and Assessment in First-year Composition. Paper presented at Computers and Writing 2006, Lubbock, Texas, May 25–29, 2006.

Semire Dikli. 2006. An overview of automated scoring of essays. *Journal of Technology, Learning, and Assessment*, 5(1):4-35. ejournals.bc.edu/ojs/index.php/jtla (last accessed on February 22, 2012).

ETS. 2011a. GRE®: *Introduction to the Analytical Writing Measure*. Educational Testing Service. www.ets.org/gre/revised_general/prepare/analytical_writing (last accessed on March 9, 2012).

ETS. 2011b. *TOEFL® iBT® Test Content*. Educational Testing Service. www.ets.org/toefl/ibt/about/content (last accessed on March 9, 2012).

Michael Flor. 2012. A fast and flexible architecture for very large word n-gram datasets. *Natural Language Engineering*. Available on CJO 2012 doi:10.1017/S1351324911000349 journals.cambridge.org/action/displayJournal?jid=NLE

Michael Flor and Yoko Futagi. 2011. Producing an annotated corpus with automatic spelling correction. Presented at the *Learner Corpus Research 2011 Conference*, 15-17 September 2011, Louvain-la-Neuve, Belgium. Submitted for publication.

Yoko Futagi. 2010. The effects of learner errors on the development of a collocation detection tool. In *Proceedings of the Fourth Workshop on Analytics for Noisy Unstructured Text Data (AND '10)*, pages 27-34.

Sylviane Granger, Estelle Dagneaux, Fanny Meunier and Magali Paquot. 2009. *The International Corpus of Learner English*. Handbook and CD-ROM (Version 2), Presses Universitaires de Louvain, Louvain-la-Neuve.

Sylviane Granger and Martin Wynne. 1999. Optimising measures of lexical variation in EFL learner corpora. in Kirk, J. (Ed.): *Corpora Galore*, pages 249–257, Rodopi, Amsterdam.

Andrew Golding and Dan Roth. 1999. A Winnow based approach to Context-Sensitive Spelling Correction. *Machine Learning*, 34(1-3):107-130.

DJ Hovermale. 2010. An analysis of the spelling errors of L2 English learners. Presented at CALICO 2010 Conference, Amherst, MA, USA, June 10-12, 2010. Available electronically from http://www.ling.ohio-state.edu/~djh/presentations/djh_CALICO2010.pptx

Aminul Islam and Diana Inkpen. 2009. Real-word spelling correction using Google Web 1T n-gram with backoff. In *Proceedings of the IEEE International Conference on Natural Language Processing and Knowledge Engineering* (IEEE NLP-KE'09), pages 1-8.

Mark Kernighan, Kenneth Church and William Gale. 1990. A spelling correction program based on a noisy channel model. In *Proceedings of the 13th Conference on Computational Linguistics (COLING '90)*, pages 205-210.

Roland Kuhn and Renato De Mori. 1990. A cache-based natural language model for speech recognition. *IEEE Transactions on Pattern Analysis and Machine Intelligence*, 12(6):570–583.

Karen Kukich, 1992. Techniques for automatically correcting words in text. *ACM Computing Surveys*, 24:377-439.

Thomas K. Landauer, Darrell Laham and Peter Foltz. 2003. Automatic essay assessment. *Assessment in Education*, 10(3):295–308.

Claudia Leacock, Martin Chodorow, Michael Gamon, and Joel Tetreault, 2010. *Automated grammatical error detection for language learners.* Synthesis Lectures on Human Language Technologies, No. 9, Morgan & Claypool, Princeton, USA.

Vladimir Levenshtein. 1966. Binary codes capable of correcting deletions, insertions and reversals. *Soviet Physics Doklady*, 10:707-710.

Andrea A. Lunsford and Karen J. Lunsford. 2008. Mistakes Are a Fact of Life: A National Comparative Study. *College Composition and Communication*, 59(4):781-806.

Eric Mays, Fred J. Damerau and Robert L. Mercer. 1991. Context based spelling correction. *Information Processing & Management*, 27(5):517–522.

Roger Mitton. 1996. *English spelling and the computer.* Harlow, Essex: Longman Group. Available electronically from http://eprints.bbk.ac.uk/469

Roger Mitton. 2009. Ordering the suggestions of a spellchecker without using context. *Natural Language Engineering*, 15(2):173–192.

Roger Mitton and Takeshi Okada. 2007. The adaptation of an English spellchecker for Japanese writers. Presented at: *Symposium on Second Language Writing*, 15-17 Sept 2007, Nagoya, Japan. Available electronically from http://eprints.bbk.ac.uk/592

Ryo Nagata, Edward Whittaker and Vera Sheinman. 2011. Creating a manually error-tagged and shallow-parsed learner corpus. In *Proceedings of the 49th Annual Meeting of the Association for Computational Linguistics*, pages 1210–1219, Portland, Oregon: Association for Computational Linguistics.

Takeshi Okada. 2005. Spelling errors made by Japanese EFL writers: with reference to errors occurring at the word-initial and the word-final position. In V. Cook and B. Bassetti (Ed.), *Second language writing systems*, pages 164-183. Clevedon: Multilingual Matters.

Diana Pérez, Enrique Alfonseca and Pilar Rodríguez. 2004. Application of the Bleu method for evaluating free-text answers in an e-learning environment. *Proceedings of the Language Resources and Evaluation Conference* (LREC-2004), pages 1351-1354.

Lawrence Philips. 2000. The Double-metaphone Search Algorithm. *C/C++ User's Journal*, June, 2000.

Anne Rimrott and Trude Heift. 2005. Language learners and generic spell checkers in CALL. *CALICO Journal*, 23(1):17-48.

Anne Rimrott and Trude Heift. 2008. Evaluating automatic detection of misspellings in German. *Language Learning & Technology*, 12(3):73-92.

Casey Whitelaw, Ben Hutchinson, Grace Y Chung and Gerard Ellis. 2009. Using the Web for language independent spellchecking and autocorrection. In *Proceedings of the Conference on Empirical Methods in Natural Language Processing* (EMNLP 2009), pages 890-899.

Mark Warschauer and Paige Ware. 2006. Automated writing evaluation: defining the classroom research agenda. *Language Teaching Research*, 10(2):157–180.

Guoxing Yu. 2010. Lexical diversity in writing and speaking task performances. *Applied Linguistics*, 31(2):236–259.

Yang Zhang, Pilian He, Wei Xiang and Mu Li. 2006. Discriminative reranking for spelling correction. In *Proceedings of the 20th Pacific Asia Conference on Language, Information and Computation*, pages 64-71.

Judging Grammaticality with Count-Induced Tree Substitution Grammars

Francis Ferraro, Matt Post and **Benjamin Van Durme**
Department of Computer Science, and HLTCOE
Johns Hopkins University
{ferraro,post,vandurme}@cs.jhu.edu

Abstract

Prior work has shown the utility of syntactic tree fragments as features in judging the grammaticality of text. To date such fragments have been extracted from derivations of Bayesian-induced Tree Substitution Grammars (TSGs). Evaluating on discriminative coarse and fine grammaticality classification tasks, we show that a simple, deterministic, count-based approach to fragment identification performs on par with the more complicated grammars of Post (2011). This represents a significant reduction in complexity for those interested in the use of such fragments in the development of systems for the educational domain.

1 Introduction

Automatically judging grammaticality is an important component in computer-assisted education, with potential applications including large-scale essay grading and helping to interactively improve the writing of both native and L2 speakers. While n-gram models have been productive throughout natural language processing (NLP), they are obviously insufficient as models of languages, since they do not model language structure or correspondences beyond the narrow Markov context.

Context-free grammars (CFGs) address many of the problems inherent in n-grams, and are therefore intuitively much better suited for grammaticality judgments. Unfortunately, CFGs used in practice are permissive (Och et al., 2004) and make unrealistic independence and structural assumptions, resulting in "leaky" grammars that overgenerate and thus serve poorly as models of language. However, approaches that make use of the CFG productions as discriminative features have performed better. Cherry and Quirk (2008) improved upon an n-gram baseline in grammatical classification by adjusting CFG production weights with a latent SVM, while others have found it useful to use comparisons between scores of different parsers (Wagner et al., 2009) or the use of CFG productions in linear classification settings (Wong and Dras, 2010) in classifying sentences in different grammaticality settings.

Another successful approach in grammaticality tasks has been the use of grammars with an extended domain of locality. Post (2011) demonstrated that larger syntactic patterns obtained from Tree Substitution Grammars (Joshi, 1985) outperformed the Cherry and Quirk models. The intuitions underlying their approach were that larger fragments are more natural atomic units in modeling grammatical text, and that larger fragments reduce the independence assumptions of context-free generative models since there are fewer substitution points in a derivation. Their grammars were learned in a Bayesian setting with Dirichlet Process priors, which have simple formal specifications (c.f., Goldwater et al. (2009, Appendix A)), but which can become quite complicated in implementation.

In this paper, we observe that fragments used for classification do not require an underlying probabilistic model. Here, we present a simple extraction method that elicits a classic formal non-probabilistic grammar from training data by deterministically counting fragments. Whereas Post parses with his TSG and extracts the Viterbi derivation, we use an

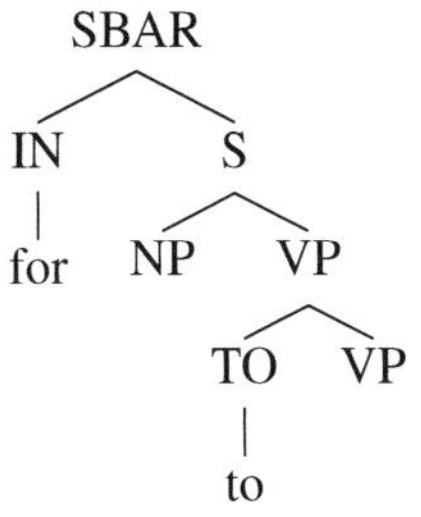

(a) A TSG fragment.

SBAR → IN S
IN → for
S → NP VP
VP → TO VP
TO → to

(b) Equivalent CFG rules.

Figure 1: Equivalent TSG fragment and CFG rules.

off-the-shelf parser and pattern match the fragments in our grammar against the tree. With enough positive and negative training data (in the form of automatic parses of good and bad sentences), we can construct classifiers that learn which fragments correlate with grammaticality. The resulting model results in similar classification accuracy while doing away with the complexity of Bayesian techniques.

2 Tree Substitution Grammars (TSGs)

Though CFGs and TSGs are weakly equivalent, TSGs permit nonterminals to rewrite as tree fragments of arbitrary size, whereas CFG rewrites are limited to depth-one productions. Figure 1 depicts an example TSG fragment and equivalent CFG rules; note that the entire internal structure of 1a is described within a single rewrite.

Unfortunately, learning probabilistic TSGs is not straight-forward, in large part because TSG-specific resources (e.g., large scale TSG-annotated treebanks) do not exist. Approaches to this problem began by taking *all* fragments $\mathcal{F}_{\text{all}}$ in a treebank (Bod, 1993; Goodman, 1996), which resulted in very large grammars composed mostly of fragments very unlikely to generalize.[1] A range of heuristic solutions reduced these grammar sizes to a much smaller, more compact subset of all fragments (Zollmann and Sima'an, 2005; Zuidema, 2007). More recently, more principled models have been proposed, taking the form of inference in Bayesian non-parametric models (Post and Gildea, 2009; Cohn et al., 2009). In addition to providing a formal model for TSGs, these techniques address the overfitting problem of all fragments grammars with priors that discourage large fragments unless there is enough evidence to warrant their inclusion in the grammar. The problem with such approaches, however, is that the sampling procedures used to infer them can be complex, difficult to code, and slow to converge. Although more general techniques have been proposed to better explore the search space (Cohn and Blunsom, 2010; Cohn et al., 2010; Liang et al., 2010), the complexity and non-determinism of these samplers remain, and there are no publicly available implementations.

The underlying premise behind these grammar learning approaches was the need for a probabilistic grammar for parsing. Post (2011) showed that the fragments extracted from derivations obtained by parsing with probabilistic TSGs were useful as features in two coarse-grained grammaticality tasks. In such a setting, fragments are needed for classification, but it is not clear that they need to be obtained from derivations produced by parsing with probabilistic TSGs. In the next section, we describe a simple, deterministic, count-based approach to learning an unweighted TSG. We will then demonstrate (§4) the effectiveness of these grammars for grammaticality classification when fragments are pattern-matched against parse trees obtained from a state-of-the-art parser.

3 Counting Common Subtrees

Rather than derive probabilistic TSGs, we employ a simple, iterative and deterministic (up to tie-breaking) alternative to TSG extraction. Our method extracts $\mathcal{F}_{\langle R,K\rangle}$, the K most common subtrees of size at most R. Though selecting the top K-most-frequent fragments from *all* fragments is computationally challenging through brute force methods, note that if $F \in \mathcal{F}_{\langle R,K\rangle}$, then all subtrees F' of F must also be in $\mathcal{F}_{\langle R,K\rangle}$.[2] Thus, we may incrementally build $\mathcal{F}_{\langle R,K\rangle}$ in the following manner: given r, for $1 \leq r \leq R$, maintain a ranking S, by frequency, of all fragments of size r; the key point is that S may be built from $\mathcal{F}_{\langle r-1,K\rangle}$. Once all fragments of size r have been considered, retain only the top K fragments of the ranked set $\mathcal{F}_{\langle r,K\rangle} = \mathcal{F}_{\langle r-1,K\rangle} \cup S$.[3]

[1]The n-gram analog would be something like storing all 30-grams seen in a corpus.

[2]Analogously, if an n-gram appears K times, then all constituent m-grams, $m < n$, must also appear at least K times.

[3]We found that, at the thresholding stage, ties may be arbitrarily broken with neglible-to-no effect on results.

Algorithm 1 EXTRACTFRAGMENTS (R, K)

Assume: Access to a treebank

$S \leftarrow \emptyset$

$\mathcal{F}_{\langle 1,K \rangle} \leftarrow$ top K CFG rules used

for $r = 2$ to R **do**

  $S \leftarrow S \cup \{$observed 1-rule extensions of $F \in \mathcal{F}_{\langle r-1,K \rangle}\}$

  $\mathcal{F}_{\langle r,K \rangle} \leftarrow$ top K elements of $\mathcal{F}_{\langle r-1,K \rangle} \cup S$

end for

Pseudo-code is provided in Algorithm 1.[4]

This incremental approach is appealing for two reasons. Firstly, our approach tempers the growth of intermediate rankings $\mathcal{F}_{\langle r,K \rangle}$. Secondly, we have two tunable parameters R and K, which can be thought of as weakly being related to the base measure and concentration parameter of (Post and Gildea, 2009; Cohn et al., 2010). Note that by thresholding at every iteration, we enforce sparsity.

4 Experiments

We view grammaticality judgment as a binary classification task: is a sequence of words grammatical or not? We evaluate on two tasks of differing granularity: the first, a coarse-grain classification, follows Cherry and Quirk (2008); the other, a fine-grain analogue, is built upon Foster and Andersen (2009).

4.1 Datasets

For the coarse-grained task, we use the BLLIP[5]-inspired dataset, as in Post (2011), which discriminates between BLLIP sentences and Kneyser-Ney trigram generated sentences (of equal length). Grammatical and ungrammatical examples are given in 1 and 2 below, respectively:

(1) The most troublesome report may be the August merchandise trade deficit due out tomorrow .

(2) To and , would come Hughey Co. may be crash victims , three billion .

For the fine-grained task we use a version of the BNC that has been automatically modified to be ungrammatical, via insertions, deletions or substitutions of grammatically important words. As has been argued in previous work, these automatically generated errors, simulate more realistic errors (Foster and Andersen, 2009). Example 3 gives an original sentence, with an italicized substitution error:

(3) The league 's promoters hope retirees and tourists will join die-hard fans like Mr. de Castro and pack *then* stands to see the seniors .

Both sets contain train/dev/test splits with an equal number of positive and negative examples, and all instances have an available gold-standard parse[6].

4.2 Models and Features

Algorithm 1 extracts common constructions, in the form of count-extracted fragments. To test the efficacy of these fragments, we construct and experiment with various discriminative models.

Given count-extracted fragments obtained from EXTRACTFRAGMENTS(R, K), it is easy to define a feature vector: for each query, there is a binary feature indicating whether a particular extracted fragment occurs in its gold-standard parse. These count-extracted features, along with the sentence length, define the first model, called COUNT.

Although our extracted fragments may help identify grammatical constructions, capturing ungrammatical constructions may be difficult, since we do not parse with our fragments. Thus, we created two augmented models, COUNT+LEX and COUNT+CFG, which built upon and extended COUNT. COUNT+LEX included all preterminal and lexical items. For COUNT+CFG, we included a binary feature for every rule that was used in the most likely parse of a query sentence, according to a PCFG[7].

Following Post (2011), we train an ℓ-2 regularized SVM using `liblinear`[8] (Fan et al., 2008) per model. We optimized the models on dev data, letting the smoothing parameter be 10^m, for integral $m \in [-4, 2]$: 0.1 was optimal for all models.

[4] Code is available at: `cs.jhu.edu/~ferraro`.

[5] LDC2000T43

[6] We parsed all sentences with the Berkeley parser (Petrov et al., 2006).

[7] We used the Berkeley grammar/parser (Petrov et al., 2006) in `accurate` mode; all other options were their default values.

[8] `csie.ntu.edu.tw/~cjlin/liblinear/`

Task	COUNT	COUNT+LEX	COUNT+CFG
coarse	86.3	86.8	**88.3**
fine	62.9	64.3	**67.0**

(a) Our count-based models, with $R = 15$, $K = 50k$.

Task	3	5	10	15
coarse	**89.2**	89.1	88.6	88.3
fine	**67.9**	67.2	67.2	67.0

(b) Performance of COUNT+CFG, with $K = 50k$ and varying R.

Table 1: Development accuracy results.

Method	coarse	fine
COUNT+CFG, $R = 3$	**89.1**	**67.2**
COUNT+CFG, $R = 15$	88.2	66.6
bigram	68.4	61.4
CFG	86.3	64.5
TSG	**89.1**	67.0

Table 2: Classification accuracy on test portions for both **coarse** and **fine**, with $K = 50k$. Chance is 50% for each task.

Our three models all have the same two tunable parameters, R and K. While we initially experimented with $R = 31, K \in \{50k, 100k\}$ — in order to be comparable to the size of Post (2011)'s extracted TSGs — we noticed that very few, if any, fragments of size greater than 15 are able to survive thresholding. Dev experimentation revealed that $K = 50k$ and $100k$ yielded nearly the same results; for brevity, we report in Table 1a dev results for all three models, with $R = 15, K = 50k$. The differences across models was stark, with COUNT+CFG yielding a two point improvement over COUNT on **coarse**, but a four point improvement on **fine**. While COUNT+LEX does improve upon COUNT, on both tasks it falls short of COUNT+CFG. These differences are not completely surprising: one possible explanation is that the PCFG features in COUNT+CFG yield useful negatively-biased features, by providing *a* generative explanation. Due to the supremacy of COUNT+CFG, we solely report results on COUNT+CFG.

In Table 1b, we also examine the effect of extracted rule depth on dev classification accuracy, where we fix $K = 50k$ and vary $R \in \{3, 5, 10, 15\}$, where the best results are achieved with $R = 3$. We evaluate two versions of COUNT+CFG: one with $R = 3$ and the other with $R = 15$ ($K = 50k$ for both).

5 Results and Fragment Analysis

We build on Post (2011)'s results and compare against bigram, CFG and TSG baselines. Each baseline model is built from the same ℓ-2 regularized SVM as above, and each is optimized on dev data. For the bigram baseline, the binary features correspond with whether a particular bigram appears in an instance, while the CFG baseline is simply the augmentation feature set used for COUNT+CFG. For the TSG baseline, the binary features correspond with whether a particular fragment is used in the most probable derivation of each input sentence (using Post's Bayesian TSGs). All baselines use the sentence length as a feature as well.

The results on the test portions of each dataset are given in Table 2. When coupled with the best parse output, our counting method was able to perform on par with, and even surpass, Post's TSGs. The simpler model ($R = 3$) ties TSG performance on **coarse** and exceeds it by two-tenths on **fine**; the more complex model ($R = 15$) gets within a point on **coarse** and four-tenths on **fine**. Note that both versions of COUNT+CFG surpass the CFG baseline on both sets, indicating that (1) encoding deeper structure, even without an underlying probabilistic model, is useful for grammaticality classifications, and (2) this deeper structure can be achieved by a simple counting scheme.

As PCFG output comprises a portion of our feature set, it is not surprising that a number of the most discriminative positive and negative features, such as flat NP and VP rules not frequent enough to survive thresholding, were provided by the CFG parse. While this points out a limitation of our non-adaptive thresholding, note that even among the highest weighted features, PCFG and count-extracted features were interspersed. Further, considering that both versions of COUNT+CFG outperformed CFGs, it seems our method adds discriminative power to the CFG rules.

	(a) Coarse			(b) Fine	
	Grammatical	**Ungrammatical**		**Grammatical**	**Ungrammatical**
1	(S NP VP (. .))	(S NP (VP (VBP are) PP))	10	(SBAR (IN if) S)	(SBAR (S VP))
2	(S (S (VP VBG NP)) VP)	(VP VBZ (S VP))	11	(NP (DT these) NNS)	(SBAR DT (S NP VP))
3	(SBAR (IN while) S)	(SBAR (S VP))	12	(VP (VBG being) VP)	(S (VP VB NP))
4	(VP (VBD called) S)	(VP VBN (S VP))	13	(PP IN (S NP (VP VBG NP)))	(S (VP VBZ NP))
5	(VP (VB give) NP NP)	(NP (NP JJ NN) SBAR)	14	(S (VP VBG VP))	(VP VB (S VP))
6	(NP NNP NNP NNP (NNP Inc.))	(VP NN (PP IN NP))	15	(PP IN (SBAR (IN whether) S))	(S (VP VBP VP))
7	(PP (IN with) (S NP VP))	(S (VP MD VP))	16	(VP (VBD had) (VP VBN S))	(S NP (VP (VBD said)))
8	(SBAR (IN for) (S NP (VP (TO to) VP)))	(SBAR (S (NP NNS) VP))	17	(VP MD (VP VB NP (PP IN NP) PP))*	(PP (PP IN NP) (CC and) PP)*
9	(PRN (-LRB- -LRB-) NP (-RRB- -RRB-))*	(S (ADJP JJ))*	18	(NP (DT no) NNS)*	(PP (IN As) NP)*

Table 3: Most discriminative count-based features for COUNT+CFG on both tasks. For comparability to Post (2011), $R = 15, K = 50k$, are shown. Asterisks (*) denote fragments hand-selected from the top 30.

Table 5 presents top weighted fragments from COUNT+CFG on both **coarse** and **fine**, respectively. Examining useful grammatical features across tasks, we see a variety of fragments: though our fragments heavily weight simple structure such as proper punctuation (ex. 1) and parentheticals (ex. 9), they also capture more complex phenomena such as lexical argument descriptions (e.g., *give*, ex. 5). Our extracted fragments also describe common constructions and transitions (e.g., 3, 8 and 15) and involved verb phrases (e.g., gerunds in 2 and 14, passives in 16, and modals in 17).

Though for both tasks some ungrammatical fragments easily indicate errors, such as sentence fragments (e.g., example 6) or repeated words (ex. 11), in general the analysis is more difficult. In part, this is because, when isolated from errors, one may construct grammatical sentences that use some of the highest-weighted ungrammatical fragments. However, certain errors may force particular rules to be inappropriately applied when acquiring the gold-standard parse. For instance, example 10 typically coordinates with larger VPs, via auxiliary verbs or expletives (e.g., *it*). Affecting those crucial words can significantly change the overall parse structure: consider that in "said *it* is too early...," *it* provides a crucial sentential link; without it, "is too early" may be parsed as a sentence, and then glued on to the former part.

6 Conclusion

In this work, we further examined TSGs as useful judges of grammaticality for written English. Using an iterative, count-based approach, along with the most likely PCFG parse, we were able to train a discriminative classifier model — COUNT+CFG — that surpassed the PCFG's ability to judge grammaticality, and performed on par with Bayesian-TSGs. Examining the highest weighted features, we saw that complex structures and patterns encoded by the count-based TSGs proved discriminatively useful. This suggests new, simpler avenues for fragment learning, especially for grammaticality judgments and other downstream tasks.

Acknowledgements Thank you to the reviewers for helpful feedback, and thanks to Johns Hopkins HLTCOE for providing support. Any opinions expressed in this work are those of the authors.

References

R. Bod. 1993. Using an annotated corpus as a stochastic grammar. In *Proceedings of the sixth conference on European chapter of the Association for Computational Linguistics*, pages 37–44. Association for Computational Linguistics.

Colin Cherry and Chris Quirk. 2008. Discriminative, syntactic language modeling through latent svms. *Proceeding of Association for Machine Translation in the America (AMTA-2008)*.

Trevor Cohn and Phil Blunsom. 2010. Blocked inference in bayesian tree substitution grammars. In *Proceedings of ACL (short papers)*, pages 225–230, Stroudsburg, PA, USA. Association for Computational Linguistics.

Trevor Cohn, Sharon Goldwater, and Phil Blunsom. 2009. Inducing compact but accurate tree-substitution grammars. In *Proceedings of Human Language Technologies: The 2009 Annual Conference of the North American Chapter of the Association for Computational Linguistics*, pages 548–556, Stroudsburg, PA, USA. Association for Computational Linguistics.

Trevor Cohn, Phil Blunsom, and Sharon Goldwater. 2010. Inducing tree-substitution grammars. *Journal of Machine Learning Research*, 11:3053–3096, December.

Rong-En Fan, Kai-Wei Chang, Cho-Jui Hsieh, Xiang-Rui Wang, and Chih-Jen Lin. 2008. Liblinear: A library for large linear classification. *Journal of Machine Learning Research*, 9:1871–1874, June.

Jennifer Foster and Oistein E. Andersen. 2009. GenERRate: generating errors for use in grammatical error detection. In *Proceedings of the Fourth Workshop on Innovative Use of NLP for Building Educational Applications*, pages 82–90.

Sharon Goldwater, Thomas L. Griffiths, and Mark Johnson. 2009. A Bayesian framework for word segmentation: Exploring the effects of context. *Cognition*, 112(1):21 - 54.

Joshua Goodman. 1996. Efficient algorithms for parsing the dop model. In *Proceedings of EMNLP*, pages 143–152.

A.K. Joshi. 1985. Tree adjoining grammars: How much context-sensitivity is required to provide reasonable structural descriptions? *Natural language parsing*, pages 206–250.

Percy Liang, Michael .I. Jordan, and Dan Klein. 2010. Type-based MCMC. In *Human Language Technologies: The 2010 Annual Conference of the North American Chapter of the Association for Computational Linguistics*. Association for Computational Linguistics.

Franz Josef Och, Daniel Gildea, Sanjeev Khudanpur, Anoop Sarkar, Kenji Yamada, Alex Fraser, Shankar Kumar, Libin Shen, David Smith, Katherine Eng, et al. 2004. A smorgasbord of features for statistical machine translation. In *Proceedings of NAACL*.

Slav Petrov, Leon Barrett, Romain Thibaux, and Dan Klein. 2006. Learning accurate, compact, and interpretable tree annotation. In *Proceedings of ACL-ICCL*, pages 433–440, Stroudsburg, PA, USA. Association for Computational Linguistics.

Matt Post and Daniel Gildea. 2009. Bayesian learning of a tree substitution grammar. In *Proceedings of ACL-IJCNLP (short papers)*, pages 45–48, Stroudsburg, PA, USA. Association for Computational Linguistics.

Matt Post. 2011. Judging grammaticality with tree substitution grammar derivations. In *Proceedings of ACL (short papers)*, pages 217–222, Stroudsburg, PA, USA. Association for Computational Linguistics.

J. Wagner, J. Foster, and J. van Genabith. 2009. Judging grammaticality: Experiments in sentence classification. *CALICO Journal*, 26(3):474–490.

Sze-Meng Jojo Wong and Mark Dras. 2010. Parser features for sentence grammaticality classification. In *Proceedings of the Australasian Language Technology Association Workshop*.

Andreas Zollmann and Khalil Sima'an. 2005. A consistent and efficient estimator for Data-Oriented Parsing. *Journal of Automata, Languages and Combinatorics*, 10(2/3):367–388.

Willem Zuidema. 2007. Parsimonious data-oriented parsing. In *Proceedings of EMNLP-CoNLL*, pages 551–560.

Scoring Spoken Responses Based on Content Accuracy

Fei Huang
CS Dept. Temple Univ.
Philadelphia, PA, 19122
tub58431@temple.edu

Lei Chen
Educational Testing Service (ETS)
Princeton, NJ, 08541
lchen@ets.org

Jana Sukkarieh
ETS
JSukkarieh@ets.org

Abstract

Accuracy of content have not been fully utilized in the previous studies on automated speaking assessment. Compared to writing tests, responses in speaking tests are noisy (due to recognition errors), full of incomplete sentences, and short. To handle these challenges for doing content-scoring in speaking tests, we propose two new methods based on information extraction (IE) and machine learning. Compared to using an ordinary content-scoring method based on vector analysis, which is widely used for scoring written essays, our proposed methods provided content features with higher correlations to human holistic scores.

1 Introduction

In recent years, there is an increasing interest of using speech processing and natural language processing (NLP) technologies to automatically score speaking tests (Eskenazi, 2009). A set of features related to speech delivery, such as fluency, pronunciation, and intonation, has been utilized in these studies. However, accuracy of an answer's content to the question being asked, important factors to be considered during the scoring process, have not been fully utilized. In this paper, we will report our initial efforts exploring content scoring in an automated speaking assessment task. To start, we will briefly describe the speaking test questions in our research.

In the test we used for evaluation, there were two types of questions. The first type, *survey*, requires a test-taker to provide answers specific to one or several key points in a survey question without any background reading/listening related to the topic of the survey. Typical questions could be *"how frequently do you go shopping?"* or *"what kind of products did you purchase recently?"* In contrast, the second type, *opinion*, requires a test-taker to speak as long as 60 seconds to present his or her opinions about some topic. An example of such questions could be, *"Do you agree with the statement that online shopping will be dominant in future or not?"* Compared to the essays in writing tests, these spoken responses could just be incomplete sentences. For example, for the *survey* questions, test-takers could just say several words. For the questions described above, some test-takers may just use phrases like "once a week" or "books". In addition, given short responding durations, the number of words in test-takers' responses is limited. Furthermore, since scoring speech responses requires speech recognition, more noisy inputs are expected. To tackle these challenges, we propose two novel content scoring methods in this paper.

The remainder of the paper is organized as follows: Section 2 reviews the related previous research efforts; Section 3 proposes the two content-scoring methods we designed for two types of questions described above; Section 4 reports the experimental results of applying the proposed methods; finally, Section 5 concludes our reported research and describes our plans for future research.

2 Related Work

For writing tests, previous content scoring investigations can be divided into the following three groups. The first group relies on obtaining and matching patterns associated with the correct answers (Leacock and Chodorow, 2003; Sukkarieh and Blackmore, 2009).

The second group of methods, also mostly used

for content-scoring, is to rely on a variety of text similarity measurements to compare a response with either pre-defined correct answers or a group of responses rated with a high score (Mohler and Mihalcea, 2009). Compared to the first group, such methods can bypass a labor intensive pattern-building step. A widely used approach to measuring text similarity between two text strings is to convert each text string into a word vector and then use the angle between these two vectors as a similarity metric. For example, Content Vector Analysis (CVA) has been successfully utilized to detect off-topic essays (Higgins et al., 2006) and to provide content-related features for essay scoring (Attali and Burstein, 2004). For this group of methods, measuring the semantics similarity between two terms is a key question. A number of metrics have been proposed, including metrics (Courley and Mihalcea, 2005) derived from WordNet, a semantics knowledge database (Fellbaum, 1998), and metrics related to terms' co-occurrence in corpora or on the Web (Turney, 2001).

The third group of methods treats content scoring as a Text Categorization (TC) task, which treats the responses being scored on different score levels as different categories. Therefore, a large amount of previous TC research, such as the many machine learning approaches proposed for the TC task, can be utilized. For example, Furnkranz et al. (1998) compared the performance of applying two machine learning methods on a web-page categorization task and found that the Repeated Incremental Pruning to Produce Error Reduction algorithm (RIPPER) (Cohen, 1995) shows an advantage concerning the feature sparsity issue.

3 Methodology

As described in Section 1, for the two types of questions considered, the number of words appearing in a response is quite limited given the short response time. Therefore, compared to written essays, when applying the content-scoring methods based on vector analysis, e.g., CVA, feature sparsity becomes a major factor negatively influencing the performance of these methods. Furthermore, there are more challenges when applying vector analysis on *survey* questions because test-takers could just use words/phrases rather than completed sentences. Also, some *survey* questions could have a very large range of correct answers. For example, if a question is about the name of a book, millions of book titles could be potential answers. Therefore, a simple phrase-matching solution cannot work.

3.1 Semi-Automatic Information Extraction

For *survey* responses, the answers should be related to the key points mentioned in the questions. For example, for the question, "*What kind of TV programs do you like to watch?*", possible correct answers should be related to TV programs. Moreover, it should be the instances of specific TV programs, like news, comedy, talk shows, etc. Note that the acceptable answers may be infinite, so it is not realistic to enumerate all possible answers. Therefore, we proposed a method to extract the potential answer candidates and then measure their semantic similarities to the answer keys that could be determined manually. In particular, the answer keys were determined by the first author based on her analysis of the test prompts. For example, for the question "*What kind of books do you like to read?*", two answer keys, "book" and "reading" were selected. After a further analysis of the questions, we found that most of the *survey* questions are about "when" "where" and "what", and the answers in the responses were usually nouns or noun phrases. Therefore, we decided to extract the noun phrases from each response and use them as potential candidates.

We use two semantic similarity metrics (SSMs) to evaluate how each candidate relates to an answer key, including PMI-IR (Turney, 2001) and a word-to-word similarity metric from WordNet (Courley and Mihalcea, 2005). The PMI-IR is a measure based on web query analysis using Pointwise Mutual Information (PMI) and Information Retrieval (IR). For an answer candidate (c) and an answer key (k), their PMI-IR is computed as:

$$SSM_{\text{PMI-IR}}(c,k) = \frac{hits(c\text{NEAR}k)}{hits(c)}$$

where the $hits(x)$ function obtains the count of term x returned by a web search engine and **NEAR** is a query operator for proximity search, searching the pages on which both k and c appear within a specified distance. Among many WordNet (WN) based SSMs summarized in Courley and Mihalcea (2005), we found that the Wu-Palmer metric proposed by Wu and Palmer (1994) worked the best in our pilot study. This metric is a score denoting how similar two word senses are, based on the depth of the two word senses in the taxonomy and their Least Common Subsumer [1] (LCS):

$$SSM_{\text{WN}}(c,k) = \frac{2 * depth(LCS)}{depth(c) + depth(k)}$$

For each answer key, we calculated two sets of SSMs ($SSM_{\text{PMI-IR}}$ and SSM_{WN}, respectively) from all candidates. Then, we selected the largest $SSM_{\text{PMI-IR}}$ and SSM_{WN} as the final SSMs for this particular answer key. For each test question, using the corresponding responses in the training set, we built a linear regression model between these SSMs for all answer keys and the human judged scores. The learned regression model was applied to the responses to this particular testing question in the testing set to convert a set of SSMs to predictions of human scores. The predicted scores were then used as a content feature. Since answer keys were determined manually, we refer to this method as semi-automatic information extraction (Semi-IE).

3.2 Machine Learning Using Smoothed Inputs

For the *opinion* responses, inspired by Furnkranz et al. (1998), we decided to try sophisticated machine learning methods instead of the simple vector-distance computation used in CVA. Due to short response-time in the speaking test being considered, the ordinary vector analysis may face a problem that the obtained vectors are too short to be reliably used. In addition, using other non-CVA machine learning methods can enable us to try other types of linguistic features. To address the feature sparsity issue, a smoothing method, which converts word-based text features into features based on other entities with a much smaller vocabulary size, is used. We use a Hidden Markov Model (HMM) based smoothing method (Huang and Yates, 2009), which induces classes, corresponding to hidden states in the HMM model, from the observed word strings. This smoothing method can use contextual information of the word sequences due to the nature of HMM.

Then, we convert word-entity vectors to the vectors based on the induced classes. TF-IDF (term frequency and inverse document frequency) weighting is applied on the new class vectors. Finally, the processed class vectors are used as input features (smoothed) to a machine learning method. In this research, after comparing several widely used machine learning approaches, such as Naive Bayes, CART, etc., we decided to use RIPPER proposed by Cohen (1995), a rule induction method, similar to Furnkranz et al. (1998).

[1] Most specific ancestor node

4 Experiments

Our experimental data was from a test for international workplace English. Six testing papers were used in our study and each individual test contains three *survey* questions (1, 2, and 3) and two *opinion* questions (4 and 5). Table 1 lists examples for these question types. From the real test, we collected spoken responses from a total of $1,838$ test-takers. $1,470$ test-takers were used for training and 368 were used for testing. Following scoring rubrics developed for this test by considering speakers' various language skill aspects, such as fluency, pronunciation, vocabulary, as well as content accuracy, the *survey* and *opinion* responses were scored by a group of experienced human raters by using a 3-point scale and a 5-point scale respectively. For the *survey* responses, the human judged scores were centered on 2; for the *opinion* responses, the human judged scores were centered on 3 and 4.

Qs.	Example
1	*How frequently do you go shopping?*
2	*What kinds of products do you buy often?*
3	*How should retailers improve their services?*
4	*Make a purchase decision based on the chart provided and justify your decision.*
5	*Do you agree with the statement that online shopping will be dominant in the future or not? Please justify your point.*

Table 1: Examples of the five kinds of questions investigated in the study

All of these non-native speech responses were manually transcribed. A state-of-the-art HMM Automatic Speech Recognition (ASR) system which was trained from a large set of non-native speech data was used. For each type of test question, acoustic and language model adaptations were applied to further lower the recognition error rate. Finally, a word error rate around 30% to 40% could be achieved on the held-out speech data. In our experiments, we used speech transcriptions in the model training stage and used ASR outputs in the testing stage. Note that we decided to use speech transcriptions, instead of noisy ASR outputs that match to the testing condition, to make sure that the learned content-scoring model are based on correct word entities related to content accuracy.

For the *survey* responses, we manually selected the key points from the testing questions. Then, using a Part-Of-Speech (POS) tagger and a sentence chunker implemented by using the OpenNLP [2] toolkit, we found all possible nouns and noun-phrases that could serve as answer candidates and applied the Semi-IE method described in Section 3.1. For *opinion* questions, based on Huang and Yates (2009), we used 80 hidden states and applied the method described in Section 3.2 for content scoring. We used JRip, a Java implementation of the RIPPER (Cohen, 1995) algorithm in the Weka (Hall et al., 2009) machine learning toolkit, in our experiments.

When measuring performance of content-related features, following many automated assessment studies (Attali and Burstein, 2004; Leacock and Chodorow, 2003; Sukkarieh and Blackmore, 2009), we used the Pearson correlation r between the content features and human scores as an evaluation metric. We compared the proposed methods with a baseline method, CVA. It works as follows: it first groups all the training responses by scores, then it calculates a TF vector from all the responses under a score level. Also, an IDF matrix is generated from all the training responses. After that, for each testing response, CVA first converts it into a TF-IDF vector and then calculates the cosine similarity between this vector with each score-level vector respectively and uses the largest cosine similarity as the content feature for that response. The experimental results, including content-features' correlations r to human scores from each proposed method and the correlation increases measured on CVA results, are shown in Table 2. First, we find that CVA, which is designed for scoring lengthy written essays, does not work well for the *survey* questions, especially on

[2] http://opennlp.sourceforge.net

Question	r_{CVA}	$r_{Semi-IE}$	$r \Uparrow$
1	0.12	0.30	150%
2	0.15	0.27	80%
3	0.21	0.26	23.8%
Question	r_{CVA}	$r_{Ripper_{HMM}}$	$r \Uparrow$
4	0.47	0.54	14.89%
5	0.33	0.39	18.18%

Table 2: Comparisons of the proposed content-scoring methods with CVA on *survey* and *opinion* responses

first two questions, which are mostly phrases (not completed sentences). By contrast, our proposed Semi-IE method can provide more informative content measurements, indicated by substantially increased r. Second, CVA works better on *opinion* questions than on *survey* questions. This is because that *opinion* questions can be treated as short spoken essays and therefore are closer to the data on which the CVA method was originally designed to work. However, even on such a well-performing CVA baseline, the HMM smoothing method allows the Ripper algorithm to outperform the CVA method in content-features' correlations to human scores. For example, on question 4, on which either a table or a chart has been provided to test-takers, the CVA achieves a r of 0.47. The proposed method can still improve the r by about 15%.

5 Conclusions and Future Works

In this paper, we proposed two content-scoring methods for the two types of test questions in an automated speaking assessment task. For particular properties of these two question types, we utilized information extraction (IE) and machine learning technologies to better score them on content accuracy. In our experiments, we compared these two methods, Semi-IE and machine learning using smoothed inputs, with an ordinary word-based vector analysis method, CVA. The content features computed using the proposed methods show higher correlations to human scores than what was obtained by using the CVA method.

For the Semi-IE method, one direction of investigation will be how to find the expected answer keys automatically from testing questions. In addition, we will investigate better ways to integrate many semantic similarly measurements (SSMs) into a single content feature. For the machine learning approach, inspired by Furnkranz et al. (1998), we will investigate how to use some linguistic features related to response structures rather than just TF-IDF weights.

References

Y. Attali and J. Burstein. 2004. Automated essay scoring with e-rater v.2.0. In *Presented at the Annual Meeting of the International Association for Educational Assessment*.

W. Cohen. 1995. Text categorization and relational learning. In *In Proceedings of the 12th International Conference on Machine Learning*.

C. Courley and R. Mihalcea. 2005. Measuring the semantic similarity of texts. In *Proceedings of the ACL Workshop on Empirical Modeling of Semantic Equivalence and Entailment*, pages 13–18.

M. Eskenazi. 2009. An overview of spoken language technology for education. *Speech Communication*, 51(10):832–844.

C. Fellbaum. 1998. *WordNet: An Electronic Lexical Database*. Bradford Books.

J. Furnkranz, T. Mitchell, and E. Riloff. 1998. A case study in using linguistic phrases for text categorization on the WWW. In *Proceedings from the AAAI/ICML Workshop on Learning for Text Categorization*, page 512.

M. Hall, E. Frank, G. Holmes, B. Pfahringer, P. Reutemann, and I. H Witten. 2009. The WEKA data mining software: An update. *ACM SIGKDD Explorations Newsletter*, 11(1):10–18.

D. Higgins, J. Burstein, and Y. Attali. 2006. Identifying off-topic student essays without topic-specific training data. *Natural Language Engineering*, 12.

F. Huang and A. Yates. 2009. Distributional representations for handling sparsity in supervised sequence-labeling. In *Proceedings of ACL*.

C. Leacock and M. Chodorow. 2003. C-rater: Automated scoring of short-answer questions. *Computers and the Humanities*, 37(4):385–405.

M. Mohler and R. Mihalcea. 2009. Text-to-text semantic similarity for automatic short answer grading. In *Proceedings of the 12th Conference of the European Chapter of the Association for Computational Linguistics*, pages 567–575.

J. Z. Sukkarieh and J. Blackmore. 2009. c-rater: Automatic content scoring for short constructed responses. In *Paper presented at the Florida Artificial Intelligence Research Society (FLAIRS) Conference, Sanibel, FL.*

P. D. Turney. 2001. Mining the Web for Synonyms: PMI-IR versus LSA on TOEFL. In *Procs. of the Twelfth European Conference on Machine Learning (ECML)*, pages 491–502, Freiburg, Germany.

Z. Wu and M. Palmer. 1994. Verbs semantics and lexical selection. In *Proceeding ACL '94 Proceedings of the 32nd annual meeting on Association for Computational Linguistics*.

Developing ARET: An NLP-based Educational Tool Set for Arabic Reading Enhancement

Mohamed Maamouri[1], Wajdi Zaghouani[1], Violetta Cavalli-Sforza[2], Dave Graff[1] and Mike Ciul[1]

[1] Linguistic Data Consortium, University of Pennsylvania, 3600 Market St., Suite 810, Philadelphia, PA 19104.

[2] School of Science and Engineering, Al Akhawayn University, Ifrane 53000, Morocco.

maamouri@ldc.upenn.edu, wajdiz@ldc.upenn.edu, v.cavallisforza@aui.ma, graff@ldc.upenn.edu, mciul@ldc.upenn.edu

Abstract

This paper describes a novel Arabic Reading Enhancement Tool (ARET) for classroom use, which has been built using corpus-based Natural Language Processing in combination with expert linguistic annotation. The NLP techniques include a widely used morphological analyzer for Modern Standard Arabic to provide word-level grammatical details, and a relational database index of corpus texts to provide word concordances. ARET also makes use of a commercial Arabic text-to-speech (TTS) system to add a speech layer (with male and female voices) to the Al-Kitaab language textbook resources. The system generates test questions and distractors, offering teachers and students an interesting computer-aided language learning tool. We describe the background and the motivation behind the building of ARET, presenting the various components and the method used to build the tools.

1 Introduction

Reading is an essential skill for learners of Modern Standard Arabic (MSA). For most of learners it is the most important skill to master in order to ensure success in learning. With strengthened reading skills, learners of Arabic tend to make greater progress in other areas of language learning. Reading should be an active, fluent process that involves the reader and the reading material in building meaning. Often, however, it is not. The average learner's second language reading ability is usually well below that of the first language. This can impede academic progress in the second language. Arabic language teachers and learners face many challenges in the classroom. Teaching students how to utilize the skills and knowledge they bring from their first language, develop vocabulary skills, improve reading comprehension and rate, and monitor their own improvement are just some of the issues that teachers must consider in preparing for an Arabic language reading class. With these issues in mind, we set out to create a web-based service that would provide efficient and pedagogically relevant access to instructional texts in Modern Standard Arabic, with the goal of creating a resource that would serve both instructors and students, by presenting novel modes of information access. We received valuable support from Georgetown University Press, which gave permission for us to use the reading passages from the 3-volume textbook publication *Al-Kitaab* (Al-Batal et al., 2001;2004 and 2006), which is the most popular publication in the USA for teaching Arabic.

2 Motivation

Using technology in classrooms can make the lessons more efficient. There are many technology tools that can be used in English as a Second Language (ESL) classes to improve foreign students' English and technology skills. According to Wang (2005) there are many advantages integrating technology in classrooms especially for ESL students. To be able to improve their language skills, like writing, reading, listening and speaking, English language learners use pedagogical computer applications to check their work and improve their language skills; they also use web browsers and e-mail to search for information, join in online discussions, publish their work, read technology texts, communicate each other even worldwide. He also says that, "Technology integration in foreign language teaching demonstrates the shift in educational paradigms from a behavioral to a constructivist learning approach" (p. 2). Gone are the days in which learning foreign language vocabulary and grammar rules relied largely on repetitive drills; more and more, foreign language learners are asked to engage directly with authentic materials and take more initiative in their learning. However, finding appropriate, authentic reading materials is a challenge for language instructors. The Web is a vast resource of texts, but most pages are not suitable for reading practice, and commercial search engines are not well suited to finding texts that satisfy pedagogical constraints such as reading level, length, text quality, and presence of target vocabulary. We present a system that uses various language technologies to facilitate the selection , presentation and study of authentic reading materials from the widely used textbook series *Al-Kitaab* (Al-Batal et al., 2001;2004 and 2006). In the next section we review some of the related work. In section 4 we discuss some of the specific challenges faced when learning the Arabic language.

3 Related work

Many studies have shown that an on-line learning environment that supplements classroom instruction with additional study materials at an appropriate level for the learner may enhance language learning and development (Ware, 2004; Chiu et al., 2007; Yuan, 2003; Wang, 2005;). As a result, a number of recent projects have aimed to dynamically provide a supply of accessible authentic texts to language learners by drawing from online resources. WERTi (Meurers et al. 2010) is an intelligent automatic workbook that uses texts from the Web to increase knowledge of English grammatical forms and functions. READ-X (Miltsakaki and Troutt, 2007) is a tool for finding texts at specified reading levels. SourceFinder (Sheehan et al.,2007) is an authoring tool for finding suitable texts for standardized test items on verbal reasoning and reading comprehension. Project REAP (Reader-Specific Lexical Practice) (Brown and Eskenazi, 2004; Heilman et al., 2006) takes a different approach. Rather than teachers choosing texts, in REAP the system selects individualized practice readings from a digital library according to specific lexical constraints. Readings are chosen to contain vocabulary words that a given student needs to learn, while limiting the number of words the student does not know. The choice of texts is therefore driven by a curriculum model, informed by a student model, and constrained by the availability of suitable texts, as described by their text model.

While a user-adapted tool has the potential to better match individual needs, since each student can work with different texts, a drawback of this approach is that instructors may have difficulty coordinating group discussion about readings and integrating the tool into their curriculum. An advantage of a tool containing a search system, however, is that teachers can find texts that match the needs and interests of the class as a whole. While some degree of individualization is lost, the advantages of better coordinated support from teachers and classroom integration are gained. In the early stages of this project, we had planned to use REAP software after adapting it to handle the complex morphology of MSA. Unfortunately, while the system was already being tested in the field, REAP project leaders did not consider the code base mature enough to be released to other research groups. As a result, we chose to develop our own database and access method to texts, foregoing adaptation to individual users.

4 Challenges of Arabic reading

It has never been an easy transition from 'learning to read' to 'reading to learn' for Arabs and other Arabic learners. In Meynet (1971) and according to father Anastase Al-Karmali, a member of the Arabic Language Academy in Cairo, Egypt. "The Arabs study the rules of the Arabic language in order to learn to read, whereas others read in order to learn …". Indeed, reading in Arabic as a first or second language presents special challenges due to its script and its rich and complex morphology. Also, Arabic texts lack short vowels and other diacritics that distinguish words and grammatical functions. These linguistic complexities result in significant reading difficulties. Typically, Arabic as a second language learners face difficulties in word recognition, word disambiguation and the acquisition of decoding skills, including recognizing letter and word boundaries, decoding unvocalized words and identifying these words. In order to understand Arabic text, the novice reader must learn to insert short vowels and other diacritics based on grammatical rules not yet learned. The ambiguity associated with a lack of diacritization is shown for instance in the lemma علم /Elm/ which has the following nine possible reading interpretations shown in Table 1.

عِلْم	'Science, learning'
عَلَم	'flag'
عَلِمَ	3rd P. Masc. Sing. Perf. V. (MSA V. I) 'he learned/knew'
عُلِمَ	3rd P. Sing. Pass. V. (MSA V. I) 'it/he was learned'
عَلَّمَ	Intensifying, Caus. V. (MSA V. II) 'he taught
عَلَّمَ	Causative V. Pass (MSA V. II) 'he was taught'
عِلْمٌ/عِلْمُ	(NOM Noun + Definite and Indefinite)
عِلْمَ	(ACCU Noun + Definite)
عِلْمِ/عِلْمٍ	(GEN Noun + Definite and Indefinite)

Table 1. Various interpretations for the lemma علم

5 The Arabic reading enhancement tools

To address these challenges, we developed an Arabic Reading Enhancement Tool (ARET) for classroom use with support from the U.S. Department of Education's International Research Study Program (IRS). The ARET tool is rather similar in intent to the foreign language learning tool, GLOSSER-RuG built by Nerbonne and Smit (1996) for Dutch, but targets explicitly the particularities of MSA. ARET has two subparts tools : the Arabic Reading Facilitation Tool (ARFT) and the Arabic Reading Assessment Tool (ARAT). A major achievement of this project was to create a collection of fully annotated texts for learners of Arabic, using materials included in an authoritative textbook series that spans several competence levels. In this section, we describe the creation, structure and content of the Arabic corpus/lexicon database, and then describe the ARFT and ARAT tools in more detail.

5.1 The Al-Kitaab corpus database

The ARET system uses the full text of Arabic reading passages from the Georgetown University Press *Al-Kitaab* textbook series, which represents a 60,000 word corpus. Each passage was submitted to a combined automatic/manual annotation process in order to create a version of the text that was completely diacritized and thoroughly segmented and labeled to identify all morphemes for each word, including their part-of-speech labels and English glosses.

We first applied the Standard Arabic Morphological Analyzer (SAMA) (Maamouri et al., 2010), to enumerate all possible solutions for each word token in a given passage. The entire passage, with the full set of possible SAMA solutions for each word token, was then presented to a native Arabic speaker experienced in the morphological analysis of MSA, and their task was to select the particular SAMA solution for each word based on their understanding of the context; where necessary, the annotator would manually edit the details of POS tags or glosses to fill gaps in SAMA's coverage of the vocabulary. This is a standard approach used in the annotation of numerous Arabic text corpora, including the Arabic Treebank Project (Maamouri and Bies 2004). As described in section 5.2, the resulting annotation was fully reviewed by expert Arabic linguists using our reading facilitation tool, to identify and repair errors.

A relational database was created to store the corpus and annotations. Separate tables were used to enumerate (a) the reading passages (keeping track of the book volume, chapter and page number of each passage), (b) the sequence of sentences in each passage, (c) the word token sequence for each sentence, (d) the inventory of distinct word types (i.e. orthographic word forms with their context-dependant analyses), and (e) the inventory of distinct "headwords" (lemmas) and affix morphemes (clitics).

Using this relational table structure, a full passage could be assembled for display by querying for the sequence of sentences and the word tokens for each sentence. The information returned by the query could include, for each word token, the original and/or diacritized spelling, and an index for looking up the context-dependent morphological analysis plus gloss for the token. This in turn also provided access to a dictionary entry for the lemma from which the token was derived. Table 2 summarizes the contents of the database. The number of distinct lemmas refers to the number of citation forms for content words (nouns, verbs, etc) that are referenced by the all the inflected stems found in the reading texts; the number of glossary entries refers to the manually edited dictionary descriptions for lemmas / citation forms, including their consonantal roots. In cases where a lemma does not have a corresponding glossary entry, the fully-detailed morphological analysis provides an English gloss (but not the root) for each word token containing the lemma.

Type	**No. of Entries**
Sentences, titles and sub-headings	3,692
Arabic word tokens	53,411
Distinct undiacritized Arabic orthographic forms	17,209
Distinct diacritized orthographic forms	20,725
Distinct morphology/POS/gloss annotations on word forms	22,304
Distinct clitic and inflected-stem morphemes	16,774
Distinct lemmas	6,829
Glossary entries for lemmas	3,436

Table 2. Corpus quantities in ARET database

5.2 The Arabic reading facilitation tool

The Arabic Reading Facilitation Tool (ARFT) provides the user with direct access to the *Al-Kitaab* text corpus, organized by volume, chapter and page number. In addition to presenting the full text for a given passage, the user can click on any word in the passage to bring up in a side-bar the full morphological analysis and gloss for the word in that context, along with a glossary entry for the associated lemma, and a summary of other Arabic citation forms that are related by root. Two other important functions are also provided: (a) toggling the presence vs. absence of all diacritic marks in the full display of the reading passage, and (b) the ability to view a concordance of all occurrences for any selected word. The tool also provides a "tool-tip" pop-up window whenever the mouse cursor hovers over an Arabic word in the text passage; if the page is showing undiacritized text, the pop-up shows the diacritized form of the word, and vice-versa. This is a very useful feature for the new learners of the Arabic language.

As soon as the annotated version of the corpus was loaded into the database, there was a sustained effort involving native Arabic speakers and Arabic faculty to carefully review the database content, as displayed by the ARFT, and validate it against the original textbook content. This effort involved numerous repairs of all sorts that stemmed from all stages of corpus preparation: typing mistakes from the original keyboarding of the text, problems in morphological annotation, and difficulties in the loading of the tables. Customized tools and procedures were developed to facilitate the updates that were needed to apply all the corrections directly to the database.

A glossary for use in the ARFT was added to the database, with the relational linkage needed to support glossary lookups triggered by the user clicking on any word in a text passage. The word-to-glossary relation is based on the "lemma_ID" of the stem in each word. The lemma_ID is a string identifier assigned by the Standard Arabic Morphological Analyzer (SAMA), which was used for the morphological annotation of the entire corpus; all verbs in a given conjugation paradigm share the same lemma_ID, as do all nouns or adjectives in a given declensional (case) paradigm, so every distinct inflected form of a noun, adjective or verb is linked by the annotation to its corresponding glossary entry. The glossary table (with indexing by Semitic root) was a special, additional annotation specifically for ARFT, so not all lemmas were covered in the glossary; when a term not in the glossary is clicked, the side-bar display area in the ARFT shows the message "Refer to Morphology Information"; the morphology information is the full set of annotation data for each word based on SAMA, and this always includes an English gloss for the stem (except in the case of proper nouns, which always have "Proper Noun" as their part-of-speech label).

The ARFT is intended for use with a modern web browser over a reasonably fast internet connection. The tool has a flexible and intuitive web interface to navigate the texts via several key features:

1. Source Panel, featuring *Al-Kitaab* text
2. Highlighted Sentence
3. Highlighted Word
4. Audio Player for highlighted sentence
5. Audio Player for highlighted word
6. Morphological Data Panel
7. Lexical Data Panel
8. Tabbed browsing for convenient access to multiple screens

Figure 1. below illustrates an example of the tool using a passage of text from Al-Kitab Volume 2, Page 61.

Figure 1. Arabic Reading Facilitation Tool featuring function labels

5.3 The Text to speech module

An Arabic Text-to-Speech technology module was licensed from RDI[1]. This technology has been used to add an audio feature to the ARFT, and can be used to render audio of arbitrary Arabic text. So the users will be able to listen to individual words or passages of text spoken by a high quality synthesized voice. The RDI module, reads text files or literal text in Windows Arabic encoding and generates WAV audio data either as files or for direct output to an audio device. It has a C++ API that may be employed in Microsoft Visual Studio. The voice rendering quality is excellent. Moreover, the module analyzes diacritized or undiacritized Arabic text to determine pronunciation, rhythm and inflection of speech. Many variables of speech production can be controlled, most significantly the gender of the speaker. We developed a simple console-based executable that reads a list of Arabic text files and generates a WAV file of speech corresponding to each one, using a male voice, female voice, or one of each.

5.4 The Arabic Reading Assessment Tool (ARAT)

In order to support the creation of tests and quizzes for specific Arabic reading skills the Arabic Reading Assessment Tool (ARAT) has been built around an existing open-source web application framework called Moodle (http://moodle.org). This framework was developed as a "Content Management System", and provides built-in support for many of the 'infrastructure' functions that ARAT would need, including: registration of faculty and student user accounts; creation of courses with schedule plans and content-based resources; creation, presentation and scoring of tests and quizzes; and overall record-keeping of resources, activities and test scores. Custom software modules were developed to augment the Moodle code base in order to provide functions that are specific to the ARAT:

- communicating with and importing data from the annotated *Al-Kitaab* passage database;
- defining specialized question types (the first three types described below) based on annotations in the database, such that answers to the questions can be scored automatically by reference to the corpus annotations.

The three types of annotation-based questions were defined and implemented in the prototype ARAT:

- Cloze-Test Question: given a reading passage in Arabic, one or more words are chosen as test items and are replaced in the text by an underlined empty slot; the student is given a multiple-choice question to identify the correct Arabic word to fill each slot.
- English Gloss Question: given a reading passage, one or more words are chosen as test items and highlighted in the text; the student is given a mul-

[1]<http://www.rdi-eg.com/Technologies/speech.htm>

tiple-choice question to identify the correct English gloss for each test word.

- Case-Ending Question: given reading passage, one or more nouns and/or adjectives are chosen as test items and highlighted in the text; the student is given a multiple-choice question of the six possible cases in Arabic to identify the correct case ending for each test word. Mood ending could also be considered for verbs.
- Yes/No questions: these are fully developed by teachers, who must enter questions and answers into the program in order to have Moodle give the student/teacher the appropriate final scores and correct answers feedback.

The implementation allows an instructor to select what text passage to use for a given quiz, and also allows for either manual and automatic selection of words to use as test items from the text, as well as either manual or automatic selection of distractor items for the Cloze and Gloss tests. By providing automatic selection of test items and distractors based on available annotations in the corpus database, ARAT allows a student to practice each task any number of times on a given text passage, be challenged by novel questions on each attempt, and receive a tally of right and wrong answers, without the instructor having to create or score each attempt as shown in Figure 2.

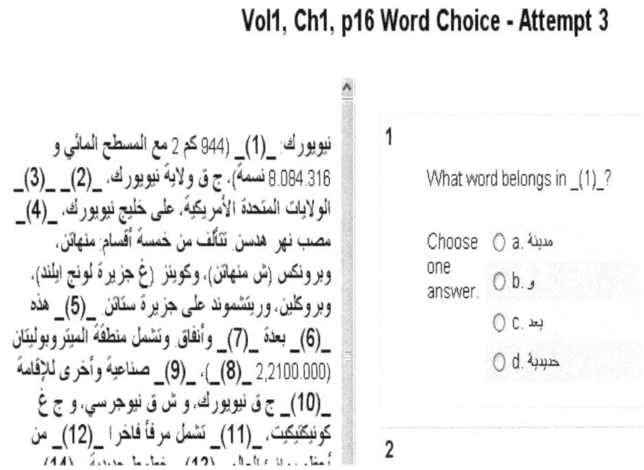

Figure 2. A sample question created with ARAT

5.5 The test set creation procedure

The procedure for creating a test set within ARAT breaks down to the following 'top-level' steps:

1. Provide or select a text passage to be used as the source from which test questions are derived.

2. For questions that will be based on specific word tokens in the text, identify the tokens that will be basis for test questions; these token-specific questions will always involve a particular task with a multiple-choice response, so for each selected token: select the task (word choice, gloss choice, case-ending), identify a correct answer and provide or select a set of three distractors.

3. For questions not based on specific tokens, the instructor must supply the following: prompting text for the question, the type of response (y/n, t/f, type-in, multiple choice) and the correct answer (and three distractors for multiple choice). Figure 3 shows the test set main screen.

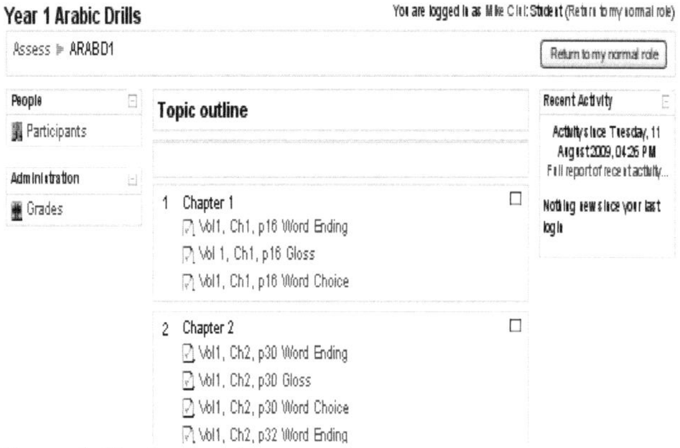

Figure 3. Test set main screen.

6 Classroom usage and tool evaluation

The ARFT was presented to Arabic faculty at the University of Pennsylvania; the tool was announced in Arabic courses and students were asked to use it. Several lists of student enrollments for many Arabic courses have been imported into the Moodle-based system.

An informal evaluation was also performed, in the Summer of 2010, with Arabic instructors teaching in the ARAbic and North African Studies (ARANAS) program at Al Akhawayn University, in Ifrane, Morocco. Unfortunately, due to the very rushed schedule and time pressure that instructors work under during this intensive program, the tools did not receive the desired attention. Only a handful of instructors actually explored the tools. Two instructors filled out an evaluation questionnaire concerning various aspects of the tools and their use of computer technology for language teaching in general. The feedback was generally positive and included some detailed suggestion for improving the tools; they also revealed some issues with inconsistent response time (partly due to the network infrastructure of the university at that time) and ease of use (for non technology-savy instructors). The biggest obstacles to using the tools, however, appeared to be lack of time on the part of the instructors to acquire sufficient familiarity with the tools and devise effective ways of introducing them in the curriculum. We are investigating the possibility of using the tools with exchange students during the regular academic year, even though the numbers in Arabic classes at all levels is much lower than in the Summer program.

Recently, the use of the ARFT and its companion the ARAT has been mandated by the Arabic Section at the University of Pennsylvania and we hope that a more consistent use is going to be made. As of now, 118 students are registered representing four 1st Year classes (total: 63 students), two 2nd Year classes (total:3 students), one 3rd Year class (total: 13 students) and One 4th Year class (11students).At this point, the tool impact on the classroom has not been evaluated, but it is in our future plans to do a comprehensive classroom evaluation of the tool.

As part of the effort to introduce the ARFT and the ARAT to faculty, we obtained three short reading passage texts, totaling 1022 Arabic word tokens, selected by a faculty member from news sources. These were submitted to annotation to disambiguate and diacritize the content based on SAMA analysis, just as was done for the *Al-Kitaab* passages. The annotated texts have been added into the database corpus and are available for use in the ARAT, but are not accessible for general browsing via the ARFT. The annotation and database import went quickly, demonstrating that these procedures have matured, and providing resources for building quizzes and tests based on materials that are 'unseen' by students who use both the ARFT and the ARAT.

7 Conclusion

We have described computational tools and linguistic resources that enable students to enhance their Arabic reading skills by helping them with the difficulties they face in word recognition, word disambiguation and general decoding skills during the Arabic reading process. These computational tools and resources provide the needed correct and meaningful vocalizations by using natural language processing (NLP) technologies namely a Standard Arabic Morphological Analyzer (SAMA), a concordance, a Text-to-Speech module and various interfaces. The time gained by students who use our Reading Enhancement Tools could be put to good use in the current ASL (Arabic as a Second Language) classroom which, following the ACTFL proficiency movement puts a primary emphasis on communication with less concern for accuracy as reflected in morphology or syntax, particularly at the initial stages of ASL learning. We reiterate at this point that our choice of the GUP *Al-Kitaab* textbook series was not fortuitous. We could have chosen any other pedagogical text but Al-Kitaab distinguishes itself by being widely used in the United States and abroad, and providing an extensive curriculum with a wide variety of texts. We are thankful that GUP gave us permission to use this resource, as it enabled us to create a tool that can accompany many English-speaking students studying MSA in many classrooms around the world.

In addition to answering learners' reading needs in MSA, our efforts went beyond the specificities of this language by allowing us to demonstrate that our tools and the methodology we followed was in fact 'portable' to other languages which had a morphologically complex nature such as, for instance, the Nahuatl Learning Environment (NLE) project based on the ARET infrastructure [2]. Future efforts will continue experimentation of the use of available and robust Arabic NLP technologies to extend the enhancement of Arabic reading to better understanding of authentic reading text that the reader could download from the Internet for instance. Progress in that direction is desirable and possible because it would increase the motivation of Modern Standard Arabic learners and will boost access by students and other professionals to authentic real world language text in new genres and topics. In this way, the contribution of NLP tech-

[2] The Nahuatl learning tool project prepared by Jonathan Amith (n.d) and a team of Nahuatl speakers can be accessed online through a Beta version of the Nahuatl Learning Environment at the LDC : http://nahuatl.ldc.upenn.edu/.

nologies to the teaching and learning of languages may become more significant and more compelling to all concerned, teachers, learners and computer NLP specialists alike.

Acknowledgements

We gratefully acknowledge the sponsorship of the U.S. Department of Education, whose International Research Study (IRS) Grant No. P017A050040-07-05 supported our work on this project. The views, opinions and/or findings contained in this article are those of the authors and should not be interpreted as representing the official views or policies, either expressed or implied, of the U.S. Department of Education's International Research Study program. We also acknowledge the help and support of Georgetown University Press who allowed us to use their Al-Kitaab series as a testing ground for our tools. Thanks and appreciation go Professor Roger Allen and his team of Arabic teachers at the University of Pennsylvania for their warm reception of our tools in their teaching structure. Thanks go finally, to all the programmers and annotators who worked on the project. They are numerous and we cannot give them all the credit they deserve but without them our achievement would not have been so significant.

References

Mahmoud Al-Batal, Kristen Brustad & Abbas Al-Tonsi. 2006. *Al-Kitaab fii tacallum al-cArabiyya*, Volume II (with DVDs, Second Edition).Washington, D.C.: Georgetown University Press, 2006.

Mahmoud Al-Batal, Kristen Brustad & Abbas Al-Tonsi. 2004. *Al-Kitaab fii tacallum al-cArabiyya*, A Textbook for Beginning Arabic, Volume I (with DVDs, Second Edition). Washington, D.C.: Georgetown University Press, 2004.

Mahmoud Al-Batal, Kristen Brustad & Abbas Al-Tonsi. 2001. *Al-Kitaab fii tacallum al-cArabiyya*,Volume III.Washington, D.C.: Georgetown University Press, 2001.

Jonathan Amith. n.d. *Nahuatl Learning Environment.* Available online at : http://nahuatl.ldc.upenn.edu/.

Jon Brown and Maxine Eskenazi. 2004. Retrieval of authentic documents for reader-specific lexical practice. In *Proceedings of* InSTIL/ICALL Symposium 2004. Venice, Italy.

Tsuo-Lin Chiu, Hsien-Chin Liou and Yuli Yeha. 2007. A study of web-based oral activities enhanced byautomatic speech recognition for EFL college learning. Computer Assisted Language Learning, 20 (3), 209–233.

Michael Heilman, Kevyn Collins-Thompson, Jamie Callan, and Maxine Eskenazi. 2006. Classroom success of an Intelligent Tutoring System for lexical practice and reading comprehension. In *Proceedings of* the Ninth International Conference on Spoken LanguageProcessing. Pittsburgh, PA.

Mohamed Maamouri, David Graff, Basma Bouziri, Sondos Krouna, Ann Bies and Seth Kulick. 2010. Standard Arabic Morphological Analyzer (SAMA) Version 3.1. Linguistic Data Consortium, Catalog No.: LDC2010L01.

Mohamed Maamouri and Ann Bies. 2004. Developing an Arabic Treebank: Methods, Guidelines, Procedures, and Tools. In *Proceedings of* the Workshop Computational Approaches to Arabic Script-based Languages. Pages 2-9./20th International Conference on Computational Linguistics/. COLING Geneva, Switzerland.

Detmar Meurers, Ramon Ziai, Luiz Amaral, Adriane Boyd, Aleksandar Dimitrov, Vanessa Metcalf, Niels Ott. 2010. Enhancing Authentic Web Pages for Language Learners. In *Proceedings of* the 5th Workshop on Innovative Use of NLP for Building Educational Applications, NAACL-HLT 2010, Los Angeles.

Roland Meynet. 1971. *L'écriture arabe en question: les projets de l'Académie de Langue Arabe du Caire de 1938 à 1968*.Beirut: Dar el-Machreq, 1971. 142 pp

Eleni Miltsakaki and Audrey Troutt. 2007. Read-X: Automatic Evaluation of Reading Difficulty of Web Text. In *Proceedings of* E-Learn 2007, sponsored by the Association for theAdvancement of Computing in Education. Quebec, Canada.

John Nerbonne and Petra Smit. 1996. GLOSSER-RuG: in Support of Reading. In *Proceedings of* the 16th International Conference on Computational Linguistics (COLING 1996).

Kathleen M. Sheehan, Irene Kostin, Yoko Futagi. 2007. SourceFinder: A Construct-Driven Approach for Locating Appropriately Targeted Reading Comprehension Source Texts. In *Proceedings of* the SLaTE Workshop on Speech and Language Technology in Education.Carnegie Mellon University and International Speech Communication Association (ISCA).

Li Wang. 2005. The advantages of using technology in second language education. T.H.E. Journal, 32 (10), 1-6.

Paige D. Ware. 2004. Confidence and competition online: ESL student perspectives on web based discussions in the classroom. Computers and Composition, 21, 451–468.

Yi Yuan. 2003. The use of chat rooms in an ESL setting. Computers and Composition, 20, 194–206.

Generating Diagnostic Multiple Choice Comprehension Cloze Questions

Jack Mostow and Hyeju Jang
Project LISTEN (www.cs.cmu.edu/~listen)
Carnegie Mellon University
RI-NSH 4103, 5000 Forbes Avenue
Pittsburgh, PA 15213-3890, USA
mostow@cs.cmu.edu, hyejuj@cs.cmu.edu

Abstract

This paper describes and evaluates DQGen, which automatically generates multiple choice cloze questions to test a child's comprehension while reading a given text. Unlike previous methods, it generates different types of distracters designed to diagnose different types of comprehension failure, and tests comprehension not only of an individual sentence but of the context that precedes it. We evaluate the quality of the overall questions and the individual distracters, according to 8 human judges blind to the correct answers and intended distracter types. The results, errors, and judges' comments reveal limitations and suggest how to address some of them.

1 Introduction

This paper presents an automated method to check a reader's comprehension of a given text while reading it, and to diagnose comprehension failures. In contrast to testing reading comprehension skill, for which there are published tests with well-established psychometric properties (e.g., Wiederholt & Bryant, 1992; Woodcock, 1998), testing comprehension during reading of a given text requires generating a test for that specific text.

A widely used solution is to replace some of the words with blanks for the student to fill, typically by selecting from multiple candidates. Such multiple choice fill-in-the-blank questions are called cloze questions. They are trivial to score because the correct answer is simply the original text word.

Cloze questions test the ability to decide which word is consistent with the surrounding context. Thus it taps the comprehension processes that judge various types of consistency, such as syntactic, semantic, and inter-sentential.

In a nutshell, these processes successively encode sentences, integrate them into an overall representation of meaning, notice gaps and inconsistencies, and repair them (see, e.g., Kintsch, 1993, 2005; van den Broek, Everson, Virtue, Sung, & Tzeng, 2002). The reader's resulting *situation model* represents "the content or microworld that the text is about" (Graesser & Bertus, 1998).

In this paper, we introduce DQGen (Diagnostic Question Generator), a system that uses natural language processing to generate diagnostic cloze questions that check the comprehension of someone reading a given text. DQGen differs from previous methods for generating cloze questions in that it is designed to minimize disruption to the reading process, and to diagnose different types of comprehension failure.

The intended application context that motivated the development of DQGen is an automated reading tutor that listens to children read aloud and helps them build their oral reading fluency (Mostow, 2008). Periodic comprehension checks should deter children from reading as fast as they can and ignoring what the text means. When the child answers incorrectly, the wrong answers should provide clues to why they are wrong.

The rest of this article is organized as follows. Section 2 describes the generated questions. Section 3 describes how DQGen generates distracters. Section 4 reports a pilot evaluation of it. Section 5 analyzes errors. Section 6 relates DQGen to prior work. Section 7 concludes.

2 Form of Generated Cloze Questions

Generating cloze questions requires deciding:

1. Which sentences to make cloze questions?
2. Which words to delete from them?
3. How many distracters to provide for them?
4. What types of distracters?

To illustrate the results of DQGen's decisions, Figure 1 shows one of the better questions it generated:

> *Some of those cells patrol your body. They are hungry, and they eat germs! Some stop the trouble germs make. Others make antibodies. They stick to germs. That helps your body find and kill _____ .*
>
> *a) are*
> *b) intestines*
> *c) terrorists*
> *d) germs*

Figure 1. An example of a generated question

The four decisions enumerated above involve tradeoffs among preserving the flow of reading, encouraging comprehension, and assessing it accurately. As this example illustrates, DQGen inserts cloze questions as comprehension checks at the end of paragraphs, where there are natural breaks, in order to minimize disruption to the flow of reading. If the last sentence is shorter than four words or DQGen fails to find an acceptable distracter of each type, it simply leaves the last sentence unchanged rather than turn it into a bad cloze question.

DQGen deletes the last word of the sentence, in order to allow normal reading up till that point and thereby minimize disruption to the flow of reading. Deleting a word earlier in the sentence would force the reader to skip the deleted word and read ahead to answer the cloze question. Indeed, a review of of comprehension assessments (Pearson & Hamm, 2005) indicates that end-of-sentence multiple choice cloze questions are widely used: "Delete words at the end of sentences and provide a set of choices from which examinees are to pick the best answer (this tack is employed in several standardized tests, including the Stanford Diagnostic Reading Test and the Degrees of Reading Power)."

The number of distracters involves a tradeoff. On the one hand, the more distracters, the less chance of lucky guesses, and the more types of distracters possible. On the other hand, offering more distracters lengthens the disruption to the flow of reading and raises the cognitive load on the reader to remember the paragraph when reading the distracters. As a compromise, DQGen adds three distracters, for a total of four choices to present in randomized order – typical for multiple choice questions on educational tests for children.

DQGen uses three types of distracters. Each type of distracter indicates a different type of comprehension failure when chosen incorrectly by the reader as the answer. By aggregating children's performance over questions with these same three types of distracters, we hope not only to test their comprehension, but to profile the difficulties encountered by a given child or posed by a given text.

2.1 Ungrammatical distracters

The first and presumably easiest type of distracter renders the completed sentence ungrammatical. Syntactic processing is part of comprehension but not necessarily well-developed in children. Analysis of children's responses to 69,000 multiple cloze questions automatically generated, presented, and scored by the Reading Tutor (Mostow et al., 2004) found that children's performance decreased as the number of distracters with the same part of speech as the correct answer increased. However, this effect was weaker for lower-level readers, indicating less sensitivity to syntax (Hensler & Beck, 2006). Choosing an ungrammatical distracter indicates failure to detect a syntactic inconsistency. The ungrammatical distracter, e.g., *are* in Figure 1, has a different part of speech (POS) than the correct answer *germs*.

2.2 Nonsensical distracters

The second type of distracter makes the completed sentence grammatical but nonsensical. Choosing a nonsensical distracter indicates failure to detect a local semantic inconsistency with the rest of the sentence. The nonsensical distracter has the same

	Ungrammatical	Nonsensical	Plausible
Source of candidates	Other words in paragraph	List of words at grade level up to 4	Matching Google N-grams
Same as correct answer?	No	No	No (94.96%)
Related to words earlier in paragraph?	–	–	No (lowest score)
Related to words earlier in sentence?	–	–	Yes (55.77%)
Contains a space?	–No	No (100%)	–No
Frequent enough for children to know?	–Yes	–Yes	Yes (96.15%)
Passes grammar checker?	No (65.48%)	Yes (52.62%)	Yes (92.31%)*
Same POS as answer?	–No	Yes (26.67%)	–
Matches a Google N-gram?	No (95.83%)	No (91.67%)	–Yes

Table 1. Sources and constraints for each distracter type, in order tested (with % satisfied in pilot data). Constraints guaranteed to be satisfied or violated without explicit testing are marked –Yes or –No.
* We added this test after the pilot evaluation because Google N-grams aren't always grammatical.

POS as the correct answer, but plugging it into the sentence forms a context not found in the Google N-grams corpus. For example, the nonsensical distracter in Figure 1 is *intestines*.

2.3 Plausible distracters

The third and hardest type of distracter makes the completed sentence meaningful in isolation but inconsistent with the preceding global context. This type of distracter is essential in testing inter-sentential processing, i.e. "understanding that reaches across sentences in a passage," because otherwise "an individual's ability to fill in cloze blanks does not depend on passage context" – a frequent criticism of cloze questions (Pearson & Hamm, 2005). A plausible distracter has the same POS as the correct answer, like a nonsensical distracter, but the sentence it forms when plugged into the blank sounds reasonable – in isolation. That is, it ends with an N-gram that occurs in the Google N-grams corpus. However, it doesn't make sense in the context of the preceding sentences, because the distracter is unrelated to the words in the preceding sentences. For example, *terrorists* in Figure 1 is a plausible distracter.

3 Generating and Filtering Distracters

DQGen uses generate-and-test to construct each type of distracter: it chooses randomly from a source of candidates and backtracks if the chosen candidate violates a constraint on that type of distracter. If none of the candidates that satisfy a constraint survive subsequent tests, DQGen drops the constraint and considers candidates that violate it. The source and constraints vary by distracter type (ungrammatical, nonsensical, plausible). Table 1 summarizes the tests and the order they are applied. Sections 3.1-3.3 discuss them in further detail.

3.1 Lexical constraints on distracters

Three constraints apply at the word level.

No spaces: We constrain all three types of distracters to be words rather than phrases. This constraint is guaranteed for paragraph words and Google N-grams, DQGen's respective sources of ungrammatical and plausible distracters. However, our source of nonsensical distracters is a table (Biemiller, 2009) that specifies the grade level not only of words but also of some phrases, such as *barbeque sauce*, which DQGen therefore filters out. Table 2 shows an excerpt from the table used.

Word	Meaning	Level	...
barbecue sauce	flavored sauce for meat	2	
intestines	guts	4	
intimate	close, friendly	10	
intimate	a close friend	10	

Table 2. Excerpt from Biemiller's (2009) table

Distinct: DQGen explicitly excludes the correct answer as a distracter. Other constraints on different types of distracters are mutually exclusive with each other. Consequently, no answer choice can appear twice.

Familiar: Distracters must be familiar to children. DQGen satisfies this constraint for ungrammatical and nonsensical distracters by choosing them from the paragraph and a grade-leveled word list (Biemiller, 2009), respectively. These sources suffice to provide candidates, but they are not comprehensive enough to test candidates from another source, such as the Google N-grams used to generate plausible distracters. To exclude words likely to be unfamiliar to children, DQGen filters out candidates whose unigram frequency falls below 5,000,000. We tuned this threshold by informal trial and error; higher thresholds proved too stringent to allow any distracters from the limited source of candidate plausible distracters.

3.2 Constraints on completed sentences

Three constraints pertain to making completed sentences sensible or not.

Grammatical: As Table 1 shows, all three types of distracters involve grammaticality constraints. Ungrammatical distracters must make the completed sentence ungrammatical, e.g., *That helps your body find and kill are*. In contrast, nonsensical and plausible distracters must make the completed sentence grammatical, e.g., *That helps your body find and kill terrorists.*

To check grammaticality of a completed sentence, we use the Link Grammar Parser (Sleator & Temperley, 1993), a syntactic dependency parser, as a grammar checker. As a grammar checker, the Link Grammar Parser usually accepts grammatical sentences and rejects ungrammatical ones, perhaps because sentences in children's text tend to be short. However, it sometimes fails to accept a grammatical sentence, as the last row of Table 3 illustrates.

sentence	grammatically	parser
The germs hide in food or people	correct	accepted
The germs hide in food or world	incorrect	rejected
So keep dirty hands away from cuts and your face.	correct	rejected

Table 3. Examples of grammar checking by parser

Part of speech: More than one POS may make a distracter grammatical. DQGen uses the Stanford POS Tagger (Toutanova, Klein, Manning, & Singer, 2003) to tag the correct answer and a candidate nonsensical distracter when used to complete the sentence, and requires them to have the same POS. This test is superfluous for ungrammatical distracters and unnecessary for plausible distracters.

Google N-gram: As a heuristic test of whether a completed sentence is plausible, we check whether its ending occurs in the Google N-grams corpus (Brants & Franz, 2006), which means that it appears at least 40 times on the Web. For ungrammatical and nonsensical distracters, the last 4 words of the completed sentence must not occur in this corpus. For plausible distracters, the last 4 words followed by "." must occur. To enforce this constraint, DQGen's source of candidate plausible distracters consists of Google 5-grams of the form *W X Y* __ . Here *W*, *X*, and *Y* are the words preceding the correct answer in the original sentence, e.g., *find and kill.* If there are fewer than 5 such 5-grams, DQGen allows 4-grams of the form *X Y* __ ., e.g. *and kill* __.

3.3 Relevance to context

Two constraints on distracters concern context.

Irrelevant to words earlier in paragraph: A plausible distracter should not be *too* plausible, so DQGen tries to ensure that it is unrelated to the earlier sentences and hence unlikely to make sense in context. We measure the relatedness of a distracter to words in the earlier sentences by how often it co-occurs with them *when used as in the last sentence*. DQGen therefore first pairs the candidate distracter, e.g. *terrorists*, with the last content word preceding the blank, e.g., *kill* in *That helps your body find and kill* ____. It then estimates the probability of these two words (*kill* and *terrorists*) co-occurring with the words in the earlier sentences of the paragraph, using a Naïve Bayes formula to score their relevance to that context:

$$\Pr(c,k \mid \vec{w}) \propto \Pr(c,k)\prod_{i=1}^{n}\Pr(w_i \mid c,k)$$

The formula omits $\Pr(\vec{w})$ because it's the same for all candidate plausible distracters for a given question. Here c is a candidate distracter (e.g., *terrorists*), k is the last content word before the blank (e.g., *kill*), $\vec{w}$ is a vector of the n content words earlier in the paragraph, and w_i is the ith such word.

Below are sample multiple-choice comprehension test items inserted in a text, for a student to answer while reading the text.
Each item consists of a paragraph ending in a fill-in-the-blank question, and 4 choices for how to fill in the blank.
For each item, please:

I. Score the completed sentence resulting from each choice as U, N, M, or C:
U: Ungrammatical
N: Nonsensical but grammatical
M: Meaningful but incorrect given the preceding text
C: Correct.

II. Please score the item overall as G, O, or B (assuming the student isn't guessing):
G: Good (answering requires understanding a central point of the text)
O: Ok (answering requires some level of understanding)
B: Bad (more than one correct answer, no correct answer, or deficient in some other way)

III. Please write any comments about a paragraph, cloze prompt, specific choice, or overall question next to it in the Comments column.

		Score:	Comments:
Sample question #1			
Has a cold ever gotten you down? That is no fun.			
Did your tummy ever feel twisted in _____ ?			
A)	freckles		
B)	knots		
C)	is		
D)	disgust		
Overall:			

Figure 2. Prompt for the pilot user test

DQGen scores $\Pr(w_i \mid c, k)$ based on how often word w_i co-occurs with words c and k in the same 30-word window in the British National Corpus (BNC).

The purpose of a plausible distracter is to detect failures of intersentential comprehension processes that monitor global consistency. As a heuristic to violate global consistency, DQGen picks distracters with the *lowest* relevance scores.

Relevant to words earlier in sentence: A plausible distracter should be relevant to the words earlier in the sentence. To score local relevance, DQGen uses a Naïve Bayes formula similar to its formula for global relevance:

$$\Pr(c \mid \vec{w}) \propto \Pr(c) \prod_{i=1}^{n} \Pr(w_i \mid c)$$

Here, c is a candidate distracter, $\vec{w}$ is a vector of the n content words earlier in the sentence, and w_i is the ith such word. DQGen estimates $\Pr(w_i \mid c)$ in the same way as before, but omits k because n is so much smaller for the sentence than for the paragraph context preceding it. DQGen averages these local coherence scores over the candidates, and allows only candidates whose local coherence scores are above the mean.

4 Pilot Study

How good are the generated questions? To evaluate DQGen, we asked human judges to score them. Section 4.1 explains how we evaluated questions, Section 4.2 reports inter-rater reliability, and Section 4.3 presents results.

4.1 Methodology

For the evaluation, we used DQGen to insert sample questions in an informational text for children, *The Germs*, which explains the concept of germs and their danger. Of the 18 paragraphs in this text, we rejected one because it was only two sentences long, and DQGen rejected another because the last sentence failed the grammar checker. For each of the other 16 paragraphs, DQGen generated a cloze question with ungrammatical and nonsensical distracters, but it found plausible distracters for only 13 of the questions, which we evaluated as follows.

We recruited eight human judges, members of our research team but unfamiliar with DQGen. We asked them to evaluate each question at two levels, using the form illustrated in Figure 2.

At the high level, we evaluated the overall quality of each question by asking judges to rate it as

Good, *OK*, or *Bad*. We report the percentage of generated questions rated by human judges as acceptable, defined as *Good* or *OK*. We used a 3-point scale rather than a finer-grained scale both to get higher inter-rater reliability, and because we were interested more in how many of the questions were acceptable than in precise ratings of quality.

At the low level, we evaluated how often DQGen generated the intended type of distracter. We asked the judges to categorize each of the multiple choices (correct answer plus 3 distracters) as *Ungrammatical*, *Nonsensical but grammatical*, *Meaningful but incorrect given the preceding text*, or *Correct*. To avoid biasing their responses, we did not tell them that each question was supposed to have one choice in each category.

To elicit additional feedback, the form invited judges to comment on the questions and distracters.

4.2 Inter-rater reliability

It is important to measure inter-rater reliability among human judges, especially on experimenter-designed measures such as the form we used.

The overall quality ratings involved ranked data from more than two judges, so to measure their inter-rater reliability we used Kendall's Coefficient of Concordance (Kendall & Smith, 1939). KCC for overall quality was .40 on a scale from 0 to 1. This low value reflects the considerable variation between the judges, whose average ratings of overall quality ranged from 1.3 to 2.6.

Categorization of each answer choice involved unranked data from more than two judges, so we used Fleiss' Kappa (Shrout & Fleiss, 1979) to measure its inter-rater reliability. Kappa was .58; a value of .4-.6 is considered moderate, .6-.8 substantial, and .8-1 outstanding (Landis & Koch, 1977). Figure 3 shows the Kappa values for each label by the judges.

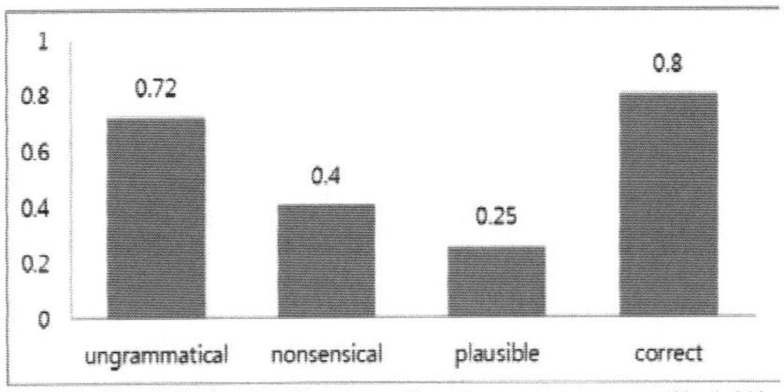

Figure 3. Fleiss's Kappa for inter-rater reliability of each type of choice

The low values of inter-rater reliability measures revealed the raters' lack of consensus, presumably due to differing interpretations of the instructions. For instance, one judge commented that instruction for rating the overall quality did not indicate whether a good question requires reading the preceding text. Another issue was missing and multiple categorical responses.

Evidently we need to specify our rating criteria more clearly, both for overall quality and for individual components, especially nonsensical and plausible distracters. A worked-out example might help judges understand each type better, but must avoid phrasing biased toward how DQGen works.

4.3 Results

We computed average ratings of overall quality and agreement with the intended category of each answer choice.

We averaged all the ratings of overall quality after converting *Bad*, *OK*, and *Good* ratings into 1, 2, and 3, respectively. Overall quality ratings averaged 2.04, which corresponds to *OK*. For agreement of judges with the intended category of each answer choice, Cohen's Kappa was .60. Note that in contrast to Section 4.2, where we used Kappa to measure inter-rater reliability, i.e., how well the judges agreed with each other on overall question quality, here we use Kappa to measure distracter quality, i.e., how well the judges agreed with DQGen on the intended type of answer choices.

Individual judges ranged from 63% to 79% agreement with the intended answer (Cohen's Kappa .51 to .72). As Figure 4 shows, agreement was stronger for correct answers and ungrammatical distracters than for nonsensical and plausible distracters. On average, judges rated 94% of the correct answers as correct and agreed with DQGen's intended distracter type for 91% of the ungrammatical distracters, 63% of the nonsensical distracters, and only 32% of the plausible distracters. Apparently correct answers are obviously right and ungrammatical answers are obviously wrong, but nonsensical and plausible distracters are harder to classify.

5 Analysis of errors

We now discuss issues revealed by errors and judges' comments, and how to address them.

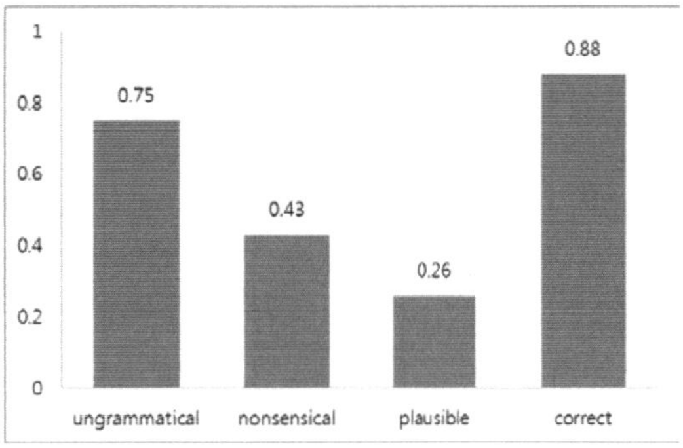

Figure 4. Cohen's Kappa for agreement with the intended type of each choice

5.1 Dependence on preceding text

The judges' most frequent comment about the quality of a question was that answering it did not require reading the preceding text. The judges rated only 32% of the intended plausible distracters as plausible. Evidently we need to identify further constraints on plausible distracters. We may also need to identify constraints on sentences where plausible distracters exist for the correct answer.

5.2 Idioms

Answer choices, whether correct answers or distracters, are problematic when they form idioms such as *twisted in knots* or *make do*. For instance, one pilot cloze question ended with *twisted in* ____, where the correct answer was *knots*. Another question ended with *get your body to make* ____, with *do* as a supposedly ungrammatical distracter.

Idioms pose multiple problems, although we found only two cases in our small pilot study. First, we want to test comprehension of the paragraph, not just knowledge of specific idioms. Second, the word that completes an idiom can be far likelier than any other choice, making it too easy to guess based solely on local context, whether correct or not. Third, because idioms have non-componential semantics, the missing word is liable to be semantically unrelated to other sentence words, causing DQGen to badly underestimate its local relevance.

Detecting idioms automatically is a research problem in its own right (Li, Roth, & Sporleder, 2010; Li & Sporleder, 2009). We might be able to recognize idioms by using the fact that its N-gram frequency is much higher than expected based on the frequency of its individual words. A simpler approach is to consult a dictionary of common phrases. Either approach would require extension to handle parameterized idioms such as *a chip on [someone's] shoulder*, or non-contiguous forms such as *Actions do in fact speak louder than words*.

5.3 Lexical issues for distracters

The pilot study exposed a number of issues affecting the suitability of words as distracters.

Same-root words

DQGen ensures that answer choices are distinct. However, one question included two forms of the same word as choices, namely *throats* as the correct answer and *throat* as a plausible distracter. We need to ensure that answer choices are not only distinct but dissimilar, unless we want questions that focus on minor differences between them.

Common verbs and modal verbs

One judge commented that we might want to avoid common verbs as distracters, such as any form of *be*, *do*, *have*, and *get*, and modal verbs, such as *can*, *cannot*, and *will*, lest children notice that they are seldom the correct answer, and therefore eliminate them without considering them. Accordingly, we plan to filter out common verbs and modal verbs.

Word difficulty

The same judge considered some words too difficult for children, such as *gauge* and *roast*. Actually, Biemiller (2009) rates noun senses of these words at grade 2, but the verb sense of *gauge* as *estimate* at grade 10. These examples illustrate a limitation of DQGen's methods to pick familiar words as distracters. It picks ungrammatical distracters from the words in the paragraph, nonsensical distracters from Biemiller's word list, and plausible distracters from Google N-grams, filtered by unigram frequency to avoid rare words. In all three cases, DQGen constrains words rather than word senses.

A more sophisticated approach would determine a distracter's word sense, or at least POS, when used to complete the sentence, and rate the familiarity of its specific sense or POS. Tagging the distracter POS is easier than determining its word sense(s) when inserted in the sentence. Rating the familiarity of different word senses would require either a grade-leveled list of them like Biemiller's (2009), or a resource with information about the frequency of different word senses or POS.

6 Relation to Prior Work

How does this research relate to previous work? There has been considerable research on automatic generation of multiple choice cloze questions to test vocabulary, grammar, and comprehension. Although these types of questions differ in purpose, they have much in common when it comes to generating them automatically.

6.1 Vocabulary and grammar cloze questions

A multiple choice cloze question to test vocabulary and grammar is constructed from a sentence selected from a corpus by deleting part of it (typically the target vocabulary word) and selecting distracters for it.

Selecting distracters with the same POS and approximate frequency as the answer word is a common strategy (Brown, Frishkoff, & Eskenazi, 2005; Coniam, 1997; Liu, Wang, & Gao, 2005).

Besides matching the correct answer's POS and frequency, Liu et al. (2005) added a culture-dependent strategy for generating distracters: choose English words with semantically similar translations in the learner's native language to the translation of the answer word.

Correia et al. (2010) generated vocabulary questions for Portuguese with three types of distracters. One type of distracter had the same POS and word level as the target word, based on its unigram frequency in Portuguese textbooks used in different grades. A second type had the lowest Levenshtein distance to the target out of all words with its POS. A third type was misspellings of the target word using a table of common spelling mistakes. Aldabe et al. (2007) also included students' common mistakes as candidate distracters.

Some work also used semantic similarity between a distracter and the answer word to choose distracters. Pino et al. (2008) selected distracters that made the completed sentence grammatical and tended to co-occur with the words in the sentence, but were semantically distant from the target word as measured by WordNet. In constrast, Smith et al. (2008) looked for distracters semantically similar to the answer word based on distributional similarity. In addition, Sumita et al. (2005) used a thesaurus for the same purpose, and then consulted the web to filter out plausible distracters.

Aldabe et al. (2009) considered context in a question sentence when choosing distracters. They used an n-gram language model to predict the probability of occurrence of a distracter with its preceding words.

Gates et al. (2011) generated phrase-type distracters, unlike other work. They generated questions from a dictionary definition of the target vocabulary word. Rather than delete the target word, they parsed the definition, deleted a phrase from it, and chose distracters with the same syntactic phrase type from definitions of other words, filtered to exclude synonyms of the target word.

6.2 Comprehension cloze questions

In contrast to vocabulary and grammar questions constructed from isolated sentences, DQGen's comprehension questions are for (and inserted into) connected text.

The most closely related work was by Mostow et al. (2004). Their Reading Tutor dynamically generated multiple choice cloze questions to test children's comprehension of randomly chosen sentences while reading a story. It randomly chose an approximate level of difficulty ('sight', 'easy', 'hard', and 'defined') for which word to delete from the sentence, and which words to choose randomly from the same story as distracters.

Goto et al. (2010) also generated questions from texts. They used a training corpus of existing cloze questions to learn how to select sentences to turn into cloze questions, words to delete, and types of distracters distinguished by their relation to the answer word: inflectional (e.g., *ask* → *asked*); derivational (e.g., *work* → *worker*); orthographic (e.g., *circulation* → *circumcision*); and semantic (e.g., synonyms and antonyms).

Aldabe et al. (2010) generated questions for learners' assessment in the science domain. To generate distracters, they measured semantic similarity by using Latent Semantic Analysis (LSA) and additional information such as semantic relationships between words. Experts discarded distracters that could form a correct answer.

DQGen differs from prior work on generating cloze questions for vocabulary and comprehension in two key respects. First, each question it generates has multiple types of distracters designed to detect different types of comprehension failure. Second, to generate plausible distracters it considers their relation not only to the clozed sentence but to the entire paragraph that contains it.

7 Conclusion

We conclude by summarizing contributions, limitations, and future work.

7.1 Contributions

This paper describes a method for generating multiple choice cloze questions to test students' comprehension while reading. Unlike previous methods, some of which also generate multiple types of distracters, DQGen's distracter types are diagnostic. It generates ungrammatical, nonsensical, and plausible distracters in order to detect failures of syntactic, semantic, and intersentential processing, respectively. Unlike prior methods, which test comprehension only of individual sentences, DQGen's plausible distracters take their preceding context into account.

We observed that candidate plausible distracters with high relevance scores tend to be surprisingly sensible answers – even though the formula doesn't "know" the correct answer or even the ungrammatical and nonsensical distracters. That is, grammaticality, N-grams, and a simple relevance measure often suffice to produce intelligent answers to a cloze question despite their shallow representation of the meaning of the paragraph – that is, without really understanding it. This finding is surprising insofar as one would expect good performance on such questions to require a deep representation such as the situation model constructed by human readers.

7.2 Limitations

Besides describing DQGen's design and implementation, we report on an evaluation of 13 generated questions by eight human judges blind to correct answer and intended distracter type. On average they rated overall question quality OK, but with a wide range from the least to most favorable judge. They agreed well with DGQen in classifying answers as ungrammatical or correct, but not as nonsensical or plausible. They criticized many questions as answerable without reading the text.

7.3 Future work

Our analysis of errors and judges' comments revealed several limitations and suggested ways to address some of them. In addition to identifying further constraints on plausible distracters, we need to identify constraints on good sentences to turn into end-of-paragraph cloze questions, beyond just the ability to generate a distracter of each type. One criterion is reliability: how well does performance on a question correlate with performance on other questions about the same text? Another criterion is informativeness: what do wrong answers reveal about comprehension?

Besides improving DQGen, we need to test it on more stories (both narrative fiction and informational text) and readers (especially children, our target population) to expose additional problems and avoid overfitting their solutions.

One possible use of DQGen is machine-assisted generation of comprehension questions, or more precisely, human-assisted machine generation, for example with the human vetting or selecting among candidate questions generated automatically, thereby reducing the amount of human effort currently required to compose comprehension questions, and producing them more systematically.

Success in getting DQGen to produce cloze questions on a large scale would have useful applications. Periodic comprehension checks should deter children from reading as fast as they can and ignoring what the text means. Diagnostic feedback based on incorrect answers should shed light on the nature of their comprehension failures and may be valuable as feedback to teachers or as guidance to the reading tutor.

Another use for large numbers of automatically generated cloze questions is to develop methods to monitor reading comprehension unobtrusively. Student responses to cloze questions could provide automated labels for data collected while they read the preceding text. Such data could include oral reading (Zhang, Mostow, & Beck, 2007) or even EEG (Mostow, Chang, & Nelson, 2011). Models trained and tested on the labeled data could estimate reading comprehension based on unlabeled data – that is, without interrupting to ask questions.

Acknowledgements

The research reported here was supported by the Institute of Education Sciences, U.S. Department of Education, through Grant R305A080157. The opinions expressed are those of the authors and do not necessarily represent the views of the Institute or the U.S. Department of Education. We thank our colleagues who judged the generated questions, and the reviewers for their helpful comments.

References

Aldabe, I., & Maritxalar, M. (2010). *Automatic Distractor Generation for Domain Specific Texts Advances in Natural Language Processing*. Paper presented at the The 7th International Conference on NLP, Reykjavk, Iceland.

Aldabe, I., Maritxalar, M., & Martinez, E. (2007). *Evaluating and Improving Distractor-Generating Heuristics*. Paper presented at the The Workshop on NLP for Educational Resources. In conjuction with RANLP07.

Aldabe, I., Maritxalar, M., & Mitkov, R. (2009). *A Study on the Automatic Selection of Candidate Sentences and Distractors*. Paper presented at the Proceedings of the 14th International Conference on Artificial Intelligence in Education (AIED2009), Brighton, UK.

Biemiller, A. (2009). *Words Worth Teaching: Closing the Vocabulary Gap*. Columbus, OH: SRA/McGraw-Hill.

Brants, T., & Franz, A. (2006). Web IT 5-gram Version 1. Philadelpha: Linguistic Data Consortium.

Brown, J. C., Frishkoff, G. A., & Eskenazi, M. (2005). *Automatic Question Generation for Vocabulary Assessment*. Paper presented at the Proceedings of Human Language Technology Conference and Conference on Empirical Methods in Natural Language Processing (HLT/EMNLP), Vancouver.

Coniam, D. (1997). A preliminary inquiry into using corpus word frequency data in the automatic generation of English language cloze tests. *CALICO Journal, 14*(2-4), 15-33.

Correia, R., Baptista, J., Mamede, N., Trancoso, I., & Eskenazi, M. (2010, September 22-24). *Automatic generation of cloze question distractors*. Paper presented at the Proceedings of the Interspeech 2010 Satellite Workshop on Second Language Studies: Acquisition, Learning, Education and Technology, Waseda University, Tokyo, Japan.

Gates, D., Aist, G., Mostow, J., Mckeown, M., & Bey, J. (2011, November 4-6). *How to Generate Cloze Questions from Definitions: a Syntactic Approach*. Paper presented at the Proceedings of the AAAI Symposium on Question Generation, Arlington, VA.

Goto, T., Kojiri, T., Watanabe, T., Iwata, T., & Yamada, T. (2010). Automatic Generation System of Multiple-Choice Cloze Questions and its Evaluation. *Knowledge Management & E-Learning: An International Journal (KM&EL), 2*(3).

Graesser, A. C., & Bertus, E. L. (1998). The Construction of Causal Inferences While Reading Expository Texts on Science and Technology. *Scientific Studies of Reading, 2*(3), 247-269.

Hensler, B. S., & Beck, J. (2006, June 26-30). *Better student assessing by finding difficulty factors in a fully automated comprehension measure [Best Paper nominee]*. Paper presented at the Proceedings of the 8th International Conference on Intelligent Tutoring Systems, Jhongli, Taiwan.

Kendall, M. G., & Smith, B. B. (1939). The Problem of m Rankings. *The Annals of Mathematical Statistics, 10*(3), 275-287.

Kintsch, W. (1993). Information Accretion and Reduction in Text Processing: Inferences. *Discourse Processes, 16*(1-2), 193-202.

Kintsch, W. (2005). An Overview of Top-Down and Bottom-Up Effects in Comprehension: The CI Perspective. *Discourse Processes A Multidisciplinary Journal, 39*(2&3), 125-128.

Landis, J. R., & Koch, G. G. (1977). The measurement of observer agreement for categorical data. *Biometrics, 33*(1), 159-174.

Li, L., Roth, B., & Sporleder, C. (2010). *Topic models for word sense disambiguation and token-based idiom detection*. Paper presented at the Proceedings of the 48th Annual Meeting of the Association for Computational Linguistics, Uppsala, Sweden.

Li, L., & Sporleder, C. (2009). *Classifier combination for contextual idiom detection without labelled data*. Paper presented at the Proceedings of the 2009 Conference on Empirical Methods in Natural Language Processing, Singapore.

Liu, C.-L., Wang, C.-H., & Gao, Z.-M. (2005). Using Lexical Constraints to Enhance the Quality of Computer-Generated Multiple-Choice Cloze Items. *Computational Linguistics and Chinese Language Processing, 10*(3), 303-328.

Liu, C.-L., Wang, C.-H., Gao, Z.-M., & Huang, S.-M. (2005). *Applications of lexical information for algorithmically composing multiple-choice cloze items*. Paper presented at the Proceedings of the second workshop on Building Educational Applications Using NLP, Ann Arbor, Michigan.

Mostow, J. (2008). Experience from a Reading Tutor that listens: Evaluation purposes, excuses, and methods. In C. K. Kinzer & L. Verhoeven (Eds.), *Interactive literacy education: facilitating literacy environments through technology* (pp. 117-148). New York: Lawrence Erlbaum Associates, Taylor & Francis Group.

Mostow, J., Beck, J. E., Bey, J., Cuneo, A., Sison, J., Tobin, B., & Valeri, J. (2004). Using automated questions to assess reading comprehension, vocabulary, and effects of tutorial interventions. *Technology, Instruction, Cognition and Learning, 2*(1-2), 97-134.

Mostow, J., Chang, K.-m., & Nelson, J. (2011, June 28 - July 2). *Toward Exploiting EEG Input in a Reading Tutor [Best Paper Nominee]*. Paper presented at the Proceedings of the 15th International Conference on Artificial Intelligence in Education, Auckland, NZ.

Pearson, P. D., & Hamm, D. N. (2005). The history of reading comprehension assessment. *S. G. Paris & S. A. Stahl (Eds.), Children's reading comprehension and assessment*, 13-69.

Pino, J., Heilman, M., & Eskenazi, M. (2008). *A selection strategy to improve cloze question quality.* Paper presented at the Proceedings of the Workshop on Intelligent Tutoring Systems for Ill-Defined Domains. 9th International Conference on Intelligent Tutoring Systems, Montreal, Canada.

Shrout, P. E., & Fleiss, J. L. (1979). Intraclass correlations: Uses in assessing rater reliability. *Psychological Bulletin, 86*(2), 420-428.

Sleator, D. D. K., & Temperley, D. (1993, August 10-13). *Parsing English with a link grammar.* Paper presented at the Third International Workshop on Parsing Technologies, Tilburg, NL, and Durbuy, Belgium.

Smith, S., Sommers, S., & Kilgarriff, A. (2008). *Learning words right with the Sketch Engine and WebBootCat: Automatic cloze generation from corpora and the web.* Paper presented at the Proceedings of the 25th International Conference of English Teaching and Learning & 2008 International Conference on English Instruction and Assessment, Lisbon, Portugal.

Sumita, E., Sugaya, F., & Yamamoto, S. (2005). *Measuring non-native speakers' proficiency of English by using a test with automatically-generated fill-in-the-blank questions.* Paper presented at the Proceedings of the second workshop on Building Educational Applications Using NLP, Ann Arbor, Michigan.

Toutanova, K., Klein, D., Manning, C., & Singer, Y. (2003). *Feature-rich part-ofspeech tagging with a cyclic dependency network.* Paper presented at the HLT-NAACL, Edmonton, Canada.

van den Broek, P., Everson, M., Virtue, S., Sung, Y., & Tzeng, Y. (2002). Comprehension and memory of science texts: Inferential processes and the construction of a mental representation. In J. L. J. Otero, & A. C. Graesser (Ed.), *The psychology of science text comprehension*. Mahwah, NJ: Erlbaum.

Wiederholt, J. L., & Bryant, B. R. (1992). *Gray Oral Reading Tests* (3rd ed.). Austin, TX: Pro-Ed.

Woodcock, R. W. (1998). *Woodcock Reading Mastery Tests - Revised (WRMT-R/NU).* Circle Pines, Minnesota: American Guidance Service.

Zhang, X., Mostow, J., & Beck, J. E. (2007, July 9-13). *Can a computer listen for fluctuations in reading comprehension?* Paper presented at the Proceedings of the 13th International Conference on Artificial Intelligence in Education, Marina del Rey, CA.

Generating Grammar Exercises

Laura Perez-Beltrachini
Université de Lorraine
LORIA, UMR 7503
Vandoeuvre-lès-Nancy
F-54500, France
laura.perez@loria.fr

Claire Gardent
CNRS, LORIA, UMR 7503
Vandoeuvre-lès-Nancy
F-54500, France
claire.gardent@loria.fr

German Kruszewski
Inria, LORIA, UMR 7503
Villers-lès-Nancy
F-54600, France
german.kruszewski@inria.fr

Abstract

Grammar exercises for language learning fall into two distinct classes: those that are based on "real life sentences" extracted from existing documents or from the web; and those that seek to facilitate language acquisition by presenting the learner with exercises whose syntax is as simple as possible and whose vocabulary is restricted to that contained in the textbook being used. In this paper, we introduce a framework (called *GramEx*) which permits generating the second type of grammar exercises. Using generation techniques, we show that a grammar can be used to semi-automatically generate grammar exercises which target a specific learning goal; are made of short, simple sentences; and whose vocabulary is restricted to that used in a given textbook.

1 Introduction

Textbooks for language learning generally include grammar exercises. *Tex's French Grammar* [1] for instance, includes at the end of each lecture, a set of grammar exercises which target a specific pedagogical goal such as *learning the plural form of nouns* or *learning the placement of adjectives*. Figure 1 shows the exercises provided by this book at the end of the lecture on the plural formation of nouns. As exemplified in this figure, these exercises markedly differ from more advanced learning activities which seek to familiarise the learner with "real world sentences". To support *in situ* learning, this latter type of activity presents the learner with sentences drawn from the Web or from existing documents thereby exposing her to a potentially complex syntax and to a diverse vocabulary. In contrast, textbook grammar exercises usually aim to facilitate the acquisition of a specific grammar point by presenting the learner with exercises made up of short sentences involving a restricted vocabulary.

As shall be discussed in the next section, most existing work on the generation of grammar exercises has concentrated on the automatic creation of the first type of exercises i.e., exercises whose source sentences are extracted from an existing corpus. In this paper, we present a framework (called *GramEx*) which addresses the generation of the second type of grammar exercises used for language learning i.e., grammar exercises whose syntax and lexicon are strongly controlled. Our approach uses generation techniques to produce these exercises from an existing grammar describing both the syntax and the semantics of natural language sentences. Given a pedagogical goal for which exercises must be produced, the *GramEx* framework permits producing *Fill in the blank* (FIB, the learner must fill a blank with an appropriate form or phrase) and *Shuffle* (given a set of lemmas or forms, the learner must use these to produce a phrase) exercises that target that specific goal.

[1] *Tex's French Grammar* http://www.laits.utexas.edu/tex/ is an online pedagogical reference grammar that combines explanations with surreal dialogues and cartoon images. Tex's French Grammar is arranged like many other traditional reference grammars with the parts of speech (nouns, verbs, etc.) used to categorize specific grammar items (gender of nouns, irregular verbs). Individual grammar items are carefully explained in English, then exemplified in a dialogue, and finally tested in self-correcting, fill-in-the-blank exercises.

```
Give the plural form of the noun indicated  in parentheses.
Pay attention to both the article and the noun.
1.      Bette aime _____ . (le bijoux)
2.      Fiona aime ______ . (le cheval)
3.      Joe-Bob aime ______ américaines. (la bière)
4.      Tex n'aime pas ______ . (le choix)
5.      Joe-Bob n'aime pas ______ difficiles. (le cours)
6.      Tammy n'aime pas ______ . (l'hôpital)
7.      Eduard aime ______. (le tableau)
8.      Bette aime ______ de Tex. (l'oeil)
9.      Tex aime ______ français. (le poète)
10.     Corey aime ______ fraîches. (la boisson)
11.     Tammy aime ______ américains. (le campus)
12.     Corey n'aime pas ______ . (l'examen)
```

Figure 1: Grammar exercises from the *Tex's French Grammar* textbook

The exercises thus generated use a simple syntax and vocabulary similar to that used in the *Tex's French Grammar* textbook.

We evaluate the approach on several dimensions using quantitative and qualitative metrics as well as a small scale user-based evaluation. And we show that the *GramEx* framework permits producing exercises for a given pedagogical goal that are linguistically and pedagogically varied.

The paper is structured as follows. We start by discussing related work (Section 2). In Section 3, we present the framework we developed to generate grammar exercises. Section 4 describes the experimental setup we used to generate exercise items. Section 5 reports on an evaluation of the exercise items produced and on the results obtained. Section 6 concludes.

2 Related Work

A prominent strand of research in Computer Aided Language Learning (CALL) addresses the automation of exercise specifications relying on Natural Language Processing (NLP) techniques (Mitkov et al., 2006; Heilman and Eskenazi, 2007; Karamanis et al., 2006; Chao-Lin et al., 2005; Coniam, 1997; Sumita et al., 2005; Simon Smith, 2010; Lin et al., 2007; Lee and Seneff, 2007). Mostly, this work targets the automatic generation of so-called objective test items i.e., test items such as multiple choice questions, fill in the blank and cloze exercise items, whose answer is strongly constrained and can therefore be predicted and checked with high accuracy. These approaches use large corpora and machine learning techniques to automatically generate the stems (exercise sentences), the keys (correct answers) and the distractors (incorrect answers) that are required by such test items.

Among these approaches, some proposals target grammar exercises. Thus, (Chen et al., 2006) describes a system called FAST which supports the semi-automatic generation of Multiple-Choice and Error Detection exercises while (Aldabe et al., 2006) presents the ArikiTurri automatic question generator for constructing Fill-in-the-Blank, Word Formation, Multiple Choice and Error Detection exercises. These approaches are similar to the approach we propose. First, a bank of sentences is built which are automatically annotated with syntactic and morpho-syntactic information. Second, sentences are retrieved from this bank based on their annotation and on the linguistic phenomena the exercise is meant to illustrate. Third, the exercise question is constructed from the retrieved sentences. There are important differences however.

First, in these approaches, the source sentences used for building the test items are selected from corpora. As a result, they can be very complex and most of the generated test items are targeted for intermediate or advanced learners. In addition, some of the linguistic phenomena included in the language schools curricula may be absent or insufficiently present in the source corpus (Aldabe et al., 2006). In contrast, our generation based approach permits controlling both the syntax and the lexicon of the generated exercices.

Second, while, in these approaches, the syntactic and morpho-syntactic annotations associated with the bank sentences are obtained using part-of-speech tagging and chunking, in our approach, these are obtained by a grammar-based generation process.

As we shall see below, the information thus associated with sentences is richer than that obtained by chunking. In particular, it contains detailed linguistic information about the syntactic constructs (e.g., cleft subject) contained in the bank sentences. This permits a larger coverage of the linguistic phenomena that can be handled. For instance, we can retrieve sentences which contain a relativised cleft object (e.g., *This is the man whom Mary likes who sleeps*) by simply stipulating that the retrieved sentences must be associated with the information *Cleft Object*).

To sum up, our approach differs from most existing work in that it targets the production of syntactically and lexically controlled grammar exercises rather than producing grammar exercises based on sentences extracted from an existing corpus.

3 Generating Exercises

Given a pedagogical goal (e.g., learning adjective morphology), *GramEx* produces a set of exercise items for practicing that goal. The item can be either a FIB or a shuffle item; and *GramEx* produces both the exercise question and the expected solution.

To generate exercise items, *GramEx* proceeds in three main steps as follows. First, a generation bank is constructed using surface realisation techniques. This generation bank stores sentences that have been generated together with the detailed linguistic information associated by the generation algorithm with each of these sentences. Next, sentences that permit exercising the given pedagogical goal are retrieved from the generation bank using a constraint language that permits defining pedagogical goals in terms of the linguistic properties associated by the generator with the generated sentences. Finally, exercises are constructed from the retrieved sentences using each retrieved sentence to define FIB and Shuffle exercises; and the sentence itself as the solution to the exercise.

We now discuss each of these steps in more detail.

3.1 Constructing a Generation bank

The generation bank is a database associating sentences with a representation of their semantic content and a detailed description of their syntactic and morphosyntactic properties. In other words, a generation bank is a set of (S_i, L_i, σ_i) tuples where S_i is a sentence, L_i is a set of linguistic properties true of that sentence and σ_i is its semantic representation.

```
Sentence realisation:
"Tammy a une voix douce"
-------------------------------------------------
Lemma-features pairs:
{"lemma": "Tammy",
"lemma-features": {anim:+,num:sg,det: +,wh:-,cat:n,
func:suj,xp: +, gen:f},
"trace": {propername}},
{"lemma": "avoir",
"lemma-features": {aux-refl:-,inv:-,cat:v,pers:3,pron:-,
num:sg,mode:ind, aspect:indet,tense:pres,stemchange:-,
flexion:irreg},
"trace": {CanonicalObject,CanonicalSubject,n0Vn1}},
{"lemma": "un",
"lemma-features": {wh:-,num:sg,mass:-,cat:d,
gen:f,def:+},
"trace": {determiner}},
{"lemma": "voix",
"lemma-features": {bar:0,wh:-,cat:n,num:sg,
mass:-,gen:f,flexion:irreg,
"trace": {noun}},
{"lemma": "doux",
"lemma-features": {num:sg,gen:f,flexion:irreg,cat:adj},
"trace": {Epith,EpithPost}}
```

Figure 2: Morphosyntactic information associated by *GraDe* with the sentence *Tammy a un voix douce*

To produce these tuples, we use the *GraDe* grammar traversal algorithm described in (Gardent and Kruszewski, 2012). Given a grammar and a set of user-defined constraints, this algorithm generates sentences licensed by this grammar. The user-defined constraints are either parameters designed to constrain the search space and guarantee termination (e.g., upper-bound on the number and type of recursive rules used or upper-bound on the depth of the tree build by *GraDe*); or linguistic parameters which permit constraining the output (e.g., by specifying a core semantics the output must verbalise or by requiring the main verb to be of a certain type). Here we use *GraDe* both to generate from manually specified semantic input; and from a grammar (in this case an existing grammar is used and no manual input need to be specified). As explained in (Gardent and Kruszewski, 2012), when generating from a semantic representation, the output sentences are constrained to verbalise that semantics but the input semantics may be underspecified thereby allowing for morpho-syntactic, syntactic and temporal variants to be produced from a single semantics. For instance, given the input semantics

L1:named(J bette_n) A:le_d(C RH SH) B:bijou_n(C) G:aimer_v(E J C), *GraDe* will output among others the following variants:

> Bette aime le bijou (*Bette likes the jewel*), Bette aime les bijoux (*Bette likes the jewels*), C'est Bette qui aime le bijou (*It is Bette who likes the jewel*), C'est Bette qui aime les bijoux (*It is Bette who likes the jewel*), Bette aimait le bijou (*Bette liked the jewel*), Bette aimait les bijoux (*Bette liked the jewels*), ...

When generating from the grammar, the output is even less constrained since all derivations compatible with the user-defined constraints will be produced irrespective of semantic content. For instance, when setting *GraDe* with constraints restricting the grammar traversal to only derive basic clauses containing an intransitive verb, the output sentences include among others the following sentences:

> Elle chante (*She sings*), La tatou chante-t'elle? (*Does the armadillo sing?*), La tatou chante (*The armadillo sings*), Chacun chante -t'il (*Does everyone sing?*), Chacun chante (*Everyone sings*), Quand chante la tatou? (*When does the armadillo sing?*), ...

Figure 2 shows the linguistic properties associated with the sentence *Tammy a une voix douce* (Tammy has a soft voice) by *GraDe*. To generate exercises, *GramEx* makes use of the morpho-syntactic information associated with each lemma i.e., the feature-value pairs occurring as values of the lemma-features fields; and of their linguistic properties i.e., the items occurring as values of the trace fields.

3.2 Retrieving Appropriate Sentences

To enable the retrieval of sentences that are appropriate for a given pedagogical goal, we define a query language on the linguistic properties assigned by *GraDe* to sentences. We then express each pedagogical goal as a query in that language; and we use these queries to retrieve from the generation bank appropriate source sentences. For instance, to retrieve a sentence for building a FIB exercise where the blank is a relative pronoun, we query the generation bank with the constraint $RelativePronoun$. This will return all sentences in the generation bank whose trace field contains the $RelativePronoun$ item i.e., all sentences containing a relative pronoun. We then use this sentence to build both the exercise question and its solution.

3.2.1 GramEx Query Language

We now define the query language used to retrieve sentences that are appropriate to build an exercise for a given pedagogical goal. Let B be a generation bank and let (S_i, L_i, σ_i) be the tuples stored in B. Then, a *GramEx* query q permits retrieving from B the set of sentences $S_i \in (S_i, L_i, \sigma_i)$ such that L_i satisfies q. In other words, *GramEx* queries permit retrieving from the generation bank all sentences whose linguistic properties satisfy those queries.

The syntax of the *GramEx* query language is as follows:

BoolExpr $\rightarrow$ BoolTerm
BoolTerm $\rightarrow$ BoolFactor | BoolTerm $\vee$ BoolFactor
BoolFactor $\rightarrow$ BoolUnary | BoolFactor $\wedge$ BoolUnary
BoolUnary $\rightarrow$ BoolPrimary | $\neg$ BoolPrimary
BoolPrimary $\rightarrow$ PrimitiveCond | (BoolExpr) | [BoolExpr]
PrimitiveCond $\rightarrow$ $traceItem$ | $feature = value$

In words: the *GramEx* query language permits defining queries that are arbitrary boolean constraints on the linguistic properties associated by *GraDe* with each generated sentence. In addition, complex constraints can be named and reused (macros); and expressions can be required to hold on a single lexical item ([BoolExpr] indicates that BoolExpr should be satisfied by the linguistic properties of a single lexical item).

The signature of the language is the set of grammatical ($traceItem$) and morpho-syntactic properties ($feature = value$) associated by *GraDe* with each generated sentence where $traceItem$ is any item occurring in the value of a `trace` field and $feature = value$ any feature/value pair occurring in the value of a `lemma-features` field (cf. Figure 2). The Table below (Table 1) shows some of the constraints that can be used to express pedagogical goals in the *GramEx* query language.

3.2.2 Query Examples

The *GramEx* query language allows for very specific constraints to be expressed thereby providing fine-grained control over the type of sentences and therefore over the types of exercises that can be produced. The following example queries illustrate this.

Grammatical Properties (traceItem)	
Argument Realisation	Cleft, CleftSUbj, CleftOBJ, ..., InvertedSubj Questioned, QuSubj, ... Relativised, RelSubj ... Pronominalised, ProSubj, ...
Voice	Active, Passive, Reflexive
Aux	tse, modal, causal
Adjective	Predicative,Pre/Post nominal
Adverb	Sentential, Verbal
Morpho-Syntactic Properties (feature=value)	
Tense	present,future,past
Number	mass, count, plural, singular
Inflexion	reg,irreg

Table 1: Some grammatical and morpho-syntactic properties that can be used to specify pedagogical goals.

(1) a. EpithAnte
Tex pense que Tammy est une jolie tatou (Tex thinks that Tammy is a pretty armadillo)

b. [Epith $\wedge$ flexion: irreg]
Tex et Tammy ont une voix douce (Tex and Tammy have a soft voice)

c. POBJinf $\wedge$ CLAUSE
POBJinf $\equiv$ (DE-OBJinf $\vee$ A-OBJinf)
CLAUSE $\equiv$ Vfin $\wedge \neg$Mod $\wedge$ $\neg$CCoord $\wedge$ $\neg$Sub
Tammy refuse de chanter (Tammy refuses to sing)

Query (1a) shows a query for retrieving sentences containing prenominal adjectives which uses the grammatical (*traceItem*) property EpithAnte associated with preposed adjectives.

In contrast, Query (1b) uses both grammatical and morpho-syntactic properties to retrieve sentences containing a postnominal adjective with irregular inflexion. The square brackets in the query force the conjunctive constraint to be satisfied by a single lexical unit. That is, the query will be satisfied by sentences containing a lexical item that is both a postnominal adjective and has irregular inflexion. This excludes sentences including e.g., a postnominal adjective and a verb with irregular inflexion.

Finally, Query (1c) shows a more complex case where the pedagogical goal is defined in terms of predefined macros themselves defined as *GramEx* query expressions. The pedagogical goal is defined as a query which retrieves basic clauses (CLAUSE) containing a prepositional infinitival object (POBJinf). A sentence containing a prepositional infinitival object is in turn defined (second line) as a prepositional object introduced either by the *de* or the *à* preposition. And a basic clause (3rd line) is defined as a sentence containing a finite verb and excluding modifiers, clausal or verb phrase coordination (CCORD) and subordinated clauses[2]

3.3 Building Exercise Items

In the previous section, we saw the mechanism used for selecting an appropriate sentence for a given pedagogical goal. *GramEx* uses such selected sentences as source or stem sentences to build exercise items. The exercise *question* is automatically generated from the selected sentence based on its associated linguistic properties. Currently, *GramEx* includes two main types of exercises namely, Fill in the blank and Shuffle exercises.

FIB questions. FIB questions are built by removing a word from the target sentence and replacing it with either: a blank (FIBBLNK), a lemma (FIBLEM) or a set of features used to help the learner guess the solution (FIBHINT). For instance, in an exercise on pronouns, *GramEx* will use the gender, number and person features associated with the pronoun by the generation process and display them to specify which pronominal form the learner is expected to provide. The syntactic representation (cf. Figure 2) associated by *GraDe* with the sentence is used to search for the appropriate key word to be removed. For instance, if the pedagogical goal is *Learn Subject Pronouns* and the sentence retrieved from the generation bank is that given in (2a), *GramEx* will produce the FIBHINT question in (2b) by searching for a lemma with category *cl* (clitic) and feature *func=subj* and using its gender value to provide the learner with a hint constraining the set of possible solutions.

(2) a. Elle adore les petits tatous
(She loves small armadillos)
b. ... adore les petits tatous (gender=fem)

Shuffle questions. Similarly to FIB questions, shuffle exercise items are produced by inspecting and using the target derivational information. More specifically, lemmas are retrieved from the list of

[2]The expressions CCoord and Sub are themselves defined rather than primitive expressions.

lemma-feature pairs. Function words are (optionally) deleted. And the remaining lemmas are "shuffled" (MSHUF). For instance, given the source sentence (2a), the MSHUF question (2b) can be produced.

(3) a. Tammy adore la petite tatou
a. tatou / adorer / petit / Tammy

Note that in this case, there are several possible solutions depending on which tense and number is used by the learner. For such cases, we can either use hints as shown above to reduce the set of possible solutions to one; or compare the learner's answer to the set of output produced by *GraDe* for the semantics the sentence was produced from.

4 Experimental Setup

We carried out an experiment designed to assess the exercises produced by *GramEx*. In what follows, we describe the parameters of this experiment namely, the grammar and lexicons used; the input and the user-defined parameters constraining sentence generation; and the pedagogical goals being tested.

4.1 Grammar and Lexicon

The grammar used is a Feature-Based Lexicalised Tree Adjoining Grammar for French augmented with a unification-based compositional semantics. This grammar contains around 1300 elementary trees and covers auxiliaries, copula, raising and small clause constructions, relative clauses, infinitives, gerunds, passives, adjuncts, wh-clefts, PRO constructions, imperatives and 15 distinct subcategorisation frames.

The syntactic and morpho-syntactic lexicons used for generating were derived from various existing lexicons, converted to fit the format expected by *GraDe* and tailored to cover basic vocabulary as defined by the lexicon used in *Tex's French Grammar*. The syntactic lexicon contains 690 lemmas and the morphological lexicon 5294 forms.

4.2 Pedagogical Goals

We evaluate the approach on 16 pedagogical goals taken from the *Tex's French Grammar* book. For each of these goals, we define the corresponding linguistic characterization in the form of a *GramEx* query. We then evaluate the exercises produced by the system for each of these queries. The pedagogical goals tested are the following (we indicate in brackets the types of learning activity produced for each teaching goal by the system):

- Adjectives: Adjective Order (MSHUF), Adjective Agreement (FIBLEM), Prenominal adjectives (FIBLEM), Present and Past Participial used as adjectives (FIBLEM), Regular and Irregular Inflexion (FIBLEM), Predicative adjectives (MSHUF)
- Prepositions: Prepositional Infinitival Object (FIBBLNK), Modifier and Complement Prepositional Phrases (FIBBLNK)
- Noun: Gender (FIBLEM), Plural form (FIBLEM), Subject Pronoun (FIBHINT).
- Verbs: Pronominals (FIBLEM), -ir Verbs in the present tense (FIBLEM), Simple past (FIBLEM), Simple future (FIBLEM), Subjunctive Mode (FIBLEM).

4.3 GraDe's Input and User-Defined Parameters

GraDe's configuration As mentioned in Section 3, we run *GraDe* using two main configurations. In the first configuration, *GraDe* search is constrained by an input core semantics which guides the grammar traversal and forces the output sentence to verbalise this core semantics. In this configuration, *GraDe* will only produce the temporal variations supported by the lexicon (the generated sentences may be in any simple tense i.e., present, future, simple past and imperfect) and the syntactic variations supported by the grammar for the same MRSs (e.g., active/passive voice alternation and cleft arguments).

Greater productivity (i.e., a larger output/input ratio) can be achieved by providing *GraDe* with less constrained input. Thus, in the second configuration, we run *GraDe* not on core semantics but on the full grammar. To constrain the search, we specify a root constraint which requires that the main verb of all output sentences is an intransitive verb. We also set the constraints on recursive rules so as to exclude the inclusion of modifiers. In sum, we ask *GraDe* to produce all clauses (i) licensed by the grammar and the lexicon; (ii) whose verb is intransitive; and (iii) which do not include modifiers. Since the number of sentences that can be produced under this configuration is very large, we restrict the experiment by using a lexicon containing a single intransitive verb (*chanter/To sing*), a single common noun and a single proper name. In this way, syntactically structurally equivalent but lexically distinct variants are excluded.

Input Semantics We use two different sets of input semantics for the semantically guided configuration: one designed to test the pedagogical coverage of the system (Given a set of pedagogical goals, can *GramEx* generate exercises that appropriately target those goals?); and the other to illustrate linguistic coverage (How much syntactic variety can the system provide for a given pedagogical goal?).

The first set (D1) of semantic representations contains 9 items representing the meaning of example sentences taken from the *Tex's French Grammar* textbook. For instance, for the first item in Figure 1, we use the semantic representation *L1:named(J bette_n) A:le_d(C RH SH) B:bijou_n(C) G:aimer_v(E J C)*. With this first set of input semantics, we test whether *GramEx* correctly produces the exercises proposed in the *Tex's French Grammar* book. Each of the 9 input semantics corresponds to a distinct pedagogical goal.

The second set (D2) of semantic representations contains 22 semantics, each of them illustrating distinct syntactic configurations namely, intransitive, transitive and ditransitive verbs; raising and control; prepositional complements and modifiers; sentential and prepositional subject and object complements; pronominal verbs; predicative, attributive and participial adjectives. With this set of semantics, we introduce linguistically distinct material thereby increasing the variability of the exercises i.e., making it possible to have several distinct syntactic configurations for the same pedagogical goal.

5 Evaluation, Results and Discussion

Using the experimental setup described in the previous section, we evaluate *GramEx* on the following points:

- Correctness: Are the exercises produced by the generator grammatical, meaningful and appropriate for the pedagogical goal they are associated with?
- Variability: Are the exercises produced linguistically varied and extensive? That is, do the exercises for a given pedagogical goal instantiate a large number of distinct syntactic patterns?
- Productivity: How much does *GramEx* support the production, from a restricted number of semantic input, of a large number of exercises?

Correctness To assess correctness, we randomly selected 10 (pedagogical goal, exercise) pairs for each pedagogical goal in Section 4.2 and asked two evaluators to say for each pair whether the exercise text and solutions were grammatical, meaningful (i.e., semantically correct) and whether the exercise was adequate for the pedagogical goal. The results are shown in Table 3 and show that the system although not perfect is reliable. Most sources of grammatical errors are cases where a missing word in the lexicon fails to be inflected by the generator. Cases where the exercise is not judged meaningful are generally cases where a given syntactic construction seems odd for a given semantics content. For instance, the sentence *C'est Bette qui aime les bijoux* (It is Bette who likes jewels) is fine but *C'est Bette qui aime des bijoux* although not ungrammatical sounds odd. Finally, cases judged inappropriate are generally due to an incorrect feature being assigned to a lemma. For instance, *avoir* (To have) is marked as an -ir verb in the lexicon which is incorrect.

Grammatical	Meaningful	Appropriate
91%	96%	92%

Table 3: Exercise Correctness tested on 10 randomly selected (pedagogical goal, exercise pairs)

We also asked a language teacher to examine 70 exercises (randomly selected in equal number across the different pedagogical goals) and give her judgment on the following three questions:

- A. Do you think that the source sentence selected for the exercise is appropriate to practice the topic of the exercise? Score from 0 to 3 according to the degree (0 inappropriate - 3 perfectly appropriate)

Nb. Ex.	1	2	4	5	6	12	17	18	20	21	23	26	31	37	138
Nb. Sem	1	4	6	1	4	3	1	1	1	1	1	1	1	1	1

Table 2: Exercise Productivity: Number of exercises produced per input semantics

- B. The grammar topic at hand together with the complexity of the source sentence make the item appropriate for which language level? A1,A2,B1,B2,C1[3]
- C. Utility of the exercise item: ambiguous (not enough context information to solve it) / correct

For Question 1, the teacher graded 35 exercises as 3, 20 as 2 and 14 as 1 pointing to similar problems as was independently noted by the annotators above. For question B, she marked 29 exercises as A1/A2, 24 as A2, 14 as A2/B1 and 3 as A1 suggesting that the exercises produced are non trivial. Finally, she found that 5 out of the 70 exercises lacked context and were ambiguously phrased.

Variability For any given pedagogical goal, there usually are many syntactic patterns supporting learning. For instance, learning the gender of common nouns can be practiced in almost any syntactic configuration containing a common noun. We assess the variability of the exercises produced for a given pedagogical goal by computing the number of distinct morpho-syntactic configurations produced from a given input semantics for a given pedagogical goal. We count as distinct all exercise questions that are derived from the same semantics but differ either in syntax (e.g., passive/active distinction) or in morphosyntax (determiner, number, etc.). Both types of differences need to be learned and therefore producing exercises which, for a given pedagogical goal, expose the learner to different syntactic and morpho-syntactic patterns (all involving the construct to be learned) is effective in supporting learning. However we did not take into account tense differences as the impact of tense on the number of exercises produced is shown by the experiment where we generate by traversing the grammar rather than from a semantics. Table 4 shows for each (input semantics, teaching goal) pair the number of distinct patterns observed. The number ranges from 1 to 21 distinct patterns with very few pairs (3) producing a single pattern, many (33) producing two patterns and a fair number producing either 14 or 21 patterns.

Nb. PG	1	2	3	4	5	6
Nb. sent	213	25	8	14	10	6

Table 6: Pedagogical Productivity: Number of Teaching Goals the source sentence produced from a given semantics can be used for

Productivity When used to generate from semantic representations (cf. Section 4.3), *GramEx* only partially automates the production of grammar exercises. Semantic representations must be manually input to the system for the exercises to be generated. Therefore the issue arises of how much *GramEx* helps automating exercise creation. Table 5 shows the breakdown of the exercises produced per teaching goal and activity type. In total, *GramEx* produced 429 exercises out of 28 core semantics yielding an output/input ratio of 15 (429/28). Further, Table 2 and 6 show the distribution of the ratio between (i) the number of exercises produced and the number of input semantics and (ii) the number of teaching goals the source sentences produced from input semantics i can be used for. Table 6 (pedagogical productivity) shows that, in this first experiment, a given input semantics can provide material for exercises targeting up to 6 different pedagogical goals while Table 2 (exercise productivity) shows that most of the input semantics produce between 2 and 12 exercises[4].

When generating by grammar traversal, under the constraints described in Section 4, from one input

[3]A1, A2, B1, B2 and C1 are reference levels established by the Common European Framework of Reference for Languages: Learning, Teaching, Assessment (cf. `http://en.wikipedia.org/wiki/Common_European_Framework_of_Reference_for_Languages`) for grading an individual's language proficiency.

[4]If the input semantics contains a noun predicate whose gender is underspecified, the exercise productivity could be doubled. This is the case for 4 of the input semantics in the dataset D2; i.e. an input semantics containing the predicates tatou_n(C) petit_a(C) will produce variations such as: *la petite tatou* (the small armadillo (f)) and *le petit tatou* (the small armadillo (m)).

Nb. SP	1	2	3	4	5	6	7	8	9	10	14	21
(S,G)	3	33	16	7	2	4	6	1	4	1	2	6

Table 4: Variability: Distribution of the number of distinct sentential patterns that can be produced for a given pedagogical goal from a given input semantics

Pedagogical Goal	FIBLEM	FIBBLNK	MSHUF	FIBHINT
Preposition	—	28	—	—
Prepositions with infinitives	—	8	—	—
Subject pronouns–il	—	—	—	3
Noun number	11	—	—	—
Noun gender	—	49	—	—
Adjective order	—	—	30	—
Adjective morphology	30	—	—	—
Adjectives that precede the noun	24	—	—	—
Attributive Adjectives	—	—	28	—
Irregular adjectives	4	—	—	—
Participles as adjectives	4	—	—	—
Simple past	78	—	—	—
Simple future	90	—	—	—
-ir verbs in present	18	—	—	—
Subjunctive mode	12	—	—	—
Pronominal verbs	12	—	—	—
Total	236	78	30	3

Table 5: Number and Types of Exercises Produced from the 28 input semantics

90 exercises are generated targeting 4 different pedagogical goals (i.e. 4 distinct linguistic phenomena).

6 Conclusion

We presented a framework (called *GramEx*) for generating grammar exercises which are similar to those often used in textbooks for second language learning. These exercises target a specific learning goal; and, they involve short sentences that make it easier for the learner to concentrate on the grammatical point to be learned.

One distinguishing feature of the approach is the rich linguistic information associated by the generator with the source sentences used to construct grammar exercises. Although space restriction prevented us from showing it here, this information includes, in addition to the morphosyntactic information and the grammatical properties illustrated in Figure 2 and Table 1 respectively, a semantic representation, a derivation tree showing how the parse tree of each sentence was obtained and optionally, an underspecified semantics capturing the core predicate/argument and modifier/modifiee relationships expressed by each sentence. We are currently exploring how this information could be used to extend the approach to transformation exercises (e.g., passive/active) where the relation between exercise question and exercise solution is more complex than in FIB exercises.

Another interesting question which needs further investigation is how to deal with exercise items that have multiple solutions such as example (3) above. Here we plan to use the fact that underspecified semantics in *GraDe* permits associating many variants with a given semantics.

Acknowledgments

We would like to thank the language teacher, Tex's French Grammar developers, and the anonymous reviewers for their useful comments. The research presented in this paper was partially supported by the European Fund for Regional Development within the framework of the INTERREG IV A Allegro Project[5].

[5] `http://www.allegro-project.eu/` and `http://talc.loria.fr/-ALLEGRO-Nancy-.html`

References

Itziar Aldabe, Maddalen Lopez de Lacalle, Montse Maritxalar, Edurne Martinez, and Larraitz Uria. 2006. Arikiturri: an automatic question generator based on corpora and nlp techniques. In *Proceedings of the 8th international conference on Intelligent Tutoring Systems*, ITS'06, pages 584–594, Berlin, Heidelberg. Springer-Verlag.

Liu Chao-Lin, Wang Chun-Hung, Gao Zhao-Ming, and Huang Shang-Ming. 2005. Applications of lexical information for algorithmically composing multiple-choice cloze items. In *Proceedings of the second workshop on Building Educational Applications Using NLP*, EdAppsNLP 05, pages 1–8, Stroudsburg, PA, USA. Association for Computational Linguistics.

Chia-Yin Chen, Hsien-Chin Liou, and Jason S. Chang. 2006. Fast: an automatic generation system for grammar tests. In *Proceedings of the COLING/ACL on Interactive presentation sessions*, COLING-ACL '06, pages 1–4, Stroudsburg, PA, USA. Association for Computational Linguistics.

David Coniam. 1997. A preliminary inquiry into using corpus word frequency data in the automatic generation of english language cloze tests. *CALICO Journal*, 14:15–33.

Claire Gardent and German Kruszewski. 2012. Generation for grammar engineering. In *11th International Conference on Natural Language Generation (ENLG)*.

Michael Heilman and Maxine Eskenazi. 2007. Application of automatic thesaurus extraction for computer generation of vocabulary questions. In *Proceedings of Speech and Language Technology in Education (SLaTE2007)*, pages 65–68.

Nikiforos Karamanis, Le An Ha, and Ruslan Mitkov. 2006. Generating multiple-choice test items from medical text: A pilot study. In *Proceedings of the Fourth International Natural Language Generation Conference*, pages 111–113, Sydney, Australia.

John Lee and Stephanie Seneff. 2007. Automatic generation of cloze items for prepositions. *Proceedings of Interspeech*, pages 2173–2176.

Yi-Chien Lin, Li-Chun Sung, and Meng Chang Chen. 2007. An Automatic Multiple-Choice Question Generation Scheme for English Adjective Understandings. In *Workshop on Modeling, Management and Generation of Problems/Questions in eLearning, the 15th International Conference on Computers in Education (ICCE 2007)*, pages pages 137–142.

Ruslan Mitkov, Le An Ha, and Nikiforos Karamanis. 2006. A computer-aided environment for generating multiple-choice test items. *Natural Language Engineering*, 12(2):177–194.

Adam Kilgarriff Simon Smith, P.V.S Avinesh. 2010. Gap-fill Tests for Language Learners: Corpus-Driven Item Generation. In *Proceedings of ICON-2010: 8th International Conference on Natural Language Processing.*

Eiichiro Sumita, Fumiaki Sugaya, and Seiichi Yamamoto. 2005. Measuring non-native speakers' proficiency of english by using a test with automatically-generated fill-in-the-blank questions. In *Proceedings of the second workshop on Building Educational Applications Using NLP*, EdAppsNLP 05, pages 61–68, Stroudsburg, PA, USA. Association for Computational Linguistics.

A Comparison of Greedy and Optimal Assessment of Natural Language Student Input Using Word-to-Word Similarity Metrics

Vasile Rus
Department of Computer Science
The University of Memphis
Memphis, TN 38152
vrus@memphis.edu

Mihai Lintean
Department of Computer Science
The University of Memphis
Memphis, TN 38152
mclinten@memphis.edu

Abstract

We present in this paper a novel, optimal semantic similarity approach based on word-to-word similarity metrics to solve the important task of assessing natural language student input in dialogue-based intelligent tutoring systems. The optimal matching is guaranteed using the sailor assignment problem, also known as the job assignment problem, a well-known combinatorial optimization problem. We compare the optimal matching method with a greedy method as well as with a baseline method on data sets from two intelligent tutoring systems, AutoTutor and iSTART.

Introduction

We address in this paper the important task of assessing natural language student input in dialogue-based tutoring systems where the primary form of interaction is natural language. Students provide their responses to tutor's requests by typing or speaking their responses. Therefore, in dialogue-based tutoring systems understanding students' natural language input becomes a crucial step towards building an accurate student model, i.e. assessing the student's level of understanding, which in turn is important for optimum feedback and scaffolding and ultimately impacts the tutoring's effectiveness at inducing learning gains on the student user.

We adopt a semantic similarity approach to assess students' natural language input in intelligent tutoring systems. The semantic similarity approach to language understanding derives the meaning of a target text, e.g. a student sentence, by comparing it with another text whose meaning is known. If the target text is semantically similar to the known-meaning text then we know the target's meaning as well.

Semantic similarity is one of the two major approaches to language understanding, a central topic in Artificial Intelligence. The alternative approach is full understanding. The full understanding approach is not scalable due to prohibitive costs to encode world and domain knowledge which are needed for full understanding of natural language.

To illustrate the problem of assessing natural language student input in dialogue-based tutoring systems using a semantic similarity approach, we consider the example below from experiments with AutoTutor (Graesser et al., 2005), a dialogue-based tutoring system.

Expert Answer: *The force of the earth's gravity, being vertically down, has no effect on the object's horizontal velocity*

Student Input: *The horizontal component of motion is not affected by vertical forces*

In this example, the student input, also called contribution, is highly similar to the correct expert answer, called expectation, allowing us to conclude that the student contribution is correct. A correct response typically triggers positive feedback from the tutor. The expert answer could also be an anticipated wrong answer, usually called a misconception. A student contribution similar to a misconception would trigger a misconception correction strategy.

We model the problem of assessing natural language student input in tutoring systems as a paraphrase identification problem (Dolan et al., 2004). The student input assessment problem has been also modeled as a textual entailment task in the past (Rus & Graesser, 2006).

Our novel method to assess a student contribution against an expert-generated answer relies on the compositionality principle and the sailor assignment algorithm that was proposed to solve the assignment problem, a well-known combinatorial optimization problem. The sailor assignment algorithm optimally assigns sailors to ships based on the fitness of the sailors' skills to the ships' needs [7, 8]. In our case, we would like to optimally match words in the student input (the sailors) to words in the expert-generated answer (the ships) based on how well the words in student input (the sailors) fit the words in the expert answer (the ships). The fitness between the words is nothing else but their similarity according to some metric of word similarity. We use the WordNet word-to-word similarity metrics (Pedersen et al., 2004) and Latent Semantic Analysis (Landauer et al., 2007).

The methods proposed so far that rely on the principle of compositionality to compute the semantic similarity of longer texts have been primarily greedy methods (Corley & Mihalcea, 2005; Lintean & Rus, 2012). To the best of our knowledge, nobody proposed an optimal solution based on the principle of compositionality and word-to-word similarity metrics for the student input assessment problem. It is important to note that the optimal method proposed here is generally applicable to compute the similarity of any texts.

We provide experimental results on two datasets provided to us by researchers developing two world-class dialogue-based tutoring systems: AutoTutor (Graesser et al., 2005) and iSTART (McNamara et al., 2004).

Background

It is beyond the scope of this work to offer an exhaustive overview of methods proposed so far to handle the task of assessing natural language student input in intelligent tutoring systems. We only describe next methods that are most relevant to our work.

Assessing student's contributions in dialogue-based tutoring systems has been approached either as a paraphrase identification task (Graesser et al., 2005), i.e. the task was to assess how similar student contributions were to expert-generated answers, or as an entailment task (Rus & Graesser, 2006), in which case the task was to assess whether student contributions were entailed by expert-generated answers. The expert answers were assumed to be true. If a correct expert answer entailed a student contribution then the contribution was deemed to be true as well.

Latent Semantic Analysis (LSA; Landauer et al., 2007) has been used to evaluate student contributions during the dialog between the student by Graesser and colleagues (2005). In LSA the meaning of a word is represented by a reduced-dimensionality vector derived by applying an algebraic method, called Singular Value Decomposition (SVD), to a term-by-document matrix built from a large collection of documents. A typical dimensionality of an LSA vector is 300-500 dimensions. To compute the similarity of two words the cosine of the word's corresponding LSA vector is computed, i.e. the normalized dot-product. A typical extension of LSA-based word similarity to computing the similarity of two sentences (or even larger texts) is to use vector algebra to generate a single vector for each of the sentences (by adding up the individual words' LSA vectors) and then compute the cosine between the resulting sentence vectors. Another approach proposed so far to compute similarities between individual words in the two sentences, greedily selects for each word its best match, and then sums the individual word-to-word similarities in order to compute the overall similarity score for the two sentences (Lintean & Rus, 2012). We do report results with LSA using the latter approach for comparison purposes. Another reason is that only the latter approach allows the application of the optimum matching method.

Extending word-to-word similarity measures to sentence level and beyond has drawn increasing interest in the last decade or so in the Natural Language Processing community. The interest has been driven primarily by the creation of standardized data sets and corresponding shared task evaluation campaigns (STECs) for the major text-to-text semantic relations of entailment (RTE; Recognizing Textual Entailment corpus by Dagan, Glickman, & Magnini, 2005), paraphrase (MSR; Microsoft Research Paraphrase corpus by Dolan, Quirk, and Brockett, 2004), and more recently for elaboration (ULPC; User Language Paraphrase Challenge by McCarthy & McNamara, 2008).

None of the existing methods for assessing the similarity of texts based on the compositional principle and word-to-word similarity metrics have proposed an optimum method.

Beyond Word-to-Word Similarity Measures

Based on the principle of compositionality, which states that the meaning of longer texts can be composed from the meaning of their individual words (which includes collocations in our case such as "free fall"), we can extend the word-to-word similarity metrics to compute the similarity of longer texts, e.g. of sentences.

In our work, we use a set of WordNet-based similarity metrics as well as LSA. We used the following similarity measures implemented in the WordNet::Similarity package and described in (Pedersen et al., 2004): LCH (Leacock and Chodorow), RES (Resnik), JCN (Jiang and Conrath), LIN (Lin), PATH, and WUP (Wu and Palmer). Some measures, e.g. PATH, are path-based, i.e. use paths of lexico-semantic relations between concepts in WordNet, while some others are gloss-based, that is, they use the text of the gloss or the definition of a concept in WordNet as the source of meaning for the underlying concept.

One challenge with the WordNet word-to-word relatedness measures is that they cannot be directly applied to larger texts such as sentences. They must be extended to larger texts, which we did as described later.

Another challenge with the WordNet word-to-word similarity metrics is the fact that texts express meaning using words and not concepts. To be able to use the word-to-word related measures we must map words in sentences to concepts in WordNet. Thus, we are faced with a word sense disambiguation (WSD) problem. It is beyond the scope of our investigation to fully solve the WSD problem, one of the hardest in the area of Natural Language Processing. Instead, we addressed the issue in two ways: (1) mapped the words in the student contribution and expert answer onto the concepts corresponding to their most frequent sense, which is sense #1 in WordNet, and (2) map the words onto all the concepts corresponding to all the senses and then take the maximum of the relatedness scores for each pair of senses. Because the ALL (all senses) method offered better results and because of space constraints we only report results with the ALL method in this paper.

Greedy versus Optimal Semantic Similarity Matching

This section describes the greedy and optimal matching methods to assess the similarity of two texts based on word-to-word similarity metrics. We assume the two texts, T1 and T2, are two sentences and regard them as bags of words (syntactic information is ignored).

The Greedy Method. In the greedy method, each word in text T1 is paired with every word in text T2 and word-to-word similarity scores are computed according to some metric. The maximum similarity score between words in T1 and any word in T2 is greedily retained regardless of the best matching scores of the other words in T1. The greedily-obtained scores are added up using a simple or weighted sum which can then be normalized in different ways, e.g. by dividing to the longest text or to the average length of the two texts. The formula we used is given in equation 1. As one would notice, this formula is asymmetric, i.e. score(T1,T2) $\neq$ score(T2,T1). The average of the two scores provides a symmetric similarity score, more suitable for a paraphrase task, as shown in Equation 2. In this paper, we do a simple non-weighted sum, i.e. all the words are equally-weighted with a weight of 1.

The obvious drawback of the greedy method is that it does not aim for a global maximum similarity score. The optimal method described next solves this issue.

$$score(T1,T2) = \frac{\sum_{v \in T1} weight(v) * \max_{w \in T2} word-sim(v,w)}{\sum_{v \in T1} weight(v)}$$

Equation 1. *Asymmetric semantic similarity score between texts T1 and T2.*

$$simScore(T1,T2) = \frac{score(T1,T2) + score(T2,T1)}{2}$$

Equation 2. *Symmetric semantic similarity score between texts T1 and T2.*

Optimal Matching. The optimal assignment problem is one of the fundamental combinatorial optimization problems and consists of finding a maximum weight matching in a weighted bipartite graph.

Given a weighted complete bipartite graph $G = X \cup Y; X \times Y)$, where edge xy has weight $w(xy)$, find a matching M from X to Y with maximum weight.

An application is about assigning a group of workers, e.g. sailors, to a set of jobs (on ships) based on the expertise level, measured by $w(xy)$, of each worker at each job. By adding dummy workers or jobs we may assume that X and Y have the same size, *n*, and can viewed as $X = \{x_1, x_2, \ldots, x_n\}$ and $Y = \{y_1, y_2, \ldots, y_n\}$. In the semantic similarity case, the workers and jobs are words from the two sentences to be compared and the weight $w(xy)$ is the word-to-word similarity between word x and y in the two sentences, respectively.

The assignment problem can be stated as finding a permutation π of {1, 2, 3, ... , n} for which $\sum_{i=1}^{n} w(x_i y_{\pi(i)})$ is maximum. Such an assignment is called optimum assignment. An algorithm, the Kuhn-Munkres method (Kuhn, 1955), has been proposed that can find a solution to the optimum assignment problem in polynomial time. For space reasons, we do not show here the algorithm in detail.

To illustrate the difference between the two methods, we use the two sentence fragments shown in Figure 1. A greedy method would pair *motion* with *motion* (similarity score of 1.00) as that is the maximum similarity between *motion* and any word in the opposite sentence and *acceleration* is paired with *speed* (similarity score of 0.69) for a total score of 1.69 (before normalization). An optimal matching would yield an overall score of 1.70 by pairing *motion* in the first sentence with *speed* (similarity of 0.75) and *acceleration* with *motion* (similarity of 0.95).

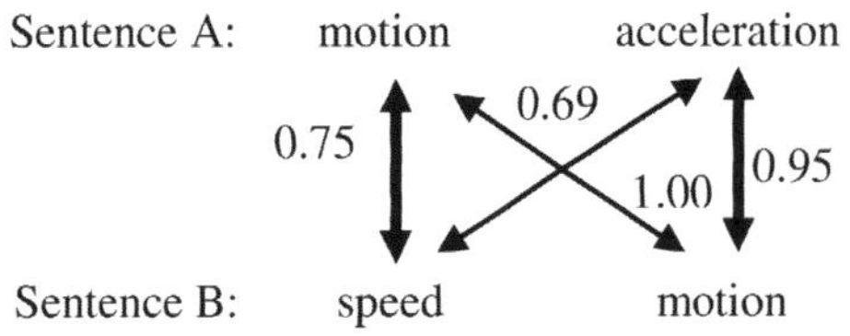

Figure 1. *Examples of two sentence fragments and word-to-word similarity scores for each of the word pairs across sentences. The bold arrows show optimal pairing.*

Experimental Setup and Results

We present in this section the datasets we used in our experiments and the results obtained. As we already mentioned, we use two datasets containing real student answers from two dialogue-based tutoring systems: AutoTutor (Graesser et al., 2005) and iSTART (McNamara et al., 2004).

The AutoTutor dataset contains 125 student contribution – expert answer pairs and the correct paraphrase judgment, TRUE or FALSE, as assigned by human experts. The target domain is conceptual physics. One expert physicist rated the degree to which particular speech acts expressed during AutoTutor training matched particular expert answers. These judgments were made on a sample of 25 physics expectations (i.e., correct expert answers) and 5 randomly sampled student answers per expectation, yielding a total of 125 pairs of expressions. The learner answers were always responses to the first hint for that expectation. The E-S pairs were graded by Physics experts on a scale of 1-4 (4 being perfect answer). This rubric could be mapped onto a binary TRUE-FALSE rubric: scores 3 and 4 equal a TRUE decision and 1 and 2 equal a FALSE decision. We ended up with 36 FALSE and 89 TRUE entailment pairs, i.e. a 28.8% versus 71.2% split (as compared to the 50-50% split of RTE data).

The iSTART data set, also known as the User Language Paraphrase Corpus (McCarty & McNamara, 2008) comprises annotations of paraphrase relations between student responses and ideal answers. The corpus contains 1998 pairs collected from previous student iSTART sessions and is divided into training (1499 instances) and testing (499 instances) subsets. The training subset contains 54% positive instances while testing contains 55% positive instances. The iSTART texts represent high school students' attempts to self-explain biology textbook texts.

To evaluate the performance of our methods, we compare the methods' judgments with the expert judgments. The percentage of matching judgments provides the accuracy of the run, i.e. the fraction of correct responses. We also report kappa statistics which indicate agreement between our methods' output and the human-expert judgments for each instance while taking into account chance agreement.

Tables 1, 2, and 3 summarize the results on the original AutoTutor data (from Rus & Graesser, 2006; Table 1), the re-annotated AutoTutor data by a second rater with inter-annotator agreement of 0.606 (Table 2), and the ULPC test subset (Table 3). For the ULPC corpus the methods have been trained on the training subset, an optimum threshold has been learned (such that scores above the threshold mean TRUE paraphrases) which is then used on the test data. Since the AutoTutor dataset is small, we only report results on it as a whole, i.e. only training. We report for each corpus a baseline method of guessing all the time the dominant class in the dataset (which is TRUE paraphrase for all three datasets), a pure greedy method (Greedy label in the first column of the tables), a greedy method applied to the words paired by the optimum method (optGreedy), and the results with the optimum matching method (Optimum).

Overall, the optimum method offered better performance in terms of accuracy and kappa statistics. The greedy method yields results that are close. In fact, when analyzed as raw scores instead of binary decisions (as is the case when computing accuracy) the greedy raw score are on average very similar to the optimum scores. For instance, for the LSA word-to-word similarity metric which provided best accuracy results on the ULPC dataset (accuracy=.643 for optimum and .615 for greedy), the average raw scores are .563 (using optimum matching) and .567 (using greedy matching). One reason for why they are so closed is that in optimum matching we have one-to-one word matches while in the greedy matching many-to-one matches are possible. That is, two words v and w from text T1 can be matched to same word y in text T2 in the greedy method. If we enforce that only one-to-one matches are possible in the greed method as in the optimum method, then we obtain the optGreedy method. The optGreedy method does work better than the pure greedy method (Greedy in the tables).

Another reason for why the raw scores are close for greedy and optimum is the fact that student input and expert answers in both the AutoTutor and ULPC corpora are sharing many words in common (>.50). This is the case because the dialogue is highly contextualized around a given, e.g. physics, problem. In the answer, both students and experts refer to the entities and interactions in the problem statement which leads to high identical word overlap. Identical words lead to perfect word-to-word similarity scores (=1.00) increasing the overall similarity score of the two sentences in both the greedy and optimum method.

Conclusions and Future Work

Overall, the optimum method offers better performance in terms of accuracy and kappa statistics than greedy and baseline methods.

The way we modeled the student assessment problem in this paper cannot deal with some type of responses. For instance, sometimes students' responses are mixed. Instead of being TRUE or FALSE responses, they contain both a correct part and an incorrect part as illustrated in the example below (Expert Answer provided for reference).

Expert Answer: The object continues to have a constant horizontal velocity component after it is released that is the same as the person horizontal velocity at the time of dropping the object.

Student Input: *The horizontal velocity will decrease while the vertical velocity increases.*

Such a mixed student input should trigger a mixed feedback from the system: "You are partially right! The vertical velocity will increase but not the horizontal velocity. Can you explain why?" We plan to address this problem in the future by proposing a more sophisticated model.

We also plan to answer the question of how much lexical versus world and domain knowledge each of these measures can capture. For instance, WordNet can be viewed as capturing some world knowledge as the concepts' definitions provide information about the world. However, it might be less rich in capturing domain specific knowledge. Indeed, WordNet seems to capture less domain knowledge at first sight. For instance, the definition of *acceleration* in WordNet does not link it to the concept of *force* but physics laws do, e.g. Newton's second law of motion.

Acknowledgments

This research was supported in part by the Institute for Education Sciences (award R305A100875). The opinions and findings reported in this paper are solely the authors'.

ID	RES	*LCH*	*JCN*	*LSA*	*Path*	*Lin*	*WUP*
Baseline	*.712*	*.712*	*.712*	*.712*	*.712*	*.712*	*.712*
Greedy	.736/.153	*.752/.204*	.760/.298	.744/.365	.752/.221	.744/.354	.760/.298
optGreedy	.744/187	*.752/.221*	.760/.298	.744/.306	.752/.309	.752/.204	.784/.349
Optimal	.744/.236	*.752/.204*	.760/.298	.744/.221	.752/.334	.752/.204	.784*/.409*

Table 1. Accuracy/kappa on AutoTutor data (* indicates statistical significance over the baseline method at p<0.005 level).

ID	RES	*LCH*	*JCN*	*LSA*	*Path*	*Lin*	*WUP*
Baseline	*.568*	*.568*	*.568*	*.568*	*.568*	*.568*	*.568*
Greedy	.616/.137	*.608/.117*	.624/.214	.632/.256	.624/.161	.608/1.34	.624/.181
optGreedy	.632/.192	*.632/.207*	.632/.229	.624/.218	.632*/.177*	.624/.165	.648*/.235*
Optimal	.624*/.153*	*.624/.169*	.640*/.208*	.640/.283	.624/.165	.624*/.148	.624/.173

Table 2. Accuracy/kappa on AutoTutor data with user annotations (* indicates statistical significance over the baseline method at p<0.005 level).

ID	RES	*LCH*	*JCN*	*LSA*	*Path*	*Lin*	*WUP*
Baseline	*.547*	*.547*	*.547*	*.547*	*.547*	*.547*	*.547*
Greedy	.619/.196	*.619/.201*	.629/.208	.615/.183	.635/.221	.629/.214	.621/.201
optGreedy	.621/.195	*.615/.201*	.629/.208	.643/.237	.623/.197	.619/.196	.613/.190
Optimal	.625/.205	*.615/.196*	.629/.208	.643/.237	.633/.215	.623/.203	.625/.214

Table 3. Accuracy/kappa on ULPC test data (all results are statistically different from the baseline at p<0.005 level).

References

Courtney Corley and Rada Mihalcea. 2005. Measures of Text Semantic Similarity. In Proceedings of the ACL workshop on Empirical Modeling of Semantic Equivalence, Ann Arbor, MI, June 2005.

Ido Dagan, Oren Glickman, and Bernando Magnini. 2005. The PASCAL recognizing textual entailment challenge. In Proceedings of the PASCAL Workshop.

Bill W. Dolan, Chris Quirk, and Chris Brockett. 2004. Unsupervised construction of large paraphrase corpora: Exploiting massively parallel news sources. In Proceedings of the 20th International Conference on Computational Linguistics, Geneva, Switzerland.

Arthur C. Graesser, Andrew Olney, Brian C. Hayes, and Patrick Chipman. 2005. Autotutor: A cognitive system that simulates a tutor that facilitates learning through mixed-initiative dialogue. In Cognitive Systems: Human Cognitive Models in System Design. Mahwah: Erlbaum.

Harold W. Kuhn. 1955. "The Hungarian Method for the assignment problem", Naval Research Logistics Quarterly, 2:83–97, 1955. Kuhn's original publication.

Thomas K. Landauer, Danielle S. McNamara, Simon Dennis, and Walter Kintsch. 2007. Handbook of Latent Semantic Analysis. Mahwah, NJ: Erlbaum.

Mihai Lintean and Vasile Rus. 2012. Measuring Semantic Similarity in Short Texts through Greedy Pairing and Word Semantics. To be presented at The Twenty-Fifth International FLAIRS Conference. Marco Island, Florida.

Philip M. McCarty and Danielle S. McNamara. 2008. User-Language Paraphrase Corpus Challenge, online.

Danielle S. McNamara, Irwin B. Levinstein, and Chutima Boonthum. 2004. iSTART: interactive strategy training for active reading and thinking. Behavioral Research Methods, Instruments, and Computers, 36(2).

Ted Pedersen, Siddharth Patwardhan, and Jason Michelizzi. 2004. WordNet::Similarity – Measuring the Relatedness of Concepts. In Proceedings of Fifth Annual Meeting of the North American Chapter of the Association for Computational Linguistics (NAACL-2004).

Vasile Rus, and Arthur C. Graesser. 2006. Deeper Natural Language Processing for Evaluating Student Answers in Intelligent Tutoring Systems, Proceedings of the Twenty-First National Conference on Artificial Intelligence (AAAI-06).

On Improving the Accuracy of Readability Classification using Insights from Second Language Acquisition

Sowmya Vajjala
Seminar für Sprachwissenschaft
Universität Tübingen
sowmya@sfs.uni-tuebingen.de

Detmar Meurers
Seminar für Sprachwissenschaft
Universität Tübingen
dm@sfs.uni-tuebingen.de

Abstract

We investigate the problem of readability assessment using a range of lexical and syntactic features and study their impact on predicting the grade level of texts. As empirical basis, we combined two web-based text sources, Weekly Reader and BBC Bitesize, targeting different age groups, to cover a broad range of school grades. On the conceptual side, we explore the use of lexical and syntactic measures originally designed to measure language development in the production of second language learners. We show that the developmental measures from Second Language Acquisition (SLA) research when combined with traditional readability features such as word length and sentence length provide a good indication of text readability across different grades. The resulting classifiers significantly outperform the previous approaches on readability classification, reaching a classification accuracy of 93.3%.

1 Introduction

Reading plays an important role in the development of first and second language skills, and it is one of the most important means of obtaining information about any subject, in and outside of school. However, teachers often find it difficult to obtain texts appropriate to the reading level of their students, on a given topic. In many cases, they end up modifying or creating texts, which takes significant time and effort. In addition to such a traditional school setting, finding texts at the appropriate reading level is also important in a wide range of real-life contexts involving people with intellectual disabilities, dyslexics, immigrant populations, and second or foreign language learners.

Readability-based text classification, when used as a ranking parameter in a search engine, can help in retrieving texts that suit a particular target reading level for a given query topic. In the context of language learning, a language aware search engine (Ott and Meurers, 2010) that includes readability classification can facilitate the selection of texts from the web that are appropriate for the students in terms of form and content. This is one of the main motivations underlying our research.

Readability assessment has a long history (DuBay, 2006). Traditionally, only a limited set of surface features such as word length and sentence length were considered to derive a formula for readability. More recently, advances in computational linguistics made it possible to automatically extract a wider range of language features from text. This facilitated building machine learning models that estimate the reading level of a text. On the other hand, there has also been an on-going stream of research on reading and text complexity in other areas such as Second Language Acquisition (SLA) research and psycholinguistics.

In SLA research, a range of measures have been proposed to study the development of complexity in the language produced by learners. These measures are used to evaluate the oral or written production abilities of language learners. The aim of readability classification, on the other hand, is to retrieve texts to be comprehended by readers at a particular level. Since we want to classify and retrieve texts for learners of different age groups, we hypothesized that these SLA-based complexity measures of learner production, when used as features for readability classification will improve the performance of the classifiers. In this paper, we show that this approach indeed results in a significant performance improvement compared to previous research.

We used the WeeklyReader website[1] as one of the text used in previous research. We combined it with texts crawled from the BBC-Bitesize website[2], which provides texts for a different age group. The combined corpus, *WeeBit*, covers a comparatively larger range of ages than covered before.

To summarize, the contributions of this paper are:

- We adapt measures from second language acquisition research to readability classification and show that the overall classification accuracies of an approach including these features significantly outperforms previous approaches.

- We extend the most widely used WeeklyReader corpus by combining it with another corpus that is graded for a different age-group, thereby creating a larger and more diverse corpus as basis for future research.

The paper is organized as follows: Section 2 describes related work on reading level classification to put our work in context. Section 3 introduces the corpora we used. Section 4 describes the features we considered in detail. Section 5 presents the approach and discusses the results. Section 6 provides a summary and points to future work.

2 Related Work

The traditional readability formulae made use of a limited number of surface features, such as the average sentence length and the average word length in characters or syllables (Kincaid et al., 1975; Coleman and Liau, 1975). Some works also made use of lists of "difficult" words, typically based on frequency counts, to estimate readability of texts (Dale and Chall, 1948; Chall and Dale, 1995; Stenner, 1996). Dubay (2006) provides a broad survey of traditional approaches to readability assessment. Although the features considered appear *shallow* in terms of linguistic modeling, they have been popular for many years and are widely used.

More recently, the developments in computational linguistics made it possible to consider various lexical and syntactic features to automatically model readability. In some of the early works on statistical readability assessment, Si and Callan (2001) and Collins-Thompson and Callan (2004) reported the impact of using unigram language models to estimate the grade level of a given text. The models were built on a United States text book corpus.

Heilman et al. (2007; 2008b; 2008a) extended this approach and worked towards retrieving relevant reading materials for language learners in the REAP[3] project. They extended the above mentioned approach to include a set of manually and later automatically extracted grammatical features.

Schwarm and Ostendorf (2005) and Petersen and Ostendorf (2009) report on classification experiments with WeeklyReader data, considering statistical language models, traditional formulae, as well as certain basic parse tree features in building an SVM-based statistical model. Feng et al. (2010) and Feng (2010) went beyond lexical and syntactic features and studied the impact of several discourse-based features, comparing their performance on the WeeklyReader corpus.

While the vast majority of approaches have targeted English texts, some work on other languages such as German, Portuguese, French and Italian (vor der Brück et al., 2008; Aluisio et al., 2010; Francois and Watrin, 2011; Dell'Orletta et al., 2011) is starting to emerge. Parse-tree-based features have also been used to measure the complexity of spoken Swedish (Roll et al., 2007).

The process of text comprehension and the effect of factors such as the coherence of texts have also been intensively studied (e.g., Crossley et al., 2007a; 2007b; Graesser et al., 2004) and measures to analyze the text under this perspective have been implemented in the CohMetrix project.[4]

The DARPA Machine Reading program created

[1] http://www.weeklyreader.com

[2] http://www.bbc.co.uk/bitesize

[3] http://reap.cs.cmu.edu

[4] http://cohmetrix.memphis.edu

a corpus of general text readability containing various forms of human and machine generated texts (Strassel et al., 2010).[5] The aim of this program is to transform natural language texts into a format suitable for automatic processing by machines and to filter out poorly written documents based on the text *quality*. Kate et al. (2010) used this data set to build a coarse grained model of text readability.

While in this paper we focus on comparing computational linguistic approaches to readability assessment and improving the state of the art on a traditional and available data set, Nelson et al. (2012) compared several research and commercially available text difficulty assessment systems in support of the Common Core Standards' goal of providing students with texts at the appropriate level of difficulty throughout their schooling.[6]

Independent of the research on readability, the complexity of the texts *produced* by language learners has been extensively investigated in Second Language Acquisition (SLA) research (Housen and Kuiken, 2009). Recent approaches have automated and compared a number of such complexity measures for learner language, specifically in English as Second Language learner narratives (Lu, 2010; Lu, 2011b). So far, there is hardly any work on using such insights in computational linguistics, though, with the notable exception of Chen and Zechner (2011) using SLA features to evaluate spontaneous non-native speech. Given that graded corpora are also intended to be used by incremental age groups, we started to investigate whether the insights from SLA research can fruitfully be applied to readability classification.

3 Corpora

We used a combined corpus of WeeklyReader and BBC-Bitesize to develop a statistical model that classifies texts into five grade levels, based on the age groups.

WeeklyReader[7] is an educational newspaper, with articles targeted at four grade levels (Level 2, Level 3, Level 4, and Senior), corresponding to children between ages 7–8, 8–9, 9–10, and 9–12 years. The articles cover a wide range of non-fiction topics, from science to current affairs, written according to the grade level of the readers. The exact criterion of graded writing is not published by the magazine. We obtained permission to use the graded magazine articles and downloaded the archives in 11/2011.[8]

Though we used the same WeeklyReader text base as the previous works, the corpus is not identical since we downloaded our version more recently. Thus the archive contained more articles per level and some preprocessing may differ. The WeeklyReader magazine issues in addition to the actual articles include teacher guides, student quizzes, images and brain teaser games, which we did not include in the corpus. The distribution of articles after this preprocessing is shown in Table 1.

Grade Level	*Age in Years*	*Number of Articles*	*Avg. Number of Sentences/Article*
Level 2	7–8	629	23.41
Level 3	8–9	801	23.28
Level 4	9–10	814	28.12
Senior	10-12	1325	31.21

Table 1: The *Weekly Reader* corpus

BBC-Bitesize[9] is a website with articles classified into four grade levels (KS1, KS2, KS3 and GCSE), corresponding to children between ages 5–7, 8–11, 11–14 and 14–16 years. The Bitesize corpus is freely available on the web, and we crawled it in 2009. Most of the articles at KS1 consisted of images and flash files and other audio-visual material, with little text. Hence, we did not include KS1 in our corpus. We also excluded pages that contained only images, audio, or video files without text.

To cover a broad range of non-overlapping age groups, we used Level 2, Level 3 and Level 4 from WeeklyReader and KS3 and GCSE from Bitesize data respectively and built a combined corpus covering learners aged 7 to 16 years. Note that while KS2 covers the age group of 8–11 years, Levels 2, 3, and

[5]The corpus is apparently intended to be available for public use, but does not yet seem to be so; we so far were unsuccessful in obtaining more information from the authors.

[6]`http://www.corestandards.org`

[7]`http://www.weeklyreader.com`

[8]A license to use the texts on the website for research can be obtained for a small fee from *support@weeklyreader.com*. To support comparable research, we will share the exact corpus we used with other researchers who have obtained a license to use the WeeklyReader materials.

[9]`http://www.bbc.co.uk/bitesize`

4 together cover ages 7–10 years. Similarly, the Senior Level overlaps with Level 4 and KS3. Hence, we excluded KS2 and Senior from the combined corpus. We will refer to the combined five-level corpus we created in this way as **WeeBit**. The distribution of articles in the combined *WeeBit* corpus after preprocessing and removing the overlapping grade levels, is shown in Table 2.

Grade Level	*Age in Years*	*Number of Articles*	*Avg. Number of Sentences/Article*
Level 2	7–8	629	23.41
Level 3	8–9	801	23.28
Level 4	9–10	814	28.12
KS3	11–14	644	22.71
GCSE	14–16	3500	27.85

Table 2: The *WeeBit* corpus

To avoid a classification bias towards a class with more training examples during, for each level in the *WeeBit* corpus, 500 documents were taken as training set and 125 documents were taken as test set. In total, we trained on a set of 2500 documents and used a test set of 625 documents, spanning across five grade levels.

4 Features

To build our classification models, we combined features used in previous research with other parse tree features as well as lexical richness and syntactic complexity features from SLA research. We group the features into three broad categories: lexical, syntactic and traditional features.

4.1 Lexical Features

Word n-grams have been frequently used as lexical features in the previous research (Collins-Thompson and Callan, 2004; Schwarm and Ostendorf, 2005).[10] POS n-grams as well as POS-tag ratio features have also been used in some of the later works (Feng et al., 2010; Petersen and Ostendorf, 2009).

In the SLA context, independent of the readability research, Lu (2011a) studied the relationship of **lexical richness** to the quality of English as Second Language (ESL) learners' oral narratives and analyzed the distribution of three dimensions of lexical richness (lexical density, sophistication and variation) in them using various metrics proposed in the language acquisition literature. Those measures were used to analyze a large scale corpus of Chinese learners of English. We adapted some of the metrics from this research as our lexical features:

Type-Token Ratio (TTR) is the ratio of number of word types (T) to total number word tokens in a text (N). It has been widely used as a measure of lexical diversity or lexical variation in language acquisition studies. However, since it is dependent on the text size, various alternative transformations of TTR came into existence. We considered Root TTR (T/$\sqrt{N}$), Corrected TTR (T/$\sqrt{2N}$), Bilogarithmic TTR (Log T/Log N) and Uber Index ($Log^2T/Log(N/T)$).

Another recent TTR variant we considered, which is not a part of Lu (2011a), is the Measure of Textual Lexical Diversity (MTLD; McCarthy and Jarvis, 2010). It is a TTR-based approach that is not affected by text length. It is evaluated sequentially, as the mean length of string sequences that maintain a default Type-Token Ratio value. That is, the TTR is calculated at each word. When the default TTR value is reached, the MTLD count increases by one and TTR evaluations are again reset. McCarthy and Jarvis (2010) considered the default TTR as 0.72 and we continued with the same default.

Considering nouns, adjectives, non-modal and non-auxiliary verbs and adverbs as lexical items, Lu (2011a) studied various syntactic category based word ratio measures. *Lexical variation* is defined as the ratio of the number of lexical types to lexical tokens. Other variants of lexical variation studied in Lu (2011a) included noun, adjective, modifier, adverb and verb variations, which represent the proportion of the words of the respective categories compared to all lexical words in the document. Alternative measures of verb variation, namely Verb Variation-1 (T_{verb}/N_{verb}), Squared Verb Variation-1 (T^2_{verb}/N_{verb}) and Corrected Verb Variation-1 ($T_{verb}/\sqrt{2N_{verb}}$) are also studied in the literature. We considered all these measures of lexical variation as a part of our lexical features. We have also included *Lexical Density*, which is the ratio of the number of lexical items in relation to the total number of words in a text.

[10] In the readability literature, n-grams are traditionally discussed as lexical features. N-grams beyond unigrams naturally also encode aspects of syntax.

In addition to these measures from the SLA literature, in our lexical features we included the average number of syllables per word (NumSyll) and the average number of characters per word (NumChar), which are used as word-level indicators of text complexity in various traditional formulae (Kincaid et al., 1975; Coleman and Liau, 1975).

Finally, we included the proportion of words in the text which are found on the *Academic Word List* as another lexical feature. It refers to the word list created by Coxhead (2000), which contains a list of most frequent words found in the academic texts.[11] The list does not include the most frequent words in the English language as such. The words in this list are specific to academic contexts. It was intended to be used both by teachers and students as a measure of vocabulary acquisition. We use it as an additional lexical feature in our work – and it turned out to be one of the most predictive features.

All the lexical features we considered in this work are listed in Table 3. The SLA based lexical features are referred to as SLALEX in the table. Of these, six features *CTTR, RTTR, SVV1, CVV1, AdvV, ModV* were shown by Lu (2011b) to correlate best with the learner data. We will refer to them as BESTLEX-SLA, highlighted in italics in the table.

Lexical Features from SLA research (SLALEX)
- Lexical Density (LD)
- Type-Token Ratio (TTR)
- *Corrected TTR (CTTR)*
- *Root TTR (RTTR)*
- Bilogarithmic TTR (LogTTR)
- Uber Index (Uber)
- Lexical Word Variation (LV)
- Verb Variation-1 (VV1)
- *Squared VV1 (SVV1)*
- *Corrected VV1 (CVV1)*
- Verb Variation 2 (VV2)
- Noun Variation (NV)
- Adjective Variation (AdjV)
- *Adverb Variation (AdvV)*
- *Modifier Variation (ModV)*
- Mean Textual Lexical Density (MTLD)

Other Lexical Features
- Proportion of words in AWL (AWL)
- Avg. Num. Characters per word (NumChar)
- Avg. Num. Syllables per word (NumSyll)

Table 3: Lexical Features (LEXFEATURES)

[11] `http://en.wikipedia.org/wiki/Academic_Word_List`

4.2 Syntactic Features

Schwarm and Ostendorf (2005) implemented four parse tree features (average parse tree height, average number of SBARs, NPs per sentence and VPs per sentence) in their work. Feng (2010) considered more syntactic features, adding the average lengths of phrases (NP, VP and PP) per sentence in words and characters, and the total number of respective phrases in the document. In our work, we started with reconsidering the above mentioned syntactic features.

In addition, we included measures of syntactic complexity from the SLA literature. Lu (2010) selected 14 measures from a large set of measures used to monitor the syntactic development in language learners. He then used these measures in the analysis of syntactic complexity in second language writing and showed that some of them correlate well with the syntactic development of adult Chinese learners of English. They are grouped into five broad categories:

The first set consists of three measures of syntactic complexity based on the length of a unit at the sentential, clausal and T-unit level respectively. The definitions for sentence, clause and T-unit were adapted from the SLA literature. While a *sentence* is considered to be a group of words delimited with punctuation mark, a *clause* is any structure with a subject and a finite verb. Finally, a *T-unit* is characterized as one main clause plus any subordinate clause or non-clausal structure that is attached to or embedded in it.

The second type of measure targets sentence complexity. Clauses per sentence is considered as a sentence complexity measure.

The third set of measures reflect the amount of subordination in the sentence. They include clauses per T-unit, complex T-units per T-unit, dependent clauses per clause and dependent clauses per T-unit. A *complex T-unit* is considered as any T-unit that contains a dependent clause.

The fourth type of measures measured the amount of co-ordination in a sentence. They consist of co-ordinate phrases per clause and co-ordinate phases per T-unit. Any adjective, verb, adverb or noun phrase that dominates a co-ordinating conjunction is considered a co-ordinate phrase.

The fifth type of measures represented the relationship between specific syntactic structures and larger production units. They include complex nominals per clause, complex nominals per T-unit and verb phrases per T-unit. Complex nominals are comprised of a) nouns plus adjective, possessive, prepositional phrase, relative clause, participle or appositive, b) nominal clauses, c) gerunds and infinitives in subject positions.

We implemented these 14 syntactic measures as features in building our classification models, in addition to existing features. Eight of these features *(MLC, MLT, CP/C, CP/T, CN/C, CN/T, MLS, VP/T)* were argued to correlate best with language development. We refer to this subset of eight as BESTSYN-SLA, shown in italics in Table 4. We will see in section 5 that a set including those features also holds good predictive power for classifying graded texts.

We also included the number of dependent clauses, complex T-units, and co-ordinate phrases per sentence as additional syntactic features. Table 4 summarizes the syntactic features used in this paper.

Syntactic features from SLA research (SLASYN)
- *Mean length of clause (MLC)*
- *Mean length of a sentence (MLS)*
- *Mean length of T-unit (MLT)*
- Num. of Clauses per Sentence (C/S)
- Num. of T-Units per sentence (T/S)
- Num. of Clauses per T-unit (C/T)
- Num. of Complex-T-Units per T-unit (CT/T)
- Dependent Clause to Clause Ratio (DC/C)
- Dependent Clause to T-unit Ratio (DC/T)
- *Co-ordinate Phrases per Clause (CP/C)*
- *Co-ordinate Phrases per T-unit (CP/T)*
- *Complex Nominals per Clause (CN/C)*
- *Complex Nominals per T-unit (CN/T)*
- *Verb phrases per T-unit (VP/T)*

Other Syntactic features
- Num. NPs per sentence (NumNP)
- Num. VPs per sentence (NumVP)
- Num. PPs per sentence (NumPP))
- Avg. length of a NP (NPSize)
- Avg. length of a VP (VPSize)
- Avg. length of a PP (PPSize)
- Num. Dependent Clauses per sentence (NumDC)
- Num. Complex-T units per sentence (NumCT)
- Num. Co-ordinate Phrases per sentence (CoOrd)
- Num. SBARs per sentence (NumSBAR)
- Avg. Parse Tree Height (TreeHeight)

Table 4: Syntactic features (SYNFEATURES)

4.3 "Traditional" Features

The average number of characters per word (NumChar), the average number of syllables per word (NumSyll), and the average sentence length in words (MLS) have been used to derive formulae for readability in the past. We refer to them as *Traditional Features* below. We included MLS in the syntactic features and NumChar, and NumSyll in the Lexical features. We also included two popular readability formulae, Flesch-Kincaid score (Kincaid et al., 1975) and Coleman-Liau readability formula (Coleman and Liau, 1975), as additional features. The latter will be referred as *Coleman* below, and both formulas together as *Traditional Formulae*.

5 Experiments and Evaluation

We used the Berkeley Parser (Petrov and Klein, 2007) with the standard model they provide for building syntactic parse trees and defined the patterns for extracting various syntactic features from the trees using the Tregex pattern matcher (Levy and Andrew, 2006). More details about the patterns from the SLA literature and their definitions can be found in Lu (2010). We used the OpenNLP[12] tagger to get POS tag information and calculate Lexical Richness features. We used the WEKA (Hall et al., 2009) toolkit for our classification experiments. We explored different classification algorithms such as Decision Trees, Support Vector Machines, and Logistic Regression. The Multi-Layer Perceptron (MLP)-classifier performed best with various combinations of features, so we focus on reporting the results for that algorithm.

[12] http://opennlp.apache.org

Feature set	# Features	Classifier Performance	
		Accuracy	RMSE
Traditional Formulae	2	38.8%	0.36
Traditional Features	3	70.3%	0.25
Trad. Features + Trad. formulae	5	72.3%	0.32
SLALEX	16	68.1%	0.29
SLASYN	14	71.2%	0.28
SLALEX + SLASYN	30	**82.3%**	0.23
BEST10SYN	10	69.9%	0.28
All Syntactic Features	25	75.3%	0.27
BEST10LEX	10	82.4%	0.22
All Lexical Features	19	86.7%	0.20
BEST10ALL	10	89.7%	0.18
All features	46	**93.3%**	0.15

Table 5: Classification results for WeeBit Corpus

5.1 Evaluation Metrics

We report our results in terms of classification accuracy and root mean square error.

Classification accuracy refers to the percentage of instances in the test set that are classified correctly. The correct classifications include both true positives and true negatives. However, accuracy does not reflect how close the prediction is to the actual value. A difference between expected and predicted values of one grade level is treated the same way as the difference of, e.g., four grade levels.

Root mean square error (RMSE) is a measure which gives a better picture of this difference. RMSE is the square root of empirical mean of the squared prediction errors. It is frequently used as a measure to estimate the deviation of an observed value from the expected value. In readability assessment, it can be understood as the average difference between the predicted grade level and the expected grade level.

5.2 Feature Combinations

Complementing our experiments comparing the different lexical and syntactic features and their combination, we also used WEKA's information-gain-based feature selection algorithm, and selected the Top-10 best features using the ranker method.

When all features were considered, the top 10 most predictive features were found to be: (*NumChar, NumSyll, MLS, AWL, ModVar, CoOrd, Coleman, DC/C, CN/C,and AdvVar*), which are referred to as BEST10ALL in the table.

Considering the 25 syntactic features alone, the 10 most predictive features were: (*MLS, CoOrd, DC/C, CN/C, CP/C, NumPP, VPSize, C/T, CN/T and NumVP*), referred to as BEST10SYN in the table.

The 10 most predictive features amongst all the lexical features were: (*NumChar, NumSyll, AWL, ModV, AdvV, AdjV, LV, VV1, NV and SVV1*). They are referred to as BEST10LEX in the table.

Although the traditionally used features (*NumChar, NumSyll, MLS*) seem to be the most predictive, it can be seen from the other top ranked features, that there is significant overlap between the best features identified by WEKA and the features which Lu (2010; 2011b) identified as correlating best with language development (shown in italics in Table 3 and Table 4), which supports our hypothesis that the SLA-based measures are useful features for readability classification of non-learner text too.

5.3 Results

Table 5 shows the results of our classification experiments using WEKA's Multi-Layer Perceptron algorithm with different combinations of features. Combining all features results in the best accuracy of 93.3%, which is a large improvement over the current state of the art in readability classification reported on the WeeklyReader corpus (74.01% by Feng et al., 2010). It should, however, be kept

	# Features	Highest reported accuracy
Previous work (on WeeklyReader)		
(Feng et al., 2010)	122	74.01%
(Petersen and Ostendorf, 2009)	25	63.18%
Syntactic features only (Petersen and Ostendorf, 2009)	4	50.91%
Our Results (on WeeklyReader alone)		
Syntactic features from (Petersen and Ostendorf, 2009)	4	50.68%
All our Syntactic Features	25	64.3%
All our Lexical Features	19	84.1%
All our Features	46	91.3%
Our Results (on WeeBit)		
All our Syntactic Features	25	75.3%
All our Lexical Features	19	86.7%
All our Features	46	93.3%

Table 6: Overall Results and Comparison with Previous Work

in mind that the improvement is achieved on the WeeBit corpus which is an extension of the WeeklyReader corpus previously used. Interestingly, the result of 89.7% for BEST10ALL, the top 10 features chosen by the WEKA ranker, are quite close to our best result, with a very small number of features.

Lexical features seem to perform better than syntactic features when considered separately. However, this better performance of lexical features was mainly due to the addition of the traditionally used features *NumChar* and *NumSyll*. So it is no wonder that these shallow features have been used in the traditional readability formulae for such a long time; but the predictive power of the traditional formulae as features by themselves is poor (38.8%), in line with the conclusions drawn in previous research (Schwarm and Ostendorf, 2005; Feng et al., 2010) about the Flesch-Kincaid and Dale-Chall formulae. Interestingly, *Coleman*, which was not considered in those previous approaches, was ranked among the Top-10 most predictive features by the WEKA ranker. So it holds a good predictive power when used as one of the features for the classifier.

We also studied the impact of SLA based features alone on readability classification. The performance of the SLA based lexical features (SLALEX) and syntactic features (SLASYN) when considered separately are still in a comparable range with the previously reported results on readability classification (68.1% and 71.2% respectively). However, combining both of them resulted in an accuracy of 82.3%, which is a considerable improvement over previously reported results. It again adds weight to the initial hypothesis that SLA based features can be useful for readability classification.

5.4 Comparison with previous work

Table 6 provides an overall comparison of the accuracies obtained for the key features sets in our work with the best results reported in the literature for the WeeklyReader corpus. However, since our classification experiments were carried out with a newly compiled corpus extending the WeeklyReader data, such a direct comparison is not particularly meaningful by itself. To address this issue, we explored two avenues.

Firstly, we ran additional experiments, training and testing on the WeeklyReader data only, including the four levels used in previous work on that corpus. A summary of the results can be seen in Table 6. Our approach with 46 features results in 91.3% accuracy on the WeeklyReader corpus, compared to 74.01% as the best previous WeeklyReader result, reported by Feng et al. (2010) for their much larger feature set (122 features).

In order to verify the impact of our choice of features, we also did a replication of the parsed syntactic feature measures reported by (Schwarm and Ostendorf, 2005) on the WeeklyReader corpus and obtained essentially the same accuracy as the one published (50.7% vs. 50.91%), supporting the comparability of the WeeklyReader data used. The significant performance increase we reported thus seems to be due to the new features we integrated from the SLA literature.

Secondly, we were interested in the impact of the training size on the results. We therefore investigated how good our best approach (using all features) is on a training corpus that is comparable to the WeeklyReader corpus used in previous work in terms of the number of documents per class. When we took 1400 WeeklyReader documents distributed into four classes as described in Feng et al. (2010), we obtained an accuracy of 84.2%, compared to the 74.01% they reported as best result. Using 2500 documents distributed into four classes as in Petersen and Ostendorf (2009) we obtained 88.4%, compared to their best result of 63.18%. Given that the original corpora used are not available, these WeeklyReader corpora with the same source, number of documents, and size of classes are as close as we can get to a direct comparison. In the future, the availability of the WeeBit corpus will support a more direct comparison of approaches.

In sum, the above experiments seem to indicate that the set of features and classifier used in our approach play an important role in the resulting significant increase in accuracy.

6 Conclusion and Discussion

We created a new corpus, *WeeBit*, by combining texts from two graded web sources WeeklyReader and BBC Bitesize. The resulting text corpus is larger and covers more grade levels, spanning the age group between 7 and 16 years. We hope that the availability of this graded corpus will be useful as an empirical basis for future studies in automatic readability assessment.[13]

We studied the impact of various lexical and syntactic features and explored their performance in combination with features encoding syntactic complexity and lexical richness that were inspired by Second Language Acquisition research. Our experiments show that not only the full set of features, but also specific manually or automatically selected subsets of features provide results significantly improving on the previously published state of the art in automatic readability assessment. There also seems to be a clear correlation between the good predictors according to SLA research on language learning and those that performed well in text classification.

Although the exact criteria based on which the individual corpora (WeeklyReader, BBC-Bitesize) were created is not known, it is possible that they were created with the well-known, traditional readability formulae in mind. It would be surprising if the two corpora, compiled in the US and Britain by different companies, were created with the same set of measures in mind, so the WeeBit corpus should be less affected. Still, it is possible that the reason the traditional features NumChar, NumSyll and MLS held such a strong predictive power is that these measures were considered when the texts were written. But removing these traditional features only strengthens the role of the other features and thereby the main point of the paper arguing for the usefuless of SLA developmental measures for readability classification.

As a part of our future work, we intend to revisit and study the impact of further classes of features employed in psycholinguistics and cognitive science research, such as those studied in Coh-Metrix (Graesser et al., 2004) or in the context of retrieving texts for specific groups of readers (Feng, 2010).

In terms of our overall application goal, we are currently studying the ability of the classification models we built to generalize to web data. We then plan to add the classification model to a language aware search engine (Ott and Meurers, 2010). Such a search engine may then also be able to integrate user feedback on the readability levels of webpages, to build a dynamic, online model of readability.

7 Acknowledgements

We thank the anonymous reviewers and workshop organizers for their feedback on the paper. The research leading to these results has received funding from the European Commission's 7th Framework Program under grant agreement number 238405 (CLARA).[14]

[13]As mentioned above, we will make the WeeBit corpus available to all researchers who have obtained the inexpensive research license from WeeklyReader.

[14]http://clara.uib.no

References

Sandra Aluisio, Lucia Specia, Caroline Gasperin, and Carolina Scarton. 2010. Readability assessment for text simplification. In *Proceedings of the NAACL HLT 2010 Fifth Workshop on Innovative Use of NLP for Building Educational Applications*, pages 1–9, Los Angeles, California, June.

Jeanne S. Chall and Edgar Dale. 1995. *Readability Revisted: The New Dale-Chall Readability Formula*. Brookline Books.

Maio Chen and Klaus Zechner. 2011. Computing and evaluating syntactic complexity features for automated scoring of spontaneous non-native speech. In *Proceedings of the 49th Annual Meeting of the Association for Computational Linguistics*, pages 722–731, Portland, Oregon, June.

Meri Coleman and T.L. Liau. 1975. A computer readability formula designed for machine scoring. *Journal of Applied Psychology*, 60:283–284.

Kevyn Collins-Thompson and Jamie Callan. 2004. A language modeling approach to predicting reading difficulty. In *Proceedings of HLT/NAACL 2004*, Boston, USA.

Averil Coxhead. 2000. A new academic word list. *Teachers of English to Speakers of Other Languages*, 34(2):213–238.

Scott A. Crossley, David F. Dufty, Philip M. McCarthy, and Danielle S. McNamara. 2007a. Toward a new readability: A mixed model approach. In Danielle S. McNamara and Greg Trafton, editors, *Proceedings of the 29th annual conference of the Cognitive Science Society*. Cognitive Science Society.

Scott A. Crossley, Max M. Louwerse, Philip M. McCarthy, and Danielle S. McNamara. 2007b. A linguistic analysis of simplified and authentic texts. *The Modern Language Journal*, 91(1):15–30.

Edgar Dale and Jeanne S. Chall. 1948. A formula for predicting readability. *Educational research bulletin; organ of the College of Education*, 27(1):11–28.

Felice Dell'Orletta, Simonetta Montemagni, and Giulia Venturi. 2011. Read-it: Assessing readability of italian texts with a view to text simplification. In *Proceedings of the 2nd Workshop on Speech and Language Processing for Assistive Technologies*, pages 73–83.

William H. DuBay. 2006. *The Classic Readability Studies*. Impact Information, Costa Mesa, California.

Lijun Feng, Martin Jansche, Matt Huenerfauth, and Noémie Elhadad. 2010. A comparison of features for automatic readability assessment. In *In Proceedings of the 23rd International Conference on Computational Linguistics (COLING 2010), Beijing, China.*

Lijun Feng. 2010. *Automatic Readability Assessment*. Ph.D. thesis, City University of New York (CUNY).

Thomas Francois and Patrick Watrin. 2011. On the contribution of mwe-based features to a readability formula for french as a foreign language. In *Proceedings of Recent Advances in Natural Language Processing*, pages 441–447.

Arthur C. Graesser, Danielle S. McNamara, Max M. Louweerse, and Zhiqiang Cai. 2004. Coh-metrix: Analysis of text on cohesion and language. *Behavior Research Methods, Instruments and Computers*, 36:193–202.

Mark Hall, Eibe Frank, Geoffrey Holmes, Bernhard Pfahringer, Peter Reutemann, and Ian H. Witten. 2009. The weka data mining software: An update. *The SIGKDD Explorations*, 11(1).

Michael Heilman, Kevyn Collins-Thompson, Jamie Callan, and Maxine Eskenazi. 2007. Combining lexical and grammatical features to improve readability measures for first and second language texts. In *Human Language Technologies 2007: The Conference of the North American Chapter of the Association for Computational Linguistics (HLT-NAACL'07)*, pages 460–467, Rochester, New York.

Michael Heilman, Kevyn Collins-Thompson, and Maxine Eskenazi. 2008a. An analysis of statistical models and features for reading difficulty prediction. In *Proceedings of the 3rd Workshop on Innovative Use of NLP for Building Educational Applications*, Columbus, Ohio.

Michael Heilman, Le Zhao, Juan Pino, and Maxine Eskenazi. 2008b. Retrieval of reading materials for vocabulary and reading practice. In *Proceedings of the Third Workshop on Innovative Use of NLP for Building Educational Applications (BEA-3) at ACL'08*, pages 80–88, Columbus, Ohio.

Alex Housen and Folkert Kuiken. 2009. Complexity, accuracy, and fluency in second language acquisition. *Applied Linguistics*, 30(4):461–473.

Rohit J. Kate, Xiaoqiang Luo, Siddharth Patwardhan, Martin Franz, Radu Florian, Raymond J. Mooney, Salim Roukos, and Chris Welty. 2010. Learning to predict readability using diverse linguistic features. In *23rd International Conference on Computational Linguistics (COLING 2010)*.

J. P. Kincaid, R. P. Jr. Fishburne, R. L. Rogers, and B. S Chissom. 1975. Derivation of new readability formulas (Automated Readability Index, Fog Count and Flesch Reading Ease formula) for Navy enlisted personnel. Research Branch Report 8-75, Naval Technical Training Command, Millington, TN.

Roger Levy and Galen Andrew. 2006. Tregex and tsurgeon: tools for querying and manipulating tree data structures. In *5th International Conference on Language Resources and Evaluation*, Genoa, Italy.

Xiaofei Lu. 2010. Automatic analysis of syntactic complexity in second language writing. *International Journal of Corpus Linguistics*, 15(4):474–496.

Xiaofei Lu. 2011a. A corpus-based evaluation of syntactic complexity measures as indices of college-level esl writers' language development. *TESOL Quarterly*, 45(1):36–62, March.

Xiaofei Lu. 2011b. The relationship of lexical richness to the quality of esl learners' oral narratives. *The Modern Languages Journal*. in press.

Philip McCarthy and Scott Jarvis. 2010. Mtld, vocd-d, and hd-d: A validation study of sophisticated approaches to lexical diversity assessment. *Behavior Research Methods*, 42(2):381–392.

J. Nelson, C. Perfetti, D. Liben, and M. Liben. 2012. Measures of text difficulty: Testing their predictive value for grade levels and student performance. Technical report, The Council of Chief State School Officers.

Niels Ott and Detmar Meurers. 2010. Information retrieval for education: Making search engines language aware. *Themes in Science and Technology Education. Special issue on computer-aided language analysis, teaching and learning: Approaches, perspectives and applications*, 3(1–2):9–30.

Sarah E. Petersen and Mari Ostendorf. 2009. A machine learning approach to reading level assessment. *Computer Speech and Language*, 23:86–106.

Slav Petrov and Dan Klein. 2007. Improved inference for unlexicalized parsing. In *Human Language Technologies 2007: The Conference of the North American Chapter of the Association for Computational Linguistics; Proceedings of the Main Conference*, pages 404–411, Rochester, New York, April.

Mikael Roll, Johan Frid, and Merie Horne. 2007. Measuring syntactic complexity in spontaneous spoken swedish. *Language and Speech*, 50(2).

Sarah Schwarm and Mari Ostendorf. 2005. Reading level assessment using support vector machines and statistical language models. In *Proceedings of the 43rd Annual Meeting of the Association for Computational Linguistics (ACL'05)*, pages 523–530, Ann Arbor, Michigan.

Luo Si and Jamie Callan. 2001. A statistical model for scientific readability. In *Proceedings of the 10th International Conference on Information and Knowledge Management (CIKM)*, pages 574–576. ACM.

A. Jackson Stenner. 1996. Measuring reading comprehension with the lexile framework. In *Fourth North American Conference on Adolescent/Adult Literacy*.

Stephanie Strassel, Dan Adams, Henry Goldberg, Jonathan Herr, Ron Keesing, Daniel Oblinger, Heather Simpson, Robert Schrag, and Jonathan Wright. 2010. The darpa machine reading program - encouraging linguistic and reasoning research with a series of reading tasks. In *Language Resources and Evaluation (LREC)*, Malta.

Tim vor der Brück, Sven Hartrumpf, and Hermann Helbig. 2008. A readability checker with supervised learning using deep syntactic and semantic indicators. *Informatica*, 32(4):429—-435.

An Interactive Analytic Tool for Peer-Review Exploration

Wenting Xiong[1,2], Diane Litman[1,2], Jingtao Wang[1,2] and Christian Schunn[2]
[1] Department of Computer Science & [2] Learning Research and Development Center
University of Pittsburgh, Pittsburgh, PA, 15260
wex12@cs.pitt.edu

Abstract

This paper presents an interactive analytic tool for educational peer-review analysis. It employs data visualization at multiple levels of granularity, and provides automated analytic support using clustering and natural language processing. This tool helps instructors discover interesting patterns in writing performance that are reflected through peer reviews.

1 Introduction

Peer review is a widely used educational approach for coaching writing in many domains (Topping, 1998; Topping, 2009). Because of the large number of review comments to examine, instructors giving peer review assignments find it difficult to examine peer comments. While there are web-based peer-review systems that help instructors set up peer-review assignments, no prior work has been done to support instructors' comprehension of the textual review comments.

To address this issue, we have designed and developed an interactive analytic interface (RevExplore) on top of SWoRD[1] (Cho and Schunn, 2007), a web-based peer-review reciprocal system that has been used by over 12,000 students over the last 8 years. In this paper, we show how RevExplore visualizes peer-review information in multiple dimensions and various granularity levels to support investigative exploration, and applies natural language processing (NLP) techniques to facilitate review comprehension and comparison.

[1] https://sites.google.com/site/swordlrdc/

2 Design Goals

Instructors face challenges when they try to make sense of the peer-review data collected by SWoRD for their assignments. Instructors we have interviewed have complained that peer reviews are time-consuming to read and almost "impossible" to interpret: 1) to understand the pros and cons of one student's paper, they need to synthesize all the peer reviews received by that student by reading them one by one; 2) furthermore, if instructors would like to discover general patterns regarding students' writing performance, they have to additionally compare peer reviews across multiple students which requires their simultaneously remembering various opinions for many students; 3) in the initial stage of peer review analysis, instructors have no clear idea of what potential patterns they should be looking for ("cold start").

These challenges motivate our design of RevExplore, a peer-review analytic tool that is a plugin to SWoRD. We set our design goals to address the challenges mentioned above, respectively: 1) create a simple and informative representation of peer-review data which automatically aggregates peer-reviews at the level of student; 2) provide intelligent support of text mining and semantic abstraction for the purpose of comparison; 3) enable an overview of key characteristics of peer reviews for initial exploration.

To fulfill our design goals, we design an interactive visualization system to ease the exploration process, following the pattern of overview plus detail (Card et al., 1999). In the overview, RevExplore provides a high level of visualization of overall peer-review information at the student level for initial exploration. In the detail-view, RevExplore automatically abstracts the semantic information of peer reviews at the topic-word level, with the original texts visible on demand. In addition, we introduce clustering and NLP techniques to support automated analytics.

3 Related Work

One major goal of peer review studies in educational research is to understand how to better improve student learning, directly or indirectly. Empirical studies of textual review comments based on manual coding have discovered that certain review features (e.g., whether the solution to a problem is explicitly stated in a comment) can predict both whether the problem will be understand and the feedback implemented (Nelson and Schunn, 2009). Our previous studies used machine learning and NLP techniques to automatically identify the presence of such useful features in review comments (Xiong et al., 2010); similar techniques have also been used to determine review comment helpfulness (Xiong and Litman, 2011; Cho, 2008). With respect to paper analysis, Sándor and Vorndran (2009) used NLP to highlight key sentences, in order to focus reviewer attention on important paper aspects. Finally, Giannoukos et al. (2010) focused on peer matching based on students' profile information to maximize learning outcomes, while Crespo Garcia and Pardo (2010) explored the use of document clustering to adaptively guide the assignment of papers to peers. In contrast to the prior work above, the research presented here is primarily motivated by the needs of instructors, instead of the needs of students. In particular, the goal of RevExplore is to utilize the information in peer reviews and papers, to help instructors better understand student performance in the peer-review assignments for their courses.

Many computer tools have already been developed to support peer review activities in various types of classrooms, from programming courses (Hyyrynen et al., 2010) to courses involving writing in the disciplines (Nelson and Schunn, 2009; Yang, 2011). Within the writing domain, systems such as SWoRD (Cho and Schunn, 2007) mainly assist instructors by providing administrative management support and/or (optional) automatic grading services. While peer review systems especially designed for instructors do exist, their goal is typically to create a collaborative environment for instructors to improve their professional skills (Fu and Hawkes, 2010). In terms of artificial intelligence support, to our knowledge no current peer review system has the power to provide instructors with insights about the semantic content of peer reviews, due to the diversity and complexity of the textual review comments. For example, SWoRD currently provides teachers a numerical summary view that includes the number of reviews received for each paper, and the mean and standard deviation of numerical reviewing ratings for each paper. SWoRD also allows instructors to automatically compute a grade based on a student's writing and reviewing quality; the grading algorithm uses the numerical ratings but not the associated text comments. In this work, we attempted to address the lack of semantic insight both by having humans in the loop to identify points of interest for interactive data exploration, and by adapting existing natural language processing techniques to the peer review domain to support automated analytics.

4 RevExplore

As an example for illustration, we will use data collected in a college level history class (Nelson and Schunn, 2009): the instructor created the writing assignment through SWoRD and provided a peer-review rubric which required students to assess a history paper's quality on three dimensions (logic, flow and insight) separately, by giving a numeric rating on a scale of 1-7 in addition to textual comments. While reviewing dimensions and associated guidelines (see below) are typically created by an instructor for a particular assignment, instructors can also set up their rubric using a library provided by SWoRD.

For instance, the instructor created the following guidance for commenting on the "logic" dimension: "*Provide specific comments about the logic of the author's argument. If points were just made without support, describe which ones they were. If the support provided doesn't make logical sense, explain what that is. If some obvious counter-argument was not considered, explain what that counter-argument is. Then give potential fixes to these problems if you can think of any. This might involve suggesting that the author change their argument.*"

Instructor guidance for numerically rating the logical arguments of the paper based on the comments was also given. For this history assignment, the highest rating of 7 ("Excellent") was described as "*All arguments strongly supported and no logical flaws in the arguments.*" The lowest rating of 1 ("Disastrous") was described as "*No support presented for any arguments, or obvious flaws in all arguments.*"

24 students submitted their papers online through SWoRD and then reviewed 6 peers' papers assigned to them in a "double blind" manner (review examples are available in Figure 2). When peer review is finished, RevExplore loads all papers and peer reviews, both textual comments and numeric ratings, and then goes through several text processing steps to prepare for interactive analytics. This preprocessing includes computing the domain words, sentence simplification, domain-word masking, syntactic analysis, and key noun-phrase extraction.

4.1 Overview – Student Clustering

RevExplore starts with a student-centric visualization overview. It uses a visual node of a bar chart to represent each student, visualizing the average of the student's peer ratings in gray, as well as the rating histogram with gradient colors (from red to blue) that are mapped to the rating scale from 1 to 7 (denoted by the legend in Figure 1).

To investigate students' writing performance, instructors can manually group similar nodes together into one stacked bar chart, or use automatic grouping options that RevExplore supports to inform initial hypotheses about peer review patterns. In the auto-mode, RevExplore can group students regarding a certain property (e.g. rating average); it can also cluster students using standard clustering algorithms[2] based on either rating statistics or Bag-Of-Words extracted from the relevant peer reviews.

If a instructor is curious about the review content for certain students during exploration, the instructor can read the main issues, in the form of noun phrases (NPs) of a student's peer reviews in a tooltip by mouse hovering on the bar squares which the student corresponds to. For example, Figure 1 shows that the peer reviews received by this student are mainly focused on the argumentation and the introduction part of the paper.

To extract peer-review main issues, RevExplore syntactically simplifies each review sentence (Heilman and Smith, 2010), parses each simplified sentence using the Stanford dependency parser (de Marneffe et al., 2006), and then traverses each dependency tree to find the key NP in a rule-based manner.[3] Due to reviewers' frequent references to the relevant paper, most of the learned NPs are domain related facts used in the paper, rather than evaluative texts that suggest problems or suggestions. To avoid the interference of the domain content, we apply domain-word masking (explained in Section 4.2) to the simplified sentences before parsing, and eliminate any key NP that contains the mask.

4.2 Detail-View – Topic Comparison

When two groups of students are selected in the overview, their textual peer reviews can be further

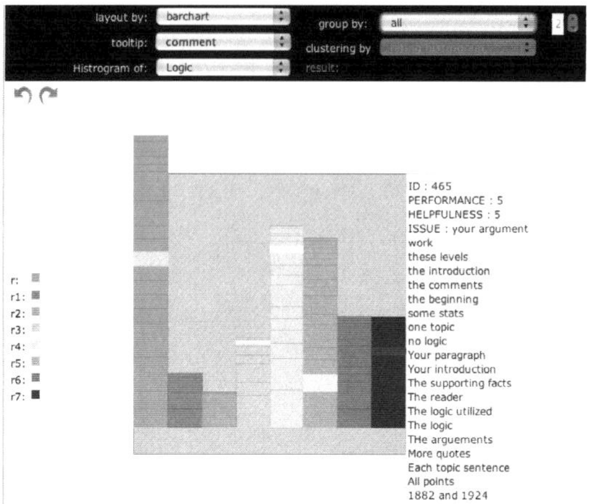

Figure 1: RevExplore overview. Stacked bar charts represent student groups. The tooltip shows the ID of the current student, writing *performance* (average peer ratings), review *helpfulness* (average helpfulness ratings), as well as the main *issues* in the descending order of their frequency, which are extracted from the peer reviews received by a highlighted student using NLP techniques.

[2]RevExplore implements both K-Means and a hierarchical clustering algorithm.

[3]Rules are constructed purely based on our intuition.

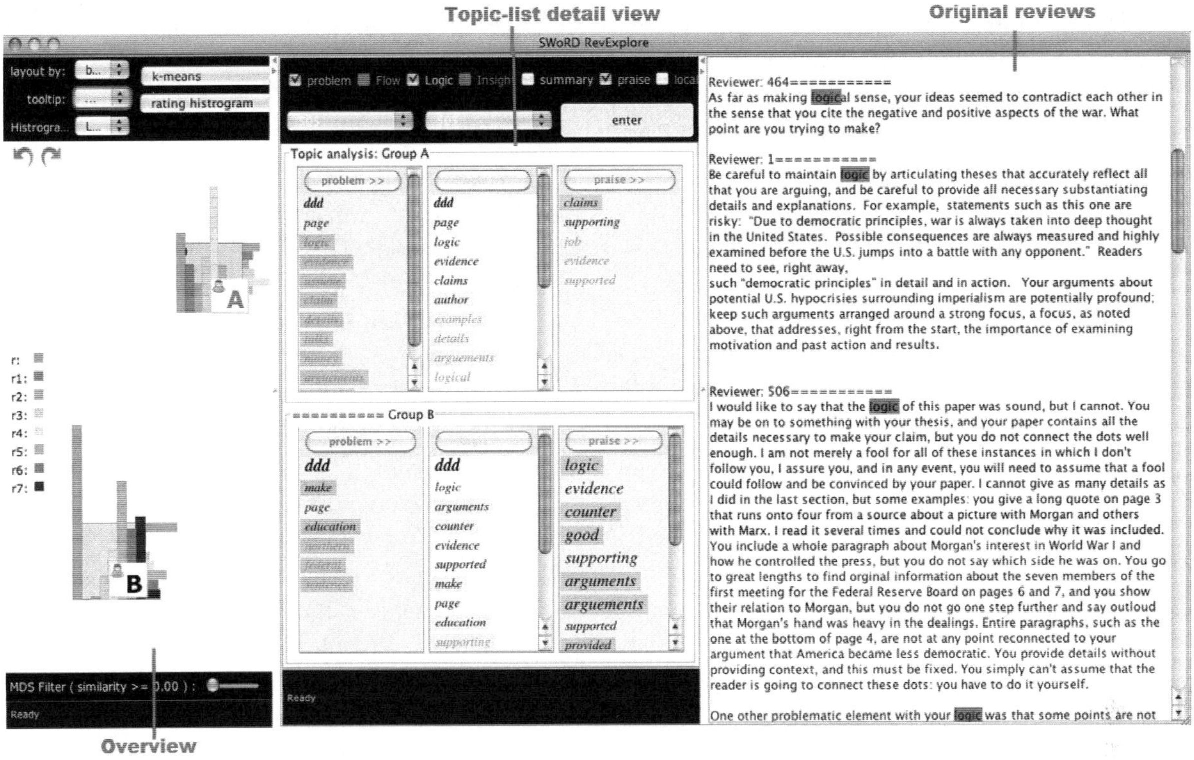

Figure 2: Peer-review exploration using RevExplore, for mining differences between strong and weak students.

compared with respect to specific reviewing dimensions using a list of topic words that are automatically computed in real-time.

Extracting topic words of peer reviews for comparison purposes is different from most traditional topic-word extraction tasks that are commonly involved in text summarization. In traditional text summarization, the informativeness measurement is designed to extract the common themes, while in our case of comparison, instructors are more concerned with the uniqueness of each target set of peer reviews compared to the others. Thus a topic-signature acquisition algorithm (Lin and Hovy, 2000), which extracts topic words through comparing the vocabulary distribution of a target corpus against that of a generic background corpus using a statistic metric, suits our application better than other approaches, such as probabilistic graphical models (e.g. LDA) and frequency based methods. Therefore, RevExplore considers topic signatures as the topic words for a group of reviews, using all peer reviews as the background corpus.[4] Again, to minimize the impact of the domain content of the relevant papers, we apply topic-masking which replaces all domain words[5] with "ddd" before computing the topic signatures.

As the software outputs topic signatures together with their associated weights which reflect signature importance, RevExplore uses this weight information to order the topic words as a list, and visualizes the weight as the font size and foreground color of the relevant topic word. These lists are placed in two rows regarding their group membership dimension by dimension. For each dimension, the corresponding lists of both rows are aligned vertically with the same background color to indicate that dimension (e.g. Topic-list detail view of Figure 2). To further facilitate the comparison within a dimension, RevExplore highlights the topic words that are unique to one group with a darker background color.

[4]We use TopicS (Nenkova and Louis, 2008) provided by Annie Louis.

[5]learned from all student papers against 5000 documents from the English Gigaword Corpus using TopicS.

If the user cannot interpret the topic that an extracted word might imply, the user can click on the word to read the relevant original reviews, with that word highlighted in red (e.g. Original reviews pane of Figure 2).

5 Analysis Example

Figure 2 shows how RevExplore is used to discover the difference between *strong* and *weak* students with respect to their writing performance on "logic" in the history peer-review assignment introduced in Section 4.

First we group students into strong versus weak regarding their writing performance on logic by selecting the K-Means algorithm to cluster students into two groups based on their rating histogram on logic. As shown in the Overview pane of Figure 2, we then label them as A and B for further topic comparison.

Next, in the topic-list detail view, we check "praise" and "problem"[6], and fire the "enter" button to start extracting topic words for group A and B on every selected dimension. Note that "logic" will be automatically selected since the focus has already been narrowed down to logic in the overview.

To first compare the difference in general logic issues between these two groups, we refer to the two lists on "logic" (in the middle of the topic-list detail view, Figure 2). As we can see, the weak students' reviews (Group A) are more about the logic of statements and the usage of facts (indicated by the unique words "examples" and "details"); the strong students' peer reviews (group B) focus more on argumentation (noted by "counter" and "supporting").

To further compare the two groups regarding different review sentiment, we look at the lists corresponding to "problem" and "praise" (left and right columns). For instance, we can see that strong students' suffer more from context specific problems, which is indicated by the bigger font size of the domain-word mask. Meanwhile, to understand what a topic word implies, say, "logic" in group A's topic list on "problem", we can click the word to bring out the relevant peer reviews, in which all occurrences of "logic" are colored in red (original reviews pane in Figure 2).

[6]Although "praise" and "problem" are manually annotated in this corpus (Nelson and Schunn, 2009), Xiong et al. (2010) have shown that they can be automatically learned in a data-driven fashion.

6 Ongoing Evaluation

We are currently evaluating our work along two dimensions. First, we are interested in examining the utility of RevExplore for instructors. After receiving positive feedback from several instructors at the University of Pittsburgh, as an informal pilot study, we deployed RevExplore for some of these instructors during the Spring 2012 semester and let them explore the peer reviews of their own ongoing classes. Instructors did observe interesting patterns using this tool after a short time of exploration (within two or three passes from the overview to the topic-word detail view). In addition, we are conducting a formal user study of 40 subjects to validate the topic-word extraction component for comparing reviews in groups. Our preliminary result shows that our use of topic signatures is significantly better than a frequency-based baseline.

7 Summary and Future work

RevExplore demonstrates the usage of data visualization in combination with NLP techniques to help instructors interactively make sense of peer review data, which was almost impracticable before. In the future we plan to further analyze the data collected in our formal user study, to validate the helpfulness of our proposed topic-word approach for making sense of large quantities of peer reviews. We also plan to incorporate NLP information beyond the word and NP level, to support additional types of review comparisons. In addition, we plan to summarize the interview data that we informally collected from several instructors, and will mine the log files of their interactions with RevExplore to understand how the tool would (and should) be used by instructors in general. Last but not least, we will continue revising our design of RevExplore based on instructor feedback, and plan to conduct a more formal evaluation with instructors.

Acknowledgments

Thanks to Melissa Patchan for providing the history peer-review corpus. We are also grateful to LRDC for financial support.

References

Stuart K. Card, Jock D. Mackinlay, and Ben Shneiderman. 1999. *Readings in information visualization: using vision to think*. San Francisco, CA, USA.

Kwangsu Cho and Christian D. Schunn. 2007. Scaffolded writing and rewriting in the discipline: A web-based reciprocal peer review system. *Computers and Education*, 48(3):409–426.

Kwangsu Cho. 2008. Machine classification of peer comments in physics. In *Proceedings First International Conference on Educational Data Mining*, pages 192–196.

Raquel M Crespo Garcia and Abelardo Pardo. 2010. A supporting system for adaptive peer review based on learners' profiles. In *Proceedings of Computer Supported Peer Review in Education Workshop*, pages 22–31.

Marie-Catherine de Marneffe, Bill MacCartney, and Christopher D. Manning. 2006. Generating typed dependency parses from phrase structure parses. In *LREC 2006*.

Hongxia Fu and Mark Hawkes. 2010. Technology-supported peer assessment as a means for teacher learning. In *Proceedings of the 2010 Workshop on Computer Supported Peer Review in Education*.

Ioannis Giannoukos, Ioanna Lykourentzou, Giorgos Mpardis, Vassilis Nikolopoulos, Vassilis Loumos, and Eleftherios Kayafas. 2010. An adaptive mechanism for author-reviewer matching in online peer assessment. In *Semantics in Adaptive and Personalized Services*, pages 109–126.

Michael Heilman and Noah A. Smith. 2010. Extracting simplified statements for factual question generation. In *Proceedings of the 3rd Workshop on Question Generation*.

Ville Hyyrynen, Harri Hämäläinen, Jouni Ikonen, and Jari Porras. 2010. Mypeerreview: an online peer-reviewing system for programming courses. In *Proceedings of the 10th Koli Calling International Conference on Computing Education Research*, pages 94–99.

Chin-Yew Lin and Eduard Hovy. 2000. The automated acquisition of topic signatures for text summarization. In *Proceedings COLING*.

Melissa M. Nelson and Christian D. Schunn. 2009. The nature of feedback: how different types of peer feedback affect writing performance. *Instructional Science*, 37:375–401.

Ani Nenkova and Annie Louis. 2008. Can you summarize this? Identifying correlates of input difficulty for generic multi-document summarization. In *Proceedings of Association for Computational Linguistics*.

Ágnes Sándor and Angela Vorndran. 2009. Detecting key sentences for automatic assistance in peer reviewing research articles in educational sciences. In *Proceedings of the 2009 Workshop on Text and Citation Analysis for Scholarly Digital Libraries*, pages 36–44, Suntec City, Singapore, August. Association for Computational Linguistics.

Keith Topping. 1998. Peer assessment between students in colleges and universities. *Review of Educational Research*, 68(3):249–276.

Keith J. Topping. 2009. Peer assessment. *Theory Into Practice*, 48(1):20–27.

Wenting Xiong and Diane Litman. 2011. Automatically predicting peer-review helpfulness. In *Proceedings of the 49th Annual Meeting of the Association for Computational Linguistics: Human Language Technologies: short papers - Volume 2*, HLT '11, pages 502–507.

Wenting Xiong, Diane J. Litman, and Christian D. Schunn. 2010. Assessing reviewers performance based on mining problem localization in peer-review data. In *Proceedings Third International Conference on Educational Data Mining*.

Yu-Fen Yang. 2011. A reciprocal peer review system to support college students' writing. *British Journal of Educational Technology*, 42(4):687–700.

Vocabulary Profile as a Measure of Vocabulary Sophistication

Su-Youn Yoon, Suma Bhat*, Klaus Zechner
Educational Testing Service, 660 Rosedale Road, Princeton, NJ, USA
{syoon,kzechner}@ets.org
* University of Illinois, Urbana-Champaign, IL, USA
sumapramod@gmail.com

Abstract

This study presents a method that assesses ESL learners' vocabulary usage to improve an automated scoring system of spontaneous speech responses by non-native English speakers. Focusing on vocabulary sophistication, we estimate the difficulty of each word in the vocabulary based on its frequency in a reference corpus and assess the mean difficulty level of the vocabulary usage across the responses (vocabulary profile).

Three different classes of features were generated based on the words in a spoken response: coverage-related, average word rank and the average word frequency and the extent to which they influence human-assigned language proficiency scores was studied. Among these three types of features, the *average word frequency* showed the most predictive power. We then explored the impact of vocabulary profile features in an automated speech scoring context, with particular focus on the impact of two factors: genre of reference corpora and the characteristics of item-types.

The contribution of the current study lies in the use of vocabulary profile as a measure of lexical sophistication for spoken language assessment, an aspect heretofore unexplored in the context of automated speech scoring.

1 Introduction

This study provides a method that measures ESL (English as a second language) learners' competence in vocabulary usage.

Spoken language assessments typically measure multiple dimensions of language ability. Overall proficiency in the target language can be assessed by testing the abilities in various areas including fluency, pronunciation, and intonation; grammar and vocabulary; and discourse structure. With the recent move toward the objective assessment of language ability (spoken and written), it is imperative that we develop methods for quantifying these abilities and measuring them automatically.

A majority of the studies in automated speech scoring have focused on fluency (Cucchiarini et al., 2000; Cucchiarini et al., 2002), pronunciation (Witt and Young, 1997; Witt, 1999; Franco et al., 1997; Neumeyer et al., 2000), and intonation (Zechner et al., 2011). More recently, Chen and Yoon (2011) and Chen and Zechner (2011) have measured syntactic competence in speech scoring. However, only a few have explored features related to vocabulary usage and they have been limited to type-token ratio (TTR) related features (e.g., Lu (2011)). In addition, Bernstein et al. (2010) developed vocabulary features that measure the similarity between the vocabulary in the test responses and the vocabulary in the pre-collected texts in the same topic. However, their features assessed content and topicality, not vocabulary usage.

The speaking construct of vocabulary usage comprises two sub-constructs: sophistication and precision. The aspect of vocabulary that we intend to measure in this paper is that of lexical sophistication, also termed lexical diversity and lexical richness in second language studies. Measures of lexical sophistication attempt to quantify the degree to which a varied and large vocabulary is used (Laufer and Nation, 1995). In order to assess the degree of lexical sophistication, we employ a vocabulary profile-based approach (partly motivated from the results of a previous study, as will be explained in Section 2).

By a vocabulary profile, it is meant that the frequency of each vocabulary item is calculated from a reference corpus covering the language variety of the target situation. The degree of lexical sophistication is captured by the word frequency - low frequency words are considered to be more difficult, and therefore more sophisticated. We then design features that capture the difficulty level of vocabulary items in test takers' responses. Finally, we perform correlation analyses between these new features and human proficiency scores and assess the feature's importance with respect to the other features in an automatic scoring module. The novelty of this study lies in the use of vocabulary profile in an automatic scoring set-up to assess lexical sophistication.

This paper will proceed as follows: we will review related work in Section 2. Data and experiment setup will be explained in Section 3 and Section 4. Next, we will present the results in Section 5, discuss them in Section 6, and conclude with a summary of the importance of our findings in Section 7.

2 Related Work

Measures of lexical richness have been the focus of several studies involving assessment of L1 and L2 language abilities (Laufer and Nation, 1995; Vermeer, 2000; Daller et al., 2003; Kormos and Denes, 2004). The types of measures considered in these studies can be grouped into quantitative and qualitative measures.

The quantitative measures give insight into the number of words known, but do not distinguish them from one another based on their category or frequency in language use. They have evolved to make up for the widely applied measure type-token-ratio (TTR). However, owing to its sensitivity to the number of tokens, TTR has been considered as an unstable measure in differing proficiency levels of language learners. The Guiraud index, Uber index, and Herdan index (Vermeer, 2000; Daller et al., 2003; Lu, 2011) are some measures in this category mostly derived from TTR as either simpler transformations of the TTR or its scaled versions to ameliorate the effect of differing token cardinalities.

Qualitative measures, on the other hand, distinguish themselves from those derived from TTR since they take into account distinctions between words such as their parts of speech or difficulty levels. Adding a qualitative dimension gives more insight into lexical aspects of language ability than the purely quantitative measures such as TTR-based measures. Some measures in this category include a derived form of the limiting relative diversity (LRD) given by $\sqrt{D(verbs)/D(nouns)}$ using the D-measure proposed in (Malvern and Richards, 1997), Lexical frequency profile (LFP) (Laufer and Nation, 1995) and P-Lex (Meara and Bell, 2003).

LFP uses a vocabulary profile (VP) for a given body of written text or spoken utterance and gives the percentage of words used at different frequency levels (such as from the one-thousand most common words, the next thousand most common words) where the words themselves come from a pre-compiled vocabulary list, such as the Academic Word List (AWL) with its associated frequency distribution on words by Coxhead(1998). *Frequency level* refers to a class of words (or appropriately chosen word units) that are grouped based on their frequencies of actual usage in corpora. P-Lex is another approach that uses the frequency level of the words to assess lexical richness. These measures are based on the differing frequencies of lexical items and hence rely on the availability of frequency lists for the language being considered.

These two different types of measures have been used in the analysis of essays written by second language learners of English (ESL). Laufer and Nation (1995) have shown that LFP correlates well with an independent measure of vocabulary knowledge and that it is possible to categorize learners according to different proficiency levels using this measure. In another study seeking to understand the extent to which VP based on students' essays predicted their academic performance (Morris and Cobb, 2004), it was observed that students' vocabulary profile results correlated significantly with their grades. Additionally, VP was found to be indicative of finer distinctions in the language skills of high proficiency nonnative speakers than oral interviews can cover.

Furthermore, these measures have been employed in automated essay scoring. Attali and Burstein

(2006) used average word frequency and average word length in characters across the words in the essay. In addition to the average word frequency measure, the average word length measure was implemented to assess the average difficulty of the word used in the essay under the assumption that the words with more characters were more difficult than the words with fewer characters. These features showed promising performance in estimating test takers' proficiency levels.

In contrast to qualitative measures, quantitative measures did not achieve promising performance. Vermeer (2000) showed that quantitative measures achieve neither the validity nor the reliability of the measures, regardless of the transformations and corrections.

More recently, the relationship of lexical richness to ESL learners' speaking task performance has been studied by Lu (2011). The comprehensive study was aimed at measuring lexical richness along the three dimensions of lexical density, sophistication, and variation, using 25 different metrics (belonging to both the qualitative and quantitative categories above) available in the language acquisition literature. His results, based on the manual transcription of a spoken corpus of English learners, indicate that a) lexical variation (the number of word types) correlated most strongly with the raters' judgments of the quality of ESL learners' oral narratives, b) lexical sophistication only had a very small effect, and c) lexical density (indicative of proportion of lexical words) in an oral narrative did not appear to relate to its quality.

In this study, we seek to quantify vocabulary usage in terms of measures of lexical sophistication: VP based on a set of reference word lists. The novelty of the current study lies in the use of VP as a measure of lexical sophistication for spoken language assessment. It derives support from other studies (Morris and Cobb, 2004; Laufer and Nation, 1995) but is carried out in a completely different context, that of automatic scoring of proficiency levels in spontaneous speech, an area not explored thus far in existing literature.

Furthermore, we investigate the impact of the genre of the reference corpus on the performance of these lexical measures. For this purpose, three different corpora will be used to generate reference frequency levels. Finally, we will investigate how the characteristics of the item types influence the performance of these measures.

3 Data

The AEST balanced data set, a collection of responses from the AEST, is used in this study. AEST is a high-stakes test of English proficiency, and it consists of 6 items in which speakers are prompted to provide responses lasting between 45 and 60 seconds per item, yielding approximately 5 minutes of spoken content per speaker.

Among the 6 items, two items elicit information or opinions on familiar topics based on the examinees' personal experience or background knowledge. These constitute the *independent* (IND) items. The four remaining items are integrated tasks that include other language skills such as listening and reading. These constitute the *integrated* (INT) items. Both sets of items extract spontaneous and unconstrained natural speech. The primary difference between the two elicitation types is that IND items only provide a prompt whereas INT items provide a prompt, a reading passage, and a listening stimulus. The size, purpose, and speakers' native language information for each dataset are summarized in Table 1. All items extract spontaneous, unconstrained natural speech.

Each response was rated by a trained human rater using a 4-point scoring scale, where 1 indicates a low speaking proficiency and 4 indicates a high speaking proficiency. The scoring guideline is summarized in the AEST rubrics.

Since none of the AEST balanced data was double-scored, we estimate the inter-rater agreement ratio of the corpus by using a large double-scored dataset which used the same scoring guidelines and scoring process; using the 41K double-scored responses collected from AEST, we calculate the Pearson correlation coefficient to be 0.63, suggesting a reasonable agreement. The distribution of scores for this data can be found in Table 2.

4 Experiments

4.1 Overview

In this study, we developed vocabulary profile features. From a reference corpus, we pre-compiled

Corpus name	Purpose	# of speakers	# of responses	Native languages	Size (Hrs)
AEST balanced data	Feature evaluation, Scoring model training and evaluation	480	2880	Korean (15%), Chinese (14%), Japanese (7%), Spanish (9%), Others (55%)	44

Table 1: Data size and speakers' native languages

Size	Score1	Score2	Score3	Score4
Number of files	141	1133	1266	340
(%)	5	40	45	12

Table 2: Distribution of proficiency scores in the dataset

multiple sets of vocabulary lists (e.g., a list of the 100 most frequent words in a reference corpus). Next, for each test response, a transcription was generated using the speech recognizer. For each response with respect to each reference word list, vocabulary profile features were calculated. In addition to vocabulary profile features, type-token ratio (TTR) was calculated as a baseline feature. Despite its instability, TTR has been employed in the automated speech scoring systems such as (Zechner et al., 2009), and its use here allows a direct comparison of the performance of the features with the results of previous studies.

4.2 Vocabulary list generation

The three reference corpora we used in this study are presented in Table 3: The General Service List (GSL), the TOEFL 2000 Spoken and Written Academic Language Corpus (T2K-SWAL) and the AEST data.

Corpus	Genre	Tokens	Types
GSL	Written	-	2,284
T2K-SWAL	Spoken	1,869,346	28,855
AEST data	Spoken	5,520,375	23,165

Table 3: Three reference corpora used in this study

GSL (West, 1953) comprises 2,284 words selected to be of "general service" to learners of English. In this study, we used the version with frequency information from (Bauman, 1995). The original version did not include word frequency and was 'enhanced' by John Bauman and Brent Culligan with the frequency information obtained from the Brown Corpus, a collection of written texts.

T2K-SWAL (Biber et al., 2002) is a collection of spoken and written texts covering a broad language variety and use in the academic setting. In this study, only its spoken texts were used. The spoken corpus included manual transcriptions of discussions, conversations, and lectures that occurred in class sessions, study-group meetings, office hours, and service encounters.

Finally, AEST data is a collection of manual transcriptions of spoken responses from the AEST for non-native English speakers. Although there was no overlap between AEST data and the evaluation data (AEST balanced data), the vocabulary lists in AEST data might be a closer match to the vocabulary lists in the evaluation data since both of them come from the same test products. From a content perspective, this dataset is likely to better reflect characteristics of non-native English speakers than the other two reference corpora.

For T2K-SWAL and AEST, all transcriptions were normalized; all the tokens were further decapitalized and removed of all non-alphanumeric characters except for dash and quote. The morphological variants were considered as different words. All words were sorted by the word occurrences in the corpus, and a set of 6 lists were generated: top-100 words (TOP1), word frequency ranks 101-300 (TOP2), ranks 301-700 (TOP3), ranks 701-1500 (TOP4), ranks 1501-3000 (TOP5), and all other words with ranks of 3001 and above (TOP6). For GSL, a set of 5 lists was generated; TOP6 was not generated since GSL only included about 2200 words.

Compared to written texts, speakers tended to use a much smaller vocabulary in speech. For instance, the percentage of words within the top-1000 words on the total word types of AEST data responses was over 90% on average, and they were similar across proficiency levels. This is the reason why we subclassified the top 1000 words into three lists, unlike the vocabulary profile features using top-1000 words as one list like (Morris and Cobb, 2004), which did not have any power to differentiate between proficiency levels.

4.3 Transcription generation for evaluation data

A Hidden Markov Model (HMM) speech recognizer was trained on the AEST dataset, approximately 733 hours of non-native speech collected from 7872 speakers. A gender independent triphone acoustic model and a combination of bigram, trigram, and four-gram language models was used. The word error rate (WER) on the held-out test dataset was 27%. For each response in the evaluation partition, an ASR-based transcription was generated using the speech recognizer.

4.4 Feature generation

Each response comprised less than 60 seconds of speech with an average of 113 word tokens. Due to the short response length, there was wide variation in the proportion of low-frequency word types for the same speaker. In order to address this issue, for each speaker, two responses from the same item-type (IND/INT) were concatenated and used as one large response. As a result, three concatenated responses (one IND response and two INT responses) were generated for each speaker, yielding a total of 480 concatenated responses for IND items and 960 concatenated responses for INT items for our experiment.

First, a list of word types was generated from the ASR hypothesis of each concatenated response. IND items provide only a one-sentence prompt, while INT items provide stimuli including a prompt, a reading passage, and a listening stimulus. In order to minimize the influence of the vocabulary in the stimuli on that of the speakers, we excluded the content words that occurred in the prompts or stimuli from the word type list[1].

Table 4: List of features.

Feature	# of features	Feature type	Description
TTR	1	Ratio	Type-token ratio
TOPn	5 or 6[a]	Listrel	Proportion of types that occurred both the response and TOPn list in the total types of the response.
aRank	1	Rank	Avg. word rank[b]
aFreq	1	Freq	Avg. word freq.[c]
lFreq	1	Freq	Avg. log(word freq)[d]

[a] For GSL, five different features were created using TOP1-TOP5 lists, but TOP6 was not created. For T2K-SWAL and AEST data, six different features were created using TOP1-TOP6 lists separately.

[b] "rank" is the ordinal number of words in a list that is sorted in descending order of word frequency; words not present in the reference corpus get the default rank of RefMaxRank+1.

[c] Avg. word frequency is the sum of the word-frequencies of word types in the reference corpus divided by the total number of words in the reference corpus; words not in the reference corpus get assigned a default frequency of 1.

[d] Same as feature **aFreq**, but the logarithm of the word frequency is taken here

Next, we generated five types of features using three reference vocabulary lists. A maximum of 10 features were generated for each reference list. The feature-types are tabulated in Table 4.

All features above were generated from word types, not word tokens, i.e., multiple occurrences of the same word in a response were only counted once.

Below we delineate the step-by-step process with a sample response that leads to the feature generation outlined in Table 5.

- Step 1: Generate ASR hypothesis for the given speech response. e.g: *Every student has different perspective about how to relax. Playing xbox.*

- Step 2: Generate type list from ASR hypothesis. For the response above we get the list - *about, how, different, xbox, to, relax, every, perspective, student, has, playing.*

[1] This process prevents to measure the content relevance; whether the response is off-topic or not. However, this is not problematic since the features in this study will be used in the conjunction with the features that measure the accuracy of the aspects of content and topicality such as (Xie et al., 2012)'s features.

	word freq. in reference corpus	word rank in the reference corpus	TOPn
about	25672	30	TOP1
how	8944	96	TOP1
has	18105	53	TOP1
to	218976	2	TOP1
different	5088	153	TOP2
every	2961	236	TOP2
playing	798	735	TOP4
perspec tive	139	1886	TOP5
xbox	1	20000	No

Table 5: An example of feature calculation.

- Step 3: Generate type list excluding words that occurred in the prompt - *about, how, different, xbox, to, every, perspective, has, playing*.

From the ASR hypotheses (result of Step 1), the corresponding type list was generated (Step 2) and two words ('student', 'relax') were excluded from the final list due to overlap with the prompt. The final word list used in the feature generation has 9 types (Step 3).

Next, for each word in the above type list, if it occurs in the reference corpus (a list of words sorted by frequency), its word frequency, word rank and the TOPn information (whether the word belonged to the TOPn list or not) are obtained. If it did not occur in the reference corpus, the default frequency (1) and the default word rank (20000) were assigned. In 5, the default values were assigned for 'xbox' since it was not in the reference corpus.

Finally, the average of the word frequencies and the average of the the word ranks were calculated (aFreq and aRank). For lFreq, the log value of each frequency was calculated and then averaged. For TOPn features, we obtain the proportion of the word types that belong to the TOPn category. For the above sample, the TOP1 feature value was 0.444 since 4 words belong to TOP1 and the total number of word types was 9 (4/9=0.444).

5 Results

5.1 Correlation

We analyzed the relationship between the proposed features and human proficiency scores to assess their influence on predicting the proficiency score. The reference proficiency score for a concatenated response was estimated by summing up the two scores of the constituent responses. Thus, the new score scale was 2-8. Table 6 presents Pearson correlation coefficients (r).

The best performing feature was **aFreq** followed by **TOP1**. Both features showed statistically significant negative correlations with human proficiency scores. **TOP6** also showed statistically significant correlation with human scores, but it was 10-20% lower than **TOP1**. This suggests that a human rater more likely assigned high scores when the vocabulary of the response was not limited to a few most frequent words. However, the use of difficult words (low-frequency) shows a weaker relationship with the proficiency scores.

Features based on AEST data outperformed features based on T2K-SWAL or GSL. The correlation of the AEST data-based **aFreq** feature was -0.61 for the IND items and -0.51 for the INT items; they were approximately 0.1 higher than the correlations of T2K-SWAL or GSL-based features. A similar tendency was found for the TOP1-TOP6 features, although differences between AEST data-based features and other reference-based features were less salient overall.

For top-performing vocabulary profile features including **aFreq** and **TOP1**, the correlations of INT items were weaker than those of the IND items. In general, the correlations of INT items were 10-20% lower than those of the IND items in absolute value.

aFreq and **TOP1** consistently achieved better performance than TTR across all item-types.

5.2 Scoring model building

To arrive at an automatic scoring model, we included the new vocabulary profile features with other features previously found to be useful in a multiple linear regression (MLR) framework. A total of 80 features were generated by the automated speech proficiency scoring system from Zechner et al. (2009),

	Reference	TTR	TOP1	TOP2	TOP3	TOP4	TOP5	TOP6	aRank	aFreq	lFreq
IND	GSL	-.147	-.347	.027	.078	.000	.053	-	.266	-.501	-.260
	T2K-SWAL	-.147	-.338	.085	.207	.055	.020	.168	.142	-.509	-.159
	ATEST	-.147	-.470	.014	.275	.172	.187	.218	.236	-.613	-.232
INT	GSL	-.245	-.255	-.086	-.019	-.068	-.031	-	.316	-.404	-.318
	T2K-SWAL	-.245	-.225	.010	.094	.047	.079	.124	.087	-.405	-.198
	ATEST	-.245	-.345	-.092	.156	.135	.188	.194	.214	-.507	-.251

Table 6: Correlations between features and human proficiency scores

and they were classified into 5 sub-groups: fluency, pronunciation, prosody, vocabulary complexity, and grammar usage. For each sub-group, at least one feature that correlated well with human scores but had a low inter-correlation with other features was selected. A total of following 6 features were selected and used in the base model (**base**):

- **wdpchk** (fluency): Average chunk length in words; a chunk is a segment whose boundaries are set by long silences
- **tpsecutt** (fluency): Number of types per sec.
- **normAM** (pronunciation): Average acoustic model score normalized by the speaking rate
- **phn_shift** (pronunciation): Average absolute distance of the normalized vowel durations compared to standard normalized vowel durations estimated on a native speech corpus
- **stretimdev** (prosody): Mean deviation of distance between stressed syllables in sec.
- **lmscore** (grammar): Average language model score normalized by number of words

We first calculated correlations between these features and human proficiency scores and compared them with the most predictive vocabulary profile features. Table 7 presents Pearson correlation coefficients (r) of these features.

In both item-types, the most correlated features represented the aspect of fluency in production. While **tpsecutt** was the best feature in IND items and the correlation with human scores was approximately 0.66, in INT items, **wdpchk** was the best feature and the correlation was even higher, 0.73.

The performance of **aFreq** was particularly high in IND items; it was the second best feature and only marginally lower than the best feature (by 0.04). **aFreq** also achieved promising performance in INT;

Features	IND	INT
wdpchk	.538	.612
tpsecutt	.659	.729
normAM	.467	.429
phn_shift	-.503	-.535
stretimemdev	-.442	-.397
lmscore	.257	.312
aFreq	-.613	-.507
TOP1	-.470	-.345
TTR	-.147	-.245

Table 7: Comparison of feature-correlations with human-assigned proficiency scores.

it was the fourth best feature. However, the performance was considerably lower than the the best feature, and the difference between the best feature and **aFreq** was approximately 22%.

We compared the performances of this **base** model with an augmented model (**base + TTR + all vocabulary profile features**) whose feature set was the **base** augmented with our proposed measures of vocabulary sophistication. Item-type specific multiple linear regression models were trained using five-fold cross validation. The 480 IND responses 960 INT responses were partitioned into five sets, separately. In each fold, an item-type specific regression model was trained using four of these partitions and tested on the remaining one.

The averages of the five-fold models are summarized in Table 8, showing weighted kappa to indicate agreement between automatic scores and human-assigned scores and also the Pearson's correlation (r) of the unrounded (un-rnd) and rounded (rnd) scores with the human-assigned scores. We used the correlation and weighted kappa as performance evaluation measures to maintain the consistency with the previous studies such as (Zechner et al., 2009). In addition, the correlation metric matches better with our goal to investigate the relationship between the predicted scores and the actual scores rather than the difference between the predicted scores and the actual scores.

	Features	un-rnd corr.	rnd corr.	weighted kappa
IND	base	0.66	0.62	0.55
	base + TTR	0.66	0.63	0.56
	base + TTR + all	0.66	0.64	0.57
INT	base	0.76	0.73	0.69
	base + TTR	0.76	0.74	0.70
	base + TTR + all	0.77	0.74	0.70

Table 8: Performance of item-type specific multiple linear regression based scoring models.

The new scores show slightly better agreement with human-assigned scores, but the improvement was small in both item-types, approximately 1%.

6 Discussion

In general, we found that the test takers used a fairly small number of vocabulary items in the spoken responses. On average, the total types used in the responses was 87.21 for IND items and 98.52 for INT items. Furthermore, the proportions of high frequency words on test takers' spoken responses were markedly high. The proportion of top-100 words was almost 50% and the proportion of top-1500 words (summation of TOP1-TOP4) was over 89% on average. This means that only 1500 words represent almost 90% of the active vocabulary of the test takers in their spontaneous speech. Figure 1 presents the average TOP1-TOP6 features across all proficiency levels.

The values of INT items were similar to IND items, but the TOP3-TOP6 values were slightly higher than IND items; INT items tended to include more low frequency words. In order to investigate the impact of the higher proportion of low frequency words in INT items, we selected two features (aFreq and TOP1) and further analyzed them.

Table 9 provides the mean of **aFreq** and **TOP1** for each score level. The features were generated using AEST as a reference.

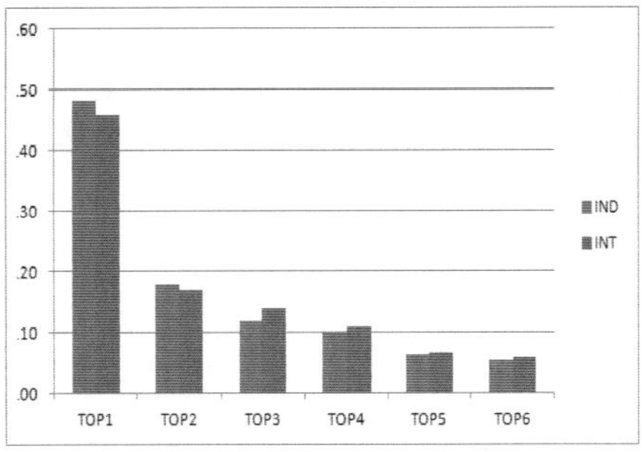

Figure 1: Proportion of top-N frequent words on average

Score	aFreq		TOP1	
	IND	INT	IND	INT
2	43623	36175	.60	.52
3	38165	32493	.55	.49
4	33861	28884	.51	.48
5	30599	27118	.49	.46
6	28485	26327	.46	.45
7	27358	25093	.45	.43
8	26065	24711	.43	.43

Table 9: Mean of vocabulary profile features for each score level

On average, the differences between adjacent score levels in INT items were smaller than those in IND items. The weaker distinction between score levels may result in the lower performance of vocabulary profile features in INT items. Particularly, the differences were smaller in lower score levels (2-4) than in higher score levels (5-8). The relatively high proportion of low frequency words in the low score level reduced the predictive power of vocabulary profile features.

This difference between the item-types strongly supports item-type-specific modeling. We combined the IND and INT item responses and computed a correlation between the features and the proficiency scores over the entirety of data sets. Despite increase in sample sizes, the correlations were lower than both the corresponding correlations of the IND items and the INT items. For instance, the correlation of the T2K-SWAL-based **aFreq** feature was -0.393, and that of the AEST data-based **aFreq** was -0.50, which was approximately 3% lower than the INT items and 10% lower than the IND items. The difference in the vocabulary distributions between the two item-types decreased the performance of the features.

In this study, AEST data-based features outperformed T2K-SWAL-based features. Although no items in the evaluation data overlapped with items in AEST data, the similarity in the speakers' proficiency levels and task types might have resulted in a better match between the vocabulary and its distributions of AEST data with AEST balanced data, finally the AEST data-based features achieved the best performance.

In order to explore the degree to which AEST balanced data (test responses) and the reference corpora matched, we calculated the proportion of word types that occurred in test responses and reference corpora (the coverage of reference list). The ASR hypotheses of AEST balanced data comprised 6,024 word types. GSL covered 73%, T2K-SWAL covered 99%, and AEST data covered close to 100%. Considering the fact that, a) despite high coverage of both T2K-SWAL and AEST data, T2K-SWAL-based features achieved much lower performance than AEST data, and, b) despite huge differences in the coverage between T2K-SWAL and GSL, the performance of features based on these reference corpora were comparable, coverage was not likely to have been a factor having a strong impact on the performance. The large differences in the performance of **TOP1** across reference lists support the possibility of the strong influence of high frequency word types on proficiency; the kinds of word types that were in the TOP1 bins were an important factor that influenced the performance of vocabulary profile features. Finally, genre differences (spoken texts vs. written texts) in reference corpora did not have strong impact on the predictive ability of the features; the performance of features based on written reference corpus (GSL) were comparable to those based on a spoken reference corpus (T2K-SWAL).

Despite the high correlation shown by the individual features (such as **aFreq**), we do not see a corresponding increase in the performance of the scoring model with all the best performing features. The most likely explanation to this is the small training data size; in each fold, only about 380 responses for IND and about 760 responses for INT were used in the scoring model training. Another possibility is overlap with the existing features; the aspect that vocabulary profile features are modeling may be already covered to some extent in existing feature set. In future research, we will further investigate this aspect in details.

7 Conclusions

In this study, we presented features that measure ESL learners' vocabulary usage. In particular, we focused on vocabulary sophistication, and explored the suitability of vocabulary profile features to capture sophistication. From three different reference corpora, the frequency of vocabulary items was calculated which was then used to estimate the sophistication of test takers' vocabulary. Among the three different reference corpora, features based on AEST data, a collections of responses similar to that of the test set, showed the best performance. A total of 29 features were generated, and the average word frequency (**aFreq**) achieved the best correlation with human proficiency scores. In general, vocabulary profile features showed strong correlations with human proficiency scores, but when used in an automatic scoring model in combination with an existing set of predictors of language proficiency, the augmented feature set showed marginal improvement in predicting human-assigned scores of proficiency.

References

Yigal Attali and Jill Burstein. 2006. Automated essay scoring with e–rater R v.2. *The Journal of Technology, Learning, and Assessment*, 4(3).

John Bauman. 1995. About the GSL. Retrieved March 17, 2012 from `http://jbauman.com/gsl.html`.

Jared Bernstein, Jian Cheng, and Masanori Suzuki. 2010. Fluency and structural complexity as predictors of L2 oral proficiency. In *Proceedings of InterSpeech 2010, Tokyo, Japan, September*.

Douglas Biber, Susan Conrad, Randi Reppen, Pat Byrd, and Marie Helt. 2002. Speaking and writing in the university: A multidimensional comparison. *TESOL Quarterly*, 36:9–48.

Lei Chen and Su-Youn Yoon. 2011. Detecting structural events for assessing non-native speech. In *Proceedings of the 6th Workshop on Innovative Use of NLP for Building Educational Applications*, pages 38–45.

Miao Chen and Klaus Zechner. 2011. Computing and evaluating syntactic complexity features for automated scoring of spontaneous non-native speech. In *Pro-*

ceedings of the 49th Annual Meeting of the Association for Computational Linguistics 2011, pages 722–731.

Catia Cucchiarini, Helmer Strik, and Lou Boves. 2000. Quantitative assessment of second language learners' fluency: Comparisons between read and spontaneous speech. *The Journal of the Acoustical Society of America*, 107(2):989–999.

Catia Cucchiarini, Helmer Strik, and Lou Boves. 2002. Quantitative assessment of second language learners' fluency: Comparisons between read and spontaneous speech. *The Journal of the Acoustical Society of America*, 111(6):2862–2873.

Helmut Daller, Roeland van Hout, and Jeanine Treffers-Daller. 2003. Lexical richness in the spontaneous speech of bilinguals. *Applied Linguistics*, 24(2):197–222.

Horacio Franco, Leonardo Neumeyer, Yoon Kim, and Orith Ronen. 1997. Automatic pronunciation scoring for language instruction. In *Proceedings of ICASSP 97*, pages 1471–1474.

Judit Kormos and Mariann Denes. 2004. Exploring measures and perceptions of fluency in the speech of second language learners. *System*, 32:145–164.

Batia Laufer and Paul Nation. 1995. Vocabulary size and use: lexical richness in L2 written production. *Applied Linguistics*, 16:307–322.

Xiaofei Lu. 2011. The relationship of lexical richness to the quality of ESL learners' oral narratives. *The Modern Language Journal*.

David D. Malvern and Brian J. Richards. 1997. A new measure of lexical diversity. In *Evolving models of language: Papers from the Annual Meeting of the British Association of Applied Linguists held at the University of Wales, Swansea, September*, pages 58–71.

Paul Meara and Huw Bell. 2003. P_lex: A simple and effective way of describing the lexical characteristics of short L2 texts. *Applied Linguistics*, 24(2):197–222.

Lori Morris and Tom Cobb. 2004. Vocabulary profiles as predictors of the academic performance of teaching english as a second language trainees. *System*, 32:75–87.

Leonardo Neumeyer, Horacio Franco, Vassilios Digalakis, and Mitchel Weintraub. 2000. Automatic scoring of pronunciation quality. *Speech Communication*, pages 88–93.

Anne Vermeer. 2000. Coming to grips with lexical richness in spontaneous speech data. *Language Testing*, 17(1):65–83.

Michael West. 1953. *A General Service List of English Words*. Longman, London.

Silke Witt and Steve Young. 1997. Performance measures for phone-level pronunciation teaching in CALL. In *Proceedings of the Workshop on Speech Technology in Language Learning*, pages 99–102.

Silke Witt. 1999. *Use of the speech recognition in computer-assisted language learning*. Unpublished dissertation, Cambridge University Engineering department, Cambridge, U.K.

Shasha Xie, Keelan Evanini, and Klaus Zechner. 2012. Exploring content features for automated speech scoring. In *Proceedings of the NAACL-HLT, Montreal, July*.

Klaus Zechner, Derrick Higgins, Xiaoming Xi, and David M. Williamson. 2009. Automatic scoring of non-native spontaneous speech in tests of spoken english. *Speech Communication*, 51:883–895, October.

Klaus Zechner, Xiaoming Xi, and Lei Chen. 2011. Evaluating prosodic features for automated scoring of non-native read speech. In *IEEE Workshop on Automatic Speech Recognition and Understanding 2011, Hawaii, December*.

Short Answer Assessment: Establishing Links Between Research Strands

Ramon Ziai Niels Ott Detmar Meurers
SFB 833 / Seminar für Sprachwissenschaft
Universität Tübingen
{rziai,nott,dm}@sfs.uni-tuebingen.de

Abstract

A number of different research subfields are concerned with the automatic assessment of student answers to comprehension questions, from language learning contexts to computer science exams. They share the need to evaluate free-text answers but differ in task setting and grading/evaluation criteria, among others.

This paper has the intention of fostering synergy between the different research strands. It discusses the different research strands, details the crucial differences, and explores under which circumstances systems can be compared given publicly available data. To that end, we present results with the CoMiC-EN Content Assessment system (Meurers et al., 2011a) on the dataset published by Mohler et al. (2011) and outline what was necessary to perform this comparison. We conclude with a general discussion on comparability and evaluation of short answer assessment systems.

1 Introduction

Short answer assessment systems compare students' responses to questions with manually defined target responses or answer keys in order to judge the appropriateness of the responses, or in order to automatically assign a grade. A number of approaches have emerged in recent years, each of them with different aims and different backgrounds. In this paper, we will draw a map of the short answer assessment landscape, highlighting the similarities and differences between approaches and the data used for evaluation. We will provide an overview of 12 systems and sketch their attributes. Subsequently, we will zoom into the comparison of two of them, namely CoMiC-EN (Meurers et al., 2011a) and the one which we call the Texas system (Mohler et al., 2011) and discuss the issues that arise with this endeavor. Returning to the bigger picture, we will explore how such systems could be compared in general, in the belief that meaningful comparison of approaches across research strands will be an important ingredient in advancing this relatively new research field.

2 The short answer assessment landscape

2.1 General aspects

Researchers from all directions have settled in the landscape of short answer assessment, each of them with different backgrounds and different goals. In this section, we aim at providing an overview of these research villages, also hoping to construct a road network that may connect them.

Most approaches to short answer assessment are situated in an educational context. Some focus on GCSE[1] tests, others aim at university assessment tests in the medical domain. Another strand of approaches focuses on language teaching and learning. All of these approaches share one theme: they assess short texts written by students. These may be answers to questions that ask for knowledge acquired in a course, e.g., in computer science, or to reading comprehension questions in second language

[1]The General Certificate of Secondary Education (GCSE) is an academic qualification in the United Kingdom, usually taken at the age of 14–16.

learning. While thematically related, short answer assessment is different from essay grading. Short answers are formulated by students in a much more controlled setting. Not only are they short, they usually are supposed to contain only a few facts that answer only one question.

Another common theme of these approaches is that they compare the student answers to one or more previously defined correct answers that are either given in natural language as target answers or as a list of concepts in an answer key. The ways of technically conducting these comparisons vary widely, as we discuss below in Section 2.2.

There also are conceptual differences between the approaches. Some systems focus on assessing whether or not the student has properly answered the question. They put the spot on comparing the meaning of target answers and student answers; they aim at being tolerant of form errors such as spelling or grammar errors. Others aim at giving a grade as accurate as possible, therefore not only assessing meaning but also performing grading similar to human teachers. This can also include modules that take into account form errors.

These two views on a similar task are also reflected in the annotation of the data used in experiments: Systems performing meaning comparison usually operate with labels specifying the relations between target answers and student answers. Grading systems naturally aim at producing numerical grades. Since labels are on a nominal scale, and grades are on an ordinal scale (or even treated as being on an interval scale), the difference between meaning comparison and grading results in a whole string of other differences in methodology.

Researchers also enter the short answer landscape from different home countries: Some projects are interested in the strategies and mechanics of meaning comparison, others aim at reducing the load and costs of large-scale assessment tests, and yet others aim at improving intelligent tutoring systems, requiring additional components that provide useful feedback to students using these systems.

2.2 Approaches

Table 1 summarizes the features of the short answer assessment systems discussed hereafter.

One of the earlier systems is WebLAS, presented by Bachman et al. (2002). A human task creator feeds the system with scores for model answers. Regular expressions are then created automatically from these model answers. Since each regular expression is associated with a score, matching the expression against a student answer yields a score for that answer. Bachman et al. (2002) do not provide an evaluation study based on data.

Another earlier system is CarmelTC by Rosé et al. (2003). It has been designed as a component in the Why2 tutorial dialogue system (VanLehn et al., 2002). Even though Rosé et al. (2003) position CarmelTC in the context of essay grading, it may be considered to deal with short answers: in their data, the average length of a student response is approx. 48 words. Their system is designed to perform text classification on single sentences in the student responses, where each class of text represents one possible model response, plus an additional class for 'no match'. They combine decision trees operating on an automatic syntactic analysis, a Naive Bayes text classifier, and a bag-of-words approach. In a 50-fold cross validation experiment with one physics question, six classes and 126 student responses, hand-tagged by two annotators, CarmelTC reaches an F-measure value of 0.85. They do not report on a baseline. Concerning the quality of the gold standard, they report that conflicts in the annotation have been resolved.

C-Rater (Leacock and Chodorow, 2003) is based on a paraphrase recognition approach. It employs correct answer models consisting of essential points formulated in natural language. C-Rater aims at automatic scoring and focuses on meaning, thus tolerating form errors. Leacock and Chodorow (2003) present two pilot studies, one of them dealing with reading comprehension. From 16,625 student answers with an average length of 43 words, they drew a random sample of 100 answers to each of the seven questions. This sample was scored by one human judge using a three-way scoring system (full credit, partial credit, no credit). Their system achieved 84% agreement with the gold standard. Information about the distribution of the scoring categories is given indirectly: A baseline system that assigns scores randomly would have achieved 47% accuracy.

System	Goal	Technique	Domain	Lang.
WebLAS (Bachman et al., 2002)	Assessment of language ability	Auto-generated regular expressions	Foreign language teaching	EN
CarmelTC (Rosé et al., 2003)	Automatic grading	Text classification	Physics	EN
C-Rater (Leacock and Chodorow, 2003)	Assessment test	Paraphrase recognition	Mathematics, Reading comp.	EN
IAT (Mitchell et al., 2003)	Assessment, Automatic grading	Information extraction w/ handwritten patterns	Medical	EN
Oxford (Pulman and Sukkarieh, 2005)	Assessment, automatic grading	Information extraction w/ handwritten patterns	GCSE exams	EN
Atenea (Pérez et al., 2005)	Automatic grading	N-gram overlap, Latent Semantic Analysis	Computer science	ES
Logic-based System (Makatchev and VanLehn, 2007)	Meaning comparison	First-order logic, machine learning	Physics	EN
CAM (Bailey and Meurers, 2008), CoMiC-EN (Meurers et al., 2011a)	Meaning comparison	Alignment, machine learning	Reading comp. in foreign language	EN
Facets System (Nielsen et al., 2009)	Meaning comparison & tutoring systems	Alignment of facets, machine learning	Elementary school science classes	EN
Texas (Mohler et al., 2011)	Automatic grading	Graph alignment, semantic similarity	Computer science	EN
CoMiC-DE (Meurers et al., 2011b)	Meaning comparison	Alignment, machine learning	Reading comp. in foreign language	DE
CoSeC-DE (Hahn and Meurers, 2012)	Meaning comparison	Alignment via Lexical-Resource Semantics	Reading comp. in foreign language	DE

Table 1: Short Answer Assessment systems and their Features

Information extraction templates form the core of the Intelligent Assessment Technologies system (IAT, Mitchell et al. 2003). These templates are created manually in a special-purpose authoring tool by exploring sample responses. They allow for syntactic variation, e.g., filling the subject slot in a sentence with different equivalent concepts. The templates corresponding to a question are then matched against the student answer. Unlike other systems, IAT additionally features templates for explicitly invalid answers. They tested their approach with a progress test that has to be taken by medicine students. Approximately 800 students each plowed through 270 test items. The automatically graded responses then were moderated: Human judges streamlined the answers to achieve a more consistent grading. This step already had been done before with tests graded by humans. Mitchell et al. (2003) state that their system reaches 99.4% accuracy on the full dataset after the manual adjustment of the templates via the moderation process. Summarizing, they report an error of "between 5 and 5.5%" in inter-grader agreement and an error of 5.8% in automatic grading without the moderation step, though it is not entirely clear which data these statistics correspond to. No information on the distribution of grades or a random baseline is provided.

The Oxford system (Pulman and Sukkarieh, 2005) is another one to employ an information extraction approach. Again, templates are constructed manually. Motivated by the necessary robustness to process language with grammar mistakes and spelling errors, they use shallow analyses in their pre-processing. In order to overcome the hassle of manually constructing templates, they also investigated machine learning techniques. However, the automatically generated templates were outperformed by the manually created ones. Furthermore, they state that manually created templates can be equipped with messages provided to the student as feedback in a tutoring system. For evaluating their system, they used factual science questions and the corresponding student answers from GCSE tests. 200 graded answers for each of nine questions served as a training set, while another 60 answers served as a test set. They report that their system achieves an accuracy of 84%. With inconsistencies in the human grading removed, it achieves 93%. However, they do not report on the level of inter-grader agreement or on a random baseline.

Pérez et al. (2005) present the Atenea system, a combined approach that makes use of Latent Semantic Analysis (LSA, Landauer et al. 1998) and n-gram overlap. While n-gram overlap supports comparing target responses and student responses with differing word order, it does not deal with synonyms and related terms. Hence, they use LSA to add a component that deals with semantic relatedness in the comparison step. As a test corpus, they collected nine different questions from computer science exams. A tenth question "[consists] of a set of definitions of 'Operating System' obtained from the Internet." Altogether, they gathered 924 student responses and 44 target responses written by teachers. Since their LSA module had been trained on English but their data were in Spanish, they chose to use Altavista Babelfish to translate the data into English. They do not provide information about the distribution of scores and about inter-grader agreement. Atenea achieves a Pearson's correlation of $r = 0.554$ with the scores in the gold standard.

The approach by Makatchev and VanLehn (2007), which we refer to as the Logic-based System, enters the landscape from the direction of artificial intelligence. It is related to CarmelTC and its dataset, but follows a different route: target responses are manually encoded in first-order predicate language. Similar logic representations are constructed automatically for student answers. They explore various strategies for matching these two logic representation on the basis of 16 semantic classes. In an evaluation experiment, they tested the system on 293 "natural language utterances" with ten-fold cross validation. The test data are skewed towards the 'empty' label that indicates that none of the 16 semantic labels could be attached. They do not report on other properties of the dataset such as number of annotators or number of questions to which the student answers were given. Their winning configuration yields a F-measure value of 0.4974. While Makatchev and VanLehn (2007) position their approach in the context of the Why2 tutorial dialogue system, their use of semantic classes seems to make them more related to meaning comparison than to grading.

The Content Assessment Module (CAM) presented in Bailey (2008) and Bailey and Meurers (2008) utilizes an approach that is different from the systems discussed so far: Following a three-step strategy, the system first automatically generates linguistic annotations for questions, target responses and student responses. In an alignment phase, these annotations are then used to map from elements (words, lemmas, chunks, dependency triples) in the student responses to elements in the target responses. Finally, a machine learning classifier judges on the basis of this alignment, whether or not the student has answered the question correctly. The data used for evaluation was made available as the Corpus of Reading Comprehension Exercises in English (CREE, Meurers et al. 2011a). This corpus consists of 566 responses produced by intermediate ESL learners at The Ohio State University as part of their regular assignments. Students had access to their textbooks and typically answered questions in one to three sentences. All responses were labelled as either appropriate or inappropriate by two independent annotators, along with a detailed diagnosis code specifying the nature of the inappropriateness (missing concept, extra concept, blend, non-answer). In leave-one-out evaluation on the development set containing 311 responses to 47 different questions, CAM achieved 87% accuracy on the binary judgment (response correct/incorrect). For the test set containing 255 responses to 28 questions, the approach achieved 88%. However, the distribution of categories in the data is heavily skewed with 71% of the responses marked as correct in the development set and 84% in the test set. The best result obtained on a balanced set with leave-one-out-testing is 78%. Meurers et al. (2011a) present a re-implementation of CAM called CoMiC-EN (Comparing Meaning in Context in English), achieving an accuracy of 87.6% on the CREE development set and 88.4% on the test set.

With their Facets System, Nielsen et al. (2009) establish a connection to the field of Recognizing Textual Entailment (RTE, Dagan et al. 2009). In a number of friendly challenges, RTE research has spawned numerous systems that try to automatically answer the following question: Given a text and a hypothesis, is the hypothesis entailed by the text? Short answers assessment can be seen as a RTE task in which the target response corresponds to the text and the student response to the hypothesis. Nielsen et al. (2009) base their system on what they call facets. These facets are meaning representations of parts of sentences. They are constructed automatically from dependency and semantic parses of the target responses. Each facet in the target response is then looked up in the corresponding student response and equipped with one of five labels[2] ranging from unaddressed (the student did not mention the fact in this facet) to expressed (the student named the fact). This step is taken via machine learning. From a tutoring system in real-life operation, they gathered responses from third- to sixth-grade students answering questions for science classes. Two annotators worked on these data, producing 142,151 facets. Furthermore, all facets were looked up in the corresponding student responses and annotated accordingly, using the mentioned set of labels. The best result of the Facets System is 75.5% accuracy on one of the held-out test sets. With ten-fold cross validation on the training set, it achieves 77.1% accuracy. The majority label baselines are 51.1% and 54.6% respectively. Providing this more fine-grained analysis of facets that are searched for in student responses, Nielsen et al. (2009) claim to "enable more intelligent dialogue control" in tutoring systems. From the point of view of grading vs. meaning comparison, their approach can be counted towards the latter, since their labels can be conflated to produce a single yes/no decision.

Another recent approach is described by Mohler et al. (2011), hereafter referred to as the Texas system. Student responses and target responses are annotated using a dependency parser. Thereupon, subgraphs of the dependency structures are constructed in order to map one response to the other. These alignments are generated using machine learning. Dealing with subgraphs allows for variation in word order between the two responses that are to be compared. In order to account for meaning, they combine lexical semantic similarity with the aforementioned alignment. They make use of several WordNet-based measures and two corpus-based measures, namely Latent Semantic Analysis and Explicit Semantic Analysis (ESA, Gabrilovich and Markovitch 2007). For evaluating their system, Mohler et al. (2011) collected student responses from an online learning environment. 80 questions from ten introductory computer science assignments spread across two exams were gathered together with 2,273 student responses. These responses were graded by two human judges on a scale from zero to five. The judges fully agreed in 57% of all cases, their Pearson correlation computes to $r = 0.586$. The gold standard has been created by computing the arithmetic mean of the two judgments for each response. The Texas system achieves $r = 0.518$ and a Root Mean Square Error of 0.978 as its best result. Mohler et al. (2011) mention that "[t]he dataset is biased towards correct answers". Data are publicly available. We used these in an evaluation experiment with the CoMiC-EN system, discussed in Section 3.

While almost all short answer assessment research has targeted answers written in English, there are two recent approaches dealing with German answers. The CoMiC-EN reimplementation of CAM discussed above was motivated by the need for a modular architecture supporting a transfer of the system to German, resulting in its counterpart named CoMiC-DE (Meurers et al., 2011b). The German system utilizes the same strategies as the English one, but with language-dependent processing modules being replaced. Meurers et al. (2011b) evaluated CoMiC-DE on a subset of the Corpus of Reading Comprehension Questions in German (CREG, Ott et al. 2012), collected in collaboration with the German programs at The Ohio State University and the University of Kansas. Like in CREE, all responses are rated by two annotators with both binary and detailed diagnosis codes.[3] The aforementioned subset contains 1,032 learner responses and 223 target responses to 177 questions. Furthermore, it features an even distribution of correct and incorrect answers according to the judgement of two human

[2]In human annotation, they use eight labels, which are grouped into five broader categories as used by their system.

[3]In CREG, correct answers as well as incorrect ones can be labelled with missing concept, extra concept, or blend.

annotators. On that subset, CoMiC-DE achieved an accuracy of 84.6% in the binary classification task. CREG is freely available for research purposes under a Creative Commons by-nc-sa license.

Hahn and Meurers (2012) present the CoSeC-DE approach based on Lexical Resource Semantics (LRS, Richter and Sailer 2003). In a first step, they create LRS representations from POS-tagged and dependency-parsed data. These underspecified LRS representations of student responses and target responses are then aligned. Using A* as heuristic search algorithm, a best alignment is computed and equipped with a numeric score representing the quality of the alignment of the formulae. If this best alignment scores higher than a threshold, the system judges student response and target response to convey the same meaning. The alignment and comparison mechanism does not utilize any linguistic representations other than the LRS semantic formulae. These semantic representations abstract away from surface features, e.g., by treating active and passive voice equally. Hahn and Meurers (2012) claim that that "[semantic representations] more clearly expose those distinction which do make a difference in meaning." They evaluate the approach on the above-mentioned subset of CREG containing 1,032 learner responses and report an accuracy of 86.3%.

3 A concrete system comparison

After discussing the broad landscape of Short Answer Evaluation systems, the main characteristics and differences, we now turn to a comparison of two concrete systems, namely CoMiC-EN (Meurers et al., 2011a) and the Texas system Mohler et al. (2011), to explore what is involved in such a concrete comparison of two systems from different contexts. While CoMiC-EN was developed with meaning comparison in mind, the purpose of the Texas system is answer grading. We pick these two systems because they constitute recent and interesting instances of their respective fields and the corresponding data are freely available.

3.1 Data

In evaluating the Texas system, Mohler et al. (2011) used a corpus of ten assignments and two exams from an introductory computer science class. In total, the Texas corpus consists of 2,442 responses, which were collected using an online learning platform. Each response is rated by two annotators with a numerical grade on a 0–5 scale. Annotators were not given any specific instructions besides the scale itself, which resulted in an exact agreement of 57.7%. In order to arrive at a gold standard rating, the numerical average of the two ratings was computed. The data exist in raw, sentence-segmented and parsed versions and are freely available for research use. Table 2 presents a breakdown of the score counts and distribution statistics of the Texas corpus. A bias towards correct answers can be observed, which is also mentioned by Mohler et al. (2011).

Score	#	**Score**	#
0.000	24	3.250	1
0.500	3	3.500	187
1.000	23	3.625	1
1.500	46	3.750	1
1.750	1	4.000	220
2.000	93	4.125	2
2.250	2	4.500	310
2.500	125	4.750	1
3.000	164	5.000	1238

$\overline{x} = 4.19, s = 1.11$

Table 2: Details on the gold standard scores in the Texas corpus. Non-integer scores result from averaging between raters and normalization onto the 0–5 scale.

3.2 Approaches

CoMiC-EN uses a three-step approach to meaning comparison. *Annotation* uses NLP to enrich the student and target answers, as well as the question text, with linguistic information on different levels (words, chunks, dependency triples) and types of abstraction (tokens, lemmas, distributional vectors, etc.). *Alignment* maps elements of the learner answer to elements of the target response using annotation. The global alignment solution is computed using the Traditional Marriage Algorithm (Gale and Shapley, 1962). Finally, *Classification* analyzes the possible alignments and labels the learner response with a binary or detailed diagnosis code. The features used in the classification step are shown in Table 3.

For the Texas system, Mohler et al. (2011) used a combination of bag-of-words (BOW) features and

Features	Description
1. Keyword Overlap	Percent of keywords aligned (relative to target)
2./3. Token Overlap	Percent of aligned target/learner tokens
4./5. Chunk Overlap	Percent of aligned target/learner chunks
6./7. Triple Overlap	Percent of aligned target/learner triples
8. Token Match	Percent of token alignments that were token-identical
9. Similarity Match	Percent of token alignments that were similarity-resolved
10. Type Match	Percent of token alignments that were type-resolved
11. Lemma Match	Percent of token alignments that were lemma-resolved
12. Synonym Match	Percent of token alignments that were synonym-resolved
13. Variety of Match (0-5)	Number of kinds of token-level alignments

Table 3: Features used in the CoMiC-EN system

dependency graph alignment in connection with two different machine learning approaches. Among the BOW features are WordNet-based similarity measures such as the one by Lesk (1986) and vector space measures such as $tf * idf$ (Salton and McGill, 1983) and the more advanced LSA (Landauer et al., 1998). The dependency graph alignment approach builds on a node-to-node matching stage which computes a score for each possible match between nodes of the student and target response. In the next stage, the optimal graph alignment is computed based on the node-to-node scores using the Hungarian algorithm.

Mohler et al. (2011) also employ a technique they call "question demoting", which refers to the exclusion of words from the alignment process if they already appeared in the question string. Incidentally, the technique is also used in the earlier CAM system (Bailey and Meurers, 2008), but called "Givenness filter" there, following the long tradition of research on givenness (Schwarzschild, 1999) as a notion of information structure investigated in formal pragmatics.

To produce the final system score, the Texas system uses two machine learning techniques based on Support Vector Machines (SVMs), SVMRank and Support Vector Regression (SVR). Both techniques are trained with several combinations of the dependency alignment and BOW features. While with SVR one trains a function to produce a score on the 0–5 scale itself, SVMRank produces a ranking of student answers which does not produce a 0–5 grade. Therefore, Mohler et al. (2011) employ isotonic regression to map the ranking to the 0–5 scale.

In terms of performance, Mohler et al. (2011) report that the SVMRank system produces a better correlation measure ($r = 0.518$) while the SVR system yields a better RMSE (0.978).

3.3 Evaluation

We now turn to the evaluation of CoMiC-EN on the Texas corpus as it is a publicly available dataset. As mentioned before, CoMiC-EN performs meaning comparison based on a system of categories while the Texas system is a scoring approach, trying to predict a grade. While the former is a *classification* task, the latter is better characterized as a *regression* problem because of the desired numerical outcome. Of course, one could simply pretend that individual grades are classes and treat scoring as a classification task. However, a classification approach has no knowledge of numerical relationships, i.e., it does not 'know' that 4 is a higher grade than 3 and a much higher grade than 1 (assuming a 0–5 scale). As a result, if an evaluation metric such as Pearson correlation is used, classification systems are at a disadvantage because some misclassifications are punished more than others. We discuss this point further in Section 4.

For these reasons, to obtain a more interesting comparison, we modified CoMiC-EN to perform scoring instead of meaning comparison. This means that the memory-based learning approach CoMiC-EN had employed so far was no longer applicable and had to be replaced with a regression-capable learning strategy. We chose Support Vector Regression (SVR) using libSVM[4] since that is one of the methods employed by Mohler et al. (2011). However, all other parts of CoMiC-EN such as the processing pipeline and the alignment approach and the extracted features remained the same.

[4] `http://www.csie.ntu.edu.tw/~cjlin/libsvm`

The evaluation procedure was carried out as a 12-fold cross-validation due to the 12 assignments in the Texas corpus. For each fold, one complete assignment was held out as test set. Parameters for the SVR were determined using a grid search using the tools provided with libSVM. As kernel function, we used a linear kernel as it was also used in the evaluation of the Texas system and thus constitutes a vital part of the evaluation setup. In general, we designed to evaluation procedure to be as close as possible to the Texas one.

Table 4 presents detailed results on the 12 folds as well as the overall results and a baseline which always predicts the median value 5.

Assignment	# responses	*r*	RMSE
1	203	0.416	0.958
2	210	0.349	1.221
3	217	0.335	0.969
4	210	0.338	1.212
5	112	0.010	1.030
6	182	0.646	0.702
7	182	0.265	0.991
8	189	0.521	0.942
9	189	0.220	0.942
10	168	0.699	0.990
11 (exam)	300	0.436	1.076
12 (exam)	280	0.619	1.165
Median Baseline	2442	–	1.375
Overall	2442	0.405	1.016

Table 4: Detailed results of CoMiC-EN on Texas corpus

The CoMiC-EN system on the Texas data set does not quite reach the level achieved by the Texas system on their data set. We obtained a Pearson correlation of $r = 0.405$ and an RMSE of 1.016 over all 12 folds. However, let us keep in mind the objective of this experiment as exemplifying the process needed to directly compare two systems from different research strands on the same dataset.

4 Comparability of approaches & datasets

It seems clear that for systems to be comparable and results to be reproducible, datasets must be publicly available, as is the case with the Texas corpus. However, data availability alone does not ensure meaningful comparison. Depending on the context the corpus was drawn from, datasets will differ just like the corresponding systems:

- Data source: Reading comprehension task in language learning setting, language tutoring context, automated grading of short answer exams
- Language properties: Native vs. learner language, domain-specific language (e.g., computer science)
- Assessment scheme: nominal vs. interval scale

Especially the last point deserves some further discussion. Depending on the kind of assessment scheme, which in turn is motivated by the task, different evaluation methods may be chosen. Scoring systems are often evaluated using a correlation metric in order to capture the systems' tendency to assign similar but not necessary equal grades as the human raters. Conversely, with category-based schemes one usually reports accuracy, which expresses how many items were classified correctly.

The question that arises is how a system coming from one paradigm can be compared to one from the other paradigm in a meaningful way. One might argue that the tasks are simply too different: scoring might take form errors into account while meaning comparison by definition does not. Moreover, while classification labels say something explicit and absolute about a piece of data, grades by definition are relative to the scale they come from. It thus seems impossible to somehow unify the two schemes as they express fundamentally different ideas.

However, the strategies systems use to tackle scoring or meaning comparison are undoubtedly similar and should be comparable, as we argue in this paper. So in order for researchers to learn from other approaches and also compare their results to those of other systems which tackle a different task, changes to systems seem necessary and should be preferred over changes to the gold standard data. In the case presented here, a meaning comparison system was turned into a scoring system by changing the machine learning component from classification to regression, which requires a certain level of system modularity.

Having compared the two systems using Pearson correlation and RMSE, it also makes sense to consider the relevance of these evaluation metrics. For example, it is the case that pairwise correlation assumes a normal distribution whereas datasets like the Texas corpus are heavily skewed towards correct answers (see Table 2). Mohler et al. (2011) also note that in distributions with zero variance, correlation is undefined, which is not a problem as such but limits the use of correlation as evaluation metric. Mohler et al. (2011) propose that RMSE is better suited to the task since it captures the relative error a system makes when trying to predict scores. However, RMSE is scale-dependent and thus RMSE values across different studies cannot be compared. We can only suggest that in order to sufficiently describe a system's performance, several metrics need to be reported.

Finally, an important point concerns the quality of gold standards. Given the relatively low inter-annotator agreement in the Texas corpus ($r = 0.586, RMSE = 0.659$) it seems fair to ask whether answers without perfect agreement should be used in training and testing systems at all. In the CREE and CREG corpora, answers with disagreement among the annotators have either been excluded from experiments or resolved by an additional judge. This approach is also supported by recent literature (cf., e.g., Beigman and Beigman Klebanov 2009; Beigman Klebanov and Beigman 2009). However, for the Texas corpus, Mohler et al. (2011) have opted to use the arithmetic mean of the two graders as gold standard. While mathematically a viable solution, it seems questionable whether the mean is reliable with only two graders, especially if they have not operated on the grounds of explicit guidelines. It would be interesting to see whether in this case, a system trained on more, singly annotated data would perform better than one on less, doubly annotated data, as argued for by Dligach et al. (2010). In any case, if many disagreements occur, one should ask the question whether the annotation task is defined well enough and whether machines should really be expected to perform it consistently if humans have trouble doing so.

5 Conclusion

We discussed several issues in the comparison of short answer evaluation systems. To that end, we gave an overview of the existing systems and picked two for a concrete comparison on the same data, the CoMiC-EN system (Meurers et al., 2011a) and the Texas system (Mohler et al., 2011). In comparing the two, it was necessary to turn CoMiC-EN into a scoring system because the Texas corpus as the chosen gold standard contains numeric scores assigned by humans. Taking a step back from the concrete comparison, we gave a more general description of what is necessary to compare short answer evaluation systems. We observed that more datasets need to be publicly available in order for performance comparisons to have meaning, a point also made earlier by Pulman and Sukkarieh (2005). Moreover, we noted how datasets differ in similar aspects as systems do, such as task context and assessment scheme. We then criticized the use of correlation measures as evaluation metrics for short answer scoring. Finally, we discussed the importance of gold standard quality.

We conclude that it is interesting and relevant to compare short answer evaluation systems even if the concrete task they tackle, such as grading or meaning comparison, is not the same. However, the availability and quality of the datasets will decide to what extent systems can sensibly be compared. For progress to be made in this area, more publicly available datasets and systems are needed. The upcoming SemEval-2013 task on "Textual entailment and paraphrasing for student input assessment"[5] will hopefully become one important step into this direction (see also Dzikovska et al. 2012).

Acknowledgements

We are grateful to the three anonymous BEA reviewers for their detailed and helpful comments.

References

Lyle Bachman, Nathan Carr, Greg Kamei, Mikyung Kim, Michael Pan, Chris Salvador, and Yasuyo Sawaki. 2002. A reliable approach to automatic assessment of short answer free responses. In *Proceedings of the 19th International Conference on Computational Linguistics (COLING 2002)*, pages 1–4.

Stacey Bailey and Detmar Meurers. 2008. Diagnosing meaning errors in short answers to reading comprehension questions. In Joel Tetreault, Jill Burstein, and Rachele De Felice, editors, *Proceedings of the*

[5] `http://www.cs.york.ac.uk/semeval-2013/task4/`

3rd Workshop on Innovative Use of NLP for Building Educational Applications (BEA-3) at ACL'08, pages 107–115, Columbus, Ohio.

Stacey Bailey. 2008. *Content Assessment in Intelligent Computer-Aided Language Learning: Meaning Error Diagnosis for English as a Second Language*. Ph.D. thesis, The Ohio State University.

Eyal Beigman and Beata Beigman Klebanov. 2009. Learning with annotation noise. In *Proceedings of the Joint Conference of the 47th Annual Meeting of the ACL and the 4th International Joint Conference on Natural Language Processing of the AFNLP*, volume 1, pages 280–287. Association for Computational Linguistics.

Beata Beigman Klebanov and Eyal Beigman. 2009. From annotator agreement to noise models. *Computational Linguistics*, 35(4):495–503.

Ido Dagan, Bill Dolan, Bernardo Magnini, and Dan Roth. 2009. Recognizing textual entailment: Rational, evaluation and approaches. *Natural Language Engineering*, 15(4):i–xvii, 10.

Dmitriy Dligach, Rodney D. Nielsen, and Martha Palmer. 2010. To annotate more accurately or to annotate more. In *Proceedings of the Fourth Linguistic Annotation Workshop*, LAW IV '10, pages 64–72, Stroudsburg, PA, USA. Association for Computational Linguistics.

Myroslava O. Dzikovska, Rodney D. Nielsen, and Chris Brew. 2012. Towards effective tutorial feedback for explanation questions: A dataset and baselines. In *Proceedings of the 2012 Conference of the North American Chapter of the Association for Computational Linguistics: Human Language Technologies*.

Evgeniy Gabrilovich and Shaul Markovitch. 2007. Computing semantic relatedness using wikipedia-based explicit semantic analysis. In *Proceedings of the 20th International Joint Conference on Artificial Intelligence*, pages 6–12.

David Gale and Lloyd S. Shapley. 1962. College admissions and the stability of marriage. *American Mathematical Monthly*, 69:9–15.

Michael Hahn and Detmar Meurers. 2012. Evaluating the meaning of answers to reading comprehension questions: A semantics-based approach. In *Proceedings of the 7th Workshop on Innovative Use of NLP for Building Educational Applications (BEA-7) at NAACL-HLT 2012*, Montreal.

Thomas Landauer, Peter Foltz, and Darrell Laham. 1998. An introduction to latent semantic analysis. *Discourse Processes*, 25:259–284.

Claudia Leacock and Martin Chodorow. 2003. C-rater: Automated scoring of short-answer questions. *Computers and the Humanities*, 37:389–405.

Michael Lesk. 1986. Automatic sense disambiguation using machine readable dictionaries: how to tell a pine cone from an ice cream cone. In *Proceedings of the 5th annual international conference on Systems documentation*, pages 24–26, Toronto, Ontario, Canada.

Maxim Makatchev and Kurt VanLehn. 2007. Combining baysian networks and formal reasoning for semantic classification of student utterances. In *Proceedings of the International Conference on AI in Education (AIED)*, Los Angeles, July.

Detmar Meurers, Ramon Ziai, Niels Ott, and Stacey Bailey. 2011a. Integrating parallel analysis modules to evaluate the meaning of answers to reading comprehension questions. *IJCEELL. Special Issue on Automatic Free-text Evaluation*, 21(4):355–369.

Detmar Meurers, Ramon Ziai, Niels Ott, and Janina Kopp. 2011b. Evaluating answers to reading comprehension questions in context: Results for german and the role of information structure. In *Proceedings of the TextInfer 2011 Workshop on Textual Entailment*, pages 1–9, Edinburgh, Scotland, UK, July. Association for Computational Linguistics.

Tom Mitchell, Nicola Aldrige, and Peter Broomhead. 2003. Computerized marking of short-answer free-text responses. Paper presented at the 29th annual conference of the International Association for Educational Assessment (IAEA), Manchester, UK.

Michael Mohler, Razvan Bunescu, and Rada Mihalcea. 2011. Learning to grade short answer questions using semantic similarity measures and dependency graph alignments. In *Proceedings of the 49th Annual Meeting of the Association for Computational Linguistics: Human Language Technologies*, pages 752–762, Portland, Oregon, USA, June. Association for Computational Linguistics.

Rodney D. Nielsen, Wayne Ward, and James H. Martin. 2009. Recognizing entailment in intelligent tutoring systems. *Natural Language Engineering*, 15(4):479–501.

Niels Ott, Ramon Ziai, and Detmar Meurers. 2012. Creation and analysis of a reading comprehension exercise corpus: Towards evaluating meaning in context. In Thomas Schmidt and Kai Wörner, editors, *Multilingual Corpora and Multilingual Corpus Analysis*, Hamburg Studies in Multilingualism (HSM). Benjamins, Amsterdam. to appear.

Diana Pérez, Enrique Alfonseca, Pilar Rodríguez, Alfio Gliozzo, Carlo Strapparava, and Bernardo Magnini. 2005. About the effects of combining latent semantic analysis with natural language processing techniques for free-text assessment. *Revista signos*, 38(59):325–343.

Stephen G. Pulman and Jana Z. Sukkarieh. 2005. Automatic short answer marking. In Jill Burstein and Claudia Leacock, editors, *Proceedings of the Second*

Workshop on Building Educational Applications Using NLP, pages 9–16, Ann Arbor, Michigan, June. Association for Computational Linguistics.

Frank Richter and Manfred Sailer. 2003. Basic concepts of lexical resource semantics. In Arnold Beckmann and Norbert Preining, editors, *ESSLLI 2003 – Course Material I*, volume 5 of *Collegium Logicum*, pages 87–143, Wien. Kurt Gödel Society.

Carolyn Penstein Rosé, Antonio Roque, Dumisizwe Bhembe, and Kurt VanLehn. 2003. A hybrid approach to content analysis for automatic essay grading. In *Proceedings of the 2003 Conference of the North American Chapter of the Association for Computational Linguistics on Human Language Technology: companion volume of the Proceedings of HLT-NAACL 2003–short papers - Volume 2*, NAACL-Short '03, pages 88–90, Edmonton, Canada. Association for Computational Linguistics.

Gerard Salton and Michael J. McGill. 1983. *Introduction to modern information retrieval.* McGraw-Hill, New York.

Roger Schwarzschild. 1999. GIVENness, AvoidF and other constraints on the placement of accent. *Natural Language Semantics*, 7(2):141–177.

Kurt VanLehn, Pamela W. Jordan, Carolyn Penstein Rosé, Dumisizwe Bhembe, Michael Boettner, Andy Gaydos, Maxim Makatchev, Umarani Pappuswamy, Micheal Ringenberg, Antonio Roque, Stephanie Siler, and Ramesh Srivastava. 2002. The architecture of why2-atlas: A coach for qualitative physics essay writing. In *Proceedings of the 6th International Conference on Intelligent Tutoring Systems*, volume 2363, pages 158–167, Biarritz, France and San Sebastian, Spain, June 2-7. Springer LNCS.

Detection and Correction of Preposition and Determiner Errors in English: HOO 2012

Pinaki Bhaskar **Aniruddha Ghosh** **Santanu Pal** **Sivaji Bandyopadhyay**
Department of Computer Science and Engineering, Jadavpur University
188, Raja S. C. Mallick Road
Kolkata – 700032, India
pinaki.bhaskar@gmail.com arghyaonline@gnail.com santanu.pal.ju@gmail.com sivaji_cse_ju@yahoo.com

Abstract

This paper reports on our work in the HOO 2012 shared task. The task is to automatically detect, recognize and correct the errors in the use of prepositions and determiners in a set of given test documents in English. For that, we have developed a hybrid system of an n-gram statistical model along with some rule-based techniques. The system has been trained on the HOO shared task's training datasets and run on the test set given. We have submitted one run, which has demonstrated an F-score of 7.1, 6.46 and 2.58 for detection, recognition and correction respectively before revision and F-score of 8.22, 7.59 and 3.16 for detection, recognition and correction respectively after revision.

1 Introduction

Writing research papers or theses in English is a very challenging task for those researchers and scientists whose first language or mother tongue is not English. Depicting their research works properly in English is a hard job for them. Generally their papers, which are submitted to conferences, may be rejected not because of their research works but because of the English writing, which makes the papers harder for the reviewer to understand the intentions of author. This kind of problem will be faced in any field where someone has to provide material in a language other than his/her first language.

The mentoring service of Association for Computational Linguistics (ACL) is one part of a response. This service can address a wider range of problems than those related purely to writing. The aim of this service is that a research paper should be judged only on its research content.

The organizer of "Help Our Own" (HOO) proposed and initiated a shared task in 2011 (Dale and Kilgarriff, 2010), which attempts to tackle the problem by developing tools or techniques for the non-native speaker of English, which will automatically correct the English prose of the papers so that they can be accepted. This tools and techniques may also help native English speakers. This task is simply expressed as text-to-text generation or Natural language Generation (NLG). In the 2011 shared task, all possible errors were covered which made the task enormously huge. In 2012, the task is more specific and only deals with determiners and prepositions as described in (Dale and Kilgarriff, 2011).

For this shared task, HOO, we have developed two models, one is rule-based model and the other is the statistical model for both determiners and prepositions. Then we have combined both these models and developed our system for HOO 2012.

2 Related Work

The English language belongs to the Germanic languages branch of the Indo-European language family, widely spoken on six continents. The HOO shared task is organized to help authors with writing tasks. Identifying grammatical and linguistic errors in text is an open challenge to researchers. In recent times, researchers (Heidorn, 2000) have provided quite a benchmark for spell checker and grammar checkers, which is commonly available. In this task it is aimed to correct errors beyond the scope of these commonly available checkers i.e. detection and correction of jarring errors at part-of-speech (POS) level, syntax level and semantic level. Earlier Heidorn (1975) developed augmented phrase structure grammar. (Tetreault et. al., 2008) has dealt with error pattern with preposition by non-native speakers. Meurers and Wunsch (2010) showed a surface based state-of-the-art machine learning technique, which deals with some frequently used prepositions. (Elghafari et al., 2010) worked on Data-Driven Prediction of Prepositions in English. Boyd et al. (2011) used an n-gram based machine-learning approach. Last year we have also participated in this shared task; our system report was reported in (Bhaskar et. al., 2011).

3 Corpus Statistics

There are two sets of data, training set and test set provided by the organizer. The training set has 1000 documents, which are collected from the FCE dataset. The publicly available dataset was in the native FCE format. So, the organizer first converted it to the HOO data format. Then CUP annotators found the errors and marked them up in the dataset. This year the task is only about the errors related to prepositions and determiners. So the organizer set only six types of errors, listed in table 1, which were dealt with this year. Hence, the other errors were discarded and replace with its corresponding standoff annotation in the training set. The training set consists of 1000 documents of total 374680 words, which means 375 words per document. All the standoff annotations of training set were provided and an example of the standoff annotation is shown in the figure 1. Table 2 gives the error statistics of training set as reported in (Dale et. al., 2012).

The test dataset has another 100 documents, which contain total of 18013 words at an average of 180 words per document. The test data was processed as the training data was done, but the standoff annotation of the test documents was not provided before the task completion. The documents were provided in XML format as shown in the figure 2.

Error Type	Tag	Original	Correction
Replacement Preposition	RT	He was born **on** January	He was born **in** January
Missing Preposition	MT	Because it reminds me my childhood.	Because it reminds me **of** my childhood.
Unwanted Preposition	UT	Regarding **to** the accommodation	Regarding the accommodation
Replacement Determiner	RD	I used to going with my friends to **the** camp.	I used to going with my friends to **a** camp.
Missing Determiner	MD	That will be nice to go on 1st of July	That will be nice to go on **the** 1st of July
Unwanted Determiner	UD	The most suitable time for shopping is weekend when parents don't work and children haven't got **a** school.	The most suitable time for shopping is weekend when parents don't work and children haven't got school.

Table 1. Examples of the six types of error.

Error Type	# Training	# Test # before Revised	 # after Revised
UT	822	43	39
MT	1104	57	56
RT	2618	136	148
Prep	4545	236	243
UD	1048	53	62
MD	2230	125	131
RD	609	39	37
Det	3887	217	230
Total	**8432**	**453**	**473**
Words/ Error	44.18	39.77	38.08

Table 2. Error Statistics in the Training set.

```
<edit end="779" file="0004" in-
dex="0008" part="1" start="775"
type="UD">
  <original>the </original>
    <corrections>
      <correction>
        <empty/>
      </correction>
  </corrections>
</edit>

<edit end="1041" file="0004" in-
dex="0010" part="1" start="1039"
type="RT">
  <original>in</original>
    <corrections>
      <correction>at</correction>
  </corrections>
</edit>
```

Figure 1: An example of a standoff error annotation

```
<?xml version="1.0" encod-
ing="utf-8"?>
<HOO version="2.1">
  <HEAD sortkey="" source-
  type="FCE">
    <CANDIDATE>
      <AGE>20-30</AGE>
    </CANDIDATE>
  </HEAD>
  <BODY>
    <PART id="1">
      <P>Dear Chris</P>
      <P>I was great ...</P>
       .
       .
       .
    </PART>
  </BODY>
</HOO>
```

Figure 2: An example of the XML format of documents

4 System Description

The task is consisted of two coarse parts – Preposition and Determiner detection, recognition and correction. In our previous year's hybrid model, to resolve preposition errors, a rule-based model was developed and for determiner errors, a linear statistical method was used. There was no linear statistical model for prepositions. So this year we have induced a statistical model to incorporate larger coverage of preposition error detection, which is not detected by the appropriate preposition list described in section 4.1.2.

To resolve preposition errors and determiner errors we have built a hybrid model for both of them and used a voting technique among the rule based and statistical model for determiners and rule based post processing for prepositions. The system architecture is shown in the figure 3.

4.1 Preposition Error Detection

4.1.1 Statistical Model for Preposition

An n-gram based linear statistical model is used. From the training corpus, it was trained with 3, 5 and 7-gram models. After testing, the 5-gram model is performing best as from 3-gram, the statistical model fails to classify since probability distance is too small among the probable set to distinguish proper one while in 7-gram it fails to score high as training data set is relatively small and there are no similar occurrences. For the statistical model, different linguistic information is taken as features. Initially, surface words are only considered which actually is similar to fingerprinting technique. Due to different inflected forms, the system fails to identify possible cases for a similar type of error with different inflected forms. Hence the root form of the word is included as a feature. Chunk information is included as a feature. The preposition with same word varies with if following word is animate or inanimate. As example,

```
collaborate with SB
collaborate in/on ST
```

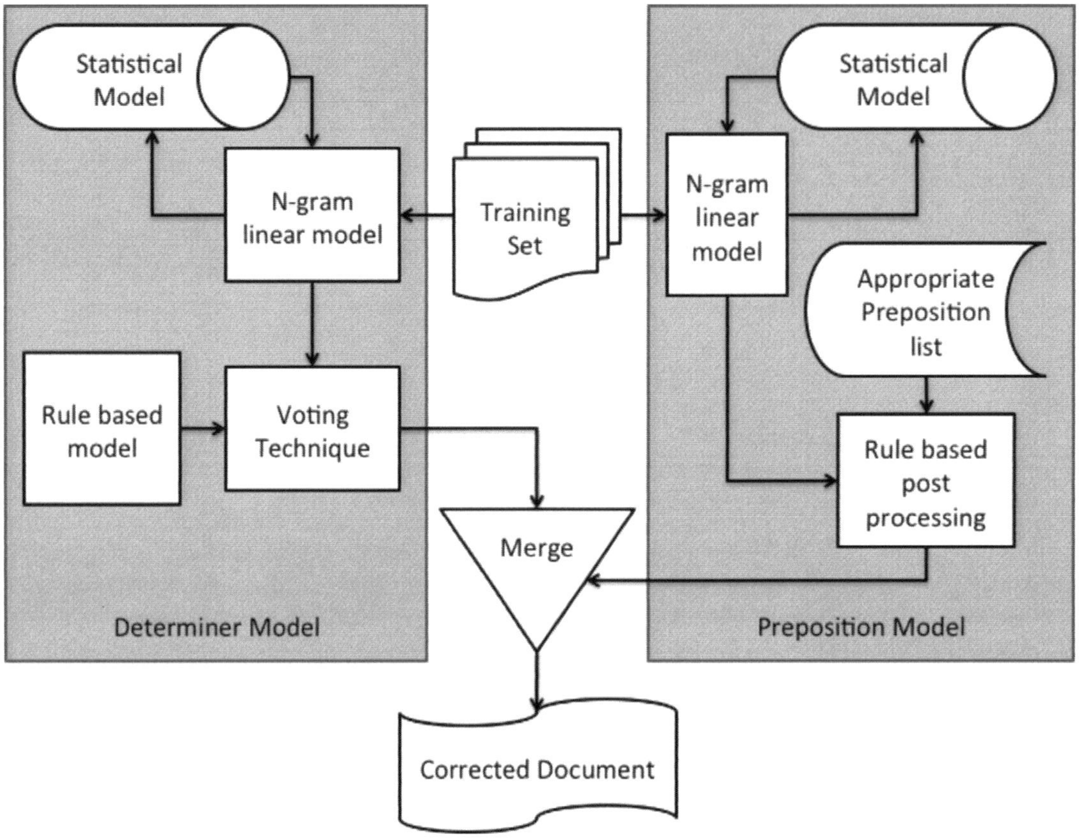

Figure 3. System Architecture

The text is parsed using the Stanford Dependency parser[1] to retrieve animate and inanimate information. After including animate and inanimate information the system didn't improve much as training data set is quite small and animate information is not correct for names. Hence, this feature is discarded from the statistical model.

4.1.2 Appropriate Preposition List

An appropriate preposition list consists of list of words along with preposition. The list is prepared in different corpus and training data. In the list, all possible formation with a word and preposition is stored. Let us take an example:

```
admit ST to SB
admit to
```

From corpus, two patterns for *admit* are found. Between admit and preposition something (ST) may come. Hence both of the entries are combined and formed in a regular expression format.

```
admit (ST)* to SB
```

4.1.3 Rule Based model for Preposition

Rule based post processing was applied on output of statistical model. For the rule based post processing, an appropriate preposition list was prepared manually. The list contains 1567 entries. The list is associated with animate and inanimate information. Hence, we aim to use dependency parser to identify subject object relation. Since the test data was in XML format, raw text was extracted from the XML document and the extracted sentences were parsed using Stanford dependency parser.

After parsing the document with the dependency parser, subject and object information was extracted. From all the sentences, proposition are detected and cross-validated with the appropriate preposition list. The preposition is dependent of the local association of the word around it. For the baseline

[1] http://nlp.stanford.edu/software/lex-parser.shtml

model, we have found that due to the list being small, few errors are being detected. Hence from the training corpus, the appropriate proposition list is enriched. The list is prepared in regular expression format. Here is an example:

```
ask * out +    invite on a date
```

In the above example, + means the two phrases have a similar meaning and * means one or more words can appear between the two words. Hence, when a match is found from the appropriate proposition list with the first word or the preposition, the words local to it are validated. Since the task is about correcting preposition errors, only words are matched with the list.

```
grateful to SB for ST
```

In the above example, *ST* means something or an object and *SB* means somebody or a subject, this information being retrieved from the dependency parser.

4.2 Determiner Error Detection

At the beginning of the determiner error detection task, we found that generation of list of rules to detect and correct the probable linguistic errors is a non-exhaustive set. Hence, we have decided to use a statistical model. After the statistical model, a rule based system is implemented with a few rules for *the* determiner devised from grammar books as for certain patterns statistical model fails to identify.

4.2.1 Statistical Model for Determiner

Similarly to preposition error detection, here a 5-gram linear statistical model is used. As same authors are prone to repeat same types of mistakes, we have decided to list out the errors from the training corpus documents. We have listed the errors document wise. In the training corpus, age information of author is mentioned. Hence documents are grouped according to age. After a close inspection of the document wise error list, the age group is prone to make similar type of errors, which depicts the attributes of the age group. Our statistical model is trained with every set of training data grouped by age separately. Hence different statistical models are prepared for different age groups. Now statistical model are applied according to the age group. It is found that age wise training incurred better result than single statistical model over whole data.

4.2.2 Rule Based Model for Determiner

It is found that statistical models works best for detecting the *a* and *an* determiner whereas performance drops for *the* determiner. Hence, rules for *the* are crafted manually from grammar books. A few rules for *a* and *an* are defined based on the first letter of the following word.
Among the determiners, usage of *the* is the most complicated one. For the rule based system different lists like nation, nationalities, unique objects, etc are produced. A few of the rules, which have been developed for the *the* determiner are mentioned below.

1. In most cases, if a sentence starts with a proper noun or common noun *the* is dropped.
2. Before a country name, *the* is dropped except if starts with *kingdom* or *republic*.
3. They system checks whether a common noun is appeared in a previous line of the document, i.e. it has already been referred to, in which case *the* is added.
4. If subject and object belong to same class i.e. they share the same hyponym class, *the* is added to the subject.
5. In case of superlatives like *best*, *worst* etc. *the* is added.
6. Before numerals, *the* is added.
7. Before unique things, *the* is added. Uniqueness is defined if a thing has single embodiment like *moon* etc.
8. It is found that if some geographical location is mentioned at a position other than start of sentence, *the* is added.

For different rules word lists are prepared such as a unique things list, superlatives, common nouns, country names, citizenships etc.

For *a* and *an* determiner correction, a list of different phonemes is prepared. Rule based system trims the first two characters and maps them into a phoneme to decide between *a* and *an*.

4.2.3 Voting Technique

The voting technique is used on the output of the rule based model and the statistical model. For *a* and *an* determiners, statistical model works best, especially in missing determiner and unnecessary determiner but for wrong determiner the rule based model performs better. For *the* determiner, the statistical model identified missing determiner and unnecessary determiner cases to some extent whereas list based rule-based system elevates the accuracy.

5 Evaluation

The system was evaluated for its performance in detecting, recognizing and correcting preposition and determiner errors in English documents. Separate scores were calculated for detection, recognition and correction for both the errors of preposition and determiner separately and then combined scores were also calculated. For all results, the organizer has provided three measures: Precision, Recall and F-Score. The precise definitions of these measures as implemented in the evaluation tool, and further details on the evaluation process are provided in (Dale and Narroway, 2012) and elaborated on at the HOO website.[4]

Each team was allowed to submit up to 10 separate runs over the test data, thus allowing them to have different configurations of their systems evaluated. Teams were asked to indicate whether they had used only publicly available data to train their systems, or whether they had made use of privately held data. We have submitted only one run (JU_run1) which has demonstrated F-scores of 7.1, 6.46 and 2.58 for detection, recognition and correction respectively before revision. And after revision it has demonstrated F-scores of 8.22, 7.59 and 3.16 for detection, recognition and correction respectively. Table 3 shows all the results of our run. We had used only publicly available data to train our systems, which are provided by the organizer as training set; we didn't use any privately held data.

6 Conclusion and Future Works

Our system has achieved F-scores of 8.22, 7.59 and 3.16 in detection, recognition and correction respectively. Our system failed to detect and correct many syntactic and semantic errors like wrong *a* determiner. Since the data consists of mostly mail conversation, it retains huge number of spelling mistakes, which misdirected the statistical, and rule based model to detect probable errors. For *the* determiner, if the size of the produced lists increases, better accuracy can be achieved with the rule-based system. Co-reference is another issue to identify, as *the* determiner is used mostly subsequent references. Anaphora resolution might therefore be of some help.

Element	Task	Before Revision			After Revision		
		Precision	Recall	F-score	Precision	Recall	F-score
Preposition	Detection	6.10	7.63	6.78	7.12	8.61	7.79
	Recognition	5.42	6.78	6.03	6.44	7.79	7.05
	Correction	3.05	3.81	3.39	3.73	4.51	4.08
Determiner	Detection	7.73	6.45	7.04	9.39	7.42	8.29
	Recognition	7.73	6.45	7.04	9.39	7.42	8.29
	Correction	1.66	1.38	1.51	2.21	1.75	1.95
Combined	Detection	6.93	7.28	**7.10**	8.19	8.25	**8.22**
	Recognition	6.30	6.62	**6.46**	7.56	7.61	**7.59**
	Correction	2.52	2.65	**2.58**	3.15	3.17	**3.16**

Table 3. Results for Preposition, Determiner and Combined (preposition and determiner) errors.

[4] See www.correcttext.org/hoo2012.

Acknowledgments

We acknowledge the support of the IFCPAR funded Indo-French project "An Advanced Platform for Question Answering Systems" and the DIT, Government of India funded project "Development of English to Indian Language Machine Translation (EILMT) System Phase II".

References

Adriane Boyd and Detmar Meurers. Data-Driven Correction of FunctionWords in Non-Native English. In 2011 Generation Challenges, HOO: Helping Our Own in the Proceedings of *the 13th European Workshop on Natural Language Generation* (ENLG), 28th – 30th September, 2011, Nancy, France.

Anas Elghafari, Detmar Meurers and Holger Wunsch, 2010. Exploring the Data-Driven Prediction of Prepositions in English. In the Proceedings of *the 23rd International Conference on Computational Linguistics*, Beijing, China, 2010.

George Heidorn. 2000. Intelligent writing assistance. In R Dale, H Moisl, and H Somers, editors, *Handbook of Natural Language Processing*, pages 181–207. Marcel Dekker Inc.

GE Heidorn. 1975. Augmented phrase structure grammars. In: BL Webber, RC Schank, eds. *Theoretical Issues in Natural Language Processing*. Assoc. for Computational Linguistics, pp.1-5.

J R Tetreault and M S Chodorow. 2008. The ups and downs of preposition error detection in ESL writing. In Proceedings of *the 22nd International Conference on Computational Linguistics*, pp-865-872, Manchester,2008.

Pinaki Bhaskar, Aniruddha Ghosh, Santanu Pal and Sivaji Bandyopadhyay. May I correct the English of your paper!!!. In 2011 Generation Challenges, HOO: Helping Our Own in the Proceedings of *the 13th European Workshop on Natural Language Generation* (ENLG), pp 250-253, 28th – 30th September, 2011, Nancy, France.

Robert Dale and A Kilgarriff. 2010. Helping Our Own: Text massaging for computational linguistics as a new shared task. In Proceedings of *the 6th International Natural Language Generation Conference*, Dublin, Ireland, pages 261–266, 7th-9th July 2010.

Robert Dale and A Kilgarriff. 2011. Helping our own: The HOO 2011 pilot shared task. In Proceedings of *the 13th European Workshop on Natural Language Generation* (ENLG), 28th – 30th September, 2011, Nancy, France.

Robert Dale and George Narroway. 2012. A framework for evaluating text correction. In Proceedings of *the Eighth International Conference on Language Resources and Evaluation* (LREC2012), 21–27 May 2012.

Robert Dale, Ilya Anisimoff and George Narroway (2012) HOO 2012: A Report on the Preposition and Determiner Error Correction Shared Task. In Proceedings of *the Seventh Workshop on Innovative Use of NLP for Building Educational Applications*, Montreal, Canada, 7th June 2012.

Informing Determiner and Preposition Error Correction with Word Clusters

Adriane Boyd **Marion Zepf** **Detmar Meurers**
Seminar für Sprachwissenschaft
Universität Tübingen
{adriane,mzepf,dm}@sfs.uni-tuebingen.de

Abstract

We extend our n-gram-based data-driven prediction approach from the Helping Our Own (HOO) 2011 Shared Task (Boyd and Meurers, 2011) to identify determiner and preposition errors in non-native English essays from the Cambridge Learner Corpus FCE Dataset (Yannakoudakis et al., 2011) as part of the HOO 2012 Shared Task. Our system focuses on three error categories: missing determiner, incorrect determiner, and incorrect preposition. Approximately two-thirds of the errors annotated in HOO 2012 training and test data fall into these three categories. To improve our approach, we developed a missing determiner detector and incorporated word clustering (Brown et al., 1992) into the n-gram prediction approach.

1 Introduction

We extend our n-gram-based prediction approach (Boyd and Meurers, 2011) from the HOO 2011 Shared Task (Dale and Kilgarriff, 2011) for the HOO 2012 Shared Task. This approach is an extension of the preposition prediction approach presented in Elghafari, Meurers and Wunsch (2010), which uses a surface-based approach to predict prepositions in English using frequency information from web searches to choose the most likely preposition in a given context. For each preposition in the text, the prediction algorithm considers up to three words of context on each side of the preposition, building a 7-gram with a preposition slot in the middle:

```
rather a question __ the scales falling
```

For each prediction task, a *cohort* of queries is constructed with each of the candidate prepositions in the slot to be predicted:

1. `rather a question` **`of`** `the scales falling`
2. `rather a question` **`to`** `the scales falling`
3. `rather a question` **`in`** `the scales falling`

...

9. `rather a question` **`on`** `the scales falling`

In Elghafari, Meurers and Wunsch (2010), the queries are submitted to the Yahoo search engine and in Boyd and Meurers (2011), the search engine is replaced with the ACL Anthology Reference Corpus (ARC, Bird et al., 2008), which contains texts of the same genre as the HOO 2011 data. If no hits are found for any of the 7-gram queries, shorter overlapping n-grams are used to approximate the 7-gram query. For instance, a 7-gram may be approximated by two overlapping 6-grams:

```
[rather a question of the scales falling]
                  ⇓
[rather a question of the scales]
      [a question of the scales falling]
```

If there are still no hits, the overlap backoff will continue reducing the n-gram length until it reaches 3-grams with one word of context on each side of the candidate correction. If no hits are found at the 3-gram level, the Boyd and Meurers (2011) approach predicts the original token, effectively making no modifications to the original text. The approach from Elghafari, Meurers and Wunsch (2010), addressing a prediction task rather than a correction task (i.e., the original token is masked), predicted the most frequent preposition *of* if no hits were found.

Elghafari, Meurers and Wunsch (2010) showed this surface-based approach to be competitive with published state-of-the-art machine learning approaches using complex feature sets (Gamon et al., 2008; De Felice, 2008; Tetreault and Chodorow, 2008; Bergsma et al., 2009). For a set of nine frequent prepositions (*of, to, in, for, on, with, at, by, from*), they accurately predicted 76.5% on native data from section J of the British National Corpus. For these nine prepositions, De Felice (2008) identified a baseline of 27% for the task of choosing a preposition in a slot (choose *of*) and her system achieved 70.1% accuracy. Humans performing the same task agree 89% of the time (De Felice, 2008).

For the academic texts in the HOO 2011 Shared Task, Boyd and Meurers (2011) detected 67% of determiner and preposition substitution errors (equivalent to detection recall in the current task) and provided the appropriate correction for approximately half of the detected cases. We achieved a detection F-score of approximately 80% and a correction F-score of 44% for the four function word prediction tasks we considered (determiners, prepositions, conjunctions, and quantifiers).

2 Our Approach

For the 2012 shared task corpus, we do not have the advantage of access to a genre-specific reference corpus such as the ARC used for the first challenge, so we instead use the Google Web 1T 5-gram Corpus (Web1T5, Brants and Franz, 2006), which contains 1-gram to 5-gram counts for a web corpus with approximately 1 trillion tokens and 95 billion sentences. Compared to our earlier approach, using the Web1T5 corpus reduces the size of available context by going from 7-grams to 5-grams, but we are intentionally keeping the corpus resources and algorithm simple. We are particularly interested in exploring the space between surface forms and abstractions by incorporating information from word clustering, an issue which is independent from the choice of a more sophisticated learning algorithm.

Rozovskaya and Roth (2011) compared a range of learning algorithms for the task of correcting errors made by non-native writers, including an averaged perceptron algorithm (Rizzolo and Roth, 2007) and an n-gram count-based approach (Bergsma et al., 2009), which is similar to our approach. They found that the count-based approach performs nearly as well as the averaged perceptron approach when trained with ten times as much data. Without access to a large multi-genre corpus even a tenth the size of the Web1T5 corpus, we chose to use Web1T5. Our longest queries thus are 5-grams with at least one word of context on each side of the candidate function word and the shortest are 3-grams with one word of context on each side. A large multi-genre corpus would improve the results by supporting access to longer n-grams, and it would also make deeper linguistic analysis such as part-of-speech tagging feasible.

Table 1 shows the sets of determiners and prepositions for each of the three categories addressed by our system: missing determiner (MD), incorrect determiner (RD), and incorrect preposition (RT). The function word lists are compiled from all single-word corrections of these types in the training data. The counts show the frequency of the error types in the test data, along with the total frequency of function word candidates.

The following sections describe the main extensions to our system for the 2012 shared task: a simple correction probability model, a missing determiner detector, and the addition of hierarchical word clustering to the prediction approach.

2.1 Correction Probability Model

To adapt the system for the CLC FCE learner data, we added a simple correction probability model to the n-gram predictor that multiplies the counts for each n-gram by the probability of a particular replacement in the training data. The model includes both correct and incorrect occurrences of each candidate, ignoring any corrections that make up less than 0.5% of the corrections for a particular token. For instance, the word *among* has the following correction probabilities: *among* 0.7895, *from* 0.1053, *between* 0.0526. Even such a simplistic probability model has a noticeable effect on the system performance, improving the overall correction F-score by approximately 3%. The preposition substitution error detection F-score alone improves by 9%.

Prior to creating the probability model, we experimented with the addition of a bias toward the original token, which we hoped would reduce the number

Category	# Errors		Candidate Corrections	# Occurrences
	Original	Revised		
MD	125	131	a, an, another, any, her, his, its, my, our, that, the, their, these, this, those, which, your	-
RD	39	37	a, an, another, any, her, his, its, my, our, that, the, their, these, this, those, which, your	1924
RT	136	148	about, after, against, along, among, around, as, at, before, behind, below, between, by, concerning, considering, during, for, from, in, into, like, near, of, off, on, onto, out, outside, over, regarding, since, through, throughout, till, to, toward, towards, under, until, via, with, within, without	2202

Table 1: Single-Word Prepositions and Determiners with Error and Overall Frequency in Test Data

of overcorrections generated by our system. Without the probability model, a bias toward the original token improves the results, however, with the probability model, the bias is no longer useful.

2.2 Word Clustering

In the 2011 shared task, we observed that data sparsity issues are magnified in non-native texts because the n-gram context may contain additional errors or other infrequent or unusual n-gram sequences. We found that abstracting to part-of-speech tags and lemmas in certain contexts leads to small improvements in system performance. For the 2012 shared task, we explore the effects of abstracting to word clusters derived from co-occurrence information (Brown et al., 1992), another type of abstraction relevant to our n-gram prediction approach. We hypothesize that replacing tokens in the n-gram context in our prediction tasks with clusters will reduce the data sparsity for non-native text.

Clusters derived from co-occurrence frequencies offer an attractive type of abstraction that occupy a middle ground between relatively coarse-grained morphosyntactic abstractions such as part-of-speech tags and fine-grained abstractions such as lemmas. For determiner and preposition prediction, part-of-speech tags clearly retain too few distinctions. For example, the choice of *a/an* before a noun phrase depends on the onset of the first word in the phrase, information which is not preserved by part-of-speech tagging. Likewise, preposition selection may be dependent on lexical specifications (e.g., phrasal verbs such as *depend on*) or on semantic or world knowledge (cf. Wechsler, 1994).

Brown et al. (1992) present a hierarchical word clustering algorithm that can handle a large number of classes and a large vocabulary. The algorithm clusters a vocabulary into C clusters given a corpus to estimate the parameters of an n-gram language model. Summarized briefly, the algorithm first creates C clusters for the C most frequent words in the corpus. Then, a cluster is added containing the next most frequent word. After the new cluster is added, the pair of clusters is merged for which the loss in average mutual information is smallest, returning the number of clusters to C. The remaining words in the vocabulary are added one by one and pairs of clusters are merged in the same fashion until all words have been divided into C clusters.

Using the implementation from Liang (2005),[1] we generate word clusters for the most frequent 100,000 tokens in the ukWaC corpus (Baroni et al., 2009). We convert all tokens to lower case, replace all lower frequency words with a single unique token, and omit from the clustering the candidate corrections from Table 1 along with the low frequency tokens. Our corpus is the first 18 million sentences from ukWaC.[2] After converting all tokens to lowercase and omitting the candidate function words, a total of 75,333 tokens are clustered.

We create three sets of clusters with sizes 500, 1000, and 2000. Due to time constraints, we did not yet explore larger sizes. Brown et al. (1992) report that the words in a cluster appear to share syntactic or semantic features. The clusters we obtained appear to be overwhelmingly semantic in nature.

[1] Available at http://cs.stanford.edu/~pliang/software

[2] Those sentences in the file ukwac_dep_parsed_01.

	Cluster ID	Selected Cluster Members
(1)	00100	was..., woz, wasn't, was, wasnt
(2)	0111110111101	definetly, definatly, assuredly, definately, undoubtedly, certainly, definitely
(3)	1001110100	extremely, very, incredibly, inordinately, exceedingly, awfully
(4)	1110010001	john, richard, peter, michael, andrew, david, stephen
(5)	11101001001	12.30pm, 7am, 2.00pm, 4.00pm, weekday, tuesdays

Table 2: Sample Clusters from ukWaC with 2000 Clusters

Table 2 shows examples from the set of 2000 clusters. Examples (1) and (2) show how tokens with errors in tokenization or misspellings are clustered with tokens with standard spelling and standard tokenization. Such clusters may be useful for the shared task by allowing the system to abstract away from spelling errors in the learner essays. Examples (3)–(5) show semantically similar clusters.

An excerpt of the hierarchical cluster tree for the cluster ID from example (3) is shown in Figure 1. The tree shows a subset of the clusters for cluster IDs beginning with the sequence 1001110. Each binary branch appends a 0 or 1 to the cluster ID as shown in the edge labels. The cluster 1001110100 (*extremely, very*) is found in the left-most leaf of the right branch. A few of the most frequent cluster members are shown for each leaf of the tree.

In our submissions to the shared task, we included five different cluster settings: 1) using the original word-based approach with no clusters, 2) using only 2000 clusters, 3) using the word-based approach initially and backing off to 2000 clusters if no hits are found, 4) backing off to 1000 clusters, and 5) backing off to 500 clusters. The detailed results will be presented in section 3.

2.3 Missing Determiner Detector

We newly developed a missing determiner detector to identify those places in the learner text where a determiner is missing. Since determiners mostly occur in noun phrases, we extract all noun phrases from the text and put them through a two-stage classifier. For a single-stage classifier, always predicting 'no error' leads to a very high baseline accuracy of 98%. Therefore, we first filter out those noun phrases which already contain a determiner, a possessive pronoun, another possessive token (e.g., *'s*), or an existential *there*, or whose head is a pronoun. This prefiltering reduces the baseline accuracy to 93.6%, but also filters out 10% of learner errors (*false negatives*), which thus cannot be detected in stage two.

In the second stage, a decision tree classifier decides for every remaining noun phrase whether a determiner is missing. From the 203 features we originally extracted to inform the classification, the chi squared algorithm selected 30. Almost all of the selected features capture properties of either the head of the noun phrase, its first word, or the token immediately preceding the noun phrase. We follow Minnen et al. (2000) in defining the head of a noun phrase as the rightmost noun, or if there is no noun, the rightmost token. As suggested by Han et al. (2004), the classifier considers the parts of speech of these three words, while the features that record the respective literal word were discarded.

We also experimented with using the entire noun phrase and its part-of-speech tag sequence as features (Han et al., 2004), which proved not to be helpful due to the limited size of the training data. We replaced the part-of-speech tag sequence with a number of boolean features that each indicate equivalence with a particular sequence. Of these features only the one that checks whether the whole noun phrase consists of a single common noun in the singular was included in the final feature set. Additionally, the selected features include countability information from noun countability lists generated by Baldwin and Bond (2003), which assign nouns to one or more countability classes: *countable*, *uncountable/mass noun*, *bipartite*, or *plural only*.

The majority of the 30 selected features refer to the position of one of the three tokens (head, first word, and preceding token) in the cluster hierarchy described in section 2.2. The set of 500 clusters proved not to be fine-grained enough, so we used

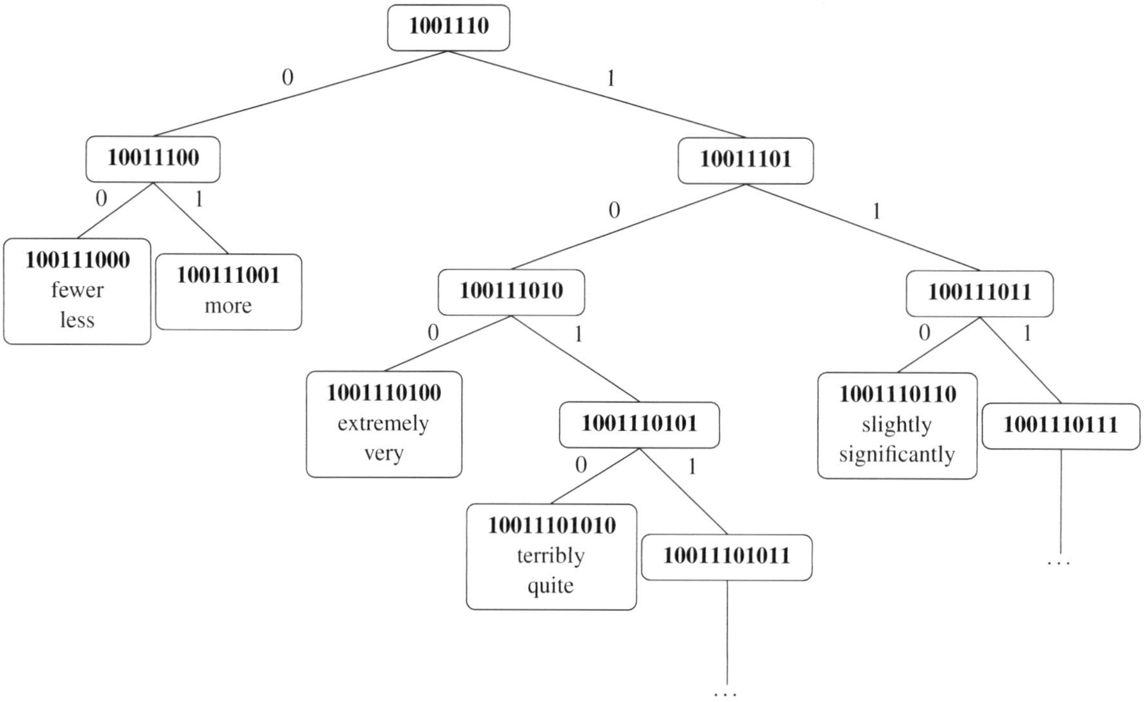

Figure 1: Hierarchical Clustering Subtree for Cluster Prefix 1001110

the set of 1000 clusters. To take full advantage of the hierarchical nature of the cluster IDs, we extract prefixes of all possible lengths (1–18 characters) from the cluster ID of the respective token. For the head and the first word, prefixes of length 3–14 were selected by the attribute selector, in addition to a prefix of length 6 for the preceding token's cluster ID.

Among the discarded features are many extracted from the context surrounding the noun phrase, including the parts of speech and cluster membership of three words to the left and right of the noun phrase, excluding the immediately preceding token. Features referring to possible sister conjuncts of the noun phrase, the next 3rd person pronoun in a following sentence, or previous occurrences of the head in the text also turned out not to be useful. The performance of the classifier was only marginally affected by the reduction in the number of features. We conclude from this that missing determiner detection is sufficiently informed by local features.

In order to increase the robustness of the classifier, we generated additional data from the written portion of the BNC by removing a determiner in 20% of all sentences. The resulting rate of errors is roughly equal to the rate of errors in the learner texts and the addition of the BNC data increases the amount of training data by a factor of 13. We trained a classifier on both datasets (referred to as *HOO-BNC* below). It achieves an F-score of 46.7% when evaluated on 30% of the shared task training data, which was held out from the classifier training data. On the revised test data, it reaches an F-score of 44.5%.

3 Results

The following two sections discuss our overall results for the shared task and our performance on the three error types targeted by our system.

3.1 Overall

Figure 2 shows the overall recognition and correction F-score for the cluster settings described in section 2.2. With the missing determiner detector *HOO-BNC* described in section 2.3, these correspond to runs #5–9 submitted to the shared task. For the unrevised data, Run #6 (2000 clusters only) gives our best result for overall detection F-score (30.26%) and Run #7 (2000 cluster backoff) for correction F-score (18.44%). For the revised data, Run

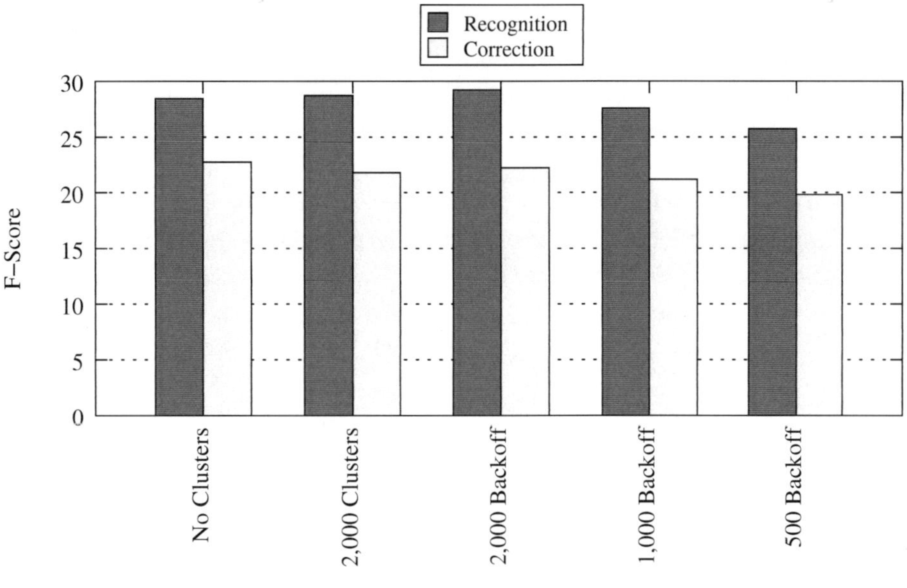

Figure 2: Recognition and Correction F-Score with Clustering

#7 (2000 cluster backoff) has our best overall detection F-score (32.21%) and Run #5 (no clusters) has our best overall correction F-score (22.46%).

Runs using clusters give the best results in two other metrics reported in the shared task results for the revised data. Run #6 (2000 clusters only) gives the best results for determiner correction F-score and Run #2 (2000 cluster backoff), which differs only from Run #7 in the choice of missing determiner detector, gives the best results for preposition detection and recognition F-scores.

The detailed results for Runs #5–9 with the revised data are shown in Figure 2. This graph shows that the differences between the systems with and without clusters are very small. The recognition F-score is best with 2000 cluster backoff and the correction F-score is best with no clusters. In both cases, the difference between the top two results is less than 0.01. There is, however, a noticeable increase in performance as the number of clusters increases, which indicates that a larger number of clusters may improve results further. The set of 2000 clusters may still retain too few distinctions for this task.

3.2 Targeted Error Types

Our system handles three of the six error types in the shared task: missing determiner (MD), incorrect determiner (RD), and incorrect preposition (RT). The recognition and correction F-scores for our best-forming run for each type are shown in Figure 3.

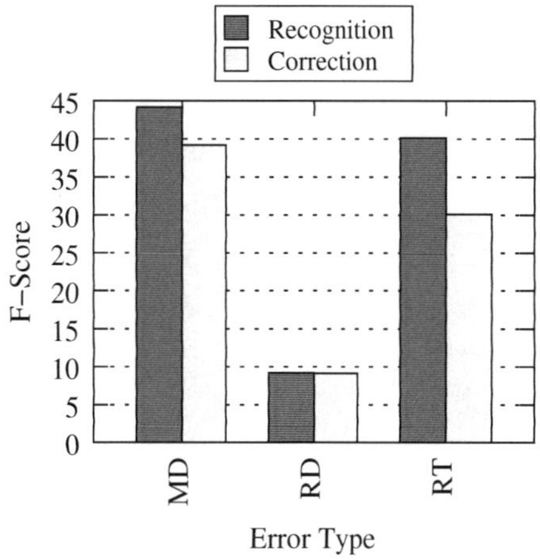

Figure 3: Recognition and Correction F-Score for the Targeted Error Types

In a comparison of performance on individual error types in the shared task, our system does best on the task for which it was originally developed, preposition prediction. We place 4th in recognition and 3rd in correction F-score for this error type. For missing determiner (MD) and incorrect determiner (RD) errors, our system is ranked similarly as in our overall performance (4th–6th).

For the sake of replicability, as the HOO 2012 test data is not publicly available, we include our results on the HOO training data for the preposition and determiner substitution errors in Table 3.

Error Type	No Clusters			
	Recognition		Correction	
	Prec	Rec	Prec	Rec
RT	32.69	29.94	24.85	22.77
RD	10.63	18.56	8.37	14.61

Error Type	2000 Backoff			
	Recognition		Correction	
	Prec	Rec	Prec	Rec
RT	25.87	35.60	18.26	25.13
RD	9.71	23.65	7.48	18.23

Table 3: Results for HOO 2012 Training Data

Results are reported for the no cluster and 2000 cluster backoff settings, which show that incorporating the cluster backoff improves recall at the expense of precision. Missing determiner errors are not reported directly as the missing determiner detector was trained on the training data, but see the evaluation at the end of section 2.3.

4 Discussion and Conclusion

The n-gram prediction approach with the new missing determiner detector performed well in the HOO 2012 Shared Task, placing 6th in terms of detection and 5th in terms of correction out of fourteen teams participating in the shared task. In our best submissions evaluated using the revised test data, we achieved a detection F-score of 32.71%, a recognition F-score of 29.21% and a correction F-score of 22.73%. For the three error types addressed by our approach, our correction F-scores are 39.17% for missing determiners, 9.23% for incorrect determiners, and 30.12% for incorrect prepositions. Information from hierarchical word clustering (Brown et al., 1992) extended the types of abstractions available to our n-gram prediction approach and improved the performance of the missing determiner detector.

For the n-gram prediction approach, word clusters IDs from the hierarchical word clustering replace tokens in the surrounding context in order to improve recall for learner texts which may contain errors or infrequent token sequences. The use of cluster-based contexts with 2000 clusters as a backoff from the word-based approach leads to a very small improvement in the overall recognition F-score for the HOO 2012 Shared Task, but our best overall correction F-score was obtained using our original word-based approach. The differences between the word-based and cluster-based approaches are quite small, so we did not see as much improvement from the word cluster abstractions as we had hoped. We experimented with sets of clusters of several sizes (500, 1000, 2000) and found that as the number of clusters becomes smaller, the performance decreases, suggesting that a larger number of clusters may lead to more improvement for this task.

Information from the word cluster hierarchy was also integrated into our new missing determiner detector, which uses a decision tree classifier to decide whether a determiner should be inserted in front of a determiner-less NP. Lexical information from the extracted noun phrases and surrounding context are not as useful for the classifier as information about the position of the tokens in the word cluster hierarchy. In particular, cluster information appears to help compensate for lexical sparsity given a relatively small amount of training data.

In future work, we plan to explore additional clustering approaches and to determine when the use of word cluster abstractions is helpful for the task of predicting determiners, prepositions, and other function words. An approach that refers to word clusters in certain contexts or in a customized fashion for each candidate correction may lead to improved performance for the task of detecting and correcting such errors in texts by non-native writers.

References

Timothy Baldwin and Francis Bond, 2003. Learning the countability of English nouns from corpus data. In *Proceedings of the 41st Annual Meeting on Association for Computational Linguistics (ACL)*. pp. 463–470.

M. Baroni, S. Bernardini, A. Ferraresi and E. Zanchetta, 2009. The WaCky Wide Web: A Collection of Very Large Linguistically Processed Web-Crawled Corpora. *Language Resources and Evaluation*, 43(3):209–226.

Shane Bergsma, Dekang Lin and Randy Goebel, 2009. Web-scale N-gram models for lexical disambiguation. In *Proceedings of the 21st international jont conference on Artifical intelligence (IJ-CAI'09)*. Morgan Kaufmann Publishers Inc., San Francisco, CA, USA.

Steven Bird, Robert Dale et al., 2008. The ACL Anthology Reference Corpus. In *Proceedings of the 6th International Conference on Language Resources and Evaluation (LREC)*. Marrakesh, Morocco.

Adriane Boyd and Detmar Meurers, 2011. Data-Driven Correction of Function Words in Non-Native English. In *Proceedings of the 13th European Workshop on Natural Language Generation – Helping Our Own (HOO) Challenge*. Association for Computational Linguistics, Nancy, France.

Thorsten Brants and Alex Franz, 2006. Web 1T 5-gram Version 1. Linguistic Data Consortium. Philadelphia.

Peter F. Brown, Peter V. deSouza, Robert L. Mercer, T. J. Watson, Vincent J. Della Pietra and Jenifer C. Lai, 1992. Class-Based n-gram Models of Natural Language. *Computational Linguistics*, 18(4):467–479.

Robert Dale and Adam Kilgarriff, 2011. Helping Our Own: The HOO 2011 Pilot Shared Task. In *Proceedings of the 13th European Workshop on Natural Language Generation*. Nancy, France.

Rachele De Felice, 2008. Automatic Error Detection in Non-native English. Ph.D. thesis, Oxford.

Anas Elghafari, Detmar Meurers and Holger Wunsch, 2010. Exploring the Data-Driven Prediction of Prepositions in English. In *Proceedings of the 23rd International Conference on Computational Linguistics (COLING)*. Beijing.

Michael Gamon, Jianfeng Gao et al., 2008. Using Contextual Speller Techniques and Language Modeling for ESL Error Correction. In *Proceedings of the Third International Joint Conference on Natural Language Processing*. Hyderabad.

Na-Rae Han, Martin Chodorow and Claudia Leacock, 2004. Detecting Errors in English Article Usage with a Maximum Entropy Classifier Trained on a Large, Diverse Corpus. In *Proceedings of the 4th International Conference on Language Resources and Evaluation (LREC)*. Lisbon.

Percy Liang, 2005. Semi-Supervised Learning for Natural Language. Master's thesis, Massachusetts Institute of Technology.

Guido Minnen, Francis Bond and Ann Copestake, 2000. Memory-based learning for article generation. In *Proceedings of the 2nd Workshop on Learning Language in Logic and the 4th Conference on Computational Natural Language Learning*. volume 7, pp. 43–48.

Nick Rizzolo and Dan Roth, 2007. Modeling Discriminative Global Inference. In *Proceedings of the First International Conference on Semantic Computing (ICSC)*. IEEE, Irvine, California, pp. 597–604.

Alla Rozovskaya and Dan Roth, 2011. Algorithm Selection and Model Adaptation for ESL Correction Tasks. In *Proceedings of the 49th Annual Meeting of the Association for Computational Linguistics: Human Language Technologies (ACL-HLT)*. Portland, Oregon.

Joel Tetreault and Martin Chodorow, 2008. Native Judgments of Non-Native Usage: Experiments in Preposition Error Detection. In *Proceedings of the 22nd International Conference on Computational Linguistics (COLING)*. Manchester.

Stephen Wechsler, 1994. Preposition Selection Outside the Lexicon. In Raul Aranovich, William Byrne, Susanne Preuss and Martha Senturia (eds.), *Proceedings of the Thirteenth West Coast Conference on Formal Linguistics*. CSLI Publications, Stanford, California, pp. 416–431.

H. Yannakoudakis, T. Briscoe and B. Medlock, 2011. A new dataset and method for automatically grading ESOL texts. In *Proceedings of the 49th Annual Meeting of the Association for Computational Linguistics: Human Language Technologies (ACL-HLT)*.

NUS at the HOO 2012 Shared Task

Daniel Dahlmeier[1], **Hwee Tou Ng**[1,2], and **Eric Jun Feng Ng**[2]
[1]NUS Graduate School for Integrative Sciences and Engineering
[2]Department of Computer Science, National University of Singapore
{danielhe,nght,eng}@comp.nus.edu.sg

Abstract

This paper describes the submission of the National University of Singapore (NUS) to the HOO 2012 shared task. Our system uses a pipeline of confidence-weighted linear classifiers to correct determiner and preposition errors. Our system achieves the highest correction F_1 score on the official test set among all 14 participating teams, based on gold-standard edits both before and after revision.

1 Introduction

Grammatical error correction is the task of automatically detecting and correcting erroneous word usage and ill-formed grammatical constructions in text. Determiner and preposition errors are the two most prominent types of errors made by non-native speakers of English. Although there has been much work on automatic correction of determiner and preposition errors over the last few years, it has so far been impossible to directly compare results because different teams have evaluated on different data sets.

The HOO 2012 shared task evaluates grammatical error correction systems for determiner and preposition errors. Participants are provided with a set of documents written by non-native speakers of English. The task is to automatically detect and correct determiner and preposition errors and produce a set of corrections (called *edits*). Evaluation is done by computing precision, recall, and F_1 score between the system edits and a manually created set of gold-standard edits. The details of the HOO 2012 shared task are described in the official overview paper (Dale et al., 2012).

In this paper, we describe the system submission from the National University of Singapore (NUS). Our system treats determiner and preposition correction as classification problems. We use confidence-weighted linear classifiers to predict the correct word from a confusion set of possible correction options. Separate classifiers are built for determiner errors, preposition replacement errors, and preposition insertion and deletion errors. The classifiers are combined into a pipeline of correction steps to form an end-to-end error correction system. Our system achieves the highest correction F_1 score on the official test set among all 14 participating teams, based on gold-standard edits both before and after revision.

The remainder of this paper is organized as follows. The next section presents our error correction system. Section 3 describes the features. Section 4 presents experimental results. Section 5 contains further discussion. Section 6 concludes the paper.

2 System Architecture

Our system consists of a pipeline of sequential steps where the output of one step serves as the input to the next step. The steps in sequence are:

1. Pre-processing
2. Determiner correction (Det)
3. Replacement preposition correction (RT)
4. Missing and unwanted preposition correction (MT, UT)

The final output after the last step forms our submission to the shared task. Each correction step (i.e., steps 2, 3, 4) involves three internal steps:

1. Feature extraction

2. Classification
3. Language model filter

Feature extraction first analyzes the syntactic structure of the input sentences (part-of-speech (POS) tagging, chunking, and parsing) and identifies relevant instances for correction (e.g., all noun phrases (NP) for determiner correction). Each instance is mapped to a real-valued feature vector. Next, a classifier predicts the most likely correction for each feature vector. Finally, the proposed corrections are filtered using a language model and only corrections that strictly increase the language model score are kept.

2.1 Confidence-Weighted Learning

As the learning algorithm for all classifiers, we choose confidence-weighted (CW) learning (Dredze et al., 2008; Crammer et al., 2009), which has been shown to perform well for natural language processing (NLP) problems with high dimensional and sparse feature spaces. Instead of keeping a single weight vector, CW learning maintains a distribution over weight vectors, parametrized by a multivariate normal distribution $\mathcal{N}(\boldsymbol{\mu}, \Sigma)$ with mean $\boldsymbol{\mu}$ and covariance matrix Σ. In practice, Σ is often approximated by a diagonal matrix (Dredze et al., 2008). CW is an online learning algorithm that proceeds in rounds over a labeled training set $((y_1, \mathbf{x}_1), (y_2, \mathbf{x}_2), \ldots, (y_n, \mathbf{x}_n))$, one example at a time. After the i-th round, CW learning updates the distribution over weight vectors such that the i-th example is predicted correctly with probability at least $0 < \eta < 1$ while choosing the update step that minimizes the Kullback-Leibler (KL) distance from the current distribution. The CW update rule is:

$$\begin{aligned}(\boldsymbol{\mu}_{i+1}, \Sigma_{i+1}) &= \\ \arg\min_{\boldsymbol{\mu},\Sigma} \mathrm{D_{KL}} & \left(\mathcal{N}(\boldsymbol{\mu}, \Sigma) || \mathcal{N}(\boldsymbol{\mu}_i, \Sigma_i)\right) \\ \text{s.t.} & \quad Pr[y_i|\mathbf{x}_i, \boldsymbol{\mu}, \Sigma] \geq \eta.\end{aligned} \tag{1}$$

Dredze *et al.* (2008) show that in the binary case, the CW update rule has a closed-form solution. In the multi-class case, there exists no closed-form solution but the solution can be efficiently approximated.

2.2 Pre-processing

Pre-processing involves sentence splitting, tokenization, re-casing, and spelling correction. We noticed that the HOO 2012 training data contained a large number of spelling mistakes and that some documents are written in all upper case. Both have a negative effect on tagging and classification accuracy. We automatically identify and re-case upper-case documents using a standard re-casing model from statistical machine translation (SMT). Re-casing is modeled as monotone decoding (without reordering) involving translation of an un-cased sentence to a mixed-case sentence. Next, we automatically correct spelling mistakes using an open-source spell checker. Words are excluded from spelling correction if they are shorter than a threshold (set to 4 characters in our work), or if they include hyphens or upper case characters inside the word. We apply a language model filter (described in the next subsection) to filter the proposed spelling corrections. Note that spelling correction is only performed to improve the accuracy of subsequent correction steps. Spelling corrections themselves are *not* part of the edits submitted for evaluation.

2.3 Determiner Correction

Determiner errors include three error types: replacement determiner (RD), missing determiner (MD), and unwanted determiner (UD). Although determiners are not limited to articles (*a, an, the, empty article* ϵ), article errors account for the majority of determiner errors. We therefore focus our efforts on errors involving only articles.

2.3.1 Correction as Classification

We treat determiner error correction as a multi-class classification problem. A classifier is trained to predict the correct article from a *confusion set* of possible article choices $\{a, the, \epsilon\}$, given the sentence context. The article *an* is normalized as *a* and restored later using a rule-based heuristic. During training, every NP in the training data generates one training example. The class $y \in \{a, the, \epsilon\}$ is the correct article as annotated by the gold standard or the observed article used by the writer if the article is not annotated (i.e., the article is correct). The surrounding context is represented as a real-valued feature vector $\mathbf{x} \in \mathcal{X}$. The features of our classifiers are described in Section 3.

One challenge in training classifiers for grammatical error correction is that the data is highly skewed.

Training examples without any error (i.e., the observed article equals the correct article) greatly outnumber those examples with an error (i.e., the observed article is different from the correct article). As the observed article is highly correlated with the correct article, the observed article is a valuable feature (Rozovskaya and Roth, 2010; Dahlmeier and Ng, 2011). However, the high correlation can have the undesirable effect that the classifier *always* predicts the observed article and never proposes any corrections. To mitigate this problem, we re-sample the training data, either by oversampling examples with an error or undersampling examples without an error. The sampling parameter is chosen through a grid search so as to maximize the F_1 score on the development data. After training, the classifier can be used to predict the correct article for NPs from new unseen sentences.

During testing, every NP in the test data generates one test example. If the article predicted by the classifier differs from the observed article and the difference between the classifier's confidence score for its first choice and the classifier's confidence score for the observed article is higher than some threshold parameter t, the observed article is replaced by the proposed correction. The threshold parameter t is tuned through a grid search so as to maximize the F_1 score on the development data. We found that using a separate threshold parameter value for each class worked better than using a single threshold value.

2.3.2 Language Model Filter

All corrections are filtered using a large language model. Only corrections that strictly increase the normalized language model score of a sentence are kept. The normalized language model score is defined as

$$score_{lm} = \frac{1}{|\mathbf{s}|} \log Pr(\mathbf{s}), \qquad (2)$$

where $\mathbf{s}$ is the corrected sentence and $|\mathbf{s}|$ is the sentence length in tokens. The final set of article corrections is applied to an input sentence (i.e., replacing the observed article with the predicted article).

2.4 Replacement Preposition Correction

Replacement preposition correction follows the same strategy as determiner correction, but with a different confusion set and different features. The confusion set consists of 36 frequent prepositions which we adopt from our previous work (Dahlmeier and Ng, 2011).[1] These prepositions account for the majority of preposition replacement errors in the HOO 2012 training data. During training, every prepositional phrase (PP) in the training data which is headed by a preposition from the confusion set generates one training example. The class y is the correct preposition. During testing, every PP in the test data which is headed by a preposition from the confusion set generates one test example.

2.5 Missing Preposition Correction

Our system corrects missing and unwanted preposition errors for the seven most frequently missed or wrongly inserted prepositions in the HOO 2012 training data. These preposition are *about, at, for, in, of, on*, and *to*. While developing our system, we found that adding more prepositions did not increase performance in our experiments.

We treat missing preposition (MT) correction as a binary classification problem.[2] For each preposition p, we train a binary classifier that predicts the presence or absence of that preposition. Thus, the confusion set consists only of the preposition p and the "empty preposition". During training, we require examples of contexts where p should be used and where it should be omitted. As prepositions typically appear before NPs, we take every NP in the training data as one training example. If the preposition p appears right in front of the NP (i.e., the preposition p and the NP form a PP), the example is a positive example, otherwise (i.e., another preposition or no preposition appears before the NP) it is a negative example. During testing, every NP which does not directly follow a preposition generates one test example. If the classifier predicts that the preposition p should have been used in this context with sufficiently high confidence and inserting p increases the normalized language model score, p is inserted before the NP.

[1] *about, along, among, around, as, at, beside, besides, between, by, down, during, except, for, from, in, inside, into, of, off, on, onto, outside, over, through, to, toward, towards, under, underneath, until, up, upon, with, within, without*

[2] Alternatively, missing preposition error correction could be treated as a multi-class problem, but we found that binary classifiers gave better performance in initial experiments.

2.6 Unwanted Preposition Correction

Unwanted preposition correction is treated as a binary classification problem similar to missing preposition correction but with different training and test examples. When training the classifier for preposition p, every PP where the writer used the preposition p is one training example. If the gold-standard annotation labels p as unwanted, the example is a positive example for deleting p, otherwise it is a negative example. During testing, every PP with the preposition p generates one test example. If the classifier predicts that p should be deleted with sufficiently high confidence and deleting p increases the normalized language model score, p is deleted.

We found that separate classifiers for missing and unwanted preposition correction gave slightly better results compared to using a single classifier for both tasks. As the test examples for missing and unwanted preposition correction of a preposition p are disjoint, both steps can be performed in parallel. This also prevents the case of the system "contradicting" itself by first inserting a preposition and later deleting it. We perform missing preposition correction and unwanted preposition correction for each preposition in turn, before moving to the next preposition.

3 Features

In this section, we describe the features used in our system. The choice of features can have an important effect on classification performance. The exact features used for determiner, replacement preposition, and missing and unwanted preposition correction are listed in Tables 1, 2, 3, and 4, respectively. The features were chosen empirically through experiments on the development data.

The most commonly used features for grammatical error correction are lexical and POS N-grams, and chunk features. We adopt the features from previous work by Han *et al.* (2006), Tetreault and Chodorow (2008), and Rozovskaya *et al.* (2011) for our system. Tetreault *et al.* (2010) show that parse features can further increase performance, and we use the dependency parse features based on their work. For all the above features, the observed article or preposition used by the writer is "blanked out" when computing the features. However, we add the observed article or preposition as an additional feature for determiner and replacement preposition correction.

The features described so far are all binary-valued, i.e., they indicate whether some feature is present in the input or not. Additionally, we can construct real-valued features by counting the log frequency of surface N-grams on the web or in a web-scale corpus (Bergsma et al., 2009). Web-scale N-gram count features can harness the power of the web in connection with supervised classification and have successfully been used for a number of NLP generation and disambiguation problems (Bergsma et al., 2009; Bergsma et al., 2010), although we are not aware of any previous application in grammatical error correction. Web-scale N-gram count features usually use N-grams of consecutive tokens. The release of web-scale parsed corpora like the WaCky project (Baroni et al., 2009) makes it possible to extend the idea to dependency N-grams of child-parent tuples over the dependency arcs in the dependency parse tree, e.g., {(child, node), (node, parent)} for bigrams, {(child's child, child, node), (child, node, parent), (node, parent, parent's parent)} for trigrams. We collect log frequency counts for dependency N-grams from a large dependency-parsed web corpus and use the log frequency count as a feature. We normalize all real-valued feature values to a unit interval $[0, 1]$ to avoid features with larger values dominating features with smaller values.

4 Experiments

In this section, we report experimental results of our system on two different data sets: a held-out test split of the HOO 2012 training data, and the official HOO 2012 test set.

4.1 Data Sets

The HOO 2012 training data consists of 1,000 documents together with gold-standard annotation. The documents are a subset of the 1,244 documents in the Cambridge Learner Corpus FCE (First Certificate in English) data set (Yannakoudakis et al., 2011). The HOO 2012 gold-standard annotation only contains edits for six determiner and preposition error types and discards all other gold edits

Feature	Example
Lexical features	
Observed article†	*the*
First word in NP†	*black*
Word i before ($i = 1, 2, 3$)†	{*on, sat, ..*}
Word i before NP ($i = 1, 2$)	{*on, sat, ..*}
Word + POS i before ($i = 1, 2, 3$)†	{*on+IN, sat+VBD, ..*}
Word i after ($i = 1, 2, 3$)†	{*black, door, ..*}
Word after NP	*period*
Word + POS i after ($N = 1, 2$)†	{*period+period, ..* }
Bag of words in NP†	{*black, door, mat*}
N-grams ($N = 2, .., 5$)‡	{*on_X, X_black, ..* }
Word before + NP†	*on+black_door_mat*
NP + N-gram after NP ($N = 1, 2, 3$)†	{ *black_door_mat+period, ..*}
Noun compound (NC)†	*door_mat*
Adj + NC†	*black+door_mat*
Adj POS + NC†	*JJ+door_mat*
NP POS + NC†	*JJ_NN_NN+door_mat*
POS features	
First POS in NP	JJ
POS i before ($i = 1, 2, 3$)	{*IN, VBD, ..*}
POS i before NP ($i = 1, 2$)	{*IN, VBD, ..*}
POS i after ($i = 1, 2, 3$)	{*JJ, NN, ..*}
POS after NP	*period*
Bag of POS in NP	{JJ, NN, NN}
POS N-grams ($N = 2, .., 4$)	{*IN_X, X_JJ, ..* }
Head word features	
Head of NP†	*mat*
Head POS	NN
Head word + POS†	*mat+NN*
Head number	*singular*
Head countable	*yes*
NP POS + head†	*JJ_NN_NN+mat*
Word before + head†	*on+mat*
Head + N-gram after NP † ($N = 1, 2, 3$)	*mat+period, ..*
Adjective + head†	*black+mat*
Adjective POS + head†	*JJ+mat*
Word before + adj + head†	*on+black+mat*
Word before + adj POS + head†	*on+JJ+mat*
Word before + NP POS + head†	*on+JJ_NN_NN+mat*
Web N-gram count features	
Web N-gram log counts $N = 3, .., 5$	{log freq(*on a black*), log freq(*on the black*), log freq(*on black*),..}
Dependency features	
Dep NP head-child†	{*mat-black-amod, ..*}
Dep NP head-parent†	*mat-on-pobj*
Dep child-NP head-parent†	{*black-mat-on-amod-pobj, ..*}
Preposition features	
Prep before + head	*on+mat*
Prep before + NC	*on+door_mat*
Prep before + NP	*on+black_door_mat*
Prep before + adj + head	*on+black+mat*
Prep before + adj POS + head	*on+JJ+mat*
Prep before + adj + NC	*on+black+door_mat*
Prep before + adj POS + NC	*on+JJ+door_mat*
Prep before + NP POS + head	*on+JJ_NN_NN+mat*
Prep before + NP POS + NC	*on+JJ_NN_NN+door_mat*

Table 1: Features for determiner correction. Example: "The cat sat on *the black door mat*." † : lexical tokens in lower case, ‡: lexical tokens in both original and lower case

Feature	Example
Verb object features	
Verb obj†	*sat_on*
Verb obj + head†	*sat_on+mat*
Verb obj + NC†	*sat_on+door_mat*
Verb obj + NP†	*sat_on+black_door_mat*
Verb obj + adj + head†	*sat_on+black+mat*
Verb obj + adj POS + head†	*sat_on+JJ+mat*
Verb obj + adj + NC†	*sat_on+black+door_mat*
Verb obj + adj POS + NC†	*sat_on+JJ+door_mat*
Verb obj + NP POS + head†	*sat_on+JJ_NN_NN+mat*
Verb obj + NP POS + NC†	*sat_on+JJ_NN_NN+door_mat*

Table 1: (continued)

from the original FCE data set. This can lead to "wrong" gold edits that produce ungrammatical sentences, like the following sentence

> There are a lot of possibilities ($\epsilon \rightarrow$ of) to earn some money ...

where the preposition *of* is inserted before *to earn*. The FCE data set contains another edit (*to earn* $\rightarrow$ *earning*) but this edit is not included in the HOO 2012 gold annotation. This necessarily introduces noise into the training data as a classifier trained on this data will learn that inserting *of* before *to earn* is correct. We sidestep this problem by directly using the FCE data set for training, and applying all gold edits except the six determiner and preposition error types. This gives us training data that only contains those types of grammatical errors that we are interested in. Note that this only applies to the training data. For our development and development test data, we use the HOO 2012 released data where the texts contain all types of errors and do not make use of the annotations in the FCE data set. For system development, we randomly select 100 documents from the HOO 2012 training data as our development set (HOO-DEV) and another 100 disjoint documents as our held-out development test set (HOO-DEVTEST). We train classifiers on the remaining 1,044 documents of the FCE data set (FCE(1044)), tune parameters on HOO-DEV, and test on HOO-DEVTEST. For our final submission, we train classifiers on all FCE documents, except those 100 documents in HOO-DEV which are used for parameter tuning. Finally, we fix all parameters and re-train the classifiers on the *complete* FCE corpus (FCE(1244)). This allows us to make maximum use of the FCE corpus as training data. The

Features	Example
Lexical and POS features	
Observed preposition†	*on*
Word i before $(i = 1, 2, 3)$†	{*sitting, cat, ..*}
Word i after $(i = 1, 2, 3)$†	{*the, mat, ..*}
N-grams $(N = 2, .., 5)$‡	{*sitting_X, X_the, ..* }
POS N-grams $(N = 2, 3)$	{*VBG_X, X_DT, ..* }
Head word features	
Head of prev VP†	*sitting*
POS head of prev VP	*VBG*
Head of prev NP†	*cat*
POS head of prev NP	*NN*
Head of next NP†	*mat*
POS head of next NP	*NN*
Head prev NP + head next NP†	*cat+mat*
POS head prev NP +POS head next NP	*NN+NN*
Head prev VP + head prev NP + head next NP†	*sitting+cat+mat*
POS head prev VP + POS head prev NP + POS head next NP	*VBG+NN+NN*
N-gram before + head of next NP $(N = 1, 2)$†	{*sitting+mat*}
Web N-gram count features	
Web N-gram log counts $N = 2, .., 5$	{log freq(*sitting at*), log freq(*sitting in*), .., log freq(*sitting on*), .., log freq(*sitting with*), ..}
Web dep N-gram log counts $N = 2, 3$	{log freq(*sitting-at*), log freq(*sitting-in*), .., log freq(*sitting-on*), .., log freq(*sitting-with*), .., log freq(*at-mat*), .., log freq(*on-mat*), .., log freq(*with-mat*), .., log freq(*sitting-at-mat*), ..., log freq(*sitting-on-mat*), ..}
Dependency features	
Dep parent†	*sitting*
Dep parent POS	*VBG*
Dep parent relation	*prep*
Dep child†	{*mat*}
Dep child POS	{*NN*}
Dep child relation	{*pobj*}
Dep parent+child†	*sitting+mat*
Dep parent POS+child POS†	*VBG+NN*
Dep parent+child POS†	*sitting+NN*
Dep parent POS+child†	*VBG+mat*
Dep parent+relation†	*sitting+prep*
Dep child+relation†	*mat+pobj*
Dep parent+child+relation†	*sitting+mat+prep+pobj*

Table 2: Features for replacement preposition correction. Example: "He saw a cat sitting *on the mat*." †: lexical tokens in lower case, ‡: lexical tokens in both original and lower case

Features	Example
Lexical and POS features	
Word i before $(i = 1, 2, 3)$†	{*sitting, cat, ..*}
Word i after $(i = 1, 2, 3)$†	{*the, mat, ..*}
N-grams $(N = 2, .., 5)$‡	{*sitting_X, X_the, ..* }
POS N-grams $(N = 2, 3)$	{*VBG_X, X_DT, ..* }
Head word features	
Head of prev VP†	*sitting*
POS head of prev VP	*VBG*
Head of prev NP†	*cat*
POS head of prev NP	*NN*
Head of next NP†	*mat*
POS head of next NP	*NN*
Head prev NP + head next NP†	*cat+mat*
POS head prev NP + POS head next NP	*NN+NN*
Head prev VP + head prev NP + head next NP†	*sitting+cat+mat*
POS head prev VP + POS head prev NP + POS head next NP	*VBG+NN+NN*
N-gram before + head of next NP $(N = 1, 2)$†	{*sitting+mat, ..*}
Web N-gram count features	
Web N-gram log counts $N = 3, .., 5$	{log freq(*sitting on the*), log freq(*sitting the*), .. ,log freq(*sitting on the mat*), .., log freq(*sitting the mat*), ..}

Table 3: Features for missing preposition correction. Example: "He saw a cat sitting *the mat*."† : lexical tokens in lower case, ‡: lexical tokens in both original and lower case

Features	Example
Web N-gram count features	
Web N-gram log counts $N = 3, .., 5$	{log freq(*went to home*), log freq(*went home*), .. ,log freq(*cat went to home*), .., log freq(*cat went home*), ..}

Table 4: Features for unwanted preposition correction. Example: "The cat went *to home*."

Data set	# Documents	# Sentences	# Tokens
FCE(1044)	1,044	22,434	339,902
FCE(1244)	1,244	28,033	423,850
HOO-DEV	100	2,798	42,347
HOO-DEVTEST	100	2,674	41,518
HOO-TEST	100	1,393	20,563

Table 5: Overview of the data sets.

official HOO 2012 test data (HOO-TEST), which is not part of the FCE corpus, is completely unobserved during system development. Table 5 gives an overview of the data. Besides the FCE and HOO 2012 data sets, we use the following corpora. The Google Web 1T 5-gram corpus (Brants and Franz, 2006) is used for language modeling and collecting N-gram counts, the PukWaC corpus from the WaCky project (Baroni et al., 2009) is used for collecting web-scale dependency N-gram counts, and the New York Times section of the Gigaword corpus[3] is used for training the re-casing model. All data sets used in our system are publicly available.

4.2 Resources

We use the following NLP resources in our system. Sentence splitting is performed with the NLTK toolkit.[4] For spelling correction, we use the free software Aspell.[5] All words that appear at least ten times in the HOO 2012 training data are added to the spelling dictionary. We use the OpenNLP tools (version 1.5.2)[6] for POS tagging, YamCha (version 0.33) (Kudo and Matsumoto, 2003) for chunking, and the MaltParser (version 1.6.1) (Nivre et al., 2007) for dependency parsing. We use RandLM (Talbot and Osborne, 2007) for language modeling. The re-casing model is built with the Moses SMT system (Koehn et al., 2007) from the Gigaword New York Times section and all normal-cased documents in the HOO 2012 training data. The CuVPlus English dictionary (Mitton, 1992) is used to determine the countability of nouns. The CW learning algorithm is implemented by our group. The source code is available from our website.[7] All resources used in our system are publicly available.

4.3 Evaluation

Evaluation is performed by computing detection, recognition, and correction F_1 score between the set of system edits and the set of gold-standard edits as defined in the HOO 2012 overview paper (Dale et al., 2012). Detection scores are very similar to recognition scores (about 1–2% higher). We omit detection scores due to space limitations. Evaluation on the official test set is performed with respect to two different gold standards: the original gold standard from Cambridge University Press and a revised version which was created in the HOO 2012 shared task in response to change requests from participating teams. All scores are computed with the official scorer. The official gold-standard edits are given in character offsets, while our system internally works with token offsets. Therefore, all token offsets are automatically mapped back to character offsets before we submit our system edits. We only submitted one run of our system.

Step	Recognition			Correction		
	P	R	F_1	P	R	F_1
Det	62.26	12.68	21.06	54.09	11.01	18.30
+ RT	64.34	22.41	33.24	57.35	19.97	29.63
+ MT/UT	60.75	28.94	**39.20**	54.84	26.12	**35.39**

Table 6: Overall precision, recall, and F_1 score on the HOO-DEVTEST data after determiner correction (Det), replacement preposition correction (RT), and missing and unwanted preposition correction (MT/UT).

Type	Recognition			Correction		
	P	R	F_1	P	R	F_1
RD	30.00	5.66	9.52	30.00	5.66	9.52
MD	69.67	41.67	52.15	59.02	35.29	44.17
UD	40.74	11.00	17.32	40.74	11.00	17.32
Det	62.26	27.73	38.37	54.09	24.09	33.33
RT	69.09	33.63	45.24	63.64	30.97	41.67
MT	53.25	35.34	42.49	49.35	32.76	39.38
UT	38.46	12.20	18.52	38.46	12.20	18.52
Prep	59.62	29.95	39.87	55.40	27.83	37.05

Table 7: Individual scores for each error type on the HOO-DEVTEST data.

4.4 Results

Tables 6 and 8 show the overall precision, recall and F_1 score of our system after each processing step on the held-out HOO-DEVTEST set and the official test set, respectively. All numbers are shown in percentages. We note that each processing step improves the overall performance. The final F_1 correction score on the official test set is 28.70% before revision and 37.83% after revision, which are the highest scores achieved by any participating team. Tables 7 and 9 show individual precision, recall, and F_1 score

[3] LDC2009T13

[4] http://www.nltk.org

[5] http://aspell.net

[6] http://opennlp.apache.org

[7] http://nlp.comp.nus.edu.sg/software

Step	Recognition			Correction		
	P	R	F_1	P	R	F_1
Det	57.76	14.79	23.55	48.28	12.36	19.68
+ RT	58.93	21.85	31.88	47.02	17.44	25.44
+ MT/UT	55.98	25.83	**35.35**	45.45	20.97	**28.70**

(a) Before revisions

Step	Recognition			Correction		
	P	R	F_1	P	R	F_1
Det	68.10	16.70	26.83	62.93	15.43	24.79
+ RT	71.43	25.37	37.44	63.10	22.41	33.07
+ MT/UT	69.38	30.66	**42.52**	61.72	27.27	**37.83**

(b) After revisions

Table 8: Overall precision, recall, and F_1 score on the HOO-TEST data after determiner correction (Det), replacement preposition correction (RT), and missing and unwanted preposition correction (MT/UT).

Type	Recognition			Correction		
	P	R	F_1	P	R	F_1
RD	33.33	2.56	4.76	33.33	2.56	4.76
MD	62.24	48.80	54.71	51.02	40.00	44.84
UD	33.33	9.43	14.71	33.33	9.43	14.71
Det	57.76	30.88	40.24	48.28	25.81	33.63
RT	61.54	23.53	34.04	44.23	16.91	24.47
MT	46.15	21.05	28.92	38.46	17.54	24.10
UT	40.00	13.95	20.69	40.00	13.95	20.69
Prep	53.76	21.19	30.40	41.94	16.53	23.71

(a) Before revisions

Type	Recognition			Correction		
	P	R	F_1	P	R	F_1
RD	100.00	8.33	15.38	66.67	5.56	10.26
MD	70.41	52.67	60.26	65.31	48.85	55.90
UD	46.67	11.29	18.18	46.67	11.29	18.18
Det	68.10	34.50	45.80	62.93	31.88	42.32
RT	78.85	27.52	40.80	63.46	22.15	32.84
MT	61.54	28.57	39.02	53.85	25.00	34.15
UT	60.00	23.08	33.33	60.00	23.08	33.33
Prep	70.97	27.05	39.17	60.22	22.95	33.23

(b) After revisions

Table 9: Individual scores for each error type on the HOO-TEST data.

for each of the six error types, and for determiners (Det: aggregate of RD, MD, UD) and prepositions (Prep: aggregate of RT, MT, UT) on the held-out HOO-DEVTEST set and the official test set HOO-TEST, respectively.

5 Discussion

The main differences between our submission to the HOO 2011 shared task (Dahlmeier et al., 2011) and to this year's shared task are the use of the CW learning algorithm, the use of web-scale N-gram count features, and the use of the observed article or preposition as a feature. The CW learning algorithm performed slightly better than the empirical risk minimization batch learning algorithm that we have used previously while being significantly faster during training. Adding the web-scale N-gram count features showed significant improvements in initial experiments. Using the observed article or preposition feature allows the classifier to learn a bias against unnecessary corrections. We believe that our good precision scores are a result of using this feature.

In our experiments, we tried adding additional training data from other text corpora: the NUS Corpus of Learner English (NUCLE) (Dahlmeier and Ng, 2011) and the Gigaword corpus. Unfortunately, we did not see any consistent improvements over simply using the FCE corpus. The general rule of thumb that "more data is better data" did not seem to hold true in this case. After the evaluation had completed, we also tried training on additional training data and tested the resulting system on the official test set but did not see improvements either. We believe that no improvements were obtained due to the similarity between the training and test data, since all of them are student essays written in response to question prompts from the Cambridge FCE exam.

6 Conclusion

We have presented the system from the National University of Singapore that participated in the HOO 2012 shared task. Our system achieves the highest correction F_1 score on the official test set among all 14 participating teams, based on gold-standard edits both before and after revision.

Acknowledgments

This research is supported by the Singapore National Research Foundation under its International Research Centre @ Singapore Funding Initiative and administered by the IDM Programme Office.

References

M. Baroni, S. Bernardini, A. Ferraresi, and E. Zanchetta. 2009. The WaCky wide web: A collection of very large linguistically processed web-crawled corpora. *Language Resources and Evaluation*, 43(3):209–226.

S. Bergsma, D. Lin, and R. Goebel. 2009. Web-scale N-gram models for lexical disambiguation. In *Proceedings of the Twenty-First International Joint Conference on Artificial Intelligence*, pages 1507–1512, Pasadena, California, USA.

S. Bergsma, E. Pitler, and D. Lin. 2010. Creating robust supervised classifiers via web-scale N-gram data. In *Proceedings of the 48th Annual Meeting of the Association for Computational Linguistics*, pages 865–874, Uppsala, Sweden.

T. Brants and A. Franz. 2006. Web 1T 5-gram corpus version 1.1. Technical report, Google Research.

K. Crammer, M. Dredze, and A. Kulesza. 2009. Multiclass confidence weighted algorithms. In *Proceedings of the 2009 Conference on Empirical Methods in Natural Language Processing*, pages 496–504, Singapore.

D. Dahlmeier and H.T. Ng. 2011. Grammatical error correction with alternating structure optimization. In *Proceedings of the 49th Annual Meeting of the Association for Computational Linguistics: Human Language Technologies*, pages 915–923, Portland, Oregon, USA.

D. Dahlmeier, H.T. Ng, and T.P. Tran. 2011. NUS at the HOO 2011 pilot shared task. In *Proceedings of the Generation Challenges Session at the 13th European Workshop on Natural Language Generation*, pages 257–259, Nancy, France.

R. Dale, I. Anisimoff, and G. Narroway. 2012. HOO 2012: A report on the preposition and determiner error correction shared task. In *Proceedings of the Seventh Workshop on Innovative Use of NLP for Building Educational Applications*, Montréal, Québec, Canada.

M. Dredze, K. Crammer, and F. Pereira. 2008. Confidence-weighted linear classification. In *Proceedings of the 25th International Conference on Machine Learning*, pages 184–191, Helsinki, Finland.

N.-R. Han, M. Chodorow, and C. Leacock. 2006. Detecting errors in English article usage by non-native speakers. *Natural Language Engineering*, 12(2):115–129.

P. Koehn, H. Hoang, A. Birch, C. Callison-Burch, M. Federico, N. Bertoldi, B. Cowan, W. Shen, C. Moran, R. Zens, C. Dyer, O. Bojar, A. Constantin, and E. Herbst. 2007. Moses: Open source toolkit for statistical machine translation. In *Proceedings of the ACL 2007 Demo and Poster Sessions*, pages 177–180, Prague, Czech Republic.

T. Kudo and Y. Matsumoto. 2003. Fast methods for kernel-based text analysis. In *Proceedings of the 41st Annual Meeting of the Association for Computational Linguistics*, pages 24–31, Sapporo, Japan.

R. Mitton. 1992. A description of a computer-usable dictionary file based on the Oxford Advanced Learner's Dictionary of Current English.

J. Nivre, J. Hall, J. Nilsson, A. Chanev, G. Eryigit, S. Kübler, S. Marinov, and M. Marsi. 2007. Malt-Parser: A language-independent system for data-driven dependency parsing. *Natural Language Engineering*, 13(2):95–135.

A. Rozovskaya and D. Roth. 2010. Training paradigms for correcting errors in grammar and usage. In *Proceedings of Human Language Technologies: The 2010 Annual Conference of the North American Chapter of the ACL*, pages 154–162, Los Angeles, California.

A. Rozovskaya, M. Sammons, J. Gioja, and D. Roth. 2011. University of Illinois system in HOO text correction shared task. In *Proceedings of the Generation Challenges Session at the 13th European Workshop on Natural Language Generation*, pages 263–266, Nancy, France.

D. Talbot and M. Osborne. 2007. Randomised language modelling for statistical machine translation. In *Proceedings of the 45th Annual Meeting of the Association of Computational Linguistics*, pages 512–519, Prague, Czech Republic.

J. Tetreault and M. Chodorow. 2008. The ups and downs of preposition error detection in ESL writing. In *Proceedings of the 22nd International Conference on Computational Linguistics*, pages 865–872, Manchester, UK.

J. Tetreault, J. Foster, and M. Chodorow. 2010. Using parse features for preposition selection and error detection. In *Proceedings of the ACL 2010 Conference Short Papers*, pages 353–358, Uppsala, Sweden.

H. Yannakoudakis, T. Briscoe, and B. Medlock. 2011. A new dataset and method for automatically grading ESOL texts. In *Proceedings of the 49th Annual Meeting of the Association for Computational Linguistics: Human Language Technologies*, pages 180–189, Portland, Oregon, USA.

VTEX Determiner and Preposition Correction System for the HOO 2012 Shared Task

Vidas Daudaravičius
VTEX
Akademijos 4
LT-08412 Vilnius, Lithuania
vidas.daudaravicius@vtex.lt

Abstract

This paper describes the system has been developed for the HOO 2012 Shared Task. The task was to correct determiner and preposition errors. I explore the possibility of learning error correcting rules from the given manually annotated data using features such as word length and word endings only. Furthermore, I employ error correction ranking based on the ratio of the sentence probabilities using original and corrected language models. Our system has been ranked for the ninth position out of thirteen teams. The best result was achieved in correcting missing prepositions, which was ranked for the sixth position.

1 Introduction

The correct usage of determiners and prepositions is one of the toughest problems in English language use for non-native speakers, especially those living in a non-English speaking environment. The issues have been explored extensively in the literature (see Leacock et al. (2010)). It was interesting to find that this error correction topic was chosen for the HOO 2012 Shared Task.

This paper describes the experimental system developed by VTEX team for this task – to correct determiner and preposition errors in CLC FCE Dataset. It explores the possibility of learning error correcting rules from the given manually annotated data using features such as word length and word endings only. Furthermore, it employs error correction ranking based on the ratio of sentence probabilities using original and corrected language models.

2 The data

The training data consisted of 1000 files drawn from the publicly available FCE dataset and converted into HOO data format (see Dale et al. (2012)). I used the HOO 2012 training and test data only. The training data had 8432 manually annotated corrections of the following six error types:

MD – Missing Determiner;

MT – Missing Preposition;

UD – Unwanted Determiner;

UT – Unwanted Preposition;

RD – Replacement Determiner;

RT – Replacement Preposition.

The total size of the training data was 374680 words. The test data consisted of 100 previously unseen files without error correction annotations. For more details about the training and test data, see (Dale et al., 2012).

I have not used any other dictionaries, corpora or language processing tools (like taggers or parsers). Thus, the system is language independent and based on supervised learning of manually annotated corrections.

3 Word length and word ending

The training corpus was small and insufficient to get complete and reliable features and statistics of error corrections based on the corrected words. Therefore I needed to find features which describe the contexts of error corrections in a more generalized way. After some experimentation, I chose word length and the word last n characters. Words in the dataset were transformed into tokens using these functions. I have tested three word transformation combinations:

word – keeps the whole word (e.g. *make* $\mapsto$ *make*);

2end – takes the length of a word and adds the last two characters (*make* $\mapsto$ *4_ke*);

1end – takes the length of a word and adds the last character (*make* $\mapsto$ *4_e*).

I have also used lists of reserved words that were used to preserve the primary form of a word:

corrections – words that were corrected to/from in HOO 2012 Gold Edits data;

mod – functional words such as: *have, has, can, not, make, made, be, was, were, am, are, and, or*;

pronouns – pronouns that were not used as corrections: *we, he, she, they, yours, ours, them.*

For instance, using 2end transformation, the incorrect sentence *I feel that festival could be even better next year* was transformed into *I 4el that 8al 5ld be 4en 6er next 4ar*, and the corrected sentence into *I 4el that the 8al 5ld be 4en 6er next 4ar.*

In Section 5, I show that the word length and ending retain a lot of information about the word.

Each participating group in HOO 2012 Shared Task was allowed to submit up to ten runs. I have submitted nine runs that differ in word length and word ending only. The different runs are:

0 – 1end: all words except reserved correction words were encoded as word length+the last character;

1 – 2end: all words except reserved correction words were encoded as word length + two last characters;

2 – word: no transformations;

3 – 1end+mod: all words except reserved correction and mod words were encoded as word length + the last character;

4 – 2end+mod: all words except reserved correction and mod words were encoded as word length + two last characters;

5 – 1end+pron: all words except reserved correction and pronoun words were encoded as word length + the last character;

6 – 2end+pron: all words except reserved correction and pronoun words were encoded as word length + two last characters;

7 – 1end+mod+pron: all words except reserved correction, pronoun and mod words were encoded as word length + the last character;

8 – 2end+mod+pron: all words except reserved correction, pronoun and mod words were encoded as word length + two last characters.

4 Error correction

Error correction consists of **the rules** that the system is able **to learn**, and **the actions** that the system is able **to apply**.

4.1 Error correction rules

Using error correction annotations from Gold Edits of the training corpus we have built the error correction rules. The error correction rule is the error correction and the context of this correction. From the training corpus I gather contextual correction rules. The context are tokens on the left- or right-hand side of the error correction. The best choice would be to take at least two tokens on the left-hand side and two tokens on the right-hand side and to express error correction rule as a 5-gram with the error correction in the middle. For instance, in the training data, the error correction of *for* to *about* of type *RT* is found within the the left-hand side context *i asked* and the right-hand side context *the discounts.*

The main problem of learning of correction rules was the small size of the training corpus.

Bigger corpora could help in learning more correction rules. But it is hard to get bigger corpora because it is very expensive to prepare them. Two or three word context on each side of a corrected fragment can produce good but rarely applicable correction rules. Therefore, I have implemented a smoothing technique for generating new rules that do not appear in the training data.

I use trigrams to generate smoothed 5-gram error correction rules. Three types of trigrams were used for the smoothing:

centered – one token on the left-hand side of the correction, then the correction and one token on the right-hand side of the correction (see line 1 in Table 1);

left – two tokens on the left-hand side of the correction and the correction (see lines 2 and 3 in Table 1);

right – two tokens on the right-hand side of the correction and the correction (see lines 4–13 in Table 1).

There are 8432 corrections in the training data. Figure 1 shows the number of distinct trigram rules for the different runs described in Section 3. Most of the trigram rules appear once. For instance,

L_2	L_1	type	original	correction	R_1	R_2
	asked	RT	for	about	the	
i	asked	RT	for	about		
to	asked	RT	for	about		
		RT	for	about	the	camp
		RT	for	about	the	discounts
		RT	for	about	the	experience
		RT	for	about	the	first
		RT	for	about	the	new
		RT	for	about	the	news
		RT	for	about	the	play
		RT	for	about	the	prise
		RT	for	about	the	terrible
		RT	for	about	the	very

Table 1: Trigram error correction rules.

- the most frequent (38 occurrences) left-context trigram rule without word encoding is *stay in* ***/a/MD***;
- the most frequent (44 occurrences) right-context trigram rule is ***on/in/RT*** *july because*; and
- the most frequent (38 occurrences) centered-context trigram rule is *travel* ***on/in/RT*** *july*.

We could expect similar generalization power for left, right or centered contexts, but in Fig. 1 we can see that the number of distinct right-hand side contexts is lower by 5% compare to

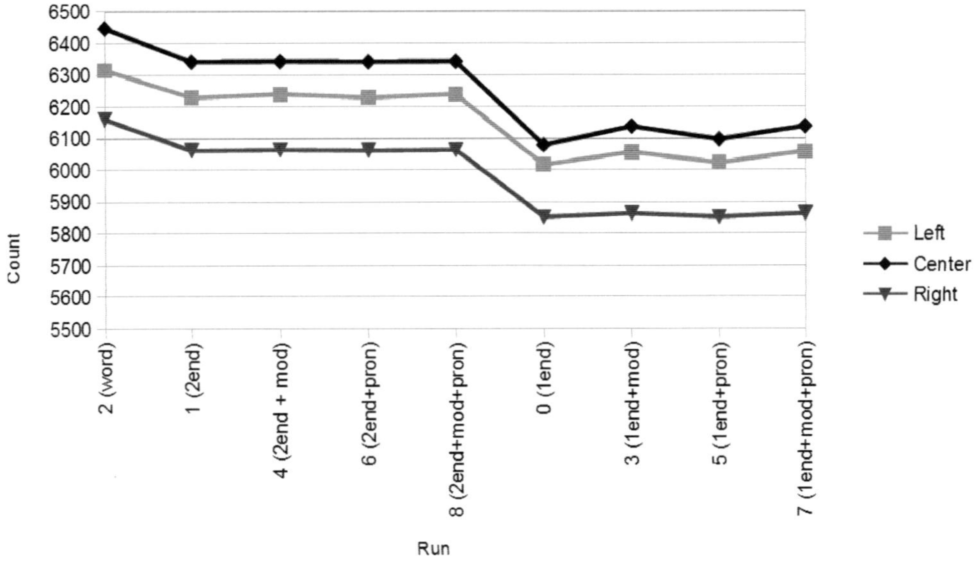

Figure 1: The number of context trigrams of error corrections for the different runs.

the number of distinct centered contexts. Surprisingly, the number of trigram rules does not degrade significantly whether the encoding `lend` is used or not.

The new smoothed 5-gram rules are extensions of the centered trigram rules. The extension on the left hand-side is the union of centered trigrams and the left trigrams when the error correction and L_1 match. And the extension on the right hand-side is the union of the centered trigrams and the right trigrams when error correction and R_1 match. For instance, the error correction of *for* to *about* of type *RT* within the the left-hand side context *i asked* and the right-hand side context *the discounts* is extended as follows:

- take centered trigram (see line 1 in Table 1);
- take left trigrams, where correction and L_1 match (see lines 2 and 3 in Table 1);
- take right trigrams, where correction and R_1 match (see lines 4–13 in Table 1);
- after that I have the following smoothed rule: L_2 = [*I, to*], L_1 = *asked*, C = *for/about/MT*, R_1 = *the*, R_2 = [*camp, discounts, experience, first, news, play, prise, terrible, very*].

This technique allows the generation of error correction rules that do not appear in the training data, e.g. in the latter example I generate 18 smoothed 5-gram rules that do not appear in the training data. The new smoothed 5-gram error correction rule is boolean operation and the rule does not contain any probabilistic information.

4.2 Error correction actions

The error correction system applies error correction rules using the following actions:

do not change – word is kept as is;

insert – missing word is inserted;

delete – unnecessary word is deleted;

replace – word is replaced by another one.

Each action is tested at each word but only one at a time. In case the context allows to apply several actions at one place then these actions are treated as alternatives. Alternative actions are not combined and no selection between

Doc ID	Run	Rules applied	OC ratio	sentence correction
2025	2	the//MD/ that/this/RD/	0.451	is the 8 th july till **the** end of **that** month , what do you think ?
		that/this/RD/	0.559	is the 8 th july till end of **that** month , what do you think ?
		the//MD/	0.633	is the 8 th july till **the** end of this month , what do you think ?
		–	0.785	is the 8 th july till end of this month , what do you think ?
	7	the//MD/ that/this/RD/	0.345	3s the 8 2h 4y till **the** 3d of **that** 5h , what 2o you 5k ?
		that/this/RD/	0.441	3s the 8 2h 4y till 3d of **that** 5h , what 2o you 5k ?
		the//MD/	0.533	3s the 8 2h 4y till **the** 3d of this 5h , what 2o you 5k ?
		–	0.683	3s the 8 2h 4y till 3d of this 5h , what 2o you 5k ?
2043	2	/for/UT/	0.976	i am writing in response to your last letter , to answer and ask you ~~for~~ some questions .
		–	1.035	i am writing in response to your last letter , to answer and ask you for some questions .
	7	/for/UT/	0.966	i am 7g in 8e to your 4t 6r , to 6r and 3k you ~~for~~ some 9s .
		a//MD/ /for/UT/	1.022	i am 7g in **a** 8e to your 4t 6r , to 6r and 3k you ~~for~~ some 9s .
		–	1.025	i am 7g in 8e to your 4t 6r , to 6r and 3k you for some 9s .
		a//MD/	1.085	i am 7g in **a** 8e to your 4t 6r , to 6r and 3k you for some 9s .

Table 2: Examples of ranking, selection and application of actions for sentence correction.

them is made at this step. The example of correction alternatives is shown in Table 2. Besides, the probability of the action can be taken into account but I do not do this and all actions are considered equally possible.

5 Language model

I use language trigram modeling to estimate the probability of a sentence. The probability of a sequence of words is estimated as the product of probabilities of trigrams:

$$p(x) = \prod_i \hat{p}(x_i \,|\, x_{i-2}, x_{i-1}).$$

To avoid zero probability I have used Kneser–Ney trigram smoothing (Kneser and Ney, 1995) technique as follows:

$$\begin{aligned}
&\hat{p}(x_i \,|\, x_{i-2}, x_{i-1}) \\
&\quad = \frac{\max[(\text{freq}(x_{i-2}, x_{i-1}, x_i) - c_3), 0]}{\max[\text{freq}(x_{i-2}, x_{i-1}), 1]} \\
&\qquad + \frac{c_3 * |x_{i-2}, x_{i-1}, \bullet|}{\max[\text{freq}(x_{i-2}, x_{i-1}), 1]} \\
&\qquad \times \frac{\max[(\text{freq}(x_{i-2}, x_{i-1}) - c_2), 0]}{\max[\text{freq}(x_{i-2}), 1]} \\
&\qquad + \frac{c_2 * |x_{i-2}, \bullet, \bullet|}{\max[\text{freq}(x_{i-2}), 1]} \\
&\qquad \times \frac{\max[(\text{freq}(x_{i-2}) - c_1), 0]}{N} + \frac{c_1 * T}{N},
\end{aligned}$$

where $c_3 = 0.8$, $c_2 = 0.6$, $c_1 = 0.4$, $T = |\bullet|$, and N is the corpus size.

I have built two language models: one for the original language and one for the corrected language. The original language model (O) was built using the corpus without corrections. The corrected language model (C) was built using the corpus with error corrections applied. The different runs yield different number of token trigrams. But the number does not degrade significantly as we might expect when words are encoded with the `1end` transformation (see Fig. 2). Thus, the `1end` transformation retains a lot of information, although, the number of trigrams of the original language model is always a little bit higher than the number of trigrams of the corrected language model.

6 The probability ratio of the original and corrected language models

The probability of a sentence depends on the length of the sentence. The longer the sentence the lower the probability. Error correction actions can change the length of a sentence. Thus, it is hard to implement the error correction system which should rank different length sentences. Therefore, I have used the ratio of the probabilities of the sentence using the original language model (O) and the corrected language

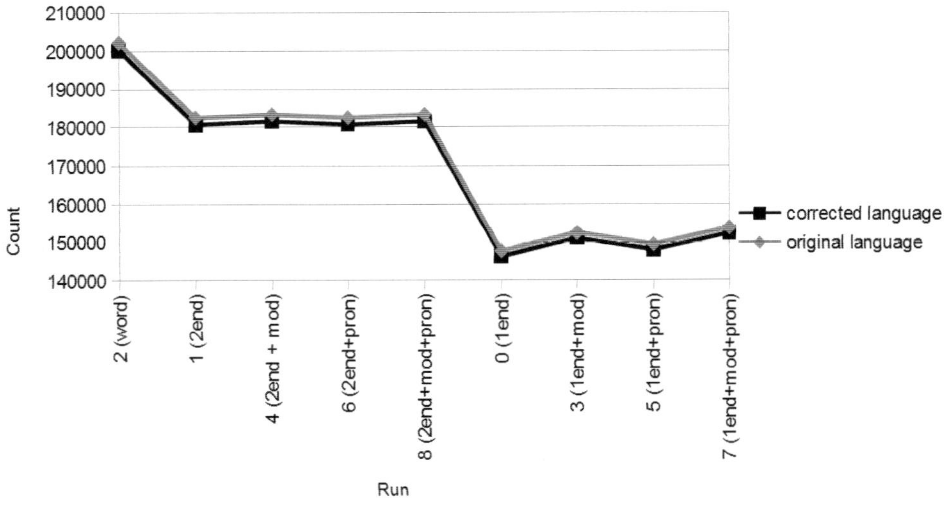

Figure 2: The number of trigrams of the original and corrected language models for different runs.

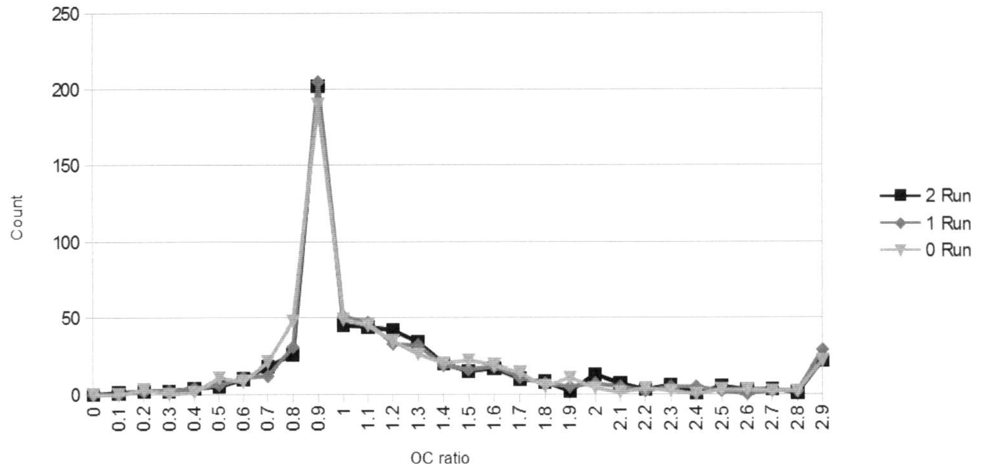

Figure 3: The histogram of *OC ratio* in the test data.

model (C):

$$OC\ ratio = \frac{\hat{p}(O)}{\hat{p}(C)},$$

where $\hat{p}(O)$ is the probability of a sentence using the original language model and $\hat{p}(C)$ is the probability of the same sentence using the corrected language model.

The lower the value of this ratio, the higher the chance that the sentence is correct, i.e. closer to corrected language rather than to original language. In Fig. 3, I show the histogram of the highest *OC ratios* of the corrected test sentences. This histogram shows that most of the ratios are close to 1, i.e. the probabilities of the sentence are almost equal using both language models. The histogram does not depend on the type of word encoding. In Table 2, I show examples of corrections and the *OC ratios* for each set of corrections. The error correction system takes corrections which are applied for the sentence with the lowest *OC ratio* (see Table 2).

7 The results and conclusions

The results for different runs of the error correction system are shown in the Table 3. The best determiner and preposition correction F-score results are achieved with *Run 5*, which is using 1end + pron encoding: all words except reserved correction and pronoun words were encoded as word length + the last character. This result was ranked for ninth position out of 14 teams.

Nevertheless, the results for different types of corrections are quite different. The error correction system was capable of performing UT, MT and MD type error corrections but hopeless for UD, RD and RT type error corrections. The best results are for:

MT – missing preposition error correction, no encoding is used;

MD - missing determiner error correction, 2end encoding is used;

UT - unwanted preposition error correction, any type of encoding except no encoding.

Surprisingly, we had to use whole words for missing preposition error correction, but never for unwanted preposition error correction. Our system was ranked at the seventh position for UT error correction using F-score.

The result for MT error correction shows that smoothed 5-gram rule generation was useful and the whole word should be used. But encoding with word length should never be used. Our system is ranked at the sixth position for MT error correction.

The result for MD error correction shows that the system degrades when encodings with fewer characters are used.

Run	All			MT			MD		
	P	R	F	P	R	F	P	R	F
0	8.15	**4.19**	5.54	4.65	3.50	4.00	7.84	**9.60**	8.63
1	24.5	2.87	5.13	12.5	**3.51**	5.48	34.8	6.40	**10.8**
2	**35.5**	2.43	4.54	**25.0**	**3.51**	**6.15**	**46.7**	5.60	10.0
3	8.41	3.75	5.19	5.56	**3.51**	4.30	8.27	8.80	8.53
4	25.0	2.87	5.15	13.3	**3.51**	5.56	34.8	6.40	**10.8**
5	8.76	**4.19**	**5.67**	5.00	**3.51**	4.12	8.57	**9.60**	9.06
6	24.5	2.87	5.14	12.5	**3.51**	5.48	34.8	6.40	**10.8**
7	9.04	3.75	5.30	5.71	**3.51**	4.35	9.17	8.80	8.98
8	25.0	2.87	5.15	13.3	**3.51**	5.56	34.8	6.40	**10.8**

Run	UT			UD			RT			RD		
	P	R	F	P	R	F	P	R	F	P	R	F
0	**100**	**4.65**	**8.89**	**4.76**	**1.89**	**2.70**	1.67	**1.47**	**2.70**	0	0	0
1	**100**	**4.65**	**8.89**	0	0	0	16.7	0.74	1.41	0	0	0
2	**100**	2.33	4.55	0	0	0	**20.0**	0.74	1.42	0	0	0
3	**100**	**4.65**	**8.89**	0	0	0	16.7	**1.47**	**2.70**	0	0	0
4	**100**	**4.65**	**8.89**	0	0	0	16.7	0.74	1.41	0	0	0
5	**100**	**4.65**	**8.89**	**4.76**	**1.89**	**2.70**	16.7	**1.47**	**2.70**	0	0	0
6	**100**	**4.65**	**8.89**	0	0	0	16.7	0.74	1.41	0	0	0
7	**100**	**4.65**	**8.89**	0	0	0	16.7	**1.47**	**2.70**	0	0	0
8	**100**	**4.65**	**8.89**	0	0	0	16.7	0.74	1.41	0	0	0

Table 3: Scores for correction of different runs.

The main conclusion is that there are no common features for all error corrections and the different systems for different error types should be implemented.

References

Robert Dale, Ilya Anisimoff, and George Narroway. 2012. Hoo 2012: A report on the preposition and determiner error correction shared task. In *Proceedings of the Seventh Workshop on Innovative Use of NLP for Building Educational Applications*, Montreal, Canada, June.

Reinhard Kneser and Hermann Ney. 1995. Improved backing-off for m-gram language modeling. In *Proceedings of the IEEE International Conference on Acoustics, Speech and Signal Processing*, volume I, pages 181–184, Detroit, Michigan, May.

Claudia Leacock, Martin Chodorow, Michael Gamon, and Joel Tetreault. 2010. *Automated Grammatical Error Detection for Language Learners.* Morgan and Claypool Publishers.

MD

Team	Run	Precision	Recall	F-Score
CU	0	83.33	8.0	14.6
KU	2	1.98	20.0	3.6
LE	0	54.43	34.4	42.16
NA	1	29.09	38.4	33.1
NU	0	51.02	40.0	44.84
TC	3	6.21	7.2	6.67
TH	3	9.54	26.4	14.01
UI	0	51.92	**43.2**	**47.16**
UT	6	36.7	32.0	34.19
VA	0	6.4	6.4	6.4
VT	1	34.78	6.4	10.81

MT

Team	Run	Precision	Recall	F-Score
CU	1	5.68	8.77	6.9
KU	1	0.51	**19.3**	1.0
LE	0	50.0	5.26	9.52
NA	3	11.43	7.02	8.7
NU	0	38.46	17.54	**24.1**
TC	3	4.65	3.51	4.0
UI	5	42.86	15.79	23.08
VA	1	1.71	7.02	2.75
VT	2	25.0	3.51	6.15

UT

Team	Run	Precision	Recall	F-Score
CU	1	4.83	**39.53**	8.61
JU	1	2.91	6.98	4.11
KU	5	60.0	13.95	22.64
LE	1	32.14	20.93	25.35
NA	3	40.91	20.93	**27.69**
NU	0	40.0	13.95	20.69
TC	9	4.69	30.23	8.13
TH	1	10.32	30.23	15.38
VA	0	12.9	18.6	15.24
VT	0	**100.0**	4.65	8.89

UD

Team	Run	Precision	Recall	F-Score
CU	3	17.86	18.87	18.35
JU	1	4.84	5.66	5.22
KU	8	26.92	13.21	17.72
LE	0	22.67	32.08	26.56
NA	5	40.0	11.32	17.65
NU	0	33.33	9.43	14.71
TC	9	5.11	16.98	7.86
TH	1	38.89	13.21	19.72
UI	2	23.38	**33.96**	**27.69**
VA	0	7.06	11.32	8.7
VT	0	4.76	1.89	2.7

Table 4: Scores for correction.

Precision Isn't Everything: A Hybrid Approach to Grammatical Error Detection

Michael Heilman and **Aoife Cahill** and **Joel Tetreault**
Educational Testing Service
660 Rosedale Road
Princeton, NJ 08541, USA
{mheilman,acahill,jtetreault}@ets.org

Abstract

Some grammatical error detection methods, including the ones currently used by the Educational Testing Service's e-rater system (Attali and Burstein, 2006), are tuned for precision because of the perceived high cost of false positives (i.e., marking fluent English as ungrammatical). Precision, however, is not optimal for all tasks, particularly the HOO 2012 Shared Task on grammatical errors, which uses F-score for evaluation. In this paper, we extend e-rater's preposition and determiner error detection modules with a large-scale n-gram method (Bergsma et al., 2009) that complements the existing rule-based and classifier-based methods. On the HOO 2012 Shared Task, the hybrid method performed better than its component methods in terms of F-score, and it was competitive with submissions from other HOO 2012 participants.

1 Introduction

The detection of grammatical errors is a challenging problem that, arguably, requires the use of both linguistic knowledge (e.g., in the form of rules or complex features) and large corpora for statistical learning. Additionally, grammatical error detection can be applied in various scenarios (e.g., automated essay scoring, writing assistance, language learning), many of which may benefit from task-specific adaptation or tuning. For example, one might want to take a different approach when detecting errors for the purpose of providing feedback than when detecting errors to evaluate the quality of writing in an essay. Thus, it seems desirable to take a flexible approach to grammatical error detection that incorporates multiple, complementary techniques.

In this paper, we extend the preposition and determiner error detection modules currently used in the Educational Testing Service's e-rater automated essay scoring system (Attali and Burstein, 2006) for the HOO 2012 Shared Task on grammatical errors (§2). We refer to this set of modules from e-rater as our "base system" (§3). While the base system uses statistical methods to learn models of grammatical English, it also leverages substantial amounts of linguistic knowledge in the form of various hand-coded filters and complex syntactic features. The base system is also tuned for high precision at the expense of recall in order to avoid a high rate of potentially costly false positives (i.e., frequent marking of correct English sentences as ungrammatical).

We apply the pre-existing base system without modifications but complement it with a large-scale n-gram method (§5) based on work by Bergsma et al. (2009). The n-gram method employs very little linguistic knowledge and instead relies almost exclusively upon corpus statistics. We also tune the resulting hybrid system with labeled training data in order to maximize the primary evaluation metric used in the HOO 2012 Shared Task: balanced F-score, or F_1 (§6). We find that the tuned hybrid system improves upon the recall and F-score of the base system. Also, in the HOO 2012 Shared Task, the hybrid system achieved results that were competitive with other submitted grammatical error detection systems (§7).

2 Task Definition

In this section, we provide a brief overview of the HOO 2012 Shared Task (Dale et al., 2012). The task focuses on prepositions and determiners only, distinguishing the following error types: preposition selection errors (coded "RT" in the data), extraneous prepositions ("UT"), missing prepositions ("MT"), determiner selection errors ("RD"), extraneous determiners ("UD"), and missing determiners ("MD").

For training and testing data, the shared task uses short essays from an examination for speakers of English as a foreign language. The data includes gold standard human annotations identifying preposition and determiner errors. These errors are represented as **edits** that transform an ungrammatical text into a grammatical one. Edits consist of start and end offsets into the original text and a correction string that should replace the original text at the specified offsets. The offsets differ by error type: word selection errors include just the word, extraneous word errors include an extra space after the word so that a blank will result in an appropriate amount of whitespace, and missing word errors specify spans of length zero.[1]

There are three subtasks: detection, recognition, and correction. Each is evaluated according to precision, recall, and F-score according to a set of gold standard edits produced by human annotation. While the correction subtask requires both correct character offsets and appropriate corrections, the detection and recognition subtasks only consider the offsets. Detection and recognition are essentially the same, except that detection allows for loose matching of offsets, which permits mismatches between the extraneous use (e.g., UT) and word selection (e.g., RT) error types. For our submission to the shared task, we chose to tune for the detection subtask, and we also chose to avoid the correction task entirely since the interface to the pre-existing base system did not give us access to possible corrections.

[1]The offsets for extraneous word errors prior to punctuation, a relatively rare occurrence, include a space before the word rather than after it. Our script for converting our system's output into the HOO 2012 format did not account for this, which may have decreased recognition performance slightly.

3 Base System

As our base system, we repurpose a complex system designed to automatically score student essays (both native and non-native and across a wide range of competency levels). The system is also used to give feedback to essay writers, so precision is favored over recall. There are three main modules in the essay-scoring system whose purpose it is to detect preposition and determiner errors (as they are defined in that system). Many of the details have been reported previously (Chodorow and Leacock, 2000; Han et al., 2004; Han et al., 2006; Chodorow et al., 2007; Tetreault and Chodorow, 2008), so here we will only give brief summaries of these modules.

It is important to note that this system was run without modification. That is, no training of new models or tuning was carried out specifically for the shared task. In addition, for the two statistical modules, we only had access to the final, boolean decisions about whether an error is present or not at a particular location in text. That is, we did not have access to confidence scores, and so task-specific tuning for F-score was not an option.

3.1 Preposition Error Detection

The base system detects incorrect and extraneous prepositions (Chodorow et al., 2007; Tetreault and Chodorow, 2008). Tetreault and Chodorow (2008) reports approximately 84% precision and 19% recall on both error types combined when evaluating the system on manually annotated non-native text.

3.1.1 Incorrect Prepositions

The module to detect incorrectly used prepositions consists of a multiclass logistic regression (i.e., "Maximum Entropy") model of grammatical usage, along with heuristic pre- and post- filters. The module works by extracting a set of features from the "context" around a preposition, generating a distribution over possible prepositions using the model of grammatical usage, and then flagging an error if the difference in probability between the text's original preposition and an alternative preposition exceeds a certain threshold. The probability for any correction also needs to exceed another minimum threshold. For this work, we used the pre-existing, manually-set thresholds.

A pre-filter prevents any contexts that contain spelling errors from being submitted to the logistic regression model. The motivation for this is that the NLP components that provide the features for the model are unreliable on such data, and since the systems favors precision over recall, no attempt is made to correct prepositions where the system cannot rely on the accuracy of those features.

The logistic regression model of correct preposition usage is trained on approximately 82 million words from the San Jose Mercury News[2] and texts for 11th to 12th grade reading levels from the MetaMetrics Lexile corpus, resulting in 7 million preposition contexts. The model uses 25 types of features: words and part-of-speech tags around the existing preposition, head verb (or noun) in the preceding VP (or NP), head noun in the following NP, among others. NPs and VPs were detected using chunking rather than full parsing, as the performance of statistical parsers on erroneous text was deemed to be too poor.

A post-filter rules out certain candidates based on the following heuristics: (1) if the suggested correction is an antonym of the original preposition (e.g., *from* vs *to*), it is discarded; (2) any correction of the benefactive *for* is discarded when the head noun of the following NP is human (detected as a WordNet hyponym of *person* or *group*).

3.1.2 Extraneous Prepositions

Heuristics are applied to detect common occurrences of extraneous prepositions in two scenarios: (1) accidentally repeated prepositions (e.g., *with with*) and (2) insertion of unnecessary prepositions in plural quantifier constructions (e.g., *some **of** people*).

3.2 Determiner Error Detection

There are two separate components that detect errors related to determiners. The first is a filter-based model that detects determiner errors involving number and person agreement. The second is a statistical system that supplements the rule-based system and detects article errors.

[2]The San Jose Mercury News is available from the Linguistic Data Consortium (catalog number LDC93T3A).

3.2.1 Filter-based system

The filter-based system combines unsupervised detection of a set of possible errors (Chodorow and Leacock, 2000) with hand-crafted filters designed to reduce this set to the largest subset of correctly flagged errors and the smallest possible number of false positives. Chodorow and Leacock (2000) found that low-frequency bigrams (sequences of two lexical categories with a negative log-likelihood) are quite reliable predictors of grammatical errors. Text is tagged and chunked, and filters that detect likely cases of NP-internal agreement violations are applied. These filters will mark, for example, a singular determiner followed by a plural noun head and vice versa, or a number disagreement between a numeral and the noun it modifies. This system has the ability to take advantage of linguistic knowledge, which contributes to its ability to detect errors with high precision.

3.2.2 Statistical model

In addition to the hand-crafted filters described above, there is a statistical component that detects incorrect, missing and extraneous articles (Han et al., 2004; Han et al., 2006). This component consists of a multiclass logistic regression that selects an appropriate article for every NP from *a, an, the*, or ϵ. This model is trained on 31.5 million words of diverse genres from the MetaMetrics Lexile corpus (from 10th to 12th grade reading levels), or 8 million NP contexts. Again, NPs were determined by chunking. The model includes various features: words and POS tags around and within the NP, NP head information including the countability of the head noun (estimated automatically from large corpora), etc.

In a cross-validation experiment, the model achieved approximately 83% accuracy on well-edited text. In an experiment evaluated on non-native learner text, the model achieved approximately 85% agreement with human annotators.

4 Task-Specific Heuristic Filtering

There is not a one-to-one mapping between the definitions of determiner and preposition errors as used in the HOO data set and the definitions used in our base system. For example, our base system marks errors involving *every*, *many* and other quantifiers as determiner errors, while these are not marked in the current HOO 2012 Shared Task data.

To ensure that our system was aligned with the HOO 2012 Shared Task, we automatically extracted lists of the most frequently occurring determiners and prepositions in the HOO training data. Any RT, UT, RD or UD edit predicted for a word not in those lists is automatically discarded. In the training data, this resulted in the removal of 4 of the 463 RT errors and 98 of the 361 RD errors detected by the base system.

5 Large-scale n-Gram Models

In order to complement the high-precision base system and increase recall, we incorporate a large scale n-gram model into our full system. Specifically, we adapt the SUMLM method from Bergsma et al. (2009). SUMLM creates confusion sets for each preposition token in an input text and uses the Google Web 1T 5-gram Corpus to score each item in the confusion set.[3] We extend SUMLM to support determiners, extraneous use errors, and missing word errors.

Consider the case of preposition selection errors. For a preposition token at position i in an input sentence $\mathbf{w}$, we compute the following score for each possible alternative v, using Eq. 1.[4]

$$\mathrm{s}(\mathbf{w}, i, v) = \frac{\sum\limits_{n=2...5} \sum\limits_{x \in \mathrm{G}(\mathbf{w}, i, n, v)} \log(\mathrm{count}(x))}{|\mathrm{G}(\mathbf{w}, i, n, v)|} \quad (1)$$

The function $\mathrm{G}(\mathbf{w}, i, n, v)$ returns the set of n-grams in $\mathbf{w}$ that include the word at position i and replace that word, w_i, with v. For example, if $\mathbf{w}$ = *Mary and John went at the store to buy milk*, $n = 4$, $i = 4$, and v = *to*, then $\mathrm{G}(\mathbf{w}, i, n, v)$ returns the following 4-grams:

- *and John went to*
- *John went to the*
- *went to the store*
- *to the store to*

The expression $\log(\mathrm{count}(x))$ is the natural logarithm of the number of times the n-gram x occurred in the corpus.[5] $|\mathrm{G}(\mathbf{w}, i, n, v)|$ is the number of n-gram count lookups, used to normalize the scores. Note that this normalization factor is not included in the original SumLM. When v is an alternative preposition not near the beginning or end of a sentence, $|\mathrm{G}(\mathbf{w}, i, n, v)| = 14$ since there are 14 n-gram count lookups in the numerator. Or, for example, if $i = 0$, indicating that the preposition occurs at the beginning of the sentence, $|\mathrm{G}(\mathbf{w}, i, n, v)| = 4$.[6]

Next, we compute the ratio of the score of each alternative to the score for the original, using Eq. 2.

$$\mathrm{r}(\mathbf{w}, i, v) = \frac{\mathrm{s}(\mathbf{w}, i, v)}{\mathrm{s}(\mathbf{w}, i, w_i)} \quad (2)$$

We then identify the best scoring alternative, requiring that its score be higher than the original (i.e., $\mathrm{r}(\mathbf{w}, i, v) > 1$). The procedure is the same for determiners, except, of course, that the set of alternatives includes determiners rather than prepositions.

To extend the method from Bergsma et al. (2009) for extraneous prepositions and determiners, we simply set v to be a blank and sum over $j = 3 \ldots 5$ instead. $|\mathrm{G}(\mathbf{w}, i, n, v)|$ will then be 12 instead of 14, since bigrams from the original sentence, which become unigrams when replacing w_i with a blank, are excluded.

To identify positions at which to flag selection or extraneous use errors, we simply scan for words that match an item in our sets of possible prepositions and determiners. To extend the method for missing

[3]The Google Web 1T 5-gram Corpus is available from the Linguistic Data Consortium (catalog number LDC2006T13). We plan to test other corpora for n-gram counts in future work.

[4]The n-gram approach considers all of the following words to be prepositions: *to, of, in, for, on, with, at, by, as, from, about, up, over, into, down, between, off, during, under, through, around, among, until, without, along, within, outside, toward, inside, upon, except, onto, towards, besides, beside*, and *underneath*. It considers all of the following words to be determiners: *a, an*, and *the*. The sets of possible prepositions and determiners for the base system are not exactly the same. Part of speech tags are not used in the n-gram system except to identify insertion points for missing prepositions and determiners.

[5]We use the TrendStream system (Flor, 2012) to retrieve n-gram counts efficiently.

[6]Our n-gram counts do not include start- or end-of-sentence symbols. Also, all n-grams are case-normalized with numbers replaced by a special symbol.

Algorithm 1 $\texttt{tune}(\mathbf{W}, \mathbf{y}, \hat{\mathbf{y}}\ \alpha, \alpha_{min})$: The hill-climbing algorithm for optimizing the n-gram method's penalty parameters $\mathbf{q}$. $\mathbf{W}$ consists of the training set texts. $\hat{\mathbf{y}}$ is a set of candidate edits. $\mathbf{y}$ is a set of gold standard edits. α is an initial step size, and α_{min} is a minimum step size.

```
q_allbest ← 0
score_allbest ← eval(q_allbest, W, y, ŷ)
while α > α_min do
    score_best ← −∞
    q_best ← q_allbest
    for q_tmp ∈ perturb(q_best, α) do
        score_tmp ← eval(q_tmp, W, y, ŷ)
        if score_tmp > score_best then
            q_best ← q_tmp
            score_best ← score_tmp
        end if
    end for
    if score_best > score_allbest then
        q_allbest ← q_best
        score_allbest ← score_best
    else
        α ← 0.5 ∗ α
    end if
end while
return q_allbest
```

word errors, however, we apply a set of heuristics to identify potential insertion points.[7]

6 Tuning

The n-gram approach in §5 generates a large number of possible edits of different types. In this section, we describe how we filter edits using their scores and how we combine them with edits from the base system (§3).

As described above, for an alternative v to be considered as a candidate edit, the value of $\mathrm{r}(\mathbf{w}, i, v)$ in Eq. 2 must be greater than a threshold of 1, indicating that the alternative scores higher than the original word. However, we observed low precision during development when including all candidate edits and decided to penalize the ratios. Bergsma et al. (2009) discuss raising the threshold, which has a similar effect. Preliminary experiments indicated that different edits (e.g., extraneous preposition edits and preposition selection edits) should have different penalties, and we also want to avoid edits with overlapping spans. Thus, for each location with one or more candidate edits, we select the best according to Equation 3 and filter out the rest.

$$v^* = \arg\max_{v} \quad \mathrm{r}(\mathbf{w}, i, v) - \mathrm{penalty}(w_i, v) \quad (3)$$

$\mathrm{penalty}(w_i, v)$ is a function that takes the current word w_i and the alternative v and returns one of 6 values: q_{RT} for preposition selection, q_{UT} for extraneous prepositions, q_{MT} for missing prepositions, q_{RD} for determiner selection, q_{UD} for extraneous determiners, and q_{MD} for missing determiners.

If the value for $\mathrm{r}(\mathbf{w}, i, v^*) - \mathrm{penalty}(w_i, v^*)$ does not exceed 1, we exclude it from the output.

We tune the vector $\mathbf{q}$ of all the penalties to optimize our objective function (F-score, see §7) on the training set using the hill-climbing approach described in Algorithm 1. The algorithm initializes the parameter vector to all zeros, and then iteratively evaluates candidate parameter vectors that result from taking positive and negative steps of size α in each direction (steps with negative penalties are skipped). The best step is taken if it improves the current score, according to the `eval` function, which returns the training set F-score after filtering based on the current parameters.[8] This process proceeds until there is no improvement. Then, the step size α is halved, and the whole process is repeated. The algorithm proceeds as such until the step size becomes lower than a specified minimum α_{min}.

When merging edits from the base system and the n-gram approach, the hybrid system always prefers edits from the base system if any edit spans overlap, equivalent to including them in Eq. 3 and assigning them a penalty of $-\infty$.[9] Note that the set of predicted edits $\mathbf{y}$ passed as input to the `tune` algorithm

[7]The heuristics are based on those used in Gamon (2010) (personal communication).

[8]Our implementation of the tuning algorithm uses the HOO 2012 Shared Task's `evalfrag.py` module to evaluate the F-score for the error detection subtask.

[9]If the base system produces overlapping edits, we keep them all. If there are overlapping edits from the n-gram system that have the same highest value for the penalized score in Equation 3 and do not overlap with any base system edits, we keep them all.

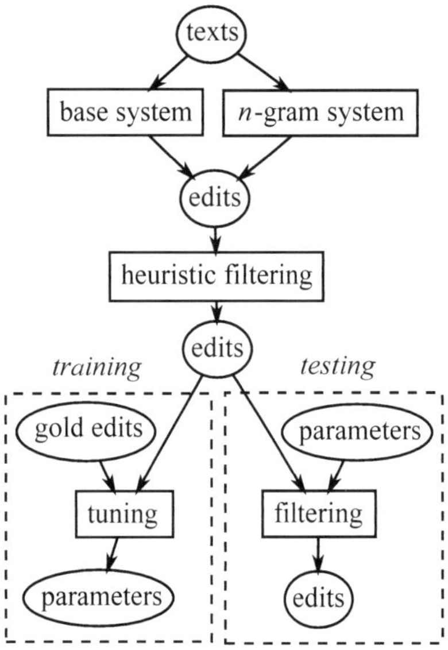

Figure 1: The architecture of the hybrid system. Different steps are discussed in different parts of the paper: "base system" in §3, "n-gram system" in §5, "heuristic filtering" in §4, and "tuning" and "filtering" in §6.

includes edits from both the base and n-gram methods.

Figure 1 illustrates the processes of training and of producing test output from the hybrid system.

7 Results

Table 1 presents results for the HOO 2012 detection subtask, including errors of all types. The results here, reproduced from Dale et al. (2012), are prior to applying participant-suggested revisions to the set of gold standard edits.[10] We include four variations of our approach: the base system (§3, labeled "base"); the n-gram system (§5, labeled "n-gram") by itself, tuned without edits from the base system; the hybrid system, tuned with edits from the base system ("hybrid"); and a variation of the hybrid system ("hybrid$_{indep}$") with the penalties tuned independently, rather than jointly, to maximize F-score for detection of each error type. For comparison, we also include the best performing run for the detection subtask in terms of F-score (labeled "UI").

	run	P	R	F
base	0	52.63	17.66	26.45
n-gram	–	25.87	37.75	30.70
hybrid	1	33.59	37.97	35.65
hybrid$_{indep}$	2	24.88	44.15	31.82
UI	8	37.22	43.71	40.20

Table 1: Precision, recall, and F-score for the combined preposition and determiner error detection subtask for various methods, before participant-suggested revisions to the gold standard were applied. All values are percentages. Official run numbers are shown in the "run" column. The "n-gram" run was not part of our official submission. For comparison, "UI" is the submission, from another team, that achieved the highest detection F-score in the HOO 2012 Shared Task.

We observe that the base and n-gram systems appear to complement each other well for this task: the base system achieved 26.45% F-score, and the n-gram system achieved 30.70%, while the hybrid system, with penalties tuned jointly, achieved 35.65%. Table 2 shows further evidence that the two systems have complementary performance. We calculate the overlap between each system's edits and the gold standard. We see that only a small number of edits are predicted by both systems (38 in total, 18 correct and 20 incorrect), and that the base system predicts 62 correct edits that the n-gram method does not predict, and similarly the n-gram method predicts 92 correct edits that the base system does not predict. The table also verifies that the base system exhibits high precision (only 68 false positives in total) while the n-gram system is tuned for higher recall (286 false positives).

Not surprisingly, when the n-gram method's penalties were tuned independently ("hybrid$_{indep}$") rather than jointly, the overall score was lower, at 31.82% F-score. However, tuning independently might be desirable if one were concerned with performance on specific error types or if macro-averaged F-score were the objective.

The hybrid system performed quite competitively

[10]After submitting our predictions for the shared task, we noticed a few minor implementation mistakes in our code related to the conversion of edits from the base system (§3) and the task-specific heuristic filtering (§4). We corrected them and retrained our system. The detection F-scores for the original and corrected implementations were as follows: 26.45% (original) versus 26.23% (corrected) for the base system, 30.70% (original) versus 30.45% (corrected) for the n-gram system, 35.65% (original) versus 35.24% (corrected) for the hybrid system, and 31.82% (original) versus 31.45% (corrected) for the hybrid$_{indep}$ system. Except for this footnote, all results in this paper are for the original system.

(1)	All models had [a]$_{\text{UD}}$ very strange long shoes made from black skin ...
(2)	I think it is a great idea to organise this sort of festival because most [of]$_{\text{UT}}$ people enjoy it.

Figure 2: Examples of errors detected by the base system and missed by the n-gram models.

(3)	We have to buy [for]$_{\text{UT}}$ some thing.
(4)	I am [ϵ]$_{\text{MD}}$ good diffender.

Figure 3: Examples of errors detected by the n-gram system and missed by the base model.

	$\in$ gold		$\notin$ gold	
	$\in$ base	$\notin$ base	$\in$ base	$\notin$ base
$\in$ n-gram	18	92	20	266
$\notin$ n-gram	62	276	48	—

Table 2: The numbers of edits that overlap in the hybrid system's output and the gold standard for the test set. The hybrid system's output is broken down by whether edits came from the base system (§3) or the n-gram method (§5). The empty cell corresponds to hypothetical edits that were in neither the gold standard or the system's output (e.g., edits missed by annotators), which we cannot count.

compared to the other HOO 2012 submissions, achieving the 3rd best results out of 14 teams for the detection and recognition subtasks. The performance of the "UI" system was somewhat higher, however, at 40.20% F-score compared to the hybrid system's 35.65%. We speculate that our hybrid system's performance could be improved somewhat if we also tuned the base system for the task.

8 Error Analysis

It is illustrative to look at some examples of edits that the base system correctly detects but the n-gram model does not, and vice versa. Figure 2 shows examples of errors detected by the base system, but missed by the n-gram system. Example (1) illustrates that the n-gram model has no concept of syntactic structure. The base system, on the other hand, carries out simple processing including POS tagging and chunking, and is therefore aware of at least some longer-distance dependencies (e.g., *a ... shoes*). Example (2) shows the effectiveness of the heuristics based on quantifier constructions mentioned in §3.1.2. These heuristics were developed by developers familiar with the kinds of errors that language learners frequently make, and are therefore more targeted than the general n-gram method.

Figure 3 shows examples of errors detected by the n-gram system but missed by the base system. Example (3) shows an example of where the base system does not detect the extraneous preposition because it only searches for these in certain quantifier constructions. Example (4) contains a spelling error, which confuses the determiner error detection system. It has not seen the misspelling often enough to be able to reliably judge whether it needs an article or not before it, and so errs on the side of caution. When *diffender* is correctly spelled as *defender*, the base system does detect that there is a missing article in the sentence.

There were a small number of cases where dialect caused a mismatch between our system's error predictions and the gold standard. For example, *an hotel* is not marked as an error in the gold standard since it is correct in many dialects. However, it was always corrected to *a hotel* by our system. Our system also often corrected determiners before the noun *camp*, since in American Standard English it is more usual to talk about *going to Summer Camp* rather than *going to a/the Summer Camp*.

Although the task was to detect preposition and determiner errors in isolation, there was sometimes interference from other errors in the sentence. This impacted the task in two ways. Firstly, in a sentence with multiple errors, it was sometimes possible to correct it in multiple ways, not all of which involved preposition or determiner errors. For example, you could correct the phrase *a women* by either changing the *a* to *the*, deleting the *a* entirely or replacing *women* with *woman*. The last change would not fall under the category of determiner error, and so there was sometimes a mismatch between the corrections predicted by the system and the gold standard corrections. Secondly, the presence of multiple errors impacted the task when a gold standard correction depended on another error in the same sentence being corrected in a particular way. For example, you could correct *I'm really excited to read the book.* as *I'm really excited about reading the book.*, however if you add the preposition *about* without correcting *to read* this correction results in the sentence becoming even more ungrammatical than the original.[11]

9 Conclusion

In this paper, we have described a hybrid system for grammatical error detection that combines a pre-existing base system, which leverages detailed linguistic knowledge and produces high-precision output, with a large-scale n-gram approach, which relies almost exclusively on simple counting of n-grams in a massive corpus. Though the base system was not tuned at all for the HOO 2012 Shared Task, it performed well in the official evaluation. The two methods also complemented each other well: many of the predictions from one did not appear in the output of the other, and the F-score of the hybrid system was considerably higher than the scores for the individual methods.

Acknowledgments

We thank Martin Chodorow for discussions about the base system, Daniel Blanchard for help with running the base system, Nitin Madnani for discussions about the paper and for its title, and Michael Flor for the TrendStream system.

[11]Many of these cases were addressed in the revised version of the gold standard data, however we feel that the issue is a more general one and deserves consideration in the design of future tasks.

References

Yigal Attali and Jill Burstein. 2006. Automated Essay Scoring with e-rater V.2. *Journal of Technology, Learning, and Assessment*, 4(3). Available from http://www.jtla.org.

Shane Bergsma, Dekang Lin, and Randy Goebel. 2009. Web-Scale N-gram Models for Lexical Disambiguation. In *Proceedings of the 21st international joint conference on Artifical intelligence*, IJCAI'09, pages 1507–1512, Pasadena, California. Morgan Kaufmann Publishers Inc.

Martin Chodorow and Claudia Leacock. 2000. An Unsupervised Method for Detecting Grammatical Errors. In *Proceedings of the First Meeting of the North American Chapter of the Association for Computational Linguistics (NAACL)*, pages 140–147, Seattle, Washington. Association for Computational Linguistics.

Martin Chodorow, Joel Tetreault, and Na-Rae Han. 2007. Detection of Grammatical Errors Involving Prepositions. In *Proceedings of the Fourth ACL-SIGSEM Workshop on Prepositions*, pages 25–30, Prague, Czech Republic. Association for Computational Linguistics.

Robert Dale, Ilya Anisimoff, and George Narroway. 2012. HOO 2012: A Report on the Preposition and Determiner Error Correction Shared Task. In *Proceedings of the Seventh Workshop on Innovative Use of NLP for Building Educational Applications*, Montreal, Canada. Association for Computational Linguistics.

Michael Flor. 2012. A fast and flexible architecture for very large word n-gram datasets. *Natural Language Engineering*, pages 1–33. doi:10.1017/S1351324911000034.

Michael Gamon. 2010. Using Mostly Native Data to Correct Errors in Learners' Writing. In *Human Language Technologies: The 2010 Annual Conference of the North American Chapter of the Association for Computational Linguistics*, pages 163–171, Los Angeles, California. Association for Computational Linguistics.

Na-Rae Han, Martin Chodorow, and Claudia Leacock. 2004. Detecting Errors in English Article Usage with a Maximum Entropy Classifier Trained on a Large, Diverse Corpus. In *Proceedings of the 4th International Conference on Language Resources and Evaluation (LREC 2004)*, pages 1625–1628, Lisbon, Portugal.

Na-Rae Han, Martin Chodorow, and Claudia Leacock. 2006. Detecting errors in English article usage by non-native speakers. *Natural Language Engineering*, 12:115–129. doi:10.1017/S1351324906004190.

Joel R. Tetreault and Martin Chodorow. 2008. The Ups and Downs of Preposition Error Detection in

ESL Writing. In *Proceedings of the 22nd International Conference on Computational Linguistics (Coling 2008)*, pages 865–872, Manchester, UK. Coling 2008 Organizing Committee.

HOO 2012 Error Recognition and Correction Shared Task: Cambridge University Submission Report

Ekaterina Kochmar
Computer Laboratory
University of Cambridge
ek358@cl.cam.ac.uk

Øistein Andersen
iLexIR Ltd
Cambridge
and@ilexir.co.uk

Ted Briscoe
Computer Laboratory
University of Cambridge
ejb@cl.cam.ac.uk

Abstract

Previous work on automated error recognition and correction of texts written by learners of English as a Second Language has demonstrated experimentally that training classifiers on error-annotated ESL text generally outperforms training on native text alone and that adaptation of error correction models to the native language (L1) of the writer improves performance. Nevertheless, most extant models have poor precision, particularly when attempting error correction, and this limits their usefulness in practical applications requiring feedback.

We experiment with various feature types, varying quantities of error-corrected data, and generic versus L1-specific adaptation to typical errors using Naïve Bayes (NB) classifiers and develop one model which maximizes precision. We report and discuss the results for 8 models, 5 trained on the HOO data and 3 (partly) on the full error-coded Cambridge Learner Corpus, from which the HOO data is drawn.

1 Introduction

The task of detecting and correcting writing errors made by learners of English as a Second Language (ESL) has recently become a focus of research.

The majority of previous papers in this area have presented machine learning methods with models being trained on well-formed native English text (Eeg-Olofsson and Knutsson, 2003; De Felice and Pulman, 2008; Gamon et al., 2008; Han et al., 2006; Izumi et al., 2003; Tetreault and Chodorow, 2008; Tetreault et al., 2010). However, some recent approaches have explored ways of using annotated non-native text either by incorporating error-tagged data into the training process (Gamon, 2010; Han et al., 2010), or by using native language-specific error statistics (Rozovskaya and Roth, 2010b; Rozovskaya and Roth, 2010c; Rozovskaya and Roth, 2011). Both approaches show improvements over the models trained solely on well-formed native text.

Training a model on error-tagged non-native text is expensive, as it requires large amounts of manually-annotated data, not currently publically available. In contrast, using native language-specific error statistics to adapt a model to a writer's first or native language (L1) is less restricted by the amount of training data.

Rozovskaya and Roth (2010b; 2010c) show that adapting error corrections to the writer's L1 and incorporating artificial errors, in a way that mimics the typical error rates and confusion patterns of non-native text, improves both precision and recall compared to classifiers trained on native data only. The approach proposed in Rozovskaya and Roth (2011) uses L1-specific error correction patterns as a distribution on priors over the corrections, incorporating the appropriate priors into a generic Naïve Bayes (NB) model. This approach is both cheaper to implement, since it does not require a separate classifier to be trained for every L1, and more effective, since the priors condition on the writer's L1 as well as on the possible confusion sets.

Some extant approaches have achieved good results on error detection. However, error correction is much harder and on this task precision remains low. This is a disadvantage for applications such as self-tutoring or writing assistance, which require feedback to the user. A high proportion of errorful suggestions is likely to further confuse learners and/or non-native writers rather than improve their writing or assist learning. Instead a system which maximizes precision over recall returning accurate suggestions for a small proportion of errors is likely to be more helpful (Nagata and Nakatani, 2010).

In section 2 we describe the data used for training and testing the systems we developed. In section 3 we describe the preprocessing of the ESL text undertaken to provide a source of features for the classifiers. We also discuss the feature types that we exploit in our classifiers. In section 4 we describe and report results for a high precision system which makes no attempt to generalize from training data. In section 5 we describe our approach to adapting multiclass NB classifiers to characteristic errors and L1s. We also report the performance of some of these NB classifiers on the training and test data. In section 6 we report the official results of all our submitted runs on the test data and also on the HOO training data, cross-validated where appropriate. Finally, we briefly discuss our main results, further work, and lessons learnt.

2 Cambridge Learner Corpus

The Cambridge Learner Corpus[1] (CLC) is a large corpus of learner English. It has been developed by Cambridge University Press in collaboration with Cambridge Assessment, and contains examination scripts written by learners of English from 86 L1 backgrounds. The scripts have been produced by language learners taking Cambridge Assessment's ESL examinations.[2]

The linguistic errors committed by the learners have been manually annotated using a taxonomy of 86 error types (Nicholls, 2003). Each error has been manually identified and tagged with an appropriate code, specifying the error type, and a suggested correction. Additionally, the scripts are linked to metadata about examination and learner. This includes the year of examination, the question prompts, the learner's L1, as well as the grades obtained. The current version of the CLC contains about 20M words of error-annotated scripts from a wide variety of examinations.

The HOO training and test datasets are drawn from the CLC. The training dataset is a reformatted 1000-script subset of a publically-available subset of CLC scripts produced by learners sitting the First Certficate in English (FCE) examination.[3] This examination assesses English at an upper-intermediate level, so many learners sitting this exam still manifest a number of errors motivated by the conventions of their L1s. The CLC-FCE subcorpus was extracted, anonymized, and made available as a set of XML files by Yannakoudakis et al. (2011).[4]

The HOO training dataset contains scripts from FCE examinations undertaken in the years 2000 and 2001 written by speakers of 16 L1s. These scripts can be divided into two broad L1 typological groups, Asian (Chinese, Thai, Korean, Japanese) and European (French, Spanish, Italian, Portuguese, Catalan, Greek, Russian, Polish). The latter can be further subdivided into Slavic (Russian, Polish) and Romance. In turn, the Romance languages differ in typological relatedness with, for example, Portuguese and Spanish being closer than Spanish and French. Error coding which is not relevant to preposition or determiner errors has been removed from the training data so that only six error type annotations are retained for training: incorrect, missing or unnecessary determiners (RD, MD, UD) and prepositions (RT, MT, UT).

One consequence of this reformatting is that the contexts of these errors often contain further errors of different types that are no longer coded. The idea is that errors should be considered in their natural habitat, and that correcting and copy-editing the surrounding text would create an artificial task. On the other hand, not correcting anything makes it difficult in some cases and nigh impossible in others to determine whether a given determiner or preposition is correct or not. The error-coding in the CLC in such cases (provided the writer's intent is deemed recoverable) depends not only on the original text, but also on the correction of nearby errors.

[1]http://www.cup.cam.ac.uk/gb/elt/catalogue/subject/custom/item3646603/Cambridge-International-Corpus-Cambridge-Learner-Corpus

[2]http://www.cambridgeesol.org/

[3]http://www.cambridgeesol.org/exams/general-english/fce.html

[4]http://ilexir.co.uk/applications/clc- fce-dataset/

Certain errors even appear as a direct result of correcting others: for instance, the phrase *to sleep in tents* has been corrected to *to sleep in a tent* in the CLC; this ends up as a 'correction' to *to sleep in a tents* in the HOO dataset. This issue is difficult to avoid given that the potential solutions are all labour-intensive (explicit indication of dependencies between error annotations, completely separate error annotation for different types of errors, or manual removal of spurious errors after extraction of the types of error under consideration), and we mention it here mainly to explain the origin of some surprising annotations in the dataset.

A more HOO-specific problem is the '[removal of] elements [from] some of [the] files [...] to dispose of nested edits and other phenomena that caused difficulties in the preprocessing of the data' (Dale et al., 2012). This approach unfortunately leads to mutilated sentences such as *I think if we wear thistoevery wherespace ships. This mean.* replacing the original *I think if we wear this clothes we will travel to every where easier than we use cars, ships, planes and space ships. This mean the engineering will find the way to useless petrol for it, so it must useful in the future.*

The HOO test set consists of 100 responses to individual prompts from FCE examinations set between 1993 and 2009, also drawn from the CLC. As a side effect of removing the test data from the full CLC, we have discovered that the distribution of L1s, examination years and exam prompts is different from the training data. There are 27 L1s exemplified, a superset of the 16 seen in the HOO training data; about half are Romance, and the rest are widely distributed with Asian and Slavic languages less well represented than in the training data.

In the experiments reported below, we make use of both the HOO training data and the full 20M words of error-annotated CLC, but with the HOO test data removed, to train our systems. Whenever we use the larger training set we refer to this as the *full CLC* below.

3 Data Preprocessing

We parsed the training and test data (see Section 2) using the Robust Accurate Statistical Parsing (RASP) system with the standard tokenization and sentence boundary detection modules and the unlexicalized version of the parser (Briscoe et al., 2006) in order to broaden the space of candidate features types. The features used in our experiments are mainly motivated by the fact that lexical and grammatical features have been shown in previous work to be effective for error detection and correction. We believe RASP is an appropriate tool to use with ESL text because the PoS tagger deploys a well-developed unknown word handling mechanism, which makes it relatively robust to noisy input such as misspellings, and because the parser deploys a hand-coded grammar which indicates ungrammaticality of sentences and markedness of constructions and is encoded entirely in terms of PoS tag sequences. We utilize the open-source version of RASP embedded in an XML-handling pipeline that allows XML-encoded metadata in the CLC and HOO training data to be preserved in the output, but ensures that unannotated text is passed to RASP (Andersen et al., 2008).

My friend was (MD: *a*) *good student*

Grammatical Relations (GRs):
(ncsubj be+ed:3_VBDZ friend:2_NN1 _)
(xcomp _ be+ed:3_VBDZ student:6_NN1)
(ncmod _ student:6_NN1 good:5_JJ)
(det friend:2_NN1 My:1_APP$)
*(det student:6_NN1 a:4_AT1)

Figure 1: RASP GR output

Relevant output of the system is shown in Figure 1 for a typical errorful example. The grammatical relations (GRs) form a connected, directed graph of typed bilexical head-dependent relations (where a non-fragmentary analysis is found). Nodes are lemmatized word tokens with associated PoS tag and sentence position number. Directed arcs are labelled with GR types. In the factored representation shown here, each line represents a GR type, the head node, the dependent node, and optional subtype information either after the GR type or after the dependent. In this example, the asterisked GR would be missing in the errorful version of the sentence. We extract the most likely analysis for each sentence based on the most probable tag sequence found by the tagger.

Extraction of the lexical and grammatical information from the parser output is easier when a determiner or preposition is present than when it is missing. During training, for all nouns, we checked for a `det` relation to a determiner, and whenever no `det` GR is present, we checked whether the noun is preceded by an MD annotation in the XML file. For missing prepositions, we have only extracted cases where a noun is governed by a verb with a `dobj` relation, and cases where a noun is governed by another noun with an `ncmod` (non-clausal modifier) relation. For example, in *It's been a long time since I last wrote you*, in absence of the preposition *to* the parser would 'recognize' a `dobj` relation between *you* and *wrote*, and this case would be used as a training example for a missing preposition, while *I trusted him* with the same `dobj` relation between *trusted* and *him* would be used as a training example to correct unwanted use of a preposition as in *I trusted *to him*.

3.1 Feature Types

In all the experiments and system configurations described below, we used a similar set of features based on the following feature templates.

For determiner errors:

- `Noun lemma`: lemma of the noun that governs the determiner
- `Noun PoS`: PoS tag of the noun
- `Distance from Noun`: distance in number of words to the governed determiner
- `Head lemma`: head lemma in the shortest grammatical relation in which the noun is dependent
- `Head PoS`: as defined above, but with PoS tag rather than lemma
- `Distance from Head`: distance in number of words to the determiner from head, as defined above (for `Head lemma`)
- `GR type to Noun`: a GR between `Head` and `Noun`.

For instance for the example shown in Figure 1, the noun lemma is *student*, the noun PoS is NN1, the distance from the noun is 2, the head lemma is *be*, the head PoS is VBDZ, and the distance from the head is 1, while the GR type to the noun is `xcomp`.

For preposition errors:

- `Preposition (P)`: target preposition
- `Head lemma (H)`: head lemma of the GR in which the preposition is dependent
- `Dependent lemma (D)`: dependent lemma of the GR in which the preposition is head.

For instance, in *I am looking forward to your reply*, `P` is *to*, `H` is *look* and `D` is *reply*.

In contrast to work by Rozovskaya and Roth, amongst others, we have not used word context features, but instead focused on grammatical context information for detecting and correcting errors. We also experimented with some other feature types, such as n-grams consisting of the head, preposition and dependent lemmas, but these did not improve performance on the cross-validated HOO training data, perhaps because they are sparser and the training set is small. However, there are many other potential feature types, such as PoS n-grams or syntactic rule types, and so forth that we don't explore here, despite their probable utility. Our main focus in these experiments is not on optimal feature engineering but rather on the issues of classifier adaption to errors and high precision error correction.

4 A Simple High Precision Correction System

We have experimented with a number of approaches to maximizing precision and have not outperformed a simple model that doesn't generalize from the training data using machine learning techniques. We leverage the large amount of error-corrected text in the full CLC to learn reliable contexts in which errors occur and their associated corrections. For the HOO shared task, we tested variants of this approach for missing determiner (MD) and incorrect preposition (RT) errors. Better performing features and thresholds used to define contexts were found by testing variants on the HOO training data. The feature types from section 3.1 deployed for the MD system submitted for the official run were `Noun` `lemma`, `Noun PoS`, `GR types to Noun` and `GR types from Noun` (set of GRs which has the noun as head). For the RT system, all three `P`, `H`, and `D` features were used to define contexts. A context is considered reliable if it occurs at least twice in the full CLC and more than 75% of the time it occurs with an error.

The performance of this system on the training data was very similar to performance on the test data (in contrast to our other runs). We also explored L1-specific and L1-group variants of these systems; for instance, we split the CLC data into Asian and European languages, trained separate systems on each, and then applied them according to the L1 metadata supplied with the HOO training data. However, all these systems performed worse than the best unadapted system.

The results for the generic, unadapted MD and RT systems appear as run 0 in Tables 4–9 below. These figures are artefactually low as we don't attempt to detect or correct UD, UT, RD or MT errors. The actual results computed from the official runs solely for MD errors are for detection, recognition and correction: 83.33 precision and 7.63 recall, which gives an F-measure of 13.99; the RT system performed at 66.67 precision, 8.05 recall and 14.37 F-measure on the detection, recognition and correction tasks. Despite the low recall, this was our best submitted system in terms of official correction F-score.

5 Naïve Bayes (NB) (Un)Adapted Multiclass Classifiers

Rozovskaya and Roth (2011) demonstrate on a different dataset that Naïve Bayes (NB) can outperform discriminative classifiers on preposition error detection and correction if the prior is adapted to L1-specific estimates of error-correction pairs. They compare the performance of an unadapted NB multiclass classifier, in which the prior for a preposition is defined as the relative probability of seeing a specific preposition compared to a predefined subset of the overall PoS class (which they call the Conf(usion) Set):

$$\text{prior}(p) = \frac{C(p)}{\sum_{q \in \text{ConfSet}} C(q)},$$

to the performance of the same NB classfier with an adapted prior which calculates the probability of a correct preposition as:

$$\text{prior}(c, p, \text{L1}) = \frac{C_{\text{L1}}(p, c)}{C_{\text{L1}}(p)},$$

where $C_{\text{L1}}(p)$ is the number of times preposition p is seen in texts written by learners with L1 as their native language, and $C_{\text{L1}}(p, c)$ is the number of times c is the correct preposition when p is used.

We applied Rozovskaya and Roth's approach to determiners as well as prepositions, and experimented with priors calculated in the same way for L1 groups as well as specific L1s. We also compared L1-adaptation to generic adaption to corrections, calculated as:

$$\text{prior}(c, p) = \frac{C(p, c)}{C(p)},$$

We have limited the set of determiners and prepositions that our classifiers aim to detect and correct, if necessary. Our confusions sets contain:

- `Determiners`: *no determiner*, *the*, *a*, *an*;
- `Prepositions`: *no preposition*, *in*, *of*, *for*, *to*, *at*, *with*, *on*, *about*, *from*, *by*, *after*.

Therefore, for determiners, our systems were only aimed at detecting and correcting errors in the use of articles, and we have not taken into account any errors in the use of possessive pronouns (*my*, *our*, etc.), demonstratives (*this*, *those*, etc.), and other types of determiners (*any*, *some*, etc.). For prepositions, it is well known that a set of about 10 of the most frequent prepositions account for more than 80% of all prepositional usage (Gamon, 2010).

We have calculated the upper bounds for the training and test sets when the determiner and preposition confusion sets are limited this way. The upper bound recall for *recognition* (i.e., ability of the classifier to recognize that there is an error, dependent on the fact that only the chosen determiners and prepositions are considered) is calculated as the proportion of cases where the incorrect, missing or unnecessary determiner or preposition is contained in our confusion set. For the training set, it is estimated at 91.95, and for the test at 93.20. Since for *correction*, the determiner or preposition suggested by the system should also be contained in our confusion set, upper bound recall for *correction* is slightly lower than that for *recognition*, and is estimated at 86.24 for the training set, and at 86.39 for the test set. These figures show that the chosen candidates distribute similarly in both datasets, and that a system aimed at recognition and correction of only these function words can obtain good performance on the full task.

The 1000 training scripts were divided into 5 portions pseudo-randomly to ensure that each portion contained approximately the same number of L1-specific scripts in order not to introduce any L1-related bias. The results on the training set presented below were averaged across 5 runs, where in each run 4 portions (about 800 scripts) were used for training, and one portion (about 200 scripts) was used for testing.

We treated the task as multi-class classification, where the number of classes equates to the size of our confusion set, and when the classifier's decision is different from the input, it is considered to be errorful. For determiners, we used the full set of features described in section 3.1, whereas for prepositions, we have tried two different feature sets: only head lemma (`H`), or `H` with the dependent lemma (`D`).

We ran the unadapted and L1-adapted NB classifiers on determiners and prepositions using the features defined above. The results of these preliminary experiments are presented below.

5.1 Unadapted and L1-adapted NB classifiers

Tables 1 to 3 below present results averaged over the 5 runs for the unadapted classifiers. We report the results in terms of recall, precision and F-score for detection, recognition and correction of errors as defined for the HOO shared task.[5]

We have experimented with two types of L1-specific classification: `classifier1` below is a combination of 16 separate multiclass NB classifiers, each trained on a specific L1 and applied to the corresponding parts of the data. `Classifier2` is a replication of the classifier presented in Rozovskaya and Roth (2011), which uses the priors adapted to the writer's L1 and to the chosen determiner or preposition at decision time. The priors used for these runs were estimated from the HOO training data.

We present only the results of the systems that use `H+D` features for prepositions, since these systems outperform systems using `H` only. Tables 1, 2 and 3 below show the comparative results of the three classifiers averaged over 5 runs, with all errors, determiner errors only, and preposition errors only, respectively.

	Detection			Recognition			Correction		
	R	P	F	R	P	F	R	P	F
U	60.69	**21.32**	**31.55**	**50.57**	**17.73**	**26.25**	**34.38**	**12.05**	**17.85**
C1	**64.51**	16.17	25.85	50.25	12.56	20.10	30.95	7.74	12.39
C2	33.74	16.51	22.15	28.50	13.96	18.72	16.51	8.10	10.85

Table 1: All errors included. Unadapted classifier (U) vs. two L1-adapted classifiers (C1 and C2). Results on the training set.

	Detection			Recognition			Correction		
	R	P	F	R	P	F	R	P	F
U	54.42	**33.25**	**41.25**	50.09	**30.60**	**30.83**	**40.70**	**24.84**	**30.83**
C1	**61.19**	20.25	30.42	**52.20**	17.27	25.94	40.57	13.43	20.17
C2	40.56	15.88	22.81	37.24	14.58	20.94	23.20	9.08	13.04

Table 2: Determiner errors. Unadapted classifier (U) vs. two L1-adapted classifiers (C1 and C2). Results on the training set.

	Detection			Recognition			Correction		
	R	P	F	R	P	F	R	P	F
U	65.71	16.89	**26.87**	**50.90**	**13.09**	**20.83**	**28.95**	**7.45**	**11.84**
C1	**66.96**	13.86	22.97	48.51	10.05	16.65	22.70	4.70	7.79
C2	27.45	**17.06**	21.00	21.00	13.07	16.09	10.79	6.73	8.27

Table 3: Preposition errors. Unadapted classifier (U) vs. two L1-adapted classifiers (C1 and C2). Results on the training set.

The results show some improvement with a combination of classifiers trained on L1-subsets in terms of recall for detection and recognition of errors, and a slight improvement in precision using L1-specific priors for preposition errors. However, in general, unadapted classifiers outperform L1-adapted classifiers with identical feature types. Therefore, we have not included L1-specific classifiers in the submitted set of runs.

5.2 Submitted systems

For the official runs, we trained various versions of the unadapted and generic adapted NB classifiers.

[5]For precise definitions of these measures see `www.correcttext.org/hoo2012`

We trained all the adapted priors on the full CLC dataset in the expectation that this would yield more accurate estimates. We trained the unadapted priors and the NB features as before on the HOO training dataset. We also trained the NB features on the full CLC dataset and tested the impact of the preposition feature `D` (dependent lemma of the GR from the preposition, i.e., the head of the preposition complement) with the different training set sizes. For all runs we used the full set of determiner features described in section 3.1.

The full set of multiclass NB classifiers submitted is described below:

- `Run1`: unadapted, trained on the HOO data. `H` feature for prepositions;
- `Run2`: unadapted, trained on the HOO data. `H` and `D` features for prepositions;
- `Run3`: a combination of the NB classifiers trained for each of the used candidate words separately. `H` and `D` features are used for prepositions;
- `Run4`: generic adapted, trained on HOO data. `H` feature for prepositions;
- `Run5`: generic adapted, trained on HOO data. `H` and `D` features for prepositions;
- `Run6`: unadapted, trained on the full CLC. `H` feature for prepositions;
- `Run7`: unadapted, trained on the full CLC. `H` and `D` features for prepositions.

The classifiers used for runs 1 and 2 differ from the ones used for runs 6 and 7 only in the amount of training data. None of these classifiers involve any adaptation. The classifiers used for runs 4 and 5 involve prior adaptation to the input determiner or preposition, adjusted at decision time. In run 3, a combination of classifiers trained on the input determiner- or preposition-specific partitions of the HOO training data are used. At test time, the appropriate classifier from this set is applied depending on the preposition or determiner chosen by the learner.

To limit the number of classes for the classifiers used in runs 1–3 and 6–7, we have combined the training cases for determiners *a* and *an* in one class *a/an*; after classification one of the variants is chosen depending on the first letter of the next word. However, for the classifiers used in runs 4–5, we used priors including confusions between *a* and *an*.

The results for these runs on the training data are shown in Tables 4 to 6 below.

	Detection			Recognition			Correction		
	R	P	F	R	P	F	R	P	F
0	5.54	**81.08**	10.37	5.32	**77.95**	9.97	4.90	**71.70**	9.17
1	60.14	18.57	28.37	48.21	14.88	22.74	32.71	10.09	15.43
2	60.69	21.32	31.55	50.57	17.73	26.25	**34.38**	12.05	17.85
3	50.09	27.54	**35.52**	45.99	25.23	**32.57**	28.78	15.80	**20.39**
4	25.39	25.48	25.39	22.10	22.23	22.13	12.23	12.33	12.26
5	31.17	22.33	25.94	26.28	18.88	21.90	14.50	10.46	12.11
6	62.41	10.73	18.31	49.95	8.57	14.63	32.66	5.60	9.57
7	**62.92**	11.60	19.59	**52.29**	9.61	16.24	34.32	6.31	10.66

Table 4: Training set results, all errors

	Detection			Recognition			Correction		
	R	P	F	R	P	F	R	P	F
0	5.02	**82.98**	9.46	5.02	**82.98**	9.46	4.81	**79.57**	9.07
1–2	54.42	33.25	41.25	50.09	30.60	30.83	40.70	24.84	30.83
3	58.50	62.22	**60.22**	**57.41**	61.07	**59.11**	**46.33**	49.25	**47.68**
4–5	34.93	31.09	32.68	33.66	30.01	31.52	19.74	17.66	18.51
6–7	**58.65**	8.11	14.24	53.90	7.43	13.06	40.61	5.60	9.84

Table 5: Training set results, determiner errors

	Detection			Recognition			Correction		
	R	P	F	R	P	F	R	P	F
0	5.87	**78.30**	10.93	5.59	**74.49**	10.40	4.97	**66.28**	9.25
1	64.71	14.04	23.06	46.54	10.11	16.61	25.86	5.61	9.22
2	**65.71**	16.89	**26.87**	**50.90**	13.09	**20.83**	**28.95**	7.45	**11.84**
3	42.63	16.53	23.81	36.18	14.04	20.22	13.74	5.35	7.70
4	16.85	19.27	17.97	12.24	14.03	13.06	5.81	6.67	6.21
5	27.49	16.89	20.88	19.96	12.30	15.19	10.03	6.20	7.65
6	64.69	14.03	23.06	46.51	10.10	16.60	25.83	5.61	9.22
7	65.68	16.89	**26.87**	50.87	13.09	**20.82**	28.92	7.44	**11.84**

Table 6: Training set results, preposition errors

The results on the training data show that use of the `D` feature improves the performance of all the preposition classifiers. Use of the full CLC for training improves recall, but does not improve precision for prepositions, while for determiners precision of the classifiers trained on the full CLC is much worse. Adaptation of the classifiers with determiner/preposition-specific priors slightly improves precision on prepositions, but is damaging for recall. Therefore, in terms of F-score, unadapted classifiers outperform adapted ones. The overall best-performing system on the cross-validated training data is Run3, which is trained on the determiner/preposition-specific data subsets and applies an input-specific classifier to test data. However, the result is due to improved performance on determiners, not prepositions.

6 Official Evaluation Results

The results presented below are calculated using the evaluation tool provided by the organizers, implementing the scheme specified in the HOO shared task. The results on the test set, presented in Tables 7–9 are from the final official run after correction of errors in the annotation and score calculation scripts.

	Detection			Recognition			Correction		
	R	P	F	R	P	F	R	P	F
0	4.86	**76.67**	9.15	4.65	**73.33**	8.75	4.65	**73.33**	8.75
1	34.46	13.04	18.92	22.83	8.64	12.54	13.53	5.12	7.43
2	35.73	14.04	**20.16**	23.47	9.22	13.24	12.26	4.82	6.92
3	19.24	12.10	14.86	14.59	9.18	11.27	5.71	3.59	4.41
4	9.51	14.95	11.63	7.19	11.30	8.79	5.29	8.31	6.46
5	15.43	14.31	14.85	10.78	10.00	10.38	6.77	6.28	6.51
6	55.60	11.15	18.58	41.86	8.40	13.99	**28.54**	5.73	**9.54**
7	**56.66**	11.59	19.24	**42.49**	8.69	**14.43**	27.27	5.58	9.26

Table 7: Test set results, all errors

	Detection			Recognition			Correction		
	R	P	F	R	P	F	R	P	F
0	4.37	**83.33**	8.30	4.37	**83.33**	8.30	4.37	**83.33**	8.30
1–2	8.73	7.61	8.13	4.80	4.18	4.47	4.37	3.80	4.07
3	6.11	11.29	7.93	5.24	9.68	6.80	5.24	9.68	6.80
4–5	6.11	9.72	7.51	4.80	7.64	5.90	4.80	7.64	5.90
6–7	**51.09**	8.53	**14.63**	**44.10**	7.37	**12.63**	**35.37**	5.91	**10.13**

Table 8: Test set results, determiner errors

	Detection			Recognition			Correction		
	R	P	F	R	P	F	R	P	F
0	5.33	**72.22**	9.92	4.92	**66.67**	9.16	4.92	**66.67**	**9.16**
1	57.79	14.29	22.91	39.75	9.83	15.76	**22.13**	5.47	8.77
2	**59.43**	15.41	**24.47**	**40.98**	10.63	**16.88**	19.67	5.10	8.10
3	29.10	11.31	16.28	23.36	9.08	13.07	6.15	2.39	3.44
4	12.71	19.75	15.46	9.43	14.65	11.47	5.74	8.92	6.98
5	24.18	16.12	19.34	16.39	10.93	13.12	8.61	5.74	6.89
6	57.79	14.29	22.91	39.75	9.83	15.76	**22.13**	5.47	8.77
7	**59.43**	15.41	**24.47**	**40.98**	10.63	**16.88**	19.67	5.10	8.10

Table 9: Test set results, preposition errors

The test set results for NB classifiers (Runs 1–7) are significantly worse than our preliminary results obtained on the training data partitions, especially for determiners. Use of additional training data (Runs 6 and 7) improves recall, but does not improve precision. Adaptation to the input preposition improves precision as compared to the unadapted classifier for prepositions (Run 4), whereas training on the determiner-specific subsets improves precision for determiners (Run 3). However, generally these results are worse than the results of the similar classifiers on the training data subsets.

We calculated the upper bound recall for our classifiers on the test data. The upper bound recall on the test data is 93.20 for recognition, and 86.39 for correction, given our confusion sets for both determiners and prepositions. However, the actual upper bound recall is 71.82, with upper bound recall on determiners at 71.74 and on prepositions at 71.90, because 65 out of 230 determiner errors, and 68 out of 243 preposition errors are not considered by our classifiers, primarily because when the parser fails to find a full analysis, the grammatical context is often not recovered accurately enough to identify missing input positions or relevant GRs. This is an inherent weakness of using only parser-extracted features from noisy and often ungrammatical input. Taking this into account, some models (Runs 1, 2, 6 and 7) achieved quite high recall.

We suspect the considerable drop in precision is explained by the differences in the training and test data. The training set contains answers from learners of a smaller group of L1s from one examination year to a much more restricted set of prompts. The well-known weaknesses of generative NB classifiers may prevent effective exploitation of the additional information in the full CLC over the HOO training data. Experimentation with count weighting schemes and optimized interpolation of adapted priors may well be beneficial (Rennie et al., 2003).

Acknowledgements

We thank Cambridge ESOL, a division of Cambridge Assessment for a partial grant to the first author and a research contract with iLexIR Ltd. We also thank them and Cambridge University Press for granting us access to the CLC for research purposes.

References

Øistein Andersen. 2011 Semi-automatic ESOL error annotation. *English Profile Journal, vol2:e1*. DOI: 10.1017/S2041536211000018, Cambridge University Press.

Øistein Andersen, Julian Nioche, Ted Briscoe, and John Carroll. 2008 The BNC parsed with

RASP4UIMA. In *6th Int. Conf. on Language Resources and Evaluation (LREC)*, Marrakech, Moroccco

Ted Briscoe, John A. Carroll, and Rebecca Watson. 2006. The second release of the RASP system. In *Proceedings of COLING/ACL*, vol 6.

Robert Dale, Ilya Anisimoff and George Narroway 2012 HOO 2012: A Report on the Preposition and Determiner Error Correction Shared Task. *In Proceedings of the Seventh Workshop on Innovative Use of NLP for Building Educational Applications* Montreal, Canada, June.

Rachele De Felice and Stephen G. Pulman. 2008. A classifier-based approach to preposition and determiner error correction in L2 English. In *Proceedings of the 22nd International Conference on Computational Linguistics (COLING 2008)*, pages 169–176, Manchester, UK, -August.

Jens Eeg-Olofsson and Ola Knutsson. 2003. Automatic grammar checking for second language learners - the use of prepositions. In *Nodalida.*

Michael Gamon, Jianfeng Gao, Chris Brockett, Alexander Klementiev, William Dolan, Dmitriy Belenko, and Lucy Vanderwende. 2008. Using contextual speller techniques and language modeling for ESL error correction. In *Proceedings of IJCNLP*, Hyderabad, India, January.

Michael Gamon. 2010. Using Mostly Native Data to Correct Errors in Learners' Writing: A Meta-Classifier Approach. In *Proceedings of NAACL 2010*, pages 163–171, Los Angeles, USA, June.

Na-Rae Han, Martin Chodorow, and Claudia Leacock. 2006. Detecting errors in English article usage by non-native speakers. *Journal of Natural Language Engineering*, 12(2):115–129.

Na-Rae Han, Joel R. Tetreault, Soo-Hwa Lee, and Jin-Young Ha. 2010. Using an Error-Annotated Learner Corpus to Develop an ESL/EFL Error Correction System. In *Proceedings of the Seventh conference on International Language Resources and Evaluation (LREC-10)*, Valletta, Malta, May.

Emi Izumi, Kiyotaka Uchimoto, Toyomi Saiga, Thepchai Supnithi, and Hitoshi Isahara. 2003. Automatic error detection in the Japanese learners' English spoken data. In *The Companion Volume to the Proceedings of 41st Annual Meeting of the Association for Computational Linguistics*, pages 145–148, Sapporo, Japan, July.

Ekaterina Kochmar. 2011. Identification of a Writer's Native Language by Error Analysis University of Cambridge, MPhil Dissertation.

Claudia Leacock, Martin Chodorow, Michael Gamon, and Joel Tetreault. 2010. *Automated Grammatical Error Detection for Language Learners.* Morgan & Claypool Publishers.

John Lee and Stephanie Seneff. 2008. An analysis of grammatical errors in non-native speech in English. In *Proceedings of the 2008 Spoken Language Technology Workshop.*

Ryo Nagata and Kazuhide Nakatani. 2010 Evaluating performance of grammatical error detection to maximize learning effect. In *Proceedings of Int. Conf. on Computational Linguistics (Coling-10), Poster Session*, pages 894–900, Beijing, China.

Diane Nicholls. 2003. The Cambridge Learner Corpus: Error coding and analysis for lexicography and ELT. In *Proceedings of the Corpus Linguistics conference*, pages 572–581.

Jason Rennie, Lawrence Shih, Jaime Teevan, and David Karger. 2003 Tackling the Poor Assumtions of Naive Bayes Text Classifiers. 20th Int. Conference on Machine Learning (ICML-2003) Washington, DC

Alla Rozovskaya and Dan Roth. 2010a. Annotating ESL Errors: Challenges and Rewards. In *Proceedings of the NAACL Workshop on Innovative Use of NLP for Building Educational Applications.*

Alla Rozovskaya and Dan Roth. 2010b. Generating Confusion Sets for Context-Sensitive Error Correction. In *of the Conference on Empirical Methods in Natural Language Processing (EMNLP).*

Alla Rozovskaya and Dan Roth. 2010c. Training Paradigms for Correcting Errors in Grammar and Usage. In *Proceedings of the Annual Meeting of the North American Association of Computational Linguistics (NAACL).*

Alla Rozovskaya and Dan Roth. 2011. Algorithm Selection and Model Adaptation for ESL Correction Tasks. In *Proceedings of the Annual Meeting of the Association of Computational Linguistics (ACL).*

Joel R. Tetreault and Martin Chodorow. 2008. The ups and downs of preposition error detection in ESL writing. In *Proceedings of the 22nd International Conference on Computational Linguistics (Coling 2008)*, pages 865–872, Manchester, UK, August.

Joel R. Tetreault, Jennifer Foster, Martin Chodorow. 2010. Using Parse Features for Preposition Selection and Error Detection. In *ACL.*

Helen Yannakoudakis, Ted Briscoe, and Ben Medlock. 2011. A New Dataset and Method for Automatically Grading ESOL Texts. In *The 49th Annual Meeting of the Association for Computational Linguistics: Human Language Technologies.*

Korea University System in the HOO 2012 Shared Task

Jieun Lee[†] and **Jung-Tae Lee**[‡] and **Hae-Chang Rim**[†]
[†]Dept. of Computer & Radio Communications Engineering, Korea University, Seoul, Korea
[‡]Research Institute of Computer Information & Communication, Korea University, Seoul, Korea
{jelee,jtlee,rim}@nlp.korea.ac.kr

Abstract

In this paper, we describe the Korea University system that participated in the HOO 2012 Shared Task on the correction of preposition and determiner errors in non-native speaker texts. We focus our work on training the system on a large collection of error-tagged texts provided by the HOO 2012 Shared Task organizers and incrementally applying several methods to achieve better performance.

1 Introduction

In the literature, there have been efforts aimed at developing grammar correction systems designed especially for non-native English speakers. A typical approach is to train statistical models on well-formed texts written by native English speakers and apply the learned models to non-native speaker texts to correct textual errors based on given context. This approach, however, fails to model the types of errors that non-native speakers usually make. Recent studies demonstrate that it is possible to improve the performance of error correction systems by training the models on error-annotated non-native speaker texts (Han et al., 2010; Dahlmeier and Ng, 2011; Gamon, 2010). Most recently, a large collection of training data consisting of preposition and determiner errors made by non-native English speakers has been released in the HOO (Helping Our Own) 2012 Shared Task, which aims at promoting the research and development of automated tools for assisting authors in writing (Dale et al., 2012).

In this paper, we introduce our error correction system that participated in the HOO 2012 Shared Task, where the goal is to correct errors in the use of prepositions and determiners by non-native speakers of English. We mainly focus our efforts on training the system using the non-native speaker texts provided in the HOO 2012 Shared Task. We also share our experience in handling some issues that emerged while exclusively using the non-native speaker texts for training our system. In the following sections, we will describe the system in detail.

2 System Architecture

The goal of our system is to detect and correct preposition and determiner errors in a given text. Our system consists of two types of classifiers, namely *edit* and *insertion* classifiers. Inputs for the two types of classifiers are noun phrases (NP), verb phrases (VP), and prepositional phrases (PP); we initially pre-process the text given for training/testing by using the Illinois Chunker[1] and the Stanford Part-of-Speech Tagger (Toutanova et al., 2003). For learning the classifiers, we use maximum entropy models, which have been successfully applied to many tasks in natural language processing. We particularly use Le Zhang's Maximum Entropy Modeling Toolkit[2] for implementation.

2.1 Edit Classifiers

The role of an edit classifier is to check the source preposition/determiner word originally chosen by the author in a given text. If the source word is incorrect, the classifier replaces it with a better choice. For every preposition/determiner word,

[1]Available at http://cogcomp.cs.illinois.edu

[2]Available at http://homepages.inf.ed.ac.uk/lzhang10/

we train a classifier using examples that are observed in training data. The choice for prepositions is limited to eleven prepositions (*about, at, as, by, for, from, in, of, on , to, with*) that most frequently occur in the training data, and the candidates for determiner choice are *the* and *a/an*. In summary, we train a total of thirteen edit classifiers, one for each source preposition or determiner. For each edit classifier, the set of candidate outputs consists of the source preposition/determiner word itself, other confusable preposition/determiner words, and *no preposition/determiner* in case the source word should be deleted. Note that the number of confusable words for each source preposition is decided flexibly, depending on examples observed in the training data; a similar approach has been proposed earlier by Rozovskaya and Roth (2010a). For a particular source preposition/determiner word in the test data, the system decides whether to correct it or not based on the output of the classifier for that source word.

2.2 Insertion Classifier

Although the edit classifiers described above are capable of deciding whether a source preposition/determiner word that appears in the test data should be replaced or removed, a large proportion of common mistakes for non-native English writers consists of missing prepositions/determiners (i.e., leaving them out by mistake). To deal with those types of errors, we train a special classifier for insertions. A training or testing event for this particular classifier is any whitespace before or after a word in a noun or verb phrase that is a potential location for a preposition or determiner. Table 1 shows the five simple heuristic patterns based on part-of-speech tags that the system uses in order to locate potential sites for prepositions/determiners. Note that s is a whitespace to be examined, an asterisk (*) means wildcard, and *NN* includes the tags that start with NN, such as NNS, NNP, and NNPS. *VB* is also treated in the same manner as *NN*. The set of candidate outputs consists of the eleven prepositions, the two determiners, and *no preposition/determiner* class. Once a candidate position for insertion is detected in the test data, the system decides whether to make an insertion or not based on the output of the insertion classifier.

Pattern	Example
s+NN	I'll give you all **information**
s+*+NN	I need **few days**
s+VB	It may seem relaxing at **beginning**
s+*+VB	Buy **new colored** clothes
VB+s	I'm looking **forward** your reply

Table 1: Patterns of candidates for insertion

2.3 Features

Both edit and insertion classifiers can be trained using three types of features described below.

- **LEX/POS/HEAD** This feature set refers to the contextual features from a window of n tokens to the right and left that are practically used in error correction studies (Rozovskaya and Roth, 2010b; Han et al., 2010; Gamon, 2010). Such features include lexical features, part-of-speech tags, and head words of the preceding and the following chunks of the source word. In this work, we set n to be 3.

- **HAN** This represents the set of features specifically used in the work of Han et al. (2010); they demonstrate that a model trained on non-native speaker texts can outperform one trained solely on well-formed texts.

- **L1**[3] L1 refers to the first language of the author. There have been some efforts to leverage L1 information for improving error correction performance. For example, Rozovskaya and Roth (2011) propose an algorithm for adapting a learned model to the L1 of the author. There have been many studies leveraging writers' L1. In this work, we propose to directly utilize L1 information of the authors as features. We also leverage additional features by combining L1 and individual head words that govern or are governed by VP or NP.

3 Additional Methods for Improvement

The training data provided in the HOO 2012 Shared Task consists of exam scripts drawn from the publicly available FCE dataset (Yannakoudakis et al.,

[3]L1 information was provided in the training data but not in the test data. Therefore, the benefits of using L1 remain inconclusive in this paper.

a/an	the	*NULL*
6028	114	203

Table 2: Training data distribution for *a/an* classifier

about	as	at	by	for	from
0	3	2510	1	2	3
in	**of**	**on**	**to**	**with**	***NULL***
75	7	20	30	3	41

Table 3: Training data distribution for *at* classifier

2011) with textual errors annotated in HOO data format. From this data, we extract examples for training our classifiers. For example, let w be a source word that we specifically want our classifier to learn. Every use of w that appears in the training data may be an example that the classifier can learn from. However, it is revealed that for all w, there are always many more examples where w is used correctly than examples where w is replaced or removed. Table 2 and Table 3 respectively show the class distributions of all examples for source words *a/an* and *at* that are observable from the whole training data for training *a/an*- and *at*-specific classifiers. We can see that various classes among the training data are unevenly represented. When training data is highly skewed as shown in the two tables, constructing a useful classifier becomes a challenging task. We observed from our preliminary experiments that classifiers learned on highly unbalanced data hardly tend to correct the incorrect choices made by non-native speakers. Therefore, we investigate two simple ways to alleviate this problem.

3.1 Filtering Examples Less Likely to be Incorrect

As mentioned above, there are many more examples where the source preposition/determiner is used without any error. One straightforward way to adjust the training data distribution is to reduce the number of examples where the source word is less likely to be replaced or removed by using language model probabilities. If a language model learned on a very large collection of well-formed texts returns a very high language model probability for a source word surrounded by its context, it may be reasonable to assume that the source word is used correctly. Therefore we build a language model trained on the English Gigaword corpus by utilizing trigrams. Before providing examples to the classifiers for training or testing, we filter out those that have very high language model probabilities above a pre-defined threshold value.

Class	Initial Distribution	After Filtering	After Adding
about	0	0	528
as	3	3	275
at	2510	2367	2367
by	1	1	207
for	2	2	1159
from	3	3	550
in	75	75	1521
of	7	7	1454
on	20	20	541
to	30	30	2309
with	3	3	727
NULL	41	41	41

Table 4: Refined data distribution for *at* classifier

3.2 Adding Artificial Errors

Our second approach is to introduce more artificial examples to the training data, so that the class distribution of all training examples becomes more balanced. For example, if we aim at adding more training examples for *a/an* classifier, we would extract correct phrases such as "*the* different actor" from the training data and artificially convert it into "*a* different actor" so that an example of *a/an* being corrected to *the* is also provided to *a/an* classifier for training. When adding aritificial examples into the training data, we avoid the number of examples belonging to each class exceeding the number of cases where the source word is not replaced or removed. Table 4 demonstrates the results of both the filtering and adding approaches for training the *a/an* classifier.

4 Experiments

4.1 Runs

This section describes individual runs that we submitted to the HOO 2012 Shared Task organizers. Table 5 represents the setting of each run.

Runs	Models	Features	Filtering Threshold	Adding
Run0	LM	n/a	n/a	
Run1	ME	LEX/POS/HEAD	X	X
Run2	ME	HAN	X	X
Run3	ME	LEX/POS/HEAD	-2	X
Run4	ME	LEX/POS/HEAD	-2	O
Run5	ME	LEX/POS/HEAD, L1	-2	O
Run6	ME	LEX/POS/HEAD, L1, age	-2	O
Run7	ME	Insertion: POS/HEAD Other: LEX/POS/HEAD	X	X
Run8	ME	LEX/POS/HEAD	-3	X

Table 5: The explanation of each runs

- **Run0** This is a baseline run that represents the language model approach proposed by Gamon (2010). We train our language model on Gigaword corpus, utilizing trigrams with interpolation and Kneser-Ney discount smoothing.

- **Run1, 2** Run1 and 2 represent our system using the LEX/POS/HEAD feature sets and HAN feature sets respectively. Neither additional method described in Section 3 is applied.

- **Run3, 8** These runs represent our system using LEX/POS/HEAD features (Run1), where examples that are less likely to be incorrect are filtered out by consulting our language model. The threshold value is set to -2 and -3 for Runs 3 and 8 respectively.

- **Run4** This particular run is one where we introduce additional errors in order to make the class distribution of the training data for the classifiers more balanced. This step is incrementally applied in the setting of Run3.

- **Run5, 6** Run5 and 6 are when we consider L1 information and age respectively as additional features for training the classifiers. The basic setup is same as Run4.

- **Run7** This run represents our system with its insertion classifier trained using POS and HEAD features only. No LEX features are used.

Runs	Precision	Recall	F-score
Run0	1.45	15.45	2.65
Run1	1.35	10.82	2.39
Run2	1.23	11.48	2.22
Run3	1.33	10.6	2.36
Run4	1.19	11.26	2.15
Run5	1.02	10.38	1.87
Run6	0.99	9.93	1.79
Run7	1.16	11.26	2.1
Run8	1.46	11.04	2.58

Table 6: Correction before test data revisions

5 Results

Table 6 shows the correction scores of the individual runs that we originally submitted. Unfortunately, we should confess that we made a vital mistake while generating the runs from 1-8; the modules implemented for learning the insertion classifier had some bugs that we could not notice during the submission time. Because of this, our system was unable to handle MD and MT type errors properly. This is the reason why the performance figures of our runs are very low. For reference, we include Tables 7-10 that illustrate the performance of our individual runs that we calculated by ourselves using the test data and the evaluation tool provided by the organizers.

We can observe that Run3 outperforms Run1 and Run4 performs better than Run3, which demonstrates that our attempts to improve the system performance by adjusting training data for classifiers

Runs	Precision	Recall	F-score
Run1	42.67	7.06	12.12
Run2	49.28	7.51	13.03
Run3	47.62	6.62	11.63
Run4	45.45	7.73	13.21
Run5	33.82	10.15	15.62
Run6	8.68	18.54	11.82
Run7	33.33	10.82	16.33
Run8	50.0	7.28	12.72

Table 7: Recognition before test data revisions (system revised)

Runs	Precision	Recall	F-score
Run1	32.0	5.3	9.09
Run2	42.03	6.4	11.11
Run3	34.92	4.86	8.53
Run4	37.66	6.4	10.94
Run5	26.47	7.94	12.22
Run6	5.68	12.14	7.74
Run7	24.49	7.95	12.0
Run8	42.42	7.28	10.79

Table 8: Correction before test data revisions (system revised)

Runs	Precision	Recall	F-score
Run1	49.33	7.82	13.50
Run2	52.17	7.61	13.28
Run3	52.38	6.98	12.31
Run4	51.95	8.46	14.55
Run5	37.5	10.78	16.75
Run6	9.29	19.03	12.5
Run7	36.73	11.42	17.42
Run8	51.52	7.18	12.62

Table 9: Recognition after test data revisions (system revised)

Runs	Precision	Recall	F-score
Run1	34.67	5.5	9.49
Run2	42.02	6.13	10.7
Run3	36.51	4.86	8.58
Run4	38.96	6.34	10.91
Run5	29.42	8.45	13.13
Run6	6.40	13.11	8.61
Run7	25.85	8.03	12.26
Run8	42.42	5.92	10.39

Table 10: Correction after test data revisions (system revised)

help. Moreover, we can also see that L1 information helps when directly used for training features.

6 Conclusion

This was our first attempt to participate in a shared task that involves the automatic correction of grammatical errors made by non-native speakers of English. In this work, we tried to focus on investigating simple ways to improve the error correction system learned on non-native speaker texts. While we had made some critical mistakes on the submitted runs, we were able to observe that our method can potentially improve error correction systems.

Acknowledgments

We would like to thank Hyoung-Gyu Lee for his technical assistance.

References

Daniel Dahlmeier and Hwee Tou Ng. 2011. Grammatical error correction with alternating structure optimization. In *Proceedings of the 49th Annual Meeting of the Association for Computational Linguistics: Human Language Technologies - Volume 1*, ACL-HLT '11, pages 915–923, Portland, Oregon.

Robert Dale, Ilya Anisimoff, and George Narroway. 2012. Hoo 2012: A report on the preposition and determiner error correction shared task. In *Proceedings of the 7th Workshop on Innovative Use of NLP for Building Educational Applications*, HOO '12, Montreal, Canada.

Michael Gamon. 2010. Using mostly native data to correct errors in learners' writing: a meta-classifier approach. In *Human Language Technologies: Proceedings of the 2010 Annual Conference of the North American Chapter of the Association for Computational Linguistics*, NAACL-HLT '10, pages 163–171, Los Angeles, California.

Na-Rae Han, Joel Tetreault, Soo-Hwa Lee, and Jin-Young Ha. 2010. Using an error-annotated learner corpus to develop an esl/efl error correction system. In *Proceedings of the 7th International Conference on Language Resources and Evaluation*, LREC '10, pages 763–770, Malta.

Alla Rozovskaya and Dan Roth. 2010a. Generating confusion sets for context-sensitive error correction.

In *Proceedings of the 2010 Conference on Empirical Methods in Natural Language Processing*, EMNLP '10, pages 961–970, Cambridge, Massachusetts.

Alla Rozovskaya and Dan Roth. 2010b. Training paradigms for correcting errors in grammar and usage. In *Human Language Technologies: Proceedings of the 2010 Annual Conference of the North American Chapter of the Association for Computational Linguistics*, NAACL-HLT '10, pages 154–162, Los Angeles, California.

Alla Rozovskaya and Dan Roth. 2011. Algorithm selection and model adaptation for esl correction tasks. In *Proceedings of the 49th Annual Meeting of the Association for Computational Linguistics: Human Language Technologies - Volume 1*, ACL-HLT '11, pages 924–933, Portland, Oregon.

Kristina Toutanova, Dan Klein, Christopher D. Manning, and Yoram Singer. 2003. Feature-rich part-of-speech tagging with a cyclic dependency network. In *Proceedings of the 2003 Conference of the North American Chapter of the Association for Computational Linguistics on Human Language Technology - Volume 1*, NAACL '03, pages 173–180, Edmonton, Canada.

Helen Yannakoudakis, Ted Briscoe, and Ben Medlock. 2011. A new dataset and method for automatically grading esol texts. In *Proceedings of the 49th Annual Meeting of the Association for Computational Linguistics: Human Language Technologies - Volume 1*, ACL-HLT '11, pages 180–189, Portland, Oregon.

A Naive Bayes classifier for automatic correction of preposition and determiner errors in ESL text

Gerard Lynch, Erwan Moreau and Carl Vogel
Centre for Next Generation Localisation
Integrated Language Technology Group
School of Computer Science and Statistics
Trinity College Dublin, Ireland
gplynch,moreaue,vogel@scss.tcd.ie

Abstract

This is the report for the CNGL ILT team entry to the HOO 2012 shared task. A Naive-Bayes-based classifier was used in the task which involved error detection and correction in ESL exam scripts. The features we use include n-grams of words and POS tags together with features based on the external Google N-Grams corpus. Our system placed 11th out of 14 teams for the detection and recognition tasks and 11th out of 13 teams for the correction task based on F-score for both preposition and determiner errors.

1 Introduction

The HOO 2012 shared task seeks to apply computational methods to the correction of certain types of errors in non-native English texts. The previous year's task, (Dale and Kilgarriff, 2011), focused on a larger scale of errors and a corpus of academic articles. This year's task focuses on six error types in a corpus of non-native speaker text. The scope of the errors is as follows:[1]

Error Code	Description	Example
RT	Replace Preposition	*When I arrived at London*
MT	Missing preposition	*I gave it John*
UT	Unnecessary preposition	*I told to John that*
RD	Replace determiner	*Have the nice day*
MD	Missing determiner	*I have car*
UD	Unnecessary determiner	*There was a lot of the traffic*

Table 1: Error types for HOO 2012 Shared Task

In Section 2, we give a brief summary of the data for the shared task and in Section 3 we explain the individual steps in the system. Section 4 details the different configurations for each of the runs submitted and finally, Section 5 presents the results.

[1] http://correcttext.org/hoo2012/errortypes.html last verified, May 10, 2012

2 Training data

The training data for this shared task has been provided by Cambridge University Press and consists of scripts from students sitting the Cambridge ESOL First Certificate in English (FCE) exams. The topics of the texts are comparable as they have been drawn from two consecutive exam years. The data is provided in XML format and contains 1000 original exam scripts, together with a standoff file containing edits of the type described in Section 1 above, also in XML format. These edits consist of offset information, edit type information and before and after text for correction. The results for the shared task were presented in this format.

The test data consists of 100 exam scripts drawn from a new corpus of exam scripts.

Some extra metadata is present in the source files, including information about the student's mother tongue and the age-range of the student, however the mother tongue data is not present in the test set.

3 Approach

The approach we have chosen for this task involves the use of supervised machine-learning algorithms in a four-part classification task.

3.1 Overview of the system

The first part of the task involves *identification* of edits in the training data, perhaps the most challenging given the large imbalance of edits vs non-edits in the data.

The next step concerns *classification* of edits into the six types described above, and the final task involves *correction* of edits, replacing or adding prepositions and determiners, and possibly in some cases removal of same.

There is a fourth step involved which reassesses the classification and correction based on some simple heuristics, using POS tags of the head word of each instance. If the headword is not a preposition and the system has marked a replace preposition error at that position, this error will be removed from the system. Likewise when the headword is not a determiner and a replace determiner error has been marked. If the replacement suggested is the same as the original text (in some cases this occurs), the edit is also removed. Another case for removal in this fashion includes an error type involving a missing determiner error where the head word is neither a noun or an adjective. In some cases the system reported and corrected an error suggesting the same text as was originally there, i.e no change. These cases are also removed from the end result.

3.2 Classification

We utilise the freely available Weka machine learning toolkit (Hall et al., 2009), and the algorithm used for classification in each step is Naive Bayes.

3.2.1 Representing the data

We represent each word in the training data as a vector of features. There are 39 basic features used in the detection process, and 42 in the classification and training step. The first 7 features contain information which is not used for classification but is used to create the edit structures, such as start offset, end offset, native language, age group and source filename and part information. These features include the current word plus the four preceding and following words, POS and spell-checked versions of each, together with bigrams of the two following and two preceding words with spell-checked and POS versions for these. Information on speaker age and native language is also included although native language information is not present in the test set.

3.2.2 Additional processing

All tokens have been lower-cased and punctuation has been removed. POS information for each token has been added. The open-source POS tagger from the OpenNLP tools package (OpenNLP, 2012) has been used to this end. Spell correction facility has been provided using the basic spellchecker in the Lucene information retrieval API(Gospodnetic and Hatcher, 2005) and the top match string as provided by this spell correcting software is used in addition to each feature. The basic maximum entropy model for English is used for the POS tagger.

We had also planned to include features based on the Google Books n-gram corpus, (Michel et al., 2011) which is freely available on the web, but unfortunately did not get to include them in the version submitted due to errors which were found in the scripts for generating the features late in the process. Nevertheless, we describe these features in Section 3.3 and present some cross-validation results from the training data for the detection step in Section 5.1.

3.3 Google N-grams Features

3.3.1 Motivation

The Google Books N-Grams[2] is a collection of datasets which consist of all the sequences of words (*n-grams*) extracted from millions of books (Michel et al., 2011). The "English Million" dataset contains more more than 500 millions distinct n-grams[3], from size 1 to 5. for every n-gram, its frequency, page frequency (number of pages containing it) and book frequency (number of books containing it) are provided.

In this Shared Task, we aim to use the Google N-grams as a reference corpus to help detecting the errors in the input. The intuition is the following: if an error occurs, comparing the frequency of the input n-grams against the frequency of other possibilities in the Google N-grams data might provide useful indication on the location/type of the error. For example, given the input *"I had to go in a library"*, The Google N-grams contain only 36,716 occurrences of the trigram *"go in a"*, but 244,098 occurrences of *"go to a"*, which indicates that the latter is more likely.

[2] `http://books.google.com/ngrams/datasets`

[3] The least frequent n-grams were discarded.

However there are several difficulties in using such a dataset:

- *Technical limitations.* Extracting information from the dataset can take a lot of time because of the size of the data, thus the range of approaches is restricted by efficiency constraints.
- *Quality of the data.* The Google N-grams were extracted automatically using OCR, which means that the dataset can contain errors or unexpected data (for example, the English dataset contains a significant number of non-English words).

This is why the Google N-grams must be used cautiously, and only as an indication among others.

3.3.2 Method

Our goal is to add features extracted from the Google N-grams dataset to the features described above, and feed the supervised classification process with these. Before computing the features, a list L of "target expressions" is extracted from the training data, which contains all the words or sequences of words (determiners and prepositions) which occur in a correction. Then, given an input sentence $A_1 \ldots A_m$ and a position n in this sentence, two types of information are extracted from the Google data:

- Specific indications of whether an error exists at this position:
  1. No change: the frequency of the input sequence $A_{n-1}A_n$ and $A_{n-1}A_nA_{n+1}$;
  2. Unnecessary word(s): the frequency of the sequence $A_{n-1}A_{n+1}$ if $A \in L$;
  3. Missing word(s): the frequency of the sequence XA_n (resp. $A_{n-1}XA_n$ for trigrams) for any target expression $X \in L$;
  4. Replacement: if $A \in L$, the frequency of XA_{n+1} (resp. $A_{n-1}XA_{n+1}$ for trigrams) for any target expression $X \in L$;
- Generic indications taking the context into account: for length N from 1 to 5 in a window $A_{n-4} \ldots A_{n+4}$, 16 combinations are computed based only on the fact the n-grams appear in the Google data; for example, one of these combinations is the normalized sum for the 4 5-grams in this window of 0 or 1 (the n-gram occurs or does not).

Additionally, several variants are considered:

- bigrams or trigrams for "specific" features;
- binary values for "specific" features: 1 if the n-gram appears, 0 otherwise;
- keep only the "generic" features and the first three features.

4 Run configurations

Ten runs were submitted to the organisers based on different configurations. Modification of the data was carried out using both instance reduction and feature selection techniques. The system facilitated the use of different training data for each of the three main classification steps.

4.1 Least frequent words filter

Before classification, the data is preprocessed by replacing all the least frequent words with a default value (actually treated as missing values by the classifier). This is intended to help the classifier focus on the most relevant indications and to prevent over-specification of the classification model.

4.2 Instance reduction filters

4.2.1 POSTrigrams filter

The POS trigrams filter works as follows: during the training stage, the sequences of POS tags for the words *current-1.current.current+1* are extracted for each instance, together with its corresponding class. Every POS trigram is then associated with the following ratio:

$$\frac{\text{Frequency of true instances}}{\text{Frequency of false instances}}$$

Then, when predicting the class, the filter is applied before running the classifier: the sequences of trigrams are extracted for each instance, and are compared against the corresponding ratio observed during the training stage; the instance is filtered out if the ratio is lower than some threshold N%. In Table

Run	Detection	Classification	Correction
0	R1	Normal	Normal
1	R20	Normal	Normal
2	Full	F12	Normal
3	R10	Normal	Normal
4	R30	Normal	Normal
5	F12	F12	Normal
6	R4new	Normal	Normal
7	R4 + F12	F12	Normal
8	R4	Normal	Normal
9	R2	Normal	Normal

Table 2: Run configurations

2, the label RN refers to the percentage (N) used as cut-off in the experiments.

This filter is intended to reduce the impact of the fact that the classes are strongly unbalanced. It permits discarding a high number of false instances, while removing only a small number of true instances. However, as a side effect, it can cause the classifier to miss some clues which were in the discarded instances.

4.2.2 CurrentPlusOrMinusOne filter

The current plusorminus one filter works as follows: A list of all *current.current+1* word bigrams is made from the error instances in the training data, along with all *current-1.current* bigrams. The non-error instances in the training data are then filtered based on whether an instance contains an occurrence of any *current.current+1* or *current-1.current* bigram in the list.

4.3 Feature selection filters

4.3.1 F12

During preliminary experiments, selecting a subset of 12 features produced classification accuracy gains in the detection and classification steps of the process using ten-fold cross validation on the training set. These twelve features were: *current, current+1.current+2, current-1.current-2, currentSC, currentPOS, current-1, current-2, current+1, current+2, current+1SC,* and *current-1SC*. The SC postfix refers to the spell-corrected token, with POS referring to the part-of-speech tag. The F12 configuration filter removes all other features except these.

5 Results

Table 3 displays the results for both preposition and determiner errors which were obtained by the system on the preliminary test set before teams submitted their revisions. Table 4 refers to the results obtained by the system after the revised errors were removed/edited.

Task	Rank	Run	Precision	Recall	F-Score
Detection	11	9	5.33	25.61	8.82
Recognition	11	9	4.18	20.09	6.92
Correction	11	9	2.66	12.8	4.41

Table 3: Overall results on original data: TC

Task	Rank	Run	Precision	Recall	F-Score
Detection	11	8	6.56	26.0	10.48
Recognition	11	8	4.91	19.45	7.84
Correction	11	8	3.09	12.26	4.94

Table 4: Overall results on revised data: TC

5.1 Some detailed results (detection)

The results reported here were obtained on the training data only, using 5-fold cross-validation, and only for the detection task. We have studied various settings for the parameters; figure 1 shows a global overview of the performance depending on several parameters (we show only a few different values in order to keep the graph readable).

The results show that the Google features contribute positively to the performance, but only slightly: the F1 score is 0.6% better on average. This overview also hides the fact that some combinations of values work better together; for instance, contrary to the fact that not filtering the POS trigrams per-

Run3	Recall	Precision	F
Detection	9.05	7.42	8.15
Correction	4.19	3.44	3.78
Recognition	9.05	7.42	8.15
Run8	**Recall**	**Precision**	**F**
Detection	22.51	5.44	8.76
Correction	11.25	2.72	4.38
Recognition	22.51	5.44	8.76
Run9	**Recall**	**Precision**	**F**
Detection	25.61	5.33	8.82
Correction	12.80	2.66	4.41
Recognition	20.09	4.18	6.92

Table 5: Top results on original test data

Figure 1: Average F-score depending on several parameters.

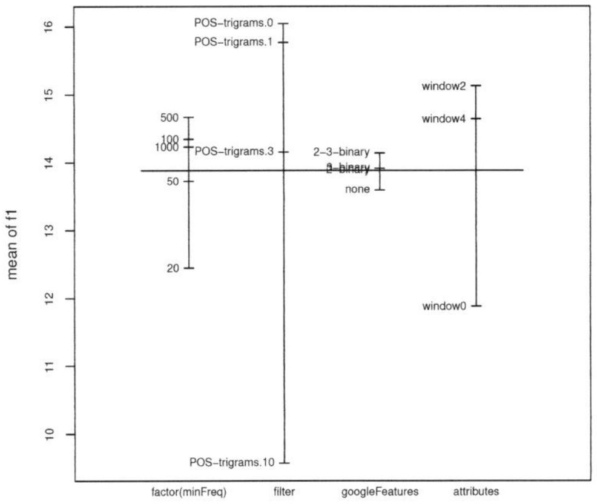

forms better on average, the best performances are obtained when filtering, as shown in figure 2.

Figure 2: F-score (%) w.r.t POS trigrams filter threshold. Parameters: window 2, Google features with bigrams and trigrams.

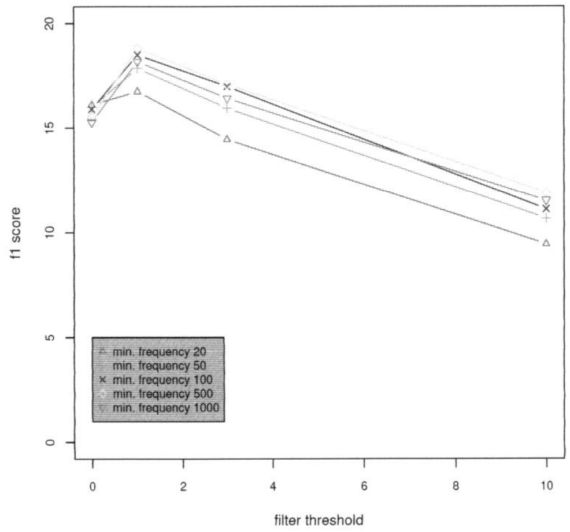

- *Minimum frequency*[4] (preprocessing, see 4.1). As shown in Figure 2, using a high threshold helps the classifier build a better model.

- *POS trigrams filter* (see 4.2.1.) Even if not filtering at all performs better on average, the best cases are obtained with a low threshold. Additionally, this parameter can be used to balance between recall and precision (when one wants to favor one or the other).

- *Size of the context window.* Results can show important differences depending on the size of the window, but no best configuration was found in general for this parameter.

- *Google features* (see 3.3.2.) The Google features help slightly in general, and are used in the best cases that we have obtained. However there is no significantly better approach between using the original frequencies, simplifying these to binary values, or even not using the list of target expressions.

6 Conclusions

The task of automated error correction is a difficult one, with the best-performing systems managing approx. 40 % F-score for the detection, recognition and correction (Dale et al., 2012). There are several areas where our system's performance might be improved. The spellcheck dictionary which was used

[4]Remark: the values used as "minimum frequencies" reported in this paper can seem unusually high. This is due to the fact that, for technical reasons, the thresholds were applied globally to the data after it had been formatted as individual instances, each instance containing a context window of 9 words. As a consequence a threshold of N means that a given word must occur at least N/9 times in the original input data.

was a general one and this resulted in many spelling corrections which were out of context. A more tailored dictionary employing contextual awareness information could be beneficial for the preprocessing step.

Multi-word corrections were not supported by the system due to how the instances were constructed and these cases were simply ignored, to the detriment of the results.

In the basic feature set, the majority of features were based on word unigrams, however more n-gram features could improve results as these were found to perform well during classification.

There were many different ways to exploit the Google N-Grams features and it may be the case that better combinations of features can be found for each of the classification steps.

Finally, very little time was spent tuning the datasets for the classification and correction step as opposed to the detection phase, this is another part of the system where fine-tuning parameters could improve performance.

Acknowledgments

This material is based upon works supported by the Science Foundation Ireland under Grant No.[SFI 07/CE/I 1142.].

References

Robert Dale and Adam Kilgarriff. 2011. Helping Our Own: The HOO 2011 pilot shared task. In *Proceedings of the 13th European Workshop on Natural Language Generation*, Dublin, Ireland.

Robert Dale, Ilya Anisimoff, and George Narroway. 2012. HOO 2012: A Report on the Preposition and Determiner Error Correction Shared Task. In *Proceedings of the Seventh Workshop on Innovative Use of NLP for Building Educational Applications*, Montreal, Canada.

O. Gospodnetic and E. Hatcher. 2005. *Lucene*. Manning.

M. Hall, E. Frank, G. Holmes, B. Pfahringer, P. Reutemann, and I.H. Witten. 2009. The WEKA data mining software: an update. *ACM SIGKDD Explorations Newsletter*, 11(1):10–18.

J.B. Michel, Y.K. Shen, A.P. Aiden, A. Veres, M.K. Gray, J.P. Pickett, D. Hoiberg, D. Clancy, P. Norvig, J. Orwant, et al. 2011. Quantitative analysis of culture using millions of digitized books. *Science*, 331(6014):176.

OpenNLP. 2012. Website: http://opennlp. apache. org.

KU Leuven at HOO-2012: A Hybrid Approach to Detection and Correction of Determiner and Preposition Errors in Non-native English Text

Li Quan, Oleksandr Kolomiyets, Marie-Francine Moens
Department of Computer Science
KU Leuven
Celestijnenlaan 200A
3001 Heverlee, Belgium
`li.quan@student.kuleuven.be`
`{oleksandr.kolomiyets, sien.moens}@cs.kuleuven.be`

Abstract

In this paper we describe the technical implementation of our system that participated in the Helping Our Own 2012 Shared Task (HOO-2012). The system employs a number of preprocessing steps and machine learning classifiers for correction of determiner and preposition errors in non-native English texts. We use maximum entropy classifiers trained on the provided HOO-2012 development data and a large high-quality English text collection. The system proposes a number of highly-probable corrections, which are evaluated by a language model and compared with the original text. A number of deterministic rules are used to increase the precision and recall of the system. Our system is ranked among the three best performing HOO-2012 systems with a precision of 31.15%, recall of 22.08% and F_1-score of 25.84% for correction of determiner and preposition errors combined.

1 Introduction

The Helping Our Own Challenge (Dale and Kilgarriff, 2010) is a shared task that was proposed to address automated error correction of non-native English texts. In particular, the Helping Our Own 2012 Shared Task (HOO-2012) (Dale et al., 2012) focuses on determiners and prepositions as they are well-known sources for errors produced by non-native English writers. For instance, Bitchener et al. (2005) reported error rates of respectively 20% and 29%.

Determiners are in particular challenging because they depend on a large discourse context and world knowledge, and moreover, they simply do not exist in many languages, such as Slavic and South-East Asian languages (Ghomeshi et al., 2009). The use of prepositions in English is idiomatic and thus very difficult for learners of English. On the one hand, prepositions connect noun phrases to other words in a sentence (e.g. ... *by bus*), on the other hand, they can also be part of phrasal verbs such as *carry on*, *hold on*, etc.

In this paper we describe our system implementation and results in HOO-2012. The paper is structured as follows. Section 2 gives the task definition, errors addressed, data resources and evaluation criteria and metrics. Section 3 shows some background and related work. Section 4 gives the full system description, while Section 5 reports and discusses the results of the experiments. Section 6 concludes with an error analysis and possible further improvements.

2 HOO-2012 Tasks and Resources

2.1 Tasks

In the scope of HOO-2012 the following six possible error types[1] are targeted:

- Replace determiner (RD):
  Have ***the*** *nice day.* → *Have* ***a*** *nice day.*
- Missing determiner (MD):
  That is great idea. → *That is* ***a*** *great idea.*
- Unnecessary determiner (UD):
  I like ***the*** *pop music.* → *I like pop music.*

[1] The set of error tags is based on the Cambridge University Press Error Coding System, fully described in (Nicholls, 2003).

- Replace preposition (RT):
  ***In** the other hand...* → ***On** the other hand...*

- Missing preposition (MT):
  She woke up 6 o'clock. → *She woke up **at** 6 o'clock.*

- Unnecessary preposition (UT):
  *He must go **to** home.* → *He must go home.*

2.2 Data

The HOO development dataset consists of 1000 exam scripts drawn from a subset of the CLC FCE Dataset (Yannakoudakis et al., 2011). This corpus contains texts written by students who attended the Cambridge ESOL First Certificate in English examination in 2000 and 2001. The entire development dataset comprises 374680 words, with an average of 375 words per file. The test data consists of a further 100 files provided by Cambridge University Press (CUP), with 18013 words, and an average of 180 words per file.

Type	# Dev	# Test A	# Test B
RD	609	38	37
MD	2230	125	131
UD	1048	53	62
Det	3887	217	230
RT	2618	136	148
MT	1104	57	56
UT	822	43	39
Prep	4545	236	243
Total	8432	453	473
Words/Error	44.18	39.77	38.08

Table 1: Data error statistics.

Counts of the different error types are provided in Table 1. The table shows counts for the development dataset ('Dev') and two versions of the gold standard test data: the original version as derived from the CUP-provided dataset ('Test A'), and a revised version ('Test B') which was compiled in response to requests for corrections from participating teams. The datasets and the revision process are further explained in (Dale et al., 2012).

2.3 Evaluation Criteria and Metrics

For evaluation in the HOO framework, a distinction is made between scores and measures. The complete evaluation mechanism is described in detail in (Dale and Narroway, 2012) and on the HOO-2012 website.[2]

Scores Three different scores are used:

1. Detection: does the system determine that an edit of the specified type is required at some point in the text?

2. Recognition: does the system correctly determine the extent of the source text that requires editing?

3. Correction: does the system offer a correction that is identical to that provided in the gold standard?

Measures For each score, three measures are calculated: precision (1), recall (2) and F-score (3).

$$precision = \frac{tp}{tp + fp} \tag{1}$$

$$recall = \frac{tp}{tp + fn} \tag{2}$$

where tp is the number of true positives (the number of instances that are correctly found by the system), fp the number of false positives (the number of instances that are incorrectly found), and fn the number of false negatives (missing results).

$$F_\beta = (1 + \beta^2)\frac{precision \cdot recall}{\beta^2 \cdot precision + recall} \tag{3}$$

where β is used as a weight factor regulating the trade-off between recall and precision. We use the balanced F-score, i.e. $\beta = 1$, such that recall and precision are equally weighted.

Combined We provide results on prepositions and determiners combined, and for each of these two subcategories separately. We also report on each of the different error types separately.

[2]See http://www.correcttext.org/hoo2012.

3 Related Work

HOO-2012 follows on from the HOO-2011 Shared Task Pilot Round (Dale and Kilgarriff, 2011). That task targeted a broader range of error types, and used a much smaller dataset.

Most work on models for determiner and preposition generation has been developed in the context of machine translation output (e.g. (Knight and Chander, 1994), (Minnen et al., 2000), (De Felice and Pulman, 2007) and (Toutanova and Suzuki, 2007)). Some of these methods depend on full parsing of text, which is not reliable in the context of noisy non-native English texts.

Only more recently, models for automated error detection and correction of non-native texts have been explicitly developed and studied. Most of these methods use large corpora of well-formed native English text to train statistical models, e.g. (Han et al., 2004), (Gamon et al., 2008) and (De Felice and Pulman, 2008). Yi et al. (2008) used web counts to determine correct article usage, while Han et al. (2010) trained a classifier solely on a large error-tagged learner corpus for preposition error correction.

4 System Description

4.1 Global System Workflow

The system utilizes a hybrid approach that combines statistical machine learning classifiers and a rule-based system. The global system architecture is presented in Figure 1. This section describes the global system workflow. The subsequent sections elaborate on the machine learning classifiers and heuristics implemented in the system.

The system workflow is divided in the following processing steps:

1. Text Preprocessing: The system performs a *preliminary text analysis* by automated spelling correction and subsequent syntactic analysis, such as tokenization and part-of-speech (POS) tagging.

2. Error Detection, Recognition and Correction: The system identifies if a correction is needed, and the type and extent of that correction. Two families of error correction tasks that separately address determiners and prepositions are performed in parallel.

3. Correction validation: Once a correction has been proposed, it is *validated* by a language model derived from a large corpus of high-quality English text.

4.1.1 Text Preprocessing

In HOO-2012, texts submitted for automated corrections are written by learners of English. Besides the error types that are addressed in HOO-2012, misspellings are another type of highly-frequent errors. For example, one student writes the following: *In my point of vue, Internet is the most important discover of the 2000 centery.*

When using automated natural language processing tools, incorrect spelling (and grammar) can introduce an additional bias. To reduce the bias propagated from the preprocessing steps, the text is first automatically corrected by the open-source spell checker GNU Aspell.[3]

At the next step, the text undergoes a shallow syntactic analysis that includes sentence boundary detection, tokenization, part-of-speech tagging, chunking, lemmatization, relation finding and prepositional phrase attachment. These tasks are performed by MBSP (De Smedt et al., 2010).[4]

4.1.2 Error Detection, Recognition and Correction

In general, the task of automated error correction is addressed by a number of subtasks of finding the position in text, recognizing the type of error, and the proposal for a correction. In our implementation we approach these tasks in a two-step approach as proposed in (Gamon et al., 2008). With two families of errors, the system therefore employs four classifiers in total.

For determiner error corrections, a classifier (C1 in Figure 1) first predicts whether a determiner is required in the observed context. If it is required, another classifier (C2 in Figure 1) estimates which one. The same approach is employed for the preposition error correction task (classifiers C3 and C4 in Figure 1). The details on how the classifiers were implemented are highlighted in Section 4.2.

[3] `http://aspell.net/`

[4] MBSP is a text analysis system based on the TiMBL and MBT memory based learning applications developed at CLiPS and ILK (Daelemans and van den Bosch, 2005).

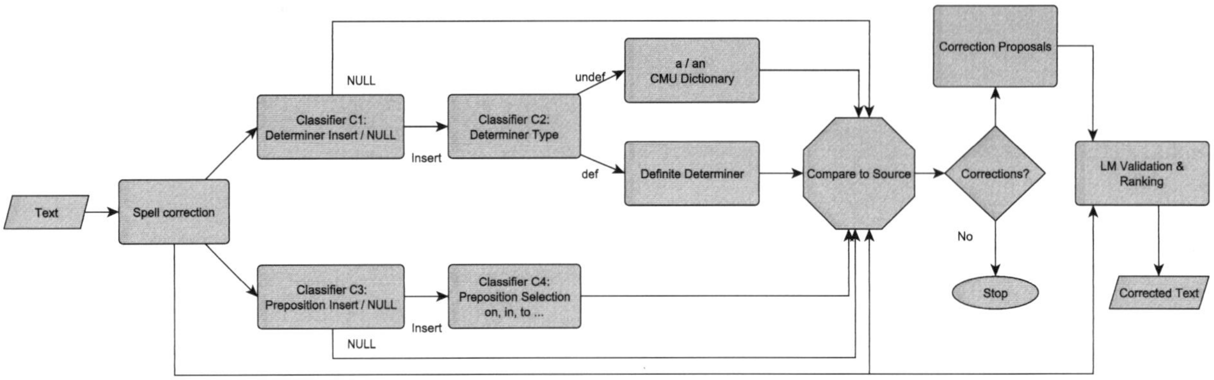

Figure 1: System architecture.

4.1.3 Correction Validation

Our error correction system implements a correction validation mechanism as proposed in (Gamon et al., 2008). The validation mechanism makes use of a language model that is derived from a large corpus of English. We use a trigram language model trained on the English Gigaword corpus with a 64K-word vocabulary (using interpolated Kneser-Ney smoothing with a bigram cutoff of 3 and trigram cutoff of 5).

The language model serves to increase the precision at the cost of recall as false positives can be confusing for learners for English. The original sentence and the error-corrected version are passed to the language model. Only if the difference in probability of being generated by the language model exceeds a heuristic threshold (estimated using a tuning set) is the correction finally accepted.

4.2 Machine Learning Classifiers

As already mentioned, the system employs four machine learning classifiers in total (C1–C4 — two for each family of errors). Classifiers C1 and C3 respectively estimate the presence of determiners and prepositions in the observed context. If one is expected, the second set of classifiers estimates which one is the most likely.

For the determiner choice classifier (C2), we restrict the determiner choice class values to the *indefinite* and *definite* articles: *a/an* and *the*. The preposition choice class values for the preposition choice classifier (C4) are restricted to set of the following 10 common prepositions: *on*, *in*, *at*, *for*, *of*, *about*, *from*, *to*, *by*, *with* and (*other*).

All the classifiers are implemented by discriminative maximum entropy classification models (ME) (Ratnaparkhi, 1998). Such models have been proven effective for a number of natural language processing tasks by combining heterogeneous forms of evidence (Ratnaparkhi, 2010).

Training Classifiers and Inference As training instances we consider each noun phrase (NP) in every sentence of the training data. For the binary classifiers (C1 and C3), a positive example is a noun phrase that follows a determiner/preposition, and a negative example is one that does not. The multiclass classifiers (C2 and C4) are trained respectively to distinguish specific instances of determiners (definite and indefinite for C2) and the set of prepositions mentioned above. For each classifier, a training instance is represented by the following features:

- Tokens in NP.
- Tokens' POS tags in NP.
- Tokens' lemmas in NP.
- Tokens in a contextual window of 3 tokens to the left and to the right from the potential correction position.
- Tokens' POS tags in a contextual window of 3 tokens from the potential correction position.
- Tokens' lemmas in a contextual window of 3 tokens from the potential correction position.
- Trigrams of concatenated tokens before and after NP.

- Trigrams of concatenated tokens' POS tags before and after NP.
- Trigrams of concatenated tokens' lemmas before and after NP.
- Head noun in NP.
- POS tag of head noun in NP.
- Lemma of head noun in NP.

Once the classification models have been derived, the classifiers are ready to be employed in the system. For the text correction task, each sentence undergoes the same preprocessing analysis as described in Section 4.1.1. Then, for each noun phrase in the input sentence, we extract the feature context, and use the models to predict the need for the presence of a determiner or preposition, and if so, which one. Our system only accepts classifier predictions if they are obtained with a high confidence. The confidence thresholds were empirically estimated from pre-evaluation experiments with a tuning dataset (Section 5.1).

4.3 Rule-based Modules

Our system also has a number of rule-based modules. The first rule-based module is in charge of making the choice between *a* and *an* if the determiner type classifier (C2) predicts the presence of an indefinite determiner. The choice is determined by a lookup in the CMU pronouncing dictionary[5] (*a/an* CMU Dictionary in Figure 1). In this dictionary each word entry is mapped to one or a number of pronunciations in the phonetic transcription code system Arpabet. If the pronunciation of the word that follows the estimated correction position starts with a consonant, *a* is used; if it starts with a vowel, *an* is selected.

The second rule-based module corrects confusion errors of determiner-noun agreement, e.g. *this/these* and *that/those* (Definite Determiner in Figure 1). It is implemented by introducing rules with patterns based on whether the noun was tagged as singular or plural.

The third rule-based module is used to filter out unnecessary corrections proposed by the classifiers (C1-C4) and augmented by the already described rule-based modules. Each correction is examined against the input text and if it yields a different text than the original input text, such a correction is considered as a necessary correction.

However, sometimes automatically proposed corrections have to be rejected because they are out of scope of the addressed errors. We do not replace possessive determiners such as *my*, *your*, *his*, *our*, *their* by the definite article *the*. Similarly, some prepositions can be grouped in opposite pairs, for example *from* and *to*, for which we do not propose any correction as it requires a deep semantic analysis of text.

[5] http://www.speech.cs.cmu.edu/cgi-bin/cmudict

5 Experiments and Results

In this section we describe the pre-evaluation experiments and the results of the final evaluation on the HOO-2012 test set. Table 2 shows the characteristics of the datasets used in the experiments.

Dataset	Sentences	Tokens
HOO training	21925	340693
HOO tuning	2560	40966
HOO held-out	2749	42325
Reuters	207083	5487021
Wikipedia	53370	1430428
HOO test	1376	20606

Table 2: Datasets used.

5.1 Pre-Evaluation Experiments

In the course of system development, we split the files in the HOO development dataset into a training set (80%), a tuning set (10%) and a held-out test set (10%). From the beginning it was clear that the provided development dataset alone was too small to address the automated error correction tasks by employing machine learning classification techniques. Additionally to that dataset, we used a set of Reuters news data and the Wikipedia corpus for training the classifiers.

Once the classification models had been derived, the system was evaluated on the tuning data and adjusted in order to increase the overall performance.

After that, the system was evaluated on the held-out test set for which the results are shown in Table 3.

Type	Precision	Recall	F_1-score
Det	64.11	14.89	24.17
Prep	52.32	16.38	25.32
All	60.19	15.38	24.50

Table 3: Correction results on held-out test set.

5.2 Final System Configuration and Evaluation Results

For the final evaluation, we retrained the models using the complete HOO development data (again, in addition to the Reuters and Wikipedia corpus mentioned above). The number of training instances are shown in Table 4.

Classifier	# Training instances
C1	1746128
C2	530885
C3	1763784
C4	706775

Table 4: Number of training instances used for the ME models.

In the HOO framework, precision and recall are weighted equally. However, in the domain of error correction for non-native writers, precision is probably more important because false positives can be very confusing and demotivating for learners of English. For this reason, we submitted two different runs which also gave us insights into the impact of the language model. 'Run 0' denotes the system excluding the language model and using lower thresholds, such that neither precision nor recall is favored in particular, while 'Run 1' focuses on precision by using the language model as a filter, and having higher thresholds. Thus, we present the results for two different runs on the final HOO test set, both before and after manual revision (see Section 2.2). Table 5 presents the results for recognition and Table 6 those for correction.

The difficulty of the HOO 2012 Shared Task is reflected by rather low system performance levels (Dale et al., 2012). Nonetheless, we observed some interesting patterns. In terms of the overall system performance, our system achieved better results for determiner errors than for preposition errors.

With respect to determiners, missing determiners are handled best by our system, while unnecessary determiners and replacement errors are more difficult. Concerning prepositions, missing prepositions are found to be the most challenging. This confirms the difficulty of choosing the right preposition due to the large number of possible alternatives, and their sometimes subtle differences in usage and meaning.

While 'Run 1' achieved a higher precision (at the cost of recall), 'Run 0' performed better in terms of overall performance (F_1-score). This result can be explained by the relative small size and limited tuning of the language model. Moreover, it also shows that the use of the F_1-score might not be the most informative evaluation metric in this context.

6 Conclusions

Determiners and prepositions present real challenges for non-native English writers. For automated determiner and preposition error correction in HOO-2012, we implemented a hybrid system that combines statistical machine learning classifiers and a rule-based system. By employing a language model for correction validation, the system achieved a precision of 42.16%, recall of 9.49% and F_1-score of 15.50%. Without the language model, a precision of 31.15%, recall of 22.08% and F_1-score of 25.84% were reached, and our system was ranked third in terms of F_1-score.

Three major bottlenecks were identified in the implementation: (i) spelling errors should first be corrected due to the noisy input texts; (ii) classifier thresholds must be carefully adjusted to minimize false positives; and (iii) overall, preposition errors are handled worse than determiner errors, although there is also a large difference among the various error types.

For future work, we will focus on models that explicitly utilize the writer's background. Also, a full evaluation of the system should include a thorough user-centric study with evaluation criteria and metrics beyond the traditional precision, recall and F-score.

Type	Precision	Recall	F_1-score
RD	17.95	17.95	17.95
MD	60.76	38.40	47.06
UD	22.67	32.08	26.56
Det	37.31	33.18	35.12
RT	55.88	13.97	22.35
MT	50.00	5.26	9.52
UT	14.77	30.23	19.85
Prep	27.34	14.83	19.23
All	33.33	23.62	27.65

(a) Run 0 (before revision)

Type	Precision	Recall	F_1-score
RD	19.44	17.95	18.67
MD	65.82	39.69	49.52
UD	26.67	32.26	29.20
Det	40.93	34.50	37.44
RT	61.76	14.09	22.95
MT	50.00	5.36	9.68
UT	15.91	35.90	22.05
Prep	29.69	15.57	20.43
All	29.47	24.74	29.47

(b) Run 0 (after revision).

Type	Precision	Recall	F_1-score
RD	37.50	7.69	12.77
MD	66.67	12.80	21.48
UD	16.67	1.89	3.39
Det	52.63	9.22	15.69
RT	51.61	11.76	19.16
MT	40.00	3.51	6.45
UT	32.14	20.93	25.35
Prep	42.19	11.44	18.00
All	46.08	10.38	16.94

(c) Run 1 (before revision).

Type	Precision	Recall	F_1-score
RD	37.50	8.33	13.64
MD	79.17	14.50	24.52
UD	33.33	3.23	5.88
Det	63.16	10.48	17.98
RT	54.84	11.41	18.89
MT	40.00	3.57	6.56
UT	35.71	25.64	29.85
Prep	45.31	11.89	18.83
All	51.96	11.21	18.43

(d) Run 1 (after revision).

Table 5: Recognition results of the runs on the test set.

Type	Precision	Recall	F_1-score
RD	17.95	17.95	17.95
MD	54.43	34.40	42.16
UD	22.67	32.08	26.56
Det	34.72	30.88	32.68
RT	50.00	12.50	20.00
MT	50.00	5.26	9.52
UT	14.77	30.23	19.85
Prep	25.78	13.98	18.13
All	31.15	22.08	25.84

(a) Run 0 (before revision)

Type	Precision	Recall	F_1-score
RD	17.95	19.44	18.67
MD	59.49	35.88	44.76
UD	26.67	32.26	29.20
Det	38.34	32.31	35.07
RT	55.88	12.75	20.77
MT	50.00	5.36	9.68
UT	15.91	35.90	22.05
Prep	28.13	14.81	19.41
All	34.27	23.26	27.71

(b) Run 0 (after revision).

Type	Precision	Recall	F_1-score
RD	37.50	7.69	12.77
MD	62.50	12.00	20.13
UD	16.67	1.89	3.39
Det	50.00	8.76	14.90
RT	41.94	9.56	15.57
MT	40.00	3.51	6.45
UT	32.14	20.93	25.35
Prep	37.50	10.17	16.00
All	42.16	9.49	15.50

(c) Run 1 (before revision).

Type	Precision	Recall	F_1-score
RD	37.50	8.33	13.64
MD	75.00	13.74	23.23
UD	33.33	3.23	5.88
Det	60.05	10.04	17.23
RT	45.16	9.40	15.56
MT	40.00	3.57	6.56
UT	35.71	25.64	29.85
Prep	40.63	10.66	16.88
All	48.04	10.36	17.04

(d) Run 1 (after revision).

Table 6: Correction results of the runs on the test set.

References

John Bitchener, Stuart Young, and Denise Cameron. 2005. The effect of different types of corrective feedback on ESL student writing. *Journal of Second Language Writing*, 14:191–205.

Walter Daelemans and Antal van den Bosch. 2005. *Memory-Based Language Processing*. Studies in Natural Language Processing. Cambridge University Press.

Robert Dale and Adam Kilgarriff. 2010. Helping Our Own: Text massaging for computational linguistics as a new shared task. In *Proceedings of the 6th International Natural Language Generation Conference*, pages 261–266, Dublin, Ireland, 7–9 July 2010.

Robert Dale and Adam Kilgarriff. 2011. Helping Our Own: The HOO 2011 pilot shared task. In *Proceedings of the 13th European Workshop on Natural Language Generation*, pages 242–249, Nancy, France, 28–30 September 2011.

Robert Dale and George Narroway. 2012. A framework for evaluating text correction. In *Proceedings of the Eight International Conference on Language Resources and Evaluation*, Istanbul, Turkey, 21–27 May 2012.

Robert Dale, Ilya Anisimoff, and George Narroway. 2012. HOO 2012: A report on the preposition and determiner error correction shared task. In *Proceedings of the Seventh Workshop on Innovative Use of NLP for Building Educational Applications*, Montreal, Canada, 3–8 June 2012.

Rachele De Felice and Stephen G. Pulman. 2007. Automatically acquiring models of preposition use. In *Proceedings of the Fourth ACL-SIGSEM Workshop on Prepositions*, pages 45–50, Prague, Czech Republic, 28 June 2007.

Rachele De Felice and Stephen G. Pulman. 2008. A classifier-based approach to preposition and determiner error correction in L2 English. In *Proceedings of the 22nd International Conference on Computational Linguistics*, pages 169–176, Manchester, United Kingdom, 18–22 August 2008.

Tom De Smedt, Vincent Van Asch, and Walter Daelemans. 2010. Memory-based shallow parser for Python. *CLiPS Technical Report Series (CTRS)*, 2.

Michael Gamon, Lucy Vanderwende, Jianfeng Gao, Chris Brockett, Alexandre Klementiev, William B. Dolan, and Dmitriy Belenko. 2008. Using contextual speller techniques and language modeling for ESL error correction. In *Proceedings of the International Joint Conference on Natural Language Processing*, pages 449–456, Hyderabad, India, 7–12 January 2008.

Jila Ghomeshi, Paul Ileana, and Martina Wiltschko. 2009. *Determiners: Universals and Variation*. Linguistik Aktuell/Linguistics Today. John Benjamins Publishing Company.

Na-Rae Han, Martin Chodorow, and Claudia Leacock. 2004. Detecting errors in English article usage with a maximum entropy classifier trained on a large, diverse corpus. In *Proceedings of the 4th International Conference on Language Resources and Evaluation*, Lisbon, Portugal, 26–28 May 2004.

Na-Rae Han, Joel Tetreault, Soo-Hwa Lee, and Jin-Young Ha. 2010. Using an error-annotated learner corpus to develop an ESL/EFL error correction system. In *Proceedings of the Seventh International Conference on Language Resources and Evaluation*, Valletta, Malta, 19–21 May 2010.

Kevin Knight and Ishwar Chander. 1994. Automatic postediting of documents. In *Proceedings of the 12th National Conference on Artificial Intelligence*, pages 779–784, Seattle, Washington, USA, 31 July–4 August 1994.

Guido Minnen, Francis Bond, and Ann Copestake. 2000. Memory-based learning for article generation. In *Proceedings of the 4th Conference on Computational Natural Language Learning and the Second Learning Language in Logic Workshop*, pages 43–48, Lisbon, Portugal, 13–14 September 2000.

Diane Nicholls. 2003. The Cambridge Learner Corpus—error coding and analysis for lexicography and ELT. In *Proceedings of the Corpus Linguistics 2003 Conference*, pages 572–581, Lancaster, UK, 29 March–2 April 2003.

Adwait Ratnaparkhi. 1998. *Maximum entropy models for natural language ambiguity resolution*. Ph.D. thesis, Philadelphia, PA, USA. AAI9840230.

Adwait Ratnaparkhi. 2010. Maximum entropy models for natural language processing. In *Encyclopedia of Machine Learning*, pages 647–651.

Kristina Toutanova and Hisami Suzuki. 2007. Generating case markers in machine translation. In *Human Language Technology Conference of the North American Chapter of the Association of Computational Linguistics*, pages 49–56, Rochester, New York, USA, 22–27 April 2007.

Helen Yannakoudakis, Ted Briscoe, and Ben Medlock. 2011. A new dataset and method for automatically grading ESOL texts. In *Proceedings of the 49th Annual Meeting of the Association for Computational Linguistics: Human Language Technologies*, pages 180–189, Portland, Oregon, USA, 19–24 June 2011.

Xing Yi, Jianfeng Gao, and William B. Dolan. 2008. A web-based English proofing system for English as a second language users. In *Proceedings of the Third International Join Conference on Natural Language Processing*, Hyderabad, India, 7–12 January 2008.

The UI System in the HOO 2012 Shared Task on Error Correction

Alla Rozovskaya **Mark Sammons** **Dan Roth**
Cognitive Computation Group
University of Illinois at Urbana-Champaign
Urbana, IL 61801
{rozovska,mssammon,danr}@illinois.edu

Abstract

We describe the University of Illinois (UI) system that participated in the Helping Our Own (HOO) 2012 shared task, which focuses on correcting preposition and determiner errors made by non-native English speakers. The task consisted of three metrics: Detection, Recognition, and Correction, and measured performance before and after additional revisions to the test data were made. Out of 14 teams that participated, our system scored first in Detection and Recognition and second in Correction before the revisions; and first in Detection and second in the other metrics after revisions. We describe our underlying approach, which relates to our previous work in this area, and propose an improvement to the earlier method, *error inflation*, which results in significant gains in performance.

1 Introduction

The task of correcting grammar and usage mistakes made by English as a Second Language (ESL) writers is difficult: many of these errors are context-sensitive mistakes that confuse valid English words and thus cannot be detected without considering the context around the word.

Below we show examples of two common ESL mistakes considered in this paper:

1. "Nowadays ∅*/*the* Internet makes us closer and closer."
2. "I can see *at**/*on* the list a lot of interesting sports."

In (1), the definite article is incorrectly omitted. In (2), the writer uses an incorrect preposition.

This paper describes the University of Illinois system that participated in the HOO 2012 shared task on error detection and correction in the use of prepositions and determiners (Dale et al., 2012). Fourteen teams took part in the the competition. The scoring included three metrics: Detection, Recognition, and Correction, and our team scored first or second in each metric (see Dale et al. (2012) for details).

The UI system consists of two components, a determiner classifier and a preposition classifier, with a common pre-processing step that corrects spelling mistakes. The determiner system builds on the ideas described in Rozovskaya and Roth (2010c). The preposition classifier uses a combined system, building on work described in Rozovskaya and Roth (2011) and Rozovskaya and Roth (2010b).

Both the determiner and the preposition systems apply the method proposed in our earlier work, which uses the error distribution of the learner data to generate artificial errors in training data. The original method was proposed for adding artificial errors when training on native English data. In this task, however, we apply this method when training on annotated ESL data. Furthermore, we introduce an improvement that is conceptually simple but very effective and which also proved to be successful in an earlier error correction shared task (Dale and Kilgarriff, 2011; Rozovskaya et al., 2011). We identify the unique characteristics of the error correction task and analyze the limitations of existing approaches to error correction that are due to these characteristics. Based on this analysis, we propose the *error inflation* method (Sect. 6.2).

In this paper, we first briefly discuss the task (Section 2) and present our overall approach (Section 3. Next, we describe the spelling correction module (Section 4). Section 5 provides an overview of the training approaches for error correction tasks. We present the inflation method in Section 6. Next, we describe the determiner error correction system (Section 7), and the preposition error correction module (Section 8). In Section 9, we present the performance results of our system in the competition. We conclude with a brief discussion (Section 10).

2 Task Description

The HOO 2012 shared task focuses on correcting determiner and preposition errors made by non-native speakers of English. These errors are some of the most common and also some of the most difficult for ESL learners (Leacock et al., 2010); even very advanced learners make these mistakes (Rozovskaya and Roth, 2010a).

The training data released by the task organizers comes from the publicly available FCE corpus (Yannakoudakis et al., 2011). The original FCE data set contains 1244 essays written by non-native English speakers and is corrected and error-tagged using a detailed error classification schema. The HOO training data contains 1000 of those files.[1] The test data for the task consists of an additional set of 100 student essays, different from the 1244 above.

Since the HOO task focuses on determiner and preposition mistakes, only annotations marking preposition and determiner mistakes were kept. Note that while the other error annotations were removed, the errors still remain in the HOO data. More details can be found in Dale et al. (2012).

3 System Overview

Our system consists of two components that address individually article[2] and preposition errors and use the same pre-processing.

[1]In addition, the participating teams were allowed to use for training the remaining 244 files of this corpus, as well as any other data. We also use a publicly available data set of native English, Google Web 1T corpus (Brants and Franz, 2006), in one of our models.

[2]We will use the terms 'article-' and 'determiner errors' interchangeably: article errors constitute the majority of determiner errors, and we address only article mistakes.

The first pre-processing step is correcting spelling errors. Since the essays were written by students of English as a Second language, and these essays were composed on-the-fly, they contain a large number of spelling errors. These errors add noise to the context around the target word (article or preposition). Good context is crucial for robust detection and correction of article and preposition mistakes.

After spelling errors are corrected, we run a sentence splitter, part-of-speech tagger[3] and shallow parser[4] (Punyakanok and Roth, 2001) on the data. Both the article and the preposition systems use features based on the output of these tools.

We made a 244-document subset of the FCE data a held-out set for development. The results in Sections 7 and 8 give performance on this held-out set, where we use the HOO data (1000 files) for training. The actual performance in the task (Section 9) reflects the system trained on the whole set of 1244 documents.

Our article and preposition modules build on the elements of the systems described in Rozovskaya and Roth (2010b), Rozovskaya and Roth (2010c) and Rozovskaya and Roth (2011). All article systems are trained using the Averaged Perceptron (AP) algorithm (Freund and Schapire, 1999), implemented within Learning Based Java (Rizzolo and Roth, 2010). Our preposition systems combine the AP algorithm with the Naïve Bayes (NB) classifier with prior parameters adapted to the learner data (see Section 5). The AP systems are trained using the *inflation* method (see Section 6.2).

We submitted 10 runs. All of our runs achieved comparable performance. Sections 7 and 8 describe our modules.

4 Correcting Spelling Errors

Analysis of the HOO data made clear the need for a variety of corrections beyond the immediate scope of the current evaluation. When a mistake occurs in the vicinity of a target (i.e. preposition or article) error, it may result in local cues that obscure the nature of the desired correction.

[3]`http://cogcomp.cs.illinois.edu/page/software_view/POS`

[4]`http://cogcomp.cs.illinois.edu/page/software_view/Chunker`

The following example illustrates such a problem: "*In my opinion your parents should be arrive in the first party of the month becouse we could be go in meeting with famous writer, travelled and journalist who wrote book about Ethiopia.*"

In this sample sentence, there are multiple errors in close proximity: the misspelled word *becouse*; the verb form *should be arrive*; the use of the word *party* instead of *part*; the verb *travelled* instead of a noun form; an incorrect preposition *in* (*in meeting*).

The context thus contains a considerable amount of noise that is likely to negatively affect system performance. To address some of these errors, we run a standard spell-checker over the data.

We use Jazzy[5], an open-source Java spell-checker. The distribution, however, comes only with a US English dictionary, which also has gaps in its coverage of the language. The FCE corpus prefers UK English spelling, so we use a mapping from US to UK English[6] to automatically correct the original dictionary. We also keep the converted US spelling, since our preposition module makes use of native English data, where the US spelling is prevalent.

The Jazzy API allows the client to query a word, and get a list of candidate corrections sorted in order of edit distance from the original term. We take the first suggestion and replace the original word. The resulting substitution may be incorrect, which may in turn mislead the downstream correction components. However, manual evaluation of the spelling corrections suggested about 80% were appropriate, and experimental evaluation on the corpus development set indicated a modest overall improvement when the spell-checked documents were used in place of the originals.

5 Training for Correction Tasks

The standard approach to correcting context-sensitive ESL mistakes follows the methodology of the *context-sensitive spelling correction* task that addresses such misspellings as *their* and *there* (Carlson et al., 2001; Golding and Roth, 1999; Golding and Roth, 1996; Carlson and Fette, 2007; Banko and Brill, 2001).

Following Rozovskaya and Roth (2010c), we distinguish between two training paradigms in ESL error correction, depending on whether the author's original word choice is used in training as a feature. In the standard *context-sensitive spelling correction* paradigm, the decision of the classifier depends only on the context around the author's word, e.g. article or preposition, and the author's word itself is not taken into consideration in training.

Mistakes made by non-native speakers obey certain regularities (Lee and Seneff, 2008; Rozovskaya and Roth, 2010a). Adding knowledge about *typical* errors to a model significantly improves its performance (Gamon, 2010; Rozovskaya and Roth, 2010c; Dahlmeier and Ng, 2011). *Typical* errors may refer both to speakers whose first language is L_1 and to specific authors. For example, non-native speakers whose first language does not have articles tend to make more articles errors in English (Rozovskaya and Roth, 2010a).

Since non-native speakers' mistakes are systematic, the author's word choice (the *source* word) carries a lot of information. Models that use the *source* word in training (Han et al., 2010; Gamon, 2010; Dahlmeier and Ng, 2011) learn which errors are typical for the learner and thus significantly outperform systems that only look at context. We call these models *adapted*. Training adapted models requires annotated data, since in native English data the source word is always correct and thus cannot be used by the classifier.

In this work, we use two methods of adapting a model to typical errors that have been proposed earlier. Both methods were originally developed for models trained on native English data: they use a small amount of annotated ESL data to generate error statistics. The **artificial errors** method is based on generating artificial errors[7] in correct native English training data. The method was implemented within the Averaged Perceptron (AP) algorithm (Rozovskaya and Roth, 2010c; Rozovskaya and Roth, 2010b), a discriminative learning algorithm, and this is the algorithm that we use in this work. The **NB-priors** method is a special adaptation technique for the Naïve Bayes algorithm (Rozovskaya and Roth, 2011). While **NB-priors** improves both precision

[5]http://jazzy.sourceforge.net/

[6]http://www.tysto.com/articles05/q1/20050324uk-us.shtml

[7]For each task, only relevant errors are generated – for example, article mistakes for the article correction task.

and recall, the **artificial errors** approach suffers from low recall due to error sparsity (Sec. 6.1).

In this work, in the preposition correction task, we use the **NB-priors** method without modifications (as described in the original paper). We use the **artificial errors** approach both for article and preposition error correction but with two important modifications: we train on annotated ESL data instead of native data, and use the proposed *error inflation* method (described in Section 6) to increase the error rate in training.

6 Error Inflation

In this section, we show why AP (Freund and Schapire, 1999), a discriminative classifier, is sensitive to the error sparsity of the data, and propose a method that addresses the problems raised by this sensitivity.

6.1 Error Sparsity and Low Recall

The low recall of the AP algorithm is related to the nature of the error correction tasks, which exhibit low error rates. Even for ESL writers, over 90% of their preposition and article usage is correct, which makes the errors very sparse (Rozovskaya and Roth, 2010c). The low recall problem is, in fact, a special case of a more general problem where there is one or a small group of dominant features that are very strongly correlated with the label. In this case, the system tends to predict the label that matches this feature, and tends to not predict it when that feature is absent. In error correction, which tends to have a very skewed label distribution, this results in very few errors being detected by the system: when training on annotated data with naturally occurring errors and using the source word as a feature, the system will learn that in the majority of cases the source word corresponds to the label, and will tend to over-predict it, which will result in low recall.

In the **artificial errors** approach, errors are simulated according to real observed mistakes. Table 1 shows a sample confusion matrix based on preposition mistakes in the FCE corpus; we show four rows, but the entire table contains 17 rows and columns, one for each preposition, and each entry shows $Prob(p_i|p_j)$, the probability that the author's preposition is p_i given that the correct preposition is p_j. The matrix also shows the preposition count for each source and label in the data set. Given the entire matrix and the counts, it is also possible to generate the matrix in the other direction and obtain $Prob(p_j|p_i)$, the probability that the correct preposition is p_j given that the author's preposition is p_i. This other matrix is used for adapting NB with the priors method.

The confusion matrix is sparse and shows that the distribution of alternatives for each source preposition is very different from that of the others. This strongly suggests that these errors are systematic. Additionally, most prepositions are used correctly, so the error rate is very low (the error rate can be estimated by looking at the matrix diagonal in the table; for example, the error rate for the preposition *about* is lower than for *into*, since 94.4% of the occurrences of label *about* are correct, but only 76.8% of label *into* are correct).

The artificial errors thus model the two properties that we mentioned: the confusability of different preposition pairs and the low error rate, and the artificial errors are similarly sparse.

6.2 The Error Inflation Method

Two extreme choices for solving the low recall problem due to error sparsity are: (1) training without the *source word* feature or (2) training with this feature, where the classifier relies on it too much. Models trained without the *source* feature have very poor precision. While the **NB-priors** method does have good recall, our expectation is that with the right approach, a discriminative classifier will also improve recall, but maintain higher precision as well.

We wish to reduce the confidence that the system has in the source word, while preserving the knowledge the model has about likely confusions and contexts of confused words. To accomplish this, we reduce the proportion of correct examples, i.e. examples where the *source* and the *label* are the same, by some positive constant < 1.0 and distribute the extra probability mass among the typical errors in an appropriate proportion by generating additional error examples. This inflates the proportion of artificial errors in the training data, and hence the error rate, while keeping the probability distribution among likely corrections the same. Increasing the error rate improves the recall, while the typical er-

Label	Sources												
	on (648)	about (700)	into (54)	with (733)	as (410)	at (880)	by (243)	for (1394)	from (515)	in (2213)	of (1954)	over (98)	to (1418)
on (598)	**0.846**	0.003	0.003	0.008	0.013	-	0.003	0.022	-	0.076	0.013	0.001	0.009
about (686)	0.004	**0.944**	-	0.007	-	-	-	0.022	0.005	0.002	0.016	0.001	-
into (55)	0.001	-	**0.768**	-	-	-	0.011	0.011	-	0.147	-	-	0.053
with (710)	0.001	0.006	-	**0.934**	-	0.001	0.007	0.004	0.001	0.027	0.003	-	0.015

Table 1: **Confusion matrix for preposition errors**. Based on data from the FCE corpus for top 17 most frequent English prepositions. The left column shows the correct preposition. Each row shows the author's preposition choices for that label and $Prob(source|label)$. The sources *among*, *between*, *under* and *within* are not shown for lack of space; they all have 0 probabilities in the matrix. The numbers next to the targets show the count of the label (or source) in the data set.

ror knowledge ensures that high precision is maintained. This method causes the classifier to rely on the *source* feature less and increases the contribution of the features based on context. The learning algorithm therefore finds a more optimal balance between the *source* feature and the context features.

Algorithm 1 shows the pseudo-code for generating training data; it takes as input training examples, the confusion matrix CM as shown in Table 1, and the inflation constant, and generates artificial source features for correct training examples.[8] An inflation constant value of 1.0 simulates learner mistakes without inflation. Table 2 shows the proportion of artificial errors created in training using the inflation method for different inflation rates.

Algorithm 1 Data Generation with Inflation

Input: Training examples E with correct sources, confusion matrix CM, inflation constant C
Output: Training examples E with artificial errors
for Example e in E **do**
  Initialize *lab* ← *e.label*, *e.source* ← *e.label*
  Randomize *targets* $\in CM[lab]$
  Initialize *flag* ← *False*
  for target *t* in *targets* **do**
    if flag equals True **then**
      Break
    end if
    if t equals lab **then**
      $Prob(t) = CM[lab][t] \cdot C$
    else
      $Prob(t) = \frac{1.0 - CM[lab][lab] \cdot C}{1.0 - CM[lab][lab]} \cdot CM[lab][t]$
    end if
    $x \leftarrow Random[0, 1]$
    if $x < Prob(t)$ **then**
      e.source ← *t*
      flag ← *True*
    end if
  end for
end for
return E

[8]When training on native English data, all examples are correct. When training on annotated learner data, some examples will contain naturally occurring mistakes.

Inflation rate					
1.0 (Regular)	0.9	0.8	0.7	0.6	0.5
7.7%	15.1%	22.6%	30.1%	37.5%	45.0%

Table 2: **Artificial errors**. Proportion of generated artificial preposition errors in training using the inflation method (based on the FCE corpus).

7 Determiners

Table 4 shows the distribution of determiner errors in the HOO training set. Even though the majority of determiner errors involve article mistakes, 14% of errors are personal and possessive pronouns.[9] Most of the determiner errors involve omitting an article. Similar error patterns have been observed in other ESL corpora (Rozovskaya and Roth, 2010a).

Our system focuses on article errors. Because the majority of determiner errors are omissions, it is very important to target this subset of mistakes. One approach would be to consider every space as a possible article insertion point. However, this method will likely produce a lot of noise. The standard approach is to consider noun-phrase-initial contexts (Han et al., 2006; Rozovskaya and Roth, 2010c).

Error type	Example
Repl. 15.7%	"Can you send me *the*/a* letter back writing what happened to you recently."
Omis. 57.5%	"Nowadays *∅*/the* Internet makes us closer and closer."
Unnec. 26.8%	"One of my hobbies is *the*/∅* photography."

Table 4: **Distribution of determiner errors in the HOO training data.**

[9]e.g. "Pat apologized to me for not keeping *the*/my* secrets."

Feature Type	Description
Word n-grams	wB, w_2B, w_3B, wA, w_2A, w_3A, $wBwA$, w_2BwB, wAw_2A, w_3Bw_2BwB, w_2BwBwA, $wBwAw_2A$, wAw_2Aw_3A, $w_4Bw_3Bw_2BwB$, w_3w_2BwBwA, $w_2BwBwAw_2A$, $wBwAw_2Aw_3A$, $wAw_2Aw_3w_4A$
POS features	pB, p_2B, p_3B , pA, p_2A, p_3A, $pBpA$, p_2BpB, pAp_2A, $pBwB$, $pAwA$, p_2Bw_2B, p_2Aw_2A, p_2BpBpA, $pBpAp_2A$, pAp_2Ap_3A
NP_1	*headWord*, *npWords*, *NC*, *adj&headWord*, *adjTag&headWord*, *adj&NC*, *adjTag&NC*, *npTags&headWord*, *npTags&NC*
NP_2	*headWord&headPOS*, *headNumber*
wordsAfterNP	*headWord&wordAfterNP*, *npWords&wordAfterNP*, *headWord&2wordsAfterNP*, *npWords&2wordsAfterNP*, *headWord&3wordsAfterNP*, *npWords&3wordsAfterNP*
wordBeforeNP	$wB\&f_i\ \forall i \in NP_1$
Verb	*verb*, $verb\&f_i\ \forall i \in NP_1$
Preposition	$prep\&f_i\ \forall i \in NP_1$

Table 3: **Features used in the article error correction system.** wB and wA denote the word immediately before and after the target, respectively; and pB and pA denote the POS tag before and after the target. *headWord* denotes the head of the NP complement. NC stands for noun compound and is active if second to last word in the NP is tagged as a noun. *Verb* features are active if the NP is the direct object of a verb. *Preposition* features are active if the NP is immediately preceded by a preposition. *adj* feature is active if the first word (or the second word preceded by an adverb) in the NP is an adjective. *npWords* and *npTags* denote all words (POS tags) in the NP.

7.1 Determiner Features

The features are presented in Table 3. The model also uses the *source* article as a feature.

7.2 Training the Determiner System

Model	Detection	Correction
AP (natural errors)	30.75	28.97
AP (inflation)	**34.62**	**32.02**

Table 5: **Article development results: AP with inflation.** The performance shows the F-Score for the 244 held-out documents of the original FCE data set. AP with inflation uses the constant value of 0.8.

The article classifier is based on the artificial errors approach (Rozovskaya and Roth, 2010c). The original method trains a system on native English data. The current setting is different, since the FCE corpus contains annotated learner errors. Since the errors are sparse, we use the *error inflation* method (Section 6.2) to boost the proportion of errors in training using the error distribution obtained from the same training set. The effectiveness of this method is demonstrated by the system performance: we obtain the top or second result in every metric. Note also that the article system does not use additional data for training.

Table 5 compares the performance of the system trained on natural errors with the performance of the system trained with the inflation method. We found that any value of the inflation constant between 0.9 and 0.5 will give a boost in performance. We use several values; the top determiner model uses the inflation constant of 0.8.

8 Prepositions

Table 6 shows the distribution of the three types of preposition errors in the HOO training data. The FCE annotation distinguishes between preposition mistakes and errors involving the infinitive marker *to*, e.g. *"He wants ∅*/to go there."*, which are annotated as verb errors. Since in the competition only article and preposition annotations are kept, these errors are not annotated, and thus we do not target these mistakes.

Error type	Example
Repl. 57.9%	"I can see *at*/on* the list a lot of interesting sports."
Omis. 24.0%	"I will be waiting ∅**/for* your call."
Unnec. 18.1%	"Despite *of**/∅ being tiring , it was rewarding"

Table 6: **Distribution of preposition errors in the HOO training data.**

To detect missing preposition errors, we use a set of rules, mined from the training data, to identify possible locations where a preposition might have been incorrectly omitted. Below we show examples of such contexts.

- "I will be waiting ∅**/for* your call."
- "But now we use planes to go ∅**/to* far places."

8.1 Preposition Features

All features used in the preposition module are lexical: word n-grams in the 4-word window around

Feature Type	Description
Word n-ngram features in the 4-word window around the target	wB, w_2B, w_3B , wA, w_2A, w_3A, $wBwA$, w_2BwB, wAw_2A, w_3Bw_2BwB, w_2BwBwA, $wBwAw_2A$, wAw_2Aw_3A, $w_4Bw_3Bw_2BwB$, w_3w_2BwBwA, $w_2BwBwAw_2A$, $wBwAw_2Aw_3A$, $wAw_2Aw_3w_4A$
Preposition complement features	*compHead*, *wB&compHead*, w_2BwB*&compHead*

Table 7: **Features used in the preposition error correction system.** wB and wA denote the word immediately before and after the target, respectively; the other features are defined similarly. *compHead* denotes the head of the preposition complement. *wB&compHead*, w_2BwB*&compHead* are feature conjunctions of *compHead* with wB and w_2BwB, respectively.

the target preposition, and three features that use the head of the preposition complement (see Table 7). The NB-priors classifier, which is part of our model, can only make use of the word n-gram features; it uses n-gram features of lengths 3, 4, and 5. AP is trained on the HOO data and uses n-grams of lengths 2, 3, and 4, the head complement features, and the author's preposition as a feature.

Model	Detection	Correction
AP (inflation)	34.64	27.51
NB-priors	38.76	26.57
Combined	**41.27**	**29.35**

Table 8: **Preposition development results: performance of individual and combined systems.** The performance shows the F-Score for the 244 held-out documents of the original FCE data set.

8.2 Training the Preposition System

We train two systems. The first one is an AP model trained on the FCE data with *inflation* (similar to the article system). Correcting preposition errors requires more data to achieve performance comparable to article error correction, due to the task complexity (Gamon, 2010). Moreover, given that the development and test data are quite different,[10] it makes sense to use a model that is independent of those, to avoid overfitting. We combine the AP model with a model trained on native English data. Our second system is an NB-priors classifier trained on the the Google Web 1T 5-gram corpus (Brants and Franz, 2006). We use training data to replace the prior parameters of the model (see Rozovskaya and Roth, 2011 for more detail). The NB-priors model does not target preposition omissions.

[10]The data contains essays written on prompts, so that the training data may contain several essays written on the same prompt and thus will be very similar in content. In contrast, we expected that the test data will likely contain essays on a different set of prompts.

The NB-priors model outperforms the AP classifier. The two models are also very different due to the different learning algorithms and the type of the data used in training. Our final preposition model is thus a combination of these two, where we take as the base the decisions of the NB-priors classifier and add the AP model predictions for cases when the base model does not flag a mistake. Table 8 shows the results. The combined model improves both the detection and correction scores. Our preposition system ranked first in detection and recognition and second in correction.

Model	Detection	Correction
AP (natural errors)	13.50	12.73
AP (inflation)	**21.31**	**32.02**

Table 9: **Preposition development results: AP with inflation.** The performance shows the F-Score for the 244 held-out documents of the original FCE data set. AP with inflation uses the constant value of 0.7.

9 Test Performance

A number of revisions were made to the test data based on the input from the participating teams after the initial results were obtained, where each team submitted proposed edits to correct annotation mistakes. We show both results.

Table 10 shows results before the revisions were made. Row 1 shows the performance of the determiner system for the three metrics. This system achieved the best score in correction, and the second best scores in detection and recognition. The system is described in Section 7.2, with the exception that the final system for the article correction is trained on the entire FCE data set.

Table 10 (row 2) presents the results on preposition error correction. The system is described in Section 8.2 and is a combined model of AP trained with inflation on the FCE data set and NB-priors model trained on the Google Web 1T corpus. The

Model	Detection			Recognition			Correction		
	Precision	Recall	F-Score	Precision	Recall	F-Score	Precision	Recall	F-Score
Articles	40.00	37.79	38.86[2]	38.05	35.94	36.97[2]	35.61	33.64	34.60[1]
Prepositions	38.21	45.34	41.47[1]	31.05	40.25	35.06[1]	20.36	24.15	22.09[2]
Combined	37.22	43.71	40.20[1]	34.23	36.64	35.39[1]	26.39	28.26	27.29[2]

Table 10: **Performance on test before revisions.** Results are shown before revisions were made to the data. The rank of the system is shown as a superscript.

Model	Detection			Recognition			Correction		
	Precision	Recall	F-Score	Precision	Recall	F-Score	Precision	Recall	F-Score
Articles	43.90	39.30	41.47[2]	45.98	34.93	39.70[2]	41.46	37.12	39.17[2]
Prepositions	41.43	47.54	44.27[1]	37.14	42.62	39.69[1]	26.79	30.74	28.63[2]
Combined	43.56	42.92	43.24[1]	38.97	39.96	39.46[2]	32.58	33.40	32.99[2]

Table 11: **Performance on test after revisions.** Results are shown after revisions were made to the data. The rank of the system is shown as a superscript.

preposition system achieved the best scores in detection and recognition, scoring second in correction.

Row 3 shows the performance of the combined system. This system was ranked first in detection and recognition, and second in correction.

Table 11 shows our performance after the revisions were applied.

10 Discussion

The HOO 2012 shared task follows the HOO 2011 pilot shared task (Dale and Kilgarriff, 2011), where the data was fully corrected and error-tagged and the participants could address any types of mistakes. The current task allows for comparison of individual systems for each error type considered. This is important, since to date it has been difficult to compare different systems due to the lack of a benchmark data set.

The data used for the shared task has many errors besides the preposition and determiner errors; the annotations for these have been removed. One undesirable consequence of this approach is that some complex errors that involve either an article or a preposition mistake but depend on other corrections on neighboring words, e.g. a noun of a verb, may result in ungrammatical sequences.

Clearly, the task of annotating all requisite corrections is a daunting task, and it is preferable to identify subsets of these corrections that can be tackled somewhat independently of the rest, and these more complex cases present a problem.

To address these conflicting needs, we propose that the scope of all "final" corrections be marked, without necessarily specifying all individual corrections necessary to transform the original text into correct English. Edits that plausibly require corrections to their context to resolve correctly could then be treated as *out of scope*, and ignored by spelling correction systems even though in other contexts, those same edits would be *in* scope.

11 Conclusion

We have demonstrated how a competitive system for preposition and determiner error correction can be built using techniques that address the error sparsity of the data and the overfitting problem. We built on our previous work and presented the error inflation method that can be applied to the earlier proposed artificial errors approach to boost recall. Our determiner system used error inflation and trained a model using only the annotated FCE corpus. Our preposition system combined the FCE-trained system with a native-data model that was adapted to learner errors, using the NB-priors approach proposed earlier. Both of the systems showed competitive performance, scoring first or second in every task ranking.

Acknowledgments

The authors thank Jeff Pasternack for his assistance and Vivek Srikumar for helpful feedback. This research is supported by a grant from the U.S. Department of Education and is partly supported by the Defense Advanced Research Projects Agency (DARPA) Machine Reading Program under Air Force Research Laboratory (AFRL) prime contract no. FA8750-09-C-018.

References

M. Banko and E. Brill. 2001. Scaling to very very large corpora for natural language disambiguation. In *Proc.*

of 39th Annual Meeting of the Association for Computational Linguistics (ACL), pages 26–33, Toulouse, France, July.

T. Brants and A. Franz. 2006. *Web 1T 5-gram Version 1*. Linguistic Data Consortium, Philadelphia, PA.

A. Carlson and I. Fette. 2007. Memory-based context-sensitive spelling correction at web scale. In *Proc. of the IEEE International Conference on Machine Learning and Applications (ICMLA)*.

A. Carlson, J. Rosen, and D. Roth. 2001. Scaling up context sensitive text correction. In *Proceedings of the National Conference on Innovative Applications of Artificial Intelligence (IAAI)*, pages 45–50.

D. Dahlmeier and H. T. Ng. 2011. Grammatical error correction with alternating structure optimization. In *Proc. of the 49th Annual Meeting of the Association for Computational Linguistics: Human Language Technologies (ACL)*, pages 915–923, Portland, Oregon, USA, June. Association for Computational Linguistics.

R. Dale and A. Kilgarriff. 2011. Helping Our Own: The HOO 2011 pilot shared task. In *Proc. of the 13th European Workshop on Natural Language Generation (ENLG)*, pages 242–249, Nancy, France.

R. Dale, I. Anisimoff, and G. Narroway. 2012. A report on the preposition and determiner error correction shared task. In *Proc. of the NAACL HLT 2012 Seventh WorkshopWorkshop on Innovative Use of NLP for Building Educational Applications*, Montreal, Canada, June. Association for Computational Linguistics.

Y. Freund and R. E. Schapire. 1999. Large margin classification using the perceptron algorithm. *Machine Learning*, 37(3):277–296.

M. Gamon. 2010. Using mostly native data to correct errors in learners' writing. In *Proc. of the 2010 Annual Conference of the North American Chapter of the Association for Computational Linguistics: Human Language Technologies (NAACL)*, pages 163–171, Los Angeles, California, June.

A. R. Golding and D. Roth. 1996. Applying Winnow to context-sensitive spelling correction. In *Proc. of the International Conference on Machine Learning (ICML)*, pages 182–190.

A. R. Golding and D. Roth. 1999. A Winnow based approach to context-sensitive spelling correction. *Machine Learning*, 34(1-3):107–130.

N. Han, M. Chodorow, and C. Leacock. 2006. Detecting errors in English article usage by non-native speakers. *Journal of Natural Language Engineering*, 12(2):115–129.

N. Han, J. Tetreault, S. Lee, and J. Ha. 2010. Using an error-annotated learner corpus to develop and ESL/EFL error correction system. In *Proc. of the Seventh conference on International Language Resources and Evaluation (LREC)*, Valletta, Malta, May. European Language Resources Association (ELRA).

C. Leacock, M. Chodorow, M. Gamon, and J. Tetreault. 2010. *Automated Grammatical Error Detection for Language Learners*. Morgan and Claypool Publishers.

J. Lee and S. Seneff. 2008. An analysis of grammatical errors in non-native speech in English. In *Proc. of the 2008 Spoken Language Technology Workshop*, Goa.

V. Punyakanok and D. Roth. 2001. The use of classifiers in sequential inference. In *The Conference on Advances in Neural Information Processing Systems (NIPS)*, pages 995–1001. MIT Press.

N. Rizzolo and D. Roth. 2010. Learning based java for rapid development of nlp systems. In *Proceedings of the International Conference on Language Resources and Evaluation (LREC)*, Valletta, Malta, 5.

A. Rozovskaya and D. Roth. 2010a. Annotating ESL errors: Challenges and rewards. In *Proc. of the NAACL HLT 2010 Fifth Workshop on Innovative Use of NLP for Building Educational Applications*, pages 28–36, Los Angeles, California, June. Association for Computational Linguistics.

A. Rozovskaya and D. Roth. 2010b. Generating confusion sets for context-sensitive error correction. In *Proceedings of the 2010 Conference on Empirical Methods in Natural Language Processing (EMNLP)*, pages 961–970, Cambridge, MA, October. Association for Computational Linguistics.

A. Rozovskaya and D. Roth. 2010c. Training paradigms for correcting errors in grammar and usage. In *Proc. of the Annual Conference of the North American Chapter of the Association for Computational Linguistics: Human Language Technologies (NAACL)*, pages 154–162, Los Angeles, California, June. Association for Computational Linguistics.

A. Rozovskaya and D. Roth. 2011. Algorithm selection and model adaptation for ESL correction tasks. In *Proc. of the 49th Annual Meeting of the Association for Computational Linguistics: Human Language Technologies (ACL)*, pages 924–933, Portland, Oregon, USA, June. Association for Computational Linguistics.

A. Rozovskaya, M. Sammons, J. Gioja, and D. Roth. 2011. University of Illinois system in HOO text correction shared task. In *Proc. of the 13th European Workshop on Natural Language Generation (ENLG)*.

H. Yannakoudakis, T. Briscoe, and B. Medlock. 2011. A new dataset and method for automatically grading esol texts. In *Proc. of the 49th Annual Meeting of the Association for Computational Linguistics (ACL)*, pages 180–189, Portland, Oregon, USA, June. Association for Computational Linguistics.

NAIST at the HOO 2012 Shared Task

Keisuke Sakaguchi, Yuta Hayashibe, Shuhei Kondo, Lis Kanashiro
Tomoya Mizumoto, Mamoru Komachi, Yuji Matsumoto
Graduate School of Information Science
Nara Institute of Science and Technology
8916-5, Takayama, Ikoma, Nara 630-0192, Japan
{ keisuke-sa, yuta-h, shuhei-k, lis-k, tomoya-m, komachi, matsu }@is.naist.jp

Abstract

This paper describes the Nara Institute of Science and Technology (NAIST) error correction system in the Helping Our Own (HOO) 2012 Shared Task. Our system targets preposition and determiner errors with spelling correction as a pre-processing step. The result shows that spelling correction improves the Detection, Correction, and Recognition F-scores for preposition errors. With regard to preposition error correction, F-scores were not improved when using the training set with correction of all but preposition errors. As for determiner error correction, there was an improvement when the constituent parser was trained with a concatenation of treebank and modified treebank where all the articles appearing as the first word of an NP were removed. Our system ranked third in preposition and fourth in determiner error corrections.

1 Introduction

Researchers in natural language processing have focused recently on automatic grammatical error detection and correction for English as a Second Language (ESL) learners' writing. There have been a lot of papers on these challenging tasks, and remarkably, an independent session for grammatical error correction took place in the ACL-2011.

The Helping Our Own (HOO) shared task (Dale and Kilgarriff, 2010) is proposed for improving the quality of ESL learners' writing, and a pilot run with six teams was held in 2011.

The HOO 2012 shared task focuses on the correction of preposition and determiner errors. There has been a lot of work on correcting preposition and determiner errors, where discriminative models such as Maximum Entropy and Averaged Perceptron (De Felice and Pulman, 2008; Rozovskaya and Roth, 2011) and/or probablistic language models (Gamon, 2010) are generally used.

In addition, it is pointed out that spelling and punctuation errors often disturb grammatical error correction. In fact, some teams reported in the HOO 2011 that they corrected spelling and punctuation errors before correcting grammatical errors (Dahlmeier et al., 2011).

Our strategy for HOO 2012 follows the above procedure. In other words, we correct spelling errors at the beginning, and then train classifiers for correcting preposition and determiner errors. The result shows our system achieved 24.42% (third-ranked) in F-score for preposition error correction, 29.81% (fourth-ranked) for determiners, and 27.12% (fourth-ranked) for their combined.

In this report, we describe our system architecture and the experimental results. Sections 2 to 4 describe the system for correcting spelling, preposition, and determiner errors. Section 5 shows the experimental design and results.

2 System Architecture for Spelling Correction

Spelling errors in second language learners' writing often disturb part-of-speech (POS) tagging and dependency parsing, becoming an obstacle for grammatical error detection and correction tasks. For example, POS tagging for learners' writing fails be-

e.g. I think it is *verey/very *convent/convenient for the group.
without spelling error correction: ... ('it', 'PRP'), ('is', 'VBZ'), ('verey', 'PRP'), ('convent', 'NN'), ...
with spelling error correction : ... ('It', 'PRP'), ('is', 'VBZ'), ('very', 'RB'), ('convenient', 'JJ'), ...

Figure 1: POS tagging for learners' writing without and with spelling error correction.

cause of misspelled words (Figure 1).[1]

To reduce errors derived from misspelled words, we conduct spelling error correction as a preprocessing task. The procedure of spelling error correction we use is as follows. First of all, we look for misspelled words and suggest candidates by GNU Aspell[2], an open-source spelling checker. The candidates are ranked by the probability of 5-gram language model built from Google N-gram (Web 1T 5-gram Version 1)[3] (Brants and Franz, 2006) with IRST LM Toolkit (Federico and Cettolo, 2007).[4] Finally, according to the rank, we changed the misspelled word into the 1-best candidate word.

In a preliminary experiment, where we use the original CLC FCE dataset,[5] our spelling error correction obtains 52.4% of precision, 72.2% of recall, and 60.7% of F-score.

We apply the spelling error correction to the training and test sets provided, and use both spelling-error and spelling-error-free sets for comparison.

3 System Architecture for Preposition Error Correction

There are so many prepositions in English. Because it is difficult to perform multi-class classification, we focus on twelve prepositions: *of, in, for, to, by, with, at, on, from, as, about, since*, which account for roughly 91% of preposition usage (Chodorow et al., 2010).

The errors are classified into three categories according to their ways of correction. First, **replacement error** indicates that learners use a wrong preposition. For instance, *with* in Example (1) is a replacement error.

I went there ~~with~~$_{by}$ bus. (1)

Second, **insertion error** points out they incorrectly inserted a preposition, such as "about" in Example (2).[6]

We discussed ~~about~~$_{NONE}$ the topic. (2)

Third, **deletion error** means they fail to write obligatory prepositions. For example, "NONE" in Example (3) is an deletion error.

This is the place to relax ~~NONE~~$_{in}$. (3)

Replacement and insertion error correction can be regarded as a multi-class classification task at each preposition occurrence. However, deletion errors differ from the other two types of errors in that they may occur at any place in a sentence. Therefore, we build two models, a combined model for replacement and insertion errors and a model for deletion errors, taking the difference into account.

For the model of replacement and insertion errors, we simultaneously perform error detection and correction with a single model.

For the model of deletion errors, we only check whether direct objects of verbs need prepositions, because it is time consuming to check all the gaps between words. Still, it covers most deletion errors.[7]

We merge the outputs of the two models to get the final output.

We used two types of training sets extracted from the original CLC-FCE dataset. One is the "gold" set, where training sentences are corrected except for preposition errors. In the gold set, spelling errors are also corrected to the gold data in the corpus. The other is the "original" set, which includes the

[1] The example is extracted from the CLC FCE dataset and part-of-speech tagged by Natural Language Toolkit (NLTK). http://www.nltk.org/

[2] GNU Aspell 0.60.6.1 http://aspell.net/

[3] http://www.ldc.upenn.edu/Catalog/CatalogEntry.jsp?catalogId=LDC2006T13

[4] irstlm5.70 http://sourceforge.net/projects/irstlm/

[5] In the CLC FCE dataset, misspelled words are corrected and tagged with a label "S".

[6] "NONE" means there are no words.

[7] 2,407 out of 5,324 preposition errors in CLC-FCE are between verbs and nouns.

Type	Name	Description (NP and PRED refer a noun phrase and a predicate.)
Lexical	Token n-gram	Token n-grams in a 2 word window around the preposition
	POS n-gram	POS n-grams in a 2 word window around the preposition
	HEAD_PREC_VP	The head verb in the preceding verb phrase
	HEAD_PREC_NP	The head noun in the preceding noun phrase
	HEAD_FOLLOW_NP	The head noun in the following noun phrase
Parsing	HEAD	Head of the preposition
	HEAD_POS	POS of the head
	COMP	Complement of the preposition
	COMPLEMENT_POS	POS of the complement
	HEAD_RELATION	Prep-Head relation name
	COMPLEMENT_RELATION	Prep-Comp relation name
Phrase Structure	PARENT_TAG	TAG of the preposition's parent
	GRANDPARENT_TAG	TAG of the preposition's grandparent
	PARENT_LEFT	Left context of the preposition parent
	PARENT_RIGHT	Right context of the preposition's parent
Web N-gram	COUNT	For the frequency $f_{\mathrm{prep,i}}$ of i (3 to 5) window size phrase including the preposition prep, the value of $\log_{100}(f_i + 1)$
	PROPORTION	The proportion $p_{\mathrm{prep,i}}$ (i is 3 to 5). $p_{\mathrm{prep,i}} = \frac{f_{\mathrm{prep,i}}}{\sum_{k \in T} f_{k,i}}$, given the set of target prepositions T.
Semantic	WORDNET_CATEGORY	WordNet lexicographer classes which are about 40 broad semantic categories for all words used as surface features. As De Felice and Pulman (2008) did not perform word sense disambiguation, neither did we.

Table 1: Baseline features for English preposition error correction.

original CLC-FCE plain sentences.

We performed sentence splitting using the implementation of Kiss and Strunk (2006) in NLTK 2.0.1rc2. We conducted dependency parsing by Stanford parser 1.6.9.[8]

We used the features described in (Tetreault et al., 2010) as shown in Table 1 with Maximum Entropy (ME) modeling (Berger et al., 1996) as a multi-class classifier. We used the implementation of Maximum Entropy Modeling Toolkit[9] with its default parameters. For web n-gram calculation, we used Google N-gram with a search system for giga-scale n-gram corpus, called SSGNC 0.4.6.[10]

4 System Architecture for Determiner Error Correction

We focused on article error correction in the determiner error correction subtask, because the errors related to articles significantly outnumber the errors unrelated to them. Though more than twenty types of determiners are involved in determiner error corrections of the HOO training set, over 90% of errors are related to three articles *a*, *an* and *the*. We defined article error correction as a multi-class classification problem with three classes, *a*, *the* and *null* article, and assumed that target articles are placed at the left boundary of a noun phrase (NP). The indefinite article *an* was normalized to *a* in training and testing, and restored to *an* later in an example-based post-processing step. If the system output was *a* and the word immediately after *a* appeared more frequently with *an* than with *a* in the training corpus, *a* was restored to *an*. If the word appeared equally frequently with *a* and *an* or didn't appear in the training corpus, *a* was restored to *an* if the word's first character was one of a, e, i, o, u.

Each input sentence was parsed using the Berkeley Parser[11] with two models, "normal" and "mixed". The "normal" model was trained on a treebank of normal English sentences. In preliminary experiments, the "normal" model sometimes misjudged the span of NPs in ESL writers' sentences due to missing articles. So we trained the "mixed" model on a concatenation of the normal treebank and a modified treebank in which all the articles appearing as the first word of an NP were removed. By

[8]http://nlp.stanford.edu/software/lex-parser.shtml

[9]https://github.com/lzhang10/maxent

[10]http://code.google.com/p/ssgnc/

[11]version 1.1, http://code.google.com/p/berkeleyparser/

Name	Description
HeadNounWord	The word form of the head noun
HeadNounTag	The POS tag of the head noun
ObjOfPrep	Indicates that the head noun is an object of a preposition
PrepWord	The word form of the preposition
PrepHeadWord	The word form of the preposition's syntactic parent
PrepHeadTag	The POS tag of the preposition's syntactic parent
ContextWindowTag	The POS tag of the words in a 3 word window around the candidate position for the article
ContextWindowWord	The word form of the word immediately following the candidate position for the article
ModByDetWord	The word form of the determiner that modifies the head noun
ModByAdjWord	The word form of the adjective that modifies the head noun
ModByAdjTag	The POS tag of the adjective that modifies the head noun
ModByPrep	Indicates that the head noun is modified by a preposition
ModByPrepWord	The word form of the preposition that modifies the head noun
ModByPossesive	Indicates that the head noun is modified by a possesive
ModByCardinal	Indicates that the head noun is modified by a cardinal number
ModByRelative	Indicates that the head noun is modified by a relative clause

Table 2: Feature templates for English determiner correction.

augmenting the training data for the parser model with sentences lacking articles, the span of NPs that lack an article might have better chance of being correctly recognized. In addition, dependency information was extracted from the parse using the Stanford parser 1.6.9.

For each NP in the parse, we extracted a feature vector representation. We used the feature templates shown in Table 2, which are inspired by (De Felice, 2008) and adapted to the CFG representation.

For the parser models, we trained the "normal" model on the WSJ part of Penn Treebank sections 02-21 with the NP annotation by Vadas and Curran (2007). The "mixed" model was trained on the concatenation of the WSJ part and its modified version. For the classification model, we used the written part of the British National Corpus (BNC) in addition to the CLC FCE Dataset, because the amount of in-domain data was limited. In examples taken from the CLC FCE Dataset, the true labels after the correction were used. In examples taken from the BNC, the article of each NP was used as the label. We trained a linear classifier using opal[12] with the PA-I algorithm. We also used the feature augmentation approach of (Daumé III, 2007) for domain adaptation.

	Subsystem Parameters		
Run	**Spelling**	**Preposition**	**Determiner**
0	no change	gold	mixed
1	no change	gold	normal
2	no change	original	mixed
3	no change	original	normal
4	corrected	gold	mixed
5	corrected	gold	normal
6	corrected	original	mixed
7	corrected	original	normal

Table 3: Distinct configurations of the system.

5 Experiment and Result

Previously undisclosed data extracted from the CLC-FCE dataset was provided as a test set by the HOO organizers. The test set includes 100 essays and each contains 180.1 word tokens on average.

We defined eight distinct configurations based on our subsystem parameters (Table 3). The official task evaluation uses three metrics (Detection, Recognition, and Correction), and three measures Precision, Recall, and F-score were computed[13] for

[12]http://www.tkl.iis.u-tokyo.ac.jp/~ynaga/opal/

[13]For details about the evaluation metrics, see http://

	Detection			Correction			Recognition		
Run	R	P	F	R	P	F	R	P	F
0	29.58	34.09	31.67	19.86	22.90	21.27	26.71	30.78	28.60
1	28.69	36.41	32.09	19.42	24.64	21.72	25.82	32.77	28.88
2*	28.91	37.21	32.54	20.97	26.98	23.60	26.26	33.80	29.56
3	28.03	40.18	33.02	20.52	29.43	24.18	25.38	36.39	29.90
4	30.24	33.66	31.86	20.75	23.09	21.86	27.37	30.46	28.83
5	29.13	35.57	32.03	19.64	23.98	21.60	26.26	32.07	28.88
6	29.35	36.23	32.43	21.41	26.43	23.65	26.26	32.42	29.02
7	28.25	38.67	32.65	20.30	27.29	23.46	25.16	34.44	29.08

Table 4: Result for preposition and determiner errors combined before revisions.

*We re-evaluated the Run2 because we submitted the Run2 with the same condition as Run0.

		Detection			Correction			Recognition		
Spelling	Preposition	R	P	F	R	P	F	R	P	F
no change	gold	25.00	34.70	29.06	14.40	20.00	16.74	20.76	28.82	24.13
no change	original	23.30	42.63	30.13	16.52	30.23	21.36	19.91	36.43	25.75
corrected	gold	26.69	34.80	30.21	15.25	19.88	17.26	22.45	29.28	25.41
corrected	original	24.57	41.13	30.76	16.52	27.65	20.68	20.33	34.04	25.46

Table 5: Result for preposition errors before revisions.

each metric.

Table 4 to Table 9 show the overall results of our systems. In terms of the effect of pre-processing, spelling correction improved the F-score of Detection, Correction, and Recognition for preposition errors after revision, whereas there were fluctuations in other conditions. This may be because there were a few spelling errors corrected in the test set.[14] Another reason why no stable improvement was found in determiner error correction is because spelling correction often produces nouns that affect the determiner error detection and correction more sensitively than prepositions. For example, a misspelled word **freewho / free who* was corrected as *freezer*. This type of error may have increased false positives. The example **National Filharmony / the National Philharmony* was corrected as *National Fleming*, where the proper noun *Fleming* does not need a determiner and this type of error increased false negatives.

As for preposition error correction, the classifier performed better when it was trained with the "original" set rather than the error-corrected (all but preposition errors) "gold" set. The reason for this is that the gold set is trained with the test set that contains several types of errors which the original CLC-FCE dataset also contains. Therefore, the "original" classifier is more optimised and suitable for the test set than the "gold" one.

For determiner error correction, the "mixed" model improved precision and F-score in the additional experiments.

5.1 Error Analysis of Preposition Correction

We briefly analyze some errors in our proposed model according to the three categories of errors.

First, most replacement errors require deep understanding of context. For instance, *for* in Example (4) must be changed to *to*. However, *modifications of* is also often used, so it is hard to decide either *to* or *of* is suitable based on the values of N-gram frequencies.

Its great news to hear you have been given extra money and that you will spend it in modifications ~~for~~$_{to}$ the cinema. (4)

Second, most insertion errors need a grammatical judgement rather than a semantic one. For instance, "in" in Example (5) must be changed to "NONE."

Their love had always been kept ~~in~~$_{NONE}$ secret (5)

In order to correct this error, we need to recog-

correcttext.org/hoo2012/eval.html

[14]There was one spelling correction per document in average.

		Detection			Correction			Recognition		
Spelling	**Determiner**	**R**	**P**	**F**	**R**	**P**	**F**	**R**	**P**	**F**
no change	mixed	34.10	33.18	33.63	25.80	25.11	25.45	33.17	32.28	32.72
no change	normal	32.25	37.43	34.65	24.88	28.87	26.73	31.33	36.36	33.66
corrected	mixed	33.64	32.30	32.95	26.72	25.66	26.18	32.71	31.41	32.05
corrected	normal	31.33	35.78	33.41	24.42	27.89	26.04	30.41	34.73	32.43

Table 6: Result for determiner errors before revisions.

	Detection			Correction			Recognition		
Run	**R**	**P**	**F**	**R**	**P**	**F**	**R**	**P**	**F**
0	31.28	37.65	34.18	22.62	27.22	24.71	28.54	34.35	31.17
1	30.44	40.33	34.69	22.19	29.41	25.30	27.69	36.69	31.56
2*	31.07	41.76	35.63	23.04	30.96	26.42	28.11	30.96	32.24
3	30.23	45.25	36.24	22.62	33.86	27.12	27.27	40.82	32.69
4	31.92	37.10	34.31	23.46	27.27	25.22	29.17	33.90	31.36
5	30.86	39.35	34.59	22.41	28.57	25.11	28.11	35.84	31.51
6	31.71	40.87	35.71	23.89	30.79	26.90	28.75	37.05	32.38
7	30.65	43.80	36.06	22.83	32.62	26.86	27.69	39.57	32.58

Table 7: Result for preposition and determiner errors combined after revisions.

*We re-evaluated the Run2 because we submitted the Run2 with the same condition as Run0.

nize "keep" takes an object and a complement; in Example (5) "love" is the object and "secret" is the complement of "keep" while the former is left-extraposed. A rule-based approach may be better suited for these cases than a machine learning approach.

Third, most deletion errors involve discrimination between transitive and intransitive. For instance, "NONE" in Example (6) must be changed to "for", because "wait" is intransitive.

I'll wait ~~NONE~~$_{for}$ your next letter. (6)

To deal with these errors, we may use rich knowledge about verbs such as VerbNet (Kipper et al., 2000) and FrameNet (Baker et al., 1998) in order to judge whether a verb is transitive or intransitive.

5.2 Error Analysis of Determiner Correction

We conducted additional experiments for determiner errors and report the results here because the submitted system contained a bug. In the submitted system, while the test data were parsed by the "mixed" model, the training data and the test data were parsed by the default grammar provided with Berkeley Parser. Moreover, though there were about 5.5 million sentences in the BNC corpus, only about 2.7 million of them had been extracted. Though these errors seem to have improved the performance, it is difficult to specify which errors had positive effects.

Table 10 shows the result of additional experiments. Unlike the submitted system, the "mixed" model contributed toward a higher precision and F-score. Though the two parser models parsed the sentences differently, the difference in the syntactic analysis of test sentences did not always led to different output by the downstream classifiers. On the contrary, the classifiers often returned different outputs even for an identically parsed sentence. In fact, the major source of the performance gap between the two models was the number of the wrong outputs rather than the number of correct ones. While the "mixed" model without spelling correction returned 146 outputs, of which 83 were spurious, the "normal" model without spelling correction produced 209 outputs, of which 143 were spurious. This may suggest the difference of the two models can be attributed to the difference in the syntactic analysis of the training data.

One of the most frequent types of errors common to the two models were those caused by misspelled words. For example, when *your letter* was misspelled to be **yours letter*, it was regarded as an

		Detection			Correction			Recognition		
Spelling	**Preposition**	**R**	**P**	**F**	**R**	**P**	**F**	**R**	**P**	**F**
no change	gold	26.63	38.23	31.40	17.62	25.29	20.77	23.36	33.52	27.53
no change	original	26.22	49.61	34.31	18.44	34.88	24.12	22.54	42.63	29.49
corrected	gold	28.27	38.12	32.47	18.44	24.86	21.17	25.00	33.70	28.70
corrected	original	27.86	48.22	35.32	19.26	33.33	24.41	24.18	41.84	30.64

Table 8: Result for preposition errors after revisions.

		Detection			Correction			Recognition		
Spelling	**Determiner**	**R**	**P**	**F**	**R**	**P**	**F**	**R**	**P**	**F**
no change	mixed	35.37	36.32	35.84	27.94	28.69	28.31	34.06	34.97	34.51
no change	normal	33.62	41.17	37.01	27.07	33.15	29.80	32.31	39.57	35.57
corrected	mixed	34.93	35.39	35.16	28.82	29.20	29.01	33.62	34.07	33.84
corrected	normal	32.75	39.47	35.79	26.63	32.10	29.11	31.44	37.89	34.36

Table 9: Result for determiner errors after revisions.

		Detection			Correction			Recognition		
Spelling	**Determiner**	**R**	**P**	**F**	**R**	**P**	**F**	**R**	**P**	**F**
no change	mixed	27.39	43.15	33.51	23.04	36.30	28.19	27.39	43.15	33.51
no change	normal	28.69	31.57	30.06	22.61	24.88	23.69	28.69	31.57	30.06
corrected	mixed	27.39	41.44	31.98	22.61	34.21	27.22	26.96	40.79	32.46
corrected	normal	30.43	33.33	31.82	24.34	26.67	25.45	30.00	32.86	31.36

Table 10: Result of additional experiments for determiner errors after revisions.

NP without a determiner resulting in a false positive such as **a yours letter*. Among the other types of errors, several seemed to be caused by the information from the context window. For instance, the system output for *It was last month and ...* was *it was *the last month and ....* It is likely that the word *last* triggered the misinsertion here. Such kind of errors might be avoided by conjunctive features of context information and the head word. Last but not least, compound errors were also frequent and probably the most difficult to solve. For example, it is quite difficult to correct **for a month* to *per month* if we are dealing with determiner errors and preposition errors separately. A more sophisticated approach such as joint modeling seems necessary to correct this kind of errors.

6 Conclusion

This report described the architecture of our preposition and determiner error correction system. The experimental result showed that spelling correction advances the performance of Detection, Correction and Recognition for preposition errors. In terms of preposition error correction, F-scores were not improved when the error-corrected dataset was used. As to determiner error correction, there was an improvement when the constituent parser was trained on a concatenation of treebank and modified treebank where all the articles appearing as the first word of an NP were removed.

Acknowledgements

This work was partly supported by the National Institute of Information and Communications Technology Japan.

References

Collin F Baker, Charles J Fillmore, and John B Lowe. 1998. The Berkeley FrameNet Project. In *Proceedings of the 36th Annual Meeting of the Association for Computational Linguistics*, pages 86–90, Montreal, Quebec, Canada.

Adam L. Berger, Vincent J. Della Pietra, and Stephen A. Della Pietra. 1996. A Maximum Entropy Approach to Natural Language Processing. *Computational Linguistics*, 22(1):39–71.

Thorsten Brants and Alex Franz. 2006. *Web 1T 5-gram Corpus Version 1.1*. Linguistic Data Consortium.

Martin Chodorow, Michael Gamon, and Joel Tetreault. 2010. The Utility of Article and Preposition Error Correction Systems for English Language Learners: Feedback and Assessment. *Language Testing*, 27(3):419–436.

Daniel Dahlmeier, Hwee Tou Ng, and Thanh Phu Tran. 2011. NUS at the HOO 2011 Pilot Shared Task. In *Proceedings of the 13th European Workshop on Natural Language Generation*, pages 257–259, Nancy, France.

Robert Dale and Adam Kilgarriff. 2010. Helping Our Own: Text Massaging for Computational Linguistics as a New Shared Task. In *Proceedings of the 6th International Natural Language Generation Conference*, pages 261–266, Trim, Co. Meath, Ireland.

Hal Daumé III. 2007. Frustratingly Easy Domain Adaptation. In *Proceedings of the 45th Annual Meeting of the Association of Computational Linguistics*, pages 256–263, Prague, Czech Republic.

Rachele De Felice and Stephen G. Pulman. 2008. A Classifier-Based Approach to Preposition and Determiner Error Correction in L2 English. In *Proceedings of the 22nd International Conference on Computational Linguistics*, pages 169–176, Manchester, UK.

Rachele De Felice. 2008. *Automatic Error Detection in Non-native English*. Ph.D. thesis, University of Oxford.

Marcello Federico and Mauro Cettolo. 2007. Efficient Handling of N-gram Language Models for Statistical Machine Translation. In *Proceedings of the Second Workshop on Statistical Machine Translation*, pages 88–95, Prague, Czech Republic.

Michael Gamon. 2010. Using Mostly Native Data to Correct Errors in Learners' Writing. In *Human Language Technologies: The 2010 Annual Conference of the North American Chapter of the Association for Computational Linguistics*, pages 163–171, Los Angeles, California.

Karin Kipper, Hoa Trang Dang, and Martha Palmer. 2000. Class-based Construction of a Verb Lexicon. In *Proceedings of the 7th National Conference on Artificial Intelligence*, pages 691–696, Austin, Texas, USA.

Tibor Kiss and Jan Strunk. 2006. Unsupervised Multilingual Sentence Boundary Detection. *Computational Linguistics*, 32(4):485–525.

Alla Rozovskaya and Dan Roth. 2011. Algorithm Selection and Model Adaptation for ESL Correction Tasks. In *Proceedings of the 49th Annual Meeting of the Association for Computational Linguistics: Human Language Technologies*, pages 924–933, Portland, Oregon, USA.

Joel Tetreault, Jennifer Foster, and Martin Chodorow. 2010. Using Parse Features for Preposition Selection and Error Detection. In *Proceedings of the 47th Annual Meeting of the Association for Computational Linguistics Short Papers*, pages 353–358, Uppsala, Sweden.

David Vadas and James Curran. 2007. Adding Noun Phrase Structure to the Penn Treebank. In *Proceedings of the 45th Annual Meeting of the Association of Computational Linguistics*, pages 240–247, Prague, Czech Republic.

Memory-based text correction for preposition and determiner errors

Antal van den Bosch
Radboud University Nijmegen
P.O. Box 9103
NL-6500 HD Nijmegen, The Netherlands
a.vandenbosch@let.ru.nl

Peter Berck
Tilburg University
P.O. Box 90153
NL-5000 LE Tilburg, The Netherlands
p.j.berck@tilburguniversity.edu

Abstract

We describe the Valkuil.net team entry for the HOO 2012 Shared Task. Our systems consists of four memory-based classifiers that generate correction suggestions for middle positions in small text windows of two words to the left and to the right. Trained on the Google 1TB 5-gram corpus, the first two classifiers determine the presence of a determiner or a preposition between all words in a text in which the actual determiners and prepositions are masked. The second pair of classifiers determines which is the most likely correction given a masked determiner or preposition. The hyperparameters that govern the classifiers are optimized on the shared task training data. We point out a number of obvious improvements to boost the medium-level scores attained by the system.

1 Introduction

Our Valkuil.net team entry, known under the abbreviation 'VA' in the HOO 2012 Shared Task (Dale et al., 2012), is a simplistic text correction system based on four memory-based classifiers. The goal of the system is to be lightweight: simple to set up and train, fast in execution. It requires a (preferably very large) corpus to train on, and a closed list of words which together form the category of interest—in the HOO 2012 Shared Task context, the two categories of interest are prepositions and determiners.

As a corpus we used the Google 1TB 5-gram corpus (Brants and Franz, 2006), and we used two lists, one consisting of 47 prepositions and one consisting of 24 determiners, both extracted from the HOO 2012 Shared Task training data. Using the Google corpus means that we restricted ourselves to a simple 5-gram context, which obviously places a limit on the context sensitivity of our system; yet, we were able to make use of the entire Google corpus.

Memory-based classifiers have been used for confusible disambiguation (Van den Bosch, 2006) and agreement error detection (Stehouwer and Van den Bosch, 2009).[1] In both studies it is argued that fast approximations of memory-based discriminative classifiers are effective and efficient modules for spelling correction, particularly because of their insensitivity to the number of classes to be predicted. They can act as simple binary decision makers (e.g. for confusible pairs: given this context, is *then* or *than* more likely?), and at the same time they can handle missing word prediction with up to millions of possible outcomes, all in the same model. Van den Bosch (2006) also showed consistent log-linear performance gains in learning curve experiments, indicating that more training data continues to be better for these models even at very large amounts of training data. The interested reader is referred to the two studies for more details.

2 System

Our system centers around four classifiers that all take a windowed input of two words to the left of the focus, and two words to the right. The focus may either be a position between two words, or a determiner or a preposition. In case of a position

[1] A working context-sensitive spelling checker for Dutch based on these studies is released under the name Valkuil.net; see `http://valkuil.net` – hence the team name.

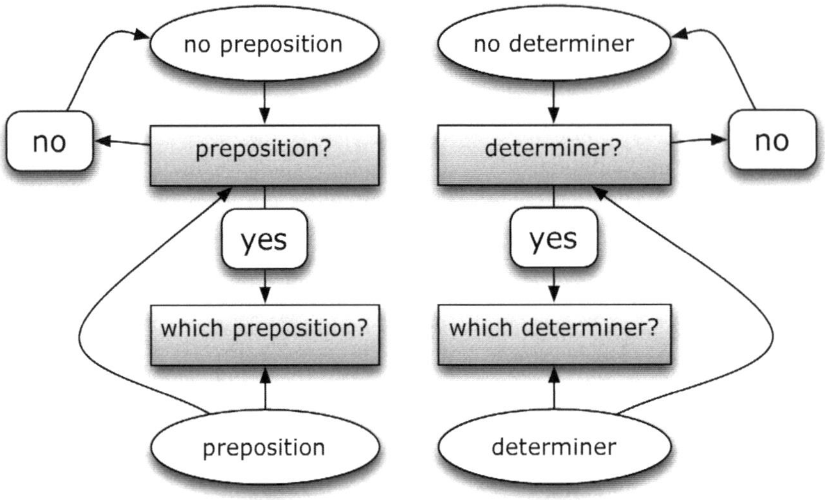

Figure 1: System architecture. Shaded rectangles are the four classifiers.

between two words, the task is to predict whether the position should actually be filled by a preposition or a determiner. When the focus is on a determiner or preposition, the task may be to decide whether it should actually be deleted, or whether it should be replaced.

The main system architecture is displayed in Figure 1. The classifiers are the shaded rectangular boxes. They are all based on IGTree, an efficient decision tree learner (Daelemans et al., 1997), a fast approximation of memory-based or k-nearest neighbor classification, implemented within the TiMBL[2] software package (Daelemans et al., 2010).

The first two classifiers, **preposition?** and **determiner?**, are binary classifiers that determine whether or not there should be a preposition or a determiner, respectively, between two words to the left and two words to the right:

- The **preposition?** classifier is trained on all 118,105,582 positive cases of contexts in the Google 1 TB 5-gram corpus in which one of the 47 known prepositions are found to occur in the middle position of a 5-gram. To enable the classifier to answer negatively to other contexts, roughly the same amount of negative cases of randomly selected contexts with no preposition in the middle are added to form a training set of 235,730,253 cases. In the participating system we take each n-gram as a single token, and ignore the Google corpus token counts. We performed a validation experiment on a single 90%-10% split of the training data; the classifier is able to make a correct decision on 89.1% of the 10% heldout cases.

- Analogously, the **determiner?** classifier takes all 132,483,802 positive cases of 5-grams with a determiner in the middle position, and adds randomly selected negative cases to arrive at a training set of 252,634,322 cases. On a 90%–10% split, the classifier makes the correct decision in 88.4% of the 10% heldout cases.

The second pair of classifiers perform the multi-label classification task of predicting which preposition or determiner is most likely given a context of two words to the left and to the right. Again, these classifiers are trained on the entire Google 1TB 5-gram corpus:

- The **which preposition?** classifier is trained on the aforementioned 118,105,582 cases of any of the 47 prepositions occurring in the middle of 5-grams. The task of the classifier is to generate a class distribution of likely prepositions given an input of the four words surrounding the preposition, with 47 possible outcomes. In a 90%-10% split experiment on the complete training set, this classifier labels 59.6% of the 10% heldout cases correctly.

[2] `http://ilk.uvt.nl/timbl`

- The **which determiner?** classifier, by analogy, is trained on the 132,483,802 positive cases of 5-grams with a determiner in the middle position, and generates class distributions composed of the 24 possible class labels (the possible determiners). On a 90%-10% split of the training set, the classifier predicts 63.1% of all heldout cases correctly.

Using the four classifiers and the system architecture depicted in Figure 1, the system is capable of detecting missing and unnecessary cases of prepositions and determiners, and of replacing prepositions and determiners by other more likely alternatives. Focusing on the preposition half of the system, we illustrate how these three types of error detection and correction are carried out.

First, Figure 2 illustrates how a missing preposition is detected. Given an input text, a four-word window of two words to the left and two words to the right is shifted over all words. At any word which is not in the list of prepositions, the binary **preposition?** classifier is asked to determine whether there should be a preposition in the middle. If the classifier says no, the window is shifted to the next position and nothing happens. If the classifier says yes beyond a certainty threshold (more on this in Section 3), the **which preposition?** classifier is invoked to make a best guess on which preposition should be inserted.

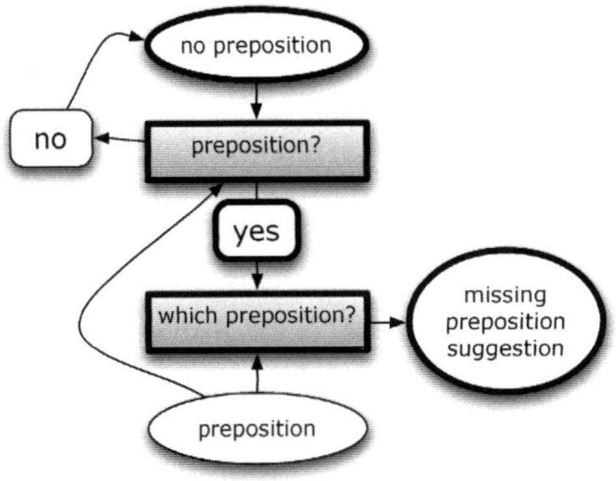

Figure 2: Workflow for detecting a missing preposition.

Second, Figure 3 depicts the workflow of how a preposition deletion is suggested. Given an input text, all cases of prepositions are sought. Instances of two words to the left and right of each preposition are created, and these context windows are presented to the **preposition?** classifier. If this classifier says no beyond a certainty threshold, the system signals that the preposition currently in focus should be deleted.

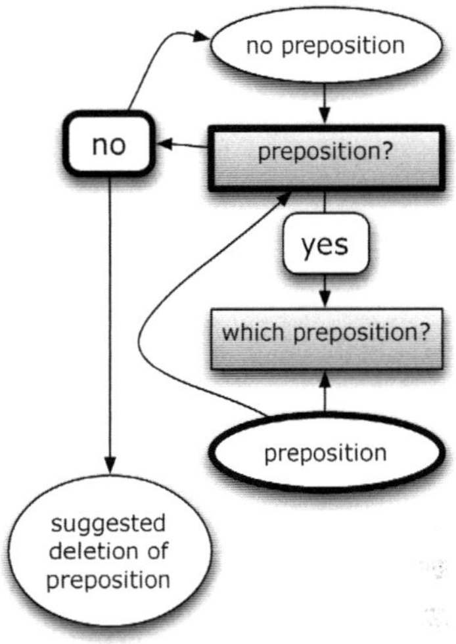

Figure 3: Workflow for suggesting a preposition deletion.

Third, Figure 4 illustrates how a replacement suggestion is generated. Just as with the detection of deletions, an input text is scanned for all occurrences of prepositions. Again, contextual windows of two words to the left and right of each found preposition are created. These contexts are presented to the **which preposition?** classifier, which may produce a different most likely preposition (beyond a certainty threshold) than the preposition in the text. If so, the system signals that the original preposition should be replaced by the new best guess.

Practically, the system is set up as a master process (implemented in Python) that communicates with the four classifiers over socket connections. The master process performs all necessary data conversion and writes its edits to the designated XML format. First, missing prepositions and determiners are traced according to the procedure sketched above; second, the classifiers are employed to find replacement errors; third, unnecessary determiners and prepositions are sought. The system does not iterate over its own output.

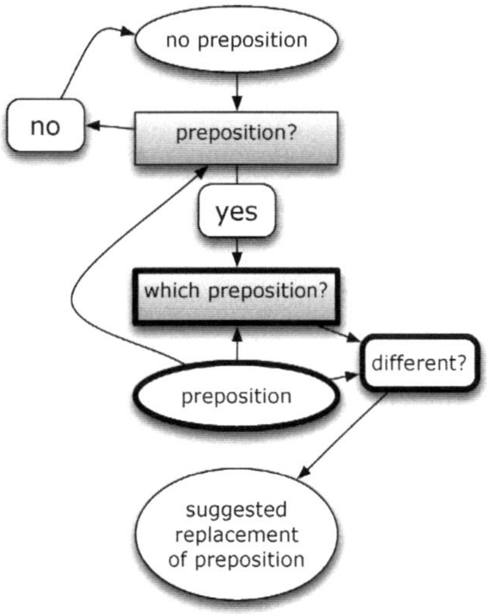

Figure 4: Workflow for suggesting a preposition replacement.

Task	Thresh.	Optimizing on Precision	Recall	F-Score
Prep.	M	30	10	20
	U	30	4	4
	DS	5	50	50
	F	50	5	5
	R	10	20	20
Det.	M	30	10	20
	U	30	2	2
	DS	5	50	20
	F	50	5	20
	R	10	20	20

Table 1: Semi-automatically established thresholds that optimize precision, recall, and F-Score. Optimization was performed on the HOO 2012 Shared Task training data.

3 Optimizing the system

When run unfiltered, the four classifiers tend to overpredict errors massively. They are not very accurate (the binary classifiers operate at a classification accuracy of 88–89%; the multi-valued classifiers perform at 60–63%). On the other hand, they produce class distributions that have properties that could be exploited to filter the classifications down to cases where the system is more certain. This enables us to tune the precision and recall behavior of the classifiers, and, for instance, optimize on F-Score. We introduce five hyperparameter thresholds by which we can tune our four classifiers.

First we introduce two thresholds for the two binary classifiers **preposition?** and **determiner?**:

M — When the two binary **preposition?** and **determiner?** classifiers are used for detecting missing prepositions or determiners, the positive class must be M times more likely than the negative class.

U — In the opposite case, when the two binary classifiers are used for signalling the deletion of an unnecessary preposition or determiner, the negative class must be U times more likely than the positive class.

For the two multi-label classifiers **which preposition?** and **which determiner?** we introduce three thresholds (which again can be set separately for determiners and prepositions):

DS — the distribution size (i.e. the number of labels that have a non-zero likelihood according to the classifier) must be smaller than DS. A large DS signals a relatively large uncertainty.

F — the frequency of occurrence of the most likely outcome in the training set must be larger than F. Outcomes with a smaller number of occurrences should be distrusted more.

R — if the most likely outcome is different from the preposition or determiner currently in the text, the most likely outcome should be at least R times more likely than the current preposition or determiner. Preferably the likelihood of the latter should be zero.

On the gold training data provided during the training phase of the HOO 2012 Shared Task we found, through a semi-automatic optimization procedure, three settings that optimized precision, recall, and F-Score, respectively. Table 3 displays the optimal settings found. The results given in Section 4 always refer to the system optimized on F-Score, listed in the rightmost column of Table 3.

The table shows that most of the ratio thresholds found to optimize F-Score are quite high; for example, the **preposition?** classifier needs to assign a likelihood to a positive classification that is at least 20 times more likely than the negative classification in order to trigger a missing preposition error. The threshold for marking unnecessary prepositions is considerably lower at 4, and even at 2 for determiners.

4 Results

The output of our system on the data provided during the test phase of the HOO 2012 Shared Task was processed through the shared task evaluation software. The original test data was revised in a correction round in which a subset of the participants could suggest corrections to the gold standard. We did not contribute suggestions for revisions, but our scores slightly improved after revisions. Table 4 summarizes the best scores of our system optimized on F-Score, before and after revisions. Our best score is an overall F-Score of 14.24 on error detection, after revisions. Our system performs slightly better on prepositions than on determiners, although the differences are small. Optimizing on F-Score implies that a reasonable balance is found between recall and precision, but overall our results are not impressive, especially not in terms of correction.

5 Discussion

We presented a preposition and determiner error detection and correction system, the focus task of the HOO 2012 Shared Task. Our system consists of four memory-based classifiers and a master process that communicates with these classifiers in a simple workflow. It takes several hours to train our system on the Google 1TB 5-gram corpus, and it takes in the order of minutes to process the 1,000 training documents. The system can be trained without needing linguistic knowledge or the explicit computation of linguistic analysis levels such as POS-tagging or syntactic analyses, and is to a large extent language-independent (it does rely on tokenization).

This simple generic approach leads to mediocre results, however. There is room for improvement. We have experimented with incorporating the n-gram counts in the Google corpus in our classifiers, leading to improved recall (post-competition). It still remains to be seen if the Google corpus is the best corpus for this task, or for the particular English-as-a-second-language writer data used in the HOO 2012 Shared Task. Another likely improvement would be to limit which words get corrected by which other words based on confusion statistics in the training data: for instance, the training data may tell that 'my' should rarely, if ever, be corrected into 'your', but our system is blind to such likelihoods.

Acknowledgements

The authors thank Ko van der Sloot for his continued improvements of the TiMBL software. This work is rooted in earlier joint work funded through a grant from the Netherlands Organization for Scientific Research (NWO) for the Vici project *Implicit Linguistics*.

References

T. Brants and A. Franz. 2006. LDC2006T13: Web 1T 5-gram Version 1.

W. Daelemans, A. Van den Bosch, and A. Weijters. 1997. IGTree: using trees for compression and classification in lazy learning algorithms. *Artificial Intelligence Review*, 11:407–423.

W. Daelemans, J. Zavrel, K. Van der Sloot, and A. Van den Bosch. 2010. TiMBL: Tilburg memory based learner, version 6.3, reference guide. Technical Report ILK 10-01, ILK Research Group, Tilburg University.

R. Dale, I. Anisimoff, and G. Narroway. 2012. HOO 2012: A report on the preposition and determiner error correction shared task. In *Proceedings of the Seventh Workshop on Innovative Use of NLP for Building Educational Applications*, Montreal, Canada.

H. Stehouwer and A. Van den Bosch. 2009. Putting the t where it belongs: Solving a confusion problem in Dutch. In S. Verberne, H. van Halteren, and P.-A. Coppen, editors, *Computational Linguistics in the Netherlands 2007: Selected Papers from the 18th CLIN Meeting*, pages 21–36, Nijmegen, The Netherlands.

A. Van den Bosch. 2006. All-word prediction as the ultimate confusible disambiguation. In *Proceedings of the HLT-NAACL Workshop on Computationally hard problems and joint inference in speech and language processing*, New York, NY.

Task	Evaluation	Before revisions Precision	Recall	F-Score	After revisions Precision	Recall	F-Score
Overall	Detection	12.5	15.23	13.73	13.22	15.43	14.24
	Recognition	10.87	13.25	11.94	11.59	13.53	12.49
	Correction	6.16	7.51	6.77	7.25	8.46	7.8
Prepositions	Detection	13.44	14.41	13.91	14.23	14.75	14.49
	Recognition	11.46	12.29	11.86	12.65	13.11	12.88
	Correction	7.51	8.05	7.77	8.7	9.02	8.85
Determiners	Detection	11.04	15.21	12.79	11.71	15.28	13.26
	Recognition	10.37	14.29	12.02	10.7	13.97	12.12
	Correction	5.02	6.91	5.81	6.02	7.86	6.82

Table 2: Best scores of our system before (left) and after (right) revisions. Scores are reported at the overall level (top), on prepositions (middle), and determiners (bottom).

Helping Our Own: NTHU NLPLAB System Description

Jian-Cheng Wu[+], Joseph Z. Chang[*], Yi-Chun Chen[+], Shih-Ting Huang[+], Mei-Hua Chen[*], Jason S. Chang[+]
[*]Institute of Information Systems and Applications, NTHU, HsinChu, Taiwan, R.O.C. 30013
[+]Department of Computer Science, NTHU, HsinChu, Taiwan, R.O.C. 30013
{wujc86, bizkit.tw, pieyaaa, koromiko1104, chen.meihua, jason.jschang}@gmail.com

Abstract

Grammatical error correction has been an active research area in the field of Natural Language Processing. In this paper, we integrated four distinct learning-based modules to correct determiner and preposition errors in leaners' writing. Each module focuses on a particular type of error. Our modules were tested in well-formed data and learners' writing. The results show that our system achieves high recall while preserves satisfactory precision.

1. Introduction

Researchers have demonstrated that prepositions and determiners are the two most frequent error types for language learners (Leacock et al, 2010). According to Swan and Smith (2001), preposition errors might result from L1 interference. Chen and Lin (2011) also reveal that prepositions are the most perplexing problem for Chinese-speaking EFL learners mainly because there are no clear preposition counterparts in Chinese for learners to refer to. On the other hand, Swan and Smith (2001) predict that the possibility of determiner errors depends on learners' native language. The Cambridge Learners Corpus illustrates that learners of Chinese, Japanese, Korean, and Russian might have a poor command of determiners.

In view of the fact that a large number of grammatical errors appear in non-native speakers' writing, more and more research has been directed towards the automated detection and correction of such errors to help improve the quality of that writing (Dale and Kilgarriff, 2010). In recent years, preposition error detection and correction has especially been an area of increasingly active research (Leacock et al, 2010). The HOO 2012 shared task also focuses on error detection and correction in the use of prepositions and determiners (Dale et al., 2012).

Many studies have been done at correcting errors using hybrid modules: implementing distinct modules to correct errors of different types. In other word, instead of using a general module to correct any kind of errors, using different modules to deal with different error types seems to be more effective and promising. In this paper, we propose four distinct modules to deal with four kinds of determiner and preposition errors (inserting missing determiner, replacing erroneous determiner, inserting missing preposition, and replacing erroneous prepositions). Four learning-based approaches are used to detect and correct the errors of prepositions and determiners.

In this paper, we describe our methods in the next section. Section 3 reports the evaluation results. Then we conclude this paper in Section 4.

2. System Description

2.1 Overview

In this sub-section, we give a general view of our system. Figure 1 shows the architecture of the integrated error detection and error correction system. The input of the system is a sentence in a learner's writing. First, the data is pre-processed using the GeniaTagger tool (Tsuruoka et al., 2005), which provides the base forms, part-of-speech tags, chunk tags and named entity tags. The tag result of the sample sentence "*This virus affects the defense system.*" is shown in Table 1. The determiner error detection module then directly inserts the missing determiners and deletes the unnecessary determiners. Meanwhile, the error determiners are replaced with predicted answers by the determiner error correction module. After finishing the determiner error correction, the preposition error detection and correction module detects and corrects the preposition errors of the modified input sentence.

In the following subsections, we first introduce the training and testing of the determiner error detection and correction modules (Section 3.2). Then in section 3.3 we focus on the training and testing of the preposition error detection and correction modules.

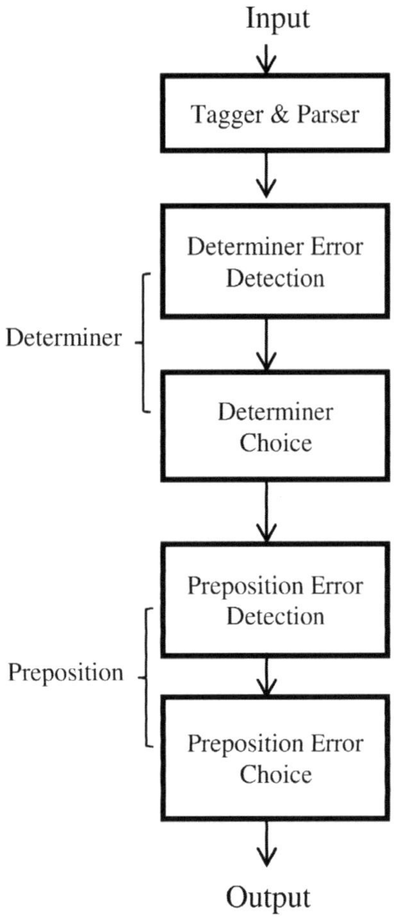

Figure 1. System Architecture (Run-Time)

Word	Base form	POS	Chunk	NE
This	This	DT	B-NP	O
virus	virus	NN	I-NP	O
affects	affect	VBZ	B-VP	O
the	the	DT	B-NP	O
defence	defence	NN	I-NP	O
system	system	NN	I-NP	O
.	.	.	O	O

Table 1. The tag result of sample sentence.

2.2 Determiners

In this section, we investigate the performance of two maximum entropy classifiers (Ratnaparkhi, 1997), one for determining whether a noun phrase has a determiner or not and the other for selecting the appropriate determiner if one is needed.

From the British National Corpus (BNC), we extract 22,552,979 noun phrases (NPs). For determining which features are useful for this task, all NPs are divided into two sets, 20 million cases as a training set and the others as a validation set.

For the classifier (named the *DetClassifier* hereafter) trained for predicting whether a NP has a determiner or not, the label set contains two labels: "Zero" and "DET." On the other hand, for the classifier (named the *SelClassifier* hereafter) which predicts appropriate determiners, the label set contains 9 labels: *the, a, an, my, your, our, one, this, their*. (In the training data, there are 7,249,218 cases with those labels.)

Both of the classifiers use contextual and syntactic information as features to predict the labels. The features include single features such as the headword of the NP, the part of speech (PoS) of the headword, the words and PoSs in the chunks before or after the NP (pre-NP, post-NP), and all words and PoSs in the NP (excluding the determiner if there was one), etc. We also combine the single features to form more specific features for better performance.

At run time, the given data are also tagged and all features for each NP in the data are extracted for classification. For testing, all determiners at the beginning of the NPs are ignored if they exist. At first, the *DetClassifier* is used to determine whether a NP needs a determiner or not. If the classifier predicts that the NP should not have a determiner but it does, there is an "UD" (Unnecessary determiner) type mistake. In contrast, if the classifier predicts that the NP should have a determiner but it does not, there is a "MD" type mistake. For both "MD" (Missing determiner) and "RD" (Replace determiner) mistake types, we would use the *SelClassifier* to predict which determiner is more appropriate for the given NP.

2.3 Prepositions

2.3.1 Preposition Error Detection

In solving other problems in natural language processing, supervised training methods suffers from the difficulty of acquiring manually labeled data. This may not be the case with grammatical language error correction. Although high quality error learner's corpora are not currently available to the public to provide negative cases, any ordinary corpus can used as positive cases at training time.

In our method, we use an ordinary corpus to train a Conditional Random Field (CRF) tagger to identify the presence of a targeted lexical category. The input of the tagger is a sentence with all words in the targeting lexical category removed. The tagger will tag every word with a *positive* or *negative* tag, predicting the presence of a word in the targeted lexical category. In this paper, we choose the top 13 most frequent prepositions: *of, to, in, for, on, with, as, at, by, from, about, like, since.*

Conditional Random Field

The sequence labeling is the task of assigning labels from a finite set of categories sequentially to a set of observation sequences. This problem is encountered not only in the field of computational linguistics, but also many others, including bioinformatics, speech recognition, and pattern recognition.

Traditionally sequence labeling problems are solved using the Hidden Markov Model (HMM). HMM is a directed graph model in which every outcome is conditioned on the corresponding observation node and only the previous outcomes.

Conditional Random Field (CRF) is considered the state-of-the-art sequence labeling algorithm. One of the major differences of CRF is that it is modeled as a undirected graph. CRF also obeys the Markov property, with respect to the undirected graph, every outcome is conditioned on its neighboring outcomes and potentially the *entire* observation sequence.

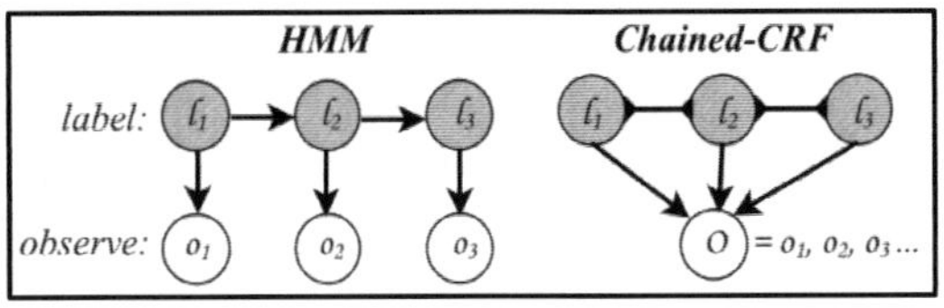

Figure 2. Simplified view of HMM and CRF

Supervised Training

Obtaining labeled training data is relatively easy for this task, that is, it requires no human labeler. For this task, we will use this method to target the lexical category *preposition.* To produce training data, we simply use an ordinary English corpus and use the presence of prepositions as the outcome, and remove all prepositions. For example, the sentence

> *"Miss Hardbroom 's eyes bored* ***into*** *Mildred like a laser-beam the moment they came* ***into*** *view ."*

will produce

> *"Miss _Hardbroom _'s _eyes _bored +Mildred _like _a _laser-beam _the _moment _they _came +view ."*

where the underscores indicate no preposition presence and the plus signs indicate otherwise. Combined with additional features described in following sections, we use the CRF model to train a preposition presence detection tagger. Features additional to the words in the sentence are their corresponding lemmas, part-of-speech tags, upper or lower case, and word suffix.

At runtime, we first remove all prepositional words in the user input sentence, generate additional features, and use the trained tagger to predict the presence of prepositions in the altered sentence. By comparing the tagged result with the original sentence, the system can output insertion and/or deletion of preposition suggestions.

The process of generating features is identical to producing the training set. To generate part-of-speech tag features at runtime, one simple approach is to use an ordinary POS tagger to generate POS tags to the tokens in the altered sentences, i.e. English sentences without any prepositions. A more sophisticated approach is to train a specialized POS tagger to tag English sentences with their prepositions removed. A state-of-the-art part-of-speech tagger can achieve around 95% precision. In our implementation, we find that using an ordinary POS tagger to tag altered sentences yield near 94% precision, whereas a specialized POS tagger performed around 1% higher precision.

We used a small portion of the British National Corpus (BNC) to train and evaluate our tagger (1M and 10M tokens, i.e. words and punctuation marks). The British National Corpus contains over 100 million words of both written (90%) and spoken (10%) British English. The written part of the BNC is sampled from a wide variety of sources, including newspapers, journals, academic books, fictions, letter, school and university essays. A separate portion of the BNC is selected to evaluate the performance of the taggers. The test set contains 322,997 tokens (31,916 sentences).

2.3.2 Preposition Error Correction

Recently, the problem of preposition error correction has been viewed as a word sense disambiguation problem and all prepositions are considered as candidates of the intended senses. In previous studies, well-formed corpora and learner corpora are both used in training the classifiers. However, due to the limited size of learner corpora, it is difficult to use the learner corpora to train a classifier. A more feasible approach is to use a large well-formed corpus to train a model in choosing prepositions. Similar to the determiner error correction, we choose the maximum entropy model as our classifier to choose appropriate prepositions underlying certain contexts. In order to cover a large variety of genres in learners' writing, we use a balanced well-formed corpus, the BNC, to train a maximum entropy model.

Our context features include four feature categories which are introduced as follows.

- **Word feature (f1)**: Word features include a window of five content words to the left and right with their positions.
- **Head feature (f2)**: We select two head words in the left and right of prepositions with their relative orders as head features. For example, in Table 2, we select the first head word, *face*, with its relative order, Rh1, as one of the head features of preposition, *to*. More specifically, "Rh1=face" denotes first head word, *face*, right of the preposition, *to*.
- **Head combine feature (f3)**: Combine any two head features described above to get six features. For example, L1R2 denotes two head words surrounding the preposition.
- **Phrase combine feature (f4)**: Combine the head words of noun phrase and verb phrase where the preposition is between the phrases. For example, V_N feature denotes the head words of verb phrase and noun phrase where the preposition is followed by noun phrase and is preceded by verb phrase.

Word Feature (f1)	Lw1=leaving, Rw1=face, Rw2= chronic, Rw3= condition
Head Feature (f2)	Lh1=them, Lh2=leaving, Rh1=face, Rh2=condition
Head Combine Feature (f3)	L1L2= them_leaving, L1R1= them_face, L1R2= them_condition, ...
Phrase Combine Feature (f4)	N_N= them_condition, V_N= leaving_condition, N_V= them_face, V_V= leaving_face

Table 2. Features example for *leaving them* ***to*** *face this chronic condition*

At run time, we extract the features of each preposition in learners' writings and ask the model to predict the preposition. The preposition error detection model described in section 2.3.1 first removes all prepositions from test sentences and then marks the "presence" and "absence" labels in every blank of a sentence. For each blank labeled "presence", the correction model predicts the preposition which best fits the blank underlying the contexts. The correction model does not predict when the blanks are labeled "absence". Although some blanks labeled "absence" may still correspond to prepositions, we decide to reduce some recall score to ensure the accuracy of the results.

3. Experimental Results

In this section, we present the experimental results of the determiner and preposition modules respectively.

3.1 Determiners

Table 3 shows the performance of the *DetClassifier* of individual feature and Table 4 shows the performance of the *SelClassifier.* We also wonder how the size of training data influences the performance of the models. Table 5 and 6 show the precision of modes of different sizes of training data with the best feature "whole words in NP and last word of pre-NP." Because the performance converges while using more than 5 million training cases, we use only 1 million training cases to investigate the performance of using multiple features. When using all features, the precision increases from 84.8% to 85.8% for *DetClassifier*, and from 39.8% to 56.0% for *SelClassifier.*

We also implement another data-driven model for determiner selection (including zero) by using the 5gram of Web 1T corpus. The basic concept of the model is to use the frequency of determiners which fit the context of the given test data to choose the determiner candidates. If the frequency of the determiner using in the given NP is lower than other candidate determiners, we would use the most frequent one as the suggestion. However, according to our observation during testing, we find that the model tends to cause false alarms. To reduce the probability of false alarm, we set a high threshold for the ratio f_1/f_2 where f_1 is the frequency of the used determiner and f_2 is the frequency of the most frequent determiner. The suggestion is accepted only when the ratio exceeds the threshold.

The major limitation of the proposed method is that some errors are ignored due to parsing errors. For example, the given data "the them" should be considered as one NP with the "UD" type error. However, the parser would give the chunk result "*the [B-NP] them [B-NP]*" and the error would not be recognized. It might need some rules to handle these exceptions. Another weakness of the proposed methods is that the less frequently used determiners are usually considered as errors and suggested to be replaced with more frequently used ones. For example, possessives such as 'my' and 'your', are usually replaced with "the." We need to integrate more informative features to improve performance.

Features	Precision
head/PoS	79.1%
word/PoS of pre-NP	70.0%
word/PoS of all words in NP	85.9%
PoS of all words in NP	77.8%
word/PoS of post-NP	71.8%
whole words in NP	87.2%
last word/PoS of pre-NP and head/PoS	92.3%
whole words in NP and last word of pre-NP	96.8%

Table 3. Precision of features used in the *DetClassifier*

Features	Precision
head/PoS	55.2%
word/PoS of pre-NP	49.5%
word/PoS of all words in NP	53.9%
PoS of all words in NP	45.3%
word/PoS of post-NP	46.1%
whole words in NP	60.4%
last word/PoS of pre-NP and head/PoS	65.3%
whole words in NP and last word of pre-NP	70.8%

Table 4. Precision of features used in the *SelClassifier*

Size	Precision
1,000,000	84.8%
5,000,000	96.8%
10,000,000	96.8%
15,000,000	96.8%
20,000,000	96.8%

Table 5. Precision of different training size for the *DetClassifier*

Size	Precision
1,000,000	39.8%
3,000,000	43.2%
5,000,000	44.5%
7,000,000	61.6%
7,249,218	70.8%

Table 6. Precision of different training size for the *SelClassifier*

3.2 Prepositions

Two sets of evaluation were carried out for detection. First, we use a randomly-selected portion of the BNC containing 1 million tokens to train our tokenizer targeting the 34 highest frequency prepositions. Second, we use a larger training corpus containing 10 million tokens, also randomly selected from the BNC, and target a smaller set of the 13 highest frequency prepositions, due to the fact that these 13 prepositions can cover over 90% of the preposition errors found in the development set.

We evaluate the trained taggers using two different metrics. First we evaluate the overall tagging precision, which is defined as

$P_{overall}$ = # of correctly tagged words / # of all words

$P_{presence}$ = # correctly tagged PRESENCE / # all words labeled with PRESENCE

Since most answer tags are Non-presence, $P_{overall}$ is not informative, we therefore focus on $P_{presense}$, and further evaluate the recall of presence, defined as:

$R_{presence}$ = # correctly tagged PRESENCE / # word should be tagged with PRESENCE

We then evaluate on Precision and Recall of the PRESENCE tag using different probabilities to threshold the CRF tagging results. Then we show the result of two evaluation sets. On the left is the tagger train with 1 million tokens, targeting 34 prepositions. On the right is the tagger trained with 10 million tokens, targeting 13 prepositions. Only the latter tagger is used for producing the submitted runs.

We used the development data released as part of HOO 2012 Shared Task as the gold standard for the evaluation of our preposition correction module. In order to observe the effect of different feature sets in training, we first extracted the MT and RT instances marked by the gold standard and then ask the correction module to correct these prepositions directly. Table 7 shows the precision of the models trained on different feature sets. The definition of precision is the same as the definition in the HOO 2012 Shared Task. The results shows that the model trained using four feature sets achieved higher precision.

Features	Precision		
	MT	RT	MT+RT
f1	43.62%	39.15%	40.48%
f1+f2	**52.58%**	43.47%	46.18%
f1+f2+f3	55.20%	46.77%	49.27%
f1+f2+f3+f4	55.11%	**47%**	**49.41%**

Table 7. The feature selection and accuracy of the preposition correction module.

In addition to the evaluation on the effect of different feature sets, we also conducted an evaluation done on the development data of HOO 2012 Shared Task to observe the performance of the correction model when combined with the detection model. The correction model corrected three different types of preposition errors, MT, RT and MT+RT simultaneously (Table 8).

	MT	RT	MT+RT
Precision	1.16%	3.80%	4.96%
Recall	29.86%	41.14%	37.79%

Table 8. Precision and recall scores of the correction modules when combined with the detection module.

Note that when we only corrected the preposition errors marked MT by preposition error detection module, the precision and recall are both lower than that of RT. The amount of false alarm instances of detection module in MT seems to be too high, thus in this paper, we won't correct the instance marked MT to insure the higher precision of overall preposition correction.

4. Conclusion

In this paper, we integrate four learning-based methods in determiner and preposition error detection and correction. The integrated system simply parses and tags the test sentences and then corrects determiners and prepositions step by step. The training of our system relies on well-formed corpora and thus seems to be easier to re-implement it. The large well-formed corpus might also insure higher recall.

In the future, we plan to integrate the system in a more flexible way. The detection modules could pass probabilities to the correction modules. The correction modules thus could decide whether to correct the instances or not. In addition, we plan to reduce the false alarm rate of the detection module. Besides, a more considerable evaluation would be conducted in the near future.

Acknowledgements

We would acknowledge the funding support from the Project (NSC 100-2627-E-007-001) and the help of the participants. Thanks also go to the comments of anonymous reviewers on this paper.

References

Mei-Hua Chen and Maosung Lin, 2011. Factors and Analyses of Common Miscollocations of College Students in Taiwan. *Studies in English Language and Literature*, 28, pp. 57-72.

Martin Chodorow, Joel R. Tetreault, and Na-Rae Han. 2007. Detection of grammatical errors involving prepositions. In *Proceedings of the Fourth ACL-SIGSEM Workshop on Prepositions*, pp. 25-30.

Robert Dale and Adam Kilgarriff. 2010. Helping Our Own: Text massaging for computational linguistics as a new shared task. In *Proceedings of the 6th International Natural Language Generation Conference*, pp. 261–266.

Robert Dale, Ilya Anisimoff and George Narroway (2012) HOO 2012: A Report on the Preposition and Determiner Error Correction Shared Task. In *Proceedings of the Seventh Workshop on Innovative Use of NLP for Building Educational Applications.*

Rachele De Felice and Stephen G. Pulman. 2007. Automatically acquiring models of preposition use. In *Proceedings of the Fourth ACL-SIGSEM Workshop on Prepositions*, pp. 45-50.

Claudia Leacock, Martin Chodorow, Michael Gamon, and Joel Tetreault. 2010. *Automated Grammatical Error Detection for Language Learners.* Synthesis Lectures on Human Language Technologies. Morgan and Claypool.

Adwait Ratnaparkhi. 1997. A linear observed time statistical parser based on maximum entropy models. In *Proceedings of the Second Conference on Empirical Methods in Natural Language Processing*, Brown University, Providence, Rhode Island.

Michael Swan and Bernard Smith, editors. *Learner English: A teacher's guide to interference and other problems.* Cambridge University Press, 2 edition, 2001. DOI: 10.1017/CBO9780511667121 19, 23, 91

Tsuruoka Y, Tateishi Y, Kim JD, Ohta T, McNaught J, Ananiadou S, Tsujii J. 2005. Developing a robust part-of-speech tagger for biomedical text. In *Advances in Informatics, 10th Panhellenic Conference on Informatics*; 11-13 November 2005 Volos, Greece. Springer; pp. 382-392.

HOO 2012 Shared Task: UKP Lab System Description

Torsten Zesch[†‡] **and Jens Haase**[†]

[†]Ubiquitous Knowledge Processing Lab (UKP-TUDA)
Department of Computer Science, Technische Universität Darmstadt

[‡]Ubiquitous Knowledge Processing Lab (UKP-DIPF)
German Institute for Educational Research and Educational Information

www.ukp.tu-darmstadt.de

Abstract

In this paper, we describe the UKP Lab system participating in the HOO 2012 Shared Task on preposition and determiner error correction. Our focus was to implement a highly flexible and modular system which can be easily augmented by other researchers. The system might be used to provide a level playground for subsequent shared tasks and enable further progress in this important research field on top of the state of the art identified by the shared task.

1 Introduction

UKP Lab already participated in the previous HOO Shared Task in 2011. Our knowledge-based system (Zesch, 2011) was targeted towards detecting real-word spelling errors, but performed also well on a number of other error classes.[1] However, it was not competitive for article and preposition errors where supervised systems based on confusion sets constitute the state of the art. Thus, we tailor the HOO 2011 system towards correcting article and preposition errors, but also implement a supervised approach based on confusion sets (Golding and Schabes, 1996; Jones and Martin, 1997; Carlson et al., 2001).

We decided to implement a basic system that should be as flexible as possible and might serve as a basis for experiments in future rounds of the shared task. We also plan to model the most successful systems in our framework as soon as the system descriptions are made available.[2] This might provide a level playground for subsequent shared tasks and enable real progress in this important field on top of the state of the art identified by the HOO shared task.

2 Supervised Error Detection

We implement a generic framework for article and preposition error detection based on the open-source DKPro framework.[3] DKPro is a collection of software components for natural language processing based on the Apache UIMA framework (Ferrucci and Lally, 2004). It comes with a collection of ready-made modules which can be combined to form more complex applications.

Our goal is to develop a system which is as flexible as possible with respect to (i) linguistic preprocessing, (ii) the extraction of features, and (iii) the applied classification method. We will make the source code publicly available as part of the DKPro infrastructure and hope that this will lower the obstacles for participating in future rounds of the HOO Shared Task.

We also provide a reference implementation of the HOO 2012 experiments based on the DKPro Lab framework (Eckart de Castilho and Gurevych, 2011) which enables (i) parameter sweeping, (ii) modeling of interdependent tasks (like e.g. training and test cycles), (iii) generating performance reports, and (iv) storing all experimental results in a convenient manner.

[1] http://clt.mq.edu.au/research/projects/hoo/hoo2011/reports/hoo2011-UDposter.pdf

[2] We invite other participating teams to help with this effort.

[3] http://code.google.com/p/dkpro-core-asl/

2.1 Linguistic Preprocessing

For our basic implementation, we only use a few preprocessing steps. We tokenize and sentence split the data with the default DKPro segmenter, and then use TreeTagger (Schmid, 2004) to POS-tag and chunk the sentences. However, the framework allows the effortless addition of other preprocessing components, e.g. parsing or named-entity recognition.

2.2 Feature Extraction

We implement a generic feature extraction process based on the ClearTK project (Ogren et al., 2008). ClearTK provides a set of highly flexible feature extractors that access the annotations (e.g. POS tags, chunks, etc.) created by the linguistic preprocessing.

One important decision during training is to decide which instances should be used for feature extraction. In the simplest setting, each token is used to generate an instance, but this would result in a very high number of negative instances for every positive instance. For the error classes RT/UT and RD/UD, a more balanced distribution of instances can be easily enforced by only creating a positive instance if the token equals an element in the corresponding confusion set. We create a negative instance by removing or changing the article/preposition.

For articles, we use the confusion set:

{a, an, the, this}[4]

For prepositions, we use the confusion set:

{as, at, but, by, for, from, in, of, on, out, over, since, than, to, up, with}

The confusion set is a parameter to the feature extraction method and can be changed easily. This also makes it possible to apply the framework to other error classes, e.g. for correcting frequently confused words like (accept, except) or (than, then).

Table 1 lists the set of basic features implemented in the reference system. As our goal was to implement a highly flexible system, we put more effort in the overall architecture than in the feature engineering. N-gram features are computed based on the Google Web1T n-gram corpus (Brants and Franz, 2006) which is accessed using jWeb1T.[5]

The listed features can be improved in many ways, e.g. the chunk feature could also encode the type of the chunk. As the framework allows to easily add new feature extractors, we are going to integrate the most successful features from the shared task. Due to the modular architecture of ClearTK, the implemented feature extractors could even be re-used for other classification tasks unrelated to spelling correction.

2.3 Classification

ClearTK provides a wide range of adapters to well known machine learning frameworks and classification tools. As of April 2012, the following adapters are supported:

- LIBSVM[6]
- MALLET[7] (McCallum, 2002)
- OpenNLP Maxent[8]
- SVM^{light}[9] (Joachims, 1999)
- SVM^{light}-TK[10] (Moschitti, 2006)
- Weka[11] (Hall et al., 2009)

As we can easily switch the classifier, we tried a wide range of classifiers, but SVM worked generally best. For the official runs, we used SVM as implemented in the Weka toolkit with the parameter "BuildLogisticModels" which allows to base a detection decision on the confidence of the classifier in order to improve precision.

3 Knowledge-based Error Detection

Besides the supervised system described above, we also apply our knowledge-based system from the HOO 2011 Pilot Round (Zesch, 2011). We re-implemented two state-of-the-art approaches: the

[4] In the official runs, *an* was not part of the confusion set, but was specially handled in a post-processing step. In the current version of the framework, we removed this heuristic and now treat *an* as a normal part of the confusion set.

[5] code.google.com/p/jweb1t/
[6] http://www.csie.ntu.edu.tw/~cjlin/libsvm/
[7] http://mallet.cs.umass.edu/
[8] http://opennlp.apache.org/
[9] http://svmlight.joachims.org/
[10] http://disi.unitn.it/moschitti/Tree-Kernel.htm
[11] http://www.cs.waikato.ac.nz/ml/weka/

Name	Description	Range of Values / Examples
pos_{-2-1}	The neighboring POS tags. For the example we assume "IN NNP *DT* NN VBD".	IN-NNP
pos_{-2}		IN
pos_{-1}		NNP
pos_{+1}		NN
pos_{+2}		VBD
pos_{+1+2}		NN-VBD
$chunk_{-1}$	Whether the neighboring tokens are part of a chunk. For the example, we assume "in *the* [United States]".	O
$chunk_{+1}$		B
$chunk_{+2}$		I
$chunk_{+1+2}$		B-I
$vowel_{+1}$	Whether the next token starts with a vowel or not.	0/1
$cons_{+1}$	Whether the next token starts with a consonant or not.	0/1
$sign_{+1}$	Any sign that is not an alphabetic character.	0/1
n-gram($t_{-1}\{x \rightarrow y\}$)	Let f(n-gram) be the frequency of the n-gram in a certain corpus. All n-gram features are then computed as $\frac{f(xt_{+1}t_{+2})}{f(t_{+1}t_{+2})} - \frac{f(yt_{+1}t_{+2})}{f(t_{+1}t_{+2})}$	n-gram("{the → a} big house");
n-gram($\{x \rightarrow y\}t_{+1}$)		f("the big house") $= 100$;
n-gram($t_{-1}\{x \rightarrow y\}t_{+1}$)		f("a big house") $= 50$;
n-gram($t_{-2}t_{-1}\{x \rightarrow y\}$)		f("big house") $= 1000$;
n-gram($\{x \rightarrow y\}t_{+1}t_{+2}$)		$\frac{100}{1000} - \frac{50}{1000} = 0.05$

Table 1: List of features used for classification.

knowledge-based approach (Hirst and Budanitsky, 2005) and the statistical approach (Mays et al., 1991; Wilcox-OHearn et al., 2008). Both approaches measure the contextual fitness of a word and the surrounding context. For that purpose, the *knowledge-based approach* computes the semantic relatedness of a target word with all other words in a certain context window. This approach is not suitable for correcting article or preposition errors, as these word classes are not linked to the context via lexical-semantic relations. Thus, we only use the *statistical approach* that computes the probability of a sentence based on a n-gram language model. We use the Google Web1T n-gram data (Brants and Franz, 2006).

Although being generally applicable to article and preposition errors, the statistical approach needs some adaptations in order to achieve acceptable performance. In the original definition, the approach computes the probability of all alternative sentences where the target word is replaced with a word from the vocabulary that has low edit distance to the target word. This results in a very high false detection rate. Thus, we (i) limit detections to positions where an article or preposition is already present, and (ii) select the substitution candidate not from all tokens with low edit distance to the original token, but only from the appropriate confusion set.

As the statistical approach is purely based on n-gram frequencies, while this is only one feature of the supervised approach, we expect the supervised approach to outperform our adapted knowledge-based system by a wide margin.

4 Experimental Setup

We model all experiment pipelines in the previously described framework. As training data, we use the publicly available Brown corpus (Francis W. Nelson and Kuçera, 1964), but limit training to 3,700 randomly selected sentences in order to speed up the training process.

4.1 Unofficial Runs

Due to technical problems, we were not able to submit all runs in time. We therefore report also unofficial runs which we evaluated on the test data that was available for participants for a limited amount of time.[12] Although we did not tailor the unofficial runs in any way towards the test data, they have certainly a different status than the official runs. We do not consider this as a major problem, as our basic

[12]HOO 2012 test data was subject to a strict license and needed to be deleted after the evaluation period.

	Description	Run	Detection P	Detection R	Detection F	Recognition P	Recognition R	Recognition F	Correction P	Correction R	Correction F
Baselines	Always *the*	-	7.09	6.13	6.58	7.09	6.13	6.58	2.00	1.69	1.81
	Always *of*	-	11.51	28.54	16.40	11.51	28.54	16.40	1.53	3.81	2.19
Unofficial	2011 Articles; $\alpha = .005$	-	9.62	8.47	9.00	9.62	8.47	9.00	0.96	0.85	0.90
	2011 Prepositions; $\alpha = .005$	-	18.11	23.04	20.28	18.11	23.04	20.28	9.00	11.42	10.05
	2012 Naive Bayes	-	9.35	39.32	15.11	9.35	39.32	15.11	1.26	5.29	2.03
	2012 SVM	-	10.46	33.40	15.93	10.46	33.40	15.93	2.71	8.67	4.13
Official	$\theta_{RD} = 0.95; \theta_{RT} = 0.8$	UD0	8.64	7.73	8.16	4.94	4.42	4.66	1.48	1.32	1.40
	$\theta_{RD} = 0.8; \theta_{RT} = 0.7$	UD1	8.36	15.45	10.85	4.18	7.73	5.43	1.19	2.21	1.55
	$\theta_{RD} = 0.5; \theta_{RT} = 0.3$	UD2	8.94	31.13	13.88	5.51	19.21	8.57	1.20	4.19	1.87

Table 2: HOO 2012 test data: Results (in %) for article and preposition errors combined.

feature set is not competitive with the best performing systems anyway.

We implemented two baseline systems, one for articles and one for prepositions. The baselines replace every occurrence of an article/preposition with the most frequent article/preposition from the confusion set (*the* for articles, *of* for prepositions).

We also apply the adapted HOO 2011 statistical approach in two versions as described above: one adapted towards articles, and one adapted towards prepositions.

Finally, we use the new framework for supervised error correction based on the basic feature set described above with two classifiers: Naive Bayes and SVM as implemented in the Weka toolkit version 3.7.5. We treat the correction task as a multi-class problem and only target the error classes RD, RT, UD, UT. The remaining error classes MD and MT (missing articles and prepositions) are more challenging, as it is less obvious how to create good training data from a non-error annotated corpus.

4.2 Official Runs

The three runs that were officially submitted are also based on the SVM implementation in Weka, but we applied the parameter "BuildLogisticModels" which allows to base a detection decision on the confidence of the classifier in order to improve precision. We tuned parameters on the training data and report three runs for the threshold combinations $(\theta_{RD}, \theta_{RT})$ = (0.95, 0.8), (0.8, 0.7), and (0.5, 0.3).

5 Results

Table 2 summarizes the results of all runs. As expected, the basic feature set used in our experiments is not competitive with the top-performing systems in the shared task.[13] However, some observations can be made from the relative differences between the scores. The thresholds applied in the official runs are not working as expected, as precision is not influenced, while recall drops a lot. The HOO 2011 system based on the statistical approach performs quite well for prepositions, but not for articles. Its performance is comparable to the supervised runs, but this is only due to the limited feature set used in our experiment.

As mentioned above, our focus was to implement a highly flexible and modular system for supervised error correction which can be easily augmented by other researchers. We plan to model the most successful systems in our framework as soon as the system descriptions are made available, and we invite other participating teams to help with this effort. The system might provide a level playground for subsequent shared tasks and enable further progress in this important field of research.

Acknowledgments

This work has been supported by the Volkswagen Foundation as part of the Lichtenberg-Professorship Program under grant No. I/82806.

[13]The best performing systems achieve about 40% F-score for detection, 35% for recognition, and 28% for correction. See (Dale et al., 2012) for an overview of the results.

References

Thorsten Brants and Alex Franz. 2006. Web 1T 5-gram Version 1.

Andrew J Carlson, Jeffrey Rosen, and Dan Roth. 2001. Scaling Up Context-Sensitive Text Correction. In *Proceedings of IAAI*.

Robert Dale, Ilya Anisimoff, and George Narroway. 2012. HOO 2012: A Report on the Preposition and Determiner Error Correction Shared Task. In *Proceedings of the Seventh Workshop on Innovative Use of NLP for Building Educational Applications*, Montreal, Canada.

Richard Eckart de Castilho and Iryna Gurevych. 2011. A lightweight framework for reproducible parameter sweeping in information retrieval. In *Proceedings of the 2011 workshop on Data infrastructurEs for supporting information retrieval evaluation (DESIRE '11)*, New York, NY, USA. ACM.

David Ferrucci and Adam Lally. 2004. UIMA: An Architectural Approach to Unstructured Information Processing in the Corporate Research Environment. *Natural Language Engineering*, 10(3-4):327–348.

Francis W. Nelson and Henry Kuçera. 1964. Manual of information to accompany a standard corpus of present-day edited American English, for use with digital computers.

Andrew R. Golding and Yves Schabes. 1996. Combining Trigram-based and feature-based methods for context-sensitive spelling correction. In *Proceedings of the 34th annual meeting on Association for Computational Linguistics*, pages 71–78, Morristown, NJ, USA. Association for Computational Linguistics.

Mark Hall, Eibe Frank, Geoffrey Holmes, Bernhard Pfahringer, Peter Reutemann, and Ian H. Witten. 2009. The WEKA Data Mining Software: An Update. *SIGKDD Explorations*, 11(1).

Graeme Hirst and Alexander Budanitsky. 2005. Correcting real-word spelling errors by restoring lexical cohesion. *Natural Language Engineering*, 11(1):87–111, March.

Thorsten Joachims. 1999. Making large-scale SVM learning practical. In B. Scholkopf, C. Burges, and A. Smola, editors, *Advances in Kernel Methods - Support Vector Learning*.

Michael P Jones and James H Martin. 1997. Contextual spelling correction using latent semantic analysis. In *Proceedings of the Fifth Conference on Applied Natural Language Processing*, pages 166–173, Morristown, NJ, USA. Association for Computational Linguistics.

Eric Mays, Fred. J Damerau, and Robert L Mercer. 1991. Context based spelling correction. *Information Processing & Management*, 27(5):517–522.

Andrew Kachites McCallum. 2002. MALLET: A Machine Learning for Language Toolkit.

Alessandro Moschitti. 2006. Making tree kernels practical for natural language learning. In *Proceedings of the Eleventh International Conference on European Association for Computational Linguistics*, Trento, Italy.

Philip V. Ogren, Philipp G. Wetzler, and Steven Bethard. 2008. ClearTK: A UIMA Toolkit for Statistical Natural Language Processing. In *Towards Enhanced Interoperability for Large HLT Systems: UIMA for NLP workshop at Language Resources and Evaluation Conference (LREC)*.

Helmut Schmid. 2004. Efficient Parsing of Highly Ambiguous Context-Free Grammars with Bit Vectors. In *Proceedings of the 20th International Conference on Computational Linguistics (COLING 2004)*, Geneva, Switzerland.

Amber Wilcox-OHearn, Graeme Hirst, and Alexander Budanitsky. 2008. Real-word spelling correction with trigrams: A reconsideration of the Mays, Damerau, and Mercer model. In *Proceedings of the 9th international conference on Computational linguistics and intelligent text processing (CICLing)*.

Torsten Zesch. 2011. Helping Our Own 2011: UKP Lab System Description. In *Proceedings of the Helping Our Own Working Group Session at the 13th European Workshop on Natural Language Generation*, pages 260–262.

Crowdsourced Comprehension: Predicting Prerequisite Structure in Wikipedia

Partha Pratim Talukdar
Machine Learning Department
Carnegie Mellon University
ppt@cs.cmu.edu

William W. Cohen
Machine Learning Department
Carnegie Mellon University
wcohen@cs.cmu.edu

Abstract

The growth of open-access technical publications and other open-domain textual information sources means that there is an increasing amount of online technical material that is in principle available to all, but in practice, incomprehensible to most. We propose to address the task of helping readers comprehend complex technical material, by using statistical methods to model the "prerequisite structure" of a corpus — i.e., the semantic impact of documents on an individual reader's state of knowledge. Experimental results using Wikipedia as the corpus suggest that this task can be approached by crowdsourcing the production of ground-truth labels regarding prerequisite structure, and then generalizing these labels using a learned classifier which combines signals of various sorts. The features that we consider relate pairs of pages by analyzing not only textual features of the pages, but also how the containing corpora is connected and created.

1 Introduction and Motivation

Nicholas Carr has argued in his recent popular book "The Shallows" that existing Internet technologies encourage "shallow" processing of recent and popular information, at the expense of "deeper", contemplative study of less immediately-accessible information (Carr, 2011) . While Carr's hypothesis is difficult to formalize rigorously, it seems intuitively plausible. For instance, user-generated content from Twitter and Facebook is mainly comprised of short, shallow snippets of information. Most current research in AI (and more broadly in computer science) does not seem likely to reverse this trend: e.g., work in crowdsourcing has concentrated on tasks that can be easily decomposed into small pieces, and much current NLP research aims at facilitating short-term "shallow" goals, such as answering well-formulated questions (e.g., (Kwok et al., 2001)) and extracting concrete facts (e.g., (Etzioni et al., 2006; Yates et al., 2007; Carlson et al., 2010)). This raises the question: what can AI do to facilitate deep, contemplative study?

In this paper we address one aspect of this larger goal. Specifically, we consider automation of a novel task—using AI methods to facilitate the "deep comprehension" of complex technical material. We conjecture that the primary reason that technical documents are difficult to understand is lack of modularity: unlike a self-contained document written for a general reader, technical documents require certain background knowledge to comprehend—while that background knowledge may also be available in other on-line documents, determining the proper sequence of documents that a particular reader should study is difficult.

We thus formulate the problem of comprehending technical material as a probabilistic planning problem, where reading a document is an operator that will probabilistically change the state of knowledge $K(u,t)$ of a user u at time t, in a manner that depends on u's prior knowledge $K(u,t-1)$. Solving this task requires, among other things, understanding the effect of reading individual documents d — specifically, the concepts that are explained by d, and the concepts that are *prerequisites* for comprehending d. This paper addresses this problem. In particular, we consider predicting whether one page in Wikipedia is a prerequisite of another.

More generally, we define the "prerequisite struc-

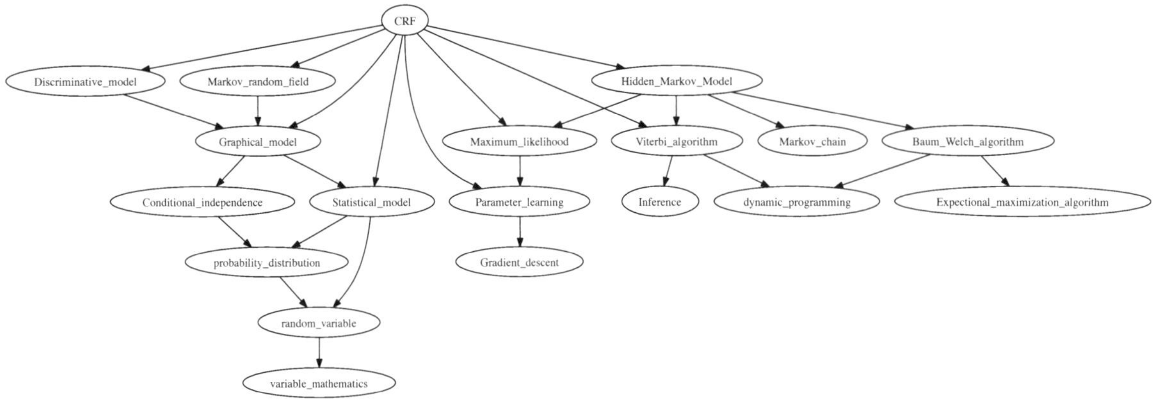

Figure 1: The prerequisite structure rooted at the page "Conditional Random Fields", omitting nodes that would already be known a typical CS graduate student.

Variable (Mathematics)	Random Variable	Probability Distribution
Conditional Independence	Statistical Model	Graphical Model
Discriminative Model	Markov Random Field	
Gradient Descent	Parameter Learning	Maximum Likelihood
Inference	Dynamic Programming	Viterbi Algorithm
Markov Chain	Expectation Maximization Algorithm	Baum Welch Algorithm
Hidden Markov Model	CRF	

Figure 2: A plan for comprehending "Conditional Random Fields" (to be read left-to-right, top-to-bottom). Horizontal lines indicate breaks between independent sections of the subgraph.

ture" for a corpus as a graph, where nodes are concepts to comprehend, and a directed edge $d \rightarrow d'$ corresponds to the assertion "understanding d' is a prerequisite to understanding d". For Wikipedia, we assume a one-to-one correspondence between document titles and concepts explicated by (i.e., post-conditions of) these documents. Figure 2 presents a small example of a prerequisite structure, and indicates how it might be used to construct a plan for comprehending a specific concept.

Focusing on Wikipedia has several advantages. First, it is densely linked, and hence a document d will likely be linked directly to any prerequisite page d'. (However, not all hyperlinks will indicate a prerequisite.) Second, Wikipedia's standardized format makes textual analysis easier. Finally, there is a great deal of social information available about how documents are used by the Wikipedia community. These properties make it easy for us to explore the informativeness of different types of information with respect to predicting prerequisite structure.

Our overall plan for producing a prerequisite structure for a corpus is first, to use crowdsourcing approaches to obtain a subset of the prerequisite structure; and second, to extrapolate this structure to the entire corpus using machine learning. Below, we first describe datasets that we have collected, based on five technical concepts in Wikipedia from five different fields. We then outline the specifics of our procedure for annotating prerequisite structure, using Amazon's Mechanical Turk, and demonstrate that meaningful signals about prerequisite structure can be obtained using a classifier that exploits several sources: graph analysis of Wikipedia's link graph; graph analysis of a bipartite graph relating Wikipedia pages to Wikipedians that have edited these pages; and textual analysis. We complete our experimental analysis of the prerequisite-structure prediction task by discussing and evaluating the degree to which prerequisite-structure prediction is domain-independent, and the degree to which different subareas of Wikipedia (e.g., biology *vs* computer science) require different predictors.

After discussing related work, we return in the concluding remarks to the overarching goal of facilitating comprehension, and discuss the relation-

Target Concept	#Nodes	#Edges	#Edits
Global Warming	19,170	501,608	1,490,967
Meiosis	19,811	444,100	880,684
Newton's Laws of Motion	15,714	436,035	795,988
Parallel Postulate	14,966	363,462	858,785
Public-key cryptography	16,695	371,104	1,003,181

Table 1: Target concepts used in the experiments.

ship of the current study to these goals. Specifically we note that facilitating comprehension also requires understanding a user's goals, and her initial state of knowledge, in addition to understanding the prerequisite structure of the corpus. We also discuss the relationship between planning and prerequisite-structure prediction and suggest that use of appropriately robust planning methods may lead to good comprehension plans, even with imperfectly predicted prerequisite structure.

2 Experiments

As discussed above, we focus in this paper on predicting prerequisite structure in Wikipedia. While most Wikipedia pages are accessible to a general reader, there are many pages that describe technical concepts, such as "conditional random fields", "cloud radiative forcing", and "Corticotropin-releasing factor". Most of these technical pages are not self-contained: for instance, to read and comprehend the page on "conditional random fields", one will have to first understand "graphical model", and so on, as suggested by Figure 1. In this section, we evaluate the following questions:

- Can we train a statistical classifier for prerequisite classification in a target domain, where the classifier is trained on out of domain (i.e., non-target domain) data annotated using Amazon Mechanical Turk service?
- What are the effects of different types of signals on the performance of such a classifier?
- How does out of domain training compare to in domain training?

2.1 Experimental Setup

For our experiments, we choose five targets from differing areas for experimentation, listed in Table 1. Several of the techniques we used are based on graph analysis. The full graphs associated with Wikipedia are unwieldy to use for experimentation because of their size: therefore, for each target concept, we extracted a moderate-sized low-conductance subgraph of Wikipedia's link graph containing the target, using a variant of the PageRank-Nibble algorithm (Andersen et al., 2006).[1]. As parameters we used $\alpha = 0.15$ and $\epsilon = 10^{-7}$, yielding graphs with approximately 15-20,000 nodes and 350-500,000 edges each. We also collected the edit history for each page in every subgraph forming a second graph for each sub-domain [2]. On average, each page from these subgraphs had been edited about 20 times, by about 8 unique editors. Details are given in Table 1.

For classification, we used a Maximum Entropy (MaxEnt) classifier. Given a pair of Wikipedia pages $x = (d, d')$ connected by a directed edge (hyperlink) from d to d', the classifier will predict with probability $p(+1|x)$ whether the main concept in page d' is a prerequisite for the main concept in page d. The classifier has the form

$$p(y|x) = \frac{\exp(\mathbf{w} \cdot \phi(x, y))}{\sum_{y' \in Y} \exp(\mathbf{w} \cdot \phi(x, y'))}, \; y \in Y = \{-1, +1\}$$

where $\phi(x, y)$ is a feature function which represents the pair of pages $x = (d, d')$ in a high dimensional space, and $\mathbf{w}$ is the parameter vector of the classifier which is estimated from training data. We use the Mallet package[3] to train and evaluate classifiers. For the experiments in this paper, we shall exploit the following types of features:

WikiHyperlinks: Features include the random walk with restart (RWR) score (Tong et al., 2006) of the target concept page d' starting from the source page d. Additional features include the PageRank score of the target and source pages.

[1]Specifically, we used the "ApproximatePageRank" method from (Andersen et al., 2006) to find a set of nodes S containing a low-conductance subgraph, but did not prune S to find the lowest-conductance subgraph of it with a "sweep". The version of Wikipedia's link graph we used was DBPedia's version 3.7 (Auer et al., 2007)

[2]Specifically, a bipartite graph connecting pages and editors. We used a version of Wikipedia's edit history extracted by other researchers (Leskovec et al., 2010), discarding edits marked as "minor" by the editor.

[3]Mallet package: http://mallet.cs.umass.edu/

Domain	Time (s) / Evaluation	Worker / HIT	# HITs	κ
Meiosis	38	3	400	0.50
Public-key Cryp.	26	3	200	0.63
Parallel Postulate	41	3	200	0.55
Newton's Laws	20	5	400	0.47
Global Warming	14	5	400	0.56
Average	27.8	-	-	0.54

Table 2: Statistics about the Gold-standard data prepared using Amazon Mechanical Turk. Also shown are the averaged κ statistics-based inter-annotator agreement in each domain. The last row corresponds to the κ value averaged across all five domains.

WikiEdits: This includes one feature—the analogous RWR score on the graph of edit information.

WikiPageContent: Features in this category are derived from the contents of the two Wikipedia pages d and d'. Examples include: the category identity of the source page; the category identity of the target page; whether the titles of d' and d are mentioned in the first sentence of d; the name of the first section in d which contains a link to d'; whether there is any overlap in categories between the two pages; whether d is also linked from d'; and the log of the number of times d' is linked form d. We use the JWPL library (http://jwpl.googlecode.com) for efficient and structured access to Wikipedia pages from a recent dump obtained on Jan 4, 2012.

2.1.1 Gold-standard Annotation from Mechanical Turk[4]

In order to evaluate different prerequisite classification systems and also to train the MaxEnt classifier, we collected gold prerequisite decisions using Amazon Mechanical Turk (AMT). Since preparing annotated gold data for entire graphs in Table 1 would be prohibitively expensive, we used the following strategy to sample a smaller subgraph from the larger domain-specific subgraph, which in turn will be used for training and evaluation purposes. Preliminary investigation suggested that most of the pages in the prerequisite structure rooted at a target concept d are connected to d via many short hyperlink paths. Hence, for each target domain, we first selected the top 20 nodes with highest RWR scores, relative to the target concept, in the subgraph for that target concept (as listed in Table 1.) We then sampled a total of 400 edges from these selected nodes, with outgoing edges from a node sampled with a frequency proportional to its RWR score. Thus, using this strategy, we selected up to 400 pairs of pages (d, d'), where each pair has a hyperlink from d to d'.

Classification of a pair of hyperlinked Wikipedia pages (d, d') into one of the four following classes constituted a Human Intelligence Task (HIT): (1) d' is a prerequisite of d; (2) d is a prerequisite of d'; (3) the two pages are unrelated; (4) Don't know. Subsequently, based on the feedback from the workers, a fifth option was also added: the two concepts are related, but they don't have any prerequisite relationship between them. Based on the available workers and turnaround time, the number of assignments per HIT (i.e., number of unique workers assigned to a particular HIT) was either 3 or 5; and the number of HITs used was either 200 or 400. Depending on the hardness of domain and availability of workers opting to work on a domain, reward per HIT assignment was varied from \$0.02 (for Global Warming and Newton's Laws) to \$0.08 (for Public-key Cryptography, Meiosis and Parallel Postulate). This data collection stage spanning all five domains was completed in about a week at a total cost of \$278. Statistics about the data are presented in Table 2[5].

Starting with the AMT data collected as above, we next created a binary-labeled training dataset, where each instance corresponds to a pair of pages. We ignored all "Don't Know" labels, treated option (1) above as vote for the corresponding prerequisite edge, and treated all other options as votes against. We then assigned the final label for a node pair using majority vote (breaking ties arbitrarily).

2.1.2 Consistency of labels

In contrast to standard setup of gold data preparation where a single annotator is guaranteed to provide feedback on every instance, the situation in case of Mechanical Turk-based annotation is different, as the workers are at liberty to choose the HITs (or instances) they want to work on. This makes

[4]Amazon Mechanical Turk: http://mturk.amazon.com

[5]The dataset is available upon request from the authors.

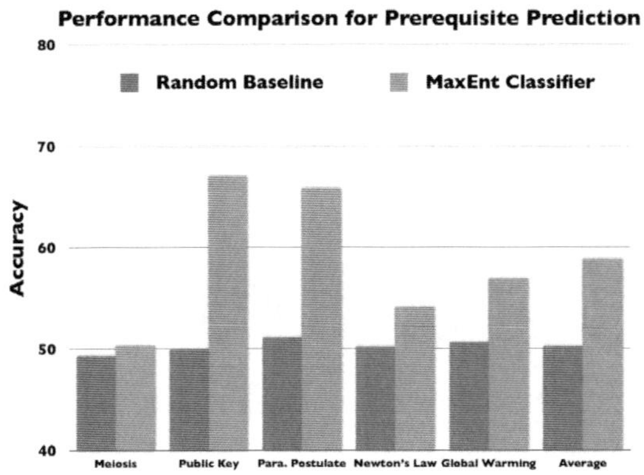

Figure 3: Comparison of performance between the MaxEnt classifier (right bar in each group) against a random baseline (left bar in each group) in all five domains. On average, the MaxEnt classifier results in an 8.6% absolute improvement in accuracy.

standard κ statistics-based inter-annotator computation (Fleiss, 1981) inapplicable in the current setting. We circumvented this problem by first selecting all workers with at least 100 feedbacks, and then computing pairwise κ statistics between all pairs of these frequent workers. These κ statistics were averaged across each domain, and also averaged across all domains. The results, also shown in Table 2, show moderate agreement (recall that $\kappa = 0$ indicates no correlation). We are encouraged to observe that moderate level of agreement is possible even in this setting, where there is no control over worker background and quality. We next explore whether this level of agreement is sufficient to train statistical classifiers.

2.2 Prerequisite Classification

In this section, we explore whether it is possible to train a MaxEnt classifier to determine prerequisite structure in a target domain, with the training performed in "leave one domain out" manner, where the training data originates from domains other than the target domain. For example, for classifications in the target domain, say "Global Warming", we train the classifier with annotated data from the remaining four domains (or whatever domains are available). We note that training on "out of domain", if it is successful, has several benefits. First, a successful training strategy in this setup removes any need to have labeled data in each target domain of interest, which is particularly relevant as labeled data is expensive to prepare. Second, a classifier trained just once can be repeatedly used across multiple domains without requiring retraining.

Accuracies of MaxEnt classifiers trained using the "leave one domain out" strategy are shown in Figure 3; we report the test accuracy on each target domain, as well as the average across domains. Performance of a random classifier is presented as a baseline. Classes in the train and test sets were balanced by oversampling the minority class. From Figure 3, we observe that it is indeed possible to train prerequisite classifiers in an out of domain setting, using data from the Amazon Mechanical Turk service; on average, the classifier outperforms the random baseline with 8.6% absolute improvement in classification accuracy. We also experimented with other rule-based classifiers[6], and in all cases, the trained MaxEnt classifier outperformed these baselines. Although more sophisticated training strategies and more clever feature engineering would likely yield further improvements, we find it encouraging that even a relatively straightforward classification technology along with a basic set of features was able to achieve significant improvement in performance on the novel task of prerequisite prediction.

2.3 Feature Ablation Experiments

The MaxEnt classifier evaluated in the previous section had access to all three types of features: WikiEdits, WikiHyperLinks, and WikiPageContent, as described in the beginning of this section. In order to evaluate the contribution of each such signal, we created ablated versions of the full MaxEnt classifier which uses only one of these three subsets. We call these thee variants: MaxEnt-WikiEdits, MaxEnt-WikiHyperLinks, and MaxEnt-WikiPageContent, respectively. Average accuracies across all five domains comparing these three variants, in comparison to the Random baseline and the full classifier (MaxEnt-Full, as in previous section) are presented in Table 3. From this, we observe that all three variants perform better than the random baseline, with maximum gains achieved by the MaxEnt-WikiPageContent classifier, which uses page content-based features exclusively. We

[6]For example, classify d' as a prerequisite for d if d' is linked from the first paragraph in d.

System	Accuracy
Random	50.22
MaxEnt-WikiEdits	51.62
MaxEnt-WikiHyperlinks	52.70
MaxEnt-WikiPageContent	57.84
MaxEnt-Full	58.82

Table 3: Comparison of accuracies (averaged across all five domains) of the full MaxEnt classifier with its ablated versions which use a subset of the features, and also the random baseline. The full classifier, which exploits all three types of signals (viz., WikiEdits, WikiHyperlinks, and WikiPageContent) achieves the highest performance.

Domain	Wiki-Edits	Wiki-HyperLinks	WikiPage-Content	All
Meiosis	**5.4**	**2.4**	**0.3**	**1**
Public-key Crypto.	-0.7	-1.8	**15.1**	**17.1**
Parallel Postulate	**3.1**	**6.1**	**11.7**	**14.7**
Newton's Laws	-0.2	**6.2**	**3.9**	**3.9**
Global Warming	-7.7	**0.1**	**5.8**	**6.8**

Table 4: Accuracy gains (absolute) relative to the Random baseline achieved by the full MaxEnt classifier as well as its ablated versions trained with three different subsets of the full classifier. Positive gains are marked in bold.

also note that the full classifier MaxEnt-Full, is able to effectively combine three types of signals improving performance even further. In Table 4, we present a per-domain breakdown of the gains achieved by these four classifiers over the random baseline. From this, we observe that the MaxEnt-WikiEdits classifier outperforms the random baseline only in 2 out of 5 domains. This might be due to the fact that the MaxEnt-WikiEdits uses uses only one feature—the RWR score of the target page relative to the source page on the Wikipedia edits graph. We hope that use of more discriminating features should further help this classifier. From Table 4, we also observe that MaxEnt-WikiHyperLinks is able to outperform the random baseline in 4 out of 5 cases, and the MaxEnt-WikiPageContent (as well as the full classifier) outperforms the random baseline in all 5 domains, sometimes with large gains (as in the case of Public-key Cryptography domain).

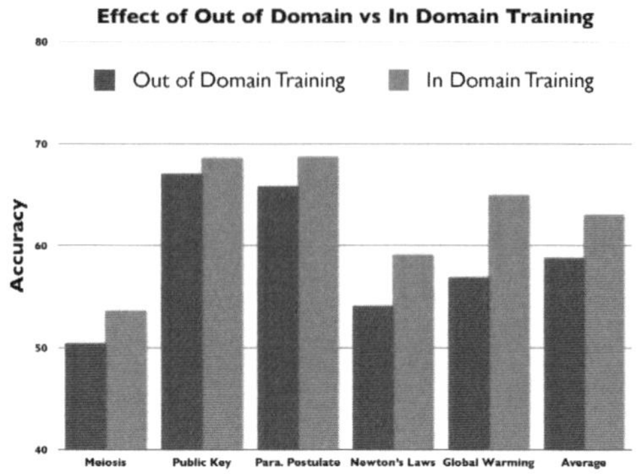

Figure 4: Accuracy comparison of out of domain (left bar in each group) and in domain training (right bar in each group) for the five domains. From this we observe that good generalization performance is possible even when there is no in domain training data available.

2.4 Effect of Out of Domain Training

All the classifiers evaluated in previous sections were trained in an out of domain setting, i.e., the training data originated from domains outside the domain in which the classifier is applied and evaluated. This has several benefits, as noted above. An alternative and more standard way to train classifiers is to have the training and evaluation data be from the same domain (below, the in-domain setting). While such a classifier will require labeled training from each domain of interest, it is nonetheless of interest to compare in-domain and out-of-domain learning. If there are substantive differences, this could be used to improve prerequisite-structure predictor in a subdomain (e.g., biology), or may suggest alternative training methods (e.g., involving transfer learning).

Motivated by this, for each domain, we compare the performances of the out-of-domain and in-domain classification performances. The results are shown in Figure 4. On average, we observe that the out-of-domain classifier is able to achieve 93% of the performance of the in-domain classifier. We note that this is encouraging for domain-independent prerequisite-structure prediction, as this suggests that for the prerequisite classification task, close to optimal (i.e., in-domain performance) is possible when the classifiers are trained in an out-of-domain setting.

3 Related Work

We believe the task of prerequisite structure prediction to be novel; however, it is clearly related to a number of other well-studied research problems.

In light of our emphasis on Wikipedia, a connection can be drawn between identifying prerequisites and measuring the semantic relatedness of concepts using Wikipedia's link structure (Yeh et al., 2009). We consider here a related but narrower question, namely whether an inter-page link will improve comprehension for a specific reader.

In the area of intelligent tutoring and educational data mining, recent research has looked at enriching textbooks with authoritative web content (Agrawal et al., 2010). Also, the problem of detecting prerequisite structure from differential student performance on tests has been considered (e.g., (Pavlik et al., 2008; Vuong et al., 2011)). Our proposal considers discovering prerequisite structure from text, rather than from exercises, and relies on different signals.

Research in adaptive hypermedia (surveyed elsewhere (Chen and Magoulas, 2005)) has goals similar to ours. Most adaptive hypermedia systems operate in narrow domains, which precludes use of some of the crowd-based signals we consider here. In this literature, a distinction is often made between "adaptability" (the ability for a user to modify a presentation of hypermedia) and "adaptivity" (the ability of a system to adapt to a user's needs.) In this framework, our project focuses on adding "adaptivity" to existing corpora via a prerequisite structure, and our principle contribution to this area is identifying techniques that learn to combine textual features and social, crowd-based signals in order to usefully guide comprehension.

Another related area is data-mining logs of Web usage, as surveyed by Pierrakos *et al* (Pierrakos et al., 2003). Our focus here is on facilitating a particular type of Web usage, comprehension, rather than more commonly-performed tasks like site navigation and purchasing.

A number of "open education" resources exist, in which information can be organized into sharable modules with known prerequisites between them (e.g., Connexions (Baraniuk, 2008)). We focus here on discovering prerequisite structure with machine-learning methods rather than simply encoding it. Similarly, a Wikimedia project[7] has developed infrastructure allowing a user to manually assemble Wikipedia pages into e-books. Our focus is on guiding the process of finding and ordering the sections of these books, not the infrastructure for generating them. We also note that one widely-used way for complex technical concepts to be broadly communicated is by writers or teams of writers, and previous researchers have investigated understanding how collaborative writers work (Noël and Robert, 2004), and even developed tools for collaborative writing (Zheng et al., 2006). Our work focuses on tools to empower readers, rather than writers.

4 Conclusion

In this paper, we motivated the goal of "crowdsourcing" the task of helping readers comprehend complex technical material, by using machine learning to predict prerequisite structure from not only document text, but also crowd-generated data such as hyperlinks and edit logs. While it is not immediately obvious that this task is feasible, our experiments suggest that relatively reliable features to predict prerequisite structure exist, and can be successfully combined using standard machine learning methods.

To achieve the broader goal of facilitating comprehension, predicting prerequisite structure is not enough. Another important subproblem is using predicted prerequisites to build a feasible plan. As part of ongoing work, we are exploring use of modern optimization methods (such as Integer Linear Programming) to compute "reading plans" that minimize a weighted linear combination of expected user effort and probability of plan "failure"[8].

We also plan to explore another major subproblem associated with facilitating comprehension—personalizing a reading plan. Clearly, even if d' is a prerequisite for d, a user interested in d need not first read a page explaining d', if she already understands d'; instead, a reading plan based on prerequisite structure should be adjusted based on what is believed about the user's prior knowledge state. In

[7]See http://en.labs.wikimedia.org/wiki/Wiki_to_print, the "Wiki to Print" project.

[8]A plan "failure" means that the plan not actually satisfy all necessary prerequisites, leading to imperfect comprehension on the part of the reader after she executes the plan.

the context of Wikipedia comprehension, one possible signal for predicting an individuals' prior knowledge is the Wikipedia edit log: if we assume that editors tend to edit things they know, the edit log indicates which concepts tend to be jointly known, and hence collaborative-filtering methods might be able to more completely predict a user's knowledge given partial information about her knowledge—just as collaborative-filtering is often used now to extrapolate user preference's from knowledge of others' joint preferences.

Besides contributing to the goal of facilitating comprehension, we believe that the specific problem of predicting prerequisite structure in Wikipedia is a task of substantial independent interest. Prerequisite structure can be thought of as a sort of explanatory discourse structure, which is overlaid on a hyperlink graph; hence, scaling up our methods and applying them to all of Wikipedia would identify a canonical broad-coverage instance of such explanatory discourse. This could be re-used for other tasks much as lexical resources like WordNet are: for instance, consider identifying explanatory discourse in an external technical text (e.g., a textbook) by soft-matching it to the Wikipedia structure, using existing techniques to match the external text to Wikipedia (Agrawal et al., 2010; Mihalcea and Csomai, 2007; Milne and Witten, 2008).

Acknowledgments

This research has been supported in part by DARPA (under contract number FA8750-09-C-0179), and Google. Any opinions, findings, conclusions and recommendations expressed in this paper are the authors' and do not necessarily reflect those of the sponsors. We are thankful to the anonymous reviewers for their constructive comments

References

Agrawal, R., Gollapudi, S., Kenthapadi, K., Srivastava, N., and Velu, R. (2010). Enriching textbooks through data mining. In *Proceedings of the First ACM Symposium on Computing for Development*, page 19. ACM.

Andersen, R., Chung, F., and Lang, K. (2006). Local graph partitioning using pagerank vectors. In *Foundations of Computer Science, 2006. FOCS'06. 47th Annual IEEE Symposium on*, pages 475–486. IEEE.

Auer, S., Bizer, C., Kobilarov, G., Lehmann, J., Cyganiak, R., and Ives, Z. (2007). Dbpedia: A nucleus for a web of open data. In Aberer, K., Choi, K.-S., Noy, N., Allemang, D., Lee, K.-I., Nixon, L., Golbeck, J., Mika, P., Maynard, D., Mizoguchi, R., Schreiber, G., and Cudr-Mauroux, P., editors, *The Semantic Web*, volume 4825 of *Lecture Notes in Computer Science*, pages 722–735. Springer Berlin / Heidelberg.

Baraniuk, R. (2008). *Challenges and opportunities for the open education movement: A Connexions case study*, pages 229–246. MIT Press, Cambridge, Massachusetts.

Carlson, A., Betteridge, J., Kisiel, B., Settles, B., Hruschka Jr, E., and Mitchell, T. (2010). Toward an architecture for never-ending language learning. In *Proceedings of the Conference on Artificial Intelligence (AAAI)*, pages 1306–1313.

Carr, N. (2011). *The shallows: What the Internet is doing to our brains*. WW Norton & Co Inc.

Chen, S. and Magoulas, G. (2005). *Adaptable and adaptive hypermedia systems*. IRM Press.

Etzioni, O., Banko, M., and Cafarella, M. (2006). Machine reading. In *Proceedings of the National Conference on Artificial Intelligence*.

Fleiss, J. (1981). The measurement of interrater agreement. *Statistical methods for rates and proportions*, 2:212–236.

Kwok, C., Etzioni, O., and Weld, D. (2001). Scaling question answering to the web. *ACM Transactions on Information Systems (TOIS)*, 19(3):242–262.

Leskovec, J., Huttenlocher, D., and Kleinberg, J. (2010). Governance in social media: a case study of the wikipedia promotion process. In *AAAI International Conference on Weblogs and Social Media (ICWSM '10)*. AAAI.

Mihalcea, R. and Csomai, A. (2007). Wikify!: linking documents to encyclopedic knowledge. In *CIKM*, volume 7, pages 233–242.

Milne, D. and Witten, I. (2008). Learning to link with wikipedia. In *Proceeding of the 17th ACM conference on Information and knowledge management*, pages 509–518. ACM.

Noël, S. and Robert, J. (2004). Empirical study on collaborative writing: What do co-authors do, use, and like? *Computer Supported Cooperative Work (CSCW)*, 13(1):63–89.

Pavlik, P., Cen, H., Wu, L., and Koedinger, K. (2008). Using item-type performance to covariance to improve the skill acquisition of an existing tutor. In *Proc. of the 1st International Conference on Educational Data Mining*.

Pierrakos, D., Paliouras, G., Papatheodorou, C., and Spyropoulos, C. (2003). Web usage mining as a tool for personalization: A survey. *User Modeling and User-Adapted Interaction*, 13(4):311–372.

Tong, H., Faloutsos, C., and Pan, J.-Y. (2006). Fast random walk with restart and its applications. In *Proceedings of the Sixth International Conference on Data Mining*, ICDM '06.

Vuong, A., Nixon, T., and Towle, B. (2011). A method for finding prerequisites within a curriculum. In *Proc. of the 4th International Conference on Educational Data Mining*.

Yates, A., Cafarella, M., Banko, M., Etzioni, O., Broadhead, M., and Soderland, S. (2007). Textrunner: Open information extraction on the web. In *Proceedings of Human Language Technologies: The Annual Conference of the North American Chapter of the Association for Computational Linguistics: Demonstrations*, pages 25–26. Association for Computational Linguistics.

Yeh, E., Ramage, D., Manning, C., Agirre, E., and Soroa, A. (2009). Wikiwalk: random walks on wikipedia for semantic relatedness. In *Proceedings of the 2009 Workshop on Graph-based Methods for Natural Language Processing*, pages 41–49. Association for Computational Linguistics.

Zheng, Q., Booth, K., and McGrenere, J. (2006). Co-authoring with structured annotations. In *Proceedings of the SIGCHI conference on Human Factors in computing systems*, pages 131–140. ACM.

Sense-Specific Lexical Information for Reading Assistance

Soojeong Eom
Georgetown University
se48@georgetown.edu

Markus Dickinson
Indiana University
md7@indiana.edu

Rebecca Sachs
Georgetown University
rrs8@georgetown.edu

Abstract

To support vocabulary acquisition and reading comprehension in a second language, we have developed a system to display sense-appropriate examples to learners for difficult words. We describe the construction of the system, incorporating word sense disambiguation, and an experiment we conducted testing it on a group of 60 learners of English as a second language (ESL). We show that sense-specific information in an intelligent reading system helps learners in their vocabulary acquisition, even if the sense information contains some noise from automatic processing. We also show that it helps learners, to some extent, with their reading comprehension.

1 Introduction and Motivation

Reading texts in a second language presents the language learner with a number of comprehension problems, including the problem of interpreting words that are unknown or are used in unfamiliar ways. These problems are exacerbated by the prevalence of lexical ambiguity. Landes et al. (1998) report that more than half the content words in English texts are lexically ambiguous, with the most frequent words having a large number of meanings. The word *face*, for example, is listed in WordNet (Fellbaum, 1998) with twelve different nominal senses; although not all are equally prevalent, there is still much potential for confusion.

To address this, we have designed an online reading assistant to provide sense-specific lexical information to readers. By *sense-specific*, we refer to information applicable only for one given sense (meaning) of a word. In this paper, we focus on the system design and whether such a system can be beneficial. Our experiment with learners illustrates the effectiveness of such information for vocabulary acquisition and reading comprehension.

The problem of lexical ambiguity in reading comprehension is a significant one. While dictionaries can help improve comprehension and acquisition (see, e.g., Prichard, 2008), lexical ambiguity may lead to misunderstandings and unsuccessful vocabulary acquisition (Luppescu and Day, 1993), as learners may become confused when trying to locate an appropriate meaning for an unknown word among numerous sense entries. Luppescu and Day showed that readers who use a (printed) dictionary have improved comprehension and acquisition, but to the detriment of their reading speed.

For electronic dictionaries as well, lexical ambiguity remains a problem (Koyama and Takeuchi, 2004; Laufer and Hill, 2000; Leffa, 1992; Prichard, 2008), as readers need specific information about a word as it is used in context in order to effectively comprehend the text and thus learn the word. Kulkarni et al. (2008) demonstrated that providing readers with sense-specific information led learners to significantly better vocabulary acquisition than providing them with general word meaning information.

We have developed an online system to provide vocabulary assistance to learners of English as a Second Language (ESL), allowing them to click on unfamiliar words and see lexical information—target word definitions and examples—relevant to that particular usage. We discuss previous online systems in section 2. Importantly, the examples we present are from the COBUILD dictionary (Sinclair, 2006), which is designed for language learners. To present these for any text, our system must map automatic word sense disambiguation (WSD) system output (using WordNet senses (Fellbaum, 1998)) to COBUILD, as covered in section 3, where we also describe general properties of the web system.

The main contribution of this work is to investigate whether high-quality sense-specific lexical information presented in an intelligent reading system helps learners in their vocabulary acquisition and reading comprehension and to investigate the effect of automatic errors on learning. We accordingly ask the following research questions:

1. Does sense-specific lexical information facilitate vocabulary acquisition to a greater extent than: a) no lexical information, and b) lexical information on all senses of each chosen word?
2. Does sense-specific lexical information facilitate learners' reading comprehension?

The method and analysis for investigating these questions with a group of 60 ESL learners is given in section 4, and the results are discussed in section 5.

2 Background

While there are many studies in second language acquisition (SLA) on providing vocabulary and reading assistance (e.g., Prichard, 2008; Luppescu and Day, 1993), we focus on outlining intelligent computer-assisted language learning (ICALL) systems here (see also discussion in Dela Rosa and Eskenazi, 2011). Such systems hold the promise of alleviating some problems of acquiring words while reading by providing information specific to each word as it is used in context (Nerbonne and Smit, 1996; Kulkarni et al., 2008). The GLOSSER-RuG system (Nerbonne and Smit, 1996) disambiguates on the basis of part of speech (POS). This is helpful in distinguishing verbal and nominal uses, for example, but is, of course, ineffective when a word has more than one sense in the same POS (e.g., *face*). More effective is the REAP Tutor (Heilman et al., 2006), which uses word sense disambiguation to provide lexicographic information and has been shown to benefit learners by providing sense-specific lexical information (Dela Rosa and Eskenazi, 2011; Kulkarni et al., 2008).

We build from this work by further demonstrating the utility of sense-specific information. What distinguishes our work is how we build from the notion that the lexical information provided needs to be tuned to the capacities of ESL learners. For example, definitions and illustrative examples should make use of familiar vocabulary if they are to aid language learners; example sentences directly taken from corpora or from the web seem less appropriate because the information in them might be less accessible (Groot, 2000; Kilgarriff et al., 2008; Segler et al., 2002). On the other hand, examples constructed by lexicographers for learner dictionaries typically control for syntactic and lexical complexity (Segler et al., 2002). We thus make use of examples from a dictionary targeting learners.

Specifically, we make use of the examples from the Collins COBUILD Student's Dictionary (Sinclair, 2006), as it is widely used by ESL learners. The content in COBUILD is based on actual English usage and derived from analysis of a large corpus of written and spoken English, thereby providing authentic examples (Sinclair, 2006). COBUILD also focuses on collocations in choosing example sentences, so that the example sentences present natural, reliable expressions, which can play an important role in learners' vocabulary acquisition and reading comprehension. We discuss this resource more in section 3.3.

3 The web system

To support vocabulary acquisition and reading comprehension for language learners, we have designed a system for learners to upload texts and click on words in order to obtain sense-appropriate examples for difficult words while reading, as shown in figure 1. Although the experiment reported upon here focused on 2 preselected texts, the system is able to present lexical information for any content words. Beyond the web interface, the system has three components: 1) a system manager, 2) a natural language processing (NLP) server, and 3) a lexical database.

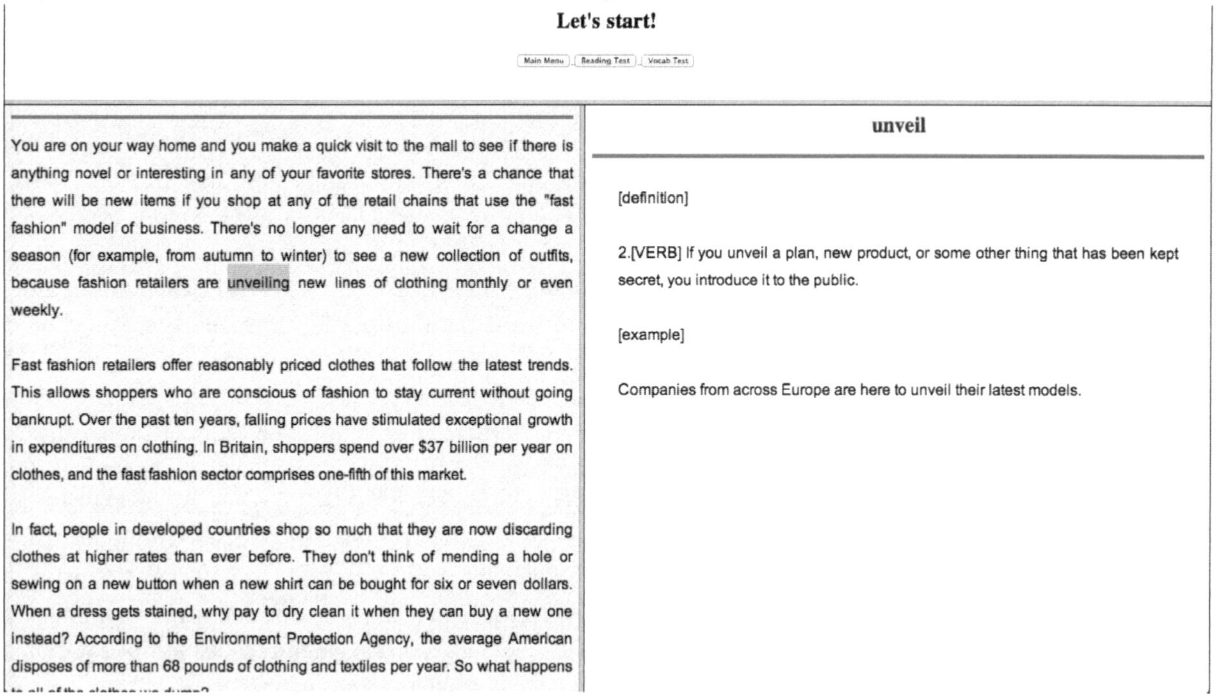

Figure 1: A screenshot showing the effect of clicking on *unveiling* and receiving sense-specific information

3.1 System manager

The system manager controls the interaction among each learner, the NLP server, and the lexical database. When the manager receives a raw text as an input from the learner, it first sends the input text to the server and returns an analyzed text (i.e., tokenized, POS-tagged, and sense-tagged) back to the learner, with content words made clickable. Then, when the learner clicks on a word while reading, the manager sends the word with its sense information to the lexical database and brings the word with its sense-specific lexical information back to the learner from the lexical database.

Upon completion of the reading, the manager sends the learner to a page of tests—i.e., a reading test and a vocabulary test, as described in section 4—and records the responses.

3.2 NLP preprocessing

To convert raw input into a linguistically-analyzed text, the system relies on several basic NLP modules for tokenizing, lemmatizing, POS tagging, and collocation identification. Although for some internal testing with different WSD systems we used other third-party software (e.g., the Stanford POS tagger (Toutanova et al., 2003)), our word sense disambiguator (see below) provides tokenization, lemmatization, and POS tagging, as well as collocation identification. Since the words making up a collocation may be basic, learners can easily overlook them, and so we intend to improve this module in the future, to reduce underflagging of collocations.

3.3 Lexical database

The lexical database is used to provide a sense-appropriate definition and example sentences of an input word to a learner. To obtain the sense-appropriate information, we must perform word sense disambiguation (WSD) on the input text. We use SenseRelate::AllWords (SR:AW) (Pedersen and Kolhatkar, 2009) to perform WSD of input texts, as this system has broad coverage of content words. Given that SR:AW does not outperform the most frequent sense (MFS) baseline, we intend to explore using the MFS in the future, as well as other WSD systems, such as SenseLearner (Mihalcea and Csomai, 2005). However, the quality of SR:AW (F-measure of 54–61% on different corpora) is sufficient to explore in our system and gives us a point to work from. Indeed, as we will see in section 5.3, while SR:AW makes errors, vocabulary learning is, in some ways, perhaps not dramatically impeded.

Even with a WSD system, pointing to appropriate examples is complicated by the fact that the database of learner-appropriate examples is from one repository (COBUILD, see section 2), while automatic WSD systems generally use senses from another (WordNet). The lexical database, then, is indexed by WordNet senses, each of which points to an appropriate corresponding COBUILD sense. While we would prefer disambiguating COBUILD senses directly, we are not aware of any systems which do this or any COBUILD sense-tagged data to train a system on. If the benefits for vocabulary acquisition gained by providing learner-friendly examples from COBUILD merit it, future work could explore building a collection of COBUILD-tagged data to train a WSD system—perhaps a semi-automatic process using the automatic system we describe next.

To build a lexical database covering all words, we built a word sense alignment (WSA) system; this is also in line with a related research agenda investigating the correspondences between sense inventories (Eom et al., 2012). Space limitations preclude a more detailed discussion, but the WSA system works by running SR:AW on COBUILD examples in order to induce a basic alignment structure between WordNet and COBUILD. We then post-process this structure, relying on a heuristic of favoring flatter alignment structures—i.e., links spread out more evenly between senses in each inventory.[1] Iteratively replacing one link with another, to give flatter structures, we weight each type of proposed alignment and accept a new alignment if the weight combined with the probability originally assigned by the WSD system is the best improvement over that of the original alignment structure. After all these steps, the alignments give the lexical database for linking WSD output to COBUILD senses.

We consider alignment structures wherein each WordNet sense maps to exactly one COBUILD sense, to match the task at hand, i.e., mapping each disambiguated WordNet sense to a single set of COBUILD examples. This assumption also makes postprocessing feasible: instead of considering an exponential number of alignment structures, we consider only a polynomial number.

Having collected alignment judgments from linguistics students and faculty, we evaluated the system against a small set of nine words, covering 63 WordNet senses (Eom et al., 2012). The WSA system had a precision of 42.7% (recall=44.5%) when evaluating against the most popular sense, but a precision of 60.7% (recall=36.5%) when evaluating against all senses that seem to be related. We focus on precision since it is important to know whether a learner is being pointed to a correct set of examples or not; whether there are other possibly relevant examples to show is less important. In Eom et al. (2012), we discuss some difficulties of aligning between the two resources in the general case; while some senses go unaligned between the resources, this was not the case for the words used in this study.

For this study, since we use pre-determined input texts, we also created gold-standard information, where each word in the text is manually given a link to the appropriate COBUILD information; note that here there is no intermediate WordNet sense to account for. This lets us gauge: a) whether the gold-standard information is helpful to learners, and b) comparatively speaking, what the effects are of using the potentially noisy information provided by the functioning system.

4 The study

We now turn to evaluating whether this set-up of providing sense-specific lexical information can lead learners to improve their vocabulary acquisition and their reading comprehension.

4.1 Method

4.1.1 Participants

The participants were recruited from three universities and a private institute in Seoul, Korea, giving 60 participants (34 male, 26 female). They ranged in age from 21 to 39 (avg.=23.8) and the length of studying English ranged from 8 to 25 years (avg.=11.32).

The 40 participants from the three universities were taking English courses to prepare for English proficiency testing. The 20 participants from the private institute were mostly university graduates

[1]The general idea is to use information about the alignment structure as a whole; flatter alignments is a convenient heuristic, in lieu of having any other additional information.

taking teacher training courses designed for elementary English teachers. All participants were intermediate-level learners, scoring between 15 and 21 on the reading section of the TOEFL iBT®. We targeted intermediate learners, so as to test the system with learners generally able to understand texts, yet still encounter many unknown words.

The 60 participants were randomly assigned to one of four groups, with 15 participants in each group. The first three received some treatment, while the fourth was a control group:

1. Gold Senses (GS): reading with support of gold standard sense-specific lexical information
2. System Senses (SS): reading with support of system-derived sense-specific lexical information
3. All Senses (AS): reading with support of lexical information of all senses of the chosen word
4. No Senses (NS): reading without any support of lexical information

For example, when presented with the example in (1), if *chains* is clicked, the GS learners see the correct sense, as in (2a), along with associated example sentences (not shown). The automatic system happens to be incorrect, so the SS learners see a related, though incorrect, sense and examples, as in (2b). The AS learners will see those two senses and examples, as well as the three others for *chain*. And the NS learners have no chance to click on a word.

(1) There's a chance that there will be new items if you shop at any of the retail **chains** that use the "fast fashion" model of business.

(2) a. **Gold:** A chain of shops, hotels, or other businesses is a number of them owned by the same person or company.

b. **System:** A chain of things is a group of them existing or arranged in a line.

4.1.2 Materials

Reading texts After piloting various reading texts and drawing on the ESL teaching experience of two of the authors, two texts deemed appropriate for learners at the (high-)intermediate level were adopted: *Fashion Victim* (adapted from *Focus on Vocabulary 1: Bridging Vocabulary* (Schmitt et al., 2011), 589 words) and *Sleep Research* (adapted from *The Official SAT Study Guide* (The College Board, 2009), 583 words).

Fashion Victim	*Sleep Research*
resilient.a, chain.n, conscience.n, cradle.n, expenditure.n, mend.v, outfit.n, sector.n, unveil.v	alternate.a, trivial.a, deliberately.r, aspect.n, fatigue.n, obedience.n, agitate.v, banish.v, indicate.v, resist.v, trigger.v

Table 1: Target words used in the study

The texts were modified to simplify their syntax, to use more ambiguous words in order to allow for a stronger test of the system, and to shorten them to about 600 words. The texts were placed in the online system, and all content words were made clickable.

Target words A total of 20 target words (9 from *Fashion Victim*, 11 from *Sleep Research*) were selected by piloting a number of possible words with 20 learners from a similar population and identifying ones which were the most unfamiliar, which also had multiple senses. They appear in table 1.

Reading comprehension tests For reading comprehension, two tests were developed, each with 4 multiple-choice and 6 true-false questions. The questions focused on general content, and participants could not refer back to the text to answer the questions. For the multiple-choice questions, more than one answer could be selected, and each choice was scored as 1 or 0 (e.g., for 5 choices, the maximum score for the question was 5); for the true-false questions, answers were scored simply 1 or 0. The maximum score for a test was 21.

Vocabulary tests There were one pretest and four immediate posttests, one of which had the same format as the pretest. The pretest and all immediate posttests had the same 30 words (20 target and 10 distractor words). Of 10 distractors, five were words appearing in the text (*obscure.a*, *correlation.n*, *intervention.n*, *discipline.v*, *facilitate.v*), and five were target words but used with a sense that was different from the one used in the reading passage (*deliberately.r*, *chain.n*, *outfit.n*, *mend.v*, *indicate.v*). Each test consisted of a word bank and sentences with blanks (cf. Kim, 2008). For the pretest, the sentences were taken from other sources, whereas the posttest sentences came from the reading texts themselves.

Although we used four posttests in order to test different kinds of vocabulary learning (giving more or fewer hints at meaning), we focus on one posttest in this paper, the one which matches the form of the pretest. Each correct answer was scored as 1; incorrect as 0.

4.1.3 Procedure

The pretest was administered two weeks before the actual experiment and posttests, so as to prevent learners from focusing on those words. Participants who knew more than 16 out of the 20 target words were excluded from the experiment.

After reading one text, learners took a reading comprehension test. Then, they did the same for the second text. After these two rounds, they took the series of vocabulary posttests.

4.1.4 Data analysis

We ran a variety of tests to analyze the data.[2] First, we ran Levene's test of homogeneity of variances, to test whether the variances of the error between groups were equal at the outset of the study. This makes it clearer that the effects from the main tests are due to the variables of interest and not from inherent differences between groups (Larson-Hall, 2010).

Secondly, to test the first research question about whether participants show better vocabulary acquisition with sense-specific lexical information, we used a repeated-measures analysis of variance (RM ANOVA). Time (pre/post) was the within-subject variable and Group (GS, SS, AS, NS) was the between-subject. Post-hoc pairwise comparisons were run in the case of significant results, to determine which groups differed from each other. We also examined the pre-post gain only for the target words which were clicked and for which we might thus expect more improvement.

Thirdly, to test the second research question about whether participants improved in reading comprehension, we used a one-way ANOVA, with reading comprehension scores as a dependent variable and the four groups as an independent variable, to explore if there was any significant main effect of the group on reading comprehension scores. Post-hoc tests were then used, in order to determine specifically which groups differed from each other.

In order to gauge the effect of automatic system errors—distinguishing the SS (System Senses) and GS (Gold Senses) conditions—on vocabulary acquisition, we also examined target words where the system gave incorrect information.

[2]We used SPSS,version 20.0, http://www-01.ibm.com/software/analytics/spss/

	Pretest		Posttest	
	Mean	SD	Mean	SD
GS	10.73 (54%)	3.43	15.93 (80%)	3.96
SS	10.93 (55%)	2.82	15.47 (77%)	3.80
AS	10.87 (54%)	3.34	13.47 (67%)	3.83
NS	10.87 (54%)	3.25	11.27 (56%)	3.39

Table 3: Descriptive statistics across groups for vocabulary acquisition (*Mean* = average, *SD* = standard deviation, percentage out of all 20 answers in parentheses)

5 Results and Discussion

5.1 Vocabulary acquisition

Since the first research question is to examine the improvement between the pretest and the posttest, the test of homogeneity of variance was carried out to ensure that the pretest/posttest scores of the participants across the four groups showed similar variances. Levene's test of homogeneity of variances suggested that the 4 groups could be considered to have similar variances on both the pretest ($F(3,55) = 0.49$, $p = 0.69$) and the post-test ($F(3,56) = 0.13$, $p = 0.94$), meaning that this assumption underlying the use of ANOVA was met.

Looking at the descriptive statistics in table 3, none of the groups differed from each other by more than a quarter of a point (or 1 percentage point) on the pretest. Thus, the groups are also comparable with respect to their levels of performance on the pre-test.

Turning to the results of the treatments in table 3, the four groups show larger differences on their posttest. The GS and SS groups show the clearest gains, suggesting greater vocabulary acquisition than the AS and NS groups, as expected. If we look at percentage gain, GS gained 26% and SS 23%,

Source	*df*	*df*2	*F*	*p*	Partial Eta^2	Obs. Power
	Test of Within-Subjects Effects					
Time	1	56	62.67	**<0.01**	0.53	1.00
Time*Group	3	56	7.20	**<0.01**	0.28	0.98
	Test of Between-Subjects Effects					
Group	3	56	1.71	**0.18**	0.08	0.42

Table 2: Results of RM ANOVA comparing vocabulary test scores across the four groups over time

while AS gained only 13% and NS 2%.

In order to examine whether the above differences among groups were statistically significant, a repeated-measures ANOVA was run on those pretest and posttest scores, with Group as the between-subject variable and Time as the within-subject variable. The results of the RM ANOVA are presented in table 2.

With respect to the within-subject variable, the effect of Time shows a statistically significant difference ($F(1,56) = 62.67$, $p < .001$, partial eta^2= 0.53). In other words, not considering Group, there is evidence of improvement from pre to posttest.

Most crucially related to the first research question about whether the groups would have different amounts of vocabulary acquisition over time, we see a significant Time*Group effect ($F(3,56) = 7.20$, $p < .001$, partial eta^2= 0.28). The partial eta^2 values for Time (0.53) and Time*Group (0.28) in table 2 represent large effect sizes which thus provide strong evidence for the differences.

Two sets of post-hoc comparisons were conducted. The first comparisons, in table 4, show significant mean differences between the pretest and posttest for three groups (GS, SS, AS), whereas no significant difference is observed in the NS group, meaning that the three groups who received lexical information showed improvement whereas the group who received no information did not.

Then, a second set of post-hoc tests were run to compare the three groups which showed significant pre-post gains (GS, SS, AS). In table 5, the Contrast Estimate (Est.) looks at the differences in the mean pre-post gains and shows that the GS group is significantly different from the AS group, whereas the difference between the mean gains of the SS and AS groups is not quite significant. (The GS-SS contrast is non-significant.) In other words, these post-hoc comparisons on the Time*Group interaction effect found a significant difference between the GS and AS groups in their vocabulary learning over time, with the GS group showing greater pretest-posttest improvement, whereas the SS's group apparent advantage over the AS group with their mean gains fell slightly short of statistical signficance.

Group	I	J	Mean Diff.	Std. Error	*p*
GS	pre	post	-5.20	0.80	**<0.01**
SS	pre	post	-4.23	0.80	**<0.01**
AS	pre	post	-2.60	0.80	**<0.01**
NS	pre	post	-0.40	0.80	0.62

Table 4: Post-hoc comparisons for Time*Group, for vocabulary acquisition

Group Contrast	Est.	Sig.
GS-AS	2.60	**0.02**
SS-AS	1.93	0.09
GS-SS	0.67	0.56

Table 5: Contrast results for Time*Group, where the dependent variable is the difference in mean pre-post gains

Clicked words In addition to analyzing learners' performance on the overall scores of their pretest and posttest, we examine their performance over their pretest and posttest only on words they clicked while reading, as well as how much they clicked. In the three treatments, we find: GS, 28.27 words clicked on average (7.00 target words); SS, 21.80 (5.93); and AS, 20.87 (5.60). Although these differences are not statistically significant, the apparent trend may suggest that the GS group realized

	Pretest		Posttest		
	Mean	SD	Mean	SD	Gain
GS	40%	32%	85%	22%	45%
SS	25%	18%	81%	25%	56%
AS	23%	25%	68%	32%	45%

Table 6: Descriptive statistics for vocabulary acquisition for clicked words (percentage correct)

they could get high-quality lexical information from clicking words and so clicked more often.

Examining only clicked target words, the test of homogeneity confirmed the error variance of all participants were equivalent at the outset of the study ($p = 0.15$). The percentages correct of the words that were clicked in the pretest and posttest are in table 6. The pre to post gain here conveys a general trend: for the words participants clicked on, they showed improvement, with larger gains than for all words (compare the best gain of 26% in table 3). As with all words, in the RM ANOVA the effect of Time shows a statistically significant difference ($F(1, 42) = 96.20$, $p < 0.01$). However, the effect of Time*Group shows no significant difference in this case ($F(2, 42) = 0.60$, $p = 0.55$).

Despite non-significance, two potentially interesting points emerge which can be followed up on in the future: 1) descriptively speaking, the SS group shows the largest gain between pretest and posttest (56%); and 2) the AS group shows as much improvement as the GS group (45%). This may come from the fact that the number of senses listed for many clicked words was small enough (e.g., 2–3) to find an appropriate sense. Future work could investigate a greater number of target words to verify and shed more light on these trends.

Discussion In sum, our results suggest a positive answer to the first research question about whether sense-specific lexical information leads learners to better vocabulary acquisition. The results from several different analyses suggest that: 1) learners provided with lexical information during reading have more vocabulary acquisition, with sense-specific information having a greater increase; 2) learning gains appear to be greater for the subset of *clicked* target words than for all words (though further research is needed to substantiate this); and 3) they seem to check the meaning more when disambiguated correctly (again needing further research).

	Mean	SD
GS	35.80 (85%)	3.98
SS	37.07 (88%)	2.46
AS	34.93 (83%)	3.08
NS	33.27 (79%)	3.69

Table 7: Descriptive statistics for reading comprehension

Source	*df*	*df*2	*F*	*p*
Group	3	56	4.01	**0.01**

Table 8: Results of one-way ANOVA for reading comprehension scores

5.2 Reading comprehension

The second research question explores whether sense-specific lexical information facilitates reading comprehension. The descriptive statistics for reading comprehension mean scores of the four groups are in table 7. The difference among the reading comprehension mean scores of the four groups was within about 4 points, corresponding to a 9% difference (SS, 88%; NS, 79%). The GS and SS groups have the highest values, but only small differences.

In order to examine whether the above differences among groups were statistically significant, a one-way ANOVA was run on reading comprehension scores. The test of homogeneity of variances confirmed the error variances were equivalent ($p = 0.42$). The results of the one-way ANOVA are in table 8.

As shown, the effect of Group shows a statistically significant difference, indicating that the groups are different in their reading comprehension ($F(3, 56) = 4.01$, $p = 0.01$). With this significant difference in reading comprehension performance, it is necessary to locate where the differences existed among the groups. Tukey post0hoc tests compared all four groups in pairs and revealed a significant difference between the SS group and the NS group ($p = 0.007$), with no significant differences between the other pairs.[3]

To some extent, the results support the idea that

[3]GS vs. SS: $p = 0.68$; GS vs. AS: $p = 0.87$; GS vs. NS: $p = 0.12$; SS vs. AS: $p = 0.24$; AS vs. NS: $p = 0.46$.

System	Pretest	Posttest	Accuracy
Appropriate	+ (16)	+ (14)	88% (14/16)
	- (42)	+ (32)	76% (32/42)
Inappropriate	+ (12)	+ (10)	83% (10/12)
	- (18)	+ (9)	**50%** (9/18)

Table 9: Pre/Posttest performance for SS condition, summed over learners, broken down by whether system sense was appropriate (+ = learner got correct; - = learner got incorrect; numbers in parentheses = actual values)

sense-specific lexical information facilitates learners' reading comprehension. Curiously, the GS group, which received more accurate sense information than the SS group, was not found to outperform the control group ($p = 0.12$)—despite descriptively showing slightly higher reading comprehension scores. This issue warrants future investigation.

5.3 Quality of sense information

We have observed some differences between the Gold Senses (GS) and System Senses (SS) conditions, but we still want to explore to what extent the learners in SS group were impacted by words which were incorrectly disambiguated. There were nine words which the automatic system incorrectly assigned senses to (*inappropriate target-sense words*),[4] and eleven words which it correctly assigned. One can see the different performance for these two types in table 9, for words that learners clicked on.

There are two take-home points from this table. First, when learners were correct in the pretest, they generally did not un-learn that information, regardless of whether they were receiving correct sense information or not (88% vs. 83%). This is important, as it seems to indicate that wrong sense information is not leading learners astray. However, the second point is that when learners were wrong in the pretest, they were in general able to learn the sense with correct information (76%), but not as effectively when given incorrect information (50%). This, unsurprisingly, shows the value of correct sense information.

[4] *aspect.n, chain.n, conscience.n, expenditure.n, sector.n, agitate.v, banish.v, indicate.v, resist.v*

6 Summary and Outlook

We have developed a web system for displaying sense-specific information to language learners and tested it on a group of 60 ESL learners. We showed that sense-specific information in an intelligent reading system can help learners in their vocabulary acquisition and, to some extent, may also help with overall reading comprehension. We also showed preliminary results suggesting that learners might learn more of the words whose definitions they check than words they simply encounter while reading. We can also be optimistic that, while there is still much room for improvement in presenting sense information automatically, errors made by the system do not seem to interfere with language learners' previously-known meanings.

There are a number of avenues to pursue in the future. One thing to note from the results was that the group receiving help in the form of all senses (AS) demonstrated relatively high performance in vocabulary acquisition and reading comprehension, at times similar to the groups receiving sense-specific information (GS, SS). This may be related to the small number of sense entries of the target words (average = 2.95), and a further study should be done on target words with more sense entries, in addition to validating some of the preliminary results presented in this paper regarding clicked words. Secondly, the word sense disambiguation methods and construction of the lexical database can be improved to consistently provide more accurate sense information. Finally, as mentioned earlier, there are preprocessing improvements to be made, such as improving the search for collocations.

Acknowledgments

We would like to thank Stephanie Dickinson and Chelsea Heaven from the Indiana Statstical Consulting Center (ISCC) for their assistance, as well as Graham Katz and the three anonymous reviewers for their useful comments.

References

Kevin Dela Rosa and Maxine Eskenazi. 2011. Impact of word sense disambiguation on ordering dictionary definitions in vocabulary learning tutors. In *Proceedings of FLAIRS 2011*.

Soojeong Eom, Markus Dickinson, and Graham Katz. 2012. Using semi-experts to derive judgments on word sense alignment: a pilot study. In *Proceedings of LREC-12*.

Christiane Fellbaum, editor. 1998. *WordNet: An Electronic Lexical Database*. The MIT Press, Cambridge, MA.

Peter J. M. Groot. 2000. Computer assisted second language vocabulary acquisition. *Language Learning and Technology*, 4(1):60–81.

Michael Heilman, Kevyn Collins-Thompson, Jamie Callan, and Maxine Eskenazi. 2006. Classroom success of an intelligent tutoring system for lexical practice and reading comprehension. In *Proceedings of the 9th International Conference on Spoken Language Processing*.

Adam Kilgarriff, Milos Husák, Katy McAdam, Michael Rundell, and Pavel Rychlý. 2008. Gdex: Automatically finding good dictionary examples in a corpus. In *Proceedings of EURALEX-08*. Barcelona.

YouJin Kim. 2008. The role of task-induced involvement and learner proficiency in L2 vocabulary acquisition. *Language Learning*, 58:285–325.

Toshiko Koyama and Osamu Takeuchi. 2004. How look-up frequency affects EFL learning: An empirical study on the use of handheld-electronic dictionaries. In *Proceedings of CLaSIC 2004*, pages 1018–1024.

Anagha Kulkarni, Michael Heilman, Maxine Eskenazi, and Jamie Callan. 2008. Word sense disambiguation for vocabulary learning. In *Ninth International Conference on Intelligent Tutoring Systems*.

Shari Landes, Claudia Leacock, and Randee I. Tengi. 1998. Building semantic concordances. In Christiane Fellbaum, editor, *WordNet: an electronic lexical database*, chapter 8, pages 199–216. MIT.

Jenifer Larson-Hall. 2010. *A guide to doing statistics in second language research using SPSS*. Routledge, New York, NY.

Baita Laufer and Monica Hill. 2000. What lexical information do L2 learners select in a CALL dictionary and how does it affect word retention? *Language Learning and Technology*, 3(2):58–76.

Vilson J. Leffa. 1992. Making foreign language texts comprehensible for beginners: An experiment with an electronic glossary. *System*, 20(1):63–73.

S. Luppescu and R. R. Day. 1993. Reading, dictionaries, and vocabulary learning. *Language Learning*, 43:263–287.

Rada Mihalcea and Andras Csomai. 2005. SenseLearner: Word sense disambiguation for all words in unrestricted text. In *Proceedings of the ACL Interactive Poster and Demonstration Sessions*, pages 53–56. Ann Arbor, MI.

John Nerbonne and Petra Smit. 1996. GLOSSER-RuG: in support of reading. In *Proceedings of COLING-96*.

Ted Pedersen and Varada Kolhatkar. 2009. WordNet::SenseRelate::AllWords - a broad coverage word sense tagger that maximizes semantic relatedness. In *Proceedings of HLT-NAACL-09*. Boulder, CO.

Caleb Prichard. 2008. Evaluating L2 readers' vocabulary strategies and dictionary use. *Reading in a Foreign Language*, 20(2):216–231.

Diane Schmitt, Norbert Schmitt, and David Mann. 2011. *Focus on Vocabulary 1: Bridging Vocabulary*. Pearson ESL, second edition.

Thomas Segler, Helen Pain, and Antonella Sorace. 2002. Second language vocabulary acquisition and learning strategies in ICALL environments. *Computer Assisted Language Learning*, 15(4):409–422.

John Sinclair, editor. 2006. *Collins COBUILD Advanced Lerner's English Dictionary*. Harper Collins.

The College Board. 2009. *The Official SAT Study Guide*. College Board, second edition.

Kristina Toutanova, Dan Klein, Christopher D. Manning, and Yoram Singer. 2003. Feature-rich part-of-speech tagging with a cyclic dependency network. In *Proceedings of HLT-NAACL 2003*, pages 252–259.

Evaluating the Meaning of Answers to Reading Comprehension Questions
A Semantics-Based Approach

Michael Hahn **Detmar Meurers**
SFB 833 / Seminar für Sprachwissenschaft
Universität Tübingen
{mhahn,dm}@sfs.uni-tuebingen.de

Abstract

There is a rise in interest in the evaluation of meaning in real-life applications, e.g., for assessing the content of short answers. The approaches typically use a combination of shallow and deep representations, but little use is made of the semantic formalisms created by theoretical linguists to represent meaning.

In this paper, we explore the use of the underspecified semantic formalism LRS, which combines the capability of precisely representing semantic distinctions with the robustness and modularity needed to represent meaning in real-life applications.

We show that a content-assessment approach built on LRS outperforms a previous approach on the CREG data set, a freely available corpus of answers to reading comprehension exercises by learners of German. The use of such a formalism also readily supports the integration of notions building on semantic distinctions, such as the information structuring in discourse, which we show to be useful for content assessment.

1 Introduction

There is range of systems for the evaluation of short answers. While the task is essentially about evaluating sentences based on their meaning, the approaches typically use a combination of shallow and deep representations, but little use is made of the semantic formalisms created by theoretical linguists to represent meaning. One of the reasons for this is that semantic structures are difficult to derive because of the complex compositionality of natural language. Another difficulty is that form errors in the input create problems for deep processing, which is required for extracting semantic representations.

On the other hand, semantic representations have the significant advantage that they on the one hand abstract away from variation in the syntactic realization of the same meaning and on the other hand clearly expose those distinctions which do make a difference in meaning. For example, the difference between *dog bites man* and *man bites dog* is still present in deeper syntactic or semantic representations, while semantic representations abstract way from meaning-preserving form variation, such as the active-passive alternation (*dog bites man – man was bitten by dog*). This suggests that sufficiently robust approaches using appropriate semantic formalisms can be useful for the evaluation of short answers.

In this paper, we explore the use of Lexical Resource Semantics (Richter and Sailer, 2003), one of the underspecified semantic formalisms combining the capability of precisely representing semantic distinctions with the robustness and modularity needed to represent meaning in real-life applications. Specifically, we address the task of evaluating the meaning of answers to reading comprehension exercises.

We will base our experiments on the freely available data set used for the evaluation of the CoMiC-DE system (Meurers et al., 2011), which does not use semantic representations. The data consists of answers to reading comprehension exercise written by learners of German together with questions and corresponding target answers.

2 Related Work

There are several systems which assess the content of short answers. Mitchell et al. (2002) use hand-crafted patterns which indicate correct answers to a question. Similarly, Nielsen et al. (2009) use manually annotated word-word relations or "facets". Pulman and Sukkarieh (2005) use machine learning to automatically find such patterns. Other systems evaluate the correctness of answers by comparing them to one or more manually annotated target answers. C-Rater (Leacock and Chodorow, 2003) and the system of Mohler et al. (2011) compare the syntactic parse to the parse of target answers. A comparison of a range of content assessment approaches can be found in Ziai et al. (2012).

The work in this paper is most similar to a line of work started by Bailey and Meurers (2008), who present a system for automatically assessing answers to reading comprehension questions written by learners of English. The basic idea is to align the student answers to a target answer using a parallel approach with several levels on which words or chunks can be matched to each other. Classification is done by a machine learning component. The CoMiC-DE system for German is also based on this approach (Meurers et al., 2011).

In terms of broader context, the task is related to the research on Recognizing Textual Entailment (RTE) (Dagan et al., 2006). In particular, alignment (e.g., MacCartney et al., 2008, Sammons et al., 2009) and graph matching approaches (Haghighi et al., 2005, Rus et al., 2007) are broadly similar to our approach.

3 General Setup

3.1 Empirical challenge: CREG

Our experiments are based on the freely available Corpus of Reading comprehension Exercises in German (CREG, Ott et al., 2012) . It consists of texts, questions, target answers, and corresponding student answers written by learners of German. For each student answer, two independent annotators evaluated whether it correctly answers the question. Answers were only assessed with respect to meaning; the assessment is in principle intended to be independent of grammaticality and orthography. The task of our system is to decide which answers correctly answer the given question and which do not.

3.2 Formal basis: Lexical Resource Semantics

Lexical Resource Semantics (LRS) (Richter and Sailer, 2003) is an underspecified semantic formalism which embeds model-theoretic semantic languages like IL or Ty2 into constraint-based typed feature structure formalisms as used in HPSG. It is formalized in the *Relational Speciate Reentrancy Language* (RSRL) (Richter, 2000).

While classical formal semantics uses fully explicit logical formulae, the idea of underspecified formalisms such as LRS is to derive semantic representations which are not completely specified and subsume a set of possible resolved expressions, thus abstracting away from ambiguities, in particular, but not exclusively, scope ambiguities.

As an example for the representations, consider the ambiguous example (1) from the CREG corpus.

(1) Alle Zimmer haben nicht eine Dusche.
all rooms have not a shower
'Not every room has a shower.'
'No room has a shower.'

The LRS representation of (1) is shown in Figure 1, where INCONT (INTERNAL CONTENT) encodes the core semantic contribution of the head, EXCONT (EXTERNAL CONTENT) the semantic representation of the sentence, and PARTS is a list containing the subterms of the representation.

$$\begin{bmatrix} \text{INCONT} & \textit{haben(e)} \\ \text{EXCONT} & \text{A} \\ \text{PARTS} & \left\langle \begin{array}{l} \text{A, haben(e), } \forall x_1(\text{B} \rightarrow \text{C}), \\ \text{zimmer}(x_1), \exists x_2\ (\text{D} \wedge \text{E}), \neg\ \text{F}, \\ \text{dusche}(x_2), \text{subj}(\text{e},x_1), \text{obj}(\text{e},x_2) \\ \exists\text{e(haben(e)} \wedge \text{subj}(\text{e},x_1) \wedge \text{obj}(\text{e},x_2)) \end{array} \right\rangle \end{bmatrix}$$

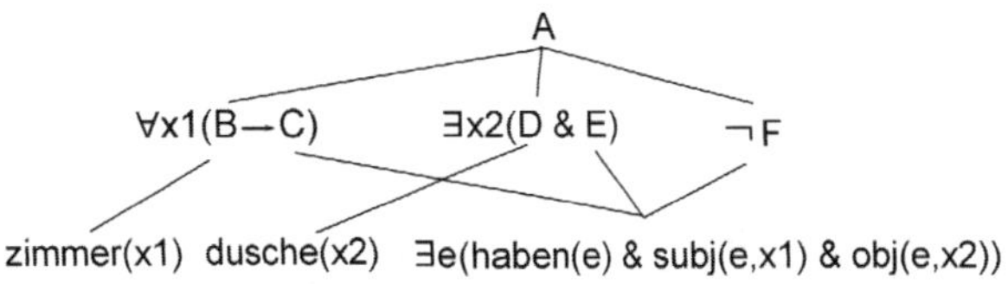

Figure 1: LRS and dominance graph for (1)

The representation also includes a set of subterm constraints, visualized as a dominance graph at the bottom of the figure. The example (1) has several readings, which is reflected in the fact that the relative scope of the two quantifiers and the negation is not specified. The different readings of the sentence can be obtained by identifying each of the meta-variables A, ..., F with one of the subformulas. Meta-variables are labels that indicate where a formula can be plugged in; they are only part of the underspecified representation and do not occur in the resolved representation.

This illustrates the main strengths of an underspecified semantic formalism such as LRS for practical applications. All elements of the semantic representation are explicitly available on the PARTS list, with dominance constraints and variable bindings providing separate control over the structure of the representation. The underspecified nature of LRS also supports partial analyses for severely ill-formed input or fragments, which is problematic for classical approaches to semantic compositionality such as Montague semantics (Montague, 1973). Another advantage of LRS as an underspecified formalism is that it abstracts away from the computationally costly combinatorial explosion of possible readings of ambiguous sentences, yet it also is able to represent fine-grained semantic distinctions which are difficult for shallow semantic methods to capture.

3.3 Our general approach

In a first step, LRS representations for the student answer, the target answer, and the question are automatically derived on the basis of the part-of-speech tags assigned by TreeTagger (Schmid, 1994) and the dependency parses by MaltParser (Nivre and Hall, 2005) in the way discussed in Hahn and Meurers (2011). In this approach, LRS structures are derived in two steps. First, surface representations are mapped to syntax-semantics-interface representations, which abstract away from some form variation at the surface. In the second step, rules map these interface representations to LRS representations. The approach is robust in that it always results in an LRS structure, even for ill-formed sentences.

Our system then aligns the LRS representations of the target answer and the student answer to each other and also to the representation of the question. Alignment takes into account both local criteria, in particular semantic similarity, and global criteria, which measure the extent to which the alignment preserves structure on the level of variables and dominance constraints.

The alignments between answers and the question are used to determine which elements of the semantic representations are *focused* in the sense of Information Structure (von Heusinger, 1999; Kruijff-Korbayová and Steedman, 2003; Krifka, 2008), an active field of research in linguistics addressing the question how the information in sentences is packaged and integrated into discourse.

Overall meaning comparison in our approach is then done based on a set of numerical scores computed from potential alignments and their quality. Given its LRS basis, we will call the system CoSeC-DE (Comparing Semantics in Context).

4 Aligning Meaning Representations

The alignment is done on the level of the PARTS lists, on which all elements of the semantic representation are available:

Definition 1. An alignment a between two LRS representations S and T with PARTS lists p_1^n and q_1^m is an injective partial function from {1,...,n} to {1,...,m}.

Requiring a to be injective ensures that every element of one representation can be aligned to at most one element of the other representation. Note that this definition is symmetrical in the sense that the direction can be inverted simply by inverting the injective alignment function.

To automatically derive alignments, we define a maximization criterion which combines three factors measuring different aspects of alignment quality. In addition to i) the similarity of the alignment links, the quality Q of the alignment a takes into account the structural correspondence between aligned elements by evaluating the consistency of alignments ii) with respect to the induced variable bindings θ and, and iii) with respect to dominance constraints:

$$\begin{aligned} Q(a, \theta|S, T) = &\ linksScore(a|S, T) \\ &\cdot variableScore(\theta) \\ &\cdot dominanceScore(a|S, T) \end{aligned} \quad (1)$$

The approach thus uses a deep representation abstracting away from the surface, but the meaning comparison approach on this deep level is flat, yet at the same time is able to take into account structural criteria. In consequence, the approach is modular because it uses the minimal building blocks of semantic representations, but is able to make use of the full expressive power of the semantic formalism.

4.1 Evaluating the Quality of Alignment Links

The quality of an alignment link between two expressions is evaluated by recursively evaluating the similarity of their components. In the base case, variables can be matched with any variable of the same semantic type:

$sim(x_\mathcal{T}, y_\mathcal{T}) = 1$

Meta-variables can be matched with any meta-variable of the same semantic type:

$sim(\mathrm{A}_\mathcal{T}, \mathrm{B}_\mathcal{T}) = 1$

For predicates with arguments, both the predicate name and the arguments are compared:

$$sim(P_1(a_1^k), P_2(b_1^k)) = sim(P_1, P_2) \cdot \prod_{i=1}^{k} sim(a_i, b_i) \quad (2)$$

If the predicates have different numbers of arguments, similarity is zero. Linguistically well-known phenomena where the number of arguments of semantically similar predicates differ do not cause a problem for this definition, because semantic roles are linked to the verbal predicate via grammatical function terms such as *subj* and *obj* predicating over a Davidsonian event variable, as in Figure 1.[1]

For formulas with generalized quantifiers, the quantifiers, the variables, the scopes and the restrictors are compared:

$$\begin{aligned} sim(Q_1 x_1(\phi \circ \psi), Q_2 x_2(\sigma \circ \tau)) = \\ sim(Q_1, Q_2) \cdot sim(x_1, x_2) \quad (3) \\ \cdot sim(\phi, \sigma) \cdot sim(\psi, \tau) \end{aligned}$$

Lambda abstraction is dealt with analogously. The similarity $sim(P_1, P_2)$ of names of predicates and generalized quantifiers takes into account several sources of evidence and is estimated as the maximum of the following quantities:

[1]In this paper, we simply use grammatical function names in place of semantic role labels in the formulas. A more sophisticated, real mapping from syntactic functions to semantic roles could usefully be incorporated.

As a basic similarity, the Levenshtein distance normalized to the interval [0,1] (with 1 denoting identity and 0 total dissimilarity) is used. This accounts for the high frequency of spelling errors in learner language.

Synonyms in GermaNet (Hamp and Feldweg, 1997) receive the score 1.

For numbers, the (normalized) difference $\frac{|n_1 - n_2|}{max(n_1, n_2)}$ is used.

For certain pairs of dissimilar elements which belong to the same category, constant costs are defined. This encourages the system to align these elements, unless the structural factors, i.e., the quality of the unifier and the consistency with dominance constraints, discourage this. Such constants are defined for pairs of grammatical function terms. Other constants are defined for pairs of numerical terms and for pairs of terms encoding affirmative and negative natural language expressions and logical negation.

Having defined how to compute the quality for single alignment links, we still need to define how to compute the combined score of the alignment links, which we define to be the sum of the qualities of the links:

$$linksScore(a|p_1^n, q_1^m) = \sum_{k=1}^{n} \begin{cases} sim(p_k, q_{a(k)}) & \text{if } a(k) \text{ is defined,} \\ \mu_{NULL} & \text{else.} \end{cases} \quad (4)$$

The quality of a given overall alignment thus is determined by the quality of the alignment links of the PARTS elements which are aligned. For those PARTS elements not aligned, a constant cost μ_{NULL} must be paid, which, however, may be smaller than a costly alignment link in another overall alignment.

4.2 Evaluating Unifiers

Alignments between structurally corresponding semantic elements should be preferred. For situations in which they structurally do not correspond, this may have the effect of dispreferring the pairing of elements which in terms of the words on the surface are identical or very similar. Consider the sentence pair in (2), where *Frau* in (2a) syntactically corresponds to *Mann* in (2b).

(2) a. Eine Frau sieht einen Mann
a woman sees a man
'A woman sees a man.'

b. Ein Mann sieht eine Frau
a man sees a woman
'A man sees a woman.'

On the level of the semantic representation, this is reflected in the correspondence between the variables x_1 and y_1, both of which occur as arguments of *subj*, as shown in Figure 2.

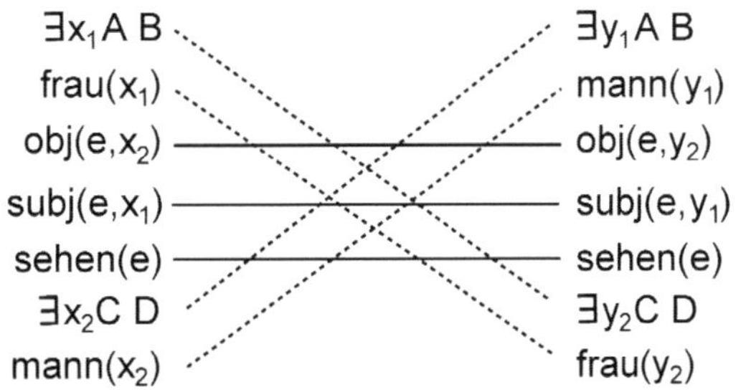

Figure 2: An excerpt of an alignment between the PARTS lists of (2a) on the left and (2b) on the right. Dotted alignment links are the ones only plausible on the surface.

Our solution to capture this distinction is to use the concept of a unifier, well-known from logic programming. A *unifier* for terms ϕ, ψ is a substitution θ such that $\phi\theta = \psi\theta$. Every alignment induces a unifier, which unifies all variables which are matched by the alignment.

The alignment in Figure 2 (without the dotted links) induces the unifier
$\theta_1 = [(x_1, y_1) \mapsto z_1; (x_2, y_2) \mapsto z_2]$.
If links between the matching predicates *mann* and *frau*, respectively, are added, one also has to unify x_1 with y_2 and x_2 with y_1 and thus obtains the unifier
$\theta_2 = [(x_1, x_2, y_1, y_2) \mapsto z]$.
Intuitively, a good unifier unifies only variables which correspond to the same places in the semantic structures to be aligned. In the case of Figure 2, choosing an alignment including the dotted links results in the unifier θ_2 which unifies x_1 and x_2 – yet they are structurally different, with one belonging to the subject and the other one to the object.

In general, it can be expected that an alignment which preserves the structure will not unify two distinct variables from the same LRS representation, since they are known to be structurally distinct. So we want to capture the information loss resulting from unification. This intuition is captured by (5), which answers the following question: Given some variable z in a unified expression, how many additional bits do we need on average[2] to encode the original pair of variables x, y in the PARTS lists p and q, respectively?

$$H(\theta) = \frac{1}{Z_{p,q}} \sum_{z \in Ran(\theta)} W_\theta(z)\, log(W_\theta(z)) \tag{5}$$

$$\text{where} \quad W_\theta(z) = |\{x \in Var(p) | x\theta = z\}| \cdot |\{y \in Var(q) | y\theta = z\}| \tag{6}$$

$$Z_{p,q} = |Var(p)| \cdot |Var(q)| \tag{7}$$

The value of a unifier θ is then defined as follows:

$$variableScore(\theta) = \left(1 - \frac{H(\theta)}{\hat{H}}\right)^k \tag{8}$$

where k is a numerical parameter with $0 \leq k \leq 1$ and $\hat{H}$ is a (tight) upper bound on $H(\theta)$ obtained by evaluating the worst unifier, i.e., the unifier that unifies all variables $\hat{H} = log(Z_{p,q})$.

4.3 Evaluating consistency with dominance constraints

While evaluating unifiers ensures that alignments preserve the structure on the level of variables, it is also important to evaluate their consistency with the dominance structure of the underspecified semantic representations, such as the one we saw in Figure 1. Consider the following pair:

(3) a. Peter kommt und Hans kommt nicht.
Peter comes and Hans comes not
'Peter comes and Hans does not come.'

b. Peter kommt nicht und Hans kommt.
Peter comes not and Hans comes
'Peter does not come and Hans comes.'

While the words and also the PARTS lists of the sentences are identical, they clearly differ in meaning. Figure 3 on the next page shows the LRS dominance graphs for the two sentences together with an

[2]For simplicity, it is assumed that every combination in $Var(p) \times Var(q)$ occurs the same number of times.

alignment between them. The semantic difference between the two sentences is reflected in the position of the negation in the dominance graph: while it dominates *kommen(e$_2$) $\wedge$ subj(e$_2$,hans)* in (3a), it dominates *kommen(f_1) $\wedge$ subj(f_1,peter)* in (3b).

To account for this issue, we evaluate the consistency of the alignment with respect to dominance constraints. An alignment a is optimally consistent with respect to dominance structure if it defines an isomorphism between its range and its domain with respect to the relation $\lhd$ 'is dominated by'.

Figure 3 shows an alignment which aligns all matching elements in (3b) and (3a). The link between the negations violates the isomorphism requirement: the negation dominates *kommen(e$_2$) $\wedge$ subj(e$_2$,hans)* in (3a), while it does not dominate the corresponding elements in (3b). An optimally consistent alignment will thus leave the negations unaligned. Unaligned negations can later be used in the overall meaning comparison as strong evidence that the sentences do not mean the same.

dominanceScore measures how "close" a is to defining an isomorphism. We use the following simple score, which is equal to 1 if and only if a defines an isomorphism:

$$dominanceScore(a|S,T) = \frac{1}{1+\sum_{i,j \in Dom(a)} \kappa \begin{pmatrix} p_i \lhd p_j, \\ p_i \rhd p_j, \\ q_{a(i)} \lhd q_{a(j)}, \\ q_{a(i)} \rhd q_{a(j)} \end{pmatrix}} \quad (9)$$

where κ is a function taking four truth values as its arguments. It measures the extent to which the isomorphism requirement is violated by an alignment. $\kappa(t_1, t_2, t_1, t_2)$ is defined as 0 because there is no violation if the dominance relation between p_i and p_j is equal to that between the elements they are aligned with, $q_{a(i)}$ and $q_{a(j)}$. For other combinations of truth values, κ should be set to values greater than zero, empirically determined on a development set.

4.4 Finding the best alignment

Because of the use of non-local criteria in the maximization criterion $Q(a, \theta|S, T)$ defined in equation (1), an efficient method is needed to find the alignment maximizing the criterion. We exploit the structure inherent in the set of possible alignments to apply the A* algorithm (Russel and Norvig, 2010). We first generalize the notion of an alignment.

Definition 2. A **partial alignment** of order i is an index i together with an alignment which does not have alignment links for any p_j with $j > i$.

A partial alignment can be interpreted as a class of alignments which agree on the first i elements.

Definition 3. The **refinements** $\rho(a)$ of the partial alignment a (of order i) are the partial alignments b such that (1) b is of order $i+1$, and (2) a and b agree on $\{1, ..., i\}$.

Intuitively, refinements of an alignment of order i are obtained by deciding how to align element $i+1$. ρ induces a tree over the set of partial alignments, whose leaves are exactly the complete alignments.

A simple optimistic estimate for the value of all complete descendants of an alignment a of order i is given by the following expression:

$$\begin{aligned} optimistic(a, \theta|S,T) &= variableScore(\theta) \\ &\cdot dominanceScore(a, S, T) \\ &\cdot (linksScore_i(a, \theta|p, q) + \\ &\sum_{k=i+1}^{n} heuristic(k, a, p_1^n, q_1^m)) \end{aligned} \quad (10)$$

where $linksScore_i$ is the sum in (4) restricted to $1 \leq k \leq i$, and $heuristic(k, a, p_1^n, q_1^m)$ is 0 if p_k is aligned and a simple, optimistic estimate for the quality of the best possible alignment link containing p_k if p_k is unaligned. It is estimated as the maximum of μ_{NULL} and $max\{sim(p_k, q_j) \mid q_j\ unaligned\}$.

The estimate in (10) is optimistic in the sense that it provides an upper bound on the values of all complete alignments below a. It defines a monotone heuristic and thus allows complete and optimal search using the A* algorithm. To obtain an efficient implementation, additional issues such as the order of elements in the PARTS lists were taken care of. As they do not play a role for the conceptualization of our approach, they are not discussed here.

The crucial part at this point of the discussion is that the A* search can determine the best alignment between two PARTS lists. As mentioned in the overview in section 3.3, we compute three such

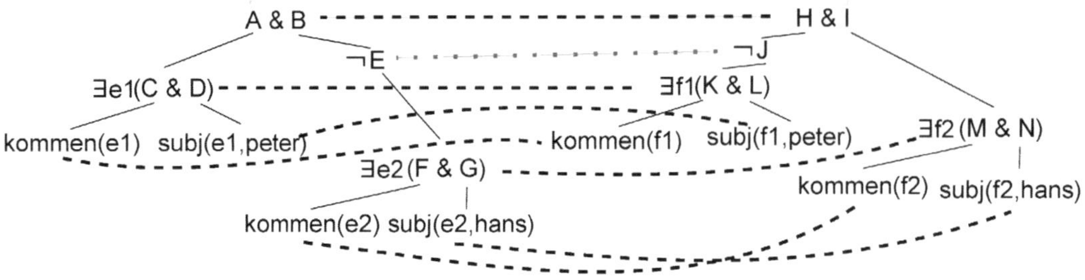

Figure 3: Alignment between the dominance graphs of (3a) and (3b). The red dotted link violates isomorphism.

alignments: between the student and the target answer, between the question and the student answer, and between the question and the target answer.

5 From Alignment to Meaning Comparison

Based on the three alignments computed using the just discussed algorithm, we now explore different options for computing whether the student answer is correct or not. We discuss several alternatives, all involving the computation of a numerical score based on the alignments. For each of these scores, a threshold is empirically determined, over which the student answer is considered to be correct.

Basic Scores The simplest score, ALIGN, is computed by dividing the alignment quality Q between the student answer and the target answer as defined in equation (1) by the number of elements in the smaller PARTS list. Two other scores are computed based on the number of alignment links between student and target answer, which for the EQUAL-Student score is divided by the number of elements of the PARTS list of the *student* answer, and for the EQUAL-Target score by those of the *target* answer.

For dealing with functional elements, i.e., predicates like *subj, obj*, quantifiers and the lambda operator, we tried out three options. The straight case is the one mentioned above, treating all elements on the PARTS list equally (EQUAL). As a second option, to see how important the semantic relations between words are, and how much is just the effect of the elements themselves, we defined a score which ignores functional elements (IGNORE). A third possibility is to weight elements so that functional and non-functional ones differ in impact (WEIGHTED).

Each of the three scores (EQUAL, IGNORE, WEIGHTED) is either divided by the number of elements of the PARTS list of the *student* answer or the *target*, resulting in six scores. In addition, three more scores result from computing the average of the student and target answer scores.

Information Structure Scores Basing meaning comparison on actual semantic representation also allows us to directly take into account Information Structure as a structuring of the meaning of a sentence in relation to the discourse. Bailey and Meurers (2008), Meurers et al. (2011), and Mohler et al. (2011) showed that excluding those parts of the answer which are mentioned (*given*) in the question greatly improves classification accuracy. Meurers et al. (2011) argue that the relevant linguistic aspect is not whether the material was mentioned in the question, but the distinction between *focus* and *background* in Information Structure (Krifka, 2008). The focus essentially is the information in the answer which selects between the set of alternatives that the question raises.

This issue becomes relevant, e.g., in the case of '*or*' questions, where the focused information determining whether the answer is correct is explicitly given in the question. This is illustrated by the question in (4) with target answer (5a) and student answer (5b), from the CREG corpus. While all words in the answers are mentioned in the question, the part of the answers which actually answer the question are the *focused* elements shown in boldface.

(4) Ist die Wohnung in einem Altbau oder
is the flat in a old building or
Neubau?
new building

(5) a. Die Wohnung ist in einem **Altbau**.
the flat is in a old.building

b. Die Wohnung ist in einem **Neubau**.
the flat is in a new.building

To realize a focus-based approach, one naturally needs a component which automatically identifies the focus of an answer in a question-answer pair. As a first approximation, this currently is implemented by a module which marks the elements of the PARTS lists of the answers for information structure. Elements which are not aligned to the question are marked as focused. Furthermore, in answers to *'or'* questions, it marks as focused all elements which are aligned to the semantic contribution of a word belonging to one of the alternatives. *'Or'* questions are recognized by the presence of *oder* ('or') and the absence of a *wh*-word.

While previous systems simply ignored all words given in the question during classification, our system aligns all elements and recognizes givenness based on the alignments. Therefore, givenness is still recognized if the surface realization is different. Furthermore, material which incidentally is also found in the question, but which is structurally different, is not assumed to be given.

Scores using information structure were obtained in the way of the BASIC scores but counting only those elements which are recognized as focused (FOCUS). For comparison, we also used the same scores with givenness detection instead of focus detection, i.e., in these scores, all elements aligned to the question were excluded (GIVEN).

Annotating semantic rather than surface representations for information structure has the advantage that the approach can be extended to cover focusing of relations in addition to focusing of entities. The general comparison approach also is compatible with more sophisticated focus detection techniques capable of integrating a range of cues, including syntactic cues and specialized constructions such as clefts, or prosodic information for spoken language answers – an avenue we intend to pursue in future research.

Dissimilar score We also explored one specialized score paying particular attention to dissimilar aligned elements, as mentioned in section 4.1. Where a focused number is aligned to a different number, or a focused polarity expression is aligned to the opposite polarity, or a logical negation is not aligned, then 0 is returned as score, i.e., the student answer is false. In all other cases, the DISSIMILAR score is identical to the WEIGHTED-Average FOCUS score, i.e., the score based on the average of the student and target scores with weighting and focus detection.

6 Experiments

6.1 Corpus

We base the experiments on the 1032 answers from the CREG corpus which are used in the evaluation of the CoMiC-DE system reported by Meurers et al. (2011). The corpus is balanced, i.e., the numbers of correct and of incorrect answers are the same. It contains only answers where the two human annotators agreed on the binary label.

6.2 Setup

The alignment algorithm contains a set of numerical parameters which need to be determined empirically, such as μ_{NULL} and the function κ. In a first step, we optimized these parameters and the weights used in the WEIGHTED scores using grid search on a development set of 379 answers. These answers are from CREG, but do not belong to the 1032 answers used for testing. We used the accuracy of the DISSIMILAR score as performance metric.

In our experiment, we explored each score separately to predict which answers are correct and which not. For each score, classification is based on a threshold which is estimated as the arithmetic mean of the average score of correct and the average score of incorrect answers. Training and testing was performed using the leave-one-out scheme (Weiss and Kulikowski, 1991). When testing on a particular answer, student answers answering the same question were excluded from training.

6.3 Results

Figure 4 shows the accuracy results obtained in our experiments together with the result of CoMiC-DE on the same dataset. With an accuracy of up to 86.3%, the WEIGHTED-Average FOCUS score outperform the 84.6% reported for CoMiC-DE (Meurers et al., 2011) on the same dataset. This is remarkable given that CoMiC-DE uses several (but comparably shallow) levels of linguistic abstraction for finding alignment links, whereas our approach is exclusively based on the semantic representations.

Score	BASIC	GIVEN	FOCUS
ALIGN	77.1		
EQUAL			
Student	69.8	75.3	75.2
Target	70.0	75.5	75.2
Average	76.6	80.8	80.7
IGNORE			
Student	75.8	80.1	80.3
Target	77.2	82.2	82.3
Average	79.8	84.7	84.9
WEIGHTED			
Student	75.0	80.6	80.7
Target	76.1	83.3	83.3
Average	80.9	86.1	**86.3**
DISSIMILAR	85.9		
CoMiC-DE	84.6		

Figure 4: Classification accuracy of CoSeC-DE

The fact that WEIGHTED-Average outperforms the IGNORE-Average scores shows that the inclusion of functional element (i.e., predicates like *subj, obj*), which are not available to approaches based on aligning surface strings, improves the accuracy.[3] On the other hand, the lower performance of EQUAL shows that functional elements should be treated differently from content-bearing elements.

Of the 13.7% answers misclassified by WEIGHTED-Average FOCUS, 53.5% are false negatives and 46.5% are false positives.

We also investigated the impact of grammaticality on the result by manually annotating a sample of 220 student answers for grammatical well-formedness, 66% of which were ungrammatical. On this sample, grammatical and ungrammatical student answers were evaluated with essentially the same accuracy (83% for ungrammatical answers, 81% for grammatical answers).

The decrease in accuracy of the COMBINED score over the best score can be traced to some yes-no-questions which have an unaligned negation but are correct. On the other hand, testing only on answers with focused numbers results in an accuracy of 97%.

The performance of GIVEN and FOCUS scores compared to BASIC confirms that information structuring helps in targeting the relevant parts of the answers. Since CoMiC-DE also demotes given material, the better GIVEN results of our approach must result from other aspects than the information structure awareness. Unlike previous approaches, the FOCUS scores support reference to the material focused in the answers. However, since currently the FOCUS scores only differs from the GIVEN scores for alternative questions, and the test corpus only contains seven answers to such '*or*' questions, we see no serious quantitative difference in accuracy between the FOCUS and GIVENNESS results.

While the somewhat lower accuracy of the score ALIGN shows that the alignment scores are not sufficient for classification, the best-performing scores do not require much additional computation and do not need any information that is not in the alignments or the automatic focus annotation.

7 Future Work

The alert reader will have noticed that our approach currently does not support many-to-many alignments. As is known, e.g., from phrase-based machine translation, this is an interesting avenue for dealing with non-compositional expressions, which we intend to explore in future work. The alignment approach can be adapted to such alignments by adding a factor measuring the quality of many-to-many links to $linkScore$ (4) and $optimistic$ (10).

8 Conclusion

We presented the CoSeC-DE system for evaluating the content of answers to reading comprehension questions. Unlike previous content assessment systems, it is based on formal semantics, using a novel approach for aligning underspecified semantic representations. The approach readily supports the integration of important information structural differences in a way that is closely related to the information structure research in formal semantics and pragmatics. Our experiments showed the system to outperform our shallower multi-level system CoMiC-DE on the same CREG-1032 data set, suggesting that formal semantic representations can indeed be useful for content assessment in real-world contexts.

[3] We also evaluated IGNORE scores using parameter values optimized for these scores, but their performance was still below those of the corresponding WEIGHTED-Average scores.

Acknowledgements

We are grateful to the three anonymous BEA reviewers for their very encouraging and helpful comments.

References

Stacey Bailey and Detmar Meurers. 2008. Diagnosing meaning errors in short answers to reading comprehension questions. In Joel Tetreault, Jill Burstein, and Rachele De Felice, editors, *Proceedings of the 3rd Workshop on Innovative Use of NLP for Building Educational Applications (BEA-3) at ACL'08*, pages 107–115, Columbus, Ohio.

Ido Dagan, Oren Glickman, and Bernardo Magnini. 2006. The PASCAL Recognising Textual Entailment Challenge. In J. Quionero-Candela, I. Dagan, B. Magnini, and F. d'Alch Buc, editors, *Machine Learning Challenges*, volume 3944 of *Lecture Notes in Computer Science*, pages 177–190. Springer.

Aria D. Haghighi, Andrew Y. Ng, and Christopher D. Manning. 2005. Robust textual inference via graph matching. In *Proceedings of the conference on Human Language Technology and Empirical Methods in Natural Language Processing*, pages 387–394. Association for Computational Linguistics.

Michael Hahn and Detmar Meurers. 2011. On deriving semantic representations from dependencies: A practical approach for evaluating meaning in learner corpora. In Kim Gerdes, Eva Hajicov, and Leo Wanner, editors, *Depling 2011 Proceedings*, pages 94–103, Barcelona.

Birgit Hamp and Helmut Feldweg. 1997. GermaNet - a Lexical-Semantic Net for German. In *Proceedings of ACL workshop Automatic Information Extraction and Building of Lexical Semantic Resources for NLP Applications*, pages 9–15.

Manfred Krifka. 2008. Basic notions of information structure. *Acta Linguistica Hungarica*, 55(3):243–276.

Ivana Kruijff-Korbayová and Mark Steedman. 2003. Discourse and information structure. *Journal of Logic, Language and Information (Introduction to the Special Issue)*, pages 249–259.

Claudia Leacock and Martin Chodorow. 2003. C-rater: Automated scoring of short-answer questions. *Computers and the Humanities*, 37(4):389–405.

Bill MacCartney, Michel Galley, and Christopher D. Manning. 2008. A phrase-based alignment model for natural language inference. In *Proceedings of the Conference on Empirical Methods in Natural Language Processing*, pages 802–811. Association for Computational Linguistics.

Detmar Meurers, Ramon Ziai, Niels Ott, and Janina Kopp. 2011. Evaluating answers to reading comprehension questions in context: Results for German and the role of information structure. In *Proceedings of the TextInfer 2011 Workshop on Textual Entailment*, pages 1–9, Edinburgh, Scotland, UK, July. Association for Computational Linguistics.

Tom Mitchell, Terry Russell, Peter Broomhead, and Nicola Aldridge. 2002. Towards robust computerised marking of free-text responses. In *Proceedings of the 6th International Computer Assisted Assessment (CAA) Conference*.

Michael Mohler, Razvan Bunescu, and Rada Mihalcea. 2011. Learning to grade short answer questions using semantic similarity measures and dependency graph alignments. In *Proceedings of the 49th Annual Meeting of the Association for Comnputational Linguistics*, pages 752–762.

Richard Montague. 1973. The Proper Treatment of Quntification in Ordinary English. In Jaakko Hintikka, Julius Moravcsik, and Patrick Suppes, editors, *Approaches to Natural Language*, pages 221–242. Reidel, Dordrecht.

Rodney D. Nielsen, Wayne Ward, and James H. Martin. 2009. Recognizing entailment in intelligent tutoring systems. *Natural Language Engineering*, 15(4):479–501.

Joakim Nivre and Johan Hall. 2005. Maltparser: A language-independent system for data-driven dependency parsing. In *Proceedings of the Fourth Workshop on Treebanks and Linguistic Theories*, pages 13–95.

Niels Ott, Ramon Ziai, and Detmar Meurers. 2012. Creation and analysis of a reading comprehension exercise corpus: Towards evaluating meaning in context. In Thomas Schmidt and Kai Wrner, editors, *Multilingual Corpora and Multilingual Corpus Analysis*, Hamburg Studies in Multilingualism (HSM). Benjamins, Amsterdam.

Stephen G. Pulman and Jana Z. Sukkarieh. 2005. Automatic short answer marking. In *Proceedings of the 2nd Workshop on Building Educational Applications Using NLP*, pages 9–16.

Frank Richter and Manfred Sailer. 2003. Basic Concepts of Lexical Resource Semantics. In Arnold Beckmann and Norbert Preining, editors, *ESSLLI 2003 – Course Material I*, volume 5 of *Collegium Logicum*, pages 87–143, Wien. Kurt Gödel Society.

Frank Richter. 2000. *A Mathematical Formalism for Linguistic Theories with an Application in Head-Driven Phrase Structure Grammar*. Phil. dissertation, Eberhard-Karls-Universität Tüingen.

Vasile Rus, Arthur Graesser, and Kirtan Desai. 2007. Lexico-syntactic subsumption for textual entailment.

Recent Advances in Natural Language Processing IV: Selected Papers frp, RANLP 2005, pages 187–196.

Stuart Russel and Peter Norvig. 2010. *Artificial Intelligence. A Modern Approach*. Pearson, 2nd edition.

Mark Sammons, V.G.Vinod Vydiswaran, Tim Vieira, Nikhil Johri, Ming-Wei Chang, Dan Goldwasser, Vivek Srikumar, Gourab Kundu, Yuancheng Tu, Kevin Small, Joshua Rule, Quang Do, and Dan Roth. 2009. Relation Alignment for Textual Entailment Recognition. In *Text Analysis Conference (TAC)*.

Helmut Schmid. 1994. Probabilistic part-of-speech tagging using decision trees. In *Proceedings of the International Conference on New Methods in Language Processing*, pages 44–49.

Klaus von Heusinger. 1999. *Intonation and Information Structure. The Representation of Focus in Phonology and Semantics*. Habilitationssschrift, Universität Konstanz, Konstanz, Germany.

Sholom M. Weiss and Casimir A. Kulikowski. 1991. *Computer systems that learn*. Morgan Kaufmann, San Mateo, CA.

Ramon Ziai, Niels Ott, and Detmar Meurers. 2012. Short answer assessment: Establishing links between research strands. In *Proceedings of the 7th Workshop on Innovative Use of NLP for Building Educational Applications (BEA-7) at NAACL-HLT 2012*, Montreal.

Author Index